PART FIRST.

GAZETTEER

—of—

Hampshire County, Mass.,

1654-1887.

COMPILED AND EDITED BY

W. B. GAY,

AUTHOR OF SIMILAR WORKS FOR RUTLAND, ADDISON, CHITTENDEN, FRANKLIN, GRAND ISLE, LAMOILLE, ORLEANS, WINDSOR, ESSEX, CALEDONIA, AND WINDHAM COUNTIES, IN VERMONT, BERKSHIRE COUNTY, MASS., AND CHESHIRE AND GRAFTON COUNTIES, IN NEW HAMPSHIRE.

PERMANENT OFFICE,   -   -   -   SYRACUSE, N. Y.

" He that hath much to do, will do something wrong, and of that wrong must suffer the consequences ; and if it were possible that he should always act rightly, yet when such numbers are to judge of his conduct, the bad will censure and obstruct him by malevolence, and the good sometimes by mistake."—SAMUEL JOHNSON.

PUBLISHED BY

W. B. GAY & Co.,

SYRACUSE, N. Y.

Facsimile Reprint
Published 1993 by
HERITAGE BOOKS, INC.
1540-E Pointer Ridge Place, Bowie, Maryland 20716
(301) 390-7709

ISBN 1-55613-809-1

A Complete Catalog Listing Hundreds of Titles on
Genealogy, History, and Americana
Available Free on Request

INTRODUCTION.

In presenting to the public the "Gazetteer and Business Directory" of Hampshire county, we desire to return our sincere thanks to *all* who have kindly aided in obtaining the information it contains, and rendered it possible to present it in the brief space of time in which it is essential such works should be completed. Especially are our thanks due to the editors and managers of the county papers for the uniform kindness they have evinced in calling public attention to our efforts, and for essential aid in furnishing material for the work. We have also found valuable aid in the following: "History of Worthington,' J. C. Rice, 1854 and 1874; "History of Ware," William Hyde, 1847; "History of Easthampton," Rev. Payson W. Lyman, 1866, and "Historical Address" of 1876; "Doolittle's Sketches" of Belchertown, 1852; "History of Goshen," Hiram Barrus, 1881; "Hundredth Anniversary of Middlefield," 1883; "History of Huntington," Rev. J. H. Bisbee, 1876; "History of Hadley," Sylvester Judd, 1863; "History of Western Massachusetts," J. G. Holland; "Gazetteer of Massachusetts," Elias Mason, 1874; "Gazetteer of Massachusetts," John Hayward, 1847; Barber's "Historical Collections;" "History of the Connecticut Valley," Lewis H. Everts, 1879; "Antiquities of Northampton," Rev. Solomon Clark, 1882; "Atlas of Hampshire County," F. B. Beers & Co., 1873; "Massachusetts in the Civil War," William Shouler; "Adjutant-General's Report," and other state and county documents; and in the various pamphlets and reports of a number of societies, institutions, corporations and towns. Our thanks are also due to the clergy throughout the county, and to Rev. Payson W. Lyman, of Belchertown; B. S. Johnson, of Haydenville; S. B. Quigley, of Southampton, for valuable assistance in compiling the sketches of that town and of Northampton; also Sardis Chapman, of Southampton; F. H. Judd, of Westhampton; Rev. Joseph M. Rockwood, of Middlefield; Rt. Rev. Bishop Huntington, of Syracuse, N. Y.; Rev. Solomon Clark, of Plainfield; Rev. Pliny S. Boyd, of Granby; Chandler T. Macomber, of Chesterfield; S. G. Hubbard, of Hatfield; Miss Mary E. Dawes, of Cummington; Rev. G. H. Johnson, of Amherst; J. R. Turnbull, of Northampton, and to many others who have rendered valuable aid.

That errors have occurred in so great a number of names is probable, and that names have been omitted which should have been inserted is quite certain. We can only say that we have exercised more than ordinary diligence and care in this difficult and complicated feature of book-making. Of such as feel aggrieved in consequence of errors or omissions, we beg pardon, and ask the indulgence of the reader in noting such as have been observed in the subsequent reading of the proofs and which are found corrected in the *Errata*.

It was designed to give a brief account of all the church and other societies in the county, but owing in some cases to the negligence of those who were able to give the necessary information, and in others to the inability of any one to do so, we have been obliged to omit special notices of a few.

We would suggest that our patrons observe and become familiar with the explanations at the commencement of the Directory on page 3, part second. The names it embraces, and the information connected therewith, were obtained by actual canvass, and are as correct and reliable as the judgment of those from whom they were solicited renders possible. Each agent is furnished with a map of the town he is expected to canvass, and he is required to pass over every road and call at every dwelling and place of business in the town in order to obtain the facts from the individuals concerned whenever possible.

The margins have been left broad to enable anyone to note changes opposite the names.   •

The *Advertisers* we most cheerfully commend to the patronage of those under whose observation these pages may come.

We take this occasion to express the hope that the information found in the book will not prove devoid of interest and value, though we are fully conscious that the brief description of the county the scope of the work enables us to give is by no means an exhaustive one, and can only hope that it may prove an aid to future historians, who will be the better able to do full justice to the subject.

While thanking our patrons and friends generally for the cordiality with which our efforts have been seconded, we leave the work to secure that favor which earnest endeavor ever wins from a discriminating public, hoping they will bear in mind, should errors be noted, that "he who expects a perfect work to see, expects what ne'er was, is, nor yet shall be."

W. B. GAY.

M. F. ROBERTS.

GAZETTEER

OF

HAMPSHIRE COUNTY, MASS.

CHAPTER I.

" Thou who wouldst see the lovely and the wild
Mingled in harmony on Nature's face,
Ascend our rocky mountains. Let thy foot
Fail not with weariness, for on their tops
The beauty and the majesty of earth,
Spread wide beneath, shall make thee to forget
The steep and toilsome way."—BRYANT.

MT. HOLYOKE AND MT. TOM NAMED—MARY PYNCHON AND ELIZUR
HOLYOKE—THE OLD BAY PATH—VIEW FROM MT. HOLYOKE—SCEN-
ERY—THE PILGRIMS--SPRINGFIELD SETTLED—OLD HAMPSHIRE COUNTY
INCORPORATED—AREA CURTAILED--COUNTY DIVIDED—PRESENT AREA
AND BOUNDARIES.

" " DO YOU see that blue mountain top at the north, just lifting itself above the intervening forests?'"

" 'Yes.'"

" 'Let that be *Mt. Holyoke* for ever!' said Mary, stretching out her hand."

" 'Amen!' responded Holyoke, 'and I shall see that your authority in be-stowing the name is fully honored. But what shall be done with the lonely mountain westward of mine? It would be unkind to leave that nameless.'"

" ' Let it be named in honor of the poor pet that lies yonder,' said Mary, pointing to the grave of poor Tom.'"

" ' Let it be *Mt. Tom* for ever!' said Holyoke.'"

And "for ever," doubtless, will these twin mountains bear the names they then received, bestowed by these two as they imbibed the intoxicating draught made up of love, youth, and the surrounding unfading beauties of

2*

nature in the "Old Bay Path" two hundred and fifty years ago—Mary Pynchon and Elizur Holyoke.*

Let us ascend the "steep and toilsome" side of this mountain which perpetuates the pioneer's name and glance at the lovely territory of which it is the purpose of this work to treat. What a view of "mingled harmony on Nature's face" greets the eye ! The grand primeval solitudes of two hundred and fifty years since to be sure are not here ; but the works of man and the works of the Creator are most harmoniously blended, in a scene transcending the powers of description or of imagination. †

Mr. Ruskin has formulated the law that, "that country is always the most beautiful which is made up of the most curves." He then applies this law in his ideal description or characterization of the "picturesque blue country" of England; that is, a country having a blue distance of mountains. Let us see if this description will not fit the view from Mt. Holyoke : "Its first and most distinctive peculiarity," he says, "is its grace ; it is all undulation and variety of line, one curve passing into another with the most exquisite softness, rolling away into faint and far outlines of various depths and decision, yet none hard or harsh ; and, in all probability, rounded off in the near ground into mossy forms of partially wooded hill, shaded downward into winding dingles or cliffy ravines, each form melting imperceptably into the next, without an edge or angle.　　*　　*　　*　　Every line is voluptuous, floating and waving in its form ; deep, rich and exquisitely soft in its color; drowsy in its effect, like slow, wild music ; letting the eye repose upon it, as on a wreath of cloud, without one feature of harshness to hurt, or of contrast to awaken."

Surely, Mr. Ruskin might have said this of Hampshire county as seen from Holyoke or the Eyrie ! Except for the green stretch of "meadows" that border the Connecticut, what a labyrinth of interlacing curves is presented. Not a harsh or ungraceful line is to be seen. Even the Connecticut bends to Nature's sweet mood with broad, sweeping curves or lace-like loops, often "flowing several miles to travel one," till lost as a wavy, silver thread in the blue distance. Even the countless brooks which swell its tide forget not to assume the same luxurious, sinuous course. Upon either hand, the cultivated

---

* This version, from Holland's *Bay Path,* may have emanated purely from the poet's brain, but unlike many traditions, equally unreliable, it has the merit of beauty ; for in his *History of Western Massachusetts,* he says : "The most probable account of the manner in which these mountains received their names is to the effect that, some five or six years after the settlement of Springfield, a company of the planters went northward to explore the country. One party, headed by Elizur Holyoke, went up the east side of the river, and another, headed by Rowland Thomas, went up on the west side. The parties arriving abreast, at the narrow place in the river below Hockanum, at what is now called Rock ferry, Holyoke and Thomas held a conversation with one another across the river, and each, then and there, gave his own name to the mountain at whose foot he stood. The name of Holyoke remains uncorrupted and without abbreviation, while Mt. Thomas has been curtailed to simple and homely Mt. Tom."

† In the earlier editions of *Webster's Dictionary* the view from Mt. Holyoke is cited as a practical illustration in defining the word "picturesque."

knolls, wooded hills and grassy slopes have been carefully carved by the glacier hand. Even the shadows, the passing cloud-flecks and the dim, blue mountains in the distance reproduce again and again Hogarth's "line of beauty." Variety, the most marvelous, but without confusion, forbids the sense to tire. Colors, the richest, softest and most delicate, charm the eye, and vary with the ever-changing conditions of the atmosphere. Fertile farms and frequent villages imbue the scene with the warmth of generous life ; while over all hangs the subdued grandeur which may well have pervaded the souls of the great and good men who have made this territory their home since that bright day when Elizur Holyoke and Mary Pynchon talked of love beneath the shadows of the " Old Bay Path," two hundred and fifty years ago.

But let us turn back over the " Old Bay Path," adown the vista of faded years, and hastily glance at the links in the strong chain that unites us with that little band whose bended knees devoutly pressed old Plymouth's frozen shore on that dreary December day in 1620—that band who had braved persecution and the rigors of a winter sea that they " might walk with God and with one another in the enjoyment of the ordinances of God, according to the Primitive fashion," and now, on this dreary 21st of December, began their stern fight with the elements, with famine, and with a savage foe, to found one of the greatest nations upon which the sun has ever shone. A God-fearing, law-loving, fearless, industrious people were this little Puritan band, the " noblest men that ever founded a nation." Of their many trials in those early days it is not necessary to speak—they are familiar to all. Accessions to the new settlement were soon made, other colonies were established, and it was not long before emigration began its steady march towards the West, a march that even now, though more than two and a half centuries have intervened, is not ended. Cotton Mather quaintly speaks of these times as follows :—

"It was not long before the Massachusetts colony was become like an hive overstocked with bees, and many of the new inhabitants entertained thoughts of swarming into plantations extended further into the country. The colony might fetch its own descriptions from the dispensations of the great God unto his ancient Israel, and say : 'O God of hosts ! thou hast brought a vine out of England ; thou hast cast out the heathen and planted it ; thou preparest room before it, and didst cause it to take deep root, and it filled the land ; the hills were covered with the shadow of it, and the boughs thereof were like the goodly cedars ; she sent out her boughs unto the sea.' But still there was one strand wanting for the complete accommodations of the description, to wit : she sent forth her branches unto the river, and this, therefore, is to be next attained. The fame of Connecticut river, a long, fresh, rich river, had made a little nilus of it, in the expectation of the good people about the Massachusetts bay, whereupon many of the planters, belonging especially to the towns of Cambridge, Watertown and Roxbury, took up resolutions to travel an hundred miles westward from those towns, for a further settlement upon this famous river."

In 1631 the Connecticut first became known to the colonists, and in 1636 William Pynchon and his little band came down the "Old Bay Path" to found what is now the flourishing city of Springfield. With this event begins the authentic history of Western Massachusetts. A little over a quarter of a century later old Hampshire county was incorporated, the settlements here having increased to such an extent that this act had become necessary. The act of incorporation reads as follows :—

" Forasmuch as the inhabitants of this jurisdiction are much increased, so that now they are planted far into the country, upon Connecticut river, who by reason of their remoteness cannot conveniently be annexed to any of the counties already settled ; and that public affairs may with more facility be transacted according to laws now established ; it is ordered by the court, and authority thereof, that henceforth Springfield, Northampton and Hadley shall be, and hereby are, constituted as a county, the bounds of limits on the south to be the south line of the patent, the extent of other bounds to be fully thirty miles distant from any or either of the aforesaid towns ; and what towns or villages soever shall hereafter be erected within the aforesaid limits to be and belong to the said county. And further, that the said county shall be called Hampshire, and shall have and enjoy the liberties and privileges of any other county ; that Springfield shall be the shire town there, and the courts be kept one time in Springfield and another time at Northampton ; the like order to be observed for their shire meetings, that is to say, one year at one town and the next year at the other town, from time to time. The deputies have passed this, with reference to the consent of the honored magistrates.

" 16th day of 3d month, 1662.

"WILLIAM TORREY, Clericus."

It will thus be seen that Hampshire county, as first erected, although containing within its limits only three towns, Springfield, Northampton and Hadley, covered nearly half of the state that then belonged to the Colony of Massachusetts Bay. It included the western tier of towns of what is now Worcester county, and the whole of what are now the counties of Franklin, Hampshire, Hampden and Berkshire.

This large area was retained until July 10, 1731, when the following act of the general court took effect, curtailing the territory as expressed therein :—

" Be it enacted by His Excellency the Governor, Council, and Representatives, in General Court assembled, and by the authority of the same, that the towns and places hereinafter named and expressed, that is to say, Worcester, Lancaster, Rutland, and Lunenburgh, all in the county of Middlesex ; Mendon, Woodstock, Oxford, Sutton, including Hassanamisco, Uxbridge, and the land lately granted to several petitioners of Medfield, all in the county of Suffolk; Brookfield in the county of Hampshire, and the south town laid out for the Narragansett soldiers, and all other lands lying within the said townships, with the inhabitants thereon, shall from and after the tenth day of July, which will be in the year of our Lord one thousand seven hundred and thirty-one, be and remain one entire and distinct county by the name of Worcester, of which Worcester to be the county or shire town, and the said county to have, use and enjoy all such powers, privileges, and immunities as by law other counties within this province have and do enjoy."

The second curtailment of the territory occurred June 30, 1761, when the following act went into effect:—

"Be it therefore enacted by the Governor, Council, and House of Representatives, that the towns and plantations hereinafter mentioned, that is to say, Sheffield, Stockbridge, Egremont, New Marlborough, Poontoosack, New Framingham, West Hoosack, number one, number three and number four, and all other lands included in the following limits, viz.: Beginning at the western line of Granvil, where it touches the Connecticut line, to run northerly as far as said west line of Granvil runs, thence easterly to the southwest corner of Blandford, and to run by the west line of the same town to the northeast corner thereof, from thence northerly in a direct line to the southeast corner of number four, and so running by the easterly line of said number four to the northeast corner thereof, and thence in a direct course to the southeast corner of Charlemont, and so northerly in the corner of the west line of the same town till it comes to the north bound of the province, and northerly on the line between this province and the province of New Hampshire, southerly on the Connecticut line, and on the west by the utmost limits of this province, shall from and after the thirtieth day of June, one thousand seven hundred and sixty-one, be and remain one entire and distinct county by the name of Berkshire, of which Sheffield for the present to be the county or the shire town; and the said county to have, use and enjoy all such powers, privileges and immunities as by law other counties in this province have and do enjoy."

After Berkshire was severed, no changes in area were made for half a century. In the meantime, the county had increased its number of towns to sixty-three. On June 24, 1811, twenty-four of these towns were set off towards forming the county of Franklin; and during the following year, February 20, 1812, eighteen towns more were taken to form with other townships the county of Hampden. Since then two other towns have been added, Enfield and Prescott, and one township, Northampton, has advanced to the dignity of an incorporated city.

The county now has an area of about 524 square miles, bounded north by Franklin county; east by Worcester county; south by Hampden county; and west by Berkshire county. It has twenty-two towns and one city, incorporated as follows: Amherst, February 13, 1759; Belchertown, June 30, 1761; Chesterfield, June 11, 1762; Cummington, June 23, 1779; Easthampton, June 17, 1785; Enfield, February 16, 1816; Goshen, May 14, 1784; Granby, June 11, 1768; Greenwich, April 20, 1754; Hadley, May 20, 1661; Hatfield, May 31, 1670; Huntington, June 29, 1773; Middlefield, March 11, 1783; Pelham, January 15, 1742; Plainfield, March 16, 1785; Prescott, January 28, 1822; South Hadley, April 12, 1753; Southampton, January 5, 1753; Ware, November 25, 1761; Westhampton, September 29, 1778; Williamsburg, April 24, 1771; Worthington, June 30, 1761; and the City of Northampton, organized as a township October 18, 1654, and as a city January 7, 1884.

*CHAPTER II.

Topography—Geological Features—Crystalline Rocks—Gneiss—
Feldspathic Mica Schist — Hornblende Schist — Hydro-Mica
Schist—Calciferous Mica Schist—Fibrolite Gneiss and Schist—
Eruptive Rocks of the Older Series—Granite—Syenite—Min-
eral Veins—The Trias—Glacial Period—Flood Period—The
Connecticut Lake.

THE topography of so limited an area as the one under discussion can hardly be fruitfully examined without some reference to the larger region of which it forms a part. The salient points in the topography of Hampshire county are :—

(*a.*) The broad Connecticut valley, extending through its middle.

(*b.*) The high grounds bordering this valley on the east, which may be looked upon as the western border of the plateau of Worcester county, but deeply notched by several valleys running north and south parallel to the main valley.

(*c.*) The western highland border of the valley, which is the eastern extension of the Berkshire hills, and which, in contrast with the eastern half of the county, is a more continuous body of high land, rising gradually to the western border of the county and beyond, of very irregular surface, but not notched by any north-south valleys extending, like those on the east, far beyond the borders of the county.

(*d.*) The "L" shaped Holyoke–Mt. Tom range, which blocks up the central valley, and which the geologist almost unconsciously expects his hearer to look upon as much younger than the valley it adorns.

From the high ground of Worcester county, on the east, there is a very rapid descent to the peculiar flat-bottomed valley which runs down through Greenwich, Enfield, and the west of Ware. On the east of this valley, in the eastern half of the town of Ware, is the only portion of the county which, in strictness, belongs topographically to the high plateau of Worcester county. West of this first valley and very near it, so near indeed that they unite for a little way just west of the village of Enfield, is the deep, narrow valley of the west branch of Swift river, continued south of the point where the two valleys unite by the channel-way of the Swift river proper. Next west, Jabish brook, rising in Pelham, becomes important, as it flows across Belchertown. Going west over the high ground of Belchertown and Pelham, we come on the broad valley of the Connecticut, which extends from the west line of

---

* Prepared by Prof. Ben K. Emerson, of Amherst College.

these towns across to a line drawn diagonally from the northeast to the south-west corner of Northampton, and continued north across Hatfield, and south across Southampton. In this broad valley Mt. Warner rises as a native, Mt. Holyoke as an immigrant of early date, while all the hills around Amherst and Northampton are comparatively late arrivals.

Farther west, a branch of the Westfield river passes as a pleasant brook across Cummington, runs in a deep cañon to West Chesterfield, and thence in a narrow valley south across Huntington to join the main stream, whose deep valley borders the county only for a short distance along the south line of Huntington and Middlefield. It is a peculiarity of this portion of the state that the main drainage trunks into the Connecticut valley lie in two pairs, opposite each other, one pair to the north and one to the south of this county—Miller's and Deerfield rivers on the north, Chicopee and Westfield rivers on the south. As the valleys of the county all run north and south, so all the drainage of the county goes north or south to these streams in order to reach the Connecticut. The exceptions are Fort river in Amherst, and Mill river and Manhan river in Northampton and Easthampton. These are small streams, heading back in only the first range of hills.

As a result of its topography, the county's western highlands have not been penetrated by railroads, while each of the deeper valleys on the east is occupied by a separate road.

This brief résumè of the topography of the county may serve as an intro-duction to a description of its geology, and the latter must in its turn explain the main topographic features.

GEOLOGICAL FEATURES.

If we could sweep the loose material—clay, sand, gravel and hardpan—from the surface of the county, we should find the eastern and western highlands little changed. Within the limits set above to the Connecticut val-ley, however, the changes would be greater. Many of the hills around the towns of Amherst, Northampton and Easthampton—the College hill, and Castor and Pollux in Amherst, and Round and Hospital hills in Northamp-ton, for instance—would be removed to their bases, while across the Hadley and Northampton meadows, as far north as the Northampton bridge, the clay would be removed more than a hundred feet down, that is, to below the level of the sea. If we were to examine the rocky surface thus exposed, we should find the boundaries of the valley set above, viz.: a diagonal line across Hat-field, Northampton and Easthampton, on the west, and the west line of Pel-ham and Belchertown, on the east, to be still topographical and geological lines of primary importance. First, as bounding a valley somewhat deeper than before ; and second, as limiting approximately the area covered by coarse red and buff sandstones, out of which the great ridges of black trap (the Hol-yoke and Mt. Tom ranges) would still rise unchanged, except that their north-ern and western faces would be higher and steeper even than now.

If now we were further to imagine the sandstones and traps removed, we should look from the high ground of Westhampton or Pelham upon a deep, broad valley; in places, and perhaps everywhere, more than a half-mile deeper than the present valley, and thus more than a half-mile below the present sea level.   The Holyoke and Mt. Tom ranges would be gone, and we should look across a valley fifteen miles wide and detect no marked elevation except Mt. Warner and the rocky ridge on which Amherst is built.   The same ancient crystalline rocks which make the eastern and western highlands would then form also the bottom of the deeper valley.

These considerations mark out the threefold division natural to our subject, viz.:—

  I. (*a.*) The character and origin of the ancient crystalline rocks which underlie everything else in the valley, and form the high lands on either side.

  (*b.*) The changes of folding and erosion by which the deep valley and the bordering highlands were made.

 II. (*a.*) The character and origin of the sandstones and traps.

  (*b.*) The erosion by which they were planed down to their present surface.

III. (*a.*) The character and origin of the hardpan, gravels and clays.

  (*b.*) The erosions by which they have been affected, down to the present time.

The rocks of the first series were deposited probably as marine sediments, with intercalated eruptive rocks, in that earliest period of the earth's history, from which no certain vestiges of life have come down to us (Azoic, Eozoic or Archaean), and their formation continued through an unknown portion of the second great period (Paleozoic).   The remainder of this period was taken up with the completion of the folding, and with the erosion of much of that which had been brought together in the first portion.

The rocks of the second series (the sandstones) were laid down in the deep valley formed by the erosion of the latter portion of the second period, this valley becoming for a time a fjord which stretched north across Connecticut to the north line of Massachusetts, at the beginning of the third great era of the earth's history (the Mesozoic), and during the remainder of this period and the early portion of the next and last of these great ages (the Cenozoic) an erosion of enormous duration swept out of the valley the major portion of the sandstone which had been gathered in it, and left the trap beds like the ribs of a great skeleton stretched across the valley.

The rocks of the third series, the hardpan, gravel, sand, and clay, were deposited when the county was again submerged, this time beneath the frozen waters of the great glacier, and when, on the recession thereof, all its valleys were filled with the superabundant waters from the melting of the ice, which waters as they sank towards the dimensions of the present rivers, changed gradually from filling up to eroding agents, carving out the terraces along the river sides, which form the last charm of the valley scenery.

The history of the area has been thus, in brief: first, a huge submergence, perhaps not uninterrupted, during which the oldest and the main body of its rocks (new crystalline) were deposited; second, a huge dry-land period of erosion, when the main contours of the region were blocked out; third, a second fjord period of submergence, for the valley alone, when the sandstones were laid down, and a transcient series of volcanoes diversified the scenery; fourth, a second erosion, which formed down the broad valley the narrow channel-way of the pre-glacial Connecticut river; fifth, a third submergence beneath the ice and succeeding floods of the glacial and post-glacial ages, which spread the loose material over the surface; sixth, by the terrace-making period, of which the "meadows" are the most valuable contributions.

THE CRYSTALLINE ROCKS.

The time-honored comparison of the folded rocks which make the earth's crust, to a pile of strips of cloth of various colors which have been laid upon a flat surface and then crumpled into close parallel folds by horizontal pressure, is quite adequate to make clear the present position of the oldest rocks in the county, if we suppose that the crumpling force worked from west to east, and that erosion has cut the whole down to the present upper surface of these rocks. The result of this is that the rocks cross the county in bands, from north to south, and dip, for the most part, steeply to east or west. The important members which make up this series are as follows, in the order of their age, the newest above:—

The calciferous mica schist.

The hydromica schist.

The hornblende schist.

The feldspathic mica schist.

The gneiss.

The Gneiss.—This is the well-known and excellent quarry stone of Becket, Pelham and Monson. It is made up of quartz, feldspar and mica. The feldspar is largely plagioclose, and is marked by delicate striation of the cleavage faces. It is in fresh, colorless, transparent grains, often difficultly distinguishable from the quartz, the two minerals together making a colorless granular mass in which the fresh black scales of the biotite, or the jet-black grains of the hornblende are strongly contrasted, and blend to form the clear gray of the rock. Much of the rock is sub-porphyritic in three ways. It is blotched by large grains or rounded aggregations of orthoclase, by distant aggregations of biotite, or by quite large, squarish crystals of hornblende. Very often it is "stretched," that is, on the surface of the broad slabs into which it splits naturally, the black mica flakes or the feldspar blotches are seen to be strewed along in parallel lines and long narrow streaks across the surface as if the whole had been stretched when in a plastic condition. Pyroxene, titanite and garnet are occasionally found, the second quite commonly. Zircon, rutile and apatite are common microscopic constituents.

The western band of the rock occupies the western portion of the county, west of a north and south line drawn through the village of Middlefield, and contains the important quarries of this town and Becket. A portion of this gneiss, in the extreme northwestern corner of the town, lies unconformably below the rest, and is apparently considerably the older. It is a coarser, more compact, flesh-colored or grey gneiss, which contains, in the neighboring town of Hinsdale, a bed of coarse crystalline limestone, with chondrodite, discovered by Prof. J. D. Dana. This mineral occurs apparently only in the oldest rocks. It is true, however, that a band of limestone, occurring where the railroad crosses Cole's brook in the upper portion of the gneiss, also contains chondrodite, in part changed to serpentine.

The second band of the gneiss crosses Shutesbury and Pelham, and ends just south of the village of Belchertown, against a great block of an eruptive rock which occupies the whole southern portion of the town. The gneisses of this band are characterized by a nearly horizontal foliation, and they are thinner bedded and more uniformly "stretched" than those of the other bands. A thick bed of an actinolitic quartzite can be traced in a curiously complex course across the band, dividing it into an upper and an under portion.

At the "Asbestus mine" in Pelham and in the middle of Shutesbury, occur two lenticular beds of an olivine-enstatite rock, associated with massive anorthite and tourmaline, with biotite containing hornblende and corundum, and with many products of the decomposition of these minerals, ending with asbestus, vermiculite and serpentine.

The third band runs down through the Prescott—Greenwich—Enfield—Ware valley, and in its southward continuation are the celebrated quarries of Monson. It is in the portion extending across the county more contorted and complexly twisted in its foliation than the other bands. It is distinguished from the other bands by its position at the bottom of a valley, and by the absence of the accessory beds described as occurring in them. I am inclined to explain this lower position by assuming the gneiss to have been faulted down into its present position, rather than entirely by the more rapid disintegration and removal of the gneiss.

The assumption that these three bands are parts of one and the same sheet, is in a degree hypothetical, as they are not seen in contact. I have, however, little doubt that they are continuous beneath the newer rocks ; that like a letter " w " the band in the west of the county goes beneath the newer rocks, comes up in the Pelham band, and again rises in the Enfield band. In these two folds the later beds are included like nests of boxes of very unequal widths, and of very unequal degrees of complexity, for the one extends from Middlefield across to Pelham, and the newer beds have several subordinate folds, while the other band extends north and south in a narrow strip through the towns of Ware, Enfield and Greenwich.

The Feldspathic Mica Schist.—This appears in a band running east of the village of Middlefield, and along the west line of Worthington, and it reappears apparently in greatly altered form along the western foot-hills of Pelham and Belchertown, and in Amherst. It is a coarse schist, mainly composed of quartz and muscovite, the latter often hydrated, carrying considerable feldspar, and characterized by large garnets often changed to chlorite.

It is represented in the eastern band by a bed of an arenaceous muscovite-biotite gneiss, which lies between the biotite gneiss below, and the hornblende schist above, on each side of the band.

The Hornblende Schist.—Next inward is the hornblende schist, which, in the western band, enters the county just where the road between Chester and Middlefield enters the latter town. It is in Chester a broad band, making the whole of West mountain above the town, and having the famous emery bed on its eastern border. Where it enters Middlefield it is almost wholly replaced by a great bed of serpentine, which runs, with a width of above a hundred rods and a length of above a mile, up nearly to the middle of the town, and in its further course it is accompanied by several other similar beds of serpentine, which seems in each case within the limits of the county to be derived from the hornblende schist itself. Other beds associated with the schist beyond the limits of the county are derived from pyroxene and enstatite rocks.

The hornblende schist is a heavy, black rock, generally thin fissile, with the fine black needles of hornblende having mostly a common direction. It is very constantly epidotic, quartzose, and non-feldspathic.

On the eastern border, the band of this rock is not exposed continuously across the county. I have found it just south of North Amherst station, and traced it thence to Belchertown, where it folds over the gneiss and is continuous with the western strip of the same rock bordering the eastern band on its western side. This junction of the two rocks takes place through the village of Belchertown, and the further southward extension of both bands is cut off by the intrusion of the Belchertown syenite, whose contact influence upon this and the surrounding beds will be described later. The schist is lithologically identical in the two bands.

The Hydromica Schist.—This is the " chlorite schist" of earlier writings. It extends in a north-south band across the county, occupying the eastern part of Middletown and the western part of Worthington, Cummington and Plainfield.

It is a gray schist, generally quartzose, and splitting into flat flags which have a soft feel from the altered muscovite, and very often carry large garnets, which are in twenty-four sided forms and are often changed more or less into a green chlorite, and other small patches of the same green chlorite occur commonly in the rock.

As a result of a subordinate fold, it crops out just west of the village of Goshen, and comes up on the eastern border of the basin in Williamsburg, where it is, in a limited way, associated with hornblende schist, but where it is for the most part replaced by granite.

In the eastern band two strips run across the county with some loops and minor irregularities. In Quabin Mt., south of Enfield, it is represented by a fine fire stone, the muscovite being silvery white and scanty, while farther north, across Enfield and Prescott, some biotite is associated with the muscovite, making a " two mica quartzite," which, at times, graduates into a gneiss. Toward the south it graduates into a rock not distinguishable from the type described above for the western band, as may be seen a little beyond the limit of the county, in the high hill southwest of Palmer depot.

The Calciferous Mica Schist.—From a line drawn through the middle of Plainfield, Cummington and Worthington, the whole region east to the border of the valley is occupied by the rocks of this series, crumpled into several subordinate folds, except where, in Goshen and Williamsburg, the older rocks protrude, and where, in the towns last mentioned and in North—West—and Southampton, great areas are occupied by granite.

It is a muscovite schist, generally dark colored from an admixture of finely divided carbon, barren in its lower portions, but in the upper full of garnet, staurotite, kyanite, and small biotite crystals, set transversely to the bedding. It splits into thin flags and is used for paving. Subordinate beds of a fine-grained arenaceous biotite schist (whetstone schist) afford the finest scythe stones.

Other beds of a fine-grained granitoid gneiss occur, and beds of a black biotitic hornblendic limestone, bounded above and below by a thin layer of hornblende schist, so that when blocks of the limestone have been exposed to long weathering, the limestone wears away more rapidly than the cappings of schist, and the curious anvils and tables found now and then are produced. On the east side of the basin, much of the schist of Mt. Warner and underlying Amherst is of this or the preceding type, but so changed by impregnation with granite that the two cannot be separated. This closes the series in the western basin. In the eastern, only the lower barren mica schist separates in a narrow strip the two bands of the last described rock ; but a little north and south of the county the strip becomes wider and is then the same dark biotite-spangled ganetiferous mica schist as in the western area. It contains everywhere fibrolite, generally in small amount.

The Fibrolite Gneiss and Schist.—I have thus described two synclinals, or downward folds of a series of rocks into the gneiss. Just on the eastern border of the county, in Ware and just entering Greenwich, is a third repetition of the same series in the same order; two mica gneisses, hornblende schists, mica schists, but all become abundantly fibrolitic. I have mentioned above that, in the eastern of the two series there described, fibrolite occurs commonly in the mica schists, and I have traced these two bands northwesterly beyond the limits of the county, to where, in the north of Orange, they bend round the gneiss and unite, so that the fibrolite band is only a somewhat more altered form of the same series we have already described.

THE ERUPTIVE ROCKS OF THE OLDER SERIES.

Granite.—The rock we have described as gneiss is very commonly called granite, and, indeed, much of it, especially the fine quarry stone of the western band is, in the largest blocks, so entirely free from any parallel arrangement of its constituents that it quite exactly matches the more technical definition of granite. In the quarry, however, these blocks are seen to be exceptional and to graduate into the banded gneiss, which is interbedded with limestone and other rocks in such a way as to forbid us to assign to the whole a purely eruptive origin. We sometimes call such rocks bedded granites, or granite-gneisses, to distinguish them from those granites which are distinctly intruded at a later time, and in a plastic state, among the strata where they are found. The infelicity of the nomenclature matches pretty exactly the complexity of the subject.

Across Goshen, Williamsburg and Westhampton, a great portion of the surface is taken up by desolate areas of a coarse granite, consisting uniformly of quartz, orthoclase and muscovite, with rarely a little tourmaline.

In some smaller and yet massive dykes of the same rock, further west, in Chesterfield, Goshen and Huntington, are subordinate portions of abnormal constitution chemically, and, as a result, also mineralogically. These contain albite, var cleavelandite, tourmaline, vars indicolite, and rubellite, spodumene, columbite, cassiterite, zircon, microlite, beryl, tryphyllite and uranite, a most interesting association of rare minerals, which have for many years made " Clark's Ledge," the " Barras farm " and Norwich Hill places well known to mineralogists everywhere.

The Syenite.— Occupying the southwestern quarter of Belchertown is a great rounded mass of a dark eruptive rock, called syenite by President Hitchcock, which was originally a diallage granite that has now by the change of the diallage into hornblende and on into biotite come to be largely a hornblende biotite granite. It is a rather coarse, granular, dark-grey, or at times slightly amethystine rock. Under the microscope the change of the diallage to hornblende and biotite can be very clearly traced. Its contact phenomena—the changes it has wrought in the surrounding rocks with which it came in contact—are of the most interesting description.

The mica schist, the newest rock of the series described above, contains everywhere a small amount of fibrolite of the exceeding fine fibrous variety, but as it comes in contact with the syenite and sends a projection far out into the eruptive rock—from which large fragments are wholly separated and float in the once molten mass—it becomes a coarsely crystalline fibrolite schist, abounding in large crystals of garnet and fibrolite. The fire stone below is changed into a compact quartzite, the hornblende schist into a coarse pyroxenite, and in one case, where a large mass of the schist is wholly enclosed in the syenite, into a very coarse biotite-pyroxene rock.

On the west side of the valley, bordering the lake terrace, from Elizabeth rock in Northampton north through Hatfield, where it is called "The Rocks," is a broad, barren ridge of the same rocks, which, in the next town to the north, has greatly altered the argillite, a rock which is newer than any in the crystalline series we have described. This shows that the syenite is newer than the crystalline series.

These two great outcrops of eruptive rock stretch, one along the eastern and one along the western border of the broad Connecticut valley, and along the rest of these borders extend lines, or rather narrow bands, of crooked and faulted rocks impregnated with silica and hematite, which seem to mark two lines of fault within which the crystalline rocks sank down to form the deep valley.

MINERAL VEINS.

At Loudville and in Hatfield are interesting veins of quartz and barite, carrying galena, zinc blende, copper and iron pyrites. The gangue was at first largely fluor and calcite, especially at Loudville, but the fissure seems to have been opened a second time, and to have been a channel for the passage of heated waters, by which this earlier gangue was removed and replaced by quartz, often in pseudomorphs, after calcite and fluor, which are now scarcely found in the vein. At Loudville, as products of surface change in a third period, many rare minerals occur, as cerusite, pyromorphite, wulfenite, stolzite and cotunnite.

The middle period of chemical activity in the vein mentioned above may have occurred during the period of volcanic activity, in the Triassic period, or when the final tilting of the sandstone took place, as similar mineral veins occur in the sandstone at Turner's Falls.

THE TRIAS.

If one will picture the broad valley from Pelham across to Westhampton as a half-mile deeper than the present river and imagine the rocky surface of the uplands as a half-mile higher than now, with the canal-like channel filled by the fjord waters to a height above the level of Mt. Holyoke, while the bordering streams swept sand and gravel into the basin and strong currents spread the material over its bottom, he will have a rude outline of Triassic times in the valley. A long list of animals now extinct and often extremely large ; reptiles, amphibians, fishes, crustaceans and insects left their tracks upon the forming sand flats, and these, hardened in the stone, have been recovered and described in a volume which, with the great collections of the remains themselves, is one of the many monuments to the labor and genius of President Hitchcock.

Coarse sands from the granites of the west and the gneisses of the east were for a long time swept into the basin, filling it to a thickness of above half a mile certainly, and how much more I do not know. The Belden artesian well, at Northampton, is sunk wholly in these lower sandstones to a depth of over 3,000 feet. Then came the eruption of an enormous sheet of lava, which I imagine came from a fissure parallel to and about a mile southeast of the crest of the Holyoke-Tom range. It is the eroded edge of this sheet which, canted up a little by a subsequent disturbance, makes the crest of the above range.

The deposition of the coarse granitic sands continued for a time after this overflow, and covered the great bed; and then came a second period of more explosive volcanic activity, which spread a great quantity of volcanic ashes and bombs across the bottom of the basin, followed by additional deposition of sand, now finer, and of deep red color from the abundant iron derived from the volcanic dust. These ashes made what we call a volcanic ash or tufa bed, and being tipped up a little with the trap or lava bed of the Holyoke range and much eroded, its outcrop now makes a band along the southeast foot of the mountain, about a mile from its crest, extending from Belchertown to Holyoke.

There followed a third period of volcanic activity, by which a row of small craters opened along the earlier fissure and formed a line of small volcanoes, approximately coincident with the present outcrop of the tufa bed given above. Only the roots of these volcanoes are now preserved, as rounded plugs of lava in the sandstone, two in Belchertown, one far southeast of the east end of the Holyoke range, three in Granby, two in South Hadley, of which the westernmost is of exceptional size and its uncovered portion seems to have expanded beneath the superincumbent sandstones as a true laccolite, and one, finally, across the river in Northampton, north of Smith's Ferry.

The deposition of sand continued, and a series of travertine depositing springs marked the close of the volcanic activity, and formed a quite continuous stratum of limestone in the later sandstones.

The lava, called diabase, dolerite and basalt by different authors with different opinions, we may still conveniently call trap. It is a basic lava, made up of plagioclose, augite and magnetite, a little olivene and glass, and uniformly containing a green chloritic mineral (delessite) as a result of decomposition. Percolating waters have taken up the results of decomposition and deposited them in fine crystals in cavities and fissures in the rock, and when fresh exposures occur, as at the railroad excavations at Cheapside, in Deerfield, many rare and beautiful minerals (zeolites) are found. The great bed of lava of the Holyoke range is compact and fine-grained below, and has baked the sandstones on which it rests, and is porous from escaping gases above, while the volcanic plugs are compact in every part and bake the sandstones everywhere at their contact.

The percolating waters cemented the sands to sandstones, while on the recession of the waters of the fjord the streams from either side ran out over the abandoned bottom of the bay and gathered in a main trunk, which ran

down the middle of the basin to the south and commenced to lower the surface of the sandstones by erosion. This surface was then above the level of
the Holyoke range, and the trap bed was wholly concealed beneath. The
course of the ancient Connecticut being thus determined by the contour of
the fjord bottom, it cut lower and lower, and in time exposed and cut down
through the trap sheet, forming the notch through which the present Connecticut flows, while the more rapid erosion of the sandstones carved out the Holyoke–Mt. Tom range.

Of the long period occupied by this erosion, rich in event as it was elsewhere, no abiding record was made in the valley; but at the approach of the
ice period the surface of the valley nad about its present contour, only over
the uplands there were rounded surfaces of deeply-rotted granites and gneisses,
and in the valley the sandstone surface north of the Holyoke range was, I
surmise, about as high as it is south of the mountain at present, that is, two
or three hundred feet above the meadows.

THE GLACIAL PERIOD.

The work of the ice was twofold. Over the uplands it planed off the
deeply-rotted rock, so that now, when ledges are exposed, they are generally
of compact and fresh rock. It planed deeply into the sandstone, especially
north of the Holyoke range, and formed the serrated outline of the range itself.
On the other hand, as a river builds up bars, it built up great rounded hills
of stony clay, of peculiar and regular shape and great density from the great
pressure of the ice. Hence the term "hardpan." These hills are very naturally called "hog backs." They are semi-circular when seen from the direction of motion of the ice, and semi-eliptical when seen at right angles thereto.
They cluster around Northampton (Round Hill) and Amherst (Castor and
Pollux). Finally, on its melting, the mass of the material being moved along
beneath the ice, with that which had gathered in and on it, was dumped in a
confused mass of clay, stones and boulders, forming the characteristic "glacial landscape" which everywhere marks our hill towns, yielding a rocky soil,
durable, but difficult of cultivation.

THE FLOOD PERIOD.

The ice which covered the county, covered also all New England and all
its mountains, and moved southeast to the sea. On melting, its front moved
back northwest across the county, with many readvances. At a railroad cutting at the camp-meeting grounds at Northampton, I found evidence of three.

Thus the abundant waters found the water-ways obstructed by the ice and
its deposits and changed by its erosions, and the re-establishment of the
drainage was accompanied by many strange and temporary streams and lakes,
most of which extend too far beyond the limits of the county to receive treat-

ment here. For instance, the ice retreating from southeast to northwest, passed *down* the tributaries of the east side of the valleys, setting free their head waters first, and for a long time clogging their mouths and preventing their waters from freely entering the main valley, while on the west it retreated *up* the valleys. So on the east the waters were dammed back in lakes and escaped south over the lowest col, while on the west the tributary valleys were simply well scoured out by the floods. Thus the ice obstructed the narrow passage between Palmer and Three Rivers, and the waters were deflected southwardly through the deep Munson valley into the Housatonic basin.

Thus the ice rested against the entrance to the large upland basin in Pelham and formed a lake into which great bodies of sand were brought, which now lie more than 800 feet above the sea. A little later it clogged the mouth of Miller's river far to the north, and a great volume of water passed south through New Salem, Greenwich, Enfield and Ware, transporting great bodies of sand and gravel to make the broad sand plains of the flat Greenwich valley, which are continuous from Orange to Palmer.

THE CONNECTICUT LAKE.

Upon the disappearance of the ice from this section of the valley, the great volume of the waters of its melting sustained a lake, which stretched in width to the full limits of the valley, as we have given them, in length from Mt. Toby to the foot of Holyoke, and sent a broad lobe out round Mt. Tom, across Easthampton and Southampton, and on south. Its height was 300 feet above the sea and 200 above low water of the present Connecticut.

The Long Plain in Leverett, North Amherst station, the Bay road, the south spur of Mt. Warner, the Florence plain, and West Farms, are level portions of its shore flats. The first and last two are great deltas sent out into its waters. In all its deeper waters the flat, laminated clays were being deposited, while the sands of the deltas were extending out from the shore. Each layer of the clay, on an average of two-fifths of an inch thick, represents a year's deposit. The clays are, at the Northampton bridge, above 120 feet thick, and at East Street bridge above fifty feet, which would give numbers for the duration of the lake favoring the idea that the glacial period was not more than 10,000 years ago, one of the shortest estimates.

In these clays I have found an abundant glacial flora, proving that the lake succeeded immediately to the ice, and I have found indications of several re-advances of the ice ploughing up the sands of the lake.

Within the limits we have assigned to the lake, the present surface of the ground is the old lake bottom, with all its bars and ridges. A period was set to the life of the lake before it had been fully silted up, and the flooded waters subsided with remarkable rapidity to nearly the present dimensions of the Connecticut. Only the meadows represent the area over which the river has swung since its shrinkage, building up their broad, flat surfaces of fine,

3*

rich, alluvial soil by the accumulated contribution of many freshets. Mean-dering thus across its meadows, the stream has formed seven great "oxbows," three in Hatfield and four in Northampton, and then cut off six of these, two within the period of settlement. It has formed them all on its western side, betraying thus a tendency to wear more on its right bank than on its left, and this is much more strongly seen in all its tributaries as they pass across the meadows. This is believed to be due to the influence of the earth's rotation.

The great range of sand dunes which stretch across Hadley, east of the meadows, and dot the Hatfield plain, the peat and bog ore filling of the swamps, deserve notice, with the newly formed islands and the extensive ero-sions of the river, as the last geological objects and agencies of the valley.

---

*CHAPTER III.

Botany of Hampshire County — Introductory Remarks—Cata-logue of Plants Growing Wild within Thirty Miles of Amherst.

WHEN the present publishers applied to me for an article on the botany of Hampshire county, I had no idea of giving to the article the form it has finally taken. It was, however, a part of my plan to give a list of plants found growing wild within the limits of the county. Regret being expressed by my botanical acquaintances that the area of the flora should be so restricted, it has, with the consent of the publishers, been made to include that portion of Central New England within thirty miles of Amherst. The list therefore includes a number of plants not yet known to have been found in Hampshire county. Still the number of which it can be said that they probably do not grow within the county, is extremely small.

Two such lists have already been published,—Hitchcock's *Catalogue of Plants growing without cultivation in the vicinity of Amherst College*, contrib-uted.to by a number of the best botanists of the time (1829), and *A Cata-logue of Plants growing without cultivation within thirty miles of Amherst College*, by the late Prof. Edward Tuckerman, of Amherst College, in collab-oration with the late Charles C. Frost, of Brattleboro, Vt. Another prom-inent contributor to the latter list was Prof. H. G. Jesup, now of Dartmouth College. It is unnecessary to say that the preparation of the present list would have been impossible but for the labors of these predecessors in the same field.

---

*Prepared by Prof. N. A. Cobb, of Williston Seminary, Easthampton.

The first of these catalogues was long since out of date. The second excellent and well-known catalogue, with which the present list is very nearly co-extensive, was published in 1875. The publication, at a more recent date, of a number of important American works on systematic botany has rendered it desirable that a list should be made out more in accordance with the material thus made accessible. Dr. Gray's *Synoptical Flora of North America,* (Gamopetalæ, 1886), which should be in the hands of every working botanist, makes changes that should become known to the students of his *Manual;* Lesquereux & James's *Manual of the Mosses of North America* (1884) becomes at once the standard American bryological work ; the publication, in 1882, of the first part of the lamented Prof. Tuckerman's *Synopsis of the North American Lichens*, makes accessible for the first time to the general student some adequate account of our more conspicuous lichens ; the publication (1884) of Underwood's *Descriptive Catalogue of the North American Hepaticæ,* brings within the reach of all a systematic account of our liverworts. All these works make numerous changes in the nomenclature and arrangement of their respective departments. In addition to all this, the lapse of time has inevitably brought to light, in a district where botany is so assiduously cultivated, a number of species not before known as growing within its limits.

That this list compensates for the loss of a second edition of his catalogue, which, had Prof. Tuckerman's life been spared, we should have had from his own hand, is not to be hoped ; but that, in embodying the changes suggested by the above mentioned facts, it proceeds on the plan he would have adopted, is unquestionable.

Attention is called to the following points : The Phanerogamia are referred by page to Gray's *Manual;* but the Gamopetalæ are arranged according to the *Synoptical Flora of North America*, and the Polypetalæ according to Mr. Sereno Watson's useful *Bibliographical Index to North American Botany.* Where later ivestigations, either structural or bibliographical, have resulted in changing the name of a plant, the most recent name is used, (the *Manual* synonym being enclosed in parenthesis). The Filices and Ophioglossaceæ are referred by page to Gray's *Manual;* but the arrangement and nomenclature is that most recently adopted by our American authority, Prof. D. C. Eaton, of Yale University. The Musci, Hepaticæ and Lichenes are referred by page to the works hereinbefore mentioned, and the arrangement and nomenclature is that adopted in those works respectively. Those lichens not included in Tuckerman's *Synopsis*, are referred to the same author's *Genera Lichenum.* The Fungi are referred by page to Cooke's *Hand-book of the British Fungi*, which, unsatisfactory and hard to procure as it is, is the best systematic work available for the purpose. The arrangement is different from that adopted in the English work and is believed to be better.

Plants whose names are entered without annotation are to be understood as at least not uncommon. Where plants are known from only a few stations, the stations are generally given, often with the authority. Introduced species are indicated by s p a c e d t y p e.

The lists of Oophyta, Zygophyta and Protophyta make no pretensions to completeness. I have simply named such forms as I have chanced to notice while searching for specimens for my classes in biology.

My thanks are due to Mrs. Edward Tuckerman for placing at my disposal Prof. Tuckerman's notes on additional species; to Miss Henrietta Hooker, of Mt. Holyoke Seminary, for new South Hadley stations; to Dr. Asa Gray and to Prof. D. C. Eaton, for aid and correction; to the Springfield Botanical Society, especially to W. H. Chapin, M. D., for the communication of specimens of a number of species new to our area; to my wife, to whom I owe the entire rearrangement of the Gamopetalæ; and to many others, whose names will be found associated with the species upon which they have furnished notes; and I take this opportunity of expressing to all my obligations. This list must be regarded as a general contribution rather than as the work of any one individual, and if this rearranged and augmented form awakens any new interest in a favorite science, I shall be glad to have been able to make this very slight contribution to the natural history of the region where for twelve years I have botanized with so much interest.

PHANEROGAMIA.

[The numbers refer to the pages of Gray's *Manual of Botany*, edition of 1868.]

Dicotyledons or Exogens.

Angiospermæ.

POLYPETALAE.

RANUNCULACEÆ.

Clematis, L. VIRGIN's BOWER.
  verticillaris, DC. Mts. Tom and Holyoke; Greenfield. 35.
  V i o r n a, L. LEATHER-FLOWER. Brattleboro, *Frost.* 36.
  Virginiana, L. VIRGIN'S BOWER. 36.
Anemone, L. WIND FLOWER.
  cylindrica, Gray. Mt. Toby, Royalston, etc. 37.
  Virginiana, L. 37.
  dichotoma, L. South Hadley, *G. L. Goodale.* (A. Pennsylvanica, L., Man.) 37.
  nemorosa, L. WIND-FLOWER. 38.
Hepatica, L. HEPATICA. LIVERWORT. (Hepatica triloba, Chaix., Man.) 38.

acutiloba, Law. HEPATICA. LIVERWORT. (Hepatica acutiloba, DC., Man.) 38.
Thalictrum, Tourn. MEADOW-RUE.
  anemonoides, Michx. RUE-ANEMONE. 38.
  dioicum, L. 39.
  Cornuti, L. 39.
Ranunculus, L. CROWFOOT.
  aquatilis, L., var. trichophyllus, Gray. 40.
  multifidus, Pursh. 40.
  alismæfolius, Geyer. 41.
  Flammula, L., var. reptans, Meyer. 41.
  abortivus, L. 42.
  sceleratus, L. 42.
  recurvatus, Poir. 42.
  Pennsylvanicus, L. 42.
  fascicularis, Muhl. 43.
  repens, L. 43.

b u l b o s u s, L. BUTTERCUPS.
43.
a c r i s, L. 43.
Caltha, L. MARSH MARIGOLD.
palustris, L. COWSLIP. 44.
Coptis, Salisb. GOLDTHREAD.
trifolia, Salisb. 45.
Aquilegia, Tourn. COLUMBINE.
Canadensis, L. 45.
Actæa, L. BANE-BERRY.
spicata, L., var. rubra, Ait. 47.
alba, Bigel, 47.
Cimicifuga, L. BLACK SNAKE-ROOT.
racemosa, Nutt. Goshen, *E.*
Hitchcock. 48.

MAGNOLIACEÆ.

Liriodendron, L
Tulipifera, L. T U L I p-T R E E.
Deerfield, Springfield, etc. 50.

MENISPERMACEÆ.

Menispermum, L. MOONSEED.
Canadense, L. 51.

BERBERIDACEÆ.

Berberis, L. BARBERRY.
v u l g a r i s, L. 52.
Caulophyllum, Michx.
thalictroides, Michx. PAPPOOSE-
ROOT, 53.
Podophyllum, L.
peltatum, L. MAY-APPLE. S.
Amherst, *Hitchcock.* 54.

NYMPHÆACEÆ.

Brasenia, Schreb.
peltata, Pursh. 55.
Nymphæa, Tourn.
odorata, Ait. WATER-LILY. 56.
Nuphar, Smith.
advena, Ait. YELLOW WATER-
LILY. 57.
luteum, Smith. Oxbow, *Jesup.*
57.
pumilum, Smith. (N. luteum,
var. pumilum, Gray, Man.) 37.

SARRACENIACEÆ.

Sarracenia, Tourn. PITCHER-PLANT.
purpurea, L. SIDE-SADDLE FLOW-
ER. 58.

PAPAVERACEÆ.

Chelidonium, L.
m a j u s, L. CELANDINE. 60.

Sanguinaria, Dill.
Canadensis, L. BLOOD-ROOT. 60.

FUMARIACEÆ.

Adlumia, Raf.
cirrhosa, Raf. Mt. Toby, etc. 61.
Dicentra, Bork.
Cucullaria, DC. DUTCHMAN'S
BREECHES. North Amherst.
Northampton. 61.
Canadensis,DC. SQUIRREL-CORN.
Conway, *G. L. Goodale.* 61.
Corydalis, Vent.
glauca, Pursh. 61.
Fumaria, L.
officinalis, L. FUMITORY. 62.

CRUCIFERÆ.

Nasturtium, R. Br. CRESS.
officinale, R. Br. TRUE WA-
TER-CRESS. Deerfield. 64.
s y l v e s t r e, R. Br. School meadow, Hadley. 64.
palustre, DC. 64.
Armoracia, Fries. HORSE-RAD-
ISH. 65.
Dentaria, L. TOOTHWORT.
diphylla, Michx. 65.
laciniata, Muhl. Deerfield, *Hitchcock.* S. Hadley, one season;
Miss Hooker. 66.
Cardamine, L. LADY'S SMOCK.
rhomboidea, DC. 66.
hirsuta, L., & var. sylvatica,
Gray. 67.
Arabis, L. ROCK-CRESS.
hirsuta, Scop. 68.
lævigata, Poir. 68.
Canadensis. L. SICKLE-POD. 68.
perfoliata, Lam. Spencer, *Cobb.*
69.
Barbarea, R. Br. WINTER-CRESS.
vulgaris, R. Br. 69.
Erysimum, L. TREACLE-MUSTARD.
cheiranthoides, L. Mt. Toby,
Jesup. Brattleboro, *Frost.*
69.
Sisymbrium, L.
officinale, Scop. HEDGE-MUS-
TARD. 70.
Brassica, Tourn.
alba, Gray. WHITE MUSTARD.
70.

nigra, Koch. TRUE MUSTARD.
71.
Alyssum, Tourn.
calycinum, L. Amherst, rare.
72.
Camelina, Crantz.
sativa, Crantz. Amherst. 73.
Capsella, Vent.
Bursa-pastoris, Moench.
SHEPHERD'S-PURSE. 73.
Lepidium, L. PEPPERWORT.
Virginicum, L. 74.
campestre, R. Br. Amherst,
Clark. 74.
Raphanus, L. RADISH.
Raphanistrum, L. CHARLOCK.
75.

CISTACEÆ.

Helianthemum, Tourn. FROST-WORT.
Canadense. Michx. 80.
Lechea, L. PIN-WEED.
major, Michx. 81.
minor, Walt., Lam. 82.

VIOLACEÆ.

Viola, L. VIOLET.
rotundifolia, Michx. 77.
lanceolata, L. 77.
primulæfolia, L 77.
blanda, Willd. WHITE VIOLET. 77
odorata, L. Sparingly about
greenhouses and gardens. 77.
cucullata, Ait., & var. palmata,
Gray. COMMON BLUE VIOLET.
78.
sagittata, Ait. 78.
pedata, L. BIRD-FOOT VIOLET.
78.
canina, L., var. sylvestris, Regel.
DOG VIOLET. 79.
rostrata, Muhl. 79.
striata, Ait. Amherst, *Hitchcock.*
79. .
Canadensis, L. 79.
pubescens, Ait. DOWNY YELLOW
VIOLET. 79.
tricolor, L. PANSY. About
houses. 80.

POLYGALACEÆ.

Polygala, Tourn. MILK-WORT.
sanguinea, L. 121.
verticillata, L. 122.

polygama, Walter. BITTER PO-
LYGALA. 122.
paucifolia, Willd. FRINGED PO-
LYGALA. FLOWERING WINTER-
GREEN. 122.

CARYOPHYLLACEÆ.

Dianthus, L.
Armeria, L. DEPTFORD PINK.
Shores of Conn. river. 88.
Saponaria, L.
officinalis, L. SOAPWORT.
BOUNCING BET. 88.
Silene, L. CATCHFLY.
inflata, Smith. BLADDER CAM-
PION. Amherst, Spencer, etc.
89.
Pennsylvanica, Michx. 89.
antirrhina, L. 90.
noctiflora, L. 90.
Lychnis, Tourn.
dioica, L. RED CAMPION.
Roadsides.
Githago, Lam. COCKLE. 90.
Flos-cuculi, L.
Arenaria, L. SANDWORT.
serpyllifolia, L. 91.
stricta, Michx. 91.
lateriflora, L. 91.
Stellaria, L STITCHWORT.
media, Smith. CHICKWEED. 92.
longifolia, Muhl. 92.
graminea, L. Amherst, rare,
Tuckerman.
uliginosa, Murr. S. Deerfield,
Jesup. 92.
borealis, Bigel. 93.
Cerastium, L. MOUSE-EAR CHICK-
WEED.
viscosum, L. 94.
nutans, Raf. Hadley, etc. 94.
arvense, L. 94.
Sagina, L. PEARLWORT.
procumbens, L. 94.
Lepigonum, Fries.
rubrum, Fries. (Spergularia rubra, Presl., var. compestris,
Gray, Man.) 95.
Spergula, L. SPURREY.
arvensis, L. 96.
PARONYCHIEÆ.
Anychia, Michx.
dichotoma, Michx. 96.

Scleranthus, L. KNAWEL.
  annuus, L. 96.
    PORTULACACEÆ.
Portulaca, Tourn.
  oleracea, L. PURSLANE 98.
  grandiflora, Hook. Occasionally spontaneous. 98.
Claytonia, L. SPRING BEAUTY.
  Virginica, L. 98.
  Caroliniana, Michx. 98.
    HYPERICACEÆ.
Hypericum, L. ST. JOHN'S-WORT.
  pyramidatum, Ait. 84.
  ellipticum, Hook. 85.
  perforatum, L. 85.
  corymbosum, Muhl. 85.
  mutilum, L. 85.
  Canadense, L. & var. majus, Gray.
    Conway, *Jesup.* 86.
  Sarothra, Michx. 86.
Elodes, Adans.
  Virginica ,Nutt. 86.
    MALVACEÆ.
Malva, L. MALLOW.
  rotundifolia, L. DWARF MALLOW. 99.
  sylvestris, L. OFFICINAL or HIGH MALLOW. 99.
  moschata, L. MUSK MALLOW. 99.
Abutilon, Tourn. INDIAN MALLOW.
  Avicennae, GAERTN. VELVET LEAF. 101.
    TILIACEÆ.
Tilia, L. LIME-TREE.
  Americana, L. BASSWOOD. 103.
    LINACEÆ.
Linum, L. FLAX.
  Virginianum, L. FLAX. 104.
    GERANIACEÆ.
Geranium, L. CRANE'S-BILL.
  maculatum, L. 107.
  Carolinianum, L. 107.
  Robertianum, L. HERB ROBERT. 107.
Impatiens, L. BALSAM.
  pallida, Nutt. PALE TOUCH-ME-NOT. 108.
  fulva, Nutt. SPOTTED TOUCH-ME-NOT. 108.

Oxalis, L. WOOD-SORREL.
  Acetosella, L. TRUE WOOD-SORREL. Conway, and northward. 109.
  violacea, L. Amherst, and southward. 109.
  corniculata, L., var. stricta, Sav. (O. stricta, L., Man.) 109.
    RUTACEÆ.
Xanthoxylum, Colden.
  Americanum, Mill. PRICKLY ASH. Sunderland, *Hitchcock;* Norwottuck, *Clark.* 110.
Ptelia, L. HOP-TREE.
  trifoliata, L. Easthampton, *Cobb.* 110.
    ILICINEÆ.
Ilex, L., Gray. HOLLY.
  verticillata, Gray. 307.
  lævigata, Gray. Belchertown ponds, *Jesup.* 307.
Nemopanthes, Raf.
  Canadensis, DC. MOUNTAIN HOLLY. 307.
    CELASTRACEÆ.
Celastrus, L. CLIMBING STAFF-TREE.
  scandens, L. 116.
    RHAMNACEÆ.
Rhamnus, Tourn. BUCKTHORN.
  cathartica, L. TRUE BUCKTHORN. Roadsides, Leverett. 114.
  alnifolia, L'Her. Deerfield, *Hitchcock.* 115.
Ceanothus, L. NEW JERSEY TEA.
  Americanus, L. 115.
    VITACEÆ.
Vitis, Tourn. VINE.
  Labrusca, L. FOX GRAPE-VINE. 112.
  æstivalis, Michx. SUMMER GRAPE-VINE. 112.
  riparia, Michx. 113 & 679.
Ampelopsis, Michx.
  quinquefolia, Michx. VIRGINIA CREEPER. WOODBINE. 113.
    SAPINDACEÆ.
Staphylea, L.
  trifolia, L. BLADDER NUT. 117.

28   HAMPSHIRE COUNTY.

Acer, Tourn. MAPLE.
    Pennsylvanicum, L. STRIPED MA-
        PLE. 119.
    spicatum, Lam. MOUNTAIN MA-
        PLE. 119.
    saccharinum, Wang. & var. ni-
        grum, Torr. & Gray. SUGAR
        MAPLE. 119.
    dasycarpum, Ehrh. SILVER MA-
        PLE. 119.
    rubrum, L. RED MAPLE. 119.

ANACARDIACEÆ

Rhus, L. SUMAC.
    typhina, L. 111.
    glabra, L. 111.
    copallina, L. 111.
    venenata, DC. POISON SUMAC.
        DOG WOOD. 111.
    Toxicodendron, L. POISON IVY.
        111.

LEGUMINOSÆ.

Lupinus, Tourn. LUPINE.
    perennis, L. 126.
Crotalaria, L.
    sagittalis, L. 126.
Trifolium, L. TREFOIL.
    arvense, L. HARE'S-FOOT TRE-
        FOIL. 127.
    pratense, L. RED CLOVER.
        127.
    hybridum, L. PINK CLOVER.
        Roadsides, Spencer, North-
        ampton, etc. Cobb.
    repens, L. WHITE CLOVER. 127.
    agrarium, L. HOP TREFOIL.
        YELLOW CLOVER. 127.
    procumbens, L. LOW HOP-
        TREFOIL. YELLOW CLOVER.
        128.
Melilotus, Tourn. MELILOT.
    officinalis, Willd. 128.
    alba, Lam. Roadsides. 128.
Medicago, L. MEDICK.
    sativa, L. LUCERNE. Rare, G.
        L. Goodale. 128.
    lupulina, L. NONESUCH. Rare.
        128.
Robinia, L. LOCUST TREE.
    Pseudacacia, L. 131.
    viscosa, Vent. 131.
Tephrosia, Pers.

Virginiana, Pers. AMER. GOAT'S
    RUE. 131.
Desmodium, DC. TICK-TREFOIL.
    nudiflorum, DC. 135.
    acuminatum, DC. 135.
    rotundifolium, DC. 135.
    canescens, DC. 135.
    cuspidatum, Hook. 136.
    Dillenii, Darlingt. 136.
    paniculatum, DC. 136.
    Canadense, DC. 136.
    rigidum, DC. 136.
    Marilandicum, Boott. 137.
Lespedeza, Michx. BUSH-CLOVER.
    repens, Barton, (L. procumbens,
        Michx., Man. is merged in
        this). 137.
    violacea, Pers. 137.
    hirta, Ell. 138.
    capitata, Michx. 138.
Vicia, Tourn. VETCH.
    sativa, L. 138.
    Cracca, L. Deerfield, Tucker-
        man's Cat. Easthampton,
        Cobb. 139.
Lathyrus, L. VETCHLING.
    pratensis, L. W. Springfield,
        A. P. Foster. 140.
Apios, Boerh.
    tuberosa, Moench. GROUND-
        NUT. 140.
Amphicarpæa, Ell. HOG PEA-NUT.
    monoica, Ell. TWINING THREAD-
        WORT. 142.
Baptisia, Vent.
    tinctoria, R. Br. WILD INDIGO.
        143.
Cassia, L.
    Marilandica, L. WILD SENNA.
        144.
    nictitans, L. Hadley, Easthamp-
        ton, common. 144.

ROSACEÆ.

Prunus, Tourn. PLUM. CHERRY.
    Americana, Marsh. WILD PLUM-
        TREE. 148.
    pumila, L. DWARF CHERRY. 148.
    Pennsylvanica, L. WILD RED
        CHERRY. 148.
    Virginiana, L. CHOKE CHERRY.
        148.
    serotina, Ehrh. WILD CHERRY.
        149.

Spiræa, L.
  salicifolia, L. MEADOW-SWEET.
  149.
  tomentosa, L. HARDHACK. 149.
Poterium, L., Gray. BURNET.
  Canadense, Benth. & Hook.
  Hadley, Sunderland, Brook-
  field, etc. 150.
Agrimonia, Tourn. AGRIMONY.
  Eupatoria, L. 151.
Geum, L. AVENS.
  album, Gmel. 152.
  Virginianum, L. 152.
  strictum, Ait. 152.
  rivale, L. WATER AVENS. 152.
Waldsteinia, Willd.
  fragarioides, Tratt. BARREN
  STRAWBERRY. 153.
Potentilla, L. CINQUEFOIL.
  Norvegica, L. 154.
  Canadensis, L. 154.
  argentea, L. 154.
  arguta, Pursh. 154.
  fruticosa, L. 155.
  tridentata, Soland. Hoosac Mt.;
  Mt. Wachusett. 155.
  palustris, Scop. Brattleboro,
  Frost. 155.
Fragaria, Tourn. STRAWBERRY.
  Virginiana, Duchesne. 155.
  vesca, L. Mt. Holyoke, etc. 156.
Rubus, Tourn. BRAMBLE.
  Dalibarda, L. Greenfield. Warwick, *Cobb.* (Dalibarda repens,
  L., Man.) 156
  odoratus, L. FLOWERING RASP-
  BERRY. 156.
  triflorus, Richards. 157.
  strigosus, Michx. RED RASP-
  BERRY. 157.
  occidentalis, L. BLACK RASP-
  BERRY. 157.
  villosus, Ait. HIGH BLACKBERRY.
  157.
  Canadensis, L. LOW BLACKBER-
  RY. 157.
  hispidus, L. 158.
Rosa, Tourn. ROSE.
  Carolina, L. SWAMP ROSE. 158.
  lucida, Ehrh. DWARF ROSE. 158.
  blanda, Ait. Mt. Holyoke. 159.
  rubiginosa, L. SWEET BRIAR.
  159.

Gallica, L. GARDEN ROSE.
  Roadsides, and fields.
  Cinnamomea, L. CINNAMON
  ROSE. Roadsides.
Cratægus, L. HAWTHORN.
  coccinea, L. 160.
  tomentosa, L., & var. punctata,
  Gray. 160.
  Crus-Galli, L. 160.
Pirus, L. PEAR. APPLE.
  arbutifolia, L. CHOKE-BERRY.
  161.
  Americana, DC. MOUNTAIN ASH.
  161.
Amelanchier, Medic. JUNE-BERRY.
  SERVICE-BERRY. SHAD-BUSH.
  Canadensis, Torr. & Gray &
  var. oblongiflora, Torr. & Gray.
  (var. Botryapium, Gray, Man.,
  is merged in the type). 162.

SAXIFRAGACEÆ.

Ribes. L. CURRANT. GOOSEBERRY·
  Cynosbati, L. Conway, War-
  wick, etc. 164.
  oxycanthoides, L. (R. hirtelium,
  Michx., Man.) 164.
  rotundifolium, Michx. West Riv-
  er Mt., *Hitchcock.* 164.
  prostratum, L'Her. SKUNK'S CUR-
  RANT. 165.
  floridum, L'Her. BLACK CUR-
  RANT. 165.
Parnassia, Tourn. GRASS OF PAR-
  NASSUS.
  Caroliniana, Michx. 167.
Saxifraga, L. SAXIFRAGE.
  Virginiensis, Michx. 168.
  Pennsylvanica, L. 168.
Mitella, Tourn. MITRE-WORT.
  diphylla, L. BISHOP'S CAP. 170.
  nuda, L. East Amherst, *Jesup.*
  170.
Tiarella, L. FALSE MITRE-WORT.
  cordifolia, L. 170.
Chrysosplenium, Tourn. GOLDEN SAX-
  IFRAGE.
  Americanum, Schwein. 171.

CRASSULACEÆ.

Penthorum, Gronov. STONE-CROP.
  sedoides, L. 171.
Sedum, Tourn. STONE-CROP.

reflexum, L. Roadside, Leverett, *Jesup.*
Telephium, L. ORPINE. 172.

DROSERACEÆ.

Drosera, L. SUN-DEW.
rotundifolia, L. 82.
Angliana, Huds. (D. longifolia, L., Man.) 82.

HAMAMELACEÆ.

Hamamelis, L.
Virginina, L. WITCH-HAZEL. 173.
Liquidambar, L.
Styraciflua, L. SWEET GUM. Northampton, *Eaton.* 174.

HALORAGEÆ.

Myriophyllum, Vaill. WATER-MIL-FOIL.
verticillatum, L. 175.
ambiguum, Nutt. Hadley, *Jesup.* 175.
tenellum, Bigel. 175.
Proserpinaca, L. MERMAID WEED.
palustris, L. 175.

MELASTOMACEÆ.

Rhexia, L. DEER GRASS.
Virginica, L. Leverett & Shutesbury. 181.

LYTHRACEÆ.

Ammannia, Houston.
humilis, Michx. Springfield, *W. H. Chapin.* 182.
Lythrum, L. PURPLE LOOSESTRIFE.
Salicaria, L. Roadsides, etc. 183.
Nesæa, Commers.
verticillata, H. B. K. Belchertown & Sunderland. 183.

ONAGRACEÆ.

Circæa, Tourn. ENCHANTER'S NIGHTSHADE.
Lutetiana, L. 176.
alpina, L. 176.
Epilobium, L. WILLOW-HERB.
spicatum, Lam. (E. angustifolium, L., Man.) 177.
palustre, L., var. lineare, Gray. 177.
molle, Torr. 178.
coloratum, Muhl. 178.

Œnothera, L EVENING PRIMROSE.
biennis. L. TREE-PRIMROSE. 178
fruticosa, L. 179.
pumila, L. 179.
Ludwigia, L. FALSE LOOSESTRIFE.
alternifolia, L. SEED BOX. Hadley. 180.
palustris, Ell. 181.

CUCURBITACEÆ.

Sicyos, L.
angulatus, L. SINGLE-SEED CUCUMBER. 186.
Echinocystis, Torr. & Gray.
lobata, Torr. & Gray. WILD BALSAM-APPLE. 187.

FICOIDEÆ.

(Caryophylleæ, Man.) 97.
Mollugo, L.
verticillata, L. 97.

UMBELLIFERÆ.

Hydrocotyle, Tourn. MARSH PENNY-WORT.
Americana, L. 189.
Sanicula, Tourn. BLACK SNAKEROOT.
Canadensis, L. 190.
Marilandica, L. SANICLE. 190.
Daucus, Tourn.
Carota, L. CARROT. 191.
Heracleum, L. COW-PARSNIP.
lanatum, Michx. 191.
Pastinaca, Tourn.
sativa, L. PARSNIP. 192.
Archangelica, Hoffm.
atropurpurea, Hoffm. ANGELICA. 193.
Thaspium, Nutt.
aureum, Nutt. 194.
Pimpinella, L.
integerrima, Benth & Hook. Montague, *J. L. Bennett.* (Zizia integerrima, DC., Man.) 195.
Cicuta, L. COW-BANE.
maculata, L. WATER-HEMLOCK. 196.
bulbifera, L. 196.
Sium, L.
cicutaefolium, Gmelin. (S. lineare, Michx., Man.) 196.
Berula, Koch.
angustifolia, Koch. (Sium angustifolium, L., Man.) 196.

Cryptotænia, DC.
    Canadensis, DC. HONEWORT.
    197.
Osmorrhiza, Raf. SWEET CICELY.
    longistylis, DC. 197.
    brevistylis, DC. 197.
Conium, L. HEMLOCK.
    maculatum, L. POISON HEM-
    LOCK. 198.

ARALIACEÆ.

Aralia, Tourn.
    racemosa, L. SPIKENARD. 199.
    hispida, Vent. 199.
    nudicaulis, L. WILD SARSAPA-
    RILLA. 199.
    quinquefolia, Decsne & Planch.
    GINSENG. 199.
    trifolia, Decsne & Planch. 199.

CORNACEÆ.

Cornus, Tourn. CORNEL.
    Canadensis, L. DWARF CORNEL.
    200.
    florida, L. DOGWOOD. 200.
    circinata, L'Her. 200.
    sericea, L. RED-OSIER. DOG-
    WOOD. 200.
    stolonifera, Michx. 200.
    paniculata, L'Her. 201.
    alternifolia, L. 201,
Nyssa, L. TUPELO.
    multiflora, Wang. SOUR GUM.
    201.

GAMOPETALAE.

CAPRIFOLIACEÆ.

Sambucus, Tourn. ELDER.
    racemosa, L. (S. pubens, Michx.
    Man) 205.
    Canadensis, L. COMMON ELDER.
    205.
Viburnum, L. ARROW-WOOD.
    lantanoides, Michx. HOBBLE-
    BUSH. 207.
    Opulus, L. HIGH CRANBERRY.
    207.
    acerifolium, L. MAPLE-LEAVED
    ARROW-WOOD. 207.
    dentatum, L. ARROW-WOOD. 206
    nudum, L. 206.
    Lentago, L. 206.
Triosteum, L.

perfoliatum, L. FEVER-WORT.
    205.
Linnæa, Gronov.
    borealis, Gronov. TWIN-FLOWER.
    202.
Lonicera, L. HONEYSUCKLE.
    caerulea, L. Deerfield, *Hitchcock.*
    Mt. Holyoke, *Miss Hooker.*
    204.
    oblongifolia, Hook. Brattleboro,
    Frost. 204.
    ciliata, Muhl. FLY-HONEYSUCKLE
    204.
    glauca, Hill. (L. parviflora, Lam.,
    Man.) 204.
Diervilla, Tourn.
    trifida, Moench. 205.

RUBIACEÆ.

Houstonia, Gronov.
    caerulea, L. BLUETS. 213.
Cephalanthus, L. BUTTON-BUSH.
    occidentalis, L. 211.
Mitchella, L. PARTRIDGE-BERRY.
    repens, L. 211.
Galium, L. BED-STRAW.
    verum, L. YELLOW BED-STRAW.
    Grass land, Amherst, *Tuckerm.*
    210.
    Aparine, L. CLEAVERS. GOOSE-
    GRASS. 208.
    pilosum, Ait. 209.
    circaezans, Michx. WILD LIQ-
    UORICE. 209.
    lanceolatum, Torr. WILD LIQ-
    UORICE. 210.
    boreale, L. NORTHERN BED-
    STRAW. 210.
    trifidum, L. (Includes var. tincto-
    rium, Man.) SMALL BEDSTRAW.
    209.
    asprellum, Michx. ROUGH BED-
    STRAW. 209.
    triflorum, Michx. SWEET-SCENT-
    ED BED-STRAW. 209.

DIPSACEÆ.

Dipsacus, Tourn.
    sylvestris, Mill. TEASLE. Road-
    sides, occasional. 215.

COMPOSITÆ.

Vernonia, Schreb.

Noveboracensis, Willd. IRON-
WEED. 222.
Mikania, Willd.
scandens, Willd. CLIMBING HEMP-
WEED. 227.
Eupatorium, Tourn.
purpureum, L. JOE PYE WEED.
TRUMPET-WEED. 225.
hyssopifolium, L. Mt. Toby,
Jesup. 225.
teucrifolium, Wild. 225.
perfoliatum, L. THOROUGHWORT.
226.
ageratoides, L. f. WHITE SNAKE-
ROOT. 226.
Liatris, Schreb.
scariosa, Willd. BLAZING STAR.
223.
Solidago, L. GOLDEN-ROD.
squarrosa, Muhl. Mts. Holyoke
& Toby. 239.
caesia, L., & var. axillaris, Gray,
Flora. 240.
latifolia, L. 240.
bicolor, L. 240.
puberula, Nutt. Pelham. 240.
odora, Ait. SWEET GOLDEN-ROD.
244.
uliginosa, Nutt. (See Hitchcock's
Cat., S. stricta, of which Dr.
Gray says: "Doubtless S. uliginosa, Nutt." S. stricta grows
from New Jersey southward on
pine barrens. For description
of uliginosa, Nutt., see *Syn.
Flo. N. A.,* p. 151.)
speciosa, Nutt. 240.
patula, Muhl. 243.
ulmifolia, Muhl. 243.
neglecta, Torr. & Gray. 243.
arguta, Ait. (Includes S. Muhlenbergii, Torr. & Gray, Man.)
243.
serotina, Ait. & var. gigantea,
Gray. (Includes S. gigantea,
Ait., Man.; but the plant hitherto described as gigantea, Ait.
is the present serotina, Ait. and
that described as serotina, Ait.
is the present var. gigantea,
Gray). 245.
Canadensis, L. (Includes S. altissima, L., Man.) 245.

nemoralis, Ait. 244.
rigida, L. S. Hadley, *Hitchcock.*
242.
lanceolata, L. 245.
Sericocarpus, Nees.
conyzoides, Nees. 228.
solidagineus, Nees. 228.
Aster, Tourn.
corymbosus, Ait. 228.
macrophyllus, L. 229.
Novæ Angliæ, L. 235.
patens, Ait. 230.
undulatus, L. 231.
cordifolius, L. 231.
lævis, L. (vars. lævigatus & cyaneus, Man., are merged in the
type, lævis.) 230.
ericoides, L. 232.
amethystinus, Nutt. Hadley,
Tuckerman. 234.
multiflorus, Ait. 232.
dumosus, L. (Includes A. miser,
L., Ait., Man., in part.) 232.
Tradescanti, L., partly. (Includes A. miser, L., Ait., Man.,
in part.) 232.
paniculatus, Lam. (A. simplex,
Willd., Man.) 233.
salicifolius, (Lam.?), Ait. (A. carneus, Nees., Man.) 233.
Novi-Belgii, L. (A. longifolius,
Lam., Man.) 233.
puniceus, L. 234.
umbellatus, Mill. (Diplopappus
umbellatus, Torr. & Gray,
Man.) 238.
linariifolius, L. (Diplopappus linariifolius. Hook., Man.) On a
piece of open, sterile ground in
Spencer, many plants having
pure white rays appeared for
one season,—never afterward.
Cobb. 238.
acuminatus, Michx. 235.
tenuifolius, L. 233.
Erigeron, L. FLEA-BANE.
bellidifolius, Muhl. 237.
Philadelphicus, L. 237.
annuus, Pers. 237.
strigosus, Muhl. (var. discoideum,
Robbins, Man., is merged in
the type, strigosus.) 237.

Canadensis, L. CANADA FLEA-
BANE. 236.
Antennaria, Gaertn., R. Br.
plantaginifolia, Hook. 269.
Anaphalis, DC. EVERLASTING.
margaritacea, Benth. & Hook.
(Antennaria margaritacea, R.
Br., Man.) 269.
Gnaphalium, L.
polycephalum, Michx. SWEET
EVERLASTING. 268.
decurrens, Ives. 268.
uliginosum, L. COMMON CUD-
WEED. 268.
Inula, L. ELECAMPANE.
Helenium, L. 246.
Ambrosia, Tourn.
trifida, L. 251.
artemisiæfolia, L. ROMAN WORM-
WOOD. PIGWEED. 251.
Xanthium, Tourn.
strumarium, L. COCKLE-BUR.
CLOT BUR. 252.
spinosum, L. Plainfield, *Porter*.
252.
Rudbeckia, L. CONE-FLOWER.
hirta, L. 254.
laciniata, L. 254.
Helianthus, L. SUNFLOWER.
giganteus, L. 256.
divaricatus, L. 257.
strumosus, L. 257.
decapetalus, L. 257.
tuberosus, L. JERUSALEM
ARTICHOKE. Northampton.
258.
Coreopsis, L.
tinctoria, Nutt. Roadsides,
rare. 259.
Bidens, Tourn. BUR-MARIGOLD.
frondosa, L. DEVIL'S PITCH-
FORKS. BEGGAR-TICKS. STICK-
TIGHTS. 261.
connata, Muhl. 261.
chrysanthemoides, Michx. 261.
Beckii, Torr. Agawam River,
Mrs. M. L. Owen. 261.
Anthemis, L.
Cotula, L. MAY-WEED. (Maruta
Cotula, DC., Man.) 265.
Achillea, Vaill.
Millefolium, L. YARROW. 265.
Chrysanthemum, Tourn., L.

Leucanthemum, L. (Leucan-
themum vulgare, Lam., Man.)
OX-EYE DAISY. WHITE-WEED.
265.
Balsamita, L. COSTMARY. Rare.
Tanacetum, Tourn.
vulgare, L. TANSY. 266.
Artemisia, Tourn., L.
Canadensis, Michx. 267.
vulgaris, L. MUG-WORT. 267.
Tussilago, Tourn.
Farfara, L. COLTSFOOT. 227.
Petasites, Tourn.
palmata, Gray. Sunderland,
Hitchcock.
Senecio, Tourn.
aureus, L. & var. Balsamitæ,
Torr & Gray. 271.
vulgaris, L. GROUNDSEL. Am-
herst. 271.
Erechtites, Raf. FIRE-WEED.
hieracifolia, Raf. 270.
Arctium, L.
Lappa, L. BURDOCK. (Lappa
officinalis, All., Man.) 275.
Cnicus, Tourn., L., partly. (Cirsium,
Tourn., Man.)
arvensis, Hoffm. CANADA
THISTLE. 274.
lanceolatus, Hoffm. COMMON
THISTLE. 273.
pumilus, Torr. 274.
altissimus, Willd. & var. discolor,
Gray. (The variety includes C.
discolor, Spreng., Man.) 273.
muticus, Pursh. 274.
Centaurea, L. KNAP-WEED.
nigra, L. Waste places, Hard-
wick, *Hitchcock.* 272.
Krigia, Schreb.
Virginica, Willd. DWARF DAN-
DELION. 276.
amplexicaulis, Nutt. (Cynthia
Virginica, Don., Man.) 276.
Cichorium, Tourn. CHICCORY. SUC-
CORY.
Intybus, L. Amherst, Green-
field, *Tuckerm.* N. Brookfield,
Cobb. 275.
Leontodon, L. partly, Juss.
autumnalis, L. FALL DANDE-
LION. Uncommon. Amherst.
Licester, *Cobb.* 276.

Hieracium, Tourn. HAWK-WEED.
  Canadense, Michx. 277.
  paniculatum, L. 277.
  venosum, L. RATTLESNAKE-
    WEED. 277.
  scabrum, Michx. 277.
  Gronovii, L. 277.
Prenanthes, Vaill. (Nabalus, Cass.,
    Man.)
  alba, L. 278.
  serpentaria, Pursh. (Nabalus
    Fraseri, DC., Man.) 278.
  altissima, L. 278.
Taraxacum, Haller.
  officinale, Weber. (T. Dens-
    leonis, Desf., Man.) DANDE-
    LION. 280.
Lactuca, Tourn.
  Canadensis, L. WILD LETTUCE.
    280.
  integrifolia, Bigel. (L. Canadense,
    var. integrifolia, Torr. & Gray,
    Man.) 281.
  leucophæa, Gray. (Mulgedium
    leucophæum, DC., Man.) 282.
Sonchus, Tourn. SOW THISTLE.
  oleraceus, L. 282.
  asper, Vill. 282.

              LOBELIACEÆ.

Lobelia, L.
  cardinalis, L. CARDINAL-FLOW-
    ER. 283.
  Dortmanna, L. 285.
  spicata, Lam. 284.
  Kalmii, L. S. Hadley, *Hitch-
    cock*. Near Greenfield, *F. G.
    Tuckerman*. 284.
  inflata, L. INDIAN TOBACCO. 283.

              CAMPANULACEÆ.

Specularia, Heist., A. DC. VENUS'S
    LOOKING-GLASS.
  perfoliata, A. DC. 286.
Campanula, Tourn. BELL FLOWER.
  rotundifolia, L. HARE-BELL. 285.
  aparinoides, Pursh. 285.

              ERICACEÆ.

Gaylussacia, H. B. K.
  frondosa, Torr. & Gray. BLUE
    HUCKLEBERRY. 289.
  resinosa, Torr. & Gray. BLACK
    HUCKLEBERRY. 289.

Vaccinium, L.
  stamineum, L. SQUAW HUCK-
    LEBERRY. DEER-BERRY. 290.
  Pennsylvanicum, Lam.. DWARF
    BLUEBERRY. 291.
  vaccillans, Soland. LOW BLUE-
    BERRY. Pink-fruited variety,
    Spencer. *Cobb*. 291.
  corymbosum, L., var. atrococ-
    cum, Gray. HIGH BLUE-BER-
    RY. 291.
  Oxycoccus, L. SMALL CRAN-
    BERRY. 289.
  macrocarpon, Ait. CRANBERRY.
    289.
Chiogenes, Salisb.
  hispidula, Torr. & Gray. 292.
Arctostaphylos, Adans.
  Uva-ursi, Spreng. BEARBERRY.
    292.
Epigaea, L.
  repens, L. MAYFLOWER. TRAIL-
    ING ARBUTUS. 293.
Gaultheria, Kalm., L. WINTER-
    GREEN. BOXBERRY.
  procumbens, L. CHECKERBER-
    RY. 293.
Andromeda, L.
  polifolia, L. Belchertown S.
    Pond. Hampton Pond. 295.
  ligustrina, Muhl. 296.
Cassandra, Don.
  calyculata, Don. LEATHER-LEAF.
    294.
Calluna, Salisb. HEATH.
  vulgaris, Salisb. Northfield,
    Frost. 297.
Kalmia, L.
  latifolia, L. LAUREL. SPOON-
    WOOD. CALICO-BUSH. 298.
  angustifolia, L. SHEEP LAUREL.
    298.
  glauca, Ait. 298.
Rhododendron, L. SWAMP-PINK.
  viscosum, Torr. (Azalea viscosa,
    L., Man.) 299.
  nudiflorum, Torr. (Azalea nudi-
    flora, L., Man.) 299.
Rhodora, Don. RHODORA. (Rho-
    dora Canadensis, L., Man.) 300.
  maximum, L. GREAT LAUREL.
    ROSE BAY. Fitzwilliam, N.
    H., *Prof. T. E. N. Eaton*. 300.

Ledum, L. LABRADOR TEA.
 latifolium, Ait. 300.
Clethra, Gronov. SWEET PEPPER-
 BUSH.
 alnifolia, L. 297.
Chimaphila, Pursh.
 umbellata, Nutt. PIPSISSEWA.
 303.
 maculata, Pursh. SPOTTED PIP-
 SISSEWA. 303.
Moneses, Salisb.
 uniflora, Gray. Williamsburg, *Jesup.* Brattleboro, *Frost.* Spencer. *Cobb.* 303.
Pyrola, Tourn. WINTERGREEN.
 SHIN-LEAF.
 secunda. L. 302.
 chlorantha, Swartz. 302.
 elliptica, Nutt. 302.
 rotundifolia, L. & var. asarifolia,
 Hook. 301.
Pterospora, Nutt.
 Andromedea, Nutt. Easthampton, *E Hitchcock.* Brattleboro, *Frost.* 304.
Monotropa, L.
 uniflora, L. INDIAN PIPE. 304.
 Hypopitys, L. PINE-SAP. BEECH-
 DROPS. 305.

PRIMULACEÆ.

Trientalis, L. CHICKWEED WINTER-
 GREEN.
 Americana, Pursh. 314.
Steironema, Raf.
 ciliatum, Raf. (Lysimachia ciliata, L., Man.) 315.
Lysimachia, Tourn. LOOSESTRIFE.
 quadrifolia, L. 315.
 stricta, Ait. 315.
 nummularia, L. MONEYWORT.
 Spencer, *Cobb.* 316.
 punctata, L. South Amherst,
 Jesup.
 thyrsifolia, L. 315.
Samolus, Tourn.
 Valerandi, L. Brattleboro, *Frost.*
 317.

OLEACEÆ.

Ligustrum, Tourn. PRIVET.
 vulgare, L. Roadsides. 400.

Fraxinus, Tourn. ASH.
 Americana, L. WHITE ASH. 401.
 pubescens, Lam. RED ASH. 402.
 viridis, Michx. f. 402.
 sambucifolia, Lam. BLACK ASH.
 402.

APOCYNACEÆ.

Apocynum, Tourn. DOGBANE.
 androsæmifolium, L. 393.
 cannabinum, L. INDIAN HEMP.
 394.

ASCLEPIADACEÆ.

Asclepias, L. MILKWEED.
 tuberosa, L. PLEURISY-ROOT.
 397.
 purpurascens, L. 395.
 incarnata, L. 396.
 Cornuti, Decaisne. COMMON
 MILKWEED. 395.
 phytolaccoides, Pursh. 395.
 quadrifolia, L. 396.
 verticillata, L. 397.
Acerates, Ell.
 viridiflora, Ell. Worcester Co.,
 Hitchcock; probably within our
 limits. 398.
Vincetoxicum, Moench.
 nigrum, Moench. Brattleboro,
 Frost 399.

GENTIANACEÆ.

Gentiana, Tourn.
 crinita, Froel. FRINGED GEN-
 TIAN. 387.
 quinqueflora, Lam. Leverett,
 Jesup. Hoosac Mt., *Hitchcock.*
 Blandford, *Mrs. S. T. Seelye.*
 387.
 Andrewsii, Griseb. CLOSED GEN-
 TIAN. 388.
Halenia, Borkh
 deflexa, Griseb. 386.
Bartonia, Muhl.
 tenella, Muhl. 389.
Menyanthes, Tourn. BUCKBEAN.
 trifoliata, L. 390.
Limnanthemum, Gmel.
 lacunosum, Griseb. Plainfield,
 etc. 390.

HYDROPHYLLACEÆ.

Hydrophyllum, Tourn.
 Virginicum, L. 367.

36 HAMPSHIRE COUNTY.

Canadense, L. Windsor, *Hitch-cock.* 368.

BORRAGINACEÆ.

Cynoglossum, Tourn. HOUND'S TONGUE.
officinale, L. 366.
Virginicum, L. Brattleboro, *Frost.* 366.
Echinospermum, Swartz.
Virginicum, Lehm. (Cynoglossum Morisoni, DC.,Man.) 366.
lappula, Lehm. Brattleboro, *Frost* 366.
Myosotis, L. FORGET-ME-NOT.
palustris, With. Brattleboro, *Frost.* Springfield, *W. H. Chapin.* 364.
arvensis, Hoffm. *Hitchcock,* Cat. 365.
verna. Nutt. 365.
Onosmodium, Michx.
Virginianum, DC. Monson,*Hitchcock.* 362.
Symphytum, Tourn.
officinale, L. COMFREY. 361.
Lycopsis, L.
arvensis, L. Amherst and Hatfield, *Hitchcock.* 361.
Echium, Tourn.
vulgare, L. VIPER'S BURGLOSS. Roadsides near Greenfield, *F. G. Tuckerman.* Springfield, *W. H Chapin.* 361.

CONVOLVULACEÆ.

Convolvulus, L. BIND-WEED. (Calyrthegia, R. Br., Man.)
spithamaeus, L. 376.
sepium, L. 376.
Cuscuta, Tourn. DODDER.
Gronovii, Willd. 379.

SOLANACEÆ.

Solanum, Tourn.
Dulcamara, L. BITTERSWEET. 380.
nigrum, L. NIGHTSHADE. 380.
Physalis, L. GROUND CHERRY.
viscosa, L. 382.
Nicandra, Adans.
physaloides, Gaertn. APPLE OF PERU. 382.

Datura, L. THORN-APPLE.
Stramonium, L. STRAMONIUM. 383.
tatula, L. 383.

SCROPHULARACEÆ.

Verbascum, L. MULLEIN.
Thapsus, L. COMMON MULLEIN. 325.
Blattaria, L. MOTH MULLEIN. Roadsides. Not common. 325.
Linaria, Tourn. TOAD-FLAX.
Canadensis, Dumont. 326.
vulgaris, Mill. BUTTER & EGGS. 326.
Scrophularia, Tourn. FIGWORT.
nodosa, L. 327.
Chelone, L.
glabra, L. SNAKE-HEAD. 327.
Penstemon, Mitchell.
pubescens, Soland. Hadley, Springfield, etc. 328.
Mimulus, L. MONKEY-FLOWER.
ringens, L. 328.
alatus, Soland. 328.
Gratiola, L. HEDGE-HYSSOP.
Virginiana, L. 330.
aurea, Muhl. 330.
Ilysanthes, Raf. FALSE PIMPERNEL.
gratioloides, Benth. 330.
Veronica, L. SPEEDWELL.
Virginica, L. CULVER'S PHYSIC. 332.
Anagallis, L. 332.
Americana, Schwein. 332.
scutellata, L. 332.
officinalis, L. TRUE SPEEDWELL. 332.
serpyllifolia, L. 333.
peregrina, L. 333.
arvensis, L. 333.
Geradia, L.
pedicularia, L. 335.
flava, L. 335.
quercifolia, Pursh. 335.
purpurea, L. Leverett, *Tuckerm.* 334.
tenuifolia, Vahl. 335.
Castilleia, Mutis.
coccinea, Spreng. PAINTED-CUP. 336.
Schwalbea, Gronov. CHAFF-SEED.
Americana, L. Montague, *Jesup.* 336.

Pedicularis, Tourn. LOUSE-WORT.
Canadensis, L. 337.
lanceolata, Michx. Prescott, *E.
F. Bishop.* W. Springfield,
Hitchcock. 337.
Melampyrum, Tourn.
Americanum, Michx. COW-
WHEAT. 338.

OROBANCHACEÆ.

Aphyllon, Mitchell. BROOM-RAPE.
uniflorum, Gray. 323.
Conopholis, Wallr. SQUAW-ROOT.
Americana, Wallr. Mt. Holyoke,
Hitchcock. 323.
Epiphegus, Nutt. BEECH DROPS.
Virginiana, Bart. 322.

LENTIBULRIACEÆ.

Utricularia, L. BLADDERWORT.
inflata, Walt. Belchertown Ponds.
318.
vulgaris, L. 318.
minor, L. Leverett Pond. *Bishop.* Proctor's Pond, Spencer,
Cobb. 318.
gibba, L. Leverett, *Bishop.*
Springfield, *W. H. Chapin.*
319.
intermedia, Hayne. Leverett &
Belchertown. 319.
purpurea, Walt. Belchertown,
Bishop. 319.
resupinata, Greene. Belchertown, *Bishop.* 319.
cornuta, Michx. 319.

VERBENACEÆ.

Phryma, L. LOPSEED.
Leptostachya, L. 341.
Verbena, Tourn. VERVAIN.
urticaefolia, L. 340.
angustifolia, Michx. S. Hadley,
Hitchcock. Amherst, *Clark.*
340.
hastata, L. 340.

LABIATÆ.

Trichostema, Gronov. BLUE CURLS.
dichotomum, L. BASTARD PENNY-
ROYAL. 344.
Teucrium, L. GERMANDER.
Canadense, L. 343.
Collinsonia, L. HORSE-BALM.
*

Canadensis, L. 350.
Mentha, Tourn. MINT.
viridis, L. SPEARMINT. 344.
piperita, L. PEPPERMINT. 344.
Canadensis, L. HORSE-MINT. 345.
Lycopus, Tourn. WATER HORE-
HOUND.
Virginicus, L. BUGLE-WEED. 345.
sinuatus, Ell. (L. Europaeus, L.,
var. sinuatus, Gray, Man.) 346.
Pycnanthemum, Michx. MOUNTAIN
MINT.
linifolium, Pursh. 348.
lanceolatum, Pursh. 348.
muticum, Pers. 347.
incanum, Michx. Mt. Holyoke,
etc. 347.
Origanum, Tourn. MAJORAM.
vulgare, L. 348.
Calamintha, Tourn., Moench.
Clinopodium, Benth. WILD
BASIL. 349.
Melissa, Tourn. BALM.
officinalis, L. Conway, *Jesup.*
350.
Hedeoma, Pers.
pulegioides, Pers. AMERICAN
PENNYROYAL. 350.
Monarda, L.
didyma, L. Leverett, etc. 351.
fistulosa, L. Shelburn, *F. G.
Tuckerman.* 351.
Blephilia, Raf.
ciliata, Raf. Hadley Meadow,
Jesup. 352.
hirsuta, Benth. Cummington,
Hitcheock. 352.
Lophanthus. Benth. GIANT HYSSOP.
nepetoides, Benth. Deerfield,
Hitchcock. 353.
Nepeta, L.
Cataria, L. CATNIP. 353.
Glechoma, Benth. GILL-OVER-
THE-GROUND. 353.
Scutellaria, L. SKULL-CAP.
lateriflora, L. MAD-DOG SKULL-
CAP. 357.
galericulata, L. 357.
Brunella, Tourn.
vulgaris, L. SELF-HEAL. 355.
Marrubium, Tourn.
vulgare, L. WHITE HORE-
HOUND. 357.

Leonurus, L.
Cardiaca, L. MOTHERWORT.
359.
Lamium, Tourn. DEAD NETTLE.
amplexicaule, L. 359.
purpureum, L. 359.
Galeopsis, L. HEMP-NETTLE.
Tetrahit, L. 357.
Stachys, Tourn. WOUND-WORT.
palustris, L. 358.
aspera, Michx. (S. palustris, L.,
var. aspera, Gray, Man.) 358.

PLANTAGINACEÆ.

Plantago, Tourn.
major, L. COMMON PLANTAIN.
311.
lanceolata, L. RIB-GRASS. 311.
Patagonica, Jacq., var. aristata,
Gray. Springfield, *W. H.
Chapin.* 312.

APETALAE.

ARISTOLOCHIACEÆ.

Asarum, Tourn. WILD GINGER.
Canadense, L. 403.
Aristolochia, Tourn.
serpentaria, L. VIRGINIA SNAKE-
ROOT. Said to have been found
at Turner's Falls. 404.

PHYTOLACCACEÆ.

Phytolacca, Tourn.
decandra, L. POKE. 405.

CHENOPODIACEÆ.

Chenopodium, L. GOOSE-FOOT. PIG-
WEED.
album, L. 407.
hybridum, L. 407.
Botrys, L. OAK OF JERUSALEM.
407.
Blitum, Tourn. BLITE.
capitatum, L. Rare, *Hitchcock.*
408.

AMARANTACEÆ.

Amarantus, Tourn. AMARANTH.
retroflexus, L. 412.
albus, L. 412.

POLYGONACEÆ.

Polygonum, L. KNOTWEED.
orientale, L. Waste places.
PRINCE'S FEATHER. 415.

Careyi, Olney. East Amherst,
etc., *C. H. Hitchcock.* 415.
Pennsylvanicum, L. Shores of
Conn. river. 415.
incarnatum, Ell. Southwick, etc.
415.
Persicaria, L. LADY'S THUMB.
416.
Hydropiper, L. COMMON SMART-
WEED. 416.
acre, H. B. K. 416.
hydropiperoides, Michx. 416.
amphibium, L. Belchertown &
Granby, *E. F. Bishop.* Ashfield, *Jesup.* 416.
Virginianum, L. 417.
articulatum, L. JOINT-WEED.
417.
aviculare, L. & var. erectum,
Roth. KNOTGRASS. 417.
tenue, Michx. 418.
arifolium, L. HALBERD-LEAVED
TEAR-THUMB. 418.
sagittatum, L. ARROW-LEAVED
TEAR-THUMB. 418.
Convolvulus, L. BLACK
BIND-WEED. 418.
Cilinode, Michx. 418.
dumetorum, L., var. scandens,
Gray. CLIMBING BUCKWHEAT.
418.
Fagopyrum, Tourn.
esculentum, Moench. BUCK-
WHEAT. 419.
Rumex, L. DOCK.
Patientia, L. PATIENCE. Amherst, *Tuckerman,* and common northward, *Jesup.* 419.
orbiculatus, Gray. GREAT WA-
TER-DOCK. Amherst, *Jesup,*
and northward, *Frost.* 420.
verticillatus, L. 420.
crispus, L. CURLED DOCK.
421.
obtusifolius, L. BITTER
DOCK. 421.
Engelmanni, Ledeb. 421.
Acetosella, L. SHEEP'S SOR-
REL. 421.

LAURACEÆ.

Sassafras, Nees.
officinale, Nees. SASSAFRAS. 423.
Lindera, Thunb.

Benzoin, Meisn. SPICE-BUSH. 423.

THYMELEACEÆ.

Dirca, L. LEATHERWOOD.
palustris, L. 424.

SANTALACEÆ.

Comandra, Nutt. BASTARD TOAD-FLAX.
umbellata, Nutt. 425.

CERATOPHYLLACEÆ.

Ceratophyllum, L. HORNWORT.
demersum, L. 427.

CALLITRICHACEÆ.

Callitriche, L. WATER STARWORT.
verna, L. 428.

PODOSTEMACEÆ.

Podostemon, Michx.
ceratophyllus, Michx. In Conn.
river, *Hitchcock.* 429.

EUPHORBIACEÆ.

Euphorbia, L. SPURGE.
maculata, L. 432.
hypericifolia, L. 432.
Cyparissias, L. 435.
Acalypha, L. THREE-SEED MERCURY.
Virginica, L. & var. gracilens,
Gray. Greenfield, *J. L. Bennett.* 436.

URTICACEÆ.

Ulmus, L. ELM.
fulva, Mich. SLIPPERY ELM. 442.
Americana, L., Willd. COMMON
ELM. 442.
Celtis, Tourn. NETTLE-TREE.
occidentalis, L. & var. crassifolia,
Gray. 443.
Morus, Tourn. MULBERRY.
rubra, L. 444.
alba, L. Shelburn Mt., *J. L.
Bennett.* 444.
Urtica, Tourn. NETTLE.
gracilis, Ait. TALL NETTLE. 444.
urens, L. SMALL NETTLE. 444.
Laportea, Gaudich. WOOD NETTLE.
Canadensis, Gaudich. 445.
Pilea, Lindl. RICHWEED. CLEARWEED.
pumila, Gray. 445.
Boehmeria, Jacq. FALSE NETTLE.
cylindrica, Willd. 445.

Parietaria, Tourn. PELLITORY.
Pennsylvanica, Muhl. Sugar-
Loaf, etc. 446.
Cannabis, Tourn. HEMP.
sativa, L. 446.
Humulus, L. HOP.
Lupulus, L. 446.

PLATANACEÆ.

Platanus, L.
occidentalis, L. SYCAMORE. BUT-
TONWOOD. PLANE-TREE. 447.

JUGLANDACEÆ.

Juglans, L.
cinerea, L. BUTTERNUT. 447.
Carya, Nutt. HICKORY. WALNUT.
alba, Nutt. SHAG-BARK. 448.
porcina, Nutt. PIG-NUT. 449.
amara, Nutt. BITTER-NUT. 449.

CUPULIFERÆ.

Quercus, L. OAK.
alba, L. WHITE OAK. 450.
bicolor, Willd. SWAMP WHITE
OAK. 451.
Prinus, L.,var. monticola, Michx.
& var. acuminata, Michx.
CHESTNUT OAK. 451.
prinoides, Willd. DWARF CHEST-
NUT or CHINQUAPIN-OAK. 452
& 681.
ilicifolia, Wang. SCRUB OAK.
453.
coccinea, Wang. SCARLET OAK,
& var. tinctoria, Gray. BLACK
OAK. 453 & 454.
rubra, L. RED OAK. 454.
palustris, Du Roi. PIN OAK. 454.
Castanea, Tourn. CHESTNUT.
vesca, L., var. Americana, Michx.
455.
Fagus, Tourn. BEECH.
ferruginea, Ait. 455.
Corylus, Tourn. HAZEL-NUT.
Americana, Walt. 456.
rostrata, Ait. BEAKED HAZEL.
456.
Ostrya, Mich. HOP HORN-BEAM.
Virginica, Willd. IRON-WOOD.
456.
Carpinus, L. HORN-BEAM.
Americana, Michx. 457.

MYRICACEÆ.

Myrica, L.
 Gale, L. Sweet Gale. Belchertown, etc. 457.
 cerifera, L. Bayberry. Conway, etc. 457.
Comptonia, Soland.
 asplenifolia, Ait. Sweet-fern.
  458.

BETULACEÆ.

Betula, Tourn. Birch.
 lenta, L. Black birch. 458.
 lutea, Michx. f. Yellow birch.
  459.
 alba, L., var. populifolia, Spach.
  White birch. 459.
 papyracea, Ait. Canoe birch.
  459.
 pumila, L. Amherst region,
  Eaton Man. 460.
Alnus, Tourn. Alder.
 viridis, DC. Mountain Alder. Conway, Jesup. 460.
 incana, Willd. Hoary Alder.
  461.
 serrulata, Ait. 461.

SALICACEÆ.

Salix, Tourn. Willow.
 tristis, Ait. 462.
 humilis, Marsh. 462.
 discolor, Muhl. 462.
 sericea, Marsh. 463.
 purpurea, L. Near Conway,
  Jesup. 463.
 cordata, Muhl. 463.
 livida, Wahl., var. occidentalis,
  Gray. 464.
 lucida, Muhl. 464.
 nigra, Marsh. 464.
 fragilis, L. Brittle Willow. 465.
 alba, L., White Willow, &
  var. vitellina, Gray, Yellow
  Willow. 465.
 longifolia, Muhl. 465.
 myrtilloides, L. Deerfield, Tuckerman. 465.
Populus, Tourn. Poplar.
 tremuloides, Michx. Aspen. 466.
 grandidentata, Michx. Great
  Aspen. 466.
 monilifera, Ait. Cotton-wood.
  467.
 balsamifera, L. Balsam Poplar. 467.

Gymnospermæ.

CONIFERÆ.

Pinus, Tourn. Pine.
 rigida, Mill. Pitch Pine. 469.
 resinosa, Ait. Red Pine. 470.
 Strobus, L. White Pine. 470.
Abies, Tourn. Spruce.
 nigra, Poir. Black Spruce. 471.
 alba, Michx. White Spruce.
  471.
 Canadensis, Michx. Hemlock
  Spruce. 471.

 balsamea, Marsh. Balsam Fir.
  471.
Larix, Tourn. Larch.
 Americana, Michx. Hackma-
  tack. Tamarack. 472.
Juniperus, L. Juniper.
 communis, L. Common Juni-
  per. 473.
 Virginiana, L. Red Cedar. 474.
Taxus, Tourn. Yew.
 baccata, L., var. Canadensis,
  Gray. 474.

Monocotyledons or Endogens.

SPADICEÆ.

ARACEÆ.

Arisæma, Mart.
 triphyllum, Torr. Indian Tur-
  nip. Jack-in-the-pulpit. 476.

Dracontium, Schott. Green
 Dragon. Deerfield, Belcher-
 town, etc. 476.
Peltandra, Raf.
 Virginica, Raf. Belchertown.
  476.

Calla, L. WILD CALLA.
  palustris, L. 477.
Symplocarpus, Salisb.
  fœtidus, Salisb, SKUNK CAB-
    BAGE. 477.
Orontium, L.
  aquaticum, L. GOLDEN CLUB.
    Hampton Pond.   Southwick.
    Westfield Pond.   Slow Brook,
    E. of Mt. Tom. 477.
Acorus, L.
  Calamus, L. .SWEET FLAG. 478.

LEMNACEÆ.

Lemna, L. DUCKWEED.
  trisulca, L. 479.
  minor, L. 479.
  polyrrhiza, L. 479.

TYPHACEÆ.

Typha, Tourn.
  latifolia, L. CAT-TAIL. 480.
Sparganium, Tourn. BUR-REED.
  simplex, Huds. 481.

NAIADACEÆ.

Naias, L.
  flexilis, Rostk. 483.
Potamogeton, Tourn. PONDWEED.
  natans, L. 484.
  Oakesianus, Robbins. 485.
  Claytonii, Tuckerm. 485.
  Spirillus, Tuckerm. 485.
  hybridus, Michx. 486.
  rufescens, Schrad. 486.
  lonchites, Tuckerm. Conn. riv-
    er, etc. 486.
  pulcher, Tuckerm. S. Pond, Bel-
    chertown. 486.
  amplifolius, Tuckerm. 487.
  gramineus, L. 487.
  lucens, L. Leverett Pond. 487.
  prælongus, Wulf. 488.
  perfoliatus, L. 488.
  compressus, L. 488.
  obtusifolius, Mert. & Koch.
    Ford's Pond, Granby. 488.
  pauciflorus, Pursh. 489.
  pulsillus, L. & var. vulgaris, Fr
    489.
  pectinatus, L. Conn. river. 490.
  Robbinsii, Oakes. 490.

PETALOIDEÆ.

ALISMACEÆ.

Scheuchzeria, L.
  palustris, L. Belchertown Ponds.
    491.
Alisma, L.
  Plantago, L., var. Americanum,
    Gray. 492.
Sagittaria, L. ARROW-HEAD.
  variabilis, Engelm. 493.
  heterophylla. Pursh. 494.
  graminea, Michx. 494.

HYDROCHARIDACEÆ.

Anacharis, Rich. WATER-WEED.
  Canadensis, Planch. 495.
Vallisneria, Mich. TAPE-GRASS.
  EEL-GRASS.
  spiralis, L. 496.

ORCHIDACEÆ.

Orchis, L.
  spectabilis, L. SHOWY ORCHIS.
    498.
Habenaria, Willd., R. Br. ORCHIS.
  tridentata. Hook. 499.
  virescens, Spreng. 499.
  viridis, R. Br., var. bracteata,
    Reichenb. 500.
  hyperborea, R. Br. 500.
  dilatata, Gray. 500.
  Hookeri, Torr. 501.
  orbiculata, Torr. 501.
  ciliaris. R. Br. East Amherst,
    C. H. Hitchcock. Easthampton.
    502.
  blephariglottis, Hook. 502.
  lacera, R. Br. 502.
  psycodes, Gray. 502.
  fimbriata, R. Br. 503.
Goodyera, R. Br. RATTLE-SNAKE
  PLANTAIN.
  repens, R. Br. 503.
  pubescens. R. Br. RATTLE-
    SNAKE LEAF. 503.
Spiranthes, Rich. LADY'S TRESSES.
  latifolia, Torr. Amherst, *G. L.
    Goodale.* Conway, *Jesup.* 504.
  cernua, Rich. 505.
  gracilis, Bigel. 505.
Listera, R. Br. TWAYBLADE.
  cordata, R. Br. Plainfield, *Por-
    ter.* 506.

Arethusa, Gronov.
  bulbosa, L. 507.
Pogonia. Juss.
  ophioglossoides, Nutt. 507.
  pendula, Lindl. Deerfield, *Hitch-cock*. 507.
  verticillata, Nutt. 507.
Calopogon, R. Br.
  pulchellus, R. Br. 508.
Tipularia, Nutt.
  discolor, Nutt. Deerfield, *Hitch-cock*. 508.
Microstylis, Nutt. ADDER'S—MOUTH.
  ophioglossoides, Nutt. Deerfield, *Hitchcock*. Spencer, *Cobb*. 509.
Liparis, Rich. TWAYBLADE.
  liliifolia, Rich. 509.
  Loeselii, Rich. 509.
Corallorhiza, Hall. CORAL-ROOT.
  innata, R. Br. 510.
  odontorhiza, Nutt. 510.
  multiflora, Nutt. 510.
Aplectrum, Nutt PUTTY-ROOT. ADAM & EVE.
  hyemale, Nutt. Mt. Holyoke & Conway, *Hitchcock*. 511.
Cypripedium, L LADY'S SLIPPER.
  arietinum, R. Br. Mt. Toby, *Clark*. 511.
  parviflorum, Salisb. 512.
  pubescens, Willd. 512.
  spectabile, Swartz. Deerfield, *Hitchcock*. Easthampton, *Clark*. Mt. Holyoke, *Jesup*. 512.
  acaule. Ait. 512.

AMARYLLIDACEÆ.

Hypoxys, L YELLOW STAR-GRASS.
  erecta, L. 514.

HÆMODORACEÆ.

Aletris, L. STAR-GRASS.
  farinosa. L. 515.

IRIDACEÆ.

Iris, L. FLOWER DE LUCE.
  versicolor. L. 516.
Sisyrinchium, L BLUE-EYED GRASS.
  Bermudiana, L. 517.

SMILACEÆ.

Smilax, Tourn.
  rotundifolia, L. GREEN-BRIER. 519.

herbacea, L. CARRION-FLOWER. 520.

LILIACEÆ.

Trillium, L. WAKE ROBIN.
  grandiflorum, Salisb. Pelham, *Hitchcock*. 522.
  erectum, L. BIRTH ROOT. 523.
  cernuum, L. NODDING WAKE-ROBIN. 523.
  erythrocarpum, Michx. PAINTED TRILLIUM. 523.
Medeola, Gronov. INDIAN CUCUMBER.
  Virginica, L. 524.
Veratrum, Tourn.
  viride, Ait. WHITE HELLEBORE. 525.
Uvularia, L. BELLWORT.
  grandiflora, Sm. Berkshire, *Oakes;* probably within our limits. 528.
  perfoliata, L. 528.
  sessilifolia, L. 528.
Streptopus, Michx. TWISTED STALK.
  amplexifolius, DC. 529.
  roseus, Michx. Spencer, in open meadow ! *Cobb*. 529.
Clintonia, Raf.
  borealis, Raf. 529.
Smilacina, Desf. FALSE SOLOMON'S SEAL.
  racemosa, Desf. 530
  stellata, Desf. 530.
  trifolia, Desf Pelham & Cummigton, *Hitchcock*. 530.
  bifolia, Ker. 530.
Polygonatum, Tourn. SOLOMON'S SEAL.
  biflorum, Ell. 531.
  giganteum, Dietr. 531.
Asparagus, L.
  officinalis, L. GARDEN AS-PARAGUS. 531.
Lilium, L. LILY.
  Philadelphicum, L. ORANGE-RED LILY. 532.
  Canadense, L. DROOPING YEL-LOW LILY. 532.
  superbum, L. TURK'S-CAP LILY. 532.
Erythronium, L. DOG'S-TOOTH VIO-LET.
  Americanum, Smith. YELLOW ADDER'S-TONGUE. 533.

Ornithogalum, Tourn.
umbellatum, L.   STAR-OF-
BETHLEHEM.   In grass land,
Amherst.   533.
Allium, L.   ONION.
tricoccum, Ait. WILD LEEK. 534.
Canadense, Kalm.   MEADOW
GARLIC. 534.
Hemerocallis, L.   DAY-LILY.
fulva, L.   Roadsides. 535.

JUNCACEÆ.

Luzula, DC. WOOD-RUSH.
pilosa, Willd. 536.
parviflora, Desv., var. melanocarpa, Gray. Mt. Wachusett,
Cobb. 536.
campestris, DC. 536.
Juncus, L. RUSH. BOG-RUSH.
effusus, L. SOFT RUSH. 537.
filiformis, L. Hadley meadows.
537.
marginatus, Rostk. Amherst,
etc. 539.
bufonius, L. TOAD RUSH. 539.
tenuis, Willd. 540.
pelocarpus, E. Mey. Shores of
Lock's Pond, etc., *Tuckerman.*
540.
articulatus, L. Mill Hollow,
Amherst, etc. 541.
acuminatus, Michx., var. legiti-
mus, Engelm. 542.
nodosus, L. Hockanum; Whit-
more's Ferry, etc. 542.
Canadensis, J. Gay, var. longi-
caudatus, Eng., & var. coarc-
tatus, Eng. 543 & 544.

PONTEDERIACEÆ.

Pontederia, L.
cordata, L. & var. angustifolia,
Torr. PICKEREL-WEED. 545.
Schollera, Schreb. WATER STAR-
GRASS.
graminea, Willd. 545.

COMMELYNACEÆ.

Tradescantia, L.
Virginica, L. Escaped & established at Easthampton. 547.

XYRIDACEÆ.

Xyris. L. YELLOW-EYED GRASS.
flexuosa, Muhl., Chapm., & var.
pusilla, Gray. At Lock's Pond,
etc. 548.

ERIOCAULONACEÆ.

Eriocaulon, L. PIPEWORT.
septangulare, With. 550.

GLUMACEAE.

CYPERACEÆ.

SEDGES.

Cyperus, L. GALINGALE.
diandrus, Torr. 552.
erythrorhizos, Muhl. Agawam
River, *Mrs M. L. Owen.* 552.
inflexus, Muhl. 553.
dentatus, Torr. 553.
phymatodes, Muhl. 554
strigosus, L. 554.
Michauxianus, Schult. Hadley
meadows. *Jesup.* 554.
filiculmis, Vahl. 555.
Dulichium, Rich.
spathaceum, Pers. 556.
Fuirena, Rottböll, squarrosa, Michx.
Springfield, *Mrs. M. L. Owen.*
556.
Hemicarpha, Nees.
subsquarrosa, Nees. 557.
Eleocharis, R. Br. SPIKE RUSH.
Robbinsii, Oakes. Ponds. 557.
obtusa, Schult. 558.
olivacea, Torr. 558.
palustris, R. Br. 558.
intermedia, Schult. 559.
tenuis, Schult. 559.
acicularis, R. Br. 560.
Scirpus, L. CLUB-RUSH.
planifolius, Muhl. 561.
subterminalis, Torr. 561.
pungens, Vahl. 561.
Torreyi, Olney. Pond in Hadley meadows, etc., *Tuckerman.*
562.
validus, Vahl. BULL-RUSH. 562.
debilis, Pursh. 563.
atrovirens, Muhl. 564.
polyphyllus, Vahl. 564.
lineatus, Michx. Plainfield, *Porter.* 565.

Eriophorum, Michx. WOOL-
GRASS. 565.
Eriophorum, L. COTTON-GRASS.
alpinum, L. Cranberry Pond,
Leverett, etc., *Tuckerman.* 565.
vaginatum, L. Belchertown S.
pond, *Jesup.* 565.
Virginicum, L. 565.
polystachyon, L., var. angustifolium, Gray, & var. latifolium,
Gray. 566.
gracile, Koch. Leverett, etc.,
Tuckerman. 566.
Fimbristylis, Vahl.
autumnalis, Roem. & Schult. 567.
capillaris, Gray. 567.
Rhynchospora, Vahl. BEAK-RUSH.
fusca, Roem. & Schult. Leverett
Pond, *Tuckerman.* 568.
alba, Vahl. 569.
glomerata, Vahl. 569.
macrostachya, Torr. Belchertown & Leverett, *Hitchcock.*
570.
Cladium, P. Browne. TWIG-RUSH.
mariscoides, Torr. Belchertown,
Leverett. etc., *Hitchcock.* 570.
Scleria, L.
triglomerata, Michx. WHIP-
GRASS. Amherst, *Jesup.* Hadley, etc., *Hitchcock.* 570.
Carex, L. SEDGE.
pauciflora, Lightf. Ashfield; *Porter.* 573.
polytrichoides, Muhl. 573.
Backii, Boott. Mt. Tom, *Prof.
W. D. Whitney.* 574.
bromoides, Schk. 574.
siccata, Dew. Westfield, *Rev.
Dr. Davis.* 574.
teretiuscula, Good., & var. major,
Koch. Deerfield, *Hitchcock.*
474 & 475.
vulpinoidea, Michx. 575.
stipata, Muhl. 575.
sparganioides, Muhl. 576.
cephalophora, Muhl. 576.
Muhlenbergii, Schk. Hadley,
etc., *Tuckerman.* 576.
rosea, Schk. 577.
retroflexa, Muhl. 577.
tenella, Schk. 577.
trisperma, Dew. 577.

tenuiflora, Wahl. Southampton,
Chapman. 578.
canescens, L.,& var. vitilis, Gray.
578.
Deweyana, Schwein. 578.
sterilis, Willd. 578.
stellulata, L., var. scirpoides,
Boott. 579.
scoparia, Schk. 579.
lagopodioides, Schk. 579.
cristata, Sehwein., & var. mira-
bilis Boott. 580.
adusta, Boott. Hadley, etc.,
Tuckerman. 580.
straminea, Schk., & var's tenera,
Boott, aperta, Boott, & fes-
tucacea, Tuckerm. 580.
torta, Boott. 582.
stricta, Lam. 583.
crinita, Lam. 583.
limosa, L. Ashfield, *Porter.* 584.
Buxbaumii, Wahl. 585.
aurea, Nutt. Conway, *Jesup.*
585.
tetanica, Schk. Amherst, *Hitchcock.* 586.
granularis, Mulh. Amherst, *Hitchcock,* & northward, *Frost.* 587.
pallescens, L. 587.
conoidea, Schk. 587.
grisea, Wahl. 587.
glaucodea, Tuckerm. Mt. Holyoke, etc.
Davisii, Schwein. & Torr. N.
Hadley. 588.
formosa, Dew. Amherst, *Hitchcock.* 588.
gracillima, Schwein. 588.
virescens, Muhl. 588.
triceps, Michx. 588.
planteginea, Lam. Mt. Toby.
Rocky Mt., Greenfield. 589.
platyphylla, Carey. Mt. Holyoke,
etc. 589.
retrocurva, Dew. Amherst, etc.,
589.
digitalis, Willd. 589.
laxiflora, Lam. & var. plantagi-
nea, Boott, & var. blanda,
Boott. 589.
pedunculata, Muhl. Mt. Holyoke, etc. 591.
umbellata, Schk. 591.

Novæ-Angliæ, Schwein. 591.
Emmonsii, Dew. 591.
Pennsylvanica, Lam. 591.
varia, Muhl. 592.
pubescens, Muhl. 592.
miliacea, Muhl. 592.
scabrata, Schwein. 593.
arctata, Boott. Leyden, *Hitch-cock.* Spencer, Easthampton, *Cobb.* 593.
debilis, Michx. 593.
flava, L. 594.
filiformis, L. 595.
lanuginosa, Michx. 595.
vestita, Willd. 595.
polymorpha, Muhl. Westfield, *Rev. Dr. Davis.* 595.
riparia, Curt. 596.
trichocarpa, Muhl. Amherst, *Hitchcock.* 597.
comosa, Boott. 597.
hystricina, Willd. 597.
tentaculata, Muhl., & var. altior, Boott. 597.
intumescens, Rudge. 598.
lupulina, Muhl. 598.
folliculata, L. 598.
squarrosa, L. Hadley, *Hitch-cock.* 599.
retrorsa, Schwein. Plainfield, *. Hitchcock.* 599.
utriculata, Boott. 600.
Monile, Tuckerm. 601.
Tuckermani, Boott. 601.
longirostris, Torr. 602.

GRAMINEÆ.

GRASSES.

Leersia, Soland. WHITE GRASS. 607.
Virginica, Willd. 607.
oryzoides, Swartz. RICE CUT-GRASS. 607.
Zizania, Gronov. WILD RICE. Northampton. 608.
aquatica, L.
Alopecurus, L. FOX-TAIL GRASS.
pratensis, L. 608.
geniculatus, L. 608.
aristulatus, Michx. Amherst, etc., *Tuckerman.* 608.
Phleum, L. CATS-TAIL GRASS.
pratense, L. HERD'S GRASS. TIMOTHY. 608.

Vilfa, Adans., Beauv. RUSH-GRASS.
vaginæflora, Torr. 609.
Sporobolus, R. Br. DROP SEED GRASS.
serotinus, Gray. 610.
Agrostis, L. BENT-GRASS.
perennans, *Tuckerm.* 611.
scabra, Willd. 611.
vulgaris, With. RED-TOP. 612.
alba, L. WHITE-TOP. 612.
Cinna, L. WOOD REED-GRASS.
arundinacea, L. 612.
Muhlenbergia, Schreb. DROP-SEED GRASS.
sobolifera, Trin. 613.
glomerata, Trin. 613.
Mexicana, Trin. 613.
sylvatica, Torr. & Gr. 613.
Willdenovii, Trin. 614.
diffusa, Schreb. Amherst, *Jesup.* 614.
capillaris, Kunth. HAIR-GRASS.
Sugar Loaf etc., *Cooley.* 614.
Brachyelytrum, Beauv.
aristatum, Beauv. 614.
Calamagrostis, Adans. BLUE-JOINT.
Canadensis, Beauv. 615.
Nuttallaina, Steud. 615.
Oryzopsis, Michx. MOUNTAIN RICE.
melanocarpa, Muhl. 617.
asperifolia, Michx. 617.
Canadensis, Torr. 617.
Aristida, L.
dichotoma, Michx. 618.
purpurascens, Poir. Mt. Holyoke, *Hitchcock.* West Springfield, *Dr. Robbins.* 619.
Spartina, Schreb.
cynosuroides, Willd. Shores of Conn. river, *Tuckerman.* 619.
Eleusine, Gaertn. CRAB-GRASS.
Indica, Gaertn. DOG'S-TAIL. Amherst, rare, *Hitchcock.* 623.
Tricuspis, Beauv.
seslerioides, Torr. Sugar-Loaf, *Hitchcock.* 624.
Dactylis, L. ORCHARD GRASS.
glomerata, L. 625.
Eatonia, Raf.
obtusata, Gray. 626.
Pennsylvanica, Gray. 626.
Glyceria, R. Br., Trin. MANNA-GRASS.
Canadensis, Trin. 627.

46

HAMPSHIRE COUNTY.

elongata, Trin. 627.
nervata, Trin. 627.
pallida, Trin. 627.
aquatica, Smith. 627.
fluitans, R. Br. 627.
acutiflora, Torr. Amherst. 628.
Poa, L. MEADOW GRASS.
annua, L. 629.
compressa, L. 629.
serotina, Ehrh 629.
pratensis, L ENGLISH GRASS.
COMMON MEADOW GRASS. 630.
trivialis, L. 630.
flexuosa, Muhl. Amherst? P.
nemoralis of Hitchcock Catal.?
630
Eragrostis, Beauv.
reptans, Nees. 631.
poæoides, Beauv. Amherst,
Tuckrm. Easthampton, *Cobb,* &
var. megastachya, Gray. 631.
pilosa, Beauv. Amherst,
Tuckerman 631.
Purshii, (Bernh?) Schrader.
Springfield, *W. H. Chapin.*
632.
capillaris, Nees. 632.
pectinacea, Gray. 632.
Briza, L. QUAKING-GLASS.
media, L. Amherst, *Tuckerman.*
Spencer, *Cobb.* 633.
Festuca, L. FESCUE-GRASS.
tenella, Willd. 633.
ovina, L, & var. durius-
cula, Koch., & var. glauca,
Koch. SHEEP'S FESCUE. 633.
elatior, L., & var. pratensis., Gray. 634.
nutans, Willd. 634.
Bromus, L. BROME GRASS.
secalinus, L. CHESS. Wheat
fields, etc. 634.
Kalmii, Gray. 634.
ciliatus, L. 635.
Phragmites, Trin.
communis. Trin. REED. S. Amherst, *Hitchcock.* 636.
Nardus, L.
stricta, L. MAT-GRASS. In
poor grass-land, Amherst since
1871, *Tuckerman.*
Lolium, L. DARNEL.
perenne, L. 637.

Triticum, L. WHEAT.
repens, L WITCH-GRASS. 637.
caninum, L. Mt. Holyoke, Leverett, etc. 638.
Elymus, L. LYME GRASS.
Virginicus, L. 639.
Canadensis, L. 639.
striatus, Willd 639.
Gymnostichum, Schreb. BOTTLE-
BRUSH GRASS.
Hystrix, Schreb. 639.
Danthonia, DC.
spicata, Beauv. 640.
compressa, Austin. Shutesbury,
etc., *Jesup.*
sericea, Nutt. Easthampton,
Cobb. 640.
Avena, L.
striata, Michx. Spencer, *Cobb.*
640.
Trisetum, Pers.
subspicatum, Beauv., var. molle,
Gray. Nonotuck, *Tuckerm.*
641.
palustre, Torr. Amherst, *Hitchcock.* 641.
Aira, L. HAIR-GRASS.
flexuosa, L. 641.
cæspitosa, L. Hadley Meadows.
641.
Arrhenatherum, Beauv. OAT-GRASS.
avenaceum, Beauv. 642.
Holcus, L., in part. SOFT-GRASS.
lanatus, L. Grass-land, Amherst, *Tuckerman.* 642.
Anthoxanthum, L.
odoratum, L. SWEET VERNAL
GRASS. 643.
Phalaris, L. CANARY-GRASS.
Canariensis, L. Royalston,
Prof. T. E. N. Eaton. 643.
arundinacea, L. 643.
Paspalum, L.
setaceum, Michx. 645.
laeve, Michx. Spencer, *Cobb.* 645.
Panicum, L. PANIC-GRASS.
filiforme, L. 646.
glabrum, Gaud. Amherst
and Hadley. 646.
sanguinale, L. 646.
agrostoides, Spreng. 646.
proliferum, Lam. Amherst, etc.,
Tuckerman. 646.

capillare, L. OLD WITCH GRASS.
647.
virgatum, L. 647.
latifolium, L. 647.
clandestinum, L. 647.
xanthophysum,Gray. Springfield,
rare, *W. H. Chapin*. 648.
pauciflorum, Eil. ? Mt. Holyoke,
Jesup. 648.
dichotomum, L. 648.
depauperatum, Muhl. 649.
C r u s-g a l l i, L. 649.

Setaria, Beauv. FOX-TAIL.
g l a u c a, Beauv. 650.
v i r i d i s, Beauv. 650.
I t a l i c a, Kunth. 650.
Cenchrus, L.
tribuloides, L. 650.
Andropogon, L.
furcatus, Muhl. 651.
scoparius, Michx. 651.
Sorghum, Pers.
nutans, Gray. 652.

P T E R I D O P H Y T A .

SELAGINELLÆ.

Isoetes, L. QUILL-WORT.
echinospora, Durieu. 676.
riparia, Engelm. 676.
Engelmanni, Braun. 677.
Selaginella, Beauv., Spring.
rupestris, Spring. 675.
apus, Spring. 675.

LYCOPODIACEÆ.

Lycopodium, L., Spring. CLUB-MOSS.
lucidulum, Michx. 673.
inundatum, L. 673.
annotinum, L 673.
dendroideum, Michx. 674.
clavatum, L. TRUE CLUB-MOSS.
674.
complanatum, L. & v. sabinae-
folium, Gray. GROUND-PINE.
674.

FILICES.

FERNS. 43 species.

Polypodium, L.
vulgare, L. 658.
Pellaea, Link.
gracilis, Hook. Mts. Holyoke,
Toby & Tom. 659.
atropurpurea, Fée. Mts. Toby
& Tom. 660.
Pteris, L.
aquilina, L. BRAKE. 658.
Adiantum, L. MAIDENHAIR.
pedatum, L. 658.
Woodwardia, Smith.
angustifolia, Smith. 661.

Virginica, Smith. 660.
Asplenium, L.
Trichomanes, L. 661.
ebeneum, Ait. 661.
angustifolium, Michx. Mts. Toby & Tom. 662.
Ruta-muraria, L. Mt. Toby, etc.
662.
thelypteroides, Michx. 662.
Felix-foemina, Bernh. 662.
Camptosorus, Link.
rhizophyllus, Link. 663.
Phegopteris, Fée.
polypodioides, Fée. 663.
hexagonoptera, Fée. 663.
Dryopteris, Fée. 663.
Aspidium, Swartz. SHIELD-FERN.
Noveboracense, Swartz. 664.
Thelypteris, Swartz. 664.
cristatum, Swartz, & var. Clinton-
ianum, Eaton. 665.
Goldianum, Hook. 666.
marginale, Swartz. 666.
spinulosum, Swartz, & vars. vulgare, Eaton, intermedium, Eaton, & dilatatum, Hook. 664
& 665.
Bootii, Tuckerm. (A. spinulosum,
Swartz, var. Boottii, Gray,
Man.) 665.
acrostichoides, Swartz. 666.
aculeatum, Swartz, var. Braunii,
Doell. Brattleboro, *Frost*.
667.
Cystopteris, Bernh.
fragilis, Bernh. 667.
bulbifera, Bernh. 667.

Onoclea, L.
  sensibilis, L. 668.
Struthiopteris, Hoffm. (Struthiopteris, Germanica, Willd.,
  Man.) 667.
Woodsia, R. Br.
  Ilvensis, R. Br. 669.
  obtusa, Torr. 668.
Dicksonia, L' Her.
  pilosiuscula, Willd. (D. punctilo
  bula, Kunze, Man.) 669.
Lygodium, Swartz. CLIMBING FERN.
  palmatum, Swartz. 670.
Osmunda, L.
  regalis, L. 670.
  Claytoniana, L. 670.
  cinnamomea, L. 670.

OPHIOGLOSSACEÆ.

Ophioglossum, L.
  vulgatum, L. ADDER'S-TONGUE.
  672.
Botrychium, Swartz. MOON-WORT.

matricariæfolium, Milde. Conway, Springfield, etc.
lanceolatum, Angstr. Conway,
  Amherst, etc. 671.
simplex, Hitchcock. Conway,
  Springfield, etc. 671.
ternatum, Swartz, & vars. lunaroides. Milde, australe, Eaton,
  obliquum. Milde, dissectum,
  Milde, (B. lunaroides, Swartz,
  & vars., Man.) 672.
Virginianum, Swartz. 671.

EQUISETACEÆ.

Equisetum. L.
  arvense, L. 654.
  sylvaticum, L. 654.
  limosum, L. 654.
  hyemale, L. 655.
  variegatum, Schleich. Conway,
    Jesup. 655.
  scirpoides, Michx. Plainfield,
    Porter. 655.

B R Y O P H Y T A.

MUSCI.

MOSSES. 196 species. The numbers
refer to pages in Lesquereux
& James's *Manual of the Mosses of North America;* S. E.
Cassino & Co., Boston, Mass.,
1884.

SPHAGNACEÆ.

Sphagnum, Dill.
  acutifolium, Ehrh. 13.
  cuspidatum, Ehrh. 14.
  squarrcsum, Pers. 16.
  subsecundum, Nees. 19.
  cymbifolium, Ehrh. 21.

ANDREÆACEÆ.

Andreæa, Ehrh.
  rupestris, Tourn. 25.

BRYACEÆ.

Sphaerangium, Schimp.
  muticum. 40.
Phascum, L., in part.
  cuspidatum, Schreb. 42.
Pleuridium, Brid.
  subulatum, Br. & Sch. 43.
  alternifolium, Brid., in part. 44.

Bruchia, Schwaegr.
  flexuosa. 46.
Gymnostomum, Hedw.
  rupestre, Schwaegr. 53.
  curvirostrum, Hedw. 54.
Weisia, Hedw.
  viridula, Brid. 55.
Dichodontium, Schimp.
  pellucidum, Schimp. 62.
Trematodon, Michx.
  ambiguum, Hornsch. 63.
  longicollis, Michx. 63.
Dicranella, Schimp.
  varia, Schimp. 65.
  rufescens, Schimp. 66.
  heteromalla, Schimp. 66.
Dicranum, Hedw.
  flagellare, Hedw. 70.
  fulvum, Hook. 70.
  longifolium, Hedw. 70.
  scoparium, Hedw. 73.
  Drummondii, Muell. 76.
  undulatum, Turn. 76.
Fissidens, Hedw.
  bryoides, Hedw. 81.
  minutulus, Sulliv. 85.
  osmundoides, Hedw. 87.

crista-castrensis, L. 389.

molluscum, Hedw. 389.

reptile, Michx. 390.
imponens, Hedw. 393.
cupressiforme, L. 394.
curvifolium, Hedw. 396.
pratense, Koch. 397.
Haldanianum, Grev. 397.

palustre, Huds. 398.
eugyrium, Schimp. 401.
ochraceum, Turn. 401.

cordifolium, Hedw. 402.
cuspidatum, L. 403.
Schreberi, Willd. 404.
stramineum, Dicks. 405.

splendens, Hedw. 407.
umbratum, Ehrh. 407.
brevirostre, Ehrh. 408.

triquetrum, L. 409.

HEPATICÆ.

LIVERWORTS. 47 species. The numbers refer to pages of Underwood's *Catalogue of the North American Hepaticæ, North of Mexico;* Peoria, Ill., 1884.

RICCIACEÆ.

Riccia, Mich.
lutescens, Schwein. 27.
fluitans, L. 28.
natans, L. 29.

MARCHANTIACEÆ.

Marchantia, L.
polymorpha, L. 33.
Asterella, Beauv.
hemisphærica, Beauv. 37.
Conocephalus, Necker.
conicus, Dumort. 39.
Fimbriaria, Nees.
tenella, Nees. 41.

ANTHOCEROTACEÆ.

Anthoceros, L.
laevis, L. 45.
punctatus, L. 47.

JUNGERMANNIACEÆ.

Aneura, Dumort.
multifida, Dumort. 54.
palmata, Nees. 54.
Pellia, Raddi.
epiphylla, Nees. 56.
Blasia, Mich.
pusilla, L. 56.
Metzgeria, Raddi.
myriopoda, Lindbl. 58.
Frullania, Raddi.
Eboracensis, Gottsche. 61.
Virginica, Gottsche. 65.
tamarisci, Nees. 66.
Grayana, Mont. 66.
Lejeunia, Libert.
cucullata, Nees. 71.
Madotheca, Dumort.
platyphylla, Dumort. 75.
porella, Nees. 76.
Radula, Nees.
complanata, Nees. 78.
Blepharostoma, Dumort.
trichophylla, Dumort. 80.
Blepharozia, Dumort.
ciliaris, Dumort. 81.
Trichocolea, Dumort.
tomentella, Dumort. 82.
Bazzania, B. Gr.
trilobata, B. Gr. 83.
Lepidozia, Nees.
reptans, Dumort. 84.
setacea, Mitt. 84.
Calypogeia, Raddi.
trichomanis, Corda. 85.
Geocalyx, Nees.
graveolens, Nees. 86.
Chiloscyphus, Corda.
polyanthos, Corda. 87.
Lophocolea, Nees.
bidentata, Dumort. 88.
Odontoschisma, Dumort.
sphagni, Dumort. 91.
Cephalozia, Dumort.
bicuspidata, Dumort. 93.
multiflora, Lindbl. 94.
divaricata, Dumort. 94.
curvifolia, Dumort. 95.
Jungermannia, L.
Schraderi, Martins. 98.
barbata, Schreb. 100.
crenulata, Smith. 101.

excisa, Dicks. 105.
Scapania, Dumort.
  nemorosa, Nees. 109.
  exsecta, Aust. 110.
Plagiochila, Dumort.

porelloides, Lindenb. 112.
spinulosa, Nees & Mont. 113.
asplenoides, Nees & Mont. 113.
Nardia, B. Gr.
  emarginata, B. Gr. 114.

C A R P O P H Y T A .

Characeae.

CHAREAE.
Nitella, Ag.
  gracilis, Ag.
  syncarpa, Thuill.
  flexilis, Ag., & var. glomerulifera,
    Braun.

mucronata, Braun.
batrachosperma, Braun.
Chara, (L.), Ag.
  vulgaris, L.
  coronata, Ziz., var. Schweinitzii,
    Braun.

Basidiomycetes.

HYMENOMYCETES.

TOAD-STOOLS, MUSHROOMS.

Agaricus, L.
  vaginatus, Bull. 5.
  cæsareus, Scop.
  Ceciliæ, B. & Br. 6.
  vernus, Fr. 7.
  phalloides, Fr. 7.
  mappa, Batsch. 7.
  volvatus, Peck.
  excelsus, Fr. 8.
  muscarius, Fr. 8.
  strobiliformis, Fr. 9.
  rubescens, Pers. 9.
  affinis, Frost.

  procerus, Scop. 12.
  rachodes, Vitt. 12.
  excoriatus, Schaef. 13.
  mastoideus, Fr. 13.
  acutesquamosus, Wm. 14.
  clypeolarius, Bull. 15.
  felinus, Peck.
  Americanus, Peck.
  cristatus, Fr. 15.
  cepæstipes, Sow. 16.
  granulosus, Batsch. 17.

  ramentaceus, Bull. 19.
  melleus, Vahl. 19.
  ponderosus, Peck.

equestris, L. 20.
sejunctus, Sow. 21.
portentosus, Fr. 21.
compactus, Sow.
spermaticus, Fr. 22.
rubicundus, Peck.
rutilans, Schaeff. 24.
imbricatus, Fr. 25.
multipunctus, Peck.
terreus, Schaeff. 27.
albus, Fr. 33.
nudus, Fr.

nebularis, Batsch. 35.
subinvolutus, Batsch.
altus, Frost.
phyllophilus, Fr. 37.
dealbatus, Pers. 38.
elixus, Sow. 38.
illudens, Schw.
fumosus, Pers. 39.
maximus, Fr. 40.
infundibuliformis, Schaeff. 40.
geotropus, Bull. 41.
albissimus, Peck.
pinus, Frost.
abortiens, B. & C.
flaccidus, Sow. 42.
cyathiformis, Fr. 42.
anomalus, Frost.
laccatus, Scop. 44.

ulmarius, Bull. 46.
ostreatus, Jacq. 48.
salignus, Fr. 48.
petaloides, Bull. 49.
mitis, Pers. 49.
porrigens, Pers. 50.
applicatus, Batsch. 52.
stypticus, Bull.
chioneus, Pers. 52.

radicatus, Relh. 53.
platyphyllus, Fr. 54.
fusipes, Bull. 54.
butyraceus, Bull. 55.
velutipes, Curt. 55.
confluens, Pers. 56.
conigenus, Pers. 57.
cirrhatus, Schum. 57.
tuberosus, Bull. 58.
myriadophyllus, Peck.
dryophylus, Bull. 59.
tenacellus, Pers. 60.
clavus, Bull. 60.
asemus, Fr.

pelianthinus, Fr. 63.
rubromarginatus, Fr. 64.
rosellus, Fr. 65.
purus, Pers. 65.
lacteus, Pers. 66.
galericulatus, Scop. 67.
alcalinus, Fr. 69.
filipes, Bull. 70.
aureosquamosus, Frost.
galopus, Schrad. 73.
epiterygius, Scop. 73.
citrinellus, Pers. 74.
corticola, Schum. 76.
capillaris, Schum. 77.
olivarius, Peck.

pyxidatus, Bull. 78.
hepaticus, Batsch. 78.
cyanipes, Frost.
campanella, Batsch. 81.
camptophyllus, Peck.
fibula, Bull. 82.

parvulus, Weinm. 85.

cretaceus, Fr. 86.

cervinus, Schaeff. 87.
sterilimarginatus, Peck.
5*

cyaneus, Peck.
sericellus, Fr. 93.
clypeatus, L. 93.
rhodopolius, Fr. 94.
strictior, Peck.
salmoneus, Peck.

prunulus, Scop. & var. Orcella,
Bull. 96 & 31.

variabilis, Pers. 98.
chalybeus, Pers. 100.
asprellus, Fr. 101.

praecox, Pers. 105.
squarrosus, Muell. 107.
adiposus, Fr. 108.
mutabilis, Schaeff. 109.
discolor, Peck.
mycenoides, Fr. 110.
temnophyllus, Peck.

flocculentus, Poll. 114.
lacerus, Fr. 115.
rimosus, Bull. 118.
geophyllus, Sow. 119.
subochraceus, Peck.

polychrous, Berk.

mollis, Schaeff. 125.

melinoides, Fr. 128.
discomorbidus, Peck.
semiorbicularis, Bull. 129.
autumnalis, Peck.

tener, Schaeff. 133.
hypnorum, Batsch. 134.

furfuraceus, Pers. 136.

arvensis, Schaeff. 137.
campestris, L. 137.

aeruginosus, Curt. 140.
stercorarius, Fr. 142.
magnus, Frost.
semiglobatus, Batsch. 142.

sublateritius, Fr. 143.
epixanthus, Fr. 143.
lachrymabundus, Fr. 144.
perplexus, Peck.

foenisecii, Pers. 149.

fibrillosus, Pers. 152.

fimiputris, Bull.   156.
phalænarum, Fr.   156.
retirugis, Batsch.   156.
campanulatus, L.   157.
papilionaceus, Bull.   157.
fimicola, Fr.   158.

disseminatus, Fr.   160.
Coprinus, Fr.
comatus   Fr.   161.
atramentarius, Fr.   162.
fimetarius, Fr.   164.
tomentosus, Fr.   164.
niveus, Fr.   164.
micaceus, Fr.   165.
radiatus, Fr.   168.
domesticus, Fr.   168.
ephemerus, Fr.   168.
plicatilis, Fr.   169.
Bolbitus, Fr.
titubans, Fr.   170.
tener, B.   171.
Cortinarius, Fr.
caperatus, Fr.   172.
cyanipes, Fr.   173.
callochrous, Fr.   174.
cærulescens, Fr.   175.
subpurpurascens, Fr.
lilacinus, Peck.
turbinatus, Fr.   175.
orichalceus, Batsch.
scaurus, Fr.   176.
squamulosus, Peck.
collinitus, Fr.   177.
sphærophorus, Peck.
tricolor, Peck.
elatior, Fr.   177.
violaceus, Fr.   179.
pholideus, Fr.   180.
ochroleucus, Fr.   181.
tabularis, Fr.   182.
anomalus, Fr.   183.
sanguineus, Fr.   183.
cinnamomeus, Fr.   184.
armillatus, Fr.   186.
Spraguei, B. & C.
rugosus, Frost.
nigellus, Peck.
lachrymans, Frost.
speciosus, Frost.
ileopodius, Fr.   188.
castaneus, Fr.   190.
vernalis, Peck.
striatus, Frost.

Lepista, Smith.
personata, Fr.   193.
Paxillus, Fr.
involutus, Batsch.   194.
porosus, Fr.
griseo-tomentosus, Secr.
flavidus, Berk.
Hygrophorus, Fr.
chrysodon, Fr.   195.
eburneus, Fr.   196.
cossus, Fr.   196.
erubescens, Fr.
fuligneus, Frost.
flavo-discus, Frost.
tephroleucus, Fr.
virgatulus, Peck.
pratensis, Fr.   199.
virgineus, Fr.   199.
niveus, Fr.   199.
borealis, Peck
cinnabarinus, Fr.
Cantharellus, Fr.
lætus, Fr.   201.
ceraceus, Schaef.   201.
coccineus, Fr.   201.
cuspidatus, Frost.
cœrulescens, B. & C.
nitidus, B. & C.
miniatus, Fr.   202.
congelatus, Peck.
puniceus, Fr.   202.
obrusseus, Fr.   202.
conicus, Fr.   203.
psittacinus, Fr.   203.
Gomphidius, Fr.
viscidus, Fr.   205.
Lactarius, Fr.
torminosus, Fr.   207.
cilicioides, Fr.   207.
insulsus, Fr.   208.
zonarius, With.
fistulosus, Frost.
hysginus, Fr.   209.
trivialis, Fr.   210.
purpureofuscus, Frost.
politus, Frost.
flexuosus, Fr.
uvidus, Fr.   210.
leucophæus, Frost.
pyrogalus, Fr.   210.
Gerardii, Peck.
pergamenus, Sw.
fragrans, Frost.

piperatus, Fr. 212.
vellereus, Fr. 212.
deliciosus, L. 213.
Chelidonium, Peck.
Indigo, Schw.
pallidus, Fr. 213.
unicolor, Frost.
theiogalus, Fr. 214.
paludosus, Frost.
rufus, Fr. 215.
subdulcis, Fr. 217.
subfloccosus, Frost.
mordax, Frost.
pallor, Frost.
udus, Frost.
distans, Peck.
umbellæformis, Frost.
Russula, Fr.
adusta, Fr. 218.
fumosa, Frost.
compacta, Frost.
furcata, Fr. 219.
sulcata, Frost.
virescens, Pers. 220.
albocinerascens, Frost.
lepida, Fr. 221.
rubra, Fr. 221.
purpurea, Frost.
candida, Frost.
fœtans, Pers. 222.
simillima, Peck.
emetica, Fr. 223.
ochroleuca, Fr. 223.
distans, Frost.
flavida, Frost.
fragilis, Fr. 224.
decolorans, Fr. 224.
nitida, Fr. 225.
regularis, Frost.
alutacea, Fr. 225.
Cantharellus, Adams.
floccosus, Schw.
cibarius, Fr. 227.
minor, Peck.
aurantiacus, Fr. 227.
tubæformis, Fr. 228.
infundibuliformis, Fr. 229.
cinereus, Fr. 229.
muscigenus, Fr. 230
Nyctalis, Fr.
asterophora, Fr. 231.
parasitica, Fr. 231.
Marasmius, Fr.

peronatus, Fr. 232.
oreades, Fr. 233.
plancus, Fr.
archyropus, Fr. 235.
scorodonius, Fr. 235.
velutipes, B. &. Br.
rotula, Fr. 238.
campanulatus, Peck.
androsaceus, L. 239.
perforans, Fr. 239.
filipes, Peck.
opacus, B. & C.
Lentinus, Fr.
lepideus, Fr. 242.
cochleatus, Fr. 242.
Lecontei, Fr.
strigosus, Schw.
Panus, Fr.
torulosus, Fr. 244.
conchatus, Fr. 244.
operculatus, B. & C.
stypticus, Fr. 245.
Schizophyllum, Fr.
commune, Fr. 247.
Lenzites, Fr.
betulina, Fr. 247.
Klotszchii, Berk.
sepiaria, Fr. 248.
bicolor, Fr.
abietina, Fr. 248.
vialis, Peck.
Boletus, Fr.
pictus, Peck.
Ravenelii, B. & C.
salmonicolor, Frost.
serotinus, Frost.
viridarius, Frost.
flavidus, Fr.
viscosus, Frost.
collinitus, Fr.
granulatus, L. 251.
unicolor, Frost.
albus, Peck.
bovinus, L. 252.
chrysenteron, Fr. 254.
subtomentosus, L. 254.
spadiceus, Schaef.
miniatoolivaceus, Frost.
speciosus, Frost.
rubeus, Frost.
Spraguei, Frost.
luridus, Fr. 258.
Frostii, Russell.

firmus, Frost.
ampliporus, Peck.
magnisporus, Frost.
decorus, Frost.
tenuiculus, Frost.
aurisporus, Peck.
innixus, Frost.
Roxanæ, Frost.
Russellii, Frost.
affinis, Peck.
edulis, Bull.   256.
retipes, B. & C.
limatulus, Frost.
robustus, Frost.
gracilis, Peck.
piperatus, Bull.   252.
ferrugineus, Frost.
pallidus, Frost.
sordidus, Frost.
chromapus, Frost.
versipellis, Fr.   259.
scaber, Fr.   259.
felleus, Bull.   260.
castaneus, Bull.   261.
cyanescens, Bull.   260.
Strobilomyces, Berk.
strobilaceus, Berk.   261.
Polyporus, Fr.
ovinus, Schaef.
brumalis, Fr.   262.
Schweinitzii, Fr.   264.
perennis, Fr.   264.
splendens, Peck.
cæruleosporus, Peck.

varius, Fr.   266.
elegans, Fr.   266.
Boucheanus, Fr.
lucidus, Fr.   267.

giganteus, Fr.   268.
sulfureus, Fr.   268.

destructor, Fr.   270.
lacteus, Fr.
gilvus, Schw.
adustus, Fr.   271.
isabellinus, Fr.
cuticularis, Fr.   272.
spumeus, Fr.   273.
resinosus, Fr.
betulinus, Fr.   273.
conchifer, Schw.
spissus, Schw.

applanatus, Fr.   274.
fomentarius, Fr.   274.
ignarius, Fr.   275.
Ribis, Fr.   275.
pinicola, Fr.
marginatus, Fr.
cinnabarinus, Fr.
ulmarius, Fr.   276.
carneus, Nees.
radiatus, Fr.   278.
cupulæformis, B. & C.
scruposus, Fr.
salicinus, Fr.   276.
cervinus, Fr.
annosus, Fr.   277.
hirsutus, Fr.   278.
hirsutulus, Schw.
versicolor, Fr.   279.
pergamenus, Batsch.
laceratus, Berk.
abietinus, Fr.   279.

ferruginosus, Fr.   280.
incarnatus, Fr.   281.
xanthus, Fr.
medulla-panis, Fr.   282.
vulgaris, Fr.   282.
vaporarius, Fr.   284.
amorphus, Fr.   272.
incrustans, B. & C.
scutellatus, Schw.
sanguinolentus, Schw.
cucullatus, B. & C.
Trametes, Fr.
pini, Fr.   285.
suaveolens, Fr.   286.
odora, Fr.   286.
sepium, Berk.
Dædalea, Fr.
quercina, Pers.   287.
confragosa, Pers.   287.
unicolor, Fr.   288.
Merulius, Fr.
tremellosus, Schrad.   289.
incarnatus, Schw.
corium, Fr.   289.
porinoides, Fr.   290.
lachrymans, Fr.   291.
hœdinus. B. & C.
badius, B. & C.
patellæformis, B. & C.
Fistulina, Bull.
hepatica, Fr.   292.

Hydnum, L.
 imbricatum, L.   292.
 repandum. L.   292.
 compactum, Fr.   293.
 zonatum, Batsch.   293.
 diffractum, Berk.
 spadiceum, Pers.
 suaveolens, Scop.

 adustum, Schw.

 coralloides, Scop.   297.
 erinaceus, Bull.   297.

 septentrionale, Fr.
 strigosum, Sw.
 gelatinosum, Scop.   298.
 ochraceum, Pers.   298.

 niveum, Pers.   300.
 ferruginosum, Fr.   299.
 amplissimum, B. & C.
 farinaceum, Pers.   301.
Sistotrema, Fr.
 confluens, Pers.   302.
Irpex, Fr.
 pendulus, Fr.   303.
 sinuosus, Fr.
 cinnamomeus, Fr.
 cinerascens, Schw.
 pityreus, B. & C.
 deformis, Fr.
Radulum, Fr.
 molare, Fr.
 rubiginosa, Berk. & Rav.
Phlebia, Fr.
 merismoides, Fr.   305.
 radiata, Fr.   305.
 vaga, Fr.   306.
Odontia, Fr.
 fimbriata, Fr.   307.
Craterellus, Fr.
 lutescens, L.   309.
 cornucopioides, Fr.   309.
 crispus, Fr.   310.
Thelephora, Fr.
 tuberosa, Grev.   311.
 anthocephala, Fr.   311.
 caryophylla, Fr.   312.
 multipartita, Schw.
 vialis, Schw.

 palmata, Fr.   312.
 pallida, Schw.
 trifaria, B. & C.

 pteruloides, B. & C.
 terrestris, Fr.   312.

 laciniata, Pers.   313.

 sebacea, Fr.   314.
Stereum, Fr.
 purpureum, Fr.   316.
 fasciatum, Fr.
 hirsutum, Fr.   316.
 striatum, Fr.
 corrugatum, Berk.
 spadiceum, Fr.   317.
 ochraceo-flavum, Schw.
 complicatum, Fr.
 radiatum, Peck.
 rugosum, Fr.   317.
 Curtisii, Berk.
 Murraii, B. & C.
 frustulosum, Fr.
 imbricatulum, Schw.
 bicolor, Fr.
 acerinum, Fr.   317.
 obliquum, B. & C.
 albobadium, Schw.
Hymenochæte, Lev.
 rubiginosa, Lev.   318.
 tabacina, Lev.   318.
Auricularia, Fr.
 mesenterica, Bull.   319.
Corticium, Fr.
 giganteum, Fr.   320.
 arachnoideum, Berk.   321.
 evolvens, Fr.   320.
 læve, Fr.   321.
 cæruleum, Fr.   322.
 quercinum, Pers.   324.
 cinereum, Fr.   324.
 incarnatum, Fr.   324.
 Oakesii, B. & C.
 colliculosum, B. & C.
 Sambuci, Pers.   325.
 pauperculum, B. & C.
 scutellatum, B. & C.
 Auberianum, Mont.
 salicinum, Fr.
Guepina, Fr.
 spathularia, Fr.
Cyphella, Fr.
 fasciculata, B. & C.
 capula, Fr.   328.
 fulva, B. & Rav.   328.
Exobasidium, Woronin.
 Azaleæ, Peck.   MAY-APPLES

Solenia, Pers.
    candida, Hoffm.   329.
    ochracea, Hoffm.   329.
Sparasus, Fr.
    crispa, Fr.   330.
Clavaria, L.
    flava, Fr.
    botrytis, Pers.   331.
    coralloides, L.   332.
    Tuckermani, Frost.
    albo-lilacina, Frost.
    cinerea, Bull.   332.
    cristata, Holmsk.   332.
    rugosa, Bull.   332.
    macropus, Pers.
    subtilis, Pers.
    pyxidata, Pers.
    Kunzei, Fr.   333.
    aurea, Schaeff.   333.
    rufescens, Schaeff.
    Peckii, Frost.
    spinulosa, Fr.
    abietina, Schum.   333.
    stricta, Pers.   334.
    crispula, Fr.   334.
    fusiformis, Sow.   335.
    inequalis, Muell.   336.
    fragilis, Holmsk.   337.
    pistillaris, L.   337.
    ligula, Fr.
    contorta, Fr.   338.
    mucida, Pers.
    clavata, Peck.
Pterula, Fr.
    durissima, B. & C.
Calocera, Fr.
    viscosa, Fr.   339.
    cornea, Fr.   339.
    palmata, Fr.
Crinula, Fr.
    paradoxa, B. & C.
Typhula, Fr.
    phacorrhiza. Fr.   341.
    muscicola, Fr.   341.
Tremella, Fr.
    aurantia, Schw.
    lutescons, Fr.   345.
    mesenterica, Retz.   345.
    foliacea, Pers.   345.
    vesicaria, Bull.   345.
    albida, Huds.   346.
    intumescens, Sow.   346.
    enata, B. & C.

Exidia, Fr.
    glandulosa, Fr.   349.
    cinnabarina, B. & C.
    repanda, Fr.
Hirneola, Fr.
    Auricula-Judæ, Berk.   349.
Næmatelia, Fr.
    encephala, Fr.   350.
    nucleata, Fr.   350.
    atrata, Peck.
Dacrymyces, Nees.
    violaceus, Fr.   351.
    deliquescens, Duby.   351.
    stillatus, Fr.   352
    chrysosperma, B. & C.
    tortus, Fr.
Hymenula, Fr.
    umbilicata, Fr.

GASTEROMYCETES.

PUFF-BALLS.

Hymenogaster, Tul.
    vulgaris, Tul.   361.
Splanchnomyces, Corda.
    roseolus, Corda.
Phallus, L.
    impudicus, L.   364.
    duplicatus, Bosc.
    indusiatus, Vent.
    rubicundus, Fr.
Cynophallus, Fr.
    caninus, Fr.   365.
Tulostoma, Pers.
    mammosum, Fr.   368.
Geaster, Mich.
    limbatus, Fr.   370.
    fimbriatus, Fr.   370.
    hygrometricus, Pers.   371.
    minimus, Schw.
Bovista, Dill.
    plumbea, Pers.   372.
Lycoperdon, Tourn.
    albo-purpureum, Frost.
    gemmatum. Fr.   374.
    pyriforme, Schaeff.   374.
    separans, Peck.
Mitremyces, Nees.
    lutescens, Schw.
Scleroderma, Pers.
    vulgare, Fr.   374.
    Bovista, Fr.   375.

Cyathus, Pers.
    striatus, Hoffm. 409.
    vernicosus, DC. 410.

Crucibulum, Tul.
    vulgare, Tul. 411.
Sphærobolus, Tode.
    stellatus, Tode. 412.

Coniomycetes.

MOULDS, RUSTS, & SMUTS.

Many of these forms are non-autonomous and nearly all are perhaps ascomycetous.

Leptostroma, Fr.
    litigiosum, Desm. 417.
Phoma, Fr.
    scabriusculum, B. & C.
    nebulosum, Berk. 421.
    pallens, B. & C.
    Syringæ, B. & C.
    glandicola, B. & C.
    ampelinum, B. & C.
Leptothyrium, Kunze.
    Fragariæ, Lib. 423.
    Celastri, B. & C.
Sphæronema, Tode.
    spina, B & C.
Sphæropsis, Lev.
    phomatospora, B. & C.
    Platani, Peck.
    insignis, B. & C.
    Frostii, Peck.
    Viticola, B. & C.
    Plantagicola, B. & C.
    collabens, B. & C.
    mamillaris, B. & C.
    torulosa, B. & C.
    ocellata, B. & C.
Discosia, Lib.
    alnea, Lib. 439.
    grammita, B. & C.
Diplodia, Fr.
    vulgaris, Lev. 431.
    viticola, Desm. 432.
    valsoides Peck.
Vermicularia, Tode.
    Dematium, Fr. 438.
    Liliaceorum, Schw.
Hendersonia, Berk.
    Sartwelli, B. & C.
    cæspitosa, B. & C.
Septoria, Fr.
    Ulmi, Kze. 441.

    Nabali, B. & C.
    Vitis, B. & C.
    Polygonorum, Desm. 444.
    Rhoides, B. & C.
    ochroleuca, B. & C.
    Herbarum, B. & C.
    maculans, B. & C.
    plantaginicola, B. & C.
    Rubi, B. & C.
    Pyri, Curt.
    Œnotheræ, B. & C.
Depazea, Fr.
    Kalmicola, Schw.
    Pyrolæ, Fr.
    cruenta, Kze.
    circumscissa, B. & C.
    castaneæcola, Fr.
Asteroma, DC.
    reticulatum, Berk. 460.
    pomigena, Schw.
Rabenhorstia, Fr.
    Tiliæ, Fr. 461.
Micropera, Lev.
    Drupacearum, Lev. 462.
Discella, B. & Br.
    obscura, B. & C.
    carbonacea, B. & Br. 463.
Melanconium, Link.
    bicolor, Nees. 466.
    magnum, Berk. 466.
    betulinum, Schw. 818.
    varium, B. & C.
Stilbospora, Pers.
    ovata, Pers. 468.
    macrosperma, Pers. 468.
Conothecium, B. & C.
    torulosum, B. & C.
Spilocæa, Fr.
    Pomi, Fr.
Coryneum, Kunze.

pulvinatum, Kze.   469.
disciforme, B. & C.
clavæsporum, Peck.
Pestalozzia, DeNot.
    Guepini, Desm.   471.
Endobotrya.
    elegans, B. & C.
Myxosporium, DeNot.
    nitidum, B & C.
Nemaspora, Pers.
    crocea, Pers.   472.
    pruinosa, B. & C.
Glœosporium, Mont.
    concentricum, B. & Br.   474.
    crocosporum, B. & C.
Torula, Pers.
    Herbarum, Link.   478.
Bactridium, Kunze.
    flavum, Kze.   479.
Septonema, Corda.
    spilomeum, Berk.   481.
    olivaceum, Peck.
Sporidesmium, Link.
    Lepraria, B. & Br.   484.
Phragmidium, Link.
    mucronatum, Link.   490.
    speciosum, Fr.
Triphragmium, Link.
    clavellosum, Berk.
Puccinia, Pers.
    graminis, Pers. (Uredo graminis.)
        493.
    coronata, Corda.   494.
    Polygonorum, Link.   495.
    Menthæ, Pers.   496.
    mesomajalis.   Frost, Cat.
    Compositarum, Schl.   498.
    Umbelliferarum, DC.   501.
    Anemones, Pers.   503.
    Violarum, Link.   504.
    Tiarellæ, B. & C.
    Circææe, Pers.   507.
    Asteris, Schw.
    solida, Schw.
    Pyrolæ, Cooke.
    Caricis, DC.
    Xanthi, Schw.
Gymnosporangium, DC.
    Juniperi, Lk.   509.
Podisoma, Link.
    Juniperi, Fr.   510.
Ustilago, Link.
    Carbo, Tul.   512.

Urceolorum, Tul.   512.
Maydis, Corda.   513.
utriculosa, Nees.   514.
Junci, Schw.
Urocystis, Rabh.
    pompholygodes, Schlecht.   517.
    Cepulæ, Frost.
    pusilla, C. & P.
Uromyces, Link.
    appendiculata, Lev.   518.
    Lespedezæ-violacæ, Schw.
    Lespedezæ-procumbentis,   Schw.
    Hyperici, Schw.
    macrospora, B. & C.
    apiculosa, Lev.   518.
    scutellata.   Frost Cat.
    triquetra, Cooke.
    solida, B & C.
    Junci, B. & C.
Coleosporium, Lev.
    Tussilaginis, Lev.   520.
Melamspora, Cast.
    salicina, Lev.   522.
    populina, Lev.   523.
Uredo, Lev.
    Rubigo, DC.
    Solidaginis, Schw.
    Pyrolæ, Strauss.
    Caricina, DC.   493.
    Polygonorum, DC.   495.
    Potentillæ, DC.   491.
    Cichoraceum, Lev.
    Filicum, Desm.   526.
    effusa, Strauss.   492 & 520.
    Leguminosarum, Lk.
    Ari-Virginici, Schw.
    miniata, Strauss.   489.
    graveolens, B. & C.
    Vacciniorum, Johnst.
    luminata, Schw.
Trichobasis, Lev.
    Pyrolæ, B.   529.
    suaveolens, Lev.   530.
Lecythea, Lev.
    Saliceti, Lev.   532.
    ovata, Strauss.
Rœstelia, Reb.
    cornuta, Tul.   534.
    lacerata, Sow.   534.
    aurantiaca, Peck.
Peridermium, Chev.
    Cerebrum, Peck.
    Pini, Chev.   535.

Æcidium, Pers.
    quadrifidum, DC. 536.
    Epilobii, DC. 536.
    Euphorbiæ, Pers. 537.
    Berberidis, Pers. 538.
    hydnoideum, B. & C.
    Houstonianum, Schw.
    Sambuci, Schw.
    Ranunculacearum, DC. 539.
    Clematitis, Schw.
    Grossulariæ. DC. 541.
    Urticæ, DC. 541.
    Compositarum, Mart. 542.
    Violæ. Schum. 543.
    Geranii. DC. 543.
    Mariæ-Wilsoni, Peck.
    Menthæ, DC. 544.
    Rumicis, Pers.
    Lycopi, Gerard.
    Aroidatum, Schw.
    Œnotheræ, Peck.
    Asteratum, Schw.
Cronartium, Fr.
    Asclepiadeum, Fr.
Isaria, Fr.
    farinosa, Fr. 548.
    brachiata, Schum. 548.
Ceratium, A. & S.
    hydnoides, A. & S. 550.
Stilbum, Tode.
    Spraguei, B. & C.
    Rhois, B. & C.
    Polyporioum, Frost.
Stemphylium, Wallr.
    Fuligo, B. & C.
Tubercularia, Tode.
    granulata, Pers. 557.
    nigricans, DC. 558.
    vulgaris, Tode. 558.
    confluens, Pers.
    dubia, Schw.
Fusarium, Link.
    lateritium, Nees. 558.
    Berenice, B. & C.
Epicoccum, Link.
    micropus, Corda.
Illosporium, Mont.
    roseum, Fr. 560.
    coccineum, Fr. 561.
Ægerita, Pers.
    candida, Pers. 561.

Periconia, Corda.
    Calicioides, Berk. 565.
Sporocybe, Fr.
    Persicæ, Fr.
    Rhois, B. & C.
    byssoides, Fr. 566.
Helminthosporium, Link.
    macrocarpon, Corda.
    Tiliæ, Fr. 572.
Macrosporium, Fr.
    Cheiranthi, Fr. 576.
    Brassicæ, Berk. 577.
Mystrosporium, Corda.
    Spraguei, B. & C.
    ventricosum, B. & C.
Polythrincium. Kunze.
    Trifolii, Kze. 582.
Cladosporium, Link.
    Herbarum, Link. 582.
    Fumago, Link.
    epiphyllum, Nees. 583.
    cabosporum, B. & C.
Aspergillus, Mich.
    glaucus, Lk. 588.
    fuliginosus, Peck.
    roseus, Lk. 588.
    maximus, Lk.
Botrytis, Mich.
    Viticola, B. & C.
    lateritia, Fr. (as A. cinnibarinus.)
      635.
Verticillium, Link.
    nanum, B. & Br. 599.
Dactylium, Nees.
    roseum, Berk. 608.
    dendroides, Fr. 607.
Polyactis, Link.
    vulgaris, Lk. 600.
    cinerea, Berk. 601.
Zygodesmus, Corda.
    fuscus, Corda. 611.
    olivaceus, B. & C.
Streptothrix, Corda.
    atra, B & C.
Botryosporium, Corda.
    diffusum, Corda. 617.
Sepedonium, Link.
    chrysospermum, Lk. 619.
    cervinum, Fr.
Pilacre, Fr.
    faginea, B. & Br. 625.
    Petersii, B. & C. 625.

Ascomycetes.

LICHENS & MOULDS.

Some of these forms are probably non-autonomous.

L I C H E N E S.

LICHENS.

The page numbers previous to the genus Bæomyces refer to Tuckerman's *Synopsis of the North American Lichens, Part I.*; S. E. Cassino, Boston, 1882.

Ramalina, Ach., De Not.
 calicaris, (L), Fr. 25
 pollinaria, (Ach.) 26.
Cetraria, (Ach.). Fr., Müll.
 aleurites, (Ach.), Th. Fr. 32.
 ciliaris, (Ach.) 34.
 lacunosa, Ach. 35.
 glauca, (L.), Ach. 35.
 Oakesiana, Tuckerm. 36.
 aurescens, Tuckerm. 37.
Evernia, Ach., Mann.
 furfuracea, (L.), Mann. 39.
 prunastri, (L.), Ach. 39.
Usnea, (Dill.), Ach.
 barbata, (L.), Fr. & vars. florida, Fr., hirta, Fr., rubiginea, Michx., ceratina, Schaer. & dasypoga, Fr. 41.
 angulata, Ach. 42.
 trichodea, Ach. 42.
 longissima, Ach. 43.
Alectoria, (Ach.), Nyl.
 jubata, (L.) & var. chalybeiformis, Ach. 44.

Theloschistes, Norm., Emend.
 chrysophthalmus, (L.), Norm. 48.
 parietinus, (L.), Norm., var. polycarpus, (Ehrh.) 50.
 concolor, (Dicks.) 51.
Parmelia, (Ach.), DeNot.
 perlata, (L.), Ach. 53.
 perforata, (Jacq.), Ach., var. crinita, Ach. 55.
 tiliacea, (Hoffm.), Floerk. 57.
 Borreri, Turn., var. rudecta, Tuckerm. 58.

saxatilis, (L.), Fr. 59.
 physodes, (L.), Ach. 59.
 pertusa, (Schrank.), Schaer. 61.
 colpodes, (Ach.), Nyl. 61.
 olivacea, (L.), Ach, 62.
 caperata, (L.), Ach. 63.
 conspersa, (Ehrh.), Ach. 64.
Physcia, (DC., Fr.), Th. Fr.
 speciosa, (Wulf., Ach.), Nyl. & var. hypoleuca, (Muhl.), Tuckerm. 67 & 68.
 aquila, (Ach.), Nyl., var. detonsa, Tuckerm. 71.
 pulverulenta, (Schreb.), Nyl. 72.
 stellaris, (L.), & var. tribacia, (Ach.), Tuckerm. herb., & var. hispida, (Schreb., Fr.), Tuckerm. herb. 73–75.
 caesia, (Hoffm.), Nyl. 76.
 obscura, (Ehrh.), Nyl. & var., endochrysea, Nyl. 76 & 77.
 adglutinata, (Floerk.), Nyl. 77.
Pyxine, Fr., Tuckerm.
 picta, (Sw.), Tuckerm., var. sorediata, Fr. 80.

Umbilicaria, Hoffm.
 Muhlenbergii, (Ach.), Tuckerm. 86.
 Dillenii, Tuckerm. 87.
 Pennsylvanica, Hoffm. 89.
 pustulata, (L.), Hoffm. 90.

Sticta, (Schreb.), Fr.
 amplissima, (Scop.), Mass. 92.
 pulmonaria, (L.), Ach. 96.
 quercizans, (Michx.), Ach. 98.
 crocata, (L.), Ach. 100.
Nephroma, Ach.
 tomentosum, (Hoffm.), Koerb. 103.
 Helveticum, Ach. 104.
 laevigatum, Ach. 104.
Peltigera, (Willd., Hoffm.), Fée.
 venosa, (L.), Hoffm. 105.
 aphthosa, (L.), Hoffm. 106.

horizontalis, (L.), Hoffm. 106.
polydactyla. (Neck.), Hoffm. 107.
rufescens, (Neck.). Hoffm. 108.
canina, (L.), Hoffm. 109.

Physma, Mass.
luridum, (Mont.) 116.
Pannaria, Delis.
lanuginosa, (Ach.), Koerb. 117.
rubiginosa, (Thunb.), Delis., &
var. conoplea, Fr. 119 & 120.
leucosticta, Tuckerm. 120.
microphylla, (Sw.), Delis. 121.
tryptophylla, (Ach.), Mass. 123.
crossophylla, Tuckerm. 124.
molybdaea, (Pers.). Tuckerm.,
var. cronia, Nyl. 125.
flabellosa, Tuckerm. 127.
nigra, (Huds.), Nyl. 127.

Ephebe, Fr., Born.
pubescens, Fr. 132.
Omphalaria, Dur. & Mont.
phyllisca, (Wahl.), Tuckerm. 139.
Collema, (Hoffm.), Fr.
pycnocarpum, Nyl. 143.
aggregatum, Nyl. var. leptaleum,
Tuckerm. 146.
microptychium, Tuckerm. 147.
flaccidum, Ach. 147.
nigrescens, (Huds.), Ach. & var.
ryssoleum, Tuckerm. 147 &
148.
pulposum, (Bernh.), Nyl. 148.
Leptogium, Fr., Nyl.
muscicola, (Sw.), Fr. 154.
lacerum, (Sw.), Fr. 158.
pulchellum, (Ach.), Nyl. 160.
Tremelloides, (L. fil.), Fr. 161.
chloromelum, (Sw.), Nyl. 163.
myochroum, (Ehrh., Schaer.),
Tuckerm. 166.

Placodium, (DC.), Naeg. & Hepp.
cinnabarrinum, (Ach.), Anz. 173.
aurantiacum, (Lightf.), Naeg. &
Hepp. 174.
cerinum,(Hedw.), Naeg. & Hepp.
& var. sideritis, Tuckerm. 175.
ferrugineum, (Huds.), Hepp. 177.
vitellinum, (Ehrh.), Naeg. &
Hepp. 180.
Lecanora, Ach., Tuckerm.
rubina, (Vill.), Ach. 183.

muralis, (Schreb.), Schaer. 184.
pallida, (Schreb.), Schaer. 185.
subfusca, (L.), Ach. & vars. allo-
phana, Ach., argentata. Ach.,
coilocarpa, Ach. & distans,
Ach. 187 & 188.
atra, (Huds.), Ach. 189.
Willeyi, Tuckerm. 191.
varia, (Ehrh.), Nyl. & vars. sym-
micta, Ach. & saepincola, Fr.
191 & 192.
elatina, Ach., var. ochrophaea,
Tuckerm. 195.
pallescens, (L.), Schaer. 196.
tartarea, (L.), Ach. 196.
cinerea, (L.), Sommerf. 198.
epulotica, (Ach.), Leight., var.
subepulotica, Nyl. 200.
Bockii, (Fr.), Th. Fr. 200.
cervina, (Pers.), Nyl. var., rufescens, Th. Fr. & var. privigna,
(Ach.), Nyl. 202-204.
Rinodina, Mass., Stizenb., Tuckerm.
oreina, (Ach.), Mass. 206.
Ascociscana, Tuckerm. 206.
sophodes, (Ach.), Nyl. emend., &
vars. confragosa, Nyl. & exigua,
Fr. 207-208.
constans, (Nyl.), Tuckerm. 210.
Pertusaria, DC.
velata, (Turn.), Nyl. 212.
multipuncta, (Turn.), Nyl. 212.
communis, DC. 214.
leioplaca, (Ach.), Schaer. 214.
pustulata, (Ach.), Nyl. 215.
globularis, Ach. 216.
Wulfenii, DC. 216.
Conotrema, Tuckerm.
urceolatum, (Ach.), Tuckerm.
217.
Gyalecta, (Ach.), Anz.
lutea, (Dicks.), Tuckerm. 218.
Pineti, (Schrad.), Tuckerm. 218.
fagicola, (Hepp.), Tuckerm. 220.
Flotovii, Koerb. 221.
cupularis, (Hedw.), Schaer. 221.
Urceolaria, (Ach.), Flot.
scruposa, (L.), Nyl. 222.
Thelotrema, (Ach.), Eschw.
subtile, Tuckerm. 224.

Stereocaulon, Schreb.
coralloides, Fr. 231.

Melaspilea, Nyl.
  arthonioides, (Fée.), Nyl. 197.

Opegrapha, (Humb.), Ach., Nyl.
  microcyclia, Tuckerm. 199.
  varia, (Pers.), Fr. 200.
  vulgata, Ach., Nyl. 200.
Graphis, Ach., Nyl.
  scripta, (L.), Ach., & var. assimi-
    lis, Tuckerm. 207.

Arthonia, Ach., Nyl.
  pyrrhula, Nyl. 220.
  velata, Nyl. 221.
  cinereo-pruinosa, Schær. 221.
  lecideella, Nyl. 221.
  lurida, Ach. 221.
  patellulata, Nyl. 221.
  diffusa, Nyl. 222.
  lurido-alba, Nyl. 222.
  astroidea, Ach., Nyl. 222.
  spectabilis, Flot. 222.
Mycoporum, (Flot.), Nyl.
  pycnocarpum, Nyl. 224.

Acolium, (Fée). DeNot.
  viridulum, (Schær.), DeNot. Brat-
    tleboro. *Frost.* 238.
  tigillare, (Ach.), DeNot. 234 &
    238.
Calicium, Pers., Fr.
  trichiale, Ach. 240.
  chrysocephalum, (Turn.), Ach.
    240.
  lenticulare, (Hoffm.), Ach. 240.
  subtile, Fr. 240.
  trachelinum, Ach. 240.
  roscidum, Floerk., Nyl., var. tra-
    binellum, Nyl. 241.
  Curtisii. Tuckerm. 241.
  turbinatum. Pers. 242.
Coniocybe, Ach.
  furfuracea, (L.), Ach. 243.
  pallida (Pers.), Fr. 243.

Endocarpon, Hedw., Fr.
  miniatum (L.), Schær. & vars.
    complicatum, Schær. & aquati-
    cum, Schær. 249.
  arboreum, Schwein. 250.
  rufescens, Ach. 250.
  pusillum, Hedw. 251.

Staurothele, Norm.
  umbrina, (Wahl.), Tuckerm. 258.
  diffractella, (Nyl.), Tuckerm. 258.
Trypethelium, Spreng., Nyl.
  virens, Tuckerm. 260.
Sagedia, (Mass.), Koerb.
  chlorotica, (Ach.), Mass. 265.
  Cestrensis, Tuckerm. 265.
  lactea, Koerb. 266.
  oxyspora, (Nyl.), Tuckerm. 266.
Verrucaria, Pers.
  epigæa, (Pers), Ach. 268.
  margacea, Wahl., Nyl. 268.
  nigrescens, Pers. 268.
  virens, Nyl. 269.
  muralis, Ach. 269.
Pyrenula, (Ach.), Naeg. & Hepp.
  thelæna, (Ach.), Tuckerm. 272.
  punctiformis, (Ach.), Naeg. 272.
  gemmata, (Ach.), Naeg. 273.
  hyalospora, (Nyl.), Tuckerm. 273.
  leucoplaca, (Wallr.), Koerb. 274.
  glabrata, (Ach.), Mass. 274.
  nitida, Ach. 274.
  lactea, (Mass), Tuck. 275.

PYRENOMYCETES.

Phacidium, Fr.
  Pini, A. & S. 751.
  dentatum, Fr. 752.
  crustaceum, B. & C.
  coronatum, Fr. 752.
Rhytisma, Fr.
  salicinum, Fr. 755.
  acerinum, Fr. 756.
  punctatum, Fr. 756.
  Asteris, Schw.
  Solidaginis, Schw.
  Prini, Fr.
  Vaccinii, Fr.
Glonium, Mich.
  stellatum, Mich.
Hysterium, Tode.
  pulicare, Pers. 757.
  elongatum, Wahl. 759.
  Fraxini, Pers. 759.
  vulvatum, Schw.
  parvulum, Gerard.
  insidens, Schw.
  lineare, Fr. 760.
  ilicinum, DeNot. 760.
  fusiger, B. & C.
  hiascens, B. & C.

salicina, Fr. 827.
quaternata, Fr. 828.
Colliculus, Wormsk.
hapalocystis, B. & C.
Americana, B. & C.
Alni, Peck.
enteroleuca, Fr. 834.
Pini, Fr.
constellata, B. & C.
Platani, Schw.
centripeta, Fr.
Cucurbitaria, Gray.
elongata, Grev. 840.
cupularis, Fr. 842.
Massaria, DeNot.
vomitoria, B. & C.
Lophiostoma, DeNot.
nucula, Fr. 849.
Sphæria, Hall.
aquila, Fr. 853.
Desmazierii, B. & Br. 854.
Brassicæ, Klotszch. 856.
Bombarda, Batsch. 860.
spermoides, Hoffm. 861.
moriformis, Tode. 861.
pomiformis, Pers. 862.
collabens, Curr. 864.
pulvis pyrius, Pers. 865.
coprophila, Fr. 866.
pulveracea, Ehr. 868.
livida, Fr. 877.
ulmea, Schw.
Lespedezæ, Schw.
salicella, Fr. 886.
spiculosa, Pers. 882.
morbosa, Schw.
fusca, Pers. 796.
aculeans, Schw.
acuminata, Fr. 899.
complanata, Tode. 903.
Coryli, Batsch. 910.
callista, B. & C.
enteromela, Schw.
Saubeneti, Mont.
subconica, C. & P.
aculeata, Schw.
fuscella, B. & Br. 892.
limæformis, B. & C.
mutila, B. & C.
ramulicola, Peck.
lilacina, Schw.
excentrica, C. & P.
Doliolum, Pers. 902.

intercellularis, B. & C.
Spraguei, B. & C.
Sphærella, DeNot.
maculæformis, Fr., var. æqualis.
912.
punctiformis, Pers. 914.
myriadea, DC. 915.
Pinastri, Duby. 916.
Pter.dis, Desm. 919.
spleniata, C. & P.
errabunda, Desm.
Microthyrium, Desm.
paradoxum, B. & C.
microscopicum, Desm. 927.
Stigmatea, Fr.
Robertiani, Fr. 928.
Hypospila, Fr.
quercina, Fr. 930.
populina, Fr. 930.
Dichæna, Fr.
faginea, Fr.
Capnodium, Mont.
elongatum, B. & Desm. 933.
Pini, B. & C.

HELVELLACEÆ.

Morchella, Dill.
esculenta, Pers. 655.
Gyromitra, Fr.
esculenta, Pers.
Helvella, L.
crispa, Fr. 658.
elastica, Bull. 659.
lacunosa, Afz. 658.
Ephippium, Lev. 659.
Mitrula, Fr.
cucullata, Fr. 660.
paludosa, Fr. 660.
Spathularia, Pers.
flavida, Pers. 661.
Leotia, Hill
lubrica, Pers. 661.
Vibrissea, Fr.
Truncorum, Fr. 662.
lutea, Peck.
Geoglossum, Pers.
hirsutum, Pers. 663.
difforme, Pers. 664.
simile, Peck.
luteum, Peck.
Rhizina, Fr.
undulata, Fr. 664.

Peziza, L.
　Acetabulum, L.　665.
　macropus, Pers.　666.
　venosa, Pers.　666.
　cochleata, Huds.　667.
　aurantia, Fr.　668.
　vesiculosa, Bull.　670.
　violacea, Pers.
　micropus, Pers.　671.
　fascicularis, A. & S.　678.
　furfuracea, Fr.　678.
　coccinea, Jacq.　679.
　hemisphærica, Wigg.　680.
　stercorea, Pers.　683.
　myceticola, B. & C.
　virginea, Batsch.　684.
　nivea, Fr.　685.
　calycina, Schum.　685.
　cerina, Pers.　685.
　Pini, Frost.
　citrina, Batsch.　(As Helotium
　　citrinum, Fr.)　712.
　mollisiæoides, Schw.
　aurelia, Pers.　692.
　fusca, Pers.
　chlora, Fr.
　Persoonii, Moug.　698.
　cyathoidea, Bull.　699.
　episphæria, Mart.　689.
　nigrell·, Pers.
　sanguinea, Pers.　695.
　rubella, Pers.
　echinosperma, Peck.
　compressa, A. & S.　707.
　scutellata, L.
　flexella, Fr.　707.
　Resinæ Fr.　706.
　atrata, Pers.　704.
　schizospora, Phillips.
　Tiliæ, Peck.
　firma, Pers.　697.
　humosa, Fr.　676.
　succosa, Berk.　667.
　cinerea, Batsch.　701.
　vinosa, A. & S.　700.
　omphalodes, Bull.　676.
　diversicolor, Fr.
　vulgaris, Fr.　703.
　cupularis, L.　673.
Helotium, Fr.
　æruginosum. Fr.　708.
　Virgultorum, Fr.　709.
　aquaticum, Curr.　711.

　citrinum, Fr.　712.
　Schweinitzii, Fr.
　lenticulare, Fr.　712.
　Herbarum, Fr.　714.
　epiphyllum, Fr.　715.
　ferrugineum, Schum.　715.
Patellaria, Fr.
　atrata, Fr.　716.
　indigotica, Peck.
　stygia, B. & C.
　rhabarbarina, Berk.　717.
　congregata, Moreau.
　discolor, Mont.　718.
　fusispora, C. & P.
　applanata, B. & C.
Urnula, Fr.
　Craterium, Fr.
Tympanis, Tode.
　alnea, Pers.　722.
　conspersa, Fr.　723.
　picastra. B. & C.
Cenangium, Fr.
　triangulare, Fr.
　Cerasi, Fr.　724.
　Ribis, Fr.　723.
　Prunastri, Fr.　724.
　populinum, Schw.
　Pinastri, Fr.
　pithyum, B. & C.
　seriatum, Fr.
　Rubi, Fr.　725.
Ascobolus, Tode.
　furfuraceus, Pers.　727.
　glomeratus, Fr.
　ciliatus, Schm.　731.
　Trifolii, Bernh.　753.
Bulgaria, Fr.
　inquinans, Fr.　732.
　sarcoides, Fr.　733.
Stictis, Pers.
　radiata, Pers.　734.
　versicolor, Fr.　736.
　hystericina, Fr.
　rufa, B. & C.

TUBERACEÆ.

Penicillium, Link.
　crustaceum, Fr.　601.
　epigaeum, B. & C.
　candidum, Link.　602.
Elaphomyces, Nees.
　granulatus, Fr.　750.

PERISPORIACEÆ.

Beyond this point the page numbers refer to Cooke.

Onygena, Pers.
  equina, Pers. 642.
Sphærotheca, Lev.
  pruinosa, C. & P.
  Castagnei, Lev. 645.
Lasiobotrys, Kunze.
  Loniceræ, Kze. 644.
Phyllactina, Lev.
  guttata, Lev. 646.
Uncinula, Lev.
  adunca, Lev. 646.
  macrospora, Peck.
  circinata, C. & P.
  flexuosa, Peck.
  Ampelopsidis, Peck.
Oidium, Link.
  fulvum, Lk. 603.
  fructigenum, Schrad. 604.
  monilioides, Lk., as E. graminis, DC. 651.

Podosphæria, Kunze.
  Kunzei, Lev. 647.
  biuncinata, C. & P.
Microsphæria, Lev.
  Friesii, Lev. & var. Castaneæ, C. & P.
  extensa, C. & P.
  pulchra, C. & P.
  diffusa, C. & P.
  Hedwigii, Lev. 648.
  Vaccinii, C. & P.
Erysiphe, Hedw.
  communis, Schl. 652.
  lamprocarpa, C. & P.
  Martii, Link. 651.
  Ceanothi, Schw.
  Vaccinii, Schw.
Erysiphella, Peck.
  aggregata, Peck.
Chætomium, Kunze.
  chartarum, Ehb. 653.
Eurotium, Link.
  aspergillus-glaucus, DeBary. 654.

Florideae.

LEMANIACEÆ.

Lemania.

fluviatilis, Ag. Turner's Falls, *Hitchcock.*

OOPHYTA.

Coeloblasteae.

PERONOSPOREÆ.

Peronospora, DeBy.
  infestans, Mont. 593.

Cystopus, De Bary.
  candidus, Lev. 524.

Volvocineae.

Volvox, Fhrb.

globator, (L.) Ehrb.

ZYGOPHYTA.

Conjugatae.

MUCORINI.

Ascophora, Tode.
  Mucedo,Tode. (Mucor stolonifer.) 629.
6*

Mucor, Mich.
  phycomyces, Berk. 630.
  Mucedo, L. 630.
  caninus, Pers. 631.

flavidus, Pers.
inequalis, Peck.
capito-ramosus, Schw.
Pilobolus, Tode.
crystallinus, Tode. 633.
roridus, Schum. 633.

ZYGNEMACEÆ.

Mesocarpus, Hass.
scalaris, Hass.
Zygnemia.
insigne, (Hass.), Ktz.
Spirogyra, Link.
crassa, Ktz.
longata, (Vauch.), Ktz.

DIATOMACEÆ.

Navicula.
viridis.

Diatoma.
vulgare.

DESMIDIACEÆ.

Closterium, Nitsch.
Lunula, (Müll), Ehrb.
Dianæ, Ehrb.
Cosmarium, (Corda).
Botrytis, Bory.
Meneghenii, Breb.
margaritiferum, (Turp.), Mengh.
Micrasterias, Ag.
Americana, Ehrb.
furcata, Ag.
Pediastrum, Meyen.
biradiatum.

ZOOSPOREÆ.

Hydrodictyon, Roth.
utriculatum, Roth.

PROTOPHYTA.

PROTOCOCCACEÆ.

Scenodesmus, Meyen.
polymorphus, Wood.
quadricauda, (Turp.), Breb.
rotundatus, Wood.
Protococcus, Ag.

pluvialis, Ktz.
viridis.

PALMELLACEÆ.

Rhaphidium, Ktz.
polymorphum, Fresen.

Cyanophyceæ.

OSCILLATORIACEÆ.
Oscillitoria, Basc.
limosa, Agardh.

NOSTOCACEÆ.

Nostoc, Vauch.
comminutum, Ktz.

CHROOCOCCACEÆ.

Chroococcus, Naegeli.
refractus, Wood.
Gleocapsa, Ktz.
sparsa, Wood.

Saccharomycetes.

SACCHAROMYCACEÆ.
Saccharomyces.

cereviseæ.

Schizomycetes.

BACTERIACEÆ.

Spirillum, Ehrb.
  volutans, Ehrb.
  undula, Ehrb.
  tenue, Ehrb.
Spirochaete, Ehrb.
  Obermeieri, Cohn.
Vibrio, Auct. *emend,*
  serpens, Müll.
  Rugula, Müll.

Bacillus. Cohn.
  anthracis, Cohn.
  ulna, Cohn.
  subtilis, Cohn.
  tuberculosis, Cohn.

amylobacter, Van Tieghem.

Bacterium, Duj. *emend.*
  Termo, Ehrb., Duj.
  lineola, Cohn.
  xanthium, Schroeter.
  syncyanum, Schroeter.
  aeruginosum, Schroeter.

Micrococcus, (Cohn), Hallier.
  septicus, Cohn.
  diphtheriticus, Cohn.
  vaccinæ, Cohn.
  ureae, Cohn.
  crepusculum, Cohn.
  prodigiosus, Cohn.

Myxomycetes.

SLIME-MOULDS.

Arranged according to Rostafinski.
Page numbers refer to Cooke.

CALCAREÆ.

Physarum, Pers.
  Schumacheri, Spr. (Diderma citrinum, Fr.) 382.
  cinereum,(Batsch),Schw.(Didymium cinereum, Fr.) 389.
  Berkeleyi, Rtfki. (P. pulcherripes, Peck.)
  sinuosum (Bull) (Angioridium, sinuosum, Grev.) 391.
  muscicola, Schw. (an uncertain species.)
Craterium, Trent.
  Leucocephalum, Pers., Ditm. 394.
Tilmadoche, Fr.
  nutans, (Pers.) (Physarum nutans, Pers.) 389.
  gracilenta, (Fr.) (Didymium furfuraceum, Fr.) 385.
  mutabilis, Rtfki. (Physarum, aureum, Pers.) 389.

Leocarpus, Link.
  fragilis (Dicks.) (Diderma vernicosum, Pers.) 382.
Fuligo, Hall.
  varians, Sommf. (Aethalium septicum, Fr.) 380.
Didymium, Schr.
  farinaceum, Schrad. (D. melanopus, Fr.) 385.
  microcarpon, (Fr.) (D. xanthopus, Fr.) 387.
Chondrioderma, R.
  spumarioides, (Fr.) (Diderma farinaceum, Peck.)
  difforme, (Pers.) (Physarum album, Fr.) 390.
  globosum, (Pers.) (Diderma globosum, Fr.) 384.
  crustacea, (Peck.) (Diderma crustaceum, Peck.)
Diachæa, Fr.
  leucopoda, (Bull.) (Diachæa elegans, Fr.) 395.
Spumaria, Pers.
  alba, (Bull.) 380.

AMAUROCHETEÆ.

Stemonites, Gled.
    fusca, Roth.   396.
    ferruginea, Ehrb.   396.
Brefeldia, R.
    maxima, (Fr.) (Reticularia max-
      ima, Fr.)   379.

ANEMEÆ.

Tubulina, Pers.
    cylindrica, Bull.   (Licea cylin-
      drica, Fr.)   407.

HETERODERMEÆ.

Dictydium, Schrad.
    cernuum, (Pers.), Schw. (D. um-
      bilicatum, Schrad.)   399.
Cribraria, Pers.
    purpurea, Schrad.
    microcarpa, (Schrad.) (Dictydium
      microcarpon, Schrad.)
    intricata, Schrad.   399.

RETICULARIÆ.

Reticularia, Bull.
    lycoperdon, Bull.   (R. umbrina,
      Fr.)   379.

CALONENEMEÆ.

Trichia, Hall.
    fallax, Pers.   404.
    fragilis, Sow.   (T.   serotina,
      Schrad.)   404.
    varia, Pers., var. genuina.   406.
    chrysosperma, Bull.   (T. turbi-
      nata, With.)   405.
Hemiarcyria, R.
    rubiformis, (Pers) (Trichia pyri-
      formis, Hoffm.)   403.
    clavata, (Pers.) (Trichia clavata,
      Pers.)   404.
    serpula, (Scop.) (Trichia serpula,
      Pers.)   406.
Arcyria, Hill.
    punicea, Pers.   400.
    stricta, R.   (A. cinerea, Schum.)
      401.
    nutans, (Bull.), Curt.   401
Lachnobolus, Fr.
    globosus, (Schw.) (Arcyria glo-
      bosa, Schw.)
Lycogala, Mich.
    epidendrum, (Buxb.)   379.
Perichæna, Fr.
    corticalis, (Batsch.)   (P. popu-
      lina, Fr.)   407.
    flavida, Peck. (uncertain species.)

CHAPTER IV.

SOIL FORMATIONS — AGRICULTURAL STATISTICS — MANUFACTURES —
    STATISTICS.

A GENERAL idea of the formation of the soil of the county has been
given in our chapter on the geology.   Still, the soil and productions
differ materially in different parts of the county ; hence, detailed descriptions properly belong in connection with the several town sketches,
where we have accordingly placed them.   A general idea of the county's resources in this direction as a whole, however, may be derived from the following statistics, shown by the census reports of 1880: The county then
had 3,113 farms, representing an area of 205,802 acres of improved land,
valued, including buildings, etc., at $9,214,543.00, while its total debt, bonded

and floating, was $1,127,282.00. These farms supported 4,885 horses, four mules, 1,137 working oxen, 11,930 milch cows, 11,193 other cattle, 7,290 sheep, and 6,327 swine. The stock products for the year were 35,123 pounds of wool, 725,548 gallons of milk, 1,358,495 pounds of butter, and 65,316 pounds of cheese. The products of the farms were 1,983 bushels of barley, 6,338 bushels of buckwheat, 220,232 bushels of Indian corn, 49 263 bushels of oats, 33,584 bushels of rye, 1,756 bushels of wheat, 59,684 tons of hay, 237,668 bushels of potatoes, 2,305,442 pounds of tobacco, and orchard products to the value of $54,534.00.

Hampshire, while it is an extensive farming district, is also eminently a manufacturing county. The principal manufacture is cloth and its kindred, elastic fabric, thread, yarn, etc., though wooden ware and lumber in its various branches ; paper, cigars, brass and iron work, including cutlery ; whips, brooms, straw goods, etc., furnish employment to thousands of hands. As we shall give in each township a sketch of each one of its manufactories, however, we will dismiss the subject at this point with the following statistics from the census reports of 1880, though many of the totals are doubtless at this time much larger. There were then 333 manufacturing establishments in the county, representing an invested capital of $7,283,518.00, and giving employment to 8,112 hands, to whom were paid $2,419,401.00 in wages. The total value of materials used was $6,603,887.00, and the total product $11,786,406.00.

CHAPTER V.

Origin of the Indians—Antiquity of—Ancients Visit this Continent—Fatal Epidemic—Algonquins—Nipmucks—Roger Williams —Indian Habits—Nonotucks—Their Claims—Indian Forts— Nonotucks Depart.

THE origin of the North American Indian is a subject which, though it has engrossed the attention of learned men for over two hundred years, must ever remain open to debate, and the question, " By whom was America peopled ?" will doubtless ever remain without a satisfactory answer. In 1637 Thomas Morton wrote a book to prove that the Indians were of late origin. John Joselyn held, in 1638, that they were of Tartar descent. Cotton Mather inclined to the opinion that they were Scythians. James Adair seems to have been fully convinced that they were decendants of the Israelites, the lost tribes ; and after thirty years' residence among them, published, in 1775, an account of their manners and customs, from which he deduced his conclusions.   Dr. Mitchell, after considerable investigation, concluded that, "the three races, Malays, Tartars, and Scandinavians, contributed to make up the great American population, who were the authors of the various works and antiquities found on the continent."   De Witt Clinton held that, " the probability is, that America was peopled from various quarters of the old world, and that its predominant race is the Scythian or Tartarian."   Calmet, a distinguished author, brings forward the writings of Hornius, son of Theodosius the Great, who affirms that, "at or about the time of the commencement of the Christian era, voyages from Africa and Spain into the Atlantic ocean were both frequent and celebrated," and holds that, "there is strong probability that the Romans and Carthagenians, even 300 B. C., were acquainted with the existence of this country," adding that there are "tokens of the presence of the Greeks, Romans, Persians and Carthagenians in many parts of the continent."   The story of Madoc's voyage to America, in 1170, has been reported by every writer upon the subject, and actual traces of Welch colonization are affirmed to have been discovered in the language and customs of a tribe of Indians living on the Missouri.   Then the fact is stated that "America was visited by some Norwegians," who had made a settlement in Greenland, in the 10th century.   Priest, in his *American Antiquities*, states that his observations had led him " to the conclusion that the two great continents, Asia and America, were peopled by similar races of men."   But it is not necessary to enlarge upon this catalogue. Charlevoix and other later writers have entered into elaborate disquisitions on this subject, and the curious reader may find much to interest, if not to instruct him.

Some time anterior to the landing of the Pilgrims, the aboriginal occupants had been visited by a fatal disease, which greatly diminished their numbers; and there is no certain data for determining how many then dwelt within the limits of Massachusetts, though it is estimated that there were between thirty and forty thousand.

Bancroft tells us that the *Algonquin* race occupied the whole Atlantic coast, from the gulf of St. Lawrence to Cape Fear.   The Indians of the interior were known and called among the tribes upon the sea-shore by the general name of *Nipmucks*, or fresh-water Indians, and, true to their name, the *Nipmucks* usually had their residences upon places of fresh water, the ponds, lakes, and rivers of the interior.   The *Nipmuck* Indians, then, were the aboriginal occupants of the territory under consideration.

The *Nipmucks* were decidedly nomadic in their habits, seldom remaining long in one place, but wandered back and forth from clearing to clearing, where they would raise a little Indian corn and perhaps a few beans and squashes, and change from one hunting or fishing-ground to another.   Thus Roger Williams tells us:—

"From thick, warm valleys where they winter they remove a little nearer to their summer fields.   When it is warm spring they remove to their fields, where they plant corn. In middle summer, because of the abundance of fleas which the dust of the house breeds, they will fly and remove on a sudden to a fresh place. And sometimes having fields a mile or two or many miles asunder, when the work of one field is over they remove hence to the other. If death call in amongst them, they presently remove to a fresh place. If an enemy approach they remove to a thicket or swamp, unless they have some fort to remove into. Sometimes they remove to a hunting-house in the end of the year and forsake it not until the snow lies thick ; and then will travel home, men, women and children, through the snow thirty, yea, fifty or sixty miles. But their great remove is from their summer fields to warm and thick woody bottoms where they winter. They are quick, in a half-day, yea, sometimes in a few hours' warning, to be gone, and the house is up elsewhere, especially if they have a few stakes ready pitched for their mats. I once in my travels lodged at a house at which in my return I hoped to have lodged again the next night, but the house was gone in that interim, and I was glad to lodge under a tree."

In the chapter on the geology of the county we have spoken of several ox-bows and islands having once been formed in the Connecticut river here. The *Nipmucks* who occupied this region derived their name from these islands and peninsulas, viz.: *Nonotucks,* meaning " in the middle of the river." This name, formerly written *Noen-tuk,* or *No-ah-tuk,* is still familiar in the vicinity and is borne by a part of Mt. Tom.

The *Nonotucks* claimed all the country on both sides of the river, from the head of the South Hadley falls to the south side of *Mt. We-quomps,* now Sugar-Loaf mountain. They had several villages and forts on both sides of the river, and numerous corn-planting fields of from twelve to sixteen acres each. Their principal fort was on a high bank near the mouth of Half-way brook, between Northampton and Hadley. This fort was occupied until the night of the 24th of August, 1675, when *Um-pan-cha-la,* chief sachem of the *Nonotucks,* left the land with all his tribe for some far-off western home, no one knows whither. Another fort, containing about an acre inclosed, was occupied by another *Nonotuck* sachem, called *Quon-quont.* It stood on the east side of the river, in Hadley, on a ridge between East and West School meadow.

CHAPTER VI.

First Visit of Europeans—First Official Record—Petition for
Grant of Land—Petition Granted—Indian Purchase—Extent
of Purchase—First Settlers—Statistics.

ON page six we quoted Holland's version of the tradition of the naming of Mt. Tom and Mt. Holyoke. Supposing this version to be
authentic, we have then the first visit of Europeans to the territory
now included within the limits of Hampshire county. But be this as it may,
in 1653 we find the first official intimation of a settlement north of Springfield, or Agawam, as it was then known, when " Mr. Samuel Cole, of Boston,"
was granted 400 acres of land at Nonotuck. About the same time the following petition was sent in to the general court, asking the privilege of making a settlement at Nonotuck, viz. :—

" Your highly honored, the General Court of the Massachusetts. The
humble petition of John Pynchon, Eleazur Holliock, and Samuel Chapin,
Inhabitants of Springfield, sheweth. We hartyly desire the continuance of
your peace. And in exercise of your *subrich* in these parts, In order where
unto we humbly tender o^r desire of that liberty may be granted to erect a plantation, About fifteen miles Above us, on this river of Connecticut, if it be the
will of the Lord, the place being, as we think, very commodious,—*sideratis
con Sixondo sor,*—the containing Large quantities of excellent land and
meadow, and tillable ground sufficient for two long plantations, and work,
w^{ch}, if it should go on, might, as we conceive, prove greatly Advantagous to
your Common Wealth,—to wch purpose there are divers mour Neighboring
plantatur that have a desire to remove thither, with your approbation thereof,
to the number of twenty-five families, at least, that Already appear, whereof
many of them are of considerable quality for Estates and for the matter for a
church, when it shall please God to find opportunity that way : it is the humble desire that by this Hon^d Corte some power may be established or some
course appointed for the regulating, at their 1st proceedings, as concerning
whome to admit and other occurrences that to the glory of God may be furthered, And your peace and happiness not retarded. And the Inducement
to us in these desires is not Any similar respect of our owne, but that we,
being Alone, may by this means may have som more neighborhood of your
jurisdiction. thus, not doubting your acceptance of our desires, w^d thus
entreat the Lord to sit among you in All your counsels, And remain your most
humble servts.

" Springfield, the 5th of ye 3d Mo. 1653.

                                        " John Pynchon,
                                        " Elezer Holliok,
                                        " Sam'l Chapin."

This petition seems to have been favorably received by the general court,
and the prayer thereof granted in the following words :—

" Att a General Court of Election held at Boston the 18 day May, 1653,
In answer to the inhabitants of Springfield's petition and others thereabouts,

this Court doth order, that Mr. John Pinchon, Mr. Holyoke, and some other of the petition[rs] should be appoynted a committee to divide the land petitioned for into two plantations and that the petition[rs] make choice of one of them, where they shall have liberty to plant themselves ; provided, they shall not appropriate to any planter above one hundred acors of all sorts of land, whereof not above twenty acres to be meddow, till twenty inhabitants have planted there, whereof twelve to be freemen, or more, which said freemen shall have power to distribute the land and give out proportions of land to the severall inhabitants as in other townes of this jurisdiction, and that the land be divided according to estates or eminent qualifications, and that Samuel Chapin be joined with Mr. Pynchon and Mr. Holyoke for the dividing of the towns."

In pursuance of this order the commissioners appointed thereby performed the duty therein enjoined, and returned to the general court the following report, to wit :—

" Nov. 1, 1654.

" To the honored Generall Court of the Massachusetts. Wee whose names are underwritten, being appointed to divide the lands at Naotucke into two plantations, wee accordingly have granted to them that now first appeared to remove thither to plant themselves on the west side of the River Connecticott, as they desired, and have laid out theire bounds, viz. : from the little meadowe above theire plantation, which meadowe is called Capawonk or Mattaomett, doune to the head of the falls which are belowe them, reserving the land on the east side of the said river for another plantation when God, by his providence shall so dispose thereof. and still remain

" your humble servants,

" JOHN PINCHON,
" ELIZER HOLYOKE.
" SAMUEL CHAPIN."

The land purchased of the Indians embraced the four Hamptons and parts of Hatfield and Montgomery. It comprised one hundred square miles, or 64,000 acres, extending from the south part of Hatfield to South Hadley Falls, and cost about $200.00 in wampum. On the 29th of October, 1654, the settlement of the new territory was begun.[*] The names of the original settlers were as follows : Thomas Judd, John King, Joseph Parsons, Thomas Bascom, Isaac Shelden, John Strong, Thomas Ford, Edward Elmore, Aaron Cook, John Hillyer, William Hulburt, Thomas Woodford, Samuel Wright, Robert Bartlett, John Lyman, James Bridgman, Thomas Root, Alexander Edwards, William Miller, David Burt, Samuel Allen, William Hannum, Nathaniel Phelps and John Stebbins. All of these located in what is now the City of Northampton.

From this small beginning the settlement spread and has increased until we have the populous, wealthy, learned county of to-day. Details of these early settlements, the erection and growth of each one of the county's townships, and the names of their present residents may be found in the future

---

[*]There is a tradition that an English family located in Northampton in 1652, remaining during the winter.

pages of this work. The comparative growth of the territory now included
with the county since 1776, however, may be seen by the following figures.
According to the colonial census of 1776, the territory had a population of
12,154 souls. The first government census was taken in 1790, when the
population here had increased to 18,823, and for each decade since, the returns have shown, for 1800, 22,885; 1810, 24,553; 1820, 26,487; 1830,
30,254; 1840, 30,897; 1850, 35,732; 1860, 37,823; 1870, 44,388; 1880,
47,236.

CHAPTER VII.

ARRANGEMENT OF CIVIL MACHINERY—FIRST COMMITTEE'S REPORT—
NORTHAMPTON MADE SHIRE TOWN—PROVINCIAL COURTS—COMMON-
WEALTH COURTS—COURT HOUSES—JAILS—CIVIL LIST.

THE first official announcement of the proper county arrangement for
the dispensation of the law in Hampshire county, is the report of the
committee appointed by the several towns "to order and settle ye
affaires of ye county," consisting of Capt. John Pynchon, Henry Clarke,
Capt. Aaron Cooke, Lieut. David Milton and Elizur Holyoke. On April 2,
1663, this committee reported that they had—

"Agreed and determined at ye Beginning of ye yeare for ye Shire meetings
of this County shal be on ye first day of March yearely; And that ye Shire
meetings shall be each other yeare at Springfield, and each other yeare at
Northampton, in a constant course. And all our Shire meetings this yeare to
be at Northampton; Springfield having had them last yeare. Also they
agreed that ye commissioner chosen in March yearely by ye Shire commissioner to carry ye votes for Nomination of Magistrates to Boston, shall have
allowed him by the County thirty shillings, to be paid by the County Treasurer; the rest of his charges he is to beare himself; and that noe one man be
thereby overburtherned, It is determined that there be a change yearely
of ye person to carry the votes, except for necessity or convenience they
shall see cause to act otherwise."

Previous to this a county court had been established in each county, to be
held by the magistrates living in it, or any other magistrates that could attend
the same, or by such magistrates as the general court should appoint from
time to time, "together with such persons of worth, where there shall be need
as shall from time to time be appointed by the General Court." This court
had power to hear and determine all causes, civil and criminal, not extending
to life, member, or banishment, or to cases of divorce. Probate matters were
also within its jurisdiction. The first session held at Northampton, or within

the present limits of the county, was under this old dispensation, March 26, 1661.

The judicial system of the province at the time the settlement of the county was commenced, and thence down to the period of the Revolution, comprised a superior court of judicature with original and appellate jurisdiction throughout the province, corresponding in a great degree to the present superior judicial court, and holding its sessions in the several counties ; a court called the superior court of common pleas, for each county, consisting of four justices, of whom three were necessary to form a quorum, which had " cognizance of all civil actions, *   *   *   *   triable at the common law, of what nature, kind or quality, soever ; " and a court of sessions in each county, comprising all of its justices of the peace, which had a limited criminal jurisdiction, and managed the prudential affairs of the county. Justices of the peace had a separate jurisdiction in minor matters, both criminal and civil, and from their judgment there was a right of appeal to the common pleas and court of sessions. There was also a probate court, having jurisdiction as at the present time. The superior court never held any session in Berkshire, but all its causes arising in this county were heard at the term held in the county of Hampshire. Judicial business was thus equalized, though the courts with which the inhabitants of the county were most familiar were those presided over by the local magistrates. All of the judicial officers were appointed by, and held their offices at, the pleasure of the crown, or its representative, the governor of the province, with the consent of the council.

The courts of the Commonwealth of Massachusetts were established by act of July 3, 1782. These were the supreme judicial court, the court of common pleas, and court of general sessions of the peace.

The judges of the supreme judicial court, by that act, were to "hold their offices as long as they behave themselves well," and to have honorable salaries, ascertained and established by standing laws. This court was to consist of one chief and four other justices, any three of whom constituted a lawful tribunal. It was given jurisdiction in civil and criminal causes and in various other matters, and was constituted the "supreme court of probate," with appellate jurisdiction in nearly all probate matters.

A court of common pleas, established by the same act for each county, was similar to the provincial court of that name, and was superceded by the circuit court of common pleas, by act of June 21, 1811; which act divided the state into six circuits, exclusive of Dukes and Nantucket counties. This court was abolished in 1821, and a court of common pleas throughout the state established, consisting of four judges, one judge empowered to hold a court. The powers and duties of the latter court were substantially those of the circuit courts.

The court of general sessions of the peace, established by the act of 1782 for each county, was held by the justices of the peace therein, and determined matters relating to the conservation of the peace and the punishment of offenses cognizable by them at common law. After several changes and modifications its powers and duties were transferred to the circuit court of common pleas. The latter was finally abolished in 1859.

By the constitution of Massachusetts, "judges of probate of wills, and for granting letters of administration," hold their offices during good behavior, and are appointed and commissioned by the governor. By the act of March 12, 1784, probate courts were established, and their powers and duties prescribed.

When the provincial courts were established, in 1792, the court of probate was separated from the others—at least in Hampshire county. From that time until June, 1858, the officers of this court were a judge of probate and a register of probate. At the latter date the court of insolvency was placed under the jurisdiction of these officers, who have since been denominated, respectively, "judge of probate and insolvency," and "register of probate and insolvency."

The court of insolvency was established in 1856, superseding the commissioners of insolvency, who had previously the charge of insolvent matters. Horace I. Hodges was appointed judge of insolvency in June of the year named, and R. B. Hubbard, register. The latter served until January, 1857, and was succeeded by Luke Lyman, who was chosen in the fall of 1856, the office having been made elective. The duties of these officers ceased when the courts were united as above named in 1858.

A board of county commissioners was established by act of the general court, February 26, 1828. The powers and duties of the court of sessions and of commissioners of highways were transferred to the board of commissioners. The board consists of three members, one of whom is chosen annually for a term of three years. Two special commissioners are elected, each at the same time, for a term of three years.

The commissioners have the care of county property, and are empowered, among other things, to estimate and apportion county taxes, erect and repair county buildings, lay out highways, license ferries and inn-holders, appoint overseers of the house of correction, and establish rules for its government.

The special commissioners are called to act in cases of vacancy in the board, or where the commissioners are interested parties.

Five court-houses have been erected in Northampton. The first one, a building erected in 1655, stood near the intersection of Main and King streets. The second, built probably in 1738–39, stood "near the east end of the green, fronting Shop Row." This did service until 1813, when a third was erected upon the site of the present. This was destroyed by fire in November, 1822. It was re-built soon after, and the building, with several modifications, did service until taken down during the past summer to make room for the fine structure now being built.

The first jail or "prison" at Northampton stood near the present city hall, and was erected in 1704. It was twenty-four by sixteen feet in size, and had a small dwelling at one end for the keeper.

The second jail was built in 1800–01. It was principally a stone structure, located on Pleasant street, and cost $11,458.39.

The present jail and house of correction was ordered built in September, 1850, and was finished in 1852. It is of brick, consists of a central edifice, four stories or sixty-six feet in height, with basement and attic, and with ground dimensions forty-six by sixty-one feet; and two wings, each with a frontage of sixty-five feet and a width of forty-five; and fifty feet in height. The jail wing contains two departments—one for males and one for females—that for males containing twelve cells, eight by ten feet in size, and ten feet high, while that for females has twenty-two cells, four by ten feet, and ten feet high. The other wing is the "house of correction," and has fifty-four cells corresponding in size to the cells for females in the jail wing. These are all for males. The cell floors are of brick. The building contains also the keeper's residence, chapel, poor debtor's room, hospital and bathing-room. In the rear of the main building is a workshop, thirty by sixty feet, and two stories in height.

JUDICIARY AND CIVIL LIST.

Since the period of the Revolution the following citizens of the county have held positions on the bench of the superior court of judicature and supreme judicial court :—

Justices.

Simeon Strong, Amherst.................................1801–05
Charles A. Dewey,* Northampton.........................1837–66
Charles E. Forbes,† Northampton........................1848–
William Allen, Northampton.............................1872–

Court of Common Pleas.

Solomon Strong. Amherst................................1820–42
Samuel Howe, Northampton...............................1820–28
Charles E. Forbes, Northampton.........................1847–48

State Senators.

Levi Stockbridge, Hadley...............................1865–66
Edmund H. Sawyer, Easthampton..........................1867–68

*Mr. Dewey was a native of Northampton, but was appointed from Worcester.
† Resigned the same year.

Edward A. Thomas, Prescott.... 1869
Stephen M. Crosby, Williamsburg............................ 1870
Rufus D. Woods, Enfield............................ 1872–73
Francis Edson, Hadley....................................... 1874
William M. Gaylord, Northampton....... 1876
Lewis N. Gilbert, Ware 1877–78
John L. Otis, Northampton...................................1879–80
Samuel M. Cook, Granby.....................................1881–82
Alvan Barrus, Goshen.....................................1883–84
Myron P. Walker, Belchertown............................. ...1885–86·
Charles N. Clark, Northampton..............................1887–

County Treasurers.

John Pynchon	1660–81	Jonathan H. Butler	1846–49
Peter Tilton	1682–88	Charles DeLano	1850–58
John Pynchon	1689 —	Henry S. Gere	1859–76
William Pynchon	1798–1808	Watson L. Smith	1877–79
Edward Pynchon	1808–12	Lewis Warner	1880–
Daniel Stebbins	1812–45		

Sheriffs

Elisha Porter	1781–96	Samuel L. Hinckley	1844–51
Ebenezer Mattoon	1796–1811	Alfred L. Strong	1851–53
Thomas Shepard	1811–12	Henry A. Longley	1855–83
Ebenezer Mattoon	1812–16	Jairus E. Clark	1883–
Joseph Lyman	1816–44		

Judges of Probate.

John Pynchon	1692–1703	Jonathan Leavitt	1809–10
Samuel Partridge	1703–29	Joseph Lyman	1810–16
John Stoddard	1729–48	Samuel Hinckley	1816–34
Timothy Dwight	1748–64	Ithamar Conkey	1834–58
Isaac Williams	1764–74	Samuel F. Lyman	1858–73
Samuel Mather	1776–79	Samuel T. Spaulding	1873–79
Samuel Henshaw	1797–1809	William G. Bassett	1879–

Registers of Probate.

Samuel Partridge	1692–1703	John C. Williams	1776–87
John Pynchon	1703–29	Samuel Hinckley	1787–1816
Timothy Dwight	1729–48	Samuel F. Lyman	1827–55
Timothy Dwight, Jr	1748–64	Luke Lyman	1859–83
Solomon Stoddard	1764–69	Hubbard M. Abbott	1883–
Israel Williams, Jr	1769–74		

Clerks of Courts.

Elizur Holyoke......... ...1660-76
Samuel Partridge..........1676-78
John Holyoke..... 1678-93
John Pynchon..........1693-1735
Israel Williams............1735-58
William Williams..........1758-78
Robert Breck............. ...1778-98
Joseph Lyman........ 1798-1810

Joseph Dwight............1810-11
John Taylor..............1811-12
Josiah Dwight.............1812-21
Solomon Stoddard.........1821-37
Samuel Wells............ ... 1837-65
William P. Strickland......1865-82
William H. Clapp........ 1882-

Registers of Deeds.

Ebenezer Hunt.......... 1787-96
Levi Lyman...........1796-1811
Solomon Stoddard.........1811-21
Levi Lyman.............1821-30

Charles Hooker...........1830-33
C. P. Huntington.........1833-33
Giles C. Kellogg..........1833-46
Henry P. Billings..........1871-

Trial Justices.*

Horace I. Hodges........ ...1858
James W. Boyden...........1858
William S. Brockenbridge......1858
Elisha H. Brewster..........1858
Epaphras Clark....... 1858
Elijah N. Woods............1858
Franklin Dickinson 1858
Albion P. Howe.............1859
Abion P. Peck.............1860
Francis DeWitt.............1860
Franklin D. Richards.........1863
Samuel Wells................1863
Charles Richards........ 1864
Hiram Smith, Jr. 1864
Oliver Pease............. 1865
William P. Strickland.........1865

Seth Warner.................1865
R. Ogden Dwight.............1868
C. Edgar Smith...............1869
William G. Bassett.. 1869
Alfred M. Copeland..........1869
Francis H. Dawes............1870
Garry Munson 1872
Edward A. Thomas.......... ..1874
Haynes H. Chilson............1875
Nathan Morse...... 1876
Lafayette Clark...............1877
Enos Parsons................1880
John J. Reardon..............1881
Edwin R. Bridgman...........1882
Alburn J. Fargo..............1882

County Commissioners.

Charles P. Phelps..... 1828-34
Levi Lyman..............1829-30
Alvan Rice..............1829-33
Ithamar Conkey..........1830-34

Osmyn Baker............1834-37
Elisha Strong............1835-40
Joseph Cummings...... 1835-52
Chauncey B. Rising.......1838-40

---

* The jurisdiction of the trial justices of Hampshire county was terminated by act of legislature approved May 16, 1882, which formed the towns of Hampshire county into a district court, of which William P. Stickland, of Northampton, was appointed justice, A. J. Fargo, of Easthampton, and R. W. Lyman, of Belchertown, special justices, and Haynes H. Chilson, of Northampton, clerk.

Roswell Hubbard..........1838–
Israel Billings.............1841–43
Timothy A. Phelps..... ...1841–43
Mark Doolittle 1844–46
Joel Hayden..............1844–52
William Bowdoin..........1847–48
Benjamin Barrett..........1847–48
Haynes H. Chilson........1850–52
Horace I. Hodges..... ...1853–54
Elisha H. Brewster........1853–65
John Warner.............. 1853
William P. Dickinson......1855–59

Elkanah Ring, Jr..........1856–58
Daniel B. Gillett..........1859–61
Enoch H. Lyman.........1860–66
William C. Eaton..........1862–67
P. Smith Williams.........1867–69
Elisha A. Edwards*....... 1868
Justin Thayer.............1869–74
Samuel Mills Cook........1871–75
Elnathan Graves...........1875–86
Flavel Gaylord............1879–87
Emory C. Davis†..........1887–

Special County Commissioners.

Ithamar Conkey...........1828–29
Oliver Smith..............1830–34
Elisha Strong.............1830–34
Dyar Bancroft............ 1835
Ephraim Smith...........1835–40
Benjamin White...........1835–40
William Clark, Jr..........1841–43
James H. Clapp..........1841–43
Joseph Smith.............1844–48
Luther Edwards..........1844–49
John A. Morton.......... 1849
George Allen............1850–52

Elkanah Ring, Jr..........1850–52
Adolphus Strong 1853–56
Otis G. Hill..............1853–56
Charles Adams...........1857–62
Justin Thayer.............1857–68
Lorenzo S. Nash..........1863–68
Elnathan Graves..........1869–74
Austin Eastman...........1869–73
Samuel L. Parsons.........1874–83
Charles E. Blood‡.........1874–
Silas G. Hubbard..........1883–86
Charles K. Brewster‡.......1887–

* Term expires 1888.   † Term expires 1889.

‡ Term expires 1889.

CHAPTER VIII.

First Newspaper—Its Origin—Still in Existence—Newspapers of Northampton—of Amherst—of Easthampton—of Huntington—of Ware—of Belchertown.

THE year 1786 marked an important era in the history of the territory now included within the limits of the county. In the early autumn of that year the first newspaper made its appearance, at Northampton—a mark of enterprise and progress in any community. There was then no paper published nearer than Springfield, Hartford and Worcester. The troubled times of the Shays Rebellion period were at their zenith in this vicinity then, and to afford a vehicle for reaching the reason of the people, was doubtless a weighty object in starting the sheet. William Butler was the founder of the paper, and the first number appeared on the 6th of September. The Hampshire Gazette,* which, to this very day, covering a prosperous life of over one hundred years, continues to be a welcome weekly visitor and a valued friend to morality and progress.

William Butler was then a young man of twenty-two years, and a practical printer. He had served an apprenticeship at the printing business with Hudson & Goodwin, printers and publishers of Hartford. He came here in the summer of 1786, and at the time he issued his first number had no office of his own, but had planned to erect a building, and while it was being built he set up his printing office in the rear part of Benjamin Prescott's house, on the corner of Main and Pleasant streets, where the Kirkland block now stands.

The first copies say, " Printed by William Butler, a few rods east of the court-house." Soon afterward his building was completed. It stood on the northeasterly side of Pleasant street, was two stories in height, twenty feet front, and twenty-one feet deep, and is now the northwesterly part of the store of G. L. Loomis & Co. The printing office was in the second story, and Daniel Butler, brother of the printer, had a variety store below.

Mr. Butler sold the paper July 1, 1815, and William W. Clapp was his successor. Mr. Clapp changed the name of the paper, making it the *Hampshire Gazette and Publick Advertiser,* and also changed its general style and make-up, but not to the satisfaction of his patrons generally. At any rate, in December of the following year (1816) he advertised the establishment for

---

* In this chapter the names of all live papers are printed in SMALL CAPITALS, extinct papers in *italics.*

7*

sale, and January 1, 1817, it was bought by a young law firm, consisting of Isaac C. Bates and Hophni Judd. As neither of these were practical print-ers, they took into partnership with them, in the following June, Thomas Watson Shepard, who was a printer and had a job office here. From that time until April 10, 1822, the paper was published under the firm name of Thomas W. Shepard & Co., when it passed into the hands of Sylvester Judd, Jr., brother of Hophni.

Mr. Judd retained the paper until January 1, 1835. Under his manage-ment the paper rapidly inceased in value and circulation. But Mr. Judd's writings and his valuable historical labors are too well known in Hampshire county to require recapitulation at this point.

Charles P. Huntington and William A. Hawley secceeded Mr. Judd. The former was a young lawyer, and the latter just out of his seven years' appren-ticeship in the printing office of J. S. & C. Adams, of Amherst. Mr. Hun-tington was connected with the paper only about five months, when, June 3, 1835, he sold his interest to Mr. Hawley, who continued its editor and pub-lisher until March, 1853, when he sold out to Hopkins, Bridgman & Co., booksellers and publishers at the old Butler book store on Shop Row.

When the latter firm took the paper, they employed James R. Trumbull as editor, who had served a four years' apprenticeship in the *Gazette* office under Mr. Hawley. Mr. Trumbull edited the paper until January 1, 1858, when Thomas Hale, of Windsor, Vt., bought a half-interest in it, and be-came the editor. He remained in that position until October 1, 1858, when the entire establishment was sold to Mr. Trumbull, and on November 1, fol-lowing, the *Gazette* and the *Northampton Courier* were united, under the ownership and editorship of Mr. Trumbull and Henry S. Gere. This co-partnership continued until January 1, 1877, when Mr. Trumbull, through failing health, sold out to Mr. Gere, who is still the venerable old *Gazette's* editor and publisher.

Twice, for short periods, the GAZETTE has been issued daily. In 1846, while the interest in the Mexican war was at its height, Mr. Hawley issued a daily from May 27th to July 30th; and in 1861, from April 26th to May 25th, when the excitement over the war of the Rebellion was most intense, a daily was printed by Trumbull & Gere.

The GAZETTE is now published every Tuesday afternoon, and has a circula-tion of about 3,400.

The *Patriotic Gazette* was the second paper started in Northampton. It was established by Andrew Wright, April 12, 1799, and died in about a year.

The *Republican Spy*, established at Springfield in 1803, was removed to Northampton in 1804, by its publisher, Thomas Ashley. On the 14th of December, 1808, its name was changed to the *Anti-Monarchist and Repub-lican Watchman*, and subsequently, March 12, 1811, to *The Democrat.* It was discontinued about the year 1815, or soon after the close of the war of 1812.

The Hive, by T. M. Pomeroy, was established at Northampton in August, 1803. It was semi-literary in cast, and Federal in politics, at least until December 25, 1804, when it became exclusively a political journal. It was discontinued the following year, 1805.

The Oracle, Northampton's seventh paper, was established by Hiram Ferry, in 1823, It was a religious weekly, and took a decided stand on the side of total abstinence. It was continued only about three years.

The Christian Freeman was the next venture here, by Jonathan A. Saxton, who brought it from Greenfield. It was devoted to politics and Unitarianism, and had a brief existence.

The Northampton Courier first appeared in 1829, a Whig newspaper, established by Winthrop Atwill. April 8, 1840, Mr. Atwill sold out to Thomas W. Shepard, and on the 22d of the same month Mr. Shepard took into partnership Josiah W. Smith, who, on the 17th of June, became sole proprietor. On the 24th of April, 1847, Mr. Smith sold the establishment to Rev. William Tyler, a Congregational clergyman. In the following year he changed its politics to the free-soil side. In 1849, May 1st, Rev. Mr. Tyler sold to Henry S. Gere, who continued the paper until November 1, 1858, when he united it with the HAMPSHIRE GAZETTE, as we have previously stated.

The Hampshire Republican appears next in the list of Northampton newspapers. It was established by Chauncey Clark, and first appeared February 18, 1835. In 1836 he was succeeded by Oliver Warner, and he in turn by Lewis Ferry, in 1837. About this time its name was changed to the *Northampton Democrat*. From this time forward the changes in its proprietorship and management were rapid, and finally, July 1, 1847, its subscription list was purchased by the *Springfield Post*, and it was issued with its old head from that establishment until the discontinuance of the latter, in 1854.

The Temperance Banner, a temperance bi-monthly, was established here by Timothy H. Mather, February 21, 1835, and was continued by him until October, 1836.

The Hampshire Herald, an organ of the " Liberty party," was established February 4, 1845. It was owned by J. P. Williston, Northampton, and Joel Hayden, Williamsburg, and conducted by A. W. Thayer. It was continued till August 15, 1848. During its last year it was published by Henry S. Gere and Harvey J. Smith. On the 22d of August it was merged with the *Northampton Courier*.

The *Independent Citizen* was started by Henry J. Smith in 1849, only one or two numbers of which were issued.

THE HAMPSHIRE COUNTY JOURNAL.—In the history of this enterprising sheet we must turn back to the year 1860. On April 13th of that year Henry M. Burt issued the first number of the Northampton *Free Press*. This sheet had a varying fortune, and, in 1874, it was consolidated with the Northampton *Journal*, under the name of *The Journal and Free Press*. This name was retained until the proprietors took the paper, when it was changed to the HAMPSHIRE COUNTY JOURNAL. Mr. Burt's venture was in the shape of a semi-weekly sheet of four pages, 20x28 inches, five columns to the page. The new paper met with a warm reception, and the marked independence of character and managerial ability of its owner and editor soon impressed itself upon the paper which he edited, and the *Free Press* became noted for the vigor and independence of its conduct. In 1864 Mr. Burt enlarged his paper, making it 21x33 inches, and taking as partner Charles H. Lyman. This partnership, however, lasted but a few months, and Mr. Burt remained the sole conductor of the paper a few months longer, disposing of his entire interest in the sheet December 9, 1864, to Albert R. Parsons, a native of Northampton, and a graduate of Yale college. The *Free Press* was again enlarged under Mr. Parsons's management the following year, making it 23x35 inches. In December, 1869, Mr. Parsons disposed of the establishment to Calvin Porter and H. M. Converse, who gave the paper a new dress of type and improved it generally. At the beginning of the year 1871 the paper was again enlarged, and changed from a weekly to a semi-weekly. Mr. Porter severed his connection with the *Free Press* November 3d of the same year, and the new firm took the name of Converse & Burleigh, the junior partner being Le Moyne Burleigh. Mr. Converse sold his interest in the *Free Press* to Mr. Burleigh, February 1, 1873, and Mr. Burleigh continued alone the management of the paper until its consolidation with the *Journal*, the latter paper being established September 12, 1874. This was an eight-page paper, printed in old style type. Its proprietors were H. H. Bond & Co., H. H. Bond and A. M. Powell being editors. In 1875 A. G. Hill, of Florence, bought of Mr. Bond his entire inerest in the *Journal* property, and consolidated the two papers, as we have shown. George R. Edwards was publisher of the paper till November, 1876. January 1, 1877, the present proprietors, Wade, Warner & Co., took charge of the office. The JOURNAL is a large, bright, independent family newspaper, issued from its office on Court street every Friday afternoon.

Le Jean Baptiste, a French paper, was started here by Burleigh & Chatel, February 24, 1875, but on the 21st of September following, P. O. Chatel became sole proprietor. April 10, 1876, Mr. Chatel removed the paper to Holyoke. In March, 1878, he again came back to Northampton and remained for a time.

The NORTHAMPTON DAILY HERALD came into existence as follows: In the summer of 1882, Messrs. Bridgman & Gay bought out the plant of the *Holyoke Herald*, and October 1, 1882, the *Hampshire Herald* was started, printed in Holyoke as a weekly. September 1, 1883, the plant was removed to Northampton, and the DAILY HERALD established. Mr. Bridgman soon became the sole proprietor of the paper, and from February 1, 1884, to July 1, 1885, leased the paper to Carruthers & Howland, obtaining management of it again on the latter date. In September, 1885, the present proprietor, E. C. Stone, purchased the office. The paper has greatly increased in circulation and influence within the past year. It is the only daily published in Hampshire county.

AMHERST.

John B. Cotting was the editor, and Carter & Adams the proprietors, of Amherst's first venture in the newspaper business—*The Chemist and Meteorological Journal*, whose brief life began with the issue of July 1, 1826. The same proprietors began the publication of *The New England Enquirer*, December 2, 1826, a file of which is carefully preserved by S. C. Carter, the venerable treasurer of the Amherst savings bank ; its editors were Hon. Osmyn Baker (a native of the town and a member of congress, 1839–1845) and Rev. Samuel Worcester, a college professor.

The next paper was *The Amherst Gazette*, James B. Yerrington, editor and proprietor, which appeared in 1839.

The first paper which "lived to grow up" was *The Hampshire and Franklin Express*, edited by Samuel C. Nash. Its publication was begun in 1844, and has continued until the present time, though under different names, viz.: *The Hampshire and Franklin Express*, 1844–1865 ; *The Hampshire Express*, 1865-1868 ; and THE AMHERST RECORD, since May, 1868. Among its editors have been Samuel C. Nash, J. R. Trumbull, who was afterwards editor of *The Hampshire Gazette* for a quarter of a century; Leander Wetherell, William Faxon, who was both editor and proprietor as Mr. Trumbull had been before him, Mr. Wetherell having been employed by the Adams Bros. as publisher ; J. H. Brewster and Rev. Pliny H. White, J. H. Brewster and Rev. J. H. M. Leland, and Rev. J. H. M. Leland successively conducted the paper until 1858, when it was purchased by Mr. H. A. Marsh, who sold it in 1866 to Capt. J. L. Skinner. Mr. H. M. McCloud became connected with the paper in February, 1868. He was at first associated with Mr. Skinner, afterwards with Mr. Charles L. Storrs, and finally with Mr. J. E. Williams, who became connected with the paper in June, 1877, and who is at present its editor and proprietor. THE RECORD is issued every Wednesday afternoon.

A rival paper, *The Amherst Transcript*, established in 1877 by the Marsh Bros., who had the contract for the publication of the AMHERST STUDENT, a college paper. It had an independent existence of about two years, but was soon consolidated with its more successful rival.

The college publications began with *The Sprite*, in 1831, whose brief existence covered but half a dozen numbers. Its successors, *The Shrine* and *The Guest* were yearlings when they ceased to be published. The permanent papers have been *Horae Collegianae*, 1837-1840 ; *The Indicator*, 1848–1851 ; *The Experiment*, 1850-1851 ; *The Amherst Collegiate Magazine*, 1853–1857, and 1861–1862; *The Ichnolite*, 1857–1861. None of these attained the success of the present AMHERST STUDENT, which was started in 1868 and has since been regularly published. Its editors are chosen from the junior class and it is published on alternate Saturdays of the college terms.

EASTHAMPTON.

Previous to October, 1875, newspapers were published only transiently at Easthampton. On the 14th of that month appeared the first number of *The Leader*, which was destined to continue through various vicissitudes and changes in name, form and proprietorship to the present time (1886). The founder of *The Leader* was H. De Bill, a caterer, who kept a restaurant on Shop Row. It was an eight page, four column paper, published Thursdays, and devoted to local news, correspondence and miscellany. The first eight numbers were printed by the Star Printing Co., at Northampton. On the following 9th of December the form was changed to four pages, five columns, and the publication was continued in that form till May 13, 1876, when the publication day was changed to Saturdays. With the next number, May 20, the paper was enlarged to six columns. Mr. De Bill's connection with the paper closed with that month. It was sold June 1st to Mr. H. M. Converse, who at that time conducted a job printing office in Easthampton. The name was changed to *Easthampton Enterprise*, and the publication continued by Mr. Converse till September 1, 1881. With the beginning of the fourth volume, October 11, 1878, the publication day was changed from Saturday morning to Friday evening. The subscription rate was $1,50 a year.

The News Letter was started by the Torrey Brothers, L. E. and D. C. Torrey, on Wednesday, June 4, 1879. It was a diminutive sheet, four small pages of three columns each, published Wednesday and Saturday mornings at $1.00 per year. Twelve numbers were issued in this style. Then, after an interval of eleven days, *The News Letter* appeared with four pages, four columns, published weekly, Wednesday mornings, at seventy-five cents per year. With the first number of the second volume, May 12, 1880, the size was doubled to eight pages, four columns, the name changed to *The East-hampton News*, and the price put at $1.00 a year. It was continued without further change till September 1, 1881, when the Torrey Brothers purchased *The Enterprise* of Mr. Converse and merged the two papers under the title of THE EASTHAMPTON NEWS AND ENTERPRISE. The form adopted was that of the *Enterprise*, and Friday was chosen as the day of publication. It has been published continuously and with a good degree of growth and prosperity to the present time. The interest of the junior partner in the concern was purchased by the senior partner and present owner, L. E. Torrey, January 1, 1884.

HUNTINGTON.

THE VALLEY ECHO, of Huntington, is the first newspaper ever published between Westfield and Pittsfield, or in any Hampshire county town west of

Northampton. In February, 1885, two Holyoke journalists conceived the idea that a right live paper, free from the millstones which might drag down country newspapers, could be made to pay in that large stretch of territory, and accordingly steps were immediately taken to give individuality to the thirteen small towns through the instrumentality of a home organ. In the following month the first issue appeared, and was bought up with an eagerness that astonished the publishers. A thorough canvass of all the towns lying in the beautiful valley and among the rugged rocks of the adjoining towns was commenced with such good success, that in July a printing office was established in Huntington. Soon after, the increasing business compelled the publishers to start a separate edition for Chester, and in the early part of 1886 another edition was commenced, for Westfield. During this time the press work had been done by hand-power, and it had become so arduous that in May a large steam press was added, and the paper enlarged. The publishers claim that their success is due principally to these facts, viz. : that they knew their business thoroughly ; that they printed all the home news in the same manner that the daily doings are served by the enterprising dailies; that a low rate of subscription was charged ; and by "minding their own business."

WARE.

The *Village Gazette*, Ware's first newspaper, was established by Hemenway & Fisk, July 7, 1847. The firm remained thus until March 15, 1848, when Mr. Fisk disposed of his interest to Mr. Hemenway, though he remained with the paper in the capacity of editor until January 1, 1849. Later on, in the same month, Mr. Hemenway sold out to Mandell & Hathaway, who continued the paper, with an alteration of its title to *The Ware Gazette*, until the summer of 1850, when the subscription list was purchased by J. F. Downing. Mr. Downing founded upon this list the *Ware American*. The following autumn it was sold to the *Springfield Republican*.

The *Ware Offering*, a monthly publication, designed for factory operatives, was started in January, 1848, by S. F. Pepper, though only two or three issues were printed. Since that time Ware has had no purely local paper. Several, however, from Worcester, Barre and Palmer have been sent to the town as reprints, with Ware headings, and partially made up of Ware local items.

BELCHERTOWN.

The Hampshire Sentinel and Farmers' and Manufacturers' Journal was started at Belchertown in November, 1826, by J. R. Shute. Mr. Shute died March 21, 1828, and was succeeded by C. A. Warren, who, three months later, was succeeded by Warren & Wilson. They issued their first number August 6, 1828, and continued the publication till September 8, 1830, when it was published by S. W. Andrews as the *Hampshire Sentinel*, till May 4, 1831, when it was consolidated with the *Northampton Courier*.

CHAPTER IX.

CONNECTICUT RIVER A HIGHWAY FOR TRAVEL—ITS NAVIGATION IM-
PROVED—COUNTY'S FIRST INTERNAL IMPROVEMENTS—LOCKS AROUND
SOUTH HADLEY FALLS—STEAMBOAT NAVIGATION—MOREY AND FUL-
TON— NEW HAVEN AND NORTHAMPTON CANAL— TURNPIKES AND
RAILROADS—BOSTON AND ALBANY RAILROAD—CONNECTICUT RIVER
RAILROAD—NEW HAVEN AND NORTHAMPTON RAILROAD—MT. TOM
AND EASTHAMPTON RAILROAD—NEW LONDON NORTHERN RAILROAD
—WARE RIVER RAILROAD—SPRINGFIELD, ATHOL AND NORTHEASTERN
RAILROAD—MASSACHUSETTS CENTRAL RAILROAD.

IN this chapter it is our purpose to briefly review the internal improvements that have been made in the county since the days when its only
highways of travel were its several streams and a few Indian pathways.
First, then, we must turn to the noble river which rolls through the county's
beautiful valley. From time immemorial Connecticut river was a favorite
pathway of Indian travel, and later became the great highway of the white
settlers located in its valley. But with the increase of population came the
increase of commerce and travel, and it soon became apparent that the river
navigation must be improved to accommodate the increasing demand for con-
veniences. The several large falls in its course were the greatest inconvenience the boatmen encountered. Accordingly, petitions were drawn up and
presented to the legislature, and on the 23d of February, 1792, that body
passed an " act incorporating the Hon. John Worthington, Esq., and others
therein named,—for the purpose of rendering Connecticut river passable for
boats and other things from the mouth of Chicopee river northward through
this Commonwealth,--by the names of the proprietors of the Locks and Canals
on the Connecticut river."   -

Under this act of incorporation, work in constructing a canal and locks
around South Hadley falls was soon after commenced, under the superintendence of Benjamin Prescott, of Northampton, engineer. This was the first
stroke towards building up the great works of internal improvement that the
county to-day enjoys. Turnpike corporations and stage-coach lines rapidly
followed.

It soon became apparent, however, that some more convenient mode of
transportation must be devised than that afforded by the rude flat boats of
the Connecticut, or by the several stage lines which traversed the several
turnpike systems. Then followed the period of steamboat navigation on the
Connecticut.

Although steamboat navigation was never brought to a point of practical utility here, its history begins with the history of the steamboat itself, briefly as follows: About the beginning of the century there lived in the northern part of the valley two brothers Morey, Samuel and Ithamar, the former at Oxford, N. H., and the latter at Fairlee, Vt.,—Samuel with a remarkable genius for invention, and Ithamar, a skillful mechanic. The universal applicability of steam had already been demonstrated, and among those who undertook its application to navigation was Samuel Morey. Under his direction Ithamar built a steamboat, which actually navigated the waters of the Connecticut between Oxford and Fairlee. Of this steamboat, which had its machinery in its bow, Samuel took a model to New York and showed it to Fulton, who was experimenting to the same end. Fulton was pleased with the work, and suggested to Morey to change the machinery to the middle of the boat. This he returned to Fairlee to do, and then took his model again to New York, to find that Fulton had made use of his ideas and was ahead of him in getting out a patent. He returned home disappointed and with a sense of injury.

The first really practical attempt at steamboat navigation on the Connecticut, however, was not made until 1827, when the " Barnet," a strong boat seventy-five by fourteen and one-half feet, was built at Hartford, and succeeded, with some help, in ascending the river as far as Bellows Falls, Vt. This was her first and last trip, however, for she was taken back to Hartford, laid up, and finally broken to pieces. In 1829 a Mr. Blanchard built a boat called the " Blanchard," of the size of the preceding one, and another eighty feet long and fourteen feet wide, drawing only twelve or fifteen inches of water, called the " Vermont." The stroke of its piston was horizontal, and its engine was of one hundred and twenty horse power. A few experimental trips were made between Bellows Falls and Barnet, but the obstacles were so great that the undertaking, after a few other vain attempts, had to be relinquished. On the levels between the locks and canals of the several falls, however, steamboats were used with comparative success, though the passengers and freight had to be transferred at the end of each level. The flat boats, rafts, etc., made through trips, using the locks, so that the navigation was fairly good from Hartford, Conn., to Dalton, N. H.

In the meantime a new highway of commerce and travel had been developed. The project of uniting the waters of the Connecticut at Northampton with New Haven harbor was first agitated in 1822. A public meeting of the towns interested in the matter was held at Southampton, in August of that year. A committee was appointed, composed of persons from all the towns represented, of which Jonathan H. Lyman, of Northampton, was chairman, to report on the feasibility of a canal from Northampton to the state line of Connecticut, in Granby. Their report, favorable to the project, with engineer's estimates, was published in the following November. In 1823 companies were chartered in Connecticut and Massachusetts to build the canal.

The Connecticut company was called the Farmington Canal Co., and the Massachusetts, the Hampshire and Hampden Canal Co. The capital of the latter company was $300,000.00—about $80,000.00 of which was subscribed in this state. The entire work from New Haven to this town cost about $1,000,000.00. The canal was completed to Westfield in 1830, and to Northampton in 1834. The business was not profitable and the stock in both states was finally transferred to a new company, called the New Haven and Northampton Canal Co., for the sum of $300,000.00.

The canal was opened July 4, 1835, on which day the first boat came through from Westfield to Northampton, drawn by four gray horses. It arrived about 4 o'clock in the afternoon. The company was chartered in both states in 1836, and continued to do business till 1847. The line of the canal at Northampton was along what is now State street, connecting with the river just above the bridge. The present Northampton and New Haven railway follows substantially the route of the old canal.

While all this was in progress, the advent of the railroad was heralded. But let us turn back a moment, and, of the many turnpike systems that were inaugurated, speak only of one, the Pontoosuc Turnpike Company, chartered in 1825, to Jonathan Allen, Lemuel Pomeroy, Joseph Shearer, Joseph Merrick and Thomas Gold, of Pittsfield; Henry Stearns, of Springfield, and Enos Foot, of Southwick. They were granted the right of building a turnpike through Chester, Middlefield, Becket, Washington, Dalton and Pittsfield, "which route presented, of all others, the most level passage from the Hudson to the Connecticut," as was subsequently reported by those in charge of the initial survey of the Western railroad. This turnpike was completed in October, 1830, and ultimately became, practically, the route of the Western railway—the Boston and Albany railroad of to-day.

In the meantime the feasibility of building a canal from Boston to Albany was presented to the legislature, which was more seriously entertained after the successful completion of the Erie canal, in 1823, and in 1825 they appointed three commissioners and an engineer to ascertain if it were practicable. The commissioners were Nathan Willis, of Pittsfield, Elihu Hoyt, of Deerfield, and Henry A. S. Dearborn, of Boston, with Col. Laomi C. Baldwin, engineer. Several routes were tested, though their report, in 1826, favored a route across "Northern Worcester, up the Deerfield river, through the Hoosac mountain, and by the valley of the Hoosac river, to the Hudson, near Troy."

As early as 1827 the feasibility of constructing a railroad on one of the above mentioned routes was agitated, though it was then contemplated that horse-power be used. Some idea of their conception of such a road may be derived from the following extract from a committee's report before the legislature on the 16th of January, 1829:—

"It is found that the cost of a continuous stone wall, laid so deep in the ground as not to be moved by the effect of frost, and surmounted by a rail of split granite about a foot in thickness and depth, with a bar of iron placed on top of it, of sufficient thickness to form the track on which the carriage wheels shall run, is much less than that of the English iron rail, and that rails of this construction, so far as can be judged by experiments which have yet been made, possess all the advantages of durability, solidity and strength."

This impracticable idea was soon abandoned, however, as was also that of utilizing horse-power. March 15, 1833, the charter of the Western railroad corporation was granted by the legislature to Nathan Hale, David Henshaw, George Bond, Henry Williams, Daniel Denny, Joshua Clapp and Eliphalet Williams and their associates, for the purpose of constructing a railroad from Worcester, the terminus of the Boston and Worcester railroad, to the line of the state of New York, with a capital limited to $2,000,000.00. The corporation was not organized until January, 1836, when the following gentlemen were made directors: John B. Wales, Edmund Dwight, George Bliss, William Lawrence, Henry Rice, John Henshaw, Francis Jackson, Josiah Quincy, Jr., and Justice Willard. Maj. William Gibbs McNeil was engaged as chief engineer, and Capt. William H. Swift as resident engineer of the company. The organization of the directors was Thomas B. Wales, president; Josiah Quincy, treasurer; and Ellis Gray Loring, clerk.

The survey of the corporation commenced in April, 1836. Twenty miles of the road, commencing at Worcester, were put under contract in January, 1837, and work was commenced on that section in the month following. In June of the same year the road from East Brookfield to Springfield was put under contract, and the work commenced upon the section in July. On the 1st day of October, 1839, the road was opened to travel between Worcester and Springfield, and, on the 23d of that month, regular merchandise trains were established. Early in 1842 the whole line was completed through to the Hudson river, with the exception of fifteen miles within the state of New York, which was run on the track of the Hudson and Berkshire railroad. From the state line to Albany the road was nominally, at least, under the conduct of a New York corporation, with the name of the Albany and West Stockbridge railway. This section was opened for travel on the 12th of September, thus accomplishing the long looked for object. December 1, 1867, the Worcester and Western railroads were consolidated, under the name of the Boston and Albany railroad.

What is now the Connecticut River railroad was the next one built in the county, the enterprise coming about as follows: March 1, 1842, a number of the citizens of Northampton and vicinity obtained a charter to build a railroad from Northampton to Springfield, under the name of the Northampton and Springfield Railroad Company, with a capital of $400,000.00, which was afterwards increased to $500,000.00. The original route was to cross the river at Mt. Holyoke and pass down on the east side of the Connecticut. Three years afterwards, several gentlemen of Greenfield, and their associates, obtained a charter for the Greenfield and Northampton Railroad Company with $500,000.00. These two companies were consolidated on equal terms July 18,

1845, taking on the present name of the Connecticut River Railroad Company, and with authority to change the route to the one now in use, from Springfield, Mass., to South Vernon, Vt., a distance of fifty miles. The road was opened to Northampton in December, 1845, to Greenfield, November 23, 1846, and through to South Vernon, January 1, 1849.

The only branch this road has in the county is the Mt. Tom railroad, extending from Mt. Tom to Easthampton, a distance of about three and three-fourth miles. While it was intended in all respects as a branch of this road, it was necessary to procure a separate charter and be constructed by an independent company. The first train of cars passed over the road on Thanksgiving day, 1871.

The New Haven and Northampton railroad, as it is now known, was the next road built after the Connecticut River. In 1846 the canal company obtained leave from the Connecticut legislature to construct a railroad on or near the line of the canal to Granby, Conn., and also a branch to Collinsville. This road was built by the New Haven and Northampton Company. The Farmington Valley Company obtained a charter and built a road from Granby to the Massachusetts state line. In 1852 the Hampden and Hampshire Company was chartered, with a capital of $175,000.00, to build a road from Westfield to the Connecticut state line. The same year the Northampton and Westfield Railroad Company was chartered with a capital of $200,000.00, for the purpose of continuing the road to Northampton. In 1853 these two roads were united, under the name of the Hampshire and Hampden Company, with a combined capital of $375,000.00. The road was opened to Westfield in 1854, and the following year to Northampton. On the first of July, 1862, all the above named roads were merged into one corporation, under the name of the New Haven and Northampton Railroad Company. The total cost of all the roads thus merged was $2,305,204.62. From New Haven to Plainville the road was opened in January, 1848; from Plainville to Granby, in February, 1850; from Granby to Northampton, in 1857; from Northampton to Williamsburg, in February, 1868. The extention to North Adams, over the Troy and Greenfield railroad, was opened July 13th, and to Turner's Falls, October 31, 1881.

The New London Northern railroad, extending from New London, Conn., to Brattleboro, Vt., a distance of 121 miles, came into existence as follows: In May, 1847, the New London, Willimantic and Springfield Railroad Company was chartered, and in May of the following year, 1848, was changed to the New London, Willimantic and Palmer Company. The road was opened through to Willimantic in September, 1849, and to Palmer in September, 1850. It was sold under foreclosure, and re-organized as the New London Northern in 1869. The Amherst and Belchertown Railroad Company was chartered in May, 1851, and opened from Palmer to Amherst in May, 1853. October 14, 1858, it was sold under foreclosure, and re-organized as the Amherst, Belchertown and Palmer road, November 23d of the same year. In March, 1864, the road was purchased by the New London Northern Company, and extended to Miller's Falls in 1867. The Miller's Falls branch of the Vermont and Massachusetts road, extending to Brattleboro, was bought by this company May 1, 1880. The entire line is leased for twenty years from December 1, 1871, to the trustees of the Central Vermont Railroad Company. The lessee assumes all responsibilities, and pays as rental $150,000.00 a year, in quarterly installments, with an additional $15,000.00 for every $100,000.00 of gross earnings in excess of $150,000.00.

The Ware River railroad extends from Palmer to Winchendon, a distance of nearly fifty miles. The company was incorporated in 1868, and the section from Palmer to Gilbertville was built in 1870, at a cost of $250,000.00. The original company became embarrassed, and in 1873 a new one was formed, retaining the old name. The road was opened through during that year. April 1, 1873, the road was leased to the Boston and Albany Company for a period of nine hundred and ninety-nine years.

The Springfield, Athol and Northeastern railroad, extending from Springfield to Athol, now a part of the Boston and Albany railroad system, was originally the Athol and Enfield railroad, chartered in 1864-65. The first portion of the road constructed was from Athol to a connection with the New London Northern road at Barretts, whence the company's trains ran to Palmer, four miles, over the New London Northern track. In 1872 the company obtained a supplementary charter, changing the name of corporation to the Springfield, Athol and Northeastern Railroad Company, and authorizing them to build a line from Barretts to Springfield, about seventeen miles, which was constructed in 1873. It is now, as we have said, a part of the Boston and Albany system.

The project which resulted in what there is to-day of the Massachusetts Central railroad, had its beginning away back in 1867, when a charter was obtained and a state loan of $1,000,000.00 granted, conditionally, for building and operating a railroad from Williamsburg to North Adams, over the mountains, " up into Goshen and down into Cummington." The corporation was organized at North Adams in September, 1868. While this project was in agitation, however, a proposition was started to build a road east from Northampton to Sterling Junction, thus making a connection with Boston and the Hudson river. December 22, 1868, a meeting was held at Northampton, at which a committee of fifteen was appointed to secure the co-operation of the towns along the proposed route, and to obtain surveys. From this action resulted the charter, May 10, 1869, of the Central Massachusetts Railroad Company, with the right to build a road from Cambridge to Northampton, a distance of one hundred and three and one-half miles, with a branch from Amherst to West Deerfield, thirteen and one-half miles. The road was put under contract in 1871, and work was pushed vigorously from several points along the route till the panic of 1873 prevented the negotiation of its bonds, when the work stopped. October 1, 1881, the road was opened from Cambridge to Hudson, nearly twenty-four miles, and in December of the same year to Jefferson's, forty-four miles. July 1, 1882, the company made default in the payment of interest then due, and the trustees under the mortgage took possession of the property May 4, 1883. Operations were suspended May 16th, and the road was sold under foreclosure September 1, 1883. It was purchased on behalf of the bondholders, who organized the present company, the Massachusetts Central Railroad Company, November 10, 1883, under a special act of the legislature. By the terms of the charter of the new company, preferred stock is to be issued dollar for dollar in payment for the mortgage debt of the old company, this stock to have entire control of the affairs of the company until such time as the road shall earn two semi-annual dividends of four per cent. each in any one year. Common stock is to be issued share for share for the stock of the old company. It also anthorizes the extension of the road from Bondsville to the New York state line, and the leasing to, or consolidation with, the Poughkeepsie, Hartford and Boston road, or any other road connecting this line in Massachusetts or New York. In June, 1885, a special act of the legislature was passed authorizing the trustees to make a contract for the operation of the road and to issue certificates of indebtedness to the amount of $200,000.00. November 7, 1886, the road was leased to the Boston and Lowell Railroad Company for a period of ninety-nine years. It is confidently asserted that operations will be re-commenced at once, and work pushed rapidly to completion.

CHAPTER X.

REMARKS MILITARY—REVOLUTIONARY RECORDS—SHAYS REBELLION*—
WAR OF 1812-15—MEXICAN WAR—WAR OF THE UNION—ROSTER OF
FIELD, STAFF AND COMPANY OFFICERS.

WHILE we devote this chapter to the military history of Hampshire county, it is not our purpose to enter into details, unless, perhaps, it be in the outline sketch of Shays Rebellion, an uprising whose history is inseparably connected with the history of Hampshire county. Neither is an extended sketch of the early Indian troubles, the French and Indian wars, and the wars with the mother country necessary, as the part each took, its sacrifices and losses, will be spoken of farther on in the work, in connection with their respective sketches.

* For the remarks on this subject we are indebted to Rev. G. H. Johnson, of North Amherst.

None of the leading events of the great wars occurred in the county ; but its inhabitants were well up to the highest point of patriotism. Nothing, perhaps, could in a brief way give a general idea of the spirit displayed during the great war for independence than the following extracts from the town records of Northampton, viz. :—

" Dec. 26, 1774.—The inhabitants met in pursuance to adjournment, and chose a committee of twelve persons to receive, preserve & convey such articles as shall be contributed by the Inhabitants of this town for the relief of their suffering brethren in the Towns of Boston and Charlestown."

" March 4, 1776.—At this meeting a Committee of Correspondence, Inspection and Safety was chosen, consisting of fifteen persons."

" Oct. 3, 1776.—The question at this meeting was put, Whether the Town will give their Consent that the present House of Representatives of the state of the Massachusetts Bay in New England, together with the Council (if they consent), in one body with the House, and by equal voice, should consult, agree on, and enact such a Constitution & Form of Government for this state as the said House of Representatives and Council as aforesaid on the fullest and mature deliberation shall judge will most conduce to the Safety, peace and Happiness of this State in all after succession and generations ; and it passed in the affirmative."

" The Question was then put, Whether the Town would direct that the same be made Publick for the Inspection and perusal of the Inhabitants before the ratification thereof by the assembly ; and it passed in the affirmative."

" March 3, 1777.—The Town entered upon the consideration of the matter which had been debated, viz. : what methods they would take to encourage and facilitate the raising of this Town's proportion of men for the Continental Army, and passed the following votes, thereon, viz. :—

" That those persons that shall now engage in the service aforesaid, who belonged to Capt. Allen's and Capt. Chapin's Company the last year, both officers and privates, shall have full compensation for all losses by them sustained in cloaths and other articles, when such losses were unavoidable, and not through the negligence of those who sustained them.

" And as a further encouragement to them, or any other able-bodied men belonging to this town who will engage in the said service.

" The town Voted that they and each of them shall receive from the Inhabitants of the Town of Northampton the sum of fifteen pounds, which sum shall be paid to them several times, viz. : namely, five pounds before they shall march to the said Army, and five pounds more shall be paid them or to their Order in the month of April, 1778, and the other five pounds in the month of April, 1779. And, whereas, it was represented to the Town that some of the inhabitants have heretofore failed of doing their proportion in promoting the publick cause.

" The Town voted that a large Committee should be appointed to examine and consider what persons in the Town have been so delinquent, and that the said Committee make out a list of such persons, with the sums affixed to their respective names which they judge it will be necessary for them to advance, in order to their doing their full proportion with the other inhabitants of this town, and that those who are found delinquent as aforesaid, shall be required to pay the sum so affixed to their names, to such persons as the Town shall appoint to collect the same.

" The Town also voted that the sum of seventy pounds now in the hands of the Town Treasurer, being the Fines of Several persons who refused to march in the last Draughts of the Militia, be applied to the payment of the bounty aforesaid, and that what further sums shall be necessary to make up the losses and pay the Bounty as aforesaid, shall be Assessed upon the Polls and Estates of the Inhabitants of this Town at such time as the Town shall order.

"April 15, 1777, voted to increase the bounty to 30 pounds."

Following immediately upon the Revolution, or rather growing out of it, was the memorable "Shays Rebellion." This uprising in Western Massachusetts against the authorities of the state, in 1786, was not, however, strickly speaking, a rebellion; that is, it was not prompted by any spirit of disloyalty, nor was it designed or plotted with the wish to overturn the government. It was the wild and lawless expression of discontent with harsh circumstances; the natural outbreak of those who were suffering and oppressed. Nothing more clearly shows the patriotic spirit of the people than their utterly exhausted condition at the close of the Revolutionary war. The credit of the government had long since gone; the states were hardly in any better circumstances; few individuals were out of debt. Business was more than prostrated, with the exception of agriculture, it was well nigh destroyed. There was no demand for labor, and there was a continuous call for the payment of debts and taxes. In all probability the war debt of Massachusetts—including the debts of state and towns, bounties promised and arrears due to soldiers and their families—averaged nearly, if not quite, fifty dollars for every man, woman and child in the commonwealth, or an average of nearly two hundred dollars for each family in the state.* The laws of that time had never contemplated such a condition of affairs, and were exceedingly unjust in their operation. An insolvent debtor's property was divided among his creditors, not in equal proportion, but in the order in which their attachments of the property were levied. Consequently, those who were first to suspect a debtor took all his property, and those less suspicious or prompt lost all their due. The debtor who could pay nothing was put into prison with the felons and villains of the day, and their families left to want and poverty. Under such circumstances the outbreak was far less a rebellion than the inevitable outcry of suffering and distress. Had it been real rebellion—had Shays possessed either the courage or ability necessary for leadership—possibly the movement would have spread until the government was overthrown, and necessity had recalled the power of England to protect those who, after long war, had conquered her armies in battle. That such a result was feared even by Washington himself is evident from his correspondence, and how ripe the circumstances would have been for such a sad result, is evident to every student of history who can add to poverty, suffering, and injustice the elements of disloyalty at heart and of able leadership in rebellious purposes. Thank God the two last were lacking in the Shays Rebellion.

The first organizer in the lawless efforts of the day was Samuel Ely, a

* See article by John Fiske, in *Atlantic Monthly* for September, 1886, p. 382.

deposed clergyman who had come into Hampshire county from Somers, Conn. He was instrumental as early as 1781 in the gathering of conventions at which the grievances of the people were discussed and when lawless acts were suggested, if not encouraged. As the courts and lawyers were instrumental in the foreclosure of mortgages, the distraining of personal property and the imprisonment of debtors, the popular outcry and rage was largely directed against the officials of law and justice. The first outbreak was at Northampton, in April, 1782, when Ely gathered a mob of sufficiently threatening aspect to disturb the sessions of the courts. For this he was arrested and tried; and pleading guilty, he was sentenced to imprisonment at Springfield. A second mob set him free; the ringleaders of this mob were arrested and imprisoned at Northampton; a mob came down from Hatfield demanding their release, and they were finally liberated upon their promise to submit to the decision of the general court in their case. The general court took no action concerning them, and the impression prevailed that there was no power able to suppress or punish such uprisings. Towns which had loyally devoted themselves to the support of the long war with England, became so sympathetic with the discontent of the times that delegates to the various conventions were not only chosen in open town meetings, but the town treasurer was instructed to pay them out of the town treasury for time spent at these conventions and for the expense of traveling.* These conventions were held at Shutesbury, January 30, 1782; at Hatfield, in the following summer; and at other towns in the county. The discussions and resolutions of these conventions; the lack of any wise measures to prevent the growing evil; the continual increase of discontent and hardship; the passionate appeals of demagogues and idle theorists—all contributed to make matters worse instead of better. Many proposed remedies were considered in the lower branch of the general court, but the conservatism of the senate crushed the hopes of many a supposed panacea; forthwith the senate was denounced by the mischief makers and the ignorant, and there was a demand that the legislature consist of but a single house, which should immediately by its size and method of election represent the people. One favorite scheme for relieving the needs of money was the issue of paper money by the state. This had already been done recklessly in Rhode Island, North Carolina and South Carolina, more cautiously in Virginia, Pennsylvania and New York, while Maryland had failed to do so by the refusal of the senate to pass a house bill for this purpose, and in New Jersey the issuing of such money was delayed only a single year by the veto of Governor Livingston. In every state the value of such money had rapidly decreased, and when it was proposed that Massachusetts should follow their example, the movers in the matter calmly proposed that the law allowing the issue of the paper money should also regulate its decline in value, making it worth ninety cents on a dollar at first,

*See publication of Amherst town records, page 87.

8*

seventy cents after a brief period, later fifty cents and finally nothing, when it would of course disappear from trade and commerce. This charming scheme failed of approval in the house by a vote of ninety-nine to nineteen. It was believed to be the influence of Boston merchants and men of wealth which had killed this bill, and also another, making cows and horses a legal tender for debts. Forthwith the cry went out that the legislature ought not to meet in Boston, but in some place less exposed to the influence of conservative wealth. Finally, a convention which met at Deerfield recommended the gathering of a large and representative convention which should distinctly formulate all the grievances of the people and demand their redress. This convention assembled at Hatfield, August 22, 1786, and there were present delegates from fifty towns of Hampshire county (as originally constituted) who, after a three days' discussion, "and upon mature consideration, deliberation and debate," (as their preamble declared) voted that the following articles specified "grievances and unnecessary burdens now lying upon the people," which in their opinion were "the sources of that discontent so evidently discoverable throughout this commonwealth :"—

1st. The existence of the senate.

2d. The present mode of representation.

3d. The officers of government not being annually dependent on the representatives of the people, in general court assembled, for their salaries.

4th. All the civil officers of government not being annually elected by the representatives of the people in general court assembled.

5th. The existence of the courts of common pleas and general sessions of the peace.

6th. The fee-table as it now stands.

7th. The present mode of appropriating the impost and excise.

8th. The unreasonable grants made to some of the officers of government.

9th. The supplementary aid.

10th. The present mode of paying the governmental securities.

11th. The present mode adopted for the payment and collection of the last tax.

12th. The present mode of taxation, as it operates unequally between the polls and estates and between landed and mercantile interests.

13th. The present methods of practice of the attorneys at law.

14th. The want of a sufficient medium of trade to remedy the mischiefs arising from a scarcity of money.

15th. The general court sitting in the town of Boston.

16th. The present embarrassments on the press.

The convention also recommended the towns to secure the election of such representatives as would favor the emission of paper money, "subject to depreciation," and favor also the calling of a constitutional convention for the purpose of securing desired changes in the constitution of the state. They asked each town in the county to petition the governor to call a special session of the legislature for the redress of grievances, and recommended the people to "abstain from all mobs and unlawful assemblies until a constitutional method of redress can be obtained." They sent copies of these results of deliberation to Springfield for publication and to Worcester and Berkshire counties, where similar conventions were to be held, and adjourned after directing their chairman to call another convention whenever he deemed it best.

Four days after this convention was the day appointed by law for the session of the court of common pleas at Northampton, also for the general sessions of the peace. A mob of fifteen hundred people took possession of the courthouse and grounds and succeeded in preventing any session of the court, their desire being to prevent legal proceedings necessary for the collection of debts. This mob was followed by a proclamation from the governor against "all such riotous proceedings;" but the matter had now gone too far to be suppressed by proclamations. The courts were prevented from sitting in Worcester, Middlesex and Berkshire counties, as well as in Hampshire, and the whole condition of the state was threatening in the extreme. Anarchy and chaos seemed to have taken the place of law and order.

Daniel Shays and Luke Day now came to the front as leaders of the uprising. The former was a resident of Pelham, a Revolutionary veteran, and a man of good address. He had fought bravely at Bunker Hill and shared in the campaign resulting in Burgoyne's surrender. The other leader was a native of West Springfield, noted for his proneness to make speeches. He too had served creditably in the Revolutionary war. His definition of liberty was thus given in a speech to his followers : " If you wish to know what liberty is, I will tell you. It is for every man to do what he pleases, to make other folks do as you please to have them, and to keep folks from serving the devil."

October 23, 1786, Shays sent word to the selectmen of each town in Hampshire county, requesting them to arm their militia, provide each man with sixty rounds of ammunition, and to have them ready to march at a moment's warning. The uprising had now passed in the person of Shays beyond the mere acts of discontent and resistance to wrong and hardship, but it is doubtful if the discontented and restless people were ready even now to follow their leader into rebellion. Shays called a convention at Hadley. Belchertown voted not to be represented in this convention at first, but afterwards, by a vote of thirty-five to thirty-two, decided to send delegates. Evidently the movement was going farther than many cared to follow, and the Belchertown town meeting foreshadowed the opposition to violent measures which indicated already the failure of the rebellion.

The grand jury were to meet with the supreme judicial court in Springfield, September 26, 1786. Hitherto it had been the inferior courts whose sessions had been interfered with by mobs, these courts being the chief legal instrument of collecting debts. But now, fearing indictments for their lawless acts, the followers of Shays determined to prevent the sitting of the supreme court in order that no indictments might be found.   In this they were measurably successful, for while the vigorous energy of Gen. William Shepherd, of West-field, and a small band of volunteers, and of the militia, enabled the court to go through the forms of business, yet, beyond the defaulting of a single case by reason of the non-appearance of a defendant, no business was done, and there was no report of the grand jury.   A collision between Shays's followers and Gen. Shepherd's militia was happily averted, but the real success of the effort of Shays to prevent the finding of indictments by the grand jury gave him and his followers an impulse to yet more desperate undertakings.   For-tunately, the conservative, law-abiding spirit of the people began now to awake.   The friends of government in Northampton and vicinity established the *Hampshire Gazette*, whose history we have given on another page, for the purpose of counteracting the influence of lawless tendencies.

September 27, 1786, the legislature met in special session.   The senate was in favor of vigorous action, but the house could not be brought to appro-priate money for the suppression of the law breakers, and the session accom-plished little in behalf of government.   Shays and his followers were corres-pondingly encouraged in their lawlessness, while the friends of order and stability were yet more alarmed than before.   On December 26th Shays came into Springfield at the head of about three hundred men and prevented the session of the court of common pleas appointed for that day.   At last the patience of law-abiding citizens with such violent proceedings gave way to prompt and vigorous action.   The merchants of Boston advanced the money which the legislature refused to appropriate, and the governor immediately issued orders for the raising and equipping of forty-five hundred men to enforce the authority of the state.   Twelve hundred of these were to be raised in Western Massachusetts, under direction of Gen. William Shepherd, but the chief command of the army was entrusted to Gen. Benjamin Lincoln.

As this sketch relates chiefly to the part taken by the present county of Hampshire in this "rebellion," it will suffice to state merely the result of the Springfield collision.   General Lincoln moved with unexpected vigor and celerity in spite of the winter weather.   He re-established the authority of the government at Worcester, pressed on to Springfield where Gen. Shepherd had posted his men for the defense of the United States arsenal.   Shays's followers were in need of arms, to resist Lincoln's advance, and he made his plans for an attack upon the arsenal on the 25th of January, 1787.   But Shays and Day did not co-operate.   The reaction from lawlessness had already begun, and the moment Gen. Shepherd ordered his single piece of artillery to be discharged into the ranks of the insurgents (a few discharges meant only as a warning and harmlessly aimed, had produced no good results) the mob broke and fled in terror.   Only three were killed and one mortally wounded, but the backbone of "Shays Rebellion" was thoroughly broken by that discharge of the government field-piece.   Shays wanted to rally his men and renew the attack, but it was in vain that he attempted so to do. The bubble of vanity had been pricked and it speedily collapsed. He retreated to Chicopee to reunite his scattered forces, and on the way two hundred of his men deserted. Lincoln reached Springfield and joined his forces with those under Shepherd, and Shays retreated to Amherst, a town which was full of sympathy for him, and to which Captain Billings, one of his subordinate officers, belonged. On the way they gave evidence of their utter demoralization by plundering even private houses and taking whatever they saw fit to lay hands upon, South Hadley being an especial sufferer in this respect. Lincoln hoped to intercept the retreat of the disordered mob at Amherst, but his troops, wearied with their forced march through the winter snows, failed to cut off the escape to the hills of Pelham. Amherst tradition reports that eleven loads of supplies sent to the insurgents from Berkshire county sympathizers reached Amherst just in advance of Gen. Lincoln's horsemen. The teams were hurried towards the Pelham hills, at whose foot a little guard of twenty men so displayed themselves as to give the impression of a large number of armed soldiers, an impression increased by their bold leader who rode towards Lincoln's horsemen and waved his hat defiantly as if challenging him to the contest. As the supporting infantry was three miles behind them, the horsemen dared not make an attack, and the wagons reached Shays without molestation.

There was now a cessation of hostile efforts for some days. General Lincoln's wearied troops, who had marched from Boston, rested in Hadley and vicinity, while Shays's followers were disappearing from the Pelham hills, seeking their own homes in full recognition of the failure of their efforts. Shays made several efforts to come to terms with the state officials, but they were not disposed to be lenient at this time. So numerous were the desertions from his "army," Shays determined to take them farther away from their homes, and on the afternoon of February 3d he started for Petersham, in Worcester county. Lincoln was watching his movements so closely that in spite of the efforts to deceive him he learned immediately of Shays's movement and its destination. His own troops started that evening for another forced march. Leaving Hadley at eight o'clock, they entered Amherst, turned north, and passing through North Amherst, they climbed the Shutesbury hills and continuing in spite of the falling snow and the blustering wind, without either rest or refreshment, they completed a march of thirty miles in twenty-four hours, and came upon Shays and his men just as the latter were preparing breakfast. The surprise was complete, and the "rebels" were captured or dispersed most effectually. Shays escaped to New Hampshire, but was unable to put forth any farther opposition to the legal authorities. He went from New Hamsphire to Sparta, New York, and there died in poverty, in 1825. Fourteen of his captured companions, who were considered leaders in the "rebellion," were condemned to death, but were finally pardoned by the wise clemency of Governor Hancock. Among them were Henry McCullock, of Pelham, and Daniel Luddington, of Southampton.

While the people of Hampshire county, in connection with most New Eng-landers, were from principle opposed to a second war with England and strongly advocated pacific measures, they were by no means lacking in pat-riotism nor tardy in responding to all calls made upon them. Governor Strong, of Northampton, was then governor of the state, and his wise, judi-cious course is well known as a matter of general history. The treaty of peace in 1815 was hailed with unbounded satisfaction.

The war sentiment was the same during the Mexican war of 1847–48—a regret that other measures were not used, but a willing response to the call for aid. The county furnished a regiment which performed well its part.

From this time down to 1861 our country never echoed the clash of arms. But the sun arose that 12th of April morning upon a terribly fateful day. That first shot upon Sumpter sounded the death knell of hundreds of thou-sands of noble ones ; it cast a pall of sorrow over the broad land whose shadow even now is but partially lifted. Massachusetts immediately came to the recue, and side by side with her sister states took her place at the front. She sent 159,254 of her sons into the breach, a surplus of 13,492 over all calls.

In 1860, the year before the war broke out, the census reports show Hampshire county to have had a population of 37,822 souls, and a valuation of $17,737,649.00. According to the returns made by the selectmen in 1866, the county furnished 3,793 men, which is very near the exact number. Each town furnished its full contingent upon every call made by the president for men, and at the end of the war had a surplus over and above all demands, which, in the aggregate, amounted to 344. The total amount of money ap-propriated and expended by the several towns on account of the war, exclu-sive of state aid, was $415,042.76. The total amount raised and expended during the war for state aid to soldiers' families, and which was afterwards repaid by the commonwealth, was $184,075.07, making the total expenditure $599,117.83. For the part each town furnished towards making up these large totals we refer the reader to the respective town sketches further on in this work.

ROSTER OF FIELD, STAFF AND COMPANY OFFICERS.

The following roster of those who went out from the county as commis-sioned officers, or who, enlisting as privates, were subsequently promoted to a commission, is compiled from the state adjutant-general's reports. Many officers not here recorded, who served in other divisions and went from other places, however, have made their home in Hampshire county since the war :—

Abbott Hubbard M., of Northampton, age 23, 2d Lieut. 37th Regt., Oct. 31, '63 ; 1st Lieut., Sept. 23, '64 ; Capt., May 24, '65 ; mustered out as 1st. Lieut., June 21, '65.

Allen William B., of Northampton, age 35, 1st Lieut. 10th Regt., May 19, '64; transferred to 37th Regt., June 20, '64; mustered out Oct. 18, '64.

Bartlett Joseph F., of Pelham, age 21, 2d Lieut. 37th Regt., May 24, '65; transferred to 2d Regt.; 1st Lieut. June 1, '65; mustered out July 15, '65.

Billings Henry P., of Hatfield, age 27, 2d Lieut. Co. K, 52d Regt., Oct. 11, '62; mustered out Aug. 14, '63.

Bishop Willard I., of Northampton, age 25, 2d Lieut. 10th Regt., Aug., '62; 1st Lieut., Sept. 29, '62; Capt., Sept. 23. '63; mustered out July 1, '64.

Bissell Edwin E., of Westhampton, age 30, Capt. Co. K, 52d Regt., Oct. 11, '62; mustered out Aug. 14, '63.

Bliss George L., of Northampton, age 23, Capt. Co. G, 52d Regt., Nov. 19, '62; died of wounds at Port Hudson, La., June 16, '63.

Bliss William, of Northampton, 1st Lieut. 37th Regt., Aug. 27, '62; Capt., Dec. 5, '63; resigned as 1st Lieut., Dec. 23, '63.

Bond Nelson F., of Ware, age 22, 1st Lieut. 31st Regt., Feb. 20, '62; Capt., April 15, '64; mustered out Sept. 9, '65.

Bond Sylvester B., of Ware, age 22, 2d Lieut. 31st Regt., Jan. 10, '63; 1st Lieut., Dec. 4, '63; Capt., June 7, '65; mustered out as 1st Lieut., Sept. 9, '65.

Bradford Ansel K., of Plainfield, age 37, 2d Lieut. Co. F, 52d Regt., Oct. 11, '62; 1st Lieut., Oct. 23, '62; mustered out Aug. 14, '63.

Brewster Charles H., of Northampton, age 27, 2d Lieut. 10th Regt., Dec. 5, '61; 1st Lieut., Sept. 29, '62; mustered out July 1, '64.

Bridgman Edward, of Northampton, age 45, 2d Lieut. 37th Regt., Aug. 27, '62; 1st Lieut., Jan. 29, '63; Capt., May 16, '65; mustered out as 1st Lieut., June 21, '65.

Bridgeman Elliott, of Belchertown, age 31, Capt. 31st Regt., Feb. 20, '62; Col., Oct. 9, '63.

Bridgeman Malcolm, of Granby, age 28, 2d Lieut. Co. H, 52d Regt., Oct. 11, '62; mustered out Aug. 14, '63.

Brown Henry A., of Northampton, age 24, 2d Lieut. 10th Regt., Sept. 29, '62; 1st Lieut., Jan. 25, '63; mustered out July 1, '64.

Brown Martin V. B., of Belchertown, age 23, 1st Lieut. 27th Regt., May 15, '65; mustered out July 26, '65.

Chapin Samuel, of South Hadley, age 21, 1st Lieut. 14th Battery, Lt. Art., Feb. 25, '64; mustered out June 15, '65.

Chauncey Chauncey R., of Northampton, 1st Lieut. 34th Regt., Aug. 6, '62; Capt., March 18, '64; mustered out June 16, '65.

Clapp Egbert I., of Easthampton, age 25, 2d Lieut. 31st Regt., June 7, '64; mustered out Sept. 9, '65.

Clapp Lewis, of Easthampton, age 40, 1st Lieut. Co. K, 52d Regt., Oct. 11, '62; mustered out Aug. 14, '63.

Clark Edwin C., of Northampton, age 34, 2d Lieut. 27th Regt., Oct. 16, '61; 1st Lieut. Co. C, 52d Regt., Oct. 2, '62; Qr. M. Sergt., Nov. 21, '62; Qr. M., Oct. 2, '63; mustered out Aug. 14, '63.

Clark James W., of Northampton, age 28, 2d Lieut. Co. I, 52d Regt., Oct. 11, '62; mustered out Aug. 14, '63.

Clark Luther A., of Northampton, age 23, 2d Lieut. Co. C, 52d Regt., Dec. 1, '62; mustered out Aug. 14, '63.

Clark William S., of Amherst, age 35, Maj. 21st Regt., Aug. 19, '61 ; Lieut.-Col., Feb. 28, '62 ; Col., May 16, '62 ; resigned April 22, '63.

Cole George, of Hadley, age 27, Sergt.-Maj. Co. E, 2d Regt. Heavy Art., June 23, '64 ; 2d Lieut., March 29, '65.

Conwell Russell H., of Worthington, age 21, Capt. Co. F, 46th Regt., Oct. 15, '62 ; mustered out of service July 29, '63.

Cook George E., of Amherst, age 23, 2d Lieut., Dec. 25, '63 ; died of wounds at Spottsylvania, May 12, '64.

Dennison Ami R., of Amherst, age 26, 1st Lieut. 27th Regt., Oct. 16, '61 ; Capt., Nov. 16, '62 ; resigned Feb. 16, '64.

Dunham Andrew J., of Northampton, age 24, 2d Lieut. 27th Regt., May 15, '65 ; mustered out June 26, '65.

Dyer Fordyce A., of Plainfield, age 21, 2d Lieut. Co. F, 46th Regt., Jan. 28, '63 ; 1st Lieut. 2d Regt. Heavy Art., June 8, '63 ; died Oct. 26, '64.

Edwards Charles L., of Southampton, age 33, 1st Lieut. 37th Regt., Aug. 27, '62 ; Capt., April 5, '64 ; Maj., June 26, '64 ; mustered out as Capt. June 21, '65.

Edwards Elisha A., of Southampton, age 36, Capt. 31st Regt., Feb. 20, '62 ; resigned Sept. 5, '62.

Edwards Samuel F., of Southampton, age 21, 2d Lieut. Co. D, 52d Regt., Oct. 11, '62 ; 1st Lieut., Nov. 13, '62 ; mustered out Aug. 14, '63.

Goodell Charles S., of Amherst, age 33, 2d Lieut. 36th Regt., Nov. 1, '64 ; mustered out June 8, '65.

Harris Erastus W., of Northampton, age 29, 2d Lieut. 37th Regt., Oct. 15, '62 ; 1st Lieut., June 3, '63 ; mustered out June 21, '65.

Hillman John R., of Northampton, age 32, 2d Lieut. Co. C, 52d Regt., Oct. 2, '62 ; 1st Lieut., Dec. 1, '62, ; mustered out Aug. 14, '63.

Hinckley Henry R., of Northampton, age 24, 2d Lieut. 5th Regt. Cav., March 8, '64 ; resigned May 23, '65.

Holden Daniel, of Ware, age 42, Capt. 34th Regt., Aug. 6, '62 ; resigned Nov. 8, '62.

Hooker Edward D., of Westhampton, age 23, 2d Lieut. 37th Regt., May 24, '65 ; mustered out June 21, '65.

Hopkins William S. B., of Ware, age 25, Capt. 31st Regt., Feb. 20, '62 ; Lieut.-Col., Dec. 24, '62 ; resigned April 14, '64.

Howard Oscar H., of Ware, age 22, 2d Lieut. 2d Regt., May 21, '61 ; 1st Lieut., Sept. 17, '61 ; Capt., Aug. 10, '62 ; Capt. in U. S. Sig. Corps.

Howland John W., of Amherst, age 26, 2d Lieut. 1st Regt. Cav., Jan. 16, '64; 1st Lieut., Nov. 13, '64 ; mustered out June 26, '65.

Jones George N., of Hadley, age 27, 2d Lieut. 37th Regt., Jan. 17, '63 ; 1st Lieut., Dec. 24, '63 ; Capt., Feb. 1st, '65 ; transferred to 20th Regt.

Judd John H., of Easthampton, age 22, 2d Lieut. 27th Regt., Jan. 2, '63 ; 1st Lieut., May 17, '64 ; mustered out as 2d Lieut., March 21, '65.

Kellogg Justin P., of Amherst, age 24, 2d Lieut. Co. G, 52d Regt., Oct. 11, '62 ; 1st Lieut., Nov. 10, '62 ; mustered out Aug. 14, '63.

Kirkland Charles H., of Huntington, age 34, 2d Lieut. Co. F, 46th Regt., June 9, '63 ; mustered out July 29, '63.

Lawton Joseph W., of Ware, age 23, 2d Lieut. 27th Regt., Feb. 13, '62 ; killed March 14, '62.

Lewis William E., of Ware, age 23, 2d Lieut. 37th Regt., June 26, '65; mustered out June 21, '65.

Lincoln Rufus P., of Amherst, age 23, 2d Lieut. 37th Regt., Aug. 27, '62; Capt., Oct. 15, '62; Major, July 27, '64; Lieut.-Col., March 4, '65; Col., May 19, '65; transferred to 20th Regt. as Lieut.-Col., March 4, '65; mustered out July 15, '65.

Lilley Erastus V., of Huntington, age 32, 2d Lieut. 44th Regt., Sept. 1, '64; 1st Lieut. Nov. 25, '64; mustered out May 15, '65.

Loomis Joshua A., of Northampton, age 24, 1st Lieut. 37th Regt., Aug. 27, '62; Capt., June 4, '63; discharged for disability, Nov. 19, '64.

Lyman Justus, of Easthampton, age 29, 2d Lieut. 27th Regt., Feb. 17, '64; 1st Lieut, June 5, '64; Capt., May 15, '65; mustered out as 2d Lieut., June 26, '65.

Lyman Luke, of Northampton, age 37, Lieut.-Col. 27th Regt., Sept. 17, '61; resigned May 27, '63.

Lyman Timothy P., of Goshen, age 27, 2d Lieut. 1st Regt. Cav., Sept. 3, '64; 1st Lieut., May 26, '65; mustered out June 26, '65.

Marsh William R., of Northampton, age 33, Maj. 10th Regt., June 21, '61; resigned June 14, '62.

Montague George L., of Amherst, age 28, Capt. 37th Regt., Aug. 13, '62; Maj., Aug. 27, '62; Lieut.-Col., Jan. 17, '63; mustered out for disability, March 3, '65.

Moody Marcus T., of Northampton, Capt. 37th Regt., Aug. 27, '62; Maj., Dec. 5, '63; mustered out for disability, July 26, '64.

Morrill William C., of Northampton, age 22, 2d Lieut. 37th Regt., Dec. 5, 63; 1st Lieut., Oct. 7, '64; mustered out June 21, '65.

Morse Horace F., of Southampton, age 29, 1st Lieut. 31st Regt., Feb. 20, '62; Capt., Aug. 17, '63; mustered out Nov. 18, '64.

Mott Abner R., of Ware, age 22, 2d Lieut. 21st Regt., Sept. 7, '64; transferred to 36th Regt.; 1st Lieut. Oct. 12, '64; mustered out June 8, '65.

Munyan Alanson E., of Northampton, age 24, 1st Lieut. 10th Regt., Dec. 26, '62; died of wounds May 21, '64.

Nichols Samuel E., of Northampton, age 20, 2d Lieut. 37th Regt., Aug. 30, '64; 1st Lieut., May 15, '65; mustered out of service as 2d Lieut., June 21, '65.

Page Seldon, of Hadley, age 34, 2d Lieut. 4th Regt. Heavy Art., Feb. 18, '65; mustered out June 17, '65.

Parsons Joseph B., of Northampton, age 33, Capt. 10th Regt., June 21, '61; Lieut.-Col., July 20, '62; mustered out July 1, '64.

Perkins William, of Hadley, age 41, Capt. Co. H, 52d Regt., Oct. 11, '62; mustered out Aug. 20, '63.

Polley George F., of Williamsburg, age 21, 1st Lieut. 10th Regt., May 6, '64; killed at Petersburg, Va., June 20, '64.

Rust Charles S., of Easthampton, age 25, 2d Lieut. 31st Regt., April 1, '63; 1st Lieut., Feb. 3, '64; resigned as 2d Lieut., April 20, '64.

Rust Fordyce A., of Easthampton, age 31, 1st Lieut. 31st Regt., Feb. 20, '62; mustered out Nov. 18, '64.

Sagendorph Milton, of Ware, age 22, 2d Lieut. 31st Regt., Dec. 1, '62; 1st Lieut., Aug. 17, '63; Capt., Aug. 26, '64; mustered out as 1st Lieut., Sept. 9, '65.

Sampson Orange S., of Huntington, age 29, 2d Lieut. 21st Regt., Sept. 2, '62; 1st Lieut., Oct. 30, '62; Capt., April 26, '63; killed at Poplar Grove Church, Va., Sept. 30, '64.

Shaw William, of Belchertown, age 42, 1st Lieut. Co. H, 46th Regt., Oct. 15, '62; mustered out July 29, '63.

Shaw William H., of Cummington, age 29, 2d Lieut. 37th Regt., March 4, '65; mustered out June 21, '65.

Sheldon Flavel R., of Southampton, age 32, 2d Lieut. 37th Regt., June 27, '64; 1st Lieut., March 4, '65; mustered out June 17, '65.

Shumway Solomon C., of Belchertown, age 53, 2d Lieut. 21st Regt., Aug. 21, '61; resigned May 19, '63.

Shurtleff Flavel, of Northampton, age 32, 2d Lieut. 10th Regt., June 21, '61; 1st Lieut., Dec. 5, '61; Capt., July 31, '62; mustered out July 1, '64.

Skinner J. Leander, of Amherst, age 23, 2d Lieut. 27th Regt., July 1, '62; 1st Lieut., May 29, '63; Capt., Sept. 29, '64; mustered out as 1st Lieut., Dec. 31, '64.

Sloan Timothy W., of Amherst, age 34, Capt. 27th Regt., Oct. 16, '61; re-signed Nov. 15, '62.

Smith Charles P., of Northampton, age 25, Capt. 27th Regt., June 4, '63; died of wounds May 21, '64.

Smith James W., of Hadley, age 25, 1st Lieut. 34th Regt., Aug. 6, '62; re-signed July 26, '63.

Smith H. Walworth, of Northampton, age 37, 2d Lieut. 4th Regt. Cav., Jan. 19, '64; 1st Lieut., Oct. 13, '64; Capt., April 7, '64; mustered out Nov. 14, '65.

Spaulding Mark H., of Northampton, age 34, 1st Lieut. 27th Regt., Oct. 16, '61; Capt. Co. C, 52d Regt., Oct. 2, '63; mustered out Aug. 14, '63.

Spear Asa A., of Amherst, age 21, 2d Lieut. Co. C, 52d Regt., Nov. 10, '62; mustered out Aug. 14, '63.

Stearns Frazar A., of Amherst, age 21, 1st Lieut. 21st Regt., Aug. 21, '61; killed at Newbern, N. C., March 14, '62.

Stockwell John W., of Northampton, age 24, 2d Lieut. 37th Regt., April 5, '64; 1st Lieut., Oct. 13, '64; mustered out June 21, '65.

Storrs Samuel J., of Amherst, age 25, Capt. Co. G, 52d Regt., Oct. 11, '62; Lieut. Col., Oct. 13, '62; mustered out Aug. 14, '63.

Taylor Lucius E., of Chesterfield, age 32, 1st Lieut. Co. I, 52d Regt., Oct. 11, '62; mustered out Aug. 14, '63.

Tileston Charles E., of Williamsburg, age 31, Capt. Co. I, 52d Regt., Oct. 11, '62; mustered out Aug. 14, '63.

Tower Elisha C., of Worthington, age 27, 1st Lieut. Co. K, 46th Regt., Oct. 22, '62; mustered out July 29, '63.

Tyler Mason W., of Amherst, 2d Lieut. 36th Regt., July 30, '62; 1st Lieut. 37th Regt., Aug. 13, '62; Capt., Jan. 17, '63; Maj., March 4, '65; Lieut.-Col., May 19, '65; Col., June 26, '65; transferred to 20th Regt. as Maj.

Ward William W., of Worthington, age 23, Com.-Sergt. 52d Regt., Oct. 14, '62; mustered out Aug. 14, '63.

Warner Almon M., of Plainfield, age 19, 2d Lieut. 37th Regt., June 7, '65; mustered out June 21, '65.

Wells William L., of Northampton, age 29, 2d Lieut. 2d Regt. Cav., Dec. 18, '62; died July 26, '63.

Wetherell James H., of Northampton, age 33, 1st Lieut. 10th Regt., June 21, '61; Capt., Sept. 8, '62; died of wounds June 20, '64.

Whitney Edward A., of Northampton, age 19, Qr. M. Sergt. 52d Regt., Oct. 2, '62; mustered out Aug. 14, '63.

Whitney Henry M., of Northampton, age 19, Sergt.-Maj. 52d Regt., Oct. 2, '62; mustered out Aug. 14, '63.

Whitney Edwin, of Williamsburg, age 25, 1st Lieut. 10th Regt., Nov. 26, '62; mustered out July 1, '64.

Williams S. Alonzo, of South Hadley, age 29, 1st Lieut. Co. H, 52d Regt., Oct. 11, '62; mustered out Aug. 14, '63.

Wright Frederick C., of Northampton, age 22, 2d Lieut. 27th Regt., Oct. 16, '61; 1st Lieut., Oct. 30, '62; died of wounds June 27, '64.

GAZETTEER OF TOWNS.

THE TERRITORY now known as the town of Amherst was originally the eastern portion of the town of Hadley. Religious dissensions in Connecticut caused the settlement of Hadley, and in 1659 and 1660 the "ox-bow," which the Connecticut river makes just above the present city of Northampton, was occupied by families from Hartford, Weathersfield and Windsor, Conn., who were dissatisfied with the tendencies and decisions of their ecclesiastical authorities in Connecticut. Their situation was easily defended during the troubles with the Indians, and the town of Hadley probably suffered less in the Indian wars than any other town upon the river. As soon as there was sufficient growth of population to make the narrow limits of the first settlement insufficient for their accommodation, the more resolute began to look towards the east and the south for new homes and wider fields, and in a town meeting held March 4, 1700, it was voted to divide the common land east of the "new swamp," as the lowlands between the present towns of Amherst and Hadley were called. The town measurers, Capt. Aaron Cooke, Cornet Nehemiah Dickinson and Samuel Porter, were instructed to lay out these lands into three divisions, separated from each other by a highway forty rods in width, and to assign to each householder of Hadley one fifty-pound allotment, and to each unmarried man, and to parents for each son between the ages of sixteen and twenty-one, one twenty-five pound allotment. This vote was carried out by the town measurers and gave to the new settlement the general outline which, in the essential features, it still retains. The two broad highways separating the three divisions became the West street and the East street, respectively, between which and on either side of which the town home lots were located; while from near the old church, in the broad front street of Hadley, another highway running east "goeth over New Swamp and runs down to Foot's Folly." This highway doubtless corresponded very closely with the present highway in its northern division, for it passed through the present center of Amherst, a little north of

NOTE.—For this sketch of Amherst we are largely indebted to Rev. George H. Johnson, of North Amherst.

the present location of the Amherst House, and ended near the place where the second parish church now stands, in the East street. Upon these three highways still fluctuates the main part of Amherst's business and pleasure, and mainly around them are still the homes of the town, in spite of the large number of highways which have since been opened. Each of these highways was originally laid out forty rods in width, enabling the traveler to go around mud-holes and steep ascents without trespassing on private land. One other highway of great importance in the days of stage traveling, but of much less account in these days of railroads, was situated at the extreme southern limits of the town, and was known as the "Bay Road," because it led eastward through Brookfield and on to Boston and the towns on Massachusetts bay.

In April, 1703, the town measurers recorded their assignments of land in these three divisions as made by drawing lots, and the student of history may still find upon the Hadley records, and in older histories, the names of those who received lots of land, and also the location and measurement of the lots.

The first division, located nearest to the Hadley settlement, was two hundred and forty rods in width, east and west, and extended from the Bay Road on the south to the Mill river in North Amherst, being 1,961 rods in length. This was divided into sixty lots with spaces for two additional highways parallel to the one from Hadley to "Foot's Folly." The land comprised in this division amounted to 2,760 acres.

East of this division and separated from it by the West street, lay the second division, including the land now forming the very heart of Amherst. Like the first, this division was 240 rods in width, with allowance for the extension of highways corresponding to those in the first division. Beginning at the Bay Road, in the south, this division ran north only 1,674 rods and was thus nearly three hundred rods shorter than the first; a town lot of sixty acres was reserved in this, and its thirty-seven lots comprised 2,343 acres. The number of inhabitants entitled to land in this division of the commons appears to have been ninety-seven, and the measurers ceased to lay out lots in the second division when each of those entitled had received his portion; this accounts for the second division being so much smaller than the first.

Still further east and separated from the second division by the East street, was the third of the three divisions ordered by the town. The lots in the first two divisions were evidently meant to be home lots, but those in the third division were as clearly not for homes, but for cattle, etc. The third division was two miles in width instead of being 240 rods as the others were. Its length north and south was 1,971 rods and it contained 7,884 acres, divided into ninety-three lots. In this division was included a part of the land north of Mill river, now forming the extreme northeastern limit of the town. Each citizen of Hadley of the requisite age received a lot in either the first or second division for a home, and also one in the third division for his cattle and meadow land. The town measurers had no compass to aid them in laying out these divisions. The first person who owned a compass in this vicinity was Timothy Dwight, of Northampton, grandfather of President Dwight of Yale college, and he was not born until 1694. Nearly forty years after the town ordered this division, a more accurate survey showed that the measurers of 1700-1703 had begun with a base line too far to the east, and in consequence had encroached upon the "equivalent lands" (now in Pelham and Belchertown) to so great an extent that nearly three thousand acres of land in the third division was beyond the outermost limits of Hadley. Those who lost lands by this correction of the survey, were afterwards compensated with lands situated farther north, called "Flat Hills," and adjoining the border of the present town of Shutesbury. It is a singular coincidence that the "equivalent lands" thus encroached upon by these early surveyors, were the lands which had been assigned by the province of Massachusetts to the province of Connecticut, in recompense for an error of location, whereby the southern boundary of Massachusetts was extended so far to the south as to include over an hundred thousand acres of land, and a large part of the towns of Suffield, Enfield and Woodstock, which rightly belonged to Connecticut, but owing to inaccurate surveys were long supposed to be in Massachusetts.

Of the ninety or more persons who thus became the first proprietors of the present town, very few ever occupied their lots in person. The French and Indian war of Queen Anne's reign broke out in 1703, the very year of the completion of this division, and raged until 1713. Deerfield was burned February 29, 1704, and all exposed places became unsafe for inhabitants and of slight value to their owners. A few inventories of estates taken during this war showed that the lots thus assigned were valued at one shilling per acre in the first and second divisions, and at four and sixpence per acre in the third division. After the close of the war this land advanced in value, and the best lots were considered worth three shillings per acre ; while after settlements began to be made the most desirable lots were worth from six to ten shillings per acre in proclamation money, six shillings of which would be a dollar. In the depreciated province bills the value would be apparently much higher.

Surface.—The town presents an uneven surface, being diversified by wide ranges of broken upland, and low level reaches, some of which are swampy. The village itself occupies a wide flattened ridge of considerable extent from north to south, with Mt. Pleasant at the north and the elevation occupied by the college buildings as prominent features. A large tract of wet land in the southeastern portion of the town is known as "Laurence Swamp." The Holyoke range forms the town's southern boundary, while the hills of Pelham and Shutesbury jut over the eastern border. Northward loom the rugged prominences of Sunderland and Leverett, with Amherst's intervening "Flat Hills." Westward lie the broad and fertile intervals of Hadley.

The only streams worthy of note are Fort river and Mill river. The former rises in Pelham, enters Amherst about two miles south of the northeast angle thereof, flows southerly under the Pelham hills, and thence south of west across the town, passing the western bounds into Hadley, two and a half miles from the southwest angle. Mill river rises in the hills of Shutesbury, crosses the southeast corner of Leverett, enters Amherst a short distance west of the northeast angle, traverses the town in a general southwesterly direction, and thence into Hadley, across the south line of the 800 acres added to Amherst in 1814.

First Settlers —It is not known when the first permanent settlements were made upon the lots laid out, as we have stated, but it was probably not far from 1725.* The first settlers from the mother town of Hadley, followed the course of the river and located in the present limits of South Hadley. So great seemed the peril of lonely dwellings to those who had grown up amid the alarms of the Indian wars, that tradition affirms that aged parents in Hadley wept in anguish, and prayed most fervently for Heaven's protection upon the daring youths and their brides, who sought new homes on the south side of Mt. Holyoke ; but as peace continued and families increased, more and more were new towns built up.

In 1730 the inhabitants upon these lots were sufficiently numerous to require a burying place, and January 5, 1730, the town voted a little more than an acre of land for this purpose, which was duly laid out before the next March, " in the west highway adjoining Nathaniel Church's lot on the west." One hundred and fifty years and more after this laying out of the cemetery it is still the burial ground of Amherst Center, although enlarged from its original size. In the year 1731 Hadley distributed among her citizens the " inner commons " or undivided lands within the present limits of Hadley, and in the records of this division the following persons are named as " East Inhabitants," *i. e.*, as residing in the present limits of Amherst :—

John Ingram, Sr.,	Richard Chauncey,	John Cowls,
John Ingram, Jr.,	Aaron Smith,	Jonathan Cowls,
Samuel Boltwood,	Nathaniel Smith,	Samuel Hawley,
Ebenezer Kellogg,	Ebenezer Dickinson,	John Wells,
Nathaniel Church,	John Nash, Jr.,	Joseph Wells,
Ebenezer Ingram,	Ebenezer Scoville,	Stephen Smith.

Of these, the names in the first two columns are of those who came from Hadley, while those in the third column were from Hatfield. Only four of these eighteen names are found in the allotment of lands in 1703, viz. : John Ingram, Sr., John Ingram, Jr., Samuel Boltwood, and John Cowls, (spelled " Cole," in 1703). The others must have acquired their land either

---

*Tradition asserts that a man by the name of Foote came to Amherst in 1703, located just north of the present Second Congregational church, where, for a time, he lived the life of a hermit. From this the section between the eminence on which the college buildings stand and the Pelham hills eastward took the name of " Foote's Folly Swamp ;" hence, the allusions in the early records to all this section of country in this vicinity as " Foote's Folly."

by inheritance or purchase. In 1738, the assessors' records show that the following persons had been added to the population ·—

Joseph Clary,	Nathan Moody,	Zechariah Field,
Jonathan Atherton,	Pelatiah Smith,	Joseph Hawley,
Solomon Boltwood,	John Perry,	Samuel Hawley, Jr.,
Charles Chauncey,	Moses Smith,	John Morton,
William Murray,		Ebenezer Williams.

The first nine of these came from Hadley, and those in the last column were from Hatfield, except Williams, who came from Deerfield.

The assessors' records for this year, 1738, also show that there were in the homes of those above named thirty-five taxable polls, a few householders having sons who were of age, and that their property consisted of forty-nine horses, thirty-nine oxen, fifty-two cows and three hundred and fifty acres of improved land, of which Ebenezer Kellogg owned forty-eight acres, or more than twice as much as any other person. There were also forty-three acres of improved land belonging to six non-residents, making three hundred and ninety-three acres of improved land. These persons and this property were assessed for the first £100 due the minister as follows : 35 polls, 25s. 6d. each, £44 12s. 6d. The property was assessed at one shilling per pound and valued at £1,101 11s. 6d., making £55 1s. 6d.

Of the thirty-two who thus became the first settlers of Amherst, John Wells soon removed (probably to Hardwick) ; Joseph Wells, his brother, removed later to Sunderland ; Aaron Smith, Nathaniel Church and John Perry had also left by 1745, and Ebenezer Scovil died in 1731, aged twenty-four, and Ebenezer Ingram in 1735, aged thirty-two ; John Ingram, Jr., died in 1737, Zechariah Field in 1738, and Samuel Boltwood, in 1738. Each of the last three left families, who remained in Amherst. Jonathan Atherton died in 1744.

From 1739 to 1745 there were added to the list of householders thirty-four names, and from 1745 to 1763 Judd's *History of Hadley*, page 425, records the names of sixty-nine more who had made settlement in Amherst. Of the one hundred and three names added between 1739 and 1763, twenty bore the name of Dickinson, and most of them left families, making the name of Dickinson the most numerous of any in town, and such it still continues.

The subsequent increase of population may be shown by extracts from the census tables, as follows : Colonial census, 1776, 915 inhabitants ; the United States census of 1790, 1,233 ; 1800, 1,358 ; 1810, 1,469 ; 1820, 1,917 ; 1830, 2,631 ; 1840, 2,550 ; 1850, 3,057 ; 1860, 3,206 ; 1870, 4,035 ; 1880, 4,298. The state census reports in 1855 give 2,937 ; 1865, 3,415 ; 1875, 3,937 ; 1885, 4,199.

Incorporation and Names.—The first name applied to that part of Hadley now known as Amherst, in any records now extant, is that of "New Swamp" and " Foote's Folly Swamp " ; but as people began to reside here these names gave way to " Hadley Farms," " East Farms" and "East Hadley." In June,

1734, John Ingram headed a petition to the general court that East Hadley might be incorporated as a separate precinct. The mother town not liking to have its property subject to "the minister's rate" decreased, sent an agent to Boston to oppose the granting of this petition, and it failed for the time. In December, 1734, the petition was renewed and granted by the general court December 31, the record stating its boundaries thus: "The precinct being of the contents of two miles and three-quarters in breadth, and seven miles in length, bounded westerly on a tract of land reserved by the town of Hadley to lie as common land forever, southerly on Boston road, easterly on equivalent lands, and northerly on the town of Sunderland." The name conferred by this act was "Hadley Third Precinct," the second precinct (now South Hadley) having been formed after the failure of two previous attempts in 1732. The term "precinct" was nearly equivalent to "parish" in our day. The laws required every one to pay a tax for the support of the Gospel ordinances proportioned to his property, and this tax was levied by the original church upon all the inhabitants of the town. Thus the "East Inhabitants" paid their proportion of the salary of Rev. Mr. Chauncey in Hadley until their incorporation as a precinct released them from this requirement, at the same time that it laid upon them the new requirement of supporting a "learned orthodox" minister by themselves. In 1753 the second precinct having been incorporated as the district of South Hadley, "Hadley Third Precinct" became "Hadley Second Precinct," by which name it was known until February 13, 1759, when Gov. Pownall signed the bill incorporating it as a district. The general court had left the name of the district blank in the act of incorporation, the privilege of bestowing names upon the new districts being one of the perquisites of the colonial governor. In signing the bill Gov. Pownall complimented his friend, Gen. Jeffrey Amherst (who had just been appointed by George II. to the command of the expedition against Louisburg), by naming the new district "Amherst" in the bill. The success of the campaign against Louisburg (the French stronghold upon Cape Breton island) and the subsequent rapid promotion of Gen. Amherst (afterwards made Lord Amherst for his military success) contributed, no doubt, to the popularity of the name among the inhabitants of the new district. Amherst was now politically, as well as ecclesiastically, independent of the mother town of Hadley ; except that the district could not send a representative to the legislature, that right being jealously reserved for *towns*. In all other respects the district enjoyed all the advantages of a town. The plan of restricting the right of representation was not of colonial origin, but was enjoined upon the colony by Great Britain, and when the revolutionary feeling overcame the love for the mother country, this restriction was removed, not indeed by law until 1786, when all districts incorporated before January 1, 1777, were declared towns. But practically the requirement of the government of Great Britain was done away with in 1774, when the provincial congress, which met successively at Salem, Concord and Cambridge, admitted Mr. Nathaniel

9*

Dickinson, Jr., to a seat in their body as representative from Amherst. Two years later the district openly assumed the designation of "town," the district clerk for 1775-76 commencing his record of a meeting held January 24, 1776, "At a legal meeting of the Inhabitants of the *town* of Amherst qualified to vote in *town* affairs," and while all previous records speak of the *district* of Amherst, all subsequent records speak of the *town* of Amherst, and this revolutionary assumption of withheld rights was first officially recognized in the following legislative record: "In Council Aug't 27, 1776. Ordered that the Commissary General be directed to deliver to Mr. Simon Smith one hundred and twenty-five pounds weight of gunpowder for the town of Amherst, he paying therefor at the rate of 5s a ℔ to the said Commissary."

Thus, Amherst was "Hadley Third Precinct" from December 31, 1734, until April, 1753, when it became "Hadley Second Precinct," until February 13, 1759, when it became the "District of Amherst." Legally it remained a district until March 23, 1786, but in reality the district became a town in 1776, and in accordance with this reality celebrated, in 1876, the centennial anniversary of its own (and the country's) independence.

The original area of Amherst has been somewhat enlarged since the incorporation of Hadley Third Precinct. In 1778 the town chose a committee "to take some measures for annexing the first Division of Inner Commons in the Town of Hadley to the town of Amherst." A year later the town promised Hadley to maintain "all roads and bridges within the bounds of S'd Land." In 1786 John Field and others whose lands lay within this division had petitioned the general court that they might "be Disannexed from the town of Hadley and annexed to the town of Amherst," and the town voted that the matter be referred to arbitrators mutually appointed by each town. This attempt to enlarge the area of Amherst at the expense of Hadley was a failure apparently, but in 1789 the farms of Silas Wright (father of the well known political leader of New York) and of three men by the name of Dickinson, were annexed to Amherst from Hadley. These men lived on the road from Sunderland to Amherst, and all their business and church connections were in Amherst, and they deemed it a burden to go to a more distant place and meet those who were comparatively strangers at the town meetings. For the same reason the entire section of territory border-ing on the old road from Sunderland to Amherst, and comprising between 700 and 800 acres of land, was annexed to Amherst by act of the legislature in 1814. In 1812 the southern boundary of the town was moved from the old "Bay road" to "the top of the mountain," between Amherst and Gran-by, thus increasing the town's area by about 1,700 acres; much of it was, however, mountain land.

One more addition to Amherst's territory was taken out of Hadley when the farm of Elias Smith, situated on the road to Hadley from Amherst, was annexed. The curious turn of this strip of land, measuring only sixteen by one hundred and fifteen rods, makes the traveler from Amherst to Hadley cross the boundary line three times on a straight road, the line between the towns forming a huge letter Z at this point. This annexation was the result of private quarrels. Efforts have been made at various times to annex parts of Belchertown and Pelham to Amherst, but the town has refused to receive these additional lands. The present area of the town is a little over 18,000 acres.

Miscellaneous Items from the Early Records.—When Hadley Third Precinct was incorporated, the year began March 25th instead of January 1st; the first five precinct meetings being respectively dated October 8, 1735, November 25, 1735, December 25, 1735, March 10, 1735, and September 16, 1736. But there were many authorities for beginning with January 1st even then, and the months of January, February and March were often written with double dates; thus, the third annual March meeting of the precinct is dated "March ye 14th, 1738-9." It was 1738 for those whose year began the last of March, but 1739 for those whose year began in January. The discrepancies in the dates of ancient records arise often from such double standards. The English parliament enacted a law that after 1752 the new year should begin with January 1st instead of March 25th, as previously, and the legal date soon became the customary one. The double dating passes out of Amherst's records with the recording of the precinct meeting held "Jana'r ye 18th, 1749-50." The March meeting of 1755 is, however, dated "March the 24th, 1754," but the next precinct meeting is dated "Janawr ye 12th, 1756," and the new custom was henceforth followed. The first month is spelled "Janaway" in 1761, which probably represented its pronunciation throughout New England.

The early settlers seemed to have had hard luck about getting their pound built. In the March meeting of 1743 they voted to build a pound, and appointed a committee to do it. In 1744, 1746 and 1748 they passed similar votes and chose committees each time to carry them out. Deacon Ebenezer Dickinson was on all these committees, but why nothing was done is unknown. Finally, in 1750, the precinct voted £19 10s. for building a pound, instructed Ebenezer Mattoon to do the work; "& to finish sd pound workman Like." This vote seems to have accomplished the desired object.

Like her neighboring towns, Amherst permitted "Hogs Rung & Yoakt Acording to Law to Run at Large." The time, at first unlimited, was afterwards limited by town votes. In 1763 the limit was "from the first of May to the first of September and after the middle of October till winter." In 1770 it was "from ye first of May to the middle of August."

It was customary for the town to instruct its officers to hire bulls for the use of the farmers. In 1753 the assessors were instructed "to Hire foure Bulls for ye use of this precinct for ye space one yeare." In 1754 the precinct appropriated £32 old tenor for this purpose. In 1759 the selectmen were to hire six bulls; in 1760 the appropriation for this purpose was £8.

In the early history of Hadley, mention is made of licenses for the sale of liquor, but the only mention of anything of this kind which I have found in the Amherst records is under date of March 28, 1775, "That this District Doth approve of Elisha Ingraham as a Tavern Keeper and recommend it to the selectmen that they grant him their approbation for the same."

Highways.—The first vote recorded on the records which does not relate to the meeting-house, the minister, or the choice of precinct officers, is in relation to highways. March 10, 1735–36, "Voted that yᵉ Highway work be done by heads and Teams, and yᵗ a Team shall be Equal to a hand per day." The various sums allowed for highway work fluctuated as the value of money rose or fell, and may be judged by the following votes passed by the precinct : In 1747, eight shillings per day; 1759, sixteen shillings per day from April to October, twelve shillings the rest of the year ; 1762, two shillings per day in summer, eighteen pence in fall; 1764, in summer two shillings and five pence, in fall one shilling and eight pence ; 1776, in summer two shillings and eight pence, in fall two shillings. In 1778 the town meeting voted to allow six shillings per day for work done the year preceding, but this year's work was to be paid for at the rate of fifteen shillings per day in summer, and twelve shillings per day in the fall. The allowance was the same for a man or for a team, meaning oxen and cart. At first the amount of work to be done seems to have been left to the discretion of the precinct officers, most probably the assessors. No regular surveyors were chosen until after the incorporation of the district, in 1759. In 1765 the district appropriated £30 for repairs on highways; in 1776 the appropriation was £60; in 1784 it was £70. In 1760 a county road was laid across the land of Jonathan Dickinson, and the town subsequently voted him four and three-fourths acres of town land as a compensation for damage to his estate. In 1774 the town ordered the town highways to be put in repair equally with the county roads, which indicates that previously the latter had been superior. Most of the town highways were laid out and recorded only a short time prior to the Revolution, and a large space of the town records for these years consist of the reports of the selectmen defining the limits of these roads. The great breadth, forty rods, of the original highways was first contracted in 1754, when the West street was reduced to twenty rods in width and the East to twelve. In 1788 both were narrowed to six rods, and the town disposed of the remaining lands. It must be remembered that these highways were not broad, leveled streets, like those of the present day, but were simply winding paths trodden by the feet of man and beast, very seldom cut by a passing wheel, except those of the rude ox-carts of the early settlers. Carriages came in general use after the Revolutionary war. The assessors' records show that so late as 1791 there was but a single carriage in the town of Amherst. This was a " fall-back chaise," owned by Simeon Strong. The first one-horse wagons made in this vicinity were made by Mason Abbe, of Amherst, after the year 1800, and it was twenty years later before they came into general use. Previous to the Revolutionary war almost all travel was on horseback, the men taking their wives behind them upon a pillion. There are a few yet living who remember the days when the people came to church from long distances in this manner. Rude sleds were the first vehicles drawn by horses in Hampshire county, the first one, so far as known, belonging to Timothy Eastman, Jr., of Hadley. It is mentioned in the inventory of his estate in 1733, and is valued at five shillings. It was hardly more than a large box with runners beneath it and boards across the top of it for seats. Shortly before the Revolutionary war a few of the more wealthy had vehicles which somewhat resembled a sleigh, but sleighs did not come into general use until the beginning of the present century. Goods from Boston were brought around by water and up the Connecticut river to Springfield, although goods of small bulk were sometimes brought from Boston to the Connecticut river on horseback.

In the year 1767 Simeon Smith, of Amherst, who lived upon the Bay road in the south part of the town, carried out his scheme of giving the people in this vicinity regular communication with Boston. With a large two-horse wagon he drove down and back, carrying produce and returning with goods for the traders, and with large quantities of New England rum for the grocery stores. He continued this business until the breaking out of the war, in 1775. His load probably seldom exceeded a ton's weight. His wagon was a rarity in this vicinity, although the Dutch in New York had been using two-horse wagons all the eighteenth century. In this connection it may be said that hearses for the conveying of the dead to cemeteries were not in common use in the vicinity of Amherst until about the time when stoves were placed in the churches. The town of Hadley had no hearse until 1826, and other towns about the same time probably. It is said that when Deacon Ebenezer Mattoon died, February, 1767, the snow was so deep on the ground that it was proposed to draw his body to the burying-ground (which was two miles away) upon a hand-sled; but when this was made known to his pastor, Mr. Parsons, the reverend man cried out in horror : " Such a saint as Deacon Mattoon to be dragged to his grave like a dead dog !" and then, putting into his word all the authority possessed by the clergy of that day, he said, "Never !" And the bearers were obliged to put the coffin upon their shoulders in accordance with the custom of the day, and tread their weary way to the distant burying-ground through the snow.

The Revolution.—The ravages of war have never disturbed the peace of the fields of Amherst, but the town has never lacked for patriotic sons, willing " to do, to dare, to die " in defense of their homes and their country. Two French and Indian wars raged after the settlement of Amherst, the first from 1744 to 1748, the second from 1754 to 1763. In both, men from Amherst went in quest of the foe into territory now belonging to New Hampshire, Vermont and New York ; some also joined the expedition which, in 1745, captured Louisburg, but their names have been lost. These smaller wars proved a fitting school for the sterner strife of the Revolutionary war, and some of the younger participants in the war of 1754–63 proved excellent veterans in the strife with the mother country. Reuben Dickinson, the captain of the Amherst minute-men in 1775–76, had been a sergeant in the expedition against Crown Point in 1755, and was one of the most influential men in Amherst in the trying days of the Revolution.

The first allusion to the break with England upon the town records is the vote passed January 26, 1774, "to Chews a Com'tee of Corrispondence to Refer with the Com'tee of Corrispondance in the Town of Boston." This committee, Reuben Dickinson, Joseph Williams, Moses Dickinson, Jacob McDaniel and Nathaniel Dickinson, was instructed to prepare a letter to be read in the next meeting. This letter was adopted by the town at the March meeting, and despite its length is worth reproduction, to enable us to see the spirit of the fathers of 1776. It reads as follows :—

"*To the Respectable Committee of Correspondence in the Town of Boston :—*

"GENTLEMEN : We think it needless to Recapitulate all those grievances which we suffer in Common with our opprest Brethren and Neighbors. Sufficient to Say that tho' we have been long silent we are not insensible of the oppressions we suffer and the ruin which threatens us or regardlis of the Diabolical Designs of our Mercernary and Manevolent Enemies Foreign and Domestic and are ready not onley to risque but even to Sacrifice our Lives and Properties in Defence of our just rights & liberties at Present we are only Galled not subdued and think ourselves heapy in having such vigilant and faithfull gardians of our rights in the Metropolis on hoom we Can depend to Call on us in Season to unite with our suffering Countrymen in the Common Cause of America we hope and beg that you will still Preserve in that most Honorable & important Imployment of watching over us with the Same Care and Fidelity which has hiterto Distinguishd & greatly Dignified your Character in the Estimation of all who have a just sence of that best of Blessings Liberty & an Equal abhorrence of that tame submition which tends to Entail on our Posterrity that worst of Curses Slavery.

" Every Avenue to the Royal Ear seems to be blocked up by gross falsities & Designd misrepresentations of those from some of whom at Least we might have Expected better things but there is a King who Cannot be Deceived & who will not be mocked who has pointed out a never failing resource when Petitions and Remonstrances, Truth and justice are unsuccesfully opposed to Tironey and Oppression falsehood and Corruption & when you feel that impulse which will not brook longer Delay, the wisdum of the People will naturally write in the mode of the best Appeal, to which you most Distant Brethren Expect to be summoned unless preventd by a sudding unexpected & very favorable chandge of affears their are whom Justice forbids to live but whom we would spare to Convince the world we Despise their utmost hate & malicious Cunning. the colonies united are invincibly free & we doubt not you are convinc'd that the Preservation of that union outweighs every other Consideration and is at present our most Important Concern, while that is secure we have nothing to fear but may Laugh at all attempts to Enslave us we know of no punishment which can be Inflicted on those vilens in Exalted Stations adequate to their own reflections & remorse accompanyd with our Neglect, Contempt & Detestation but at the same time should think ourselves happier if Everey banefull Noxious weed Could by any means be Eradicated from this our fair garden of Liberty. we Entirely approve & Concurr with you in every measure hitherto adopted & Conducted & return our gratefull thanks to the People of Boston & the Neighboring towns in a Perticular manner for the seasonable Indeavours & mandley opposition to prevent the Landing of the East India Companys teas which Plan we are Convinced was artefully Projected to open the gate for the admition of Tyrany & oppression with all their Rapacious followers to Stalk at Large & uncontrold to Ravage our fare & Dear bought Possessions. Every measure which shall appear Conducive to the Publick good we are warranted to asure you will always be approved and supportd by a Large Majority in this District and our [your] Continual Correspondence as Long as you shall think occation requires meet with Due respect & attention we are in behalf of the District very Respect-fully Gent'm your oblig'd & most hble servts."

The following September the town chose a standing committee of corres-pondence and also three delegates to represent them in a convention at Northampton. In October the district voted unanimously to send a delegate to the meeting of the provincial congress at Concord, and then made choice of Nathaniel Dickinson, Jr., one of. the foremost men in Amherst, in resisting the aggressions of England, a man whose earnestness of spirit and strong feeling caused him to forget the reverence then considered due to the meeting-house and the minister, and when his pastor, Mr. Parsons, persisted in saying in the pulpit, " God save the King," was provoked beyond all endurance, and spring-ing to his feet cried out, " You say God save the king ; but I say God save the Commonwealth of Massachusetts !" Mr. Dickinson was re-elected dele-gate the following year.

Early in 1775 the town voted to purchase 150 pounds weight of powder and lead, and also flints, directing the assessors to levy a rate for this purchase immediately. They also directed that all province money still in the hands of the constables should be paid to Henry Gardner, of Stow, instead of Harrison Gray, who was probably commissioned in the king's name. The district voted to indemnify the constables against all loss incurred in obeying this vote—such money as was due and not yet collected by the constables was to be borrowed on the town's credit and forwarded to Henry Gardner at once—a vote which shows both the urgent need of money by the patriotic leaders in the opening war and also the willingness of the town to contribute such money. A committee of inspection was chosen whose main duty was to exert themselves in behalf of the cause of the colonies—rendering all possible assistance "in Causing the association of the Continental Congress," which congress passed, July 4, 1776, the Declaration of Independence. As a minor duty, this committee was instructed " to suppress all Peddlers and Petty Chapmen." Another committee was appointed to circulate a subscrip-tion paper for the relief of the poor of Boston and Charlestown.

Thus Amherst showed her willingness to give both to the cause of freedom and to those who were suffering in that cause ; and also exhibited her fore-sight and breadth of information in declaring in favor of a united effort by all the colonies under direction of a continental congress. On May 4, 1775, a committee was appointed to provide stores for the support of the army at Cambridge, and a special town meeting held June 13, 1776,—three weeks

previous to the adoption of the Declaration of Independence, " Voted, That
should the Honorable Congress, for the Safety of the united Colonies in America, Declare them Independent of the Kingdom of Great Britain, we, the Inhabitants of the town of Amherst, solemnly engage with our lives and fortnnes
to support them in the measure, And that this Resolve be transmitted to our
Representative in General Assembly as instructions to him."

In 1778 the town recorded its desire for a new state constitution and chose
a committee to confer with the neighboring towns about calling a county convention to urge on all the necessity of such a constitution.   In 1779 the town
instructed their representative to vote for the calling of a state convention for
forming such a constitution, and it was adopted and went into effect in 1780.
In 1779 the town voted ℐ434 10s. "to Pay Bounties & Mileage to soldiers,"
and in 1780 ten thousand pounds was appropriated to pay for beef for the
soldiers, the price of beef being then more than four dollars per pound in the
depreciated currency of the day.   A committee appointed to see "how soldiers may be best procured to serve in the Continental army," seemed to
think the chief obstacle to enlistment was the poor credit of the continental
treasury, and advised the town to offer each soldier who would enlist for three
years in the war the sum of three pounds "hard money" per month, the soldiers to assign their continental pay to the town which should thus incur the
risk of the continental currency being redeemed.   Or, if the soldiers should
prefer, the town would guarantee to each soldier the sum of forty shillings in
hard money per month in addition to their continental pay, the town to also
promise each soldier two shirts, two pairs of stockings, and two pairs of shoes
yearly "in case he fails of the same from the Continent or State."   The town
adopted these recommendations.   A town vote of December 28, 1780, making
the town liable for money promised to soldiers by individuals, speaks of the
price of rye as being "fifty dollars per bushel."   An assessment of £460 in
"new currency" for furnishing beef and grain to the army was voted at this
time, and the next meeting voted that an unexpended balance of this money
should go towards the purchase of horses for the continental army, and this
appropriation was still further increased by the grant of the balance of school
funds.   Another purchase of beef was necessary in 1781, and the town treasurer was obliged to borrow "hard money" to procure it.   At this time the
continental bills were accepted in trade at one cent on the dollar, and falling
still lower the bills became absolutely worthless for a time and ceased to circulate.   The lack of money was a greater obstacle to the success of Washington's army than were the snows of Valley Forge and the armies of Great
Britain.

In 1781 the town was required to furnish a certain number of soldiers for
three months.   A committee was appointed to hire them, and were authorized to hire them on whatever terms they could, the town engaging to pay
whatever the committee should promise.   This was the last requisition upon
Amherst for soldiers, the surrender of Cornwallis, October 19, 1781, closing

hostilities. Like other towns, Amherst was obliged to draft soldiers once or twice during the war of 1775-1781; the names of some who were drafted and of many who volunteered for service at this time are preserved for their children and succeeding citizens to read with pride and gratitude.

Opposition to the Revolution.—The high degree of patriotic self-denial displayed by the town of Amherst throughout the long war, was by no means the unanimous expression of the town's people. There were men of rank and wealth in Amherst in 1775, and such men, having the most to lose in any dubious undertaking, are generally found opposing violent and costly changes in government and in social customs. At the head of the Amherst Tories was the long loved pastor of the church, Rev. David Parsons, Capt. Isaac Chauncey, Lieut. John Field, and Ensign John Nash, who had received royal commissions through the colonial governor, Hutchinson, were early objects of suspicion to the eager Revolutionists. Simeon Clark, one of the deacons of the church, heartily supported his pastor in opposition to "the rebels" against royal authority; and among others the influential family of the Boltwoods were prominent on the "Tory side." As early as the fall of 1774, there was a demand that all who held commissions from the king should renounce all authority derived from such commissions, and at a meeting of militia officers in Northampton, November 10 and 11, 1774, thirty-three, including the three Amherst officials, Chauncey, Field and Nash, renounced in writing all authority conferred by the royal governor. In addition to the militia officers the Revolutionists were suspicious of the justices of the peace of whom there were two in Amherst, Josiah Chauncey, father of Lieut. Isaac Chauncey, and Simeon Strong, the former having been appointed in 1758, the latter ten years later. Apparently Mr. Strong made no resistance to the patriotic demands, and after the war he regained his influence, and his high ability caused his election as state senator in 1793, and in 1800 his appointment as one of the judges of the supreme court of Massachusetts. But Mr. Chauncey fared differently. The town records of May 4, 1775, have the following account: "The town enters into the examination of Mr. Josiah Chauncey. Voted, Not satisfied with his answer to the charge laid against him. Voted, That s'd Chauncey should Burn all his Commissions he had ever received from the King, and also commit his Fire arms into the hands of the Select men of the District." The meeting adjourned for five days, when similar votes were recorded against John Nash. At this latter meeting the town "Voted that the Arms of Josiah Chauncey should be returned to him." It is said that Chauncey had given his commissions to certain leaders of the "Whigs" or Revolutionary party, by whom they were burnt in a public bonfire. But in April, 1776, Chauncey's son, Capt. Isaac Chauncey, was arrested and tried upon the charges of "insulting behavior" towards the committee of safety, and of being "an enemy to his country;" being convicted, he was confined in the jail at Northampton, whence he petitioned the general court for relief, but to no purpose. Upon his release he left his home secretly in

the following August, and the committee of safety advertised their desire that
the good people wherever he should be found would "secure him in such a
manner that he may not have it in his power to injure America." A similar
desire for the securing of Lieut. Robert Boltwood was expressed by the committee, but it is not known that either of them were arrested or that America
was injured by their escape from Amherst.

On July 7, 1777, "the Selectmen exhibited to the Town a List of the
Names of Such Persons as they supposed to be Inimical to the Interest of the
United States, viz.: L't John Field, Eben'r Boltwood, Isaac Goodale, William Boltwood." The meeting adjourned for eight days, and then voted to
erase Lieut. John Field's name from the list, but this vote was afterwards reconsidered, and Elijah Baker was appointed to procure evidence against the
accused parties. The meeting adjourned for four weeks, and then voted to
strike out of the list the names of each one of the four in succession. Evidently the prosecution of these men did not seem wise to many who were
strongly in favor of the Revolution. Yet so strong was the animosity felt
towards the sympathizers with England, that not even the love and respect
felt for the faithful pastor could secure him from much annoyance. In 1775
the proceedings at a town meeting were suspended until a committee should
go and request the attendance of Mr. Parsons, who had probably remained
away because he could not favor the wishes of a majority of the town. On
January 20, 1777, the town showed its appreciation of the religious work of
their pastor by voting him his usual salary; but they joined to this a vote
expressive of their dislike of his political influence, and " Vot'd that the conduct of the Rev'd David Parsons is not friendly with regard to the Common
Cause," and appointed a committee of five to tell him so. It seems that in
spite of the annual appropriation for the payment of his salary, Mr. Parsons
was not able to get his full dues, for in 1778 the town, in the appropriation for
his salary, instructed the assessors to pay him also the amount not paid him the
year before. On January 13, 1780, the town " Voted that Mr. Abraham Hill
be prohibited from Preaching in this Town in future," and a committee was
chosen "to write to him concerning the matter." Mr. Hill was the Shutesbury
preacher, and a very bitter Tory. Probably Mr. Parsons had exchanged with
him, and he had not concealed his feelings concerning the action of the
majority of the town, who had prohibited (March 11, 1778) " Persons not
owning Independence on the Crown of Great Britain agreeable to the Declaration of Congress" from the exercise of the freeman's right of voting in
town meetings.

War of 1812-15 *and* 1861-65.—The war with Great Britain, 1812-15,
was very unpopular throughout New England, and immediately after the declaration of war, June 18, 1812, steps were taken to hold a convention of
Hampshire county towns to give expression to the general feeling of regret
that war had been declared. Fifty-seven towns in the present counties of
Hampden, Hampshire and Franklin sent eighty-eight delegates to this con-

vention, which met at Northampton, July 14, 1812. Amherst's representatives were Ebenezer Mattoon (Revolutionary veteran and ex-member of congress), Samuel Fowler Dickinson (a prominent lawyer) and Simeon Strong (son of Judge Strong). It was an influential delegation which was sent from Amherst. The convention unanimously adopted a memorial praying that commissioners might be appointed for the speedy negotiation of terms of peace with Great Britain. This memorial was addressed to the president of the United States. The convention also recommended the meeting of a state convention to give voice to the feeling of Massachusetts. Notwithstanding the unanimity of opposition to this war, the rumor of a contemplated descent upon the coast of Massachusetts by English forces showed the willingness of the people to defend their state, and when Governor Strong called out the militia the Connecticut valley sent two regiments of infantry and one of artillery to Boston. They were encamped for six weeks at Dorchester, where they were formally reviewed by the governor; but as apprehensions of attack passed away, they were soon released from duty and returned home. This was facetiously called " Governor Strong's war."

In the civil war of 1861–65, Amherst had three hundred and fifty-two citizens in the Union army, and twenty-two in the navy. Of the three hundred and seventy-four, eleven were killed, fifteen died of wounds, thirty-two died of disease ; thirty-five others were wounded in the service. The military expenses of the town and individuals, in addition to regular taxes, were $46,237.27, of which the state refunded $1,641.27 "to equalize bounties."

Early Politics.—As already stated, Amherst was warmly in favor of adopting a state constitution in 1778 and 1779. The first election under this constitution was held Monday, September 4, 1780, when Amherst cast her first vote for governor, " The Hon'ble John Hancock, Esq'r," receiving forty-three votes, and "The Hon'ble James Bowdoin, Esq'r," eight. These two men continued to be rival candidates for five years, Bowdoin apparently growing in favor with the Amherst voters as will be seen by the following : Hancock, in the respective years, received forty-three, fifty-seven, fifty-seven, twenty-eight, and thirteen, while Bowdoin received eight, nine, twenty-three, nineteen, and twenty-one.

In 1785 John Hancock was not a candidate for the office, and James Bowdoin was elected governor. Amherst, however, favored the Hon. John Worthington, who received sixteen votes, to nine for James Bowdoin. In 1786 Governor Bowdoin was re-elected, his opponent being Benjamin Lincoln, Amherst giving Bowdoin twenty-three votes and Lincoln eleven, while John Hancock received one. In 1787 Hancock and Bowdoin were again rivals, and Amherst gave Bowdoin thirteen votes and Hancock eight, but the state went for ex-Governor Hancock. In recent years Amherst has been a strong Republican town at every election.

In 1782 the town neglected to send a representative to the legislature, and for this neglect was fined by the general court. At the town meeting, held

January 19, 1784, Simeon Strong, Esq., Nathaniel Dickinson, Jr., and Lieut. John Field were appointed a committee to secure an abatement of this fine. In 1786 and 1789 Amherst again failed to send a representative, as also in 1795. In 1788 the town sent Daniel Cooley to the convention, which considered the adoption of the proposed constitution of the United States. Mr. Cooley represented the wishes of the town, and probably of the western part of the state, when he voted against adoption. Fortunately, the majority of the convention was the other way.

Schools.—In November, 1647, the general court of Massachusetts ordered that every town having fifty families should provide a school where children might be taught to read and write, and that every town with an hundred families should provide a grammar school whose master should be able to fit young men for college. These grammar schools were not for instruction in English grammar, which was not studied in these, but for teaching Latin grammar. This law was by no means a compulsory educational law, for it did not require that these schools should be free, and for many years they were supported partly by the town and partly by the parents. Free schools did not become general in Massachusetts until a century after the landing at Plymouth. It will seem very strange to those accustomed only to modern systems of education, that the early schools were attended by so few of the girls; if a girl was taught to read and to sew her education was considered complete, and at the time Amherst was settled probably not one woman in ten could write her name; she could read the Bible, but what was the need of writing in days when the postoffice was unknown? It was not considered to be a serious drawback that a man could not write his own name, although boys were generally taught to write on account of the need of signing business documents; yet many a man of considerable social and business prominence signed his legal papers by " his mark " in the days before the Revolution. No reader of the original records of any old town needs to be told that the spelling-book was not studied in these early schools; every man spelled as he pleased, and often in the same sentence he would write the same word twice and spell it differently.

The first vote on record concerning schools in Hadley Third Precinct is at a meeting held March 13, 1749, when a committee was chosen " to Hire three Scool Dames for three or four Months In the Summer Seson to Larne children to read; sd scools to be In the most convenient places." This meant that women were hired to receive children into their own homes, or some convenient room in a private dwelling, for instruction in the New England Primer. The town of Hadley having appropriated £60 for the use of the third precinct for school purposes, it was voted, April 9, 1752, that £30 " be Improved to hire a scool Master att ye fall of yᵉ yeare ; that the other therty pounds be Improved to hire Scoole Dames in the Summer." And a school committee of nine persons was chosen. In 1753 Hadley granted £20 for school purposes, and the precinct appropriated £4 in addition ; three schools were to be kept in the precinct this year. The precinct appropriated £4 lawful money in 1754, and there is no mention of schools again until 1759, when £20 was appropriated. In January, 1760, the precinct voted £10 13s. 4d. lawful money for school purposes, and the following March £13 6s. 8d.

The first vote in relation to school-houses was January 5, 1761, when it was voted to build two school-houses at the expense of the district. The location of these buildings was not settled until the next December, when the number was increased to three; the first to be placed "in the highway that leads to Pelham, near the place where Moses Warner's house formerly stood," (near the present centre of the town); the second was to be put "in the highway that runs east and west between Joseph Church and Jon'th Coles," (somewhere near the postoffice in North Amherst); the third, in the highway south of Nathaniel Colman's lot, east of Plum brook, upon the hill, (on the road south of Mill valley in South Amherst).

Probably the location of these school-houses was a matter of some dispute not easily harmonized, for the next meeting revoked the vote locating "the midle Scool-house," and the next meeting after this "Vo't to stop all Proceedings Respecting the Scool-houses another year." In October, 1762, the district again voted to build three school-houses, and chose three committees, the first to determine "Where said Scool-houses shall be Set," the second "to wait on the aforsd Com'tt," the third "to Build the aforsd Scool-housses where the Com'tt apointed shall order." Curiosity can hardly refrain from wondering what were the duties of that second committee. Apparently, however, even these committees failed to get the school-houses built, for in December, 1764, it was voted to build four school-houses, a "North," a "South," an "East-middle" and a "West-middle." Four committees of three each were chosen to locate these houses, and it was "Vot'd that the District will abide the Determination of the aforesaid Com'ttees." Four other committees of three each were to build the school-houses. This time the work was done, for January 6, 1766, the meeting adjourned from the meeting-house "to the school-house which is near Landlord Warner's dwelling house." This school-house stood where Hunt's block now stands. There was, of course, no way for warming the meeting-house in those days, and the January day was probably cold, if the school-house was without a stove as well as the church; probably its nearness to "Landlord Warner's" made "suthin hot" accessible to the chilled voters.

The labor upon the school-houses was paid for by the day, the carpenters receiving 2s. 4d. for fall work, 2s. 8d. for summer work; the laborers received 2s. a day in summer, 1s. 6d. in fall, the last named sum being about equivalent to twenty-five cents.

Apparently the "North" school-house was in the present "City" district, and the parents in "the West St.," by the present North Amherst church, felt aggrieved at this location, for in 1767 it was voted "to keep the scool one

Month in the West St. North End," and the next year it was voted that "the North Scool to be kept one halfe the Time in the West Street." In 1771 it was "Voted that the Select Men Set up a new school at the North End of the District the space of six weeks in addition to the present school." In 1778, "Voted that a school be kept three months at the North school-house, also three months in the West St. in the Northern part of the town." But in January, 1779, the first vote in town meeting, after choice of moderator, was "That the money raised for the use of Schooling in the North part of this Town be expended in the North school-house." The controversy had its usual termination, for in January, 1786, the town voted "To Allow a reasonable reward to those Persons who built the school-house in the Northerly part of the Town on the road leading to Sunderland."

The effort to accommodate North Amherst and "the City" in a single schoolhouse was unfortunately renewed when the schools came to be graded, and while two schools were kept for primary scholars, the older children were sent to a cross street half-way between the two villages. As this location was convenient for nobody, it had the merit of being impartial, at the price of removing the children from all the salutary restraints of surrounding homes and people. In 1787 the town voted "to allow the people in the North East part of Amherst [now the City district] eighteen pounds in case they shall build for the town such a school-house as is built in the North West part of the town." Apparently the City people outdid their neighbors, for in 1788 it was "Voted to allow thirty pounds for building the school-house in the North East part of the town."

The first school of advanced grade in Amherst was taught by Josiah Pierce, who had been master of the Hadley grammar school for eighteen years. From 1766 to 1769 he taught alternately in each of the middle school-houses, keeping a private school for older scholars in the evening. He was a graduate of Harvard college, and sometimes preached in neighboring pulpits during the absence or illness of the minister. Judd's *History of Hadley* says that his salary was thirty-two shillings ($5.33) and board per month. In 1772 the district voted "to Improve M'r William Gay Ballentine for six months" as master of the grammar school. Mr. Ballentine had been a classmate at Harvard of the Rev. Mr. Parson's son, and came to Amherst to study theology with his classmate's father. In 1777 the stress of war caused the town to vote "to improve English Schoolmasters only," and the study of Latin ceased for a time. It is of course unknown to how great an extent it had been previously taught, but the fact that six Amherst boys are known to have been sent to college indicates that the master had some pupils in the dead languages. Nathaniel Dickinson, Jr., and David Parsons graduated at Harvard in 1771, Ebenezer Boltwood two years later, David Kellogg and Ebenezer Mattoon attended Dartmouth college, graduating respectively in 1775 and 1776, and Aaron Kellogg graduated at Yale in 1778. Compared with other towns Amherst has always sent an unusually large number of her sons to college, many of whom have attained a high degree of distinction and usefulness.

The early schools were of short terms, and the younger scholars attended but a single summer term in the year.   More importance was then attached to home instruction, especially in manual labor, than has been customary since.   In 1773 it was "Voted to allow five month schooling to each quarter of the town, in that part of the year when the Select men Shall Judg most profatable for the Inheabitants."   "Voted to be at the Expence of twelve month schooling for grammar schooling in the Winter ceason."   In 1780 there was to be eighteen months' schooling in the six schools or three months' at each school.   The town passed a similar vote for the next year, and this was probably the length of the school sessions for many years.   In 1778 the town voted "that the Persons who send scholars shall provide wood for the schools."   Schools were sometimes dismissed because the supply of fire-wood was exhausted.

The graded system of public schools now almost universal in the larger towns of Massachusetts was introduced into Amherst in 1860.   There was a bitter opposition to this system in town, and it was delayed for many years after its introduction in other parts of the state.   Its working has not been altogether free from the criticism made at its introduction that it would prevent the sons of workingmen from obtaining the education which had formerly been given during the winter terms when the older boys were not needed for farm work as they would be in summer.   Still, the town's schools are an object of pride to the citizens who yearly expend nearly $10,000.00 upon them.   The number of school children reported by the assessors in 1885 was 600. The appropriation of the town the same year was, for schools $8,800.00, and for school-books $2,000.00, making the average cost of the schools about eigheen dollars for each scholar.

The high school has three courses of instruction, a classical, designed to fit young men for college, an English and Latin, chiefly taken by young ladies, and an English course in which the only foreign tongue studied is French. The two former courses require each four years for their completion, and the last is completed in three years.

The school buildings are distributed in various parts of the town, the center village having two large brick structures, the high school on School street receiving the scholars of the grammar grades as well as of the high school proper ; the Amity Street school-house, containing the primary and intermediate grades.   East Amherst district has one large school-house with rooms for the various classes of the respective grades below the high school. North Amherst has three school-houses, one of them having double rooms for the grammar and intermediate grades respectively ; the other two being both of primary grade, one in the "West Street" and the other at "the City." The more scattered population south of the centre village requires five smaller schools, called respectively " Mill Valley," " South Grammar," "South Green," South East" and " South West."

Amherst College.—It was during the second war with Great Britain that Amherst academy, which was the stepping stone to Amherst college, was opened.   Even before the Revolution a movement had begun for the establishment of a college or collegiate school in Hampshire county, and as soon as the county recovered its prosperity after the financial disasters of that long war, the efforts were renewed.   Northampton was anxious to secure the honor of being an academic town, but the clergy of the vicinity seem to have favored Amherst from the commencement of the effort.   Amherst academy was opened in 1814, and formally dedicated in 1815, although it was not chartered until 1816, owing to opposition.   Samuel Fowler Dickinson, Hezekiah W. Strong and Rev. Dr. Parsons were very instrumental in founding this academy.   Dr. Parsons donated the land for the academy building, and was the first president of the board of trustees.   The state made a conditional grant of half a township of land in the present state of Maine in aid of the academy, which flourished for several years, the number of pupils being at one time one hundred and eighty, one-half of them females.   Mary Lyon, the well-known founder of Mt. Holyoke seminary, studied here in 1821, and many others of note first climbed the hill of knowledge at this academy.   The building occupied the present site of the Amity Street school-house, just west of the Amherst House.   It was never endowed, and with the passing away of the need of academies, upon the introduction of a graded system of schools and the establishment of free high schools for advanced instruction, it lost its non-resident support and was finally swallowed up by the Amherst high school. The building was torn down in 1868 to make room for the new town grammar school building.

It was through a charity fund that Amherst academy grew into Amherst college.   An effort to raise money for the educating of promising but needy youth who wished to enter the ministry, revealed the fact that friends of the movement would subscribe more readily if the establishment of an institution of higher grade was contemplated.   At the same time the desire for the removal of Williams college to a place of more convenient access seemed to be favorable to the project of a new college in Hampshire county.   The friends of Williams college at first favored Northampton for the location of this institution, but as the legislature refused to charter a new institution, it became necessary to fall back upon the charter already obtained for Amherst academy.   Fifty thousand dollars as a charity fund was quickly raised, and in 1820 the trustees of the academy began the erection of the first college building, Noah Webster delivering an address at the laying of the corner stone.   Col. Elijah Dickinson had given the land, nine acres, the present location of the Amherst college buildings, and friends of the enterprise contributed both material and labor, and in September, 1821, a brick structure four stories high and 30 x 100 feet was completed.   The trustees of the academy had already (May, 1821,) chosen Zephaniah Swift Moore as president of the " Charity Institution," as they called it, and he resigned the presidency of Williams college to accept his new position, bringing to Amherst a large number of his former pupils at Williamstown. The inauguration of the president and the dedication of the college took place September 8, 1821, the ceremonies taking place in the First church, which was located near the site of the present college observatory. Noah Webster presided and Rev. Dr. Leland, of Charleston, S. C., preached the sermon.

The college opened with forty-seven students, two of whom were sufficiently advanced to enter the senior class. There were two professors besides the president. The latter was to teach theology and moral philosophy, while the two professors, Rev. Gamaliel S. Olds and Joseph Estabrook, were respectively assigned to the departments of mathematics and natural philosophy, and that of the Latin and Greek. The present " North College " was erected during the presidency of Dr. Moore, and a president's house (now occupied by the Psi Upsilon society). At the first commencement, in 1821, there were two graduates, Pindar Field, who founded and superintended Amherst's first Sunday-school, and E. S. Snell, afterwards professor. They received Latin testimonials that they had completed a regular college course, but could not receive degrees as the charter of the academy did not authorize the conferring of degrees.

Dr. Moore's death (June 29, 1823), at the early age of fifty-two, was a severe blow to the college, but in the following October Rev. Heman Humphrey was installed as his successor, and the prospects of the institution materially brightened when, in 1825, it finally succeeded in obtaining a college charter from the legislature. It is said that one of the questions of the preceding political campaign was the granting of a charter to the college, Governor Eustis, the successful candidate, favoring, and his opponent being adverse to the granting of the charter. After an early measure of success, Dr. Humphrey's presidency became embarrassed by financial difficulties and a threatened split upon the question of slavery. He resigned in 1844, and was succeeded in 1845 by Prof. Edward Hitchcock, during whose administration the endowment funds of the college were largely increased and its prosperity permanently assured. Rev. William A. Stearns, the next president, was inaugurated November 22, 1854. During his presidency the college was the recipient of over $75,000.00 in donations, the officers of instruction increased from eleven to twenty-one, with a proportionate increase of the number of students. The new buildings erected in his administration, Williston hall, Walker hall, and the College church, were architecturally a great improvement upon those erected before. President Stearns died June 8, 1876, and Prof. Julius H. Seelye was inaugurated as his successor May 24, 1877.

The college grounds embrace about thirty acres of land, to which five more acres is to be added by a purchase now being completed (August,

10*

1886). In addition to the college buildings, technically so called, the various secret societies own a number of chapter houses, which are an ornament to the town, in addition to fulfilling their society requirements. The building used for the college library, recently enlarged and admirably fitted for its purposes, contains about 45,000 volumes. The new Pratt gymnasium enables the students to seek physical development, and affords a place of training for the various athletic exhibitions and contests, second only to the Hemingway gymnasium of Harvard college, and far surpassing the ordinary facilities of college gymnasiums. In its art museum and its collection of bird tracks named in honor of President Hitchcock, and its collection of Indian relics, the college offers unusual opportunities to the lovers of sculpture, of paleontology and of aboriginal remains to pursue their favorite lines of study. Amherst college was the first to admit the students to a share in the government of the college, and at present all cases of college discipline are referred to the "Senate," a body of students elected by their fellows and presided over by the college president. So successful has been this mode of solving many vexed questions relating to the government of college students, that in its essential features it has been adopted by nearly all of the larger colleges.

Amherst college has ever been noted for its deep religious influence, and it has been said that no class has ever graduated from its halls without having passed through a revival of religious interest. In questions of educational methods, the position of the college was tersely defined by President Seelye at the commencement dinner in 1886, "Not as eager for changes as Harvard, we are not as afraid of them as Yale." Prof. William S. Tyler has now held the professorship of the classical languages for fifty years, and in honor of this unusual event in college history the president of the institution at the commencement dinner of 1886, asked the alumni to respond to his sentiment, "O king, live forever," and the heartiness of the ovation rendered spontaneously to the genial professor left no doubt of his popularity with the many hundreds who have been taught no less by his character than by his learning.

In 1885-86 the college faculty consisted of thirty-two officers of instruction, and the students were classified as follows: resident graduates, 3 ; seniors, 77 ; juniors, 74 ; sophomores, 101 ; freshmen, 100 ; total number of students, 355. The total number of graduates from 1822 to 1881, has been 2,614. Among the large number of Amherst's sons who have rendered distinguished service to their fellow men may be mentioned as theological leaders, Profs. B. B. Edwards (1824) and George Harris (1866), of Andover Theological seminary, and President R. D. Hitchcock (1836), of Union seminary. Prof. H. B. Hackett, of the theological seminaries of Newton and Rochester, was graduated at Amherst in 1830. The college has furnished the churches with a large number of gifted and consecrated workers, at the head of whom stand Henry Ward Beecher (1834), Bishop Huntington (1839) and Rev. Richard S. Storrs (1839). William Hayes Ward, the editor of *The Independent*, graduated in 1856. Ex-Gov. Bullock, of Massachusetts (1836),

Horace Maynard, of Tennessee (1838), Galusha A. Grow, of Pennsylvania (1844), with others of Amherst's sons, have held high political offices. Francis A. Walker, president of the Massachusetts Institute of Technology, belongs to the Amherst class of 1860, as does also George L. Goodale, the professor in charge of the botanical department of Harvard university. Two hundred and sixteen graduates of the college served in the Union army or navy ; 1,024 have been ordained as clergymen, and 105 as foreign missionaries.

Massachusetts Agricultural College.—In 1864 a second college was located in Amherst by vote of the trustees of the Massachusetts Agricultural college, which had been incorporated the year before by the state legislature, and was at that time " the only college in the United States designed exclusively for the education of farmers." The nucleus for the funds of this institution was the grant of public land given by congress in 1862, for the maintenance of at least one college in each state " to teach such branches of learning as are related to agriculture and the mechanic arts." The state of Massachusetts received 360,000 acres of the public domain under this grant, one-third of which was appropriated to the institute of technology, in Boston. As an inducement for the location of the college within its limits, the town of Amherst donated $50,000.00 for the erection of buildings. The college bought 383½ acres of land from six proprietors, and the institution was formally opened in October, 1867, when a class of thirty-three students were admitted. The college has never received such private bequests from friends as have sufficed to give other institutions a permanent endowment fund, and has depended mainly for its support upon the appropriations generously made by the state legislature.

The total number of graduates is 245, non-graduates (those who have pursued a partial course) 406. Of the 650 whom this college has thus educated, 221 are now engaged in business, and 175 are in agricultural pursuits of some kind. The presidents of the college have been Hon. Henry F. French, 1864–1866 ; Rev. Dr. P. A. Chadbourne, 1866–1867 ; Col. William S. Clark, 1867–1879 ; Charles L. Flint, 1879–1880 ; Levi Stockbridge, 1880–1882 ; Rev. Dr. P. A. Chadbourne, 1882–1883 ; James C. Greenough, 1883–1886 ; H. H. Goodell, 1886.

The early success of the college was due in large measure to the active and energetic ability of Colonel Clark, who made the institution to be known not merely in this state, but also in far away Japan, whose agricultural college at Sapporo was modeled upon this, and organized by President Clark, who received a year's leave of absence to start the college, and which has ever looked to Amherst for gifted and energetic teachers. Colonel Clark is the only president who has held the office long enough to stamp his own personal influence upon the college, and much is due to his ability as an organizer and his active energy as a worker. The presidency of Dr. Chadbourne from which much was hoped, was cut short in 1867 by the failure of his health, and again in 1883 by his untimely death. President Greenough in his brief administration accomplished a great deal for the college in securing the erection of new buildings, which were greatly needed. South college, the library and chapel, and the president's house and barn, together with the buildings of the experiment station will remain as the testimony to his usefulness in furthering the interests of the college, and of the confidence of the state's representatives in his administration.

The funds of the college are the gift of land from the United States and a grant of nearly $150,000.00 by the state. In addition to the income of these funds the state has made appropriations for the various needs of the college amounting in all to $395,500.00.

The grant of $10,000.00 for free scholarships, first made in 1883, is annually made in accordance with the law of April 16, 1886. In 1885-86, the college faculty consisted of twelve instructors and the catalogued students numbered, seniors, 11 ; juniors, 27 ; sophomores, 22 ; freshmen, 23 ; total, 83—all but ten of whom were residents of Massachusetts.

In connection with the college there is an agricultural experiment station, established in 1882, where experiments are continually being made in all branches of agriculture, reports of which are published and distributed for the benefit of the farmers of the state. Prof. Charles A. Goessman, the college professor of chemistry, is the director of this station, whose board of management consists of seven persons, of whom the *ex officio* members are the governor of the state and the president of the college.

Private Schools.—Mount Pleasant Institute, a private school for boys, was organized in 1846 by John A. Nash. The buildings erected especially for a school have a beautiful and healthful location on an eminence half a mile north of the village of Amherst. In 1853 the Institute was bought by Henry C. Nash, and conducted by him until 1877. From that time to 1884 it did not exist as a school; but in 1884 W. K. Nash, son of H. C., took the school and is conducting it at the present time.

Mrs. Williams's school for young ladies and misses is located on South Prospect street. Rev. R. G. Williams and Mrs. Williams have been engaged in teaching many years, and have been in charge of large institutions. Mr. Williams's health having failed, Mrs. Williams proposes to continue her life work in Amherst. The assistance of first-class teachers in every department has been obtained, so that pupils can have the very best instruction.

Libraries.—The first public library in Amherst was begun in 1869, when the North Amherst Library association was formed by public spirited citizens of North Amherst. Its first books were purchased by subscription, and although a public library, it did not become a free public library until 1876, when the town made an appropriation for the purchase of books for this library. For many years the town has annually appropriated $100.00 for this purpose, and the citizens of North Amherst add to this from year to year by their united efforts. The number of volumes at the opening of the year 1886 was 1,189.

The library at the center village, now containing about four thousand volumes, the use of which is free to all citizens of the town, began in a book-club formed in 1872. The next year an association was formed, and a three days' fair netted over six hundred dollars for the purchase of books, etc. A small association at East Amherst united with this, and the library thus commenced contained about 750 volumes. At present the town makes a small annual appropriation for the purchase of books, and the directors of the association secure additional contributions by fairs, entertainments, or subscriptions. The library both needs and deserves the generous gifts of the public spirited, which will erect a suitable building for its accommodation, and also increase its income and its power for good.

BIOGRAPHICAL.

Not far from 1745 there came to Hadley third precinct (now Amherst), Nathan Dickinson, a native of Hatfield, where he was born in 1712. He brought with him his wife, Thankful Warner, and three children; and March 30, 1746, a fourth child was born to him at his new home in the third precinct. His wife died soon after coming to Amherst, and he married Joanna Leonard, of Westfield, and after her death he married a third wife, Judith Hosmer. He died in Amherst August 7, 1796, at the ripe age of eighty-four. Of his thirteen children all but four seemed to have lived to have families of their own. His oldest son and namesake, Nathan Dickinson, Jr., was about ten years of age at the time of his father's coming to Amherst, having been born in Hatfield in 1735. He married in Amherst, Esther Fowler, and died August 3, 1825, aged ninety years. Seven of his eight children were married, and one of them, Timothy, his oldest son, was graduated at Dartmouth college in 1785, and became pastor of the church in Holliston, where he died in 1813.

Samuel Fowler Dickinson, son of Nathan, Jr., was born in Amherst October 9, 1775. His father was a farmer in East Amherst, and his mother, Esther Fowler, was from Westchester, Conn. He fitted for college with Judge Strong, of Amherst, entered Dartmouth college at the age of sixteen years, and graduated in 1795. Though the youngest of his class he received the second appointment, the salutatory oration in Latin. After leaving college, and teaching one year in the academy at New Salem, he completed the usual term of study in the law office of Judge Strong, and then established an office of his own in his native place. He early united with the West Parish church, and at the age of twenty-one was elected one of the deacons, an office which he held nearly forty years. For fifteen years, from 1804 to 1818 inclusive, he was town clerk, was frequently employed as the agent and advocate of the town in litigated questions, and served in the legislature twelve years, in the house of representatives eleven, and in the senate one, being chosen first in 1805. He was ranked among the best lawyers in Hampshire county, and might doubtless have had a seat on the judicial bench if he had continued the practice of his profession.   But he was gradually drawn off into business for which he had a natural fondness, and he was still more deeply interested in religious movements, ecclesiastical affairs and educational enterprises.   With a large family to educate, and at the same time having at heart the general welfare, he, with a few others, established the academy of Amherst, erected the building, furnished it with apparatus and other endowments—liberal for those times—sought far and near the ablest teachers that could be found, and spared neither time nor money to make it the ablest institution of the kind in the Commonwealth.   No one was more intrusted, none bore a more important part in the founding of Amherst college than Samuel Fowler Dickinson.   The enlargement of the plan from a mere professorship in Amherst academy, into that of a separate collegiate institution, was owing expressly to his suggestion and influence.   He was among the original board of trustees of both the academy and college.   He was the chairman of the committee appointed by the board to secure a title to the land for the site of the college, to decide on a plan of the first building, to procure subscriptions, donations or contributions for defraying the expense thereof, and then to prepare the ground and erect the building.   With all the zeal and effort of numerous friends and benefactors in Amherst and the neighboring towns, the work of erecting this building would often have stopped if Mr. Dickinson had not pledged his private property at the bank to obtain money.   He hesitated at no sacrifice of his time, property or personal service, in furthering the enterprise in which he was so deeply enlisted, even to his own impoverishment—indeed, his efforts for this may be considered the best part of his life work.   Mr. Dickinson was a tall, thin man, plain in his dress and appearance, of prodigious bodily and mental activity and energy, a famous walker, a ferocious worker, a born leader, a man of ideas and principles, of rare public spirit, strong religious faith and zeal, whose whole life was one of self-denial and self-sacrifice in the public service for education and religion, for the glory of God and the good of his fellow men.   He died suddenly of pneumonia, April 22, 1838, at the age of sixty-two years.

Edward Dickinson, oldest son of Hon. Samuel Fowler Dickinson, was born in Amherst, where he always lived, on the first of January, 1803 ; was educated in the public schools of Amherst, and in Amherst academy, till he was prepared to enter college ; was a member of the first junior class in the collegiate institution at Amherst, although the other three years of his collegiate course were at Yale, where he graduated in 1823 with high honor ; studied law for two years with his father, and a third year in the then prominent and ably conducted law school at Northampton ; in 1826 opened his office in Amherst, and continued in active and successful practice to the time of his death.   In 1835 he was chosen treasurer of Amherst college, and held that office from that time to the end of his life, although he had resigned the year before, and his son, William A. Dickinson, had been elected his successor.

In 1838 and 1839, and again in 1874 he represented Amherst in the legislature; in 1842 and 1843 he was a member of the Massachusetts senate; in 1845 and 1846 he was a member of the governor's council, when George N. Briggs was governor, and in the years 1853 and 1855 he represented his district in congress, and held many other offices of trust by local election and executive appointment. He was of the old Whig party in politics, and never identified himself with any other, though acting in the main with the Republican after the Whig as such had ceased to exist, and in the era of good feeling and patriotism which prevailed and came near doing away with party lines in the state, in 1861 he was nominated by the Republicans a lieutenant-governor on the ticket with Andrew, but declined the honor.

As a lawyer he was sound, safe and the soul of uprightness. He hated pettifoggers and tricksters, believed in his profession as a high calling, and used it to promote the ends of justice and good morals. Faithful to every trust, conscientious in the discharge of every duty, of rare public spirit—like his father before him—the especial devotion of his life may well be said to have been Amherst and Amherst college. At home and abroad as well, he bore its banner proudly and defiantly aloft, and to no one citizen does it owe so much of its present local and foreign reputation for high position and character as to him. He led in every enterprise which promised to add to its growth, prosperity and attractiveness. He was especially conspicuous with labor and money in procuring the building of the New London Northern railroad, and was hardly less prominent and influential in his endeavors for the construction of the Massachusetts Central line. It was for this that he consented to become a member of the legislature again in 1873–74. His labors and anxieties for its interests in connection with the tunnel, undoubtedly were the occasion of his sudden death, he having been stricken with apoplexy while making a speech on a bill relating to this matter before the house, just after noon, June 16, 1874. Thus, and even more, was his devotion to the college. No man ever watched or tended his own child, or his own property, with more personal, jealous care, than he did the institution he so long and ably served.

He was a man "without fear and without reproach"—a man with the full courage of his convictions. His moral power made him always respected and felt, and commanded honor. In his state, and particularly in its western section, he long ranked among the few "first citizens," respected for his sturdy good sense and independence, revered for his spotless integrity and patriotic self-sacrifice to the public, and beloved by all who came near to him, for the simple truthfulness and chivalric tenderness that lay deep and broad in the base of his nature. His life and character were a rich legacy to the community in which he lived.

William Austin Dickinson, oldest child of Edward, was born in Amherst April 16, 1829, and graduated at Amherst college in 1850, and at the Harvard law school in 1854, when he was admitted to the bar in Boston. He began the practice of law in Amherst in 1855, and in 1873 was chosen treasurer of Amherst college, succeeding his father in that important trust.   He married, in 1856, Susan H. Gilbert, of Greenfield.   As a public spirited citizen, Mr. Dickinson has rendered much valuable service to his native town—one of the most conspicuous of his services being his work as president of the Village Improvement society, through whose efforts an unsightly " dumping spot for all refuse " in the very center of the village became transformed into the tasteful common which is admired by all visitors to Amherst.   Mr. Dickinson is well nigh invariably chosen moderator of the Amherst town meetings, a position for which he is well adapted, both by his legal knowledge and his firmness and decision of character.

Walter Dickinson was born in this town May 2, 1784, married Lydia Dickinson in 1806, and reared ten children, namely, Sylvester, Frederick E., Marquis F., Nathaniel A., Lydia E., Nehemiah O., Leander M., Amy S., Walter M. and Sarah M.   Mrs. Dickinson died in 1828, and Mr. Dickinson survived her till 1851.   Marquis F. resides on the farm which was first settled by his great grandfather, Nathaniel, about 1840, and is located on road 18.   He was born in 1814, married Hannah S. Williams in 1838, and has reared ten children, namely, Maurice F., who is practicing law in Boston, Walter N., Lydia J., Amelia S., Roxy E., Asa W., Walter M., Julia C., Hannah F. and Mary U.

Azariah Dickinson was born April 13, 1753, married Mary Eastman, December 22, 1785, and reared six children, viz.: Sarah I., Ransom, Austin, Daniel, Baxter and Hannah.   He died August 31, 1813.   Daniel was born in Amherst, June 13, 1793, married twice, first, Louisa Adams, February 17, 1819, who bore him two children, Mary A. and Daniel A., and died March 6, 1828.   He married for his second wife, Fannie Eastman, June 25, 1829, and reared six children, viz.: Louisa, William E., Sarah T., George, Charles R. and Edward B.   Charles R. was born October 16, 1837, Married Adelia M. Harris, August 16, 1865, and has four children, namely, Edwin H., Louisa, Laura A. and Raymond D.

Abijah Dickinson, son of Ebenezer, was born on the homestead December 7, 1781, married Mary Stetson, October 26, 1806, and had born to him five children, William E., Charlotte, Franklin, Samuel S. and E. Porter.   Samuel S. was born February 12, 1815, married Alzina Towne, March 27, 1839, and reared seven children, Abby J. (Mrs. Lewis Bartlett), Mary E., Samuel S., Emleyetta C., Alice A., John H. and Herbert S.

Leander M. Dickinson was born August 20, 1821, and Laura A., his wife, was born May 14, 1825.   They reared five children, as follows: Lydia T., Julia A., Edward L., Mason A. and Frank N.   The last mentioned was born January 15, 1866, and resides on road 1.   Leander M. died November 7, 1885.

Lieut. Enos Dickinson, son of Jonathan K. and Azubah (Coleman) Dickinson, was born in Amherst, in the house in which he died, October 23, 1785. His father and mother died in the same house—his father at the age of

Engraved by Samuel Sartain, Phil[a]

Edward Dickinson

eighty-five years, and his mother at the age of eighty-six years. He married Lois Dickinson, April 27, 1809, who died April 18, 1868, aged eighty-four years. Mr. Dickinson was a conscientious Christian and philanthropic to a marked degree. The "Dickinson Nineveh Gallery" of Amherst college is an example of the latter trait in his character. He united with the First Congregational church in 1816, and was one of the original founders of the Congregational church at South Amherst.

Noah Dickinson, son of Johathan, was born in this town, February 18, 1819, married Malah Bliss, March 17, 1857, and has had born to him four children, namely, Helen B., Frank B., Amy S. and May B. He resides on road 31.

John Dickinson was born in Shutesbury, and married Lydia Eastman, of North Amherst. His son Zebina was born in Amherst, in 1778, married Mary Watson, of Lester, Mass., and had born to him ten children. His son William W. was born August 22, 1810, married Mary L. Marsh, March 3, 1840, and has had born to him four children, namely, Ellen R., Jane W., Amy S. and Amelia.

William I. Dickinson was born on the homestead, on road 44, November 7, 1815, married twice, first, Vester Rankin, December 1, 1836, who bore him three children, Willard R., Mary E. and Frank E. He married for his second wife Harriet N. Allen, August 7, 1845, and has had born to him three children, Hattie V., Sumner L. and Alice L.

Jonathan Cowles was born in Suffield, in 1703, married Sarah Gaylord, and reared ten children, viz.: Sarah, Oliver, Jerusha, Jonathan, David, Josiah, Eleazer, Reuben, Enos and Simeon. He died March 14, 1792. His youngest son, Simeon, was born in 1755, married Sarah Dickinson, February 12, 1778, lived and died on the homestead, located on road 18, and reared nine children, viz.: Simeon, Jerusha, Orinda, Azubah, Lebina, Moses, Aaron, Sally and Eli. The mother of these children died in 1814, and Mr. Dickinson married for his second wife Polly King, who died in 1831. He also died in 1831. Simeon, Jr., married Charlotte Stetson, and reared eight children, as follows: Hiram, Esther, Nancy, Rufus, Amasa, Charlotte, Mary and Harriet. He lived on the homestead a few years after marriage, and then moved to Goshen, Mass., where he died in 1857, aged seventy-eight years. Moses, son of Simeon, married Chloe Dickinson, and spent his life on the homestead. He reared five children, namely, Henry, James, Ebenezer, Harriet and Marietta. Of these only two are living, Henry, who is a physician in Framingham, Mass., and James. Henry married Nancy K. Puffer, and has one child. James, who is living on the homestead, married Nancy Henderson, and has two children, Arthur Frederick and Mary Ellen. The former has married twice; first, Bell Kellogg, and second, Lucia Kellogg. He is now a widower and resides at home. Mary E. married Willis Tuxbury, and has one son, James F.

David Cowls was born August 11, 1741, built the house where his grandson, Jonathan, now resides, and which is probably over one hundred and twenty-five years old. He married Sarah Eastman, and reared five children, namely, David, Sally, Joseph, Silas and Jonathan. The last mentioned was born December 2, 1781, married Esther Graves, April 16, 1807, and had born to him eight children, viz.: Justin, Erastus, Louis, Ira, Esther, Sarah, Ransom and Jonathan. The last mentioned was born on the homestead, May 4, 1822, married Sarah Dickinson, July 1, 1851, and has had born to him four children, namely, Walter D., Newton E., Abby G. and Sarah J. Walter D. is now one of the selectmen of this town.

Ransom Cowls was born August 18, 1818, married Sarah Gunn, August 24, 1843, and shortly after marriage, located on the place where he now resides, on the corner of roads 5 and 6. He has had born to him eight children, as follows: Stephen, born January 15, 1845, died December, 1854; Francis I., born October 26, 1846 ; George C., Esther T., Albert R., born June 23, 1852 ; J. Edward, born July 8, 1857, and died December 18, 1865 ; Charles S., born June 14, 1856, died February 4, 1859 ; and Melville A. born November 11, 1859.

Enoch Cowles was born January 29, 1802, married Julia Brigham, June 19, 1825, and had born to him three children, Julia A., Enoch D. and Watson W. He died in April, 1883, and his widow died October 9, 1884. Enoch D. was born November 17, 1823, married three times, first, Belena B. Strickland, in 1853 ; second, Frances Dickinson, and third, Mary Harrington. They reside in Easthampton. Watson W. was born November 26, 1834, married Elizabeth Howes, January 2, 1865, and has one child, Willie, born February 24, 1867.

John Cowles came from England about 1640. was one of the original proprietors and settlers of the town of Farmington, Conn., and represented that town at the general court three sessions, and moved to Hadley, where he died in September, 1675. Clinton J., a descendant of John Cowles, was born on the homestead, in North Amherst, June 16, 1810, married Sarah E. Sanderson, October 11, 1837, and has had born to him two children, Almon E. and Edson C. The former was born November 16, 1838, married Helen L. Gilbert, July 4, 1859, and has one child, Estella, born January 23, 1860. He resides on the homestead, and is engaged in farming. Edson C. was born June 12, 1847, married Ida I. Taylor, March 2, 1864, and lives in Iowa. He has three children, namely, John E., Mary I. and Ruth E.

Chester Cowles was born in Granby, married Mary Bangs, and has reared four children, namely, William D., Hettie, Frank C. and Samuel W. Mr. Cowles sold 106 acres of land to the Agricultural college about 1864.

Nathaniel Kellogg was among the early settlers of Amherst, and died here October 30, 1750, aged eighty years. His son Ephraim died here March 16, 1777, aged sixty-seven, and Ephraim, Jr., who died here January 29, 1815, aged seventy-three years. The latter had nine children, of whom John was the eldest, born here September 23, 1762. These were the ancestors of a large portion of the many who bear this name in Amherst to-day. Willard M. Kellogg, a great-great-grandson, now occupies the old homestead, on road 21, or East street, as it is generally known. The house now occupied by him was built by his grandfather, Daniel, about one hundred years ago. His father, Rufus, was postmaster about 1821, and had his office in this house, where the mail was brought once a week. Willard M. was born December 29, 1810, married Elvira M. Marsh, of Hadley, and has had born to him eight children, as follows: Rufus, Willard, Rufus M., Catharine C., Charles, Mary, Esther M. and Joseph M.

Eleazer Kellogg, son of John, was born here March 16, 1800, married Sally McCloud Roberts, December 30, 1824, and reared eight children— Julia A., Albert, Roxey, Esther, Elizabeth C., Charles H., Sally M. and John E. He served the town as selectman many years, and in the legislature in 1836. Charles H., born May 7, 1842, married Mary W. Adams, of North Hadley, in 1868, and now resides on road 18. They have one child, Willie A.

Thomas Hastings, grandson of Lieut. Thomas Hastings, who came to Amherst from Hatfield about 1753, was born here February 6, 1782. He married Eunice Clark, November 1, 1803, who bore him thirteen children, as follows: Sophia, Mary, Mary, 2d., Lucy, Thomas, James, Henry, Harriet, Henry, William, Edmund, Lucy, 2d., Philomela. Uncle Tom, as he was called, was a farmer, a man of considerable genius and fond of writing verses. He died October 11, 1858, and his widow survived him till August 11, 1873. Their son Edmund now occupies the old homestead. He was born March 4, 1822, married Minerva Lee, of Conway, May 23, 1849, who has borne him five children, Emma A., Mary Luella, Esther M., Abbie M. and Walter L.

Ephraim Cushman was a soldier in the Revolutionary war, and was also a participator in Shays Rebellion. He died in North Amherst in 1832. His sons, Ephraim and John P., began business as paper makers in the " old mill " on the road to Still Corner, in 1835. In 1854 they obtained a patent from the government for a method of drying thick paper, whereby it was prevented from warping out of shape. In 1857 the mill at the corner of the road to Leverett, below them, was burned, and the Cushman Brothers bought the rights of Jones & Bradford, its former owners, and built, in 1859, the present red mill. In 1864 the firm was dissolved, and Ephraim Cushman, with his son, built a mill in " Factory Hollow " for the manufacture of printing and manilla paper, while John R. Cushman and his sons carried on the manufacture of leather board at the old mills, in which business he continued until the failure of the firm, in 1880. Ephraim was born in Amherst, February 26, 1799 married Wealthy Cutter in December, 1822, and reared six children, as follows: Sanford C., born May 14, 1824, married Thankful Cook, and resides in Birmingham, Conn. J. Ephraim was born January 6, 1826, and married Elizabeth Rankin ; Susan B., born October 15, 1828, married W. V. Cutter, of Amherst ; Wealthy A. was born December 4, 1830 ; John S., born January 8, 1833, resides in Connecticut; and Marshall B. was born September 23, 1839, married twice, first, Josephine Bassett; second, Hannah Gibbs, and resides in Washington, D. C.   Mrs. Cushman died January 5, 1865.   John Richmond Cushman was born at North Amherst, September 6, 1803, married Rhoda Crafts, of Whately, and had born to him ten children, four of whom died in infancy.   Of those surviving, George H., the oldest son, and Edward P., the youngest, are in business in Lynn.   The others are still residents of North Amherst.   Mr. Cushman became a member of the North church in 1839.   At the time of his death he resided with his son Avery R.

John E. Cushman was born in Amherst September 4, 1839, and married Mary Wells, of Whately, Mass., September 14, 1876.   He served in the late war, in Co. D, 27th Mass. Vols., and lost his arm at the battle of Newbern, March 28, 1862.   He now resides on road 4.

Lucius Boltwood, son of William and Eunice Boltwood, was born in Amherst, March 16, 1792, and married Fannie Haskins Shepard, August 30, 1824.   He attended the town school of Amherst, the Grammar school at Hadley, and entered Williams college in 1810, and graduated from there in 1814.   He read law with Hon. Samuel Fowler Dickinson, of this town, was admitted to the bar in August, 1817, and immediately entered into company with his instructor.   In 1820 he opened an office of his own.   He was secretary of the corporation of Amherst college from 1828 to 1864, commissioner of the charity fund of the same institution from 1833 to 1866, and was president of the Amherst bank in 1835–36.   At the time of his death, which occurred July 10, 1872, aged eighty years, he was the senior member of the Hampshire county bar.   He reared nine children, of whom two are living, Lucius M. and Samuel.   His widow resides in the house built by him in 1835.

Noah Smith was born in North Amherst, June 6, 1772, married Jerusha Cowles, of Amherst, February 20, 1806, and reared nine children, only three of whom are living, William, Spencer and Sally.   Spencer was born in Amherst, February 21, 1819, married Martha B. Potwine, of South Amherst, January 21, 1844, and has had born to him six children, viz. : Joanna, born February 13, 1845; Atwell P., born July 26, 1847; Lucia M., born February 17, 1850; William A., born July 11, 1852; Newton A., born May 10, 1856, and Nettie B., born August 16, 1864.   His father died October 27, 1847, and his mother died July 10, 1858.

Deacon Lyman Smith, son of Jonathan, and grandson of Noah, all natives of Amherst, was born in Amherst, November 10, 1801, and married three times; first, Electa Dickinson, May 25, 1825, who died April 25, 1859. She was the mother of seven children, as follows : Frederick A., Andrew A., who died in the army, Ellen Eliza and Eliza Ellen (twins), William W. H., Mary E., and Julia E., who was born September 3, 1834, and married William L. Roberts.   Mr. Smith married for his second wife, Mary M. Emerson, who died March 30, 1879, and for his third wife, Jane E. Nye, November 24, 1880. He resides on road 18.

Cotton Smith was born in Hadley, April 7, 1787, and married Sibyl Smith. His son, W. W., was born in Amherst, June 2, 1829, married Mary E., daughter of Daniel and Mary H. Cowles, April 13, 1858, and has had born to him three children, viz.: Mary H., born September 14, 1859; William H., born May 12, 1864; and Alice E., born May 8, 1870.

Frederick Williams was born in Amherst, October 3, 1803, married twice, first, Caroline Howe, who bore him six children, viz.: Chester, William F., Elizabeth, who died in infancy, Solomon H., who died in 1868, Oren B., who died in infancy, and Sarah E., who died in 1861. He married for his second wife, Cornelia Dorman, April 3, 1861. William F. resides on road 32.

George Montague, son of Luke, was born in this town, September 14, 1804, was engaged in mercantile pursuits until 1828, and was then connected with Mt. Pleasant Classical institution as accountant and instructor in book-keeping until 1831. He married twice, first, Mary A. Parsons, and second Sarah M. Seely, November 20, 1856. He has four children, George, William, Charles C. and Mary E.

Willard Haskins was born in 1804, married Rebecca Howard, of Amherst, in 1827, and had born to him five children, namely, Esther C., who died in 1847, Jonathan H., Henry W., Ira C., who died in 1835, and James E. He died in 1834. Jonathan H. was born in 1830, married Louise Graves, of Hinsdale, Mass., and has had born to him two children, John W., who died in 1884, and Mary L., who lives at home. Mr. Haskins resides on road 18.

Henry W. Haskins was born in this town November 14, 1833, married Harriet Newell, November 30, 1854, and has had born to him five children as follows: Hattie E., born February 24, 1857, married Willie E. Cushman; Sarah E., born October 7, 1858, married Loren Shumway, November 3, 1881; Ida L., born June 23, 1864, married Erwin W. Andrews, October 5, 1883; Charles H., born July 7, 1869, resides in Springfield; and Esther L., born February 24, 1876. Mr. Haskins is engaged as a contractor and builder, and resides on road 2.

Simeon Clark, son of Increase, was born October 20, 1720, married Rebecca Strong, moved to Amherst, and reared twelve children. His son, Simeon, born in 1752, married twice, first, Lucy Hubbard, who bore him three children, and second, Irene Lewis, who bore him five children. Simeon, son of Simeon and Irene (Lewis) Clark, was born October 15, 1807, married Myra Cowles, and reared nine children, namely, Juliette, Asahel L., Royal W., Zilpha C., Edwin W., Emily M., Emily A., Albert S. and Edwin W., 2d. He was justice of the peace thirty years, served as selectman, assessor and overseer of the poor for many years. He was a deacon of the First church sixteen years. His wife died June 8, 1871, and he died July 31, 1883, aged seventy-six years. His son, Edwin W., was born December 2, 1842, married twice, first, Louisa M. Kellogg, December 8, 1868, who died July 18, 1869, and second, Lizzie L. Henry, February 28, 1872. He has had born to him three children as follows: Walter Edwin, born April 13, 1874, and died July 18, 1875; Howard E., born November 17, 1876, and Fanny L., born July 29, 1881, died January 8, 1883.

William Smith Clark, son of Dr. Atherton and Harriet (Smith) Clark, was born at Ashfield, Mass., July 31, 1826, received his early education there and at Williston seminary, and graduated from Amherst college in 1848. He then returned to Williston seminary, where he taught the natural sciences from 1848 to 1850. He then went abroad, and for the next two years devoted himself to the study of chemistry and botany at Göttingen, Germany, receiving from that university the degree of Ph. D., in 1852. On his return to this country, he was elected to the chair of chemistry, botany and zoölogy in Amherst college, performing the duties of that position from 1852 to 1858, and of the chair of chemistry alone from 1858 to 1867, when he resigned to accept the presidency of the Massachusetts Agricultural college. This, and the professorship of botany and horticulture, he held from 1867 to 1879. He then became interested in the project of a "floating college," and being made president, bent all his energies during the years 1879 and 1880 to developing this scheme of uniting scientific study with a trip around the world. It was abandoned, however, on the sudden death of its originator, Mr. Woodruff. He subsequently engaged in mining operations; and the last few years of his life were spent quietly at his home in Amherst, vainly battling with the disease which had already sapped the foundation of his life. He died at his home, March 9, 1886, from an affection of the heart. He served in the late war as major and colonel. He married Harrietta Keopuolani Richards, daughter of Rev. William Richards, of the Sandwich Islands, and adopted daughter of Samuel Williston, of Easthampton, May 25, 1853. His children were as follows: Emily W., who married Frank W. Stearns, of Boston; Atherton, Fannie, who married William F. Stearns; Mary R., Eliza, Edith, Hubert L. and Bertha.

George Nutting married Julia Hastings, in December, 1809, resided in Amherst, and had born to him nine children, namely, Eli, Julia, Judith, John, Mary, Maria, Anna, Harriet and Amelia. He held many town offices, and served as town representative in 1833 and 1836. He died in 1838, aged fifty-one years, and his widow died in 1883, at the advanced age of ninety-six years.

Richard B. Bridgman was born in Amherst, January 27, 1817, and married Mary, daughter of George and Julia (Hastings) Nutting, March 22, 1843. He reared ten children, namely, Herbert L., Helen F., Raymond L., Arthur M., Loraine H., Mary L., Lauren A., Gertrude L., Clara A. and Amy S. He was engaged as a farmer, and in 1852 located on the place, on road 44, where his widow now resides. He died July 27, 1882.

Chester E. Marshall was born in Amherst, May 18, 1784, married Orinda Cowles, and had born to him six children, viz.: Electa, Joseph E., Mary,

Elvira, Sarah D. and Ansel C. The last mentioned was born August 18, 1816, married Lucy C. Palmer, December 12, 1861, and has had born to him two children, John F. and Mary E. The former married Nellie R. Kentfield, March 28, 1883. Mr. Marshall resides on road 2.

Oliver M. Clapp, great-grandson of Persevered Clapp, who was one of the first settlers of Amherst, was born in this town, October 6, 1802, married Mary Ann Reed, May 10, 1826, and has had born to him three children, namely, Anna, Elizabeth and Charles D.

Cyrus King was born in Amherst in 1804, married Miss A. Adams, and had born to him seven children, viz. : Woodbridge A., who was born April 1, 1832, married Sophia Slate, and has had born to him two children, Henry W. and Flora J. ; Clarence, who died at the age of six years ; Ebenezer A.,who was born March 1, 1839 ; Israel, Edward P., Ella C. and Emma C. Ebenezer A. married Clara Hawley, April 11, 1860, and has two children, Hattie J. and Frank A. Mr. King has served as selectman three years, and resides on road 38.

Warren F. King was born in Shutesbury, Mass., October 30, 1835, married Catherine S. Cutter, October 6, 1864, and has one child, Herbert F., born September 18, 1865. Mr. King served in the late war, in Co. D, 27th Mass. Vols., and was confined as a prisoner in Libby prison.

Isaac N. King was born in Amherst, September 12, 1841, married Mary E. Dickinson, December 20, 1864, and has had born to him two children, Homer C., born December 27, 1870, died February 9, 1877, and Mary A., born August 1, 1878. Mr. King located on road 21, where he now resides, about 1864.

Reuben Roberts was born July 26, 1805, and married three times, first, Mary Smith, of Amherst, who bore him four children, namely, William L., Manning, Catherine, and one child who died in infancy. He married for his second wife, Hannah Goddard, of Athol, Mass., August 4, 1841, who died July 12, 1850. She was the mother of four children, viz.: James B., Ann Janet, Hollis W. and Lizzie T. He married for his third wife Lydia D. Endicott, June 17, 1851, and had born to him two children, Mary E. and Catherine. James B. was born in North Amherst, October 8, 1843, married Lucy M. Ufford, May 13, 1868, and has three children, Reuben, born October 5, 1874, Esther L., born December 26, 1875, and Angie B., born April 22, 1879.

Lieut. Ebenezer Eastman was born May 31, 1749, married Mary Dickinson, November 12, 1772, and served in the Revolutionary war, after which he settled down as a farmer. He died November 7, 1820, and his widow died March 16, 1825. His son Elijah was born in this town, March 13, 1777, married Rebecca Hall, October 24, 1802, and reared seven children, viz. : Elijah L., Caroline, William, Samuel, Austin, Zebina and Baxter. Austin was born on the homestead, October 5, 1812, married Mary Spear, October 6, 1833, and has had born to him eight children, viz.: William E., Charles

A., George H., Edgar E., Lyman A., Mary C., Martha E. and Will'am N. Charles A. was born January 13, 1843, married Clara Wyatt, March 6, 1865. William N. was born December 6, 1858, married Eva E. Ward, December 25, 1879, and has two children, Estella A. and Ethel H. Baxter, son of Elijah, was born January 9, 1818, married Mary E. Bentley, and died December 9, 1860. His son Edward B. was born June 9, 1847, married Esther Wyatt, December 13, 1868, and has had born to him four children, viz.: Mary B., Fannie M., Allie T. and Lucia K. His mother resides with him on road 2.

Horace Hawley was born in Amherst, March 16, 1814, married Sarah A. Haskins, May 21, 1840, resides on road 21, and has had born to him ten children, viz.: Mary A., Susan, who died February 21, 1846, Charles, Susan, Frank E., Laura, who died March 28, 1864, Adeline, Ellen, Herbert and Dwight. Frank E. was born January 27, 1851, married Lucy A. Reed, March 31, 1875, and has one child, Alice L., born June 4, 1884.

Henry Hawley was born in this town, October 25, 1842, married Mary Kellogg, June 2, 1869, and resides on road 21. He served in the late war, in Co. D, 27th Mass. Vols.

Gideon S. Hawley was born in Floyd, N. Y., June 29, 1827, came to this town when an infant, and married Rachel H. Quance, November 26, 1852. He has had born to him seven children, viz. · William S., Mary M., who died in infancy, John J., Alice M., Henry E., who died at the age of five years, George L., and Edwin B., who died in infancy. He lives on road 21.

William Ingram was born in this town, May 12, 1816, married Betsey S. Parker, and had born to him two daughters, Harriet L., born June 12, 1841, and Jennie B., born May 2, 1843. He died August 20, 1878. His daughter Harriet married David Guertin, in 1860. The latter was born in Canada, and came to this town about 1854. He was engaged in the wholesale meat business for many years, in which he was very successful. He had born to him four children, two of whom are living, Albert, born June 6, 1865, and Solomon, born January 16, 1868. He died July 23, 1885. His widow continues in the business in which he was engaged.

John Guertin was born in Canada in 1834, and came to this town when he was sixteen years of age. He married Lizzie E. Sears in 1860, and has had born to him three children, Edward A., Cora L., who married Frank Ingram, and Lena M.

Zacheus C. Ingram was born in Amherst, September 17, 1771, married Sarah B. Hastings, and reared eleven children, namely, Solomon B., Susan C., Caroline, Mary B., Robert, William, Aaron, Lucius, Albert B., Sarah B., who died in infancy, and Sarah. Lucius was born in this town, November 2, 1823, married Lydia M. Brown, and has reared five children, namely, Elizabeth M., Lucia, Albert B., Mary L. and an adopted daughter, Carrie C. Mr. Ingram is engaged in the manufacture of brooms, and resides on road 18.

Jonathan Thayer was born in Weymouth, Mass., married Mary Dewey, and came to this town in 1806. He had born to him two children, Charles E. and Dwight R. The former died November 2, 1872, leaving a widow and one child, Herbert D., who resides in North Amherst. Jonathan died February 19, 1856, and his widow died five years after. Dwight R. was born in this town, October 15, 1842, married Emily Bishop, February 14, 1871, and has reared five children, viz.: Allie R., Charles H., Pearly E., Mary E. and Katie M.

Joseph W. Dana was born in this town, January 26, 1826, married Marion A. Nash, of Williamsburg, July 1, 1846, and has had born to him seven children, viz.: Clarence W., Joseph L., Clara, who died December 7, 1858, Edward N. and George H. (twins), both of whom died in 1858, Minnie L. and Herbert N., who died in 1871. Mr. Dana is engaged in farming, and resides on road 47.

Austin Loomis, son of Thomas, was born in Bolton, Conn., June 19, 1789, married twice, first, Hannah Dickinson, February 2, 1820, and second, Mary A. Russell. He came to Amherst about 1723, and located on the place where his son Austin D. now resides, on road 3. The latter was born here September 4, 1828, married Martha Newell, May 25, 1854, and has had born to him five children, namely, Francis E., Nellie F., Charles E., Harriet N. and Herbert R.

Sarah S. Loomis, widow of John M., was born in Irving, Mass., September 13, 1821, married Mr. Loomis October 25, 1843. They have had three children, namely, Marietta, born February 14, 1847, George M., born September 18, 1849, died August 24, 1885, and William B., born October 25, 1857. Mr. Loomis, who was born March 21, 1823, died December 12, 1862.

Emeline G. Elmer, daughter of Joseph and Ester Douglass, was born in Amherst, October 31, 1831. She was married twice, first, to Benjamin Wright, and second, to Charles Elmer. She is now a widow, and resides on road 45.

Ptolemy P. Cutler was born in Amherst in 1837, and married Clara M. Hubbard, August 15, 1860. He enlisted in Co. D, 27th Mass. Vols., as a private, was promoted to sergeant, was fatally wounded at the battle of Cold Harbor, and died in the field hospital June 4, 1864.

L. M. Hills, the pioneer designer, and successful manufacturer in the palm and straw hat trade in Amherst, was born in Ellington, Conn., in 1803. He came to Amherst, Mass., in 1829, and commenced business in the manufacture of palm hats. The first year his receipts were about $5,000.00, while those of the year 1871, were about $300,000.00, furnishing employment to over one hundred hands in the shops on the home grounds, and to probably six hundred hands at their homes in the vicinity. As a public man, Mr. Hills declined to accept political or town offices, but was first and foremost in all enterprises of a beneficial character to town and vicinity, which was evinced by his liberality and hearty interest. He was tendered and accepted the office of president of the First National bank of Amherst, at its organization, which he held until his death, in 1872. He was also for a time, presi-

11*

dent of the Amherst and Belchertown railroad corporation. Many other public enterprises in the meantime received his hearty support and liberal donations; notably the Agricultural college and First Congregational church and parish, as also a fund given by him for poor working women in Amherst and Pelham. For several years before his death the sons, Henry F. and L. D. Hills, were associated with him in business, and seem not only to have acquired his business qualities, but also his untiring energy.

Oliver H. Curtiss was born in Willington, Conn., March 30, 1811, came to Amherst in 1839, and located upon the farm which he now occupies, on road 38. He married Emily Hills, November 14, 1837, and has had born to him five children, namely, Clara, William (now deceased), Emily, Frank and Samuel.

Nathaniel L. Harlow was born in Farley, Vt., July 2, 1816, married Harriet Church, August 28, 1836, and came to Amherst in 1836. He has had born to him nine children, as follows: William F., Harriet N., Frederick, Henrietta, Julia A., Nathaniel, Norman, who died July 6, 1849, Sarah F., who died May 17, 1874, and Mary F.

Stephen Puffer was born at Berlin, Mass., February 17, 1784, married Sally Fosgate, September 15, 1812, and had born to him five children, viz.: Reuben G., Sarah E., Stephen P., Charles A. and Gilbert F. Reuben G. was born June 16, 1817, came to Amherst about 1839, married Clarissa B. Johnson, December 7, 1842, and has had born to him seven children, viz.: Ellen Jane, Sarah E., Nancy M., Frank G., Clara B., Alice L. and Herbert E. Sarah E., daughter of Stephen, was born August 16, 1819, and married Joseph C. Hastings, December 7, 1842. Stephen P., son of Stephen, was born June 22, 1822, married twice, first, Eugenia C. Strickland, and has had born to him six children, three of whom are living, namely, Charles, F., Eugene O., Clarabel L. and Edward S. He married for his second wife, Martha Blodgett, May 28, 1872, and has had born to him one child, Estella C., born September 24, 1878.

Jonathan Pierce was born in Shutesbury, Mass., November 3, 1814, married Johanna Kellogg, and came to this town about 1828. He reared two children, Nellie S., who was born January 2, 1838, married Roger P. Carlton, and died in 1860; and James A. The latter was born in Amherst, May 24, 1840, married Ellen J. Puffer, March 17, 1864, and has two children, F. Herbert, born June 29, 1867, and John E., born October 11, 1869.

Edwin H. Johnson, son of Hervey S., was born in Enfield, Conn., and came to this town when he was four years of age. He married Louisa Allen, and has had born to him two children, Frederick and May.

Mrs. Susan A. Lamb was born in Vernon, Vt., August 9, 1821, and came to Amherst in 1840. She was married twice, first, Charles H. Bangs, March 28, 1866, who died July 30, 1873. She married for her second husband, George E. Lamb, February 18, 1875, who died June 14, 1878. Mrs. Lamb resides on road 2.

Charles E. Hayward, was born in this town, September 23, 1842, married twice, first, Loretta Field, January 20, 1869, who bore him three children, Lucius F. (deceased), Lucia B. and Carrie S. He married for his second wife Elizabeth A. Smith, and has had born to him one child, Afton S., born June 13, 1882.

Dr. Israel H. Taylor was born in Pelham, Mass., commenced the practice of medicine in that town in 1842, and came to Amherst in 1851. He has had born to him two children, Helen M. and Abbie F. The former married Samuel Curtis, who is employed as a book-keeper in Hartford, Conn., where they reside. Abbie F. married C. F. Roper, who is engaged in the manufacture of iron screws at Hopedale, Mass.

Abraham Ball was born in Leverett, Mass., in 1783, married Martha Field in 1803, and reared ten children, namely, Sophronia, Martha, Havilla, Lucina, Clarissa, Edith A., Mary, Albert, Hoyt E. and Rhoda G. Hoyt E. married Mary Dodge, in 1847, and resides in North Amherst. Albert W. was born in 1820, married twice, first, Mary I. Messenger, in 1842, who died in 1854, and second, Julia A. Kellogg, June 18, 1856. He has one child, Lizzie J., born in 1867. They reside on road 18.

Gideon Stetson was born in Randolph, Mass., May 22, 1791, married Clarissa Henry, of Shutesbury, Mass., March 27, 1816, and reared nine children as follows: Luther H., Charles T., Mary A., James, Maria, Jeanette E., William B., Adeline M. and John H. Luther H. married Olive F. Upton, of New Salem, Mass., and resides in Amherst. Charles married Emily Roberts in 1841, and died in 1858, leaving one daughter. James was born in 1823, and lives at North Amherst. William B. married Kate Beals, and resides at Leverett, Mass. John H. was born in 1829, married Eliza M. Pierce, and resides on road 18.

Richard Baxter Hobart was born in Leverett, Mass., in 1822, married Mary E. Rowe, of Sunderland, Mass., May 10, 1843, and had born to him three children, namely, Mary L., Alice S. and Arthur E. Arthur E., the only one living, was born in Leverett, Mass., March 18, 1854, married Ida A. Ferry, January 3, 1877, and has had born to him two children, M. Almyra, born June 20, 1878, and Edward B., born February 1, 1882. He came to Amherst from Granby in 1878, and resides on road 18.

J. W. Hobart was born in Leverett, April 12, 1817, married twice, first, Nancy Macomber, in 1840, and had born to him four children, namely, Nancy E., Charles H., Joshua and Ella E. The mother of these children died July 24, 1851, and he married for his second wife, Harriet Macomber, a sister of his first wife, March 29, 1853, who bore him five children, viz.: George F., Willie C., Lucia B., Ellen M., who married Frank E. Spear, of this town, and Mary S. George F. was born August 19, 1854, married Lottie Fortune, October 5, 1880, and has one adopted child, Mary V., born February 18, 1885.

Franklin C. Willis was born in Boston, in 1810, married Tryphosa M. Gunn, in 1838, and came to this town about 1846. He has one child, Flora E., who married William I. Marsh, and resides with her father on road 18.

Lewis G. Cummings was born at Royalston, Mass., May 10, 1807, and came to this town in 1863. He married Lorinda Buss, of Dover, Vt., October 1, 1833, and has had born to him six children, viz. : Martha A., who married Edwin J. Fisk, of Upton, Mass., (deceased), Sarah J., who died in 1840, Gusta M., George, 1st, George, 2d, and Atta L.

Lewis A. Bartlett was born in Shutesbury, Mass., June 16, 1832, came to Amherst about 1853, and married Abbie P. Dickinson, September 3, 1862. He has had born to him two children, Cora A., born December 23, 1865, and Clayton A , born July 19, 1868.

Charles Wiley was born in Sunderland, Mass., September 2, 1847, married Clara A. Cook, of Pelham, Mass., November 25, 1868, and has two children, Edward E., born November 5, 1869, and Nettie C., born December 25, 1871.

H. A. Parsons was born in Enfield, Conn., December 20, 1860, came to Amherst in 1878, is engaged in farming and in growing fruit, and resides on road 2. He married Hattie M. Harrington, April 5, 1882, and has two children, Albert, born June 1, 1883, and Emma H., born August 15, 1885.

John F. Billings was born in Amherst, June 24, 1852, married Sophia Moore, May 10, 1881, and has one child, Samuel W., born May 12, 1884. He has a shop located on road 9½, where he carries on carriage painting. He also resides on that road.

Leonard Marsh was born in Hawley, Mass., May 15, 1811, married Louise Parker, November 27, 1834, and came to this town about 1869 and located upon the place where he now resides, on road 6. He has had born to him eight children, viz.: Jane A., who married Loren L. Ball, Theodore C., Albert E., Lucretia P., Joel W., Munroe P., William I. and Achsah S.

Stephen Matthews was born in Leverett, Mass., October 21, 1817, married Phebe A. Leonard, May 1, 1850, and came to this town about 1856, locating on road 10. He has had born to him six children, as follows: Charles W., born January 21, 1852 ; Hattie E., born October 19, 1853, died March 25, 1860 ; Flora B., who died in infancy; Flora A., born March 31, 1858; John E., born March 17, 1863; and Albert A., born March 14, 1866.

Dr. William Dwight was born in Windsor, Mass., and came to this town in 1875. He married Ellen M. Clark, and has two children, Mary E. and William G. The former married Edward Perkins, of Hartford, who died in 1876, leaving two children, Henry A. and Edward E. William G. graduated from Amherst in 1881, and is associated with W. S. Loomis in the publication of the *Transcript*, a daily and weekly newspaper of Holyoke.

Jeremiah Stockwell was born in Leverett, Mass., August 15, 1836, married Elizabeth Cummings in November, 1855, and has had born to him four children, Mary Jane, Nettie M., Charles L. and Hattie M. Mr. Stockwell served in the late war, in Co. D, 27th Mass. Vols.

Henry Stearns was born in South Hadley, June 2, 1825, married Jeanette Edgarton, of Northampton, May 26, 1849, and came to this town in 1876. He is located on road 10, and is engaged in manufacturing hand-made harnesses.

J. C. Reed was born in Shutesbury, November 25, 1820, married Miss L. B. Cummings, April 16, 1845, and came to Amherst about 1845. In 1849 he located on road 15, where he now resides. He has had born to him six children, viz.: Arthur, Martha M., Willie A., Lois B., Sarah L. and Seth J.

Nathaniel Cook was born in Pelham, Mass., June 16, 1807, married Bertha Ward, and has reared twelve children, viz.: Sarah, Horace W., Henry, Rose, Theodore, Smith, Elmyra, Fenner, Elisha, Delphia, Hattie and Mary, all of whom are living excepting Sarah, who died in April, 1885. Mr. Cook resides in Pelham. Horace W. was born in Pelham, September 10, 1836, married Mary N. Stetson, March 4, 1863, and has had born to him three children, namely, Charles S., born December 10, 1863, Emily R., born December 18, 1871, and H. Ward, born September 14, 1873.

Charles E. Wilson was born in Buckland, Mass., February 3, 1852, married Lydia Dickinson, May 3, 1876, and came to this town in 1879. He has had born to him two children, Minnie A., born December 18, 1878, and Caroline M., born September 7, 1884, and lives on road 21.

Charles A. Hyde was born in Amherst, March 1, 1831, married Harriet A. Dickinson, January 14, 1869, and has two children, Esther R., born November 13, 1872, and Charles D., born September 29, 1876. He lives on road 21.

Leprelate Dean was born in Attleborough, Mass., June 22, 1812, married Harriet E. Whitaker, January 26, 1834, and came to Amherst in 1857. He has had born to him eight children, as follows: Ellen B., who married Lansford Gates, and died June 19, 1871; Everett L., Mary E., who married Willard Kellogg; Harriet A., who married William Benton; Ann Jeanette, Mineva A., Herbert A. and Abbott L.

William F. Goodale was born in this town, February 6, 1860, married Hattie Robinson, of Pelham, Mass., May 10, 1883, and has two children, Austin A., born February 6, 1884, and Anna B., born February 6, 1886.

Charles A. Shaw was born in Northampton, April 20, 1846, married Fannie R., daughter of Edward Bridgman, November 15, 1871, and has had born to him three children, viz.: Frederick B., born April 16, 1876, Ethel E., born February 11, 1879, and Charles H., born March 1, 1883. He came to South Amherst about 1861, is postmaster, is engaged in mercantile business, and has a saw-mill located on road 55.

Edward P. Pomeroy, son of David and Mary (Atkinson) Pomeroy, was born in Hadley, August 16, 1829, married twice, first, Amelia Clapp, who was the mother of Edward E. He was engaged in farming and broom manufacturing, and lived on road 44, where Edward E. now lives. He died May 17, 1884. Edward E. was born in this town, August 7, 1859, and married Flora I. Newgeon, of New Haven, December 25, 1865.

John White was born in New York city in 1838, and came to this town when he was only seven years of age, his father being the first Irish settler in the town. He married Bridget Duley in 1856, and his children are as follows : Thomas F., John, Mary A., Peter W., George H., Matthew, Kate E., James and Martha V.

J. Eugene Sanderson was born in Franklin county, April 22, 1824, married Martha Pomeroy, of Chesterfield, in 1845, and came to this town in 1878, locating on road 53. He has reared six children, viz. : Ella F., who married Henry Chapin (deceased), Lillian M., who married Newland Merritt (deceased), Hattie P., who married Willis H. Maxson, and resides in Michigan, Mary, Arthur J. and Walter E.

T. M. Armstrong was born in Windham, Mass., November 3, 1831, and married Mary Frances, daughter of Hiram H. and Mary (Dickinson) Allen. He came to this town from Montague about 1855. Hiram H. Allen, father of Mrs. Armstrong, was born in Bakersfield, Vt., and came to Amherst about 1831, clerked for Sweetser & Cutter five years, and then started in business for himself at South Amherst, in the store now occupied by Charles A. Shaw. He died at South Amherst in 1851.

Roswell Howard was born in Washington, Vt., October 30, 1802, and moved to this county with his parents when about a year old, they locating in Hadley. When eleven years of age his father died, and he came to Amherst to reside with his grandfather, Zachariah Hawley. When about eighteen years of age he went to work for his uncle, Chester Hawley, at the brick making business, and has worked at that trade ever since. The brick-yard he now carries on, at the age of eighty-four years, he has conducted since 1835, and is the only brick manufactory in town. He married Fanny Hawley, August 29, 1824, who died June 30, 1862. The only one of his six children now living is Mrs. John Goodale, of this town.

Mrs. Lucy Crossett, widow of Samuel, was born in North Brookfield, March 28, 1786, and was the only child of Joel and Ruth Abbott. She came to this town about eighteen years ago on a visit to Dr. Taylor's. She met with an accident by falling down stairs, and was unable to return to her home in Prescott. She now resides on High street. She married Samuel Crossett, May 25, 1805, who died June 13, 1850. Five of their thirteen children are living. Mrs. Crossett is now over one hundred years of age.

Rev. George E. Fisher is a native of Harvard, Mass., graduated from Amherst college in 1846, and from the Andover Theological seminary in 1849. He was pastor at Rutland, Mass., from 1850 to 1852, at North Amherst from 1852 to 1858, at Greenville, N. H., from 1859 to 1862, at Ashburnham, Mass., from 1863 to 1867, at South Hadley Falls from 1867 to 1878, and at East Amherst from 1879 to 1886. He removed to North Amherst in 1885. He was a member of the general court of Massachusetts in 1867. He married twice, first, Harriet B. Holt, of Amherst, May 1, 1850, who died in August, 1858, and second, Ellen E. Kellogg, of North Amherst, September 7, 1859.

Rev. Charles Crombie Bruce, M. A., son of Charles F. and Mary E. Bruce, was born in Peterboro, N. H., February 5, 1854, prepared for college at Appleton academy, New Ipswich, N. H., graduated from Amherst college in 1875, and from the Andover Theological seminary in 1878. He was ordained over the First Congregational church at Rowley, Mass., July 2, 1878, installed over the Congregational church in Haydenville, Mass., December 7, 1882, and was acting pastor of the Congregational church in South Deerfield, Mass., from January 23, 1885, to August 1, 1886. He married Laura Bassett Green, March 1, 1874, and has three children, Josephine, Annie E. and Martha P. He has resided in Amherst since September 1, 1884.

Edward Tuckerman was born in Boston, December 7, 1817. He passed his youth in the same city, fitting for college at the Boston Latin school. He graduated from Union college, Schenectady, in 1837, and afterwards graduated successively from the Harvard Law school, the regular academic department of Harvard university, and the Harvard Divinity school. Throughout his life, which ended March 15, 1886, he retained his interest in the subjects indicated by the above university courses, and for a time (1854–58) occupied positions as lecturer on history in Amherst college. But his life was mainly devoted to botanical investigation, more particularly to the investigation of the difficult order of Lichens. In May, 1854, he married Sarah Eliza Sigourney Cushing, of Boston, and the same year they removed to Amherst, where Mrs. Tuckerman still resides. Prof. Tuckerman's most important works are his *Enumeratio Methodica Caricum Quarundam*, the elaboration of the difficult genus Potamsgeton, the *Synopsis of the Lichens of New England*, *Lichenes Americanæ Septentrionales Exsiccati*, and finally his *Genera Lichenum* and *Synopsis of North American Lichens, Part I.* The latter two embody the results of long and assiduous critical study by one whose genius as a systematizer is unquestioned, and they will secure for their author the grateful remembrance of all who shall hereafter tread the maze of American lichenology.

VILLAGES.

There are three post villages in the town at present. The Amherst post-office is located in the largest and most important of the villages, and is near the town's geographical centre. This village is on an elevation of land which includes the site of Amherst college and the common—a pretty stretch of green beneath stately elms lying in the very heart of the town, and which is under the care of a village improvement society. The village stores, public halls and hotels are on three sides of this common, Amherst college and various club houses and residences completing the enclosure. The main street runs from this village to the Pelham line, passing through the East village, where is a Congregational church, a store, etc.

The North Amherst postoffice is near the northern boundary of the town,

and accommodates many of the residents in the adjoining extremities of the
towns of Sunderland and Hadley. At the village is situated the North Congregational church, two stores and a neat brick school-house, containing also
a public library. Mill river passes just above this village, on its way from its
source in the Shutesbury hills to its place of *deouchure* into the Connecticut
river, just below the village of North Hadley. This river gives the town its
principal water-power. Fort river, which rises in Pelham hills and enters the
town's eastern limit about two miles below Mill river, flows in a southwesterly
direction and empties into the Connecticut below the town of Hadley. A
grist-mill upon this stream, where it crosses the West street, gives the name
of " Mill Valley " to its vicinity, which lies between two ranges of hills south
of the center village.

The postoffice in South Amherst is on the East street, and was established
in 1838 for the convenience of the farming population of this vicinity. There
is a Congregational church here also, as well as a store and school-house,
grouped about a village green. The town farm for the maintenance of the
town's poor is in this village. The farm was purchased in 1837, and contains
about one hundred and fifty acres. The buildings were burned by an incendiary fire set by one of the inmates on the evening of January 1, 1882, and
were subsequently replaced by a new and much more convenient dwelling
house and out-buildings. Henry C. Dickinson is the present warden, and
his wife the matron. In 1885–86 there were twelve inmates of this institution,
but the selectmen reported the whole number of those receiving town aid that
year as fifty-three.

In addition to the post villages there is a pretty village in the northeast
corner of the town, known as " North Amherst City." There is a Methodist
church, a brick store, and a group of clustered dwellings here. The North
Amherst station of the New London Northern railroad is also in this village,
and in the days during and succeeding the war, when business was driving at
the paper-mills, upon whose wages this village depends, the place was quite
thriving and successful. Of late years business has fallen off and the population and the value of real estate has somewhat decreased.

BANKS.

The Amherst Savings bank, largely through the efforts of the late I. F.
Conkey, Esq., was incorporated April 15, 1864, and commenced business
with a deposit of fifty dollars, on January 2, 1865. The second deposit, made
on the following day, has never been withdrawn. At the end of the first
year's business there was on deposit sixty-eight hundred and sixty-two dollars.
The following statement, made on August 1, 1886, will show how largely the
bank has prospered during the twenty-one years of its existence :—

Liabilities.

Deposits...$ 983,918.51
Profit and loss.......................................   28,775.69
Guaranty fund.......................................   23,270.15

$1,035,964.35

Assets.

Mortgage notes.......................................$ 509,878.00
Town notes...   30,700.00
Parish notes..   4,733.55
Personal notes..   46,175.00
Collateral notes......................................   3,200.00
Bank stock... 186,383.51
City and town bonds.................................   87,120.00
Railroad bonds.......................................   85,000.00
Real estate...   15,000.00
Deposits in banks on interest........................   62,000.00
Cash on hand...   5,774.29

$1,035,964.35

The officers of the institution are E. F. Cook, president; C. S. Carter, treasurer; and F. A. Hobbs, assistant treasurer.

The First National Bank of Amherst was organized in January, 1864, with a capital of $51,000.00, which has since been increased to $150,000.00, with a surplus fund of $50,000.00. Leonard D. Hills is president of the institution, and R. J. D. Westcott, cashier. The first president of the institution was Leonard M. Hills.

INDUSTRIES.

Roberts & Co.'s mill.—The earliest manufacturing in Amherst was done in Rowe's paper-mill, at North Amherst. This mill was erected as early as 1795. Soon after 1800 Rowe sold out to Roberts & Cox, and about 1809 the firm became the Roberts Brothers. Reuben and Ephraim Roberts were both natives of East Hartford, Conn., and became influential and prominent citizens in Amherst. Reuben was one of the town's representatives in the legislature in 1835. Their mill was located just above the City, on Mill river. Rags for this mill were gathered through all the western part of the state, and the products of the mill were carried by teams to Albany for market. The early paper makers of North Amherst did all their work by hand, with the exception of reducing the stock to pulp, for which purpose rude machinery was employed. From 1795 paper of one kind or another has continued to be made at this place, the present proprietors being two brothers, Lowell and Manning Roberts, who succeeded their father, Reuben Roberts, Jr., the son

of the Reuben Roberts who bought out the original owner, Rowe.   The firm
now manufactures straw and leather-board, turning out about one ton per day.

D. Graves & Co.'s sash, door and blind factory.—In 1809, or thereabouts,
the first cotton-mill was erected in " Factory Hollow " at North Amherst, a
short distance below the mill of the Roberts Brothers, and at a place where
there is an excellent water-privilege.   This mill, a three-story wooden building, was erected by Ebenezer Dickinson, a farmer who lost all his property
in an attempt to spin cotton yarn by machinery.   Tradition avers that in
his disappointment he vigorously " cursed " the Hollow, and subsequent mis-
fortunes, neither few nor far between, have frequently been attributed to
" Ebenezer's Curse."   In 1812 a company (at the head of which was Gen.
Ebenezer Mattoon) put $10,000.00 into business in this mill, manufacturing
cotton yarn and putting it out in families to be woven on hand-looms.   No
one of the company had any practical knowledge of the business, and every
dollar of the capital was finally lost.   One or two others undertook to revive
the enterprise, but without any marked success.   About 1835 Elnathan Jones
obtained possession of the property and ran the mill until 1842, when it was entirely swept away by fire.   The mill was re-built by Elnathan Jones and his brother Thomas, the latter of whom was at one time owner of three mills on this stream
and a manufacturer of Kentucky jeans.   In 1850 " The Amherst Manufacturing
Company" was formed, consisting of Edward Dickinson, L. M. Hills, G.
Cutler, William Kellogg and others, with a capital of fifty thousand dollars.
This company bought out Jones, but, like General Mattoon's company, they
lost their capital and the property passed back into the hands of Jones, who
sold it to Dana Wheelock.   Not long after this the mill was again destroyed
by fire.   The next enterprise in this place was the hat-finishing business, under charge of L. M. Hills.   His mills were washed away in the freshet of
1863.   Undismayed by this succession of calamities, Ephraim Cushman & Sons
bought the water-privilege and erected a paper-mill, at which they manufactured printing and manilla paper.   The company was financially ruined by the
destruction of their mill by fire in 1873, the third disastrous fire on this spot.
For some time the blackened ruins of the mill, its lofty chimney and huge
boilers, were an unsightly object to the dwellers in the Hollow, but at last a
new building was put up, in 1880, by the firm of Graves, Kellogg & Bangs,
for making sash, doors, blinds and other articles of wood work.   The business
of this firm was originally organized in 1868, and they seem to have broken
the " spell " of the " curse."   They employ ten hands.

Cushman's paper-mill.—The third mill on this stream was built higher up,
above the Roberts Brothers' mill, by Peter Ingram, about 1830.   It was a
small woolen-mill and the enterprise was ruined in the disastrous days of 1837.
New parties undertook to revive the business, but the mill was destroyed by
fire.   Jones & Bradford re-built it in 1845, and it was again burned in 1857.
Thomas Jones, the senior proprietor, died from the effect of excitement
brought on by this fire.   Ephraim and John R. Cushman, brothers, who had

been engaged in paper making at a mill still higher up the stream, now called "Cushman's old mill," bought the water privilege and erected the present "Red mill," just beyond "the City," in 1859. Ephraim Cushman sold out when he went into business in the Hollow, and J. R. Cushman & Sons continued the business, which is now under the management of Avery R. Cushman, manufacturer of straw and leather-board. He employs fifteen hands and turns out about two tons of goods per day.

S. E. Harrington & Son's wood-working factory.—In addition to the two Cushmans and the Roberts mills near "the City" and the unfortuate mill at the Hollow, there was a fifth mill privilege on this stream in what is known as Westville, where the planing-mill of S. E. Harrington & Son now stands. Here the Westville Company (William H. Smith, George Cutler, Luke Sweetser and Thomas Jones) built a woolen-mill in 1852, and it was burned in 1858. William H. Smith and John Wiley then erected a paper-mill on this site, but this too was burned, and the privilege remained unused until S. E. Harrington moved here from Greenfield and put up his mill for working lumber, and took his son, Frank W., into partnership with him in 1882. They get out lumber for builders, such as cornices, moldings, window frames, etc., and do also a general jobbing business.

Charles E. Hayward.—Eli Dickinson was the first manufacturer at South Amherst. His shop occupied the site of Hayward's present manufactory for children's wagons, and made wood faucets, on which he had obtained a patent. About 1835 James Kellogg bought the property and began making planes; in 1839 he moved the business to Kelloggville, where it has been carried on for many years by William Kellogg. Hayward's manufactory was established in 1844, by C. & C. F. Hayward. In 1860 the firm was changed to C. F. Hayward, and since 1865 it has been conducted by the present proprietor.

William Kellogg's plane factory, on road 38, was established by James Kellogg, his father, as stated above, about 1835. He carried on the business until about 1867, when he retired and the manufactory was taken by his son William, who still carries on the business. When the shops are in full operation they give employment to twenty men and turn out about $10,000.00 worth of goods, all kinds of carpenter's planes.

A. J. Robinson's factory.—The site now occupied by Mr. Robinson's manufactory for children's carriages was first used by Luther Fox, who manufactured wood faucets. Afterwards Ebenezer Nutting and others made planes there.

Levi E. Dickinson's wood-work factory.—Mr. Dickinson commenced business in a saw-mill at North Amherst, in 1872, doing all kinds of job work. He introduced the box-making business in 1873. In 1879 he removed to Amherst, building a factory fitted up for all kinds of job work, the manufacture of house finishings, etc., also all kinds of box-work. He began making boys' tool-chests and tools in 1882, and has facilities for making from 500 to 1,000 chests a week, according to size.

The Hills Manufacturing Co.—Near the depot the first business enterprise was the palm leaf shop of L. M. Hills & Son, which was opened in 1856. The site of this mill, which was destroyed by fire in 1880, is still occupied by the Hills Manufacturing Company, incorporated 1878, (Henry F. Hills, prest.), which employs about two hundred and fifty hands. The material used by this company comes from nearly all parts of the world.

Henry D. Fearing & Co., whose first mill was destroyed by fire at the same time with Hills's shop in 1880, have now a substantial brick mill, where straw hats are pressed and prepared for the market. This is also a large concern.

Edward P. Dickinson's machine and blacksmith shop, on road 26, was established about 1835 by his father, Porter Dickinson, who died in October, 1879. He manufactured hammers, forks and edged tools till the last fifteen years of his life, when he did nothing but general job work. His son succeeded him in 1879, and in 1885 began the manufacture of builders' molding planes.

Albert A. Thayer's grist-mill was purchased by him of the Northampton Savings bank in the spring of 1883. The mill is operated by water-power and has the capacity for grinding about one hundred bushels of grain per day. Connected with it is a saw-mill, which cuts about 200,000 feet of lumber per year. He employs six men when in full operation.

A. W. Hall's carriage and wagon shop is located on road 9½. He has carried on a successful business in this place for the last eight years. He also does general blacksmithing, employing from three to six men.

Stephen P. Puffer's grist-mill, located on road 2, was established in 1838 by M. F. and Sylvester Dickinson. Mr. Puffer commenced operating the mill in 1860. The mill is run by water-power, has three runs of stones, and capacity for grinding about three hundred bushels of grain per day.

O. M. Clapp's marble and granite works was established by Chandler Sabin, about 1830. In 1850 Mr. Clapp bought out Mr. Sabin, and has conducted the business since. The shop is located on road 21. Mr. Clapp is now eighty-four years of age, and his son, Charles D., manages the business.

S. B. Matthew's rope manufactory, on road 21, was established in 1876, by M. B. Mosier. Mr. Matthews took the business in April, 1886. The walk is 140 feet long. He also makes fish lines, window cord, garden lines, etc. Turns out about 100,000 feet of rope per day.

Roswell H. Howard's brick yard, on road 38, was established by him in 1836. He has since carried on the business, making about 500,000 bricks per year.

Anthony B. Culver's bakery, located on Pleasant street, was established by him in 1880, he having moved from Main street, where he had been since 1876. He has the capacity for turning out sixty loaves of bread per day, aside from a large quantity of cakes, etc. Mr. Culver came here from Miller's Falls, and was the first to establish the bakery business in Amherst.

The Amherst Co-operative Association was established in March, 1877. Previous to this time, for several years, the local grange had brought their goods on the co-operative plan, but at that time they concluded to start a store, and formed a stock company under the laws of Massachusetts. The stock was issued, 120 shares at $10.00 each. The first agent was F. M. Hubbard, succeeded by George H. Dana, and W. G. Town, the present agent.

J. L. Lovell's photograph gallery was established in 1850, by a Mr. Shumway, whom Mr. Lovell bought out in 1856. In 1879 he took his son, Charles O. Lovell, into partnership with him, and the firm was thus J. L. Lovell & Son till 1885, when the latter went to Northampton to engage in the business. Mr. Lovell is a master of his profession; was appointed chief photographer at the Lick Observatory, California, to take views of the transit of Venus.

ECCLESIASTICAL.

When the general court granted the prayer of Zechariah Field and others of the inhabitants of East Hadley, to form them into a precinct, it was upon the condition that they should build a meeting-house and settle a "learned orthodox" minister within three years. This permission of the general court being given December 31, 1734, a warrant was issued "in His Majestie's name" for a first precinct meeting, which was held at the house of Mr. Zechariah Field, October 8, 1735, when the necessary officers having been chosen its first vote was to "Hiere a Menestor half a yeare," and John Ingram, Jr., John Coles and Nathaniel Smith were appointed a committee to carry out this vote. Probably the East inhabitants had hired a minister for half a year before this, for in January, 1732, Hadley voted an abatement of one-fifth of the minister's rate or tax to such of them as had been at the expense of hiring a minister; and again, August 27, 1733, Hadley voted that if the East inhabitants should hire a minister for six months they should have an abatement of one-half their assessment for Rev. Mr. Chauncey's support at Hadley. But who the preacher or preachers thus hired were we have now no means of knowing.

In the March following the first precinct meeting another meeting voted to raise £15 towards the minister's rate and that the remainder of the rate should come out of the non-resident money, so that there was probably a preacher that year. In September, 1736, the precinct again voted to hire a minister for six months; and the next April it was voted "to give Mr. David Parsons, Jr., a call to Settle in ye ministry." They also "voated for his settlement to give him tow Lots of Land that was Granted heretofore by the town of Hadley for the Settlement of the Gospel in this Precinct; Voated 2d, to give him Eeighty pounds ye first year & five pounds to be yearly added until it amounts to one Hundred; Voated 3d, also towards Building a Dwelling House to set him up a frame forty foots in Length in Breth twenty-one

foots & two Storys high and Cover sd House and Build ye Chimney and Cel-
lor." Mr. parsons did not seem favorably disposed towards this call, for another meeting was held July 4, 1737, when a committee was appointed "to
try to get more Lands for his Settlement," and in September following it was
"Voated to Give Mr. David Parsons, Jnr, one Hundred and twenty pounds
sallery." The offer was unsuccessful and Mr. Parsons went to Southampton
to preach November 22, 1737, and the precinct voted to hire a minister for
five months and to pay him forty shillings a Sabbath. In March, 1738, the
precinct voted Jonathan Cowls "eight shillings for keeping Mr. Parsons upon
the Sabbath and John Cowls five shillings for keeping Mr. Parsons' hors."
This shows that Mr. Parsons had returned to Amherst from Southampton, and
December 15, 1738, it was voted to raise one hundred pounds for Mr. Parsons for preaching the year past. March 14, 1739, it was voted "to get y^e
Ministers Lots laid out." On the 12th of July following, they renewed the
call to Mr. Parsons, offering him two lots of land, one in the second division,
the other in the third, and also $\mathcal{J}175$ "of money" towards building his house.
September 28, 1739, another meeting voted that his salary should be
£100 the first year, and that as the polls and estates of the parish
increased his salary should increase accordingly until it amounted to £160; .
but this increase was to come entirely from new families which might move
into town. Following the record of this meeting in the town books is the
following :—

"Hadley 3d Precinct Septemb'r ye 28th 1739 : Complied with the Request
of the Inhabitants of ye third precinct in Hadley.

"P'r me David Parsons, Jn'r."

Mr. Parsons, who thus became the first pastor of Amherst, was born in
Malden, March 24, 1712, was the son of Rev. David Parsons, of Malden and
Leicester, was educated at Harvard college, and first preached in Amherst,
in November, 1735, six years after his graduation at college. The Harvard
catalogue shows his place in his class of twenty-three members to have been
the tenth. This place was determined not by scholarship, but in accordance with the aristocratic customs brought from England by the supposed
rank and dignity of his family. Mr. Parsons's son (and successor in the Amherst pastorate) graduated at Harvard in 1771, and was ranked as the twelfth
in a class of sixty-three members, showing that the family was one of some
prestige among the early colonists.

March 19, 1740, the precinct voted John Nash eleven pounds for providing
for Mr. Parsons's ordination. The Boston *News Letter*, the paper of that
early day, records the date of his ordination Wednesday, November 7, 1739.
He continued in the pastorate until his death, January 1, 1781. He was
deeply loved by his people, as was shown by the continual increase of his salary until it became the largest of any minister's in this vicinity, except that
of Mr. Hooker at Northampton. It was also shown in the fact that his people continued to pay his salary, though after some delay in spite of his strong

sympathy with the English arms during the Revolutionary war. Mr. Parsons's wife, Eunice, was the daughter of Gideon Wells, of Wethersfield, Conn. She was eleven years younger than her husband, and survived him fifteen years. They had eight children, two of whom died in infancy, and one, (the youngest son) died while a member of the junior class in Yale college in 1785. The oldest son graduated at Harvard college in 1771, and another son married and located in Esopus, New York. Two daughters were married, and one, unmarried, survived until 1839, when she died at the age of eighty-four.

Value of Money —The mention of Mr. Parsons's salary makes it necessary to speak of the fluctuating value of money in the colonial days. The original settlers brought with them English standards in money as in all other matters. But in 1652 Massachusetts began to coin "pine tree" shillings and pence. These coins had a pine tree on one side and were made lighter than the English coins of similar name in the vain attempt to keep them from being sent to England. The colonists would purchase English goods and were obliged to pay for them with the lighter coin, which were received by merchants at a discount of nearly twenty-five per cent., twenty pine tree shillings being valued at 15s. 6d. sterling. Commerce brought the money of other countries than Great Britain to Massachusetts, and the Spanish dollars especially seem to have circulated. These were first called "pieces of eight," because containing eight rials, the Spanish rial being worth about twelve and a half cents. They were worth 4s. 6d. apiece in English money, but in Massachusetts they passed current at first for five shillings, and after 1672 they were made legal tender for six shillings. In 1704, by proclamation of Queen Anne regulating the value of foreign coins in the colonies, "pieces of eight," or Spanish dollars, Rix dollars (a German coin) and French crowns, of the value of 4s. 6d. each in England, were declared to be of the value of six shillings each in the colonies, smaller change being correspondingly fixed in value. This was already the Massachusetts value of these coins, but receiving thus the royal approval, the money came to be called "Proclamation Money." The value of money was still further unsettled by the issue of paper money, which began in Massachusetts in 1690, to meet war expenses. At first these "bills of credits" passed among traders at a little more than two-thirds of their face value, but they finally rose to nearly par value.

"Province bills" were first issued in Massachusetts Bay in 1702, the excuse for their emission being "scarcity of money and the want of other medium of commerce." The paper money increasing in quantity, values of course decreased accordingly. In May, 1736, the province bills were ordered to be equal to coined silver at 6s. 8d. per ounce. One pound in these bills was to be equal to three pounds in the bills previously emitted. Thus arose the distinction between "old tenor" and "new tenor;" the latter being three times as valuable as the former where the face of the bills was for the same amount. In November, 1741, a new supply of bills was issued in which one pound was to be equal to four pounds old tenor. These new bills were now known as "new tenor," and the bills of 1736 were sometimes called "middle tenor." It is therefore necessary to know the standard of value in estimating any accounts kept in the eighteenth century, and the modern reader needs to be on his guard against considering the pounds, shillings and pence of the days preceding the Revolution as so much sterling or English money. The precinct meeting of September 28, 1739, which fixed Mr. Parsons's salary at one hundred pounds with an annual increase until it amounted to one hundred and sixty pounds, passed the following votes : " This salary we propose to pay in province bills of the old tenor, or one-third so much in the new, which is to be the only fixed standard until the year 1741. Second, after the year 1741, the salary shall be paid in money, *if any be passing*, or some commodity which shall be equivalent to money upon the footing money now stands ; that is to say, if the country makes good the credit of province bills agreeable to promise at the rate of six shilling and eight pence new tenor for one ounce of silver or twenty shillings old tenor the ounce ; then the above said sums to be settled by that standard. But if the country fails of their promise of the value of money above said, then the salary to be settled at the rate of twenty-six shillings the ounce, in old tenor, or a third part so much in new. The true intent of this vote is to set forth the value of money as it now stands and how it shall stand in all future payments." The precinct also voted to pay the salary annually in the month of March. In 1746 the precinct voted to give Mr. Parsons 35s. the ounce for his salary, and the next precinct meeting chose a committee to agree with their pastor upon the value of money, and a similar committee was appointed yearly for some time. In 1750 their agreement is recorded by a vote that the minister's salary shall be raised from 57s. 8d. the ounce to £3 the ounce. In 1754 voted "to add to the Rev'd Mr. David Parsons's salary for this year ninety-two pounds ten shillings old tenor." The same vote was repeated for the following year. In 1756 an addition of £13 6s. 8d. was voted, which was of course in new tenor. In 1757 the addition was £15 "lawful money," or new tenor. In 1759, '60 and '61 the town made the entire salary for each year £66 13s. 4d. lawful money. At the proportion of three to one this was much more than the £160 old tenor offered him in 1738 and as the proportion at this time was nearer four to one it shows both the increase of the ability of the people to pay and also their love for their pastor. In 1762 an addition of £13 6s. 8d. was voted to the usual £66 13s. 4d. making the entire salary £80, and in 1763 this sum for the pastor's salary was voted. The next year (1764) a committee of sixteen was appointed "to treat with the Rev'd David Parsons respecting the settlement of his salary." After interview with this committee Mr. Parsons addressed a letter to the town proposing that his salary should henceforth be £80 lawful money and firewood or £93 6s. 8d. without firewood. The district accepted the latter proposal apparently without opposition. Mr. Parsons had stipulated in his letter that if money "should be so scarce as not to be a common sufficient medium of trade " then he would accept grain and other necessaries of life at the following rate : wheat 3s. 7d. 1 far. per bushel and rye at 2s. 5d. per bushel.

Minister's Firewood.—By the terms of Mr. Parsons's settlement he was to receive his firewood in addition to his regular salary. And even before his settlement the precinct voted "yt each head and teame be Improved to get firewood for Mr. Parsons." This was during the winter preceding his settlement. In 1742 it was voted that one load of wood should be valued at eight shillings and that the minister's wood should be proportioned upon polls and estates; that is, each one was to furnish wood according to his wealth, and that, as a basis of determining the amount due, each load should count as if a tax of eight shillings had been paid. In 1742 the precinct provided sixty loads of wood. To make sure that the minister lost nothing by carelessness, a committee was appointed " to observe ye loads. In 1743 the wood supplied to Mr. Parsons was seventy loads, the next winter it was eighty, and it had risen in 1749 to ninety loads, and in 1751 to one hundred loads. The historian of Hadley (Mr. Judd) declared, " I never found in any records a minister who consumed as much wood as Mr. Parsons." He estimates each load to have been from two-thirds to three-fourths of a cord. Usually the precinct voted a sum of money for the procuring of this wood, the different sums appropriated indicating rather the fluctuating value of money than any change in the price of wood. In 1742 and '43 the wood was valued at eight shillings per load. In 1750 the value was three shillings per load, the former price being in old tenor, the latter in new tenor or lawful money. In 1763 the price was fixed at eighteen shillings per load, old tenor. In 1745 the precinct appropriated £40, old tenor. In 1747 Dea. Ebenezer Dickinson was given £36 for providing this wood; the next year Nehemiah Strong supplied the wood and received £51. In 1749 the precinct appropriated £122 10s. for the minister's firewood while a year later the appropriation was £13 10s. " lawful," thus bringing into sharp contrast the different values of old and new tenor. The town ceased to supply the minister's firewood in 1764 as recorded above.

First Meeting House.—The first vote after choosing officers at the first precinct meeting was to hire a minister. The second was " to Build a Meating House, forty-five foot in Length and thirty five in Bredth." There seems to have been quite a difference of opinion as to the best place for locating this house of worship. The meeting which voted to build decided to " Set sd house upon the Hill East of Jno. Nash's House," and appointed a building committee. The next month the precinct voted to change the location of the house and also chose a new committee. A month later a third location was assigned, but apparently little or nothing was done (although in March, 1737, it was voted to frame, raise and cover the meeting-house " this year ensuing "), for a special meeting of the precinct, held November 14, 1738, voted to set the house in the place designated by the first meeting held more

12*

than three years previously, October 8, 1735), and accordingly the first meeting-house was erected near the site of the present college observatory. The location being finally determined, rapid progress was made for a time. December 15, 1738, the precinct voted nineteen pounds to Thomas Temple for framing the meeting-house, and three pounds seventeen shillings to Evenenezer Kellogg "for Rum & Sugar," which indicates that there had been "a raising." After this the work apparently dragged. A building committee was annually chosen, and in 1740 "ye former Commity" was instructed "to go on wt ye work." In 1741 a committee was appointed to proceed in finishing the meeting-house "so farr as thay think best," and in March, 1742, the meeting house was "so farr" completed that a precinct meeting was held in it. March 25, 1743, it was voted to provide fastening for the meeting-house doors, and to secure the windows; also "to Aaron Warner thirty shillings to sweep the Meeting House and to give a Signe when to go to Meeting for one yeare." A year later ten shillings old tenor was appropriated for sweeping and twenty-eight shillings old tenor "to Sound ye Signal." November 3, 1744, it was voted to finish the outside of the meeting-house. Six years later (1750) "Voated to provide Glass to Mend ye Meeting house windows," and December 2, 1751, thirteen years after the raising, it was voted "to finish ye Meeting House this yeare Ensuing," and a committee of five was appointed "to se sd House finished." Apparently the work was now accomplished for January 23, 1753, the precinct appropriated ten pounds lawful money to pay for " finishing the meeting house."

An annual appropriation was required for sweeping the meeting-house and "to give ye signel when to meet upon ye sabbaths and Lectures." What this "signel" was is shown by the vote in 1746 "to Give John Nash forty shillings to sound ye Kunk for this year." "Ye Kunk" was of course a conch shell, and the appropriation for blowing it varied as the value of money changed. In 1748 it was twenty-eight shillings old tenor, the next year thirty shillings, the next forty shillings, while in 1750 it was two pounds fifteen shillings; in 1751 it required £4 in old tenor "to blow the Kunk," and fifteen shillings more to sweep the meeting-house. In 1752 the appropriation was ten shillings eight pence, while in 1754 it was seven pounds old tenor for sweeping and giving the signal.

Pews and Seating.—The first recorded mention of a pew in this meeting-house is in the vote of March 16, 1741, when it was "Voated to build a Pue for ye Minister's Wife, whare ye Rev'd Mr. David Parsons Shall chuse." Pews were considered aristocratic, and their introduction into many churches was violently opposed by the common people, who sat upon benches in assigned seats during the services. November 3, 1744, the precinct voted to build two pews, one on the women's side and one on the men's side, and a limited permission to build pews at their own expense was given "to sum particular persons." Probably this vote excited some feeling, for a month later both these votes were revoked. It was, however, voted to build pews round the sides of the meeting-house, and four years later the meeting voted to raise one hundred pounds toward building pews.

It is possible that this vote was not carried into effect, for August 9, 1753, it was voted to make four pews "where the hind seats are," and the next spring Ebenezer Dickinson, John Nash, Jr., and Joseph Church were given " Liberty to Build a pue whare the two hind seats are, in the front gallery on the mens side upon thare own charge." March 20, 1759, five persons were allowed to build a pew " over the stairs in the gallery on the mens side, if it didn't hinder passing in the attics and up and down stairs," and December 19, 1763, a limited permission was given to twelve men, six of whom wrote "Jr." after their names, to build a pew " in the place of the two hind seats in the upper, Teer in the Gallery." This is the last recorded permission to individuals to build pews in the old meeting-house.

Amherst was no exception to the rule of heart-burnings, jealousies and difficulties caused by attempts to "seat the meeting-house." The attempt to assign persons to certain seats, an attempt apparently made in every one of the ancient churches, could not fail to provoke human nature into some manifestation of dissatisfaction. The feeling in Hadley Third Precinct upon this matter is not recorded; but that there was bitter feeling no reader of the records of the town can doubt. The first vote on this subject was passed August 3, 1749, when it was " Voated to Seate yᵉ Meeting House, and to Seate yᵉ Males togethr and Females together, except yᵉ two pues next yᵉ East End the Pulpit. Voted 2ᵈ that the seators are Guided by the following Ruels, that is to say : by Age, Estate and Qualifications ; and for Estates to be guided by the Last year's List. Voted 3ᵈ to Make Choise of five meat Parsons to seat yᵉ Meeting House." It was, however, three weeks later before the precinct proceeded to choose the "five meat Parsons" who should say where each individual should sit in the house of God. The next January the precinct voted to seat the meeting-house "A Nue," and added four more to the committee of five appointed the previous August, instructing them to assign the seats according to "Estates, Age and Qualifications." By the first vote the choice of seats would go to the aged, by the new vote they were to be given to the heaviest tax payers, and which should have precedence, gray hairs or a large tax bill, was long a standing question in the precinct meetings. July 5, 1753, another seating was ordered, and a new committee chosen, who were to assign seats by "men's age, estate and qualifications." The next precinct meeting increased the committee from seven to eleven, but made no change in the rules, but the efforts of the eleven did not apparently satisfy the town, for at the March meeting it was voted "that the Late Seators of the Meeting House to Consider if they Can Resonably make any alteration in seating the Meeting House," and a year later the same committee were instructed to " Make Sum alterations," and the next precinct meeting voted "that the Seaters last made choise of—Make sum alteration whare sd seators think proper." In 1760 a committee to make a new assignment of seats was chosen, who was to give preference to age, but two years later a new committee was appointed and instructed to give precedence to estate. This assignment seems to have held for five years, and when a new committee was chosen for another seating (in 1767), no instructions were given them as to who should have " the chief seats in the synagogue." In 1771 voted " to make sum alterations in seeting of the Meeting Hous," and the warrant for the following meeting (March 5, 1771) includes an article "To see whether the District will accept of the report of the Com'tee Chosen to Seet the Meeting House," and also another " wheather the Destrict will Vote that Every Person Seated Shall Take their Seats where they are Seated & to be esteemed Disorderly if not & be Liable to Such a fine as the Court Judge Proper"—from which it appears that some who were dissatisfied with the action of the seaters, had refused to sit in their assigned places, probably crowding into seats which they preferred, to the great annoyance of those who were assigned there. This was by no means an unfrequent happening in other places. What action was taken under this article can hardly be now known from the brief entry in the clerk's records, " Voted to accept of the Com'tee report in the regulation of the seats in the Meeting Hous." The district had already voted " that all persons that had either Children or Prentices, or any under their care that have seats aseined them in the meeting hous, see to it that they take and keep their respective seats unless at any particular time they were for some speatial reason invited into an nother seat by the oner or oners of the same." In 1778 and again in 1780, the town ordered a re-seating of the meeting-house—both times the order of the town was to seat by age, estate and qualifications. The last term doubtless refers to titles and civic honors which a man may have received ; the man who had been appointed to some petty magistracy, or who had received a military title, or the degree of some college, seldom failed to claim precedence over his neighbor who lacked these " qualifications."

Church Troubles, and a New Pastor and Church.—Before the Revolutionary war broke out, Amherst was already of sufficient population and wealth to lead many to desire the formation of a new church. The "West Street" was seven miles in length and well filled homes along its entire length sent their representatives to the church in the center of the town, some of them traveling more than four miles each way on Sunday. In town meetings, when the north and south parts of the town were fully represented, they were often able to outvote those living in the center by a small majority. Those at the ends of the town wished that whenever a new meeting-house became necessary there might be two such built, one in the north part and one in the southern part of the town. They felt that as the center people had had the church in their midst for more than thirty years, it was no more than right that the people who had traveled for long distances each Sunday should now have their turn in living near the meeting-house and let the Center take its turn in the Sabbath day's journey to the house of God.

The first vote upon this subject in town meeting was taken January 13, 1772, when the following vote was passed " to Take Sum Measures to divide the District into two Pearishes." Upon a similar vote at the following March meeting there was a tie vote and it was declared lost. It is not known whether this vote was upon some definite "measure to divide the district," or was simply upon a renewal of the proposition voted at the previous meeting, but clearly there was ground for much contention when those who clung so tenaciously to their opinions as our fathers were so evenly divided upon so important a question. The question came up again the next year and the district voted "to build two Meeting houses," and refused to grant the petition "of Sundry of the Inheabitants to be freed from the charge of Building two Meeting Houses." Those who lived near the old meeting-house finding themselves in a minority now petitioned the general court (May, 1773) asking the court to decide if a division of the district was necessary, and if it was, to incorporate them into a new parish; seventy of the people signed this petition for a new parish in the very center of the district. The general court deferred action until the following year, when the opponents of this petition might present their case. Accordingly, the next town meeting voted that a committee should be chosen "to make answer" to this petition, and this committee of seven were given discretionary power to do in this matter "as they shall think best for the town." At the same meeting the majority still further irritated the minority by voting "to Divide the District of Amherst by an East and west line from the Center of the Meeting house as it now stands." The town records depart from their usual brevity to inform us that this vote was passed "by a large Majority." This would leave the inhabitants of the Center, whose life had been spent "beneath the eaves of the Sanctuary," on the extreme outside of two parishes. Evidently this vote provoked bitter feeling, and three weeks later (January 26, 1774) another meeting was held, at which the (outside) majority carried a vote to choose two agents to go to the general court and endeavor to get the consent of that body to the division of the district. They also voted that the town should pay the expenses of these men. The minority sent a vigorous protest to Boston, and the general court appointed a committee to visit Amherst and report what was the best thing to be done. Accordingly, another town meeting (March 14, 1774) chose a committee "to wait upon the Courts' Com'tee that is to Repare to Amherst to decide the dispute respecting the Division of Amherst." Still another meeting, May 23, 1774, voted to send Reuben Dickinson to Boston, to hear the report of this committee and to "Conduct the affear as he shall think best for the town." They also voted "to furnish the agent with money," but as only seven pounds was appropriated for this purpose it can hardly be understood as furnishing a precedent for the amount of money sometimes expended in later days to secure a majority in some legislative bodies. The town records speak of no further action on this matter, and the excitement of the opening war with its discussions of great state questions were of evident relief to those who seemed helplessly in the power of a majority, bent upon dividing the town through its very heart. Of necessity the question was postponed until it was seen what would be the issue of the war.

Before the war closed the first pastor of the "precinct," "district" and "town" had "entered into his rest," dying upon New Year's day, 1781, a few weeks before reaching his sixty-ninth birthday. A town meeting held the week following makes no allusion to his death, but the March meeting chose a committee to settle with his heirs for salaries due. In May the town appointed the selectmen a committee to provide a preacher, and in June, 1781, a meeting to consider church affairs passed several votes concerning "the Resettlement of the Gospel Ministry and Ordnances." The town no longer took upon itself the decision of the whole question of procuring a pastor, but expressed their willingness "to concur with the Church in all proper measures," and to this end they chose a committee to act with this committee of the church giving them the following instructions : " that when occasion requires they shall confer with the committee of the Church and endeavor a union and harmony in all measures." They also directed this committee "to employ Mr. David Parsons to supply the Pulpit for the present." He was the oldest son of the deceased pastor of the church, and had been graduated at Harvard college ten years previous.

In July, 1781, the town voted to pay the executor of the former pastor "the whole of the salaries Due to him on the first day of May, 1781, in gold or silver, with the interest due on the same." But in spite of this vote the debt remained unpaid, for in January, 1784, three years after their pastor's decease, the town "Voted, That the Treasurer call on the Constables to Pay the Debt Due to the Heirs of the Late Rev'd David Parsons for salaries, as soon as may be." Still the debt remained unsettled and apparently the executors brought suit against the town, for May 1, 1786, the town voted to request the continuance until the next term of court of "the action brought by the executors of the Rev'd David Parsons, Dec'd, against the town." Still another meeting instructed the selectmen "to find how much is Due to the Heirs " of Mr. Parsons, and July 13, 1786, the town appropriated the sum of £250 to pay the debts due to the heirs of the late pastor, which doubtless settled the matter legally if not satisfactorily.

This long delay in settling a salary account was no doubt due in part to the difficulties which attached to all money transactions in the time of the failure of the Continental credit and the depreciated currency of the day. Still more was it due to the feeling that Mr. Parsons's influence against the country in the hour of war had forfeited some part of his claim upon the scanty resources of the patriotic and self-denying majority of his people ; but doubtless the debt would have been paid in less than five years but for the complication of church troubles arising with his son and successor.

We have already seen that the town had instructed its committee to hire Mr. Parsons's son to preach for a limited time. A special meeting called to take action in church matters was held September 13, 1781, and voted to hire Mr. David Parsons for three months longer. Another meeting to consider church affairs was held December 17, when the committee was given " a Discretionary power in procuring a preacher " and " Directed as Soon as may be to procure a Candidate." January 7, 1782, the town voted Mr. Parsons " five dollars per Sabbath for thirty-nine Sabbaths," which probably represents the length of time he had supplied the pulpit. In April following there was another special town meeting to take action on church matters, and money was appropriated " to Pay Mr. Ely for his services," and Mr. David Parsons was invited to preach two months " on probation for settlement." Evidently Mr. Parsons was anxious to succeed his father, for that there was a decided opposition to his candidacy can hardly be doubted in view of the subsequent facts. June 17, 1782, the town " Voted, to Concur with the Church in their vote to give Mr. David Parsons an invitation to settle in the Ministry of the Gospel in this town." " Voted, to Grant him three hundred pounds for a settlement, to be paid in the following manner, to wit, one hundred pounds within one year after his settlement, and one hundred pounds within two years after his settlement, and one hundred pounds within three years after his settlement ; also to grant him ninety pounds as a salary for the first year after his Settlement, and ninety-five pounds for the second, and one hundred pounds for each year afterwards during his Ministry here." . Mr. Parsons was asked to supply the pulpit during his consideration of this offer. Possibly he was not wholly satisfied with the terms offered, for a later meeting (July 15) voted " To provide twenty-five cords of firewood for Mr. Parsons the first year, and to add five cords annually until it shall amount to forty cords, which shall be annually provided for him afterward." On the 12th of August, 1782, the citizens met in town meeting, when the following letter was read to them :—

"Gentlemen : Inasmuch as you have passed sundry Votes respecting my encouragement and support in case I should settle with you in the work of the Gospel Ministry, and as it is always expedient that the meaning of the parties in Transactions of this Nature should be well explained and clearly understood to prevent any Dispute or misunderstanding between them afterwards, I beg Leave to express to you my sense of the meaning of your Proposals as I understand them which is as follows, (viz.) The several sums which you offer me in Settlement and Salary I understand to be in Silver money, Spanish Milled Dollars at six shillings or other Silver or Gold equivalent; And as for the Payment of my Settlement I understand that you will procure me Real Estate to the value, in case any such can be procured, to my acceptance ; otherwise that you will pay me the money according to your first vote ; And as to the Article of Wood, I understand that the most I am ever to expect is forty Cords of fire wood of good quality in a year, unless the town shall voluntarily make addition on being satisfied that forty Cords is not sufficient for my reasonable use. Give me Leave further to add that I must understand it to be your intent, that no advantage shall ever be taken of any Paper Currency Depreciated, or of due act of Government that may be passed to avoid the fair, honest and equitable intent of the Contract. If this be your meaning, as I have expressed my sense of it, and if nothing more than I know of shall appear to prevent, you may expect an Answer in the Affirmative to the Church's Call. Your affectionate friend and servant,

"David Parsons."

The town accepted the "foregoing" as "the true intent and meaning" of their votes, and empowered the town treasurer to give security for the payment of the promised settlement. They also voted to pay the expenses of Mr. Parsons's ordination and chose a committee "with a Discretionary Power to make the usual and Decent Preparations for the ordination." Probably most ministers of the present day would have hesitated even longer than did Mr. Parsons in accepting a call to which there was such a bitter opposition; but Mr. Parsons clearly knew of all the animosity felt towards himself, and as in the words of his letter "nothing more than I know of" did "appear," he accepted the call and was ordained as second pastor of the church, October 2, 1782. The brief diary of one who attended the ordination tells us that "Rev. Breck preached; Hopkins gave charge; Dana prayed first; Hubbard, of Northfield, prayed to ordain; Newton prayed last; Backus gave right hand." The ministers thus designated were Rev. Robert Breck, of Springfield; Rev. Samuel Hopkins, of Hadley; Rev. John Hubbard, of Northfield; Rev. Roger Newton, of Greenfield; and Rev. Simon Backus, of Granby. How long they deliberated, or whether they consulted the opponents of Mr. Parsons, is not apparent.

At the installation it was already evident that it would be impossible to reconcile those who were opposed to Mr. Parsons, to his ministry. The opposition to him was chiefly political in the sense that he had, like his father, failed to sympathize with the spirit which prompted and carried through the Revolutionary war. The majority of the town, as we have already seen, heartily approved that war; but they had endured throughout almost its entire duration a pastor who was strongly opposed to it. Now it was proposed to settle another "Tory" minister, and those who can remember the feelings called forth by the war of 1861-65 will not wonder that the patriotic majority could hardly endure the thought of settling one who sympathized with their enemies in the stern struggle. Coupled with this fact were charges against the christian character of the new pastor, which, whether true or false, tended to prevent a full degree of confidence in him. Evidently Mr. Parsons desired the call and wanted to live in Amherst, and many a minister has since sympathized with him in this respect; but perhaps he would not have accepted his call nor the council have advised his settlement had it not been for the feeling that Amherst was large enough to support two churches, and that it was better that those so completely estranged from one another should be separated ecclesiastically rather than that the old strife as to the location of new meeting-houses and the dividing of the parish should be renewed. It is difficult to see on what other basis Mr. Parsons accepted his call or the council consented to his settlement. Tradition declares that the opponents of

Mr. Parsons were so nearly a majority of the town that when the question between the two parties was decided in town meeting, the vote was taken by the two parties passing out of the meeting house and forming in two lines in front of the house, and it was not certain that Mr. Parsons's friends had the larger number in line until almost the last man had taken his place, so nearly were the people evenly divided. At the head of Mr. Parsons's opponents was General Ebenezer Mattoon, who had rendered faithful service in the army during the war, and at this time was one of the influential men of the town, a graduate of Dartmouth college in 1776. He was one of the most ardent " Whigs" and represented Amherst in the state convention at Concord the year of his graduation; was the Amherst delegate to the convention of 1779 which formed the state constitution, and was afterwards representative, senator, presidential elector, and member of congress. At the house of this man there met, September 30, 1782, two days before Mr. Parsons's settlement, an ecclesiastical council "to advise the agrieved party." It was made up of the pastors of Southampton, Williamsburg, Whately, Hatfield, Northampton and Westhampton churches, with a lay delegate from each church except Williamsburg. This council "began to hear" on the evening of September 30th. They continued to "hear and consult" throughout October 1st. The next day they attended Mr. Parsons's installation, and consulted until midnight; October 3d they came to some unknown result and dissolved. It is probable that this council advised the formation of a new church, for October 15th twenty-two of Mr. Parsons's opponents bound themselves together to form a new church. Another council, composed of clergy and delegates from the churches of Southampton, Montague, Whately, Hatfield and Westhampton met at Amherst October 28 and 29, adjourned until November 11, and came to a decision November 12. In this decision the council approved an offer now unknown made to Mr. Parsons and his church by his opponents, but consider the proposals made by the church and pastor "unequal and insufficient," and they therefore advised General Mattoon and his associates to proceed with the organization of a new church unless the old church would agree within four weeks to a mutual council. This the old church appears to have declined to do, although the town in special meeting " voted, To Concur with the Church in their Vote to invite an Ecclesiastical Council to look into the affairs of the Church and give their advice respecting the Brethren who stile themselves the aggrieved, and have withdrawn themselves from the Communion of the Church." This council was doubtless an *exparte* council on behalf of the old church, as the former one had been on behalf of the new. In the following year (1783) the legislature formally incorporated "the second church and parish in Amherst," and from that time the reunion of the two churches became impossible, in spite of many efforts made in this direction both during Mr. Parsons's ministry and after his dismissal. It should be said that the old church long claimed that the organization of the new church was irregular and therefore void of effect; that Dr. Parsons refused to recognize their minister as a brother pastor; and that the old church even went so far as to attempt to "discipline" the members of the second church as being disorderly and unmindful of their covenant obligations to the First church. And it was not until May 21, 1810, twenty-eight years after the trouble began, that the First church formally removed the ecclesiastical censures they had voted upon the members of the Second church. Even at this late day, after the centennial of the Second church has been celebrated, the Amherst visitor may still hear the story of the bitter feelings "the warm contentions and unfriendly dispositions, which were lasting," of which Mr. Judd speaks in his *History of Hadley*. These have indeed been now long dead and buried; but their bitterness causes the recital of their curious incidents. It is said that the people of North Amherst, most of whom attended the new church, desired that a new road should be laid out which should enable them to attend their church without being obliged to go through the center of the town. This was bitterly opposed in town meeting by the First church people, but was finally voted. When the road was laid out it was the present Triangle street running from the National bank to Henry D. Fearing's residence. The First church people refused to unite in the work of making it, and made it a point of honor never to set foot upon the street. At a muster the command of a company devolved upon an ardent supporter of the Second church, who undertook to march his command through this street, only to find that religious prejudice was more powerful than military obedience, while the delighted landlord of the tavern, who was watching the maneuver, offered free liquor to those who fell out of the ranks rather than obey the command to march through the hated street.

The incorporation of the Second Parish marked the end of the town's support of the gospel ordinances, and the history of both these organizations belongs henceforth not to the town as such, but to their respective bodies. It is probable that for some time after the formation of the Second church it was the larger and the stronger body.

The First Congregational church edifice is located on the south side of Main street. This is a stone structure and the fourth building the society has erected. The corner stone was laid September 21, 1867, and the building was completed and dedicated September 23, 1868. The second building was erected in 1788, third in 1828. The society now has 450 members, with Rev. G. S. Dickerman, pastor.

The Second Congregational church has a fine building located on the north side of Main street. It was built in 1839. The society's first church building, erected in 1790, stood in the center of old East street. The society now has 200 members, with Rev. Francis J. Fairbanks, pastor.

The North Congregational Church of Amherst was organized November 15, 1826, and is an enduring monument to the memory of Oliver Dickinson, through whose generosty, zeal and faith the church property was secured, the people brought to believe in their own power to sustain a church, and a stream of good influences put in motion. "Landlord Oliver," as his neighbors called the tavern keeper in North Amherst in the early days of the present century, was a man of some property in those days of comparative poverty, and being childless was able to bestow his property where he set his heart; and never was man's heart more firmly "sot" on anything than was his on the church in North Amherst. When he was told by objectors that the little village of farmers could not maintain preaching, even if a church was formed, he replied by drawing up a paper pledging the subscribers to give towards a fund which he desired to have sufficiently large to enable the income to pay the modest salary required for the parson in those days. This paper he headed with a cash subscription of eight hundred dollars, and when he had gathered all the cash subscriptions he could, he headed another paper giving land with the gift of a farm belonging to him, whose value he estimated at a thousand dollars. In this way he gathered the fund which the church still holds, and of which the income only has been used. This fund is not large enough to make the church an entirely free church, but it annually paid one-half of the salary of the first pastor, and at present yields about one-sixth part of the money required to support the church. Its management is entrusted to the care of a board of seven trustees, legally incorporated, who are chosen by the parish and hold office for life. They may be held personally responsible for any loss in the property entrusted to them, and thanks to their wise management the fund remains intact sixty years after its collection.

When Oliver Dickinson was told that the gathering of this fund had exhausted the ability of the people, and that it would be impossible to build a meeting-house, he responded by becoming personally liable for every obligation for both material and labor requisite to the building of a convenient house of worship. He personally superintended the entire work, and so closely did he inspect every contribution of the people to the erection of the house that it was said that he "not only examined every shingle and clapboard put upon the house, but also every nail that was to hold them in place, in order to be sure that none but the best were used." His determination was "that from sill to rafter not one crooked or defective timber should enter into the composition of the house of the Lord," and many are the tales told of his contests with "such as would defraud the Lord by bringing to his service inferior material." When he had built the house of worship, Mr. Dickinson sold the pews and in this way obtained a partial remuneration for his expenditures. The house was of wood and still remains in use by the church, though it has been several times extensively repaired and its interior aspect greatly changed. Its present value is about eight thousand dollars.

The parish was not organized until after the completion of the meeting-house, and all the pew deeds given by Oliver Dickinson described him as "being sole owner and proprietor of a meeting-house lately erected." This exclusive right enabled him to attach to the property two conditions, which seemed to him and to his associates proper enough, but will hardly meet the approval of later generations. His desire for "the best" in the house of the Lord extended even to the people who should sit in the pews, and his "imperative dictation" secured the attachment of the following condition to every pew deed: "that if the said grantee, his heirs or assigns, or any person or persons claiming under them, or either of them, shall let the said pew, or any part thereof to any negro or mulatto, or in any way admit any negro or mulatto to the possession or the occupancy of the same, then the said pew or pews, or such share thereof so let or occupied shall in every such case be forfeited and become the property of the other proprietors of said meeting-house."

The second condition attached to the meeting-house by Oliver Dickinson, was one that expressed his extreme dislike of the Unitarian movement then just in the very flush of its early success. He formally deeded the pulpit of the meeting-house to the first pastor of the church and his successor "for and in consideration of the sum of one dollar," upon the express condition that these ministers should themselves believe, and in their preaching should inculcate the "principles of the gospel as contained in the Westminster Assembly's shorter catechism, and if he (the first pastor), or they (his successors), shall depart from said standard of faith in their preaching or belief," the deed was to be forfeited. When he deeded his rights in the meeting-house to the parish, a similar condition was attached to the conveyance. One of like import was inserted in the rules regulating the control of the church fund, and the communion service was similarly conditioned, being "loaned" to the church while such condition should be observed. Unnecessary and arbitrary as this last condition may seem to-day, there was a good and sufficient reason for it at that time, inasmuch as there was a large and influential number of persons connected with the parish who were avowedly Unitarians in their sympathies, and had property been given simply to the parish, it would have at once become a bone of contention between the Orthodox and Unitarian brethren. Being placed by this condition out of the reach of such contest, the parish was, from the first, heartily harmonious, and that even the Unitarians felt no grievance was shown by the fact that they gave generously to the new society's treasury, and at the first parish meeting, three of the officers chosen to manage the society's business, were Unitarians.

It was not until several years had elapsed that the parish was able to change this proviso in the pew deeds, but when the property passed out of the hands of its former "sole owner," and became the property of the incorporated society, the pew owners surrendered their deeds to the parish and received in return other deeds in which this condition was omitted, and even the once "sole owner and proprietor" was persuaded just before his death, in 1843, to consent to this action of the society. The Sunday before this sketch was written, the pulpit of the same meeting-house was occupied by a negro who preached with heartiest acceptance and approbation of a large congregation. So greatly do the times change.

When the fund for the support of preaching was thus collected, and the meeting house ready for service, the church was formally organized and reorganized by an ecclesiastical council, November 15, 1826. It consisted of forty-seven members dismissed from the neighboring churches for this purpose. The house was formally dedicated the same day and the next Sunday.

Rev. William W. Hunt began his ministry. He was a young man, a native of the neighboring town of Belchertown. He endeared himself greatly to the people, and after "supplying the pulpit" during the winter, he was formally ordained as first pastor of the church the following March. He was a vigorous man, although in feeble health all his time of service here, and the success of the church for the past sixty years is largely due to him for the wise and sure laying of substantial foundations of success. In his ministry of nearly eleven years, he received into church membership one hundred and eleven persons. Mr. Hunt was one of the first and foremost in the early band of abolitionists, and his zeal in this cause brought upon him the only criticisms and ill-will whose memory lives in the traditions of the parish. He died October 5, 1837, and was buried amidst those whom he had loved and served so faithfully.

Rev. George Cooke was his successor, being ordained as second pastor January 15, 1839, and continued in office until failing health necessitated his dismissal, May 20, 1852. Mr. Cooke was a thorough scholar and a faithful pastor. One hundred and five persons joined the church during his ministry, and his interest in the young, his influence in the town which he served as a committee on school management, and the general love and confidence which he won from all who knew him, were all of great advantage to the church which still cherishes most warmly a love for its second pastor, although thirty-four years have elapsed since his dismissal. Mr. Cooke became president of the University of East Tennessee, after leaving North Amherst, and now resides with his only child at Winchester, Mass.

The successors of pastors Hunt and Cooke have not continued in office as long as these early workers in the church, but the church has never lacked for both able and successful ministers. The names of subsequent pastors are, Rev. George E. Fisher (1852–1857), in whose ministry occurred the greatest revival of the church's history, ninety persons being added to the church in a single year; Rev. John W. Underhill (1859–1862), whose work was cut short by his early death; Rev. Daniel H. Rogan (1865–1866), now pastor of a Unitarian church in Athol, Mass.; Rev. William D. Herrick (1867–1874), whose ministry witnessed another powerful revival, bringing over fifty into the church; Rev. George F. Humphrey (1875–1875), whose troubled pastorate lasted but a single year. The present pastor of the church is Rev. George H. Johnson, a native of Worcester, Mass., and a graduate of Harvard college. This is his first pastorate, and he is now in his eighth year of service, having commenced his labors here in September, 1878. He has received eighty-three persons into the church, his ministry having been blessed with a revival of religious interest in the winter of 1884–1885. Mr. Johnson has taken great interest in the local history of North Amherst, and his researches have recovered to knowledge many little but interesting items concerning the early history of the church and village, which were fast passing into oblivion by the death of one after another of those who had attained to advanced age.

The South Congregational church, located at South Amherst, was organized October 24, 1824, and re-organized in 1858. The society was organized with forty-eight members and now has one hundred and fifty-five. Their church building, a wooden structure, was erected in 1825, re-modeled in 1843, and quite extensively repaired at other times, so that it is now valued at about $5,000.00, and will accommodate about 250 persons. The society's pastors have been as follows : Revs. H. B. Chapin, 1825–29 ; Aaron Gates, 1832–37 ; Gideon Dana, 1838–40 ; Dana Goodsell, 1841–46 ; James L. Merrick, 1849–64 ; Walter Barton, 1864–66 ; George Lyman, 1869–73, F. B. Pullan, 1875 ; Charles S. Walker, 1876, the present pastor.

The Baptist church, located on Pleasant street, was organized as a branch of the New Salem and Prescott church, November 8, 1827, removed its connection from the church in New Salem and Prescott to the church in Northampton in October, 1830, and was re-organized as the " First Baptist Church of Christ in Amherst," August 3, 1832. It then had forty members, and the first pastor was Rev. Mason Bell. The church building was erected soon after the organization and is still in use, though it has been extensively repaired and remodeled several times. The society is now in a flourishing condition, with Rev. Jonathan Childs, pastor.

The Grace Episcopal church, located on Maple street, was organized by Bishop Huntington, September 12, 1864, with thirty-seven members. The first rector was Rev. S. P. Parker, D.D., who was installed January 11, 1864. Services were held in the hall of the old academy until March 2, 1866, when they moved into the basement of their new church, which was consecrated on September 1st of the same year. This is a handsome stone edifice capable of seating four hundred and eighty persons. It cost, including grounds, etc., $40,000.00, about its present value. The society now has one hundred members, with Rev. Samuel Snelling, rector.

The Methodist church at " North Amherst City," was organized March 9, 1849, although Methodist services were held here by Rev. E. S. Potter and others as early as 1842. The church building was dedicated January 1, 1845, though it has been repaired and enlarged twice since, in 1867–68 and 1874–75. The church is now fairly sustained, with Rev. H. A. Jones, pastor.

The Wesleyan Methodist Episcopal Society.—In 1868 a Methodist society was formed at Amherst village, which existed about a year, with Rev. E. Frank Pitcher, pastor. In the winter of 1874, Rev. S. L. Rogers, who was supplying the Methodist church at North Amherst, formed a class at Amherst with twelve members, and appointed Cummings Fish, leader. In the summer of 1875 the church was again organized, Rev. S. L. Rogers being the first pastor. The church building, a brick structure, was erected in 1878–79. The present pastor of the society is Rev. John Emerson.

St. Bridget's Roman Catholic church.—Previous to 1869 meetings of Roman Catholics in this vicinity were held at " Palmer's Hall," under the ministration of pastors from Northampton. In that year, however, their present lot on Pleasant street was purchased, and in 1870–71 their church building was erected. The society's first resident pastor, Rev. Francis Brennan, served until the spring of 1878, a period of six years. The present pastor is Rev. Father E. M. Barry.

The Zion Congregational church, (colored) was formed by its first pastor, Rev. S. L. Hobbs, in 1876, though the society had been in existence without formal oaganization since the autumn of 1862. The chapel, on Parsons street, was built in 1868. There is kept up no regularly organized society connected with the chapel, however, those (colored) persons who wish to unite with the church are simply received into the membership of the College church, which is responsible for the salary of the clergyman in charge of the chapel services, the Rev. D. W. Marsh, D.D., a retired clergyman living in Amherst.

BELCHERTOWN, in area the largest town in the county, lies in the eastern part of the same, and is bounded north by Pelham, east by Pelham, Enfield and Ware, south by the county line and west by Granby and Amherst. The bounds thus roughly stated include, as we have said, the largest area of any township in the county, and we might also have added among the largest of the state, it being about twelve miles in length, north and south, and five miles in width, thus giving it an area of sixty square miles.

Surface.—The surface of the town is amply diversified, affording many choice bits of scenery and enchanting views. The town is noted for its charming drives, while its salubrious climate attracts many summer residents. In our chapter on the county's geology, page 10, we have given a description of the geological formation of this section, and outlined the causes which carved out the town's present contour. In the northern part the country is broken and rough, often rocky, though the soil is usually good and strong, but not easily cultivated ; while the soutnern part of the town is more level, with considerable sandy plain. Still, the town is hilly throughout nearly its entire extent.

Settlement.—The territory now included within the limits of Belchertown, Ware and Pelham was early known as the "Equivalent Lands," and was

noted as an excellent hunting ground. Later on, when settlements had
sprung up in the vicinity of Northampton, the highway of travel for these
settlers in their visits to Boston or points in the eastern part of the colony,
lay directly across these "Equivalent Lands." In what is now Belchertown,
near the present Cyrus Bartlett farm, and directly in the course of this highway, was a copious spring at which the travelers used to stop for rest and
refreshment. Thus the section in that vicinity took on the name of "Cold
Spring." This name lingered even after settlements had been effected here,
and hence the territory of Belchertown, down to the time the town was
legally incorporated, bore the name of "Cold Spring."

The title of "Equivalent Lands" was obtained through circumstances as
follows: The first grant made of lands in Connecticut by the Plymouth
Council to the Earl of Warwick in 1630, and which the Earl soon assigned
to Lord Say or Seal, Lord Brook and others, was very indefinite; the territory conveyed was very imperfectly known. John Mason, as agent for the
Colony of Connecticut, in 1661, bought of the Indians all lands which had
not been previously purchased by particular towns, and made a surrender of
them to the colony. The colonists then petitioned the crown for a charter
confirming their rights to the land. In 1662 Charles II. issued his letters
patent in compliance with their request, and fixed the boundaries as follows :—

"All that part of his Majesty's Domains in New England, in America,
bounded East by Narragansett river, commonly called Narragansett Bay,
where the river falleth into the sea; and on the north by the line of Massachusetts plantation, and on the south by the sea, and in longitude as the
line of the Massachusetts colony, running from east to west, that is to say,
from the said Narragansett Bay on the east to the south sea on the west part,
with the islands thereto belonging."

The north line of this grant, as well as of others, was still undefined.
Settlements were springing up on the line of the two governments at Enfield,
Somers, Woodstock and Suffield, which were supposed to lie within the limits
of Massachusetts, and its government accordingly extended its jurisdiction over
them, protecting them during the Indian wars. This state of things continued till Indian hostilities had subsided, English settlements multiplied, and
the lands attained considerable value, when it became necessary to ascertain
the true line between Massachusetts and Connecticut. The survey was
made, when it was found that the towns we have mentioned lay really within
the limits of Connecticut. Enfield was granted by the general court of Massachusetts to Springfield, in 1648, and in 1670 the court granted Suffield to
Maj. John Pynchon. Lines corresponding with these grants placed Somers
and Woodstock within the limits of Massachusetts, and this government
claimed jurisdiction over them. Connecticut consented to this, upon condition that Massachusetts grant to Connecticut a jurisdiction over an equal extent within its territory as an equivalent. A treaty of this description was
carried into effect, and thus it was that a large tract, including the present
territory of Belchertown, came to be known as the "Equivalent Lands."

In 1727 the portion of these lands which was destined to ultimately become the town of which we write was sold by Connecticut to seven persons who resided in Boston and its vicinity, in six equal divisions, as follows: The first division to Paul Dudley, two-thirds, and Col. John Wainwright, one-third; second division, to John Caswell, one-sixth; third division, to Col. Thomas Fitch, one-sixth; fourth division, to Adington Devenport, one-sixth; fifth division, to Jonathan Belcher, one-sixth; sixth division, to William Clark's heirs, one-sixth.

In October and November of the same year Col. Timothy Dwight, of Northampton, who had been employed to survey and lay out the territory, completed his task. According to this survey, the purchase included 27,390 acres of land. With the sale of this land, Connecticut transferred her powers of jurisdiction over it to Massachusetts. At the time the town was incorporated, it had increased its territory so that it had an additional territory to the north of that embraced by Col. Dwight's amounting to 12,000 acres, a part of which has since been taken to make up the township of Enfield.

As a natural sequence, the proprietors once in possession of their lands, they immediately began to look about for a means of procuring their settlement. It is very probable that transient settlements had been made, for the section was, as we have said, noted as a hunting ground; and not only this, but during the summer season it was used by the people in Northampton and vicinity as a place for their cattle to browse, while it abounded in pine trees which were valuable on two accounts—for "candle-wood" and turpentine. In Northampton the authorities had early recognized the value of the two latter commodities, and had passed a law that "no candle-wood should be gathered within seven miles of the meeting-house," and "no trees boxed for turpentine within three miles of the same." This would naturally drive seekers of these commodities to more remote places, and hence into the territory of Belchertown.

The proprietors of course were conversant with these facts, and were not slow to take advantage of the opportunities they offered for influencing settlers to come in. Accordingly they offered gratuitous grants of land to such of the settlers in the older districts as would come on to their tract and make permanent settlements thereon. This proposal was accepted, and several families from Northampton, Hatfield and Hadley moved here in 1731, of whom the pioneers, locating here in July, were as follows: Samuel Bascom, Benjamin Stebbins and a man by the name of Hooker. Later on in the same year Aaron Lyman came on from Northampton, and in 1732 John Bardwell and Jonathan Graves, from Hatfield, joined them.

No records are left of the settlers' affairs down to 1739, and while it is known that the settlement increased but slowly, it is difficult to determine just what the increase was. A petition addressed to the general court in 1737, however, throws some light upon the matter. This petition says they "had twenty families, and more expected soon." They pray the general court to
13*

grant them a land tax to aid them, for they " are about settling a minister and building a meeting-house." In another petition, dated November, 1738, the petitioners say : " We have agreed with Mr. Noah Merrick to settle with us in the gospel ministry, and pray for the privileges of a township." But Mr. Merrick did not settle here, and in January, 1739, another petition prays for the same privilege. Another petition, under date of November, 1740, says the petitioners are "greatly in debt for building a meeting-house, outside covered and glazed, and a minister settled; we are but twenty families, and owe Judge Dudley and others over £200 for lands for our minster's settlement, and to our minister between £200 and £300 for salary and settlement. We have sustained preaching five or six years, and have advanced the estates of the proprietors more than our own by settling Cold Spring." This was a prayer for the taxation of non-resident land owners. The names attached to these petitions, other than those mentioned, were John Smith, Ebenezer Bridgman, Moses Hannum, Eliakim Phelps, Joseph Bardwell, Nathaniel Dwight. Abner Smith, Joseph Bridgman, Benjamin Billings, Stephen Crawfoot, Thomas Graves, Joseph King and Robert Brown.

Thus from these petions we deduce the following : A permanent settlement was commenced at Cold Spring in July, 1731; up to and including the year 1736 the settlement had increased to twenty familes ; that in November, 1740, the settlement still numbered twenty families, who had built a church, sustained preaching five or six years, and were then greatly embarrassed by debt in consequence thereof.

During the next twelve years, however, the population more than doubled, for in 1752 the town had " more than fifty families." In 1776 the population amounted to 972 souls. The government census reports for each decade from 1790 to 1880 show the population to have been as follows : 1790, 1,485 ; 1800, 1,878 ; 1810, 2,270 ; 1820, 2,426 ; 1830, 2,491 ; 1840, 2,554 ; 1850, 2,680 ; 1860, 2,709 ; 1870, 2,428 ; 1880, 2,346.

Organization —The first meeting of the settlers of " Cold Spring," held under legislative authority for the purposes of electing precinct officers and for transacting general prudential business for the settlement, was convened April 28, 1740. The precinct organization continued until the legal organization of the town, twenty-one years later.

As early as 1757 measures were taken to obtain an act of incorporation with town privileges. The settlers had no power to tax non-resident land owners for parochial charges, to pay a minister or build a meeting-house; that could be done only by special authority from the general court ; this had embarrassed them from their first settlement. There was a conflicting interest between resident and non-resident proprietors on this subject. Resident proprietors, in a petition dated December, 1754, say they are destitute of a minister and unable to go through with the expense of settling one, and pray for leave to assess a small tax on all lands. This was opposed by non-resident proprietors. By way of remonstrance, February 26, 1755, they say :—

"This tract was equivalent land and purchased without any conditions or limitations. One-third was sold to persons to bring forward a settlement, but they culled out the best; their own one-third is in fact equal to all the rest; yet proprietors (non-resident) agreed to be taxed for meeting-house and minister. A meeting-house was built, and Mr. Billing settled. After a long controversy and debate Mr. Billing was dismissed. And now the inhabitants petition for a tax to settle another. We think this unreasonable, as we were not obliged originally to pay anything, and pray that no power be given to raise a tax."

This remonstrance prevailed, and no tax was then granted. A similar petition was made to the general court in 1756. In January, 1757, the power was given by the legislature, and a tax of half a penny per acre was assessed. This greatly relieved and encouraged the people.

The greatest obstacle in the way of the prosperity of the place, and which was most embarrassing to the settlers, was this inability to tax the property here for the support of their religious institutions, making that support unequal and troublesome. So long as that inability existed they were not successful; lands were not taken, population was stationary and the people discouraged; when the difficulty was removed and power given for a general tax, the people prospered.

At a precinct meeting held December 29, 1760, a committee was appointed to present a petition to the general court for an act of incorporation as a town. In March, 1761, it was presented, and on June 23d an act was passed incorporating the town under the name of Belchertown. A warrant was issued by the general court for calling the first meeting, and appointing Eleazer Porter, Esq., to warn the same.

The name Belchertown was given in honor of Jonathan Belcher, whom we have mentioned as one of the original proprietors. He was a prominent man, having served the province as governor from 1730 to 1740.

Pursuant to warrant authorizing the inhabitants to convene for organization and election of officers, a meeting was held September 30, 1761, when the following list of town officers was elected: Nathaniel Dwight, moderator and clerk; Dea. Aaron Lyman, Lieut. Abner Smith and Joseph Bridgman, selectmen and assessors; Nathaniel Dwight, treasurer; Joseph Graves and James Walker, constables and collectors; Sergt. Hezekiah Root and Sergt. Daniel Smith, wardens; Joseph Smith and Israel Cowles, surveyors of highways; Joseph Bardwell and Moses Hannum, tythingmen; Benjamin Morgan and Ebenezer Warner, fence viewers; Lieut. Abner Smith, clerk of the market; Joseph Bridgman, sealer of leather; Benjamin Morgan, deer-reeve; and Caleb Clark and John Cowles, hog-reeves.

BIOGRAPHICAL.

In the early records the following names are met with frequently, and hence may be looked upon as the fathers of the town: John Smith, Joseph King, William, Samuel and Moses Hannum, Abner Smith, Benjamin Stebbins,

Ebenezer Warner, Moses Warner, Thomas, John and Jonathan Graves, Benjamin Morgan, Ebenezer Bridgman, Joseph Bridgman, Samuel Bascom, Hezekiah Root, Robert Brown, Stephen Crawfoot, Israel Towne, Benjamin Billings, Thomas Graves, Walter Fairfield, Nathan Parsons, Eliakim Phelps, Joseph Bardwell, Israel and John Cowles, Thomas Brown, Nathaniel Dwight, Daniel Worthington, James Walker, Elihu Lyman and Aaron Lyman.

Of the distinguished ones who have been born here may be mentioned Ethan Smith, an able divine and theological writer; Erastus Worthington, politician and lawyer; Samuel Stillman Greene, able teacher and author; and Josiah Gilbert Holland, distinguished journalist, author, poet.

John Smith was the son of Joseph Smith, and grandson of Joseph Smith, who came from England and settled in Hartford, Conn., about 1651. He married Elizabeth Hovey, of Hadley, in 1709, and removed to Hatfield in 1711, where he was chosen deacon of the church. He settled in Belchertown in 1736, and was chosen first deacon of the church at its organization in 1737. He was a prominent actor in the religious and civil affairs of the town, and was authorized by the general court to call the first meeting ever called by legislative authority of the settlers of Belchertown for police purposes, raising money to support the Gospel, and for other prudential affairs. The church records say of him: "A valuable man in his day." He died in 1777, at the age of ninety-one years. Several of his sons settled in town.

Dea. Aaron Lyman (formerly spelled " Limon") was a grandson of John Lyman, of Northampton, whose name occurs there as early as 1661. He settled in Belchertown in 1731, and married Eunice, daughter of Nathaniel Dwight, the following year. He was chosen deacon in the church at its organization, and died in 1780, aged seventy-five years. His descendants have disappeared from the town.

The Bridgman family were among the very early settlers of Hampshire county. As early as 1640 James Bridgman appears to have settled in Hartford, Conn., and to have moved to Northampton in 1655, where he died in 1676. His children, who lived to adult age, were John, Mary and Martha. John was born in Springfield, July 7, 1645, married Mary Sheldon, December 11, 1670, and reared seven sons and six daughters. He died April 7, 1712. His son Ebenezer was born in Northampton, in 1686, married Mary Parsons in 1710, came to Cold Spring in 1732, reared four children, and lived here till he died, in 1760. Joseph, son of Ebenezer, was born in 1712, married Elizabeth Warner, and had born to him two sons, Oliver, born December 28, 1738, and Joseph, born January 4, 1745. The latter married Ruth Wright, of Northampton, June 21, 1770, and reared four sons and two daughters, viz.: Wright, Joseph, Theodore, Mary, Sarah and Jonathan. He died in 1826, aged eighty years. Wright was born June 3, 1772, married Irene Smith, December 15, 1796, and reared nine children, as follows: Wright, Henry, Mary C., John B., Wright, 2d, Porter, Phineas S., Calvin and Helen M. Phineas S. was born June 20, 1810, married Sarah Stebbins, July

22, 1828, who bore him eight children, as follows : Jane A., Frederick B., Sophronia S., William E., Eugene, Edward S., Frank H. and Arthur.

Nathaniel Dwight was a native of Northampton, and a son of Nathaniel Dwight, who located at Northampton in 1689. His great-grandfather, John Dwight, came from England in 1636, and located at Dedham. Nathaniel settled in Belchertown in 1732, married Hannah Lyman, a sister of Aaron Lyman, and was a prominent man in all civil and religious affairs. He served as a captain in the French and Indian war, 1755–60, was active and useful in the Revolutionary war, and did much to advance the interests of the town. He died in 1784, aged seventy-two years. The family is still represented. A second branch settled about 1775, in the person of Henry Dwight, from Weston (now Warren), Mass.

Eliakim Phelps was born in Northampton, in 1709, and was a descendant of Nathaniel Phelps, one of the first settlers of that place, and of William Phelps, who was one of the first settlers of Windsor, Conn., in 1640. He was the sixth settler in Belchertown, in 1731 or 1732. He lived an honorable and useful life, leaving descendants, and died in the year 1777, at the age of sixty-nine years. For his first wife he married Elizabeth Rust, of Northampton, who bore him six children, and died in 1752, at the age of forty years ; and for his second, Elizabeth Davis, of Springfield, who died in 1778, aged sixty-four years, and by whom he had several children.

John Bardwell was a son of Robert Bardwell, who came from London to Boston about the year 1670. He settled in Belchertown in 1732, and was one of the first settlers. He had three sons, Martin, Joseph and Jonathan, who came with their father. The family has been active and influential, and is still represented in the town. Bardwell village bears their name.

Moses and Ebenezer Warner were brothers, sons of Ebenezer Warner, of Hatfield, and grandsons of Daniel Warner, one of the first settlers of Hatfield, in 1684. Moses, the eldest, was born in 1717, and Ebenezer in 1729. The former married Sarah Porter in 1739, and died in 1759, at the age of forty-two years, leaving descendants. Ebenezer married Dinah Phelps, and died in the year 1812, at the age of eighty-three years. Moses settled in the town about 1747 ; Ebenezer in 1752.

William and Samuel Hannum were brothers, and came to Belchertown with families in 1732. They were sons of John Hannum, and grandsons of William Hannum, one of the earliest settlers in Northampton. William was born in 1690, and died in 1756, leaving three sons. Samuel Hannum died in 1780, aged eighty-eight years, leaving two sons.

The Graves family settled prior to 1735, in the persons of Thomas, John and Jonathan, who came from Hatfield, and were lineal descendants of Thomas Graves, one of the first settlers of that place. Jonathan was born in 1702, and passed his life in Belchertown, dying in 1787 at the age of eighty-six years, leaving descendants. Thomas and John were brothers, and sons of Samuel Graves. The former married a daughter of Isaac Graves, a cousin, and died in 1784, at the age of eighty-two years. The latter was born in 1719, and died in 1793, at the age of eighty years. The family is not now represented in the town.

Israel and John Cowles, sons of John Cowles, were natives of Hatfield, and born, the former in 1726 and the latter in 1731. They settled in Belchertown about the year 1752. Both engaged in the French and Indian war, and went to the relief of Fort William Henry in 1757. Israel died in town in 1797, aged nearly seventy-one years, leaving two sons. John died in 1811, aged eighty years.

The Towne family are descended from William Towne, who came to this country and settled at Salem about 1640. Israel, son of Israel, purchased a farm in Belchertown and settled in 1749, being then twenty-two years of age. He married Naomi, daughter of Benjamin Stebbins, in 1754. He died in 1805, aged seventy-eight years, and his wife in 1827, aged ninety-two years. They left a family of ten children, of whom a number settled in town, and intermarried with some of the oldest and best families. The family is still represented.

Walter Fairfield, a native of Lenox, or Ipswich, was an early settler ; located about 1742, and died in 1756, aged eighty-three years.

Nathan Parsons settled about 1746, and was a brother of Rev. David Parsons, the first settled minister in Amherst. He raised a family, and died in 1806, at the age of eighty-six years.

Hezekiah Root was a native of Northampton, and a lineal descendant of Thomas Root, one of the first settlers of Northampton. He settled prior to 1736, married, and raised a family. His brother Orlando also settled, and died in 1805, at the age of seventy-two years, leaving descendants. Hezekiah died at the age of seventy-eight years.

Benjamin Morgan settled probably in 1750, passed his life in Belchertown and had three sons, Benjamin, Titus and Gad, and one daughter, Sarah, who married Benjamin Billings. Morgan was the last survivor of those who acted in town at the time of the settlement of Rev. Mr. Forward, in 1756. He died August 21, 1812, aged ninety-three years. His descendants are still represented in town.

Benjamin Billings was born in Hatfield in 1704, and was one of the first settlers in Belchertown. He married Mary Hastings, passed his life in the town, where he raised a family, and died in 1782, aged seventy-eight years.

Stephen Crawfoot, from Northampton, was an early settler, before 1737. He served in the French war from Belchertown, and died in 1765, at the age of fifty-five years.

Daniel Worthington, a native of Colchester, Conn., settled in town in 1753. He was a soldier in the French war, and was out in Capt. Nathaniel Dwight's company for the relief of Fort William Henry in 1757. He died at Woodstock, Vt., in 1830, at the age of ninety-eight years.

Capt. James Walker was born in Weston, in November, 1732, and was a son of Nathaniel Walker. He settled in Belchertown in 1755, was twice married, and had eight sons, of whom James, Hezekiah, Silas, Jason and Nathaniel lived to advanced ages in town. He served in the French war in 1757, and died in 1806, aged seventy-four years.

Col. Myron P. Walker, one of the best known of Belchertown's sons at the present time, was born February 18, 1845 ; was educated in the public schools. At the age of fourteen he was accepted as the drummer boy of the first Connecticut valley Massachusetts regiment, the famous 10th. With it he was in all the hard fought campaigns of the army of the Potomac, frequently at the front and under fire. Returning, after three years' service, he went into a country store, from whence he took a clerkship in Springfield. At majority he struck out for the Pacific slope. He went into a Sacramento life insurance company, whose cashiership he at length resigned for the secretaryship of a new corporation, to which was given the Pacific coast business of the great New York Life Insurance Company. While in California he won the reputation of a sound, skillful and successful insurance man. Able at length to select a residence, irrespective of business considerations, he returned to his native town and has developed a fine country seat. In the fall of 1884 he was placed in nomination for the Hampshire senatorship, and was handsomely elected, leading every candidate on the ticket, whether state or national. His own town gave him all but twenty-nine of her 392 votes, and at his re-election the following year all but eleven, a wholly unprecedented occurrence. This time he led his ticket by 700 votes. During his two terms he has held the chairmanship of the insurance committee and has been a member of the military and of the treasury committees. One of his most important services was the passage of a law regulating assessment insurance. The bill, which was mainly his work, became a law with scarcely a word of debate, and is regarded as the best existing law on the subject. In military and agricultural matters he has won the cordial regard of those especially interested. His record in legislation is an honorable one, and has gained him many friends. He is now assistant adjutant-general on the staff of Gov. Robinson, with the rank of colonel, and was last year on the staff of the national commander of the G. A. R. For two years or more he has been president of his regimental association. He is, besides, a member of several military and civic bodies. As he is not yet forty years of age, it is fair to anticipate other honors and services yet to come.

Capt. Roger Clapp came to Dorchester, Mass., from England, about 1630, and was one of the most important men of the colony. His son, Preserved, was born in Dorchester, November 23, 1643, married Sarah Newbury, and died September 20, 1720. Samuel, son of Preserved, was born in Northampton in 1677, and died in 1761. He married three times, first, Sarah Bartlett ; second, Thankful King, and third, Mary Sheldon. Ebenezer, son of William, was born in Northampton about 1707, and married Catherine Sheldon, in 1726. Ebenezer, Jr., was born in Northampton in 1730, married

Mary Tileston, and died in Pittsfield, Mass. James Harvey, son of Ebenezer, Jr., was born in Northampton, March 5, 1792, married twice, first, Marilla D. Francis, and second, Mrs. Sarah Roy, and was for many years proprietor of a line of stages between Boston and Albany. He served in the legislature three terms. In 1812 he located in Belchertown and resided here until his death, April 23, 1871. Of his nine children four are living, namely, Everett, of the firm of Rice, Clapp & Co., of New York city, Dwight P., Edward L., of the firm of Clark, Clapp, & Co., of New York city, and Mrs. Jane A. M. Gilmer, residing in Belchertown. John F., the oldest son, who died July 28, 1882, was of the firm of Simpson, Clapp & Co., of New York city. He left a fund of $40,000.00 in trust to his brothers, Everett and Dwight P., to build a library in Belchertown, with the stipulation that it be completed within the term of five years, and then given to the town. This request has been complied with, and the fine structure that now ornaments the village is the result of his generosity.

Benjamin Stebbins, son of Samuel, was born in Northampton in 1711, and is said to have been the first settler in Belchertown. He died in 1789, aged seventy-eight years. His son, Captain Gideon, was born in this town in 1740, married Mary Hinsdale in 1768, and had born to him five sons, Benjamin, who died many years ago, Darius, who died in infancy, Zenas, Samuel H. and Henry.

Joshua Barton, son of Samuel and Hannah Barton, was born in Oxford, Mass., December 24, 1697, and died February 13, 1773. His son, Reuben, was born March 28, 1728, served in the Revolutionary war, and died in Belchertown, December 22, 1819. Reuben, Jr., was born in this town, January 17, 1772, married Candace Darling, and reared seven children, viz.: Augustus, Nancy, William, Theodore, Orin, Horace and Marcus. The mother of these children lived to the great age of 102 years, the greatest age ever attained by any person in Belchertown. Theodore was born February 3, 1805, married twice. first, Rachel Cowin, November 22, 1832, and second, Electa C. Bush, February 16, 1852. Mr. Barton lived and died on the farm where his son, Myron S., now resides. The oldest child, Lydia, was born August 6, 1835, and lives in the village. Myron S. married Celestia E. Fisher, and has two children, Frederick S. and Harold E.

David Pratt came to this town from Ware, at an early day, and settled on road 23. He served in the Revolutionary war, and died in 1806. His son Elisha was born on the homestead, where he always lived, in October, 1785, married Abigail Sherman, and reared ten children, viz.: David, Hiram, Sophia, Virgil, Maria, Coolidge E., Caroline, Mary S., Experience and James H. Virgil was born in 1816, married Mary A. Randall, and has had born to him five children, two of whom are living, Homer S. and Almon L. Mr. Pratt lives on the homestead.

William Shaw, son of William, was born in this town in 1776, on the farm now owned by Edwin Kimball. He died February 14, 1859, aged eighty-four years. His son Oziel was born in 1806, married Lovina Bassett, and reared nine children, viz.: William B., George F., Francis H., Ellen L, Austin H., Elmer P., Laura A., Mary I. and Eva A. William B. married Julia M. Gamwell, and has three children, Lillian J., Ida L. and Myron A. Ellen L. married Edwin Kimball in 1862, and they have had born to them nine children, viz.: Angie E., Edwin E., William A., Clara L., Henry E., Nettie N., Austin L., Leila I. and Edith L.

Marcus L. Goodell is a son of Moses Goodell, a native of Woodstock, Conn., where he was born March 30, 1777. While an infant his parents moved to Belchertown, locating upon the farm now owned by LaFayette Goodell, where he died October 15, 1854, aged seventy-seven years, and is buried in the old cemetery near Dwight's Staton. Marcus, the fifth of his twelve children, was born on the old homestead April 24, 1807. He married for his first wife Amanda Aldrich, September 18, 1831, who bore him two children, both of whom died in infancy. For his second wife he married Dorothy Dickinson, of Amherst, November 9, 1837. She died without issue, March 2, 1870. His present wife, Julia A., daughter of Aretas Cadwell, of North Hadley, he married October 23, 1873. Mr. Goodell located upon the farm which he now occupies, on road 16, in 1831. In 1876 he built a residence in Amherst, where he resided a short time, but returned to the old farm. Mr. Goodell began as a poor boy, and has, by perseverance and good management, worked his way to wealth.

Luther Holland was born in Petersham, Mass., in 1776, and came to this town in 1808. He married Clarissa Ashley, and reared five children, namely, Nelson, George, Ashley, Luther and Clarissa. Luther, Jr., was born in 1810, married Dorothy W. Stebbins, and reared eight children, three of whom are living, Harriet, Caroline and Charles. Harriet married Horatio Holland, and has one child, Dorothy S. Caroline married Edward Fisk, of Amherst. Charles L. married Cornelia Eaton, in 1876, and has two children, Ella E. and Charles L., Jr. The farm now owned by Mr. Holland has been in the family for four generations.

Thomas Sabin, son of Thomas, was born December 22, 1783, came to this town in 1813, and purchased the farm now owned by Lyman Sabin. He married twice, first, Abigail Durfey, who bore him five children, Lewis, Laura, Sherman, Lyman and Abigail. He married for his second wife, Abigail, widow of Horace Gates, and died March 29, 1885, at the great age of 101 years. His son Lyman was born in 1813, married Lucy C. Stebbins, and has three children, namely, Maria D., widow of Joshua Longley, Abigail D. (Mrs. Lewis K. William), and Laura S., who resides with her father on the homestead, which is located on road 79. This farm was awarded the first premium as being the best managed farm in the county, in 1871, by the East Hampshire's Agricultural Society. It also affords one of the finest views along the Connecticut valley, being at an elevation of 1,000 feet.

Henry Graves was born August 19, 1793, married Selina Smith, and had born to him four children, namely, Henry, Sophia S., who married John Elliott, a dentist; William and Austin L.   Mr. Graves moved to South Hadley Falls from Williamsburg, lived there seven years, moved to Ware in 1824, built a house there, which place he exchanged for the farm where he died, which event occurred March 25, 1865.   Henry, Jr., was born in 1819, married for his first wife Hannah Wales, October 9, 1844, who bore him one son, Moses Wales, born April 1, 1846.   She died April 16, 1863, and he married for his second wife Nancy Witt, May 8, 1866.   Mr. Graves located on the farm where he now resides in 1853.   He served in the late war, enlisting August 7, 1862, and serving three years.   Mr. Graves has been deacon of the Baptist church for twenty-five years.

George Hubbard was born in Fabius, N. Y., in 1828, where he lived until he was eleven years of age, and then came to Belchertown.   He married Maria Town, and has had born to him four children, namely, Lyman, Alfred, Edwin and Jennie S.   Lyman married Malvina Burns, and has six children. Alfred married Julia Bisbee, and has two children.   Jennie S. married Jerome Draper, and has one child.

Jefferson White, son of Amos and grandson of Jesse, was born in Northbridge, Mass., in 1805, and came to Belchertown in 1841.   He was married three times, first, Abigail Eastman, who bore him eleven children, viz. : Mary J., Thomas J., Martha A., Wilbur F., Rufus B., William O., Charles A., Hannah E., Albert E., Amos L. and Eugene E.   He married for his second wife Dorcas Lorring, and for his third wife Marion Cady, in April, 1885. Mr. White lives on road 86.

Martin L. Hastings was born in East Boylston, Mass., in 1821, and resided there until he was eleven years of age, then moved with his father to Leominster.   He moved to Barre when he was nineteen years of age, and came to this town in 1856.   He married Mary Corbit, of Ware, and has had born to him one child, who died in infancy.   He worked in Smith's cotton factory in Barre three years, worked for the Thorndyke Company, in Palmer, as overseer, and was employed in Otis Company's cotton mills in Ware, for about nine months.

Isaac Prouty was born in West Boylston, Mass., married Betsey Bear, and reared seven children, viz. : James, Jane (Mrs. Elias Cook), Benjamin, Isaac, Irena, Forester and Edward.   Forester was born in Shutesbury, Mass., in 1826, married Elvira Pratt, in 1846, and has had born to him four children, three of whom are living, Emerson, Luther and Judson.

Philander Chandler, son of Jonas C., was born in Hardwick, in 1805, married Myra Keith, in 1833, and has had born to him five children, three of whom are living, namely, Minnie M., who married Arthur D. Howard, a correspondent of *The Homestead*, George F., who lives with his parents, and Susan E., who married T. W. Chapman, of this town.   Mr. Chandler came to this town in 1865, locating on the farm where he now lives.   His son Charles, who died in Boston in 1885, was a graduate of Amherst college, soon after obtaining a position on the *Boston Herald,* and eventually became assistant editor.

Russell Jenks was born in Spencer, was a manufacturer of twisted whip stocks, and had born to him thirteen children. He moved to Palmer about 1806, and settled a place which was at that time a dense wilderness. His son Russell was born in Palmer in 1820, married Minerva Cary, of Westfield, Vt., and has one child, Abbey. The latter married Orcian Feague, who carries on business in Palmer, but resides in this town.

John S. Green was born in Monson, Mass., September 27, 1806, married Arminda Jenks, who bore him six children—Rachel, Sophia, Susan, Laura, Oliver and Josiah J.—and died here in November, 1881. His grandfather, Lovell Green, came from Sheffield, England, about 1667, and settled in Monson. John S. was the seventh of the eight grandchildren, brought him by his son Reuben. Josiah J., son of John S., was born in Palmer in 1829, and located upon the farm he now occupies on road 115, in 1877. He was overseer in the Dwight Manufacturing Company's works at Chicopee twenty-five years. His son, John C., is now overseer in a cotton mill at Millbury.

George Warner, son of Martin, was born in the state of New York in 1832, and came to this town with his father in 1847. His father died here at the age of seventy years. His children were as follows: Abraham, Eliza, Sarah, Magdeline, Martha E., Maria and George. Sarah married Asa Canterbury, and has three children, George, Fred and Eva. Magdeline married Joseph N. Towne, and has four children, Edwin, Byron, Carrie and Fannie. Martha E. married Frank Brewster, of Norwich. George married twice, first, Catherine Holden, who died in 1861, and second, he married a Miss Cushman, and has four sons, Frank L., Fred E., David H. and Arthur E.

Henry D. Moulton was born in Wales, April 5, 1842, and served in the late war, enlisting in Co. K, 1st Conn. Cav., January 1, 1862; was wounded at the battle of the Rapidan in 1864, and after recovery again rejoined the army. He married Anna Dyer, who died in September, 1882, leaving four children, Carrie B. and Cora B. (twins), Fannie A. and Arthur G. Mr. Moulton married for his second wife Marion E. Hurlburt, January 1, 1884, and moved to this town in August, 1885.

David Blodgett came to this country from England, locating in East Windsor. He afterwards moved to Amherst, married a Miss Dickinson and reared six children, viz.: Asahel, Jerusha, Sabrey, Eunice, Sally and Alma. Asahel was born in Amherst, married twice, first, Eunice Calkins, who bore him eight children, namely, Israel P., Elisha B., Jerusha, Asahel, Alonzo C., David, Asahel, 2d, and Eunice. The mother of these children died January 21, 1812, and Mr. Blodgett married for his second wife Lucinda Clapp, and had born to him four children, namely, Eunice, Lucinda, Theodore and Edward S. Alonzo C. was born in Amherst, April 24, 1805, married twice, first, Rosalind Hyde, December 2, 1830, and has had born to him five children, Edward P., Mary M., Ellen M., Rosalind H., who died in infancy, and Rosalind, 2d. Mr.

Blodgett lived in South Hadley about fourteen years, and then came to this town.   His wife died November 16, 1849, and he married for his second wife Mary Pease, January 3, 1854.   He now resides near the village.

MILITARY.

The "old" French and Indian war broke out in 1744, being the fifth of the series, and there were wars and rumors of wars almost up to the time of the Revolution.   In the early colonial struggles the town bore its full part, and it taxed the people heavily.

Coming down to the Revolution, the records show that when the first provincial congress in 1774 directed the municipal tax-gatherers not to pay the incoming tax to the regular treasurer, whom they regarded as too much of a Tory, but to Henry Gardner, whom they styled receiver-general, Belchertown was the first of all the towns to pay its tax to him, thereby inaugurating a severe blow against the loyalist government.   In accordance with the advice of this congress the people of the town gathered in their meeting-house November 4, 1774, and organized a militia company with Caleb Clark as captain, Joseph Graves and John Cowles, lieutenants, and Elijah Dwight, ensign. They had previously laid in a stock of ammunition, having sent a team to Providence for powder, and at this meeting Ensign Dwight was made custodian of all their war material.   Having been thus on the alert, they were ready for the call to arms when the conflict was precipitated at Lexington. The day after that battle two companies marched from Belchertown, one of thirty-five men, under Capt. Jonathan Bardwell, and Lieut. Aaron Phelps and Silvanus Howe, was attached to the regiment led by Col. Jonathan Warner, of Hardwick.   Capt. John Cowles was at the head of the other company, Asahel Smith and Eleazer Warner being the lieutenants, and it formed a part of the regiment which Col. Ruggles Woodbridge, of South Hadley, commanded.   It contained thirty-four Belchertown and twenty-six Granby residents.   These minute-men served only a fortnight, but many of them re-enlisted and others joined them, so that Capt. Bardwell led a company in Col. David Brewer's regiment, which served over three months up to August. Moses Howe was the first lieutenant.   Capt. Cowles also commanded a company in the army for the same period.

One of Arnold's captains in this terrible expedition across the wilds of Maine the next winter was Elihu Lyman, son of Deacon Aaron Lyman, of Belchertown, who was afterward promoted to be major.   His brother, Josiah Lyman, was a captain in the regiment of Col. Elisha Porter, of Hadley.   They left Belchertown, March 22, 1776, marching to Ticonderoga, thence up Lake Champlain, by way of St. Johnsbury to Quebec.   They had a very arduous campaign, and were consequently credited, by vote of the town, with double the months during which they actually served.   Capt. Lyman was afterward major in Col. Nathan Tyler's regiment, serving in Rhode Island in 1779.   A

Belchertown company of twenty-seven men, led by Lieuts. Aaron Phelps and James Walker, marched one hundred and forty miles in July, 1777, to join Col. Porter's regiment, just before Burgoyne's surrender. This band included the leading men of the town. Bardwell's company in the same regiment contained a dozen Belchertown nine-months' men in 1779. At the Bennington alarm Capt. Elijah Dwight and Lieut. Gideon Hannum were the officers who marched at the head of the leading men of the place to repel the invaders. But as they were gone from home only five days it is fair to presume they did not reach the scene of action. Belchertown men saw considerable service around New London in 1779, the officers being Maj. Elihu Lyman, Capt. Dwight and Lieut. David Barton. Lieut. Daniel Smith served at Dorchester in the winter of 1776–77. Calls for special service were frequent, and some citizens were in the Continental army four years or more. Dr. Estes Howe, Belchertown's first physician, who practiced in the town fifty years, was a drummer in his father's company at Lake George in 1759, and he served as surgeon at two different times during the Revolution, being on General Gates's staff through the Saratoga campaign. When General La Fayette was riding through Belchertown on his way from Albany to Boston, in June, 1825, hearing that an old officer of the Saratoga army lay sick in a neighboring house, he stopped his carriage and went in to greet Dr. Howe. Capt. Joel Green was credited in the town average rolls with more service than almost any other man. He led a company in Ezra Woods's regiment at Peekskill and White Plains in 1778, and was adjutant in the regiment of Lexington minute-men which Col. Jonathan Warner, of Hardwick, commanded.

The town had little to do with the war of 1812 until Gov. Caleb Strong called out the militia, in the fall of 1814, to defend the Atlantic coast. Belchertown contributed an artillery company of fifty-four men to Col. William Edwards's regiment, the officers being Capt. Zenas Stebbins and Lieuts. Eliab Washburn and Theodore Bridgman. The company was on duty in Boston from September 8th to November 5th. An infantry company was also raised at this same time from Belchertown and vicinity of seventy-seven men, with George Gilbert as captain and Thomas Field and Samuel Rich, lieutenants. These men served at Boston from September 10th to November 7th, but none of the troops saw an enemy.

Just as soon as the war for the Union became a certainty, the Belchertown militia company was recruited to its full strength, but so many such organizations were offered for the Tenth regiment, that they could not all be accepted, and this one was broken up, although many of the members enlisted in other companies. Belchertown's soldiers were mostly found in the Tenth, Twenty-seventh, Thirty-first, Thirty-seventh and Forty-sixth regiments, although a good many sons of the town fought elsewhere, a few being members of cavalry and artillery regiments and the navy. The list of officers comprises Col. Eliot Bridgman, Twentieth corps de Afrique, Maj. Harry Walker, a cavalry officer, Dr. George F. Thomson, assistant surgeon of the Thirty-eighth, and surgeon of a regiment which served on the Canadian frontier at the close of the war, with the ranks of major; Capts. Mason Abbey and George Darling, Thirty-first; Lieut. Martin M. Pulver, Thirty-first; Lieut. M. V. Brown, Twenty-seventh; Lieut. William Shaw, Forty-sixth; Lieut. Solomon C. Shumway, Burnside's staff.

The town furnished, in all, two hundred and eighty men, being twenty over her quota under all calls. It furnished $29,000.00 to the government, aside from the $13,576.40 which was afterwards refunded by the state.

VILLAGES.

BELCHERTOWN village is located about at the geographical center of the town, on the New London Northern railway, and occupying the site of the earliest municipal enterprises of the town, is to-day, as it ever has been, the chief point of interest in the township. Lying about 1,000 feet above sea level, in the midst of much that is beautiful in nature, these beauties and salubrious climate attract many summer residents. The stores, hotels, etc., are grouped about a fine park of five acres, which was presented to the town by Col. Elijah Dwight, in 1791. It is oval in form, is nicely kept, and contains a fine band-stand and a graceful soldier's monument. At the north end of this park is the quiet, home-like, popular hotel of Mr. Dwight V. Fuller,

(BELCHER HOUSE, D. V. FULLER, PROPRIETOR.)

the Belcher House, as shown in the accompanying engraving. At the opposite end of the park is the fine summer hotel erected by Mr. B. Butler during the past season, the Highland House. This building is a wooden structure 40x170 feet, three stories in height, and surrounded by broad verandas. It is equipped with all the appliances of modern hotel art, and bids fair to become a popular resort. Just south of the latter hotel stands the town's pride, its elegant $40,000.00 library building, erected through the munificence of the late Mr. Frank Clapp, of Brooklyn. The building is of stone and a model of architectural beauty and convenience. Aside from these buildings, the village has several fine summer residences, notably those of the Messrs. Clapp and Senator Walker.

In brief, the village has three churches, a town-hall, library building, high, grammar, and intermediate schools, two hotels, eight stores, including a drug store, eight mechanic's shops and a large number of dwellings.

DWIGHT'S STATION, a hamlet in the northwestern part of the town, on the New London Northern railway, perpetuates the name of the Dwight family. It has the only postoffice in the town outside of Belchertown village. There are, however, several other hamlets, as follows :—

BARRETT'S JUNCTION, in the southern part of the town, where the Athol branch crosses the New London Northern railroad.

BARDWELL VILLAGE,, deriving its name from the Bardwell family, in the southeastern part of the town, where formerly quite a manufacturing business was carried on.

SLAB CITY, in the eastern part of the town, on Swift river.

INDUSTRIES.

Hawkes, Smith & Co.'s carriage shop.—For many years Belchertown was noted for its extensive carriage, wagon and sleigh manufactories, though of late years this business has almost entirely passed away, there being only two or three small shops in the town, of whom Hawkes, Smith & Co. do the largest business, employing seven hands.

Lyman Smith's carriage shop, on Main street, was built by Nathaniel Walker, over seventy years ago. Mr. Smith does repairing and jobbing principally.

Dore & Woodman's soap-stone factory.—The manufacture of soap-stone was commenced in the southern part of the town, at Barrett's Junction, in 1880. A large amount of money was expended in the building of a dam, canals and mill, largely by W. B. Kimball, of Enfield. The company, known as the Springfield Soap-stone Company, failed after a year or two, but the business is now carried on at the same place by the firm of Dore & Woodman, who obtain their supply of stone from Francestown, N. H. The business is in charge of A. M. Cushing, formerly of Boston, who is thoroughly acquainted with the business in all its branches, and it promises to become a large and profitable venture. The use of soap-stone is increasing, and as people come to understand its value, they will doubtless avail themselves of the opportunities presented for obtaining it, especially for fire purposes and for kitchen use.

Nathan W. Bond's grist and saw-mill, on road 99, occupies the last privilege on Jabish brook before it empties into Swift river. This site has been occupied for many years, and several mills have been destroyed by fire. In October, 1883, the mills were burned, and the present mills built during the same year. The grist-mill has one run of stones, with capacity for grinding 300 bushels of grain per day, while the saw-mill has a circular saw and the capacity for cutting 10,000 feet of lumber per day.

Fernando G. Shaw's steam saw-mill, on road 91, was built in 1883. It has a forty horse power engine, circular saw, and the capacity for sawing 10,000 feet of lumber per day.

Edwin Snow's spoke and handle factory, on Jabish brook, road 41, was originally built for a grist-mill, by Nathan Shumway, about seventy years ago. Mr. Snow purchased the property in 1879, and put in machinery for manufacturing spokes and handles. He has also added a saw-mill, cider-mill and distillery for making cider brandy.

Virgil Pratt & Son's grist, saw and shingle-mill, located on Jabish brook, road 23, was built in 1860–61. The saw-mill has the capacity for cutting about 10,000 feet of lumber per day, the shingle-mill 6,000 shingles, and the grist-mill is for grinding coarse grain.

D. Bruce & Son's saw, shingle and planing-mills, on Jabish brook, road 54, were built many years ago, at least a portion of the mills, and used as a woolen-mill. The saw-mill was built by Elijah Walker, about forty years ago, and has the capacity for turning out 10,000 feet of lumber per day. The shingle-mill was also built by Mr. Walker, about thirty-three years ago, and has the capacity for cutting 8,000 shingles per day,

Sanford & Stebbins's saw mill, on road 54, was built by a Mr. Thayer about 1820. It was purchased by the present firm in 1883. It is operated by water-power, gives employment to four hands and turns out about 300,000 feet of lumber per year.

Blackmer & Walker's saw and shingle-mill, on road 74, was built at a very early date, by Orlando Root, and is still known as the " Root mill." The present firm purchased the mill in 1872. It has the capacity for manufacturing 5,000 feet of lumber and 6,000 shingles per day. The shingle-mill was added to the saw mill in 1820, by Enos Lincoln. There is also a planing-mill connected, added by H. Root in 1855.

George B. Weston's saw-mill, on road 52, was originally built by Mr. Barton at an early date, burnt, and re-built by Mr. Weston's father in 1847, and again in 1869. The mill has the capacity for cutting 10,000 feet of lumber per day, and also has a shingle-mill connected which cuts 10,000 shingles per day.

Thomas S. Haskell's cider-mill and vinegar works, on road 54, were established by him in 1860. In 1885 he put in steam and improved apparatus for converting the cider into vinegar.

The Jabish grist-mill, off road 66, near Belchertown village, owned by Dorman & Sanford, was built in 1875, upon the site of an old mill destroyed by fire that year. It has two runs of stones and grinds about 25,000 bushels of Western corn per year, besides a considerable amount of custom work.

LaFayette W. Goodell, on road 22, is extensively engaged in growing seeds. He devotes from ten to fifteen acres to this purpose, employing from five to ten hands. He deals in all kinds of seeds, making a specialty of growing flower seeds.

Gold & Knight's saw-mill, on road 6, was built by C. T. Brown, about forty years ago. It was purchased by Mr. Knight in 1863, who took Samuel S. Livermore into partnership with him. In 1875 Mr. Gold purchased the latter's interest. They saw about 200,000 feet of lumber per year.

Levi W. Gold's wood-turning shop, on road 5, was established by him about 1867. The shop is operated by water-power. Mr. Gold does a general wood-turning business and manufactures tool-handles, spokes and hubs.

Alden A. Day's cider-mill, on road 16, was purchased by him about ten years ago. He turns out about 400 barrels of cider per year.

ECCLESIASTICAL.

The early history of the church here has already been touched upon, as in the early times the religious interests and the temporal interests of the community were so closely united that it is impossible to trace one without the other. At this point it was only necessary to remind the reader that the subject of erecting a meeting-house was brought up in 1737. A year after, the building was ready for use, though not finished till 1746, and then "done in a manner suited to their embarrassed circumstances." The house now occupied as a place of public worship was erected in 1789, the birth year of our Constitutional Republic, but it was not dedicated till September 12, 1792. In 1828, during Dr. Coleman's ministry, it was much enlarged, and the interior entirely re-constructed at an expense of over three thousand dollars. Again, in 1850, during the ministry of Dr. Wolcott, it was re-modeled and better adapted to the wants of the minister and congregation. It was put into its present condition in the summer of 1872, being re-constructed and re-furnished at a cost of seven thousand dollars. It was re-dedicated September 12, 1872, on the eightieth anniversary of its first dedication. The exercises of the occasion included a sermon by the pastor, Rev. P. W. Lyman, an historical address by Rev. G. A. Oviatt, and dedicatory prayer by Rev. H. B. Blake, former pastors.

The Brainerd church was organized September 30, 1834; between ninety and a hundred persons were then, or shortly after, dismissed from the First church to constitute it. It continued a separate existence until August 31, 1841, when, with about a hundred and eighty members, it was re-united to the parent church, its pastor, Rev. G. A. Oviatt, becoming the pastor of the

united people.   About 1,680 persons have been members of this church since
its organization.

The first pastor of this church was Rev. Edward Billing, a native of Sunderland, and a graduate of Harvard college.   He accepted the call, in a letter dated February 22, 1739, and was probably ordained in April, 1739.   He
was dismissed in April, 1752.   In 1754 he became the first pastor of the
church in Greenfield, where he died about the year 1757.

Rev. Justus Forward, the second pastor, was born in Suffield, Ct., May 11,
1730; graduated from Yale college in 1754; taught school in Hatfield,
where he studied theology; was licensed to preach in the fall of 1755, and
was ordained February 25, 1756.   He was sole pastor till March, 1812, when
a colleague was settled.   He died March 8, 1814, in the fifty-ninth year of his
ministry, and the eighty-fourth year of his age, having followed to the grave
more than nine hundred of his people.   During his ministry three hundred
and eighty members were received into the church, of whom two hundred
and ninety-four joined on profession of faith.   Several revivals of religion occurred during his connection with the church—the most remarkable of which
was in the years 1785–86.

Rev. Experience Porter, the third pastor, was a native of Lebanon, N. H.,
graduated from Dartmouth college in 1803; was tutor in Middlebury college
one year; studied theology with Rev. Asahel Hooker in Goshen, Conn.;
was ordained over the church in Winchester, N. H., November 12, 1807, and
settled over this church early in 1812.   He retained his pastorate until
March 9, 1825.   During these thirteen years four hnndred and twenty-five
persons were received into the church, three hundred and forty-five of them
on profession.   This number was about equal to the whole number added
during the previous eighty years.   Two remarkable revivals occurred during
his ministry.   In 1813 one hundred and seven persons were added to the
church upon profession, and from the fall of 1818 through 1819, two hundred
and eight persons united with it.   Mr. Porter died August 25, 1828.

Rev. Lyman Coleman, the fourth pastor, was born in Middlefield, June 14,
1796; graduated at Yale college in 1817; taught three years in the Latin
Grammar school at Hartford, Conn.; was a tutor in Yale college four years
and a half.   While there he studied theology, and was ordained here October
19, 1825, and was dismissed in September, 1832, having received one
hundred and seventy-eight persons into the church, of whom one hundred
and thirty-three were upon profession of faith.   Since his dismission he has
been principal of Burr seminary, Vermont, also of the English department
of Phillips academy in Andover, a teacher in Amherst, Mass., and Philadelphia, Pa., professor of German in Princeton college (from which he received
the degree of D.D.), and of ancient languages in Lafayette college, Easton,
Pa.   He is the author of several valuable works upon sacred geography and
subjects connected with Christian antiquities.

Rev. Jared Reid, the fifth pastor, was born in Preston, Conn., February,

1788 ; graduated at Yale college, 1817 ; studied theology at Andover ; licensed to preach, April, 1822 ; was settled in the ministry at Reading, November 20, 1823 ; dismissed in 1833 ; installed here September 4, 1833 ; was dismissed here January 6, 1841. He was afterwards at Tiverton, R. I.

Rev. George A. Oviatt, the sixth pastor, is a native of Bridgeport, Conn. ; graduated at Yale college, 1835, where he also studied theology. He was ordained pastor of the Brainerd church in this place August 28, 1838, when (upon the resignation of Mr. Reid) the two churches were re-united, he was invited to become their pastor, and was installed over this church August 31, 1841. He was dismissed July, 1845, and took the pastorate of the Suffolk Street church, Boston ; afterwards of the churches in Chicopee, Somers, Conn., and Talcotville, Conn.

Rev. John Clancey, the seventh pastor, graduated at Middlebury college, 1818 ; studied theology at Andover ; settled in the ministry at Charlton, N. Y., twenty years. He was installed here February 25, 1846, and remained until March 27, 1849, when, having been dismissed, he returned to Charlton.

Rev. Samuel Wolcott, the eighth pastor, was born in what is now South Windsor, Conn., July, 1813 ; graduated at Yale college in 1833 ; completed theological study at Andover in 1837. For two years afterward he assisted the secretary of the A. B. C. F. M. November 13, 1839, he was ordained, and went to Syria as a missionary. He continued his labors in that region till January, 1843, when, on account of the death of his wife and the unsettled condition of affairs in Syria, he returned to America. In August, 1843, he became pastor of the church in Longmeadow, from which he was dismissed in December, 1847. He was installed over this church October 2, 1849, and dismissed March 29, 1853. At that time he became pastor of a church in Providence, R. I., where he remained six and a half years ; then spent two years in connection with the New England church, in Chicago, Ill., and was then settled over a church in Cleveland, Ohio. A noteworthy revival visited the church during the first year of his ministry here, and one hundred more added to the church, eighty-nine on profession of faith.

Rev. Henry B. Blake, the ninth pastor, was born in Winchester Center, Ct., May 20, 1817 ; united with the church in 1832 ; graduated at Williams college in 1841 ; studied theology at East Windsor, Ct., and graduated in 1844. He was ordained at South Coventry, Ct., January 1, 1845 ; dismissed in May, 1855 ; installed here June 26, 1855, and dismissed at the end of ten years, June 26, 1865. He went to Wilmington, N. C., as an agent of the American Missionary association, in 1868.

Rev. W. W. Woodworth, the tenth pastor, was born at Cromwell, Ct., October 16, 1813 ; graduated at Yale college in 1838, and at Andover Theological seminary in 1841. He was pastor at Berlin, Ct., 1842–52 ; at Waterbury, Ct., 1852–58 ; stated supply at Mansfield, Ohio, 1858–60 ; at the Olivet church, Springfield, 1860–62 ; at Plymouth, Mass., 1862–64 ; at Painsville, Ohio, 1864–66 ; pastor of this church, 1866–70.

Rev. Payson W. Lyman, the present pastor, was born at Easthampton, February 28, 1842; graduated at Amherst college in 1867, and at Union Theological seminary, New York, in 1870; ordained and installed over this church, May 10, 1871, having previously preached a short time in Ashfield.

The Baptist church of Belchertown was organized June 24, 1795, by its first pastor, Rev. Samuel Bigelow, with sixteen members. In 1814 the society built a house of worship, which was used until 1842, when the present structure was purchased of the Brainerd church, which at that time re-united with the Congregational church. The building is a fine wooden structure, having been extensively repaired several times. The present pastor of the society is Rev. William Read.

The Methodist Episcopal church of Belchertown was organized by Theodore Blodgett and Thomas Haskell, with twelve members, March 29, 1865. The first pastor was Rev. William Gordon. The church building, a wooden structure erected in 1874, is valued, including grounds, at $6,000.00, and will seat 500 persons. The present pastor is Rev. William F. Lawford.

The Union church society of North Belchertown was organized during the past summer, and a neat chapel has been put up at Dwight's Station, the corner stone being laid on the 6th of October. This church is made up of the people in this vicinity, irrespective of denomination. It is the growth of years; for, while the people here desired a church, they were not sufficiently strong in any one denomination to support one, though at one time a Methodist society flourished here. As an outgrowth of this desire, the present chapel society has grown.

———

CHESTERFIELD* is one of what is known as the hill towns of the county, lying in the western-central part of the same, bounded north by Cummington and Goshen, east by Goshen and Williamsburg, south by Westhampton and Huntington, and west by Worthington. These boundaries enclose an area of 16,748 acres.

Natural Features.—The land is mountainous, the ranges running north and South, with long, pleasant intervening valleys. Through one of these valleys, in the western part of the town, flows Westfield river, making up the most characteristic feature in the town's landscape. In one place this stream has cut through a ledge of rocks a channel thirty feet deep and sixty rods in length, as symetrically as if done by art. East of this valley lies the valley of Dead Branch, which is a tributary of the Westfield river, the outlet of Dead pond in the Northern part of the town. Generally speaking, the surface of the town is rough and mountainous, better adapted to grazing than cultivation, though its valleys and hillsides afford many fine farms. Its gen-

---

* For this sketch we are largely indebted to the "Centennial address," delivered by J. D. Vinton, in 1862, and to Chandler T. Macomber.

eral geological formation is granite in the eastern and calciferous mica schist in the western part. The latter formation is rich in minerals, among which is albite, blue, green and red tourmaline, smoky quartz, spodumene, kyanite, rose-beryl, garnet, tin ore, columbite, and lithia-mica.

Original Grants.—King Philip's war broke out in 1675, and was one of the most remarkable of our Indian wars. As the reader well knows eight hundred and forty Massachusetts troops were marched through the December snows to attack Fort Narragansett at Pocasset, and a great slaughter followed. As an acknowledgment for this brave service, the general court of Massachusetts granted, June 30, 1732, seven tracts of land to the descendants of this band of eight hundred and forty. These tracts were designated as Narragansett Township Number One, Two, Three, etc. A part of Number Four was eventually embraced within the limits of the present town of Chesterfield, though the tract was primarily laid out in New Hampsire.

In the court records of Massachusetts Bay, dated December 16, 1735, is the following :—

"A petition of John Foster and Edward Shove in behalf of the grantees of the tract of land granted to the Narragansett soldiers, which lies at Amoskeag, on the west side of Merrimack river, showing, that upon their viewing the said land, in order to their laying it out into lots, they found it so poor and barren as to be altogether incapable of making settlements, and therefore praying that they may have liberty to quit it and take up the said grant in some other province land."

Their petition was granted, and February 4, 1736, we find another act confirming to them another tract of land "lying between Lambstown on the east, Swift river and the Equivalent Land on the west, Salemtown on the north, and Mr. Reed's land on the south." This grant received the name of "Quabbin Territory"—Quabbin being the Indian name—and included the town now called Greenwich, while the "Equivalent Land" was comprised in Belchertown, Pelham, Prescott and Ware, and was so called from the manner of settling the boundary between Massachusetts and Connecticut. Twelve hundred acres of this territory were confirmed to James Patterson and others, and the remainder was confirmed in the same act to the proprietors of Narragansett Township Number Four, "in part to satisfy a grant of a township made to them," meaning the New Hampshire grant. This was insufficient to make up 23,040 acres, or six miles square, therefore it was further ordered in the same act, "that a township of the contents of six miles square be laid out west of Hatfield [the part now Williamsburg] and adjoining thereto, and that so much thereof be confirmed to the proprietors of the Narragansett Town Number Four, as shall be, together with what is found to be contained in the above described land, over and above the twelve hundred acres especially granted, as shall make up and complete the contents of six miles square, formerly granted to them." The Quabbin territory contained 15,779 acres, which was confirmed to them in an act by the general court, January 9, 1737, and the remaining 7,261 acres was made over in a special act, July

7, 1739, from the above named township west of Hatfield.   In laying out this land, they were to commence at the northeast corner and run to the center or middle of the eastern line, and then to extend in a parallel line westward with the north line, so far as to contain 7,261 acres.

This township was laid out June 13, 1738, at least this is the date of its entrance upon the court records, by Nathaniel Kellogg, and contained 23,040 acres, exclusive of six hundred acres granted to one Coleman, bounded "east on Hatfield (or Williamsburg), north, south and west on unappropriated lands, beginning nine miles west of Connecticut river in the line between Hatfield and Deerfield, supposed to be Hatfield northwest corner," running west 2,160 perch, south 1,880 perch, east 1,880 perch, and thence north 90 degrees east to the first mentioned point.   This last statement must be a mistake in the records, as it is a continuation of an eastern line, whereas it really is north 10 degrees east.

The conditions of this grant were, that they should settle forty families in Quabbin, and twenty others in the township west of Hatfield, making sixty the number required to be settled in each township.   A committee was appointed by the general court to oversee the laying out of the latter tract, and they were "empowered to admit forty other settlers in said township, first giving preference to John Potter, Jonathan Tarbox, Joseph Breden, John Newhall, John Delaway, Joseph Coolings, Daniel Johnson, Samuel Newhall, and to one of the heirs of each of the following persons : William Wormwood, Zachariah Marsh, John Driver, Henry Trivet, John Page and Bartholomew Flagg."   Some of these are supposed to be the soldiers, or the descendants of the soldiers, engaged in the Canada expedition of 1690, and who served under Capt. Thomas Andrews.   Their portion of the land was located in the southern part of the township and was subsequently called "New Hingham," probably because so many of the soldiers came from Hingham.   We have but little evidence that any of the above named persons ever had a settlement in town, but there are records of the transfer of land given in some of their names.

The committee was also "directed to lay out three hundred acres for the first settled minister, another for the ministry, and another for the school, and the rest of the land (besides what is hereby confirmed to the Narragansett soldiers) to be equally divided to the other forty settlers, provided each of them shall within two years from this time build and finish a house eighteen feet square and seven feet stud, and he or one of his decendants shall continue to dwell there two years from the building such house, and bring to and put under good improvement ten acres of said land within the space of four years from this time."   Another provision was "that the settlers shall build a suitable meeting-house and settle a learned orthodox minister among them within the space of five years from this time."   Though this is the reading of the act, no meeting-house was built until thirty-two years after.

Of the Coleman grant but little has as yet been ascertained.   Why he received six hundred acres of the best land in the township, and in laying out the township there should be an allowance made of that number of acres, has not been satisfactorily explained. It is somewhat traditionary that he received the grant for services rendered in laying out lots in the township, which may be probable. We find his grant spoken of in the records of January 13, 1738, but without his given name, and this in the act concerning the boundaries of the town, which we have spoken.

In 1781 the present township of Goshen was set off from Chesterfield territory.

Settlement and Growth.—At what precise date the first family entered the town is uncertain. Gideon Bisbee came into town as early as 1755 or 1756, and chopped wood. He only staid during the week, returning to Northampton Saturday nights. How long he worked is unknown. Owing to the Indian difficulties in and about Northampton, he was prevented from doing it for any great length of time. George Buck is supposed to have been the first person who wintered here, in Ireland street, and perhaps the fact that George Buck and Prince Cowing, two of its earliest settlers, were Irishmen, is the reason for calling the street by its present name. It is related of him that he was detained an unusual length of time in Northampton by a snow storm, where he had gone for provisions, being short at home, and his family were so reduced during his absence as to be obliged to kill and eat their dog.

The settlement from this time gradually increased. In 1776 the population was 1,092 souls. The growth and fluctuation of the town's population since 1790 may be seen by the following: 1790, 1,183; 1800, 1,223; 1810, 1,408; 1820, 1,447; 1830, 1,416; 1840, 1,132; 1850, 1,014; 1855, 950; 1860, 897; 1865, 801; 1870, 811; 1875, 746; 1880, 769.

Organization.—Two sets of proprietors, the Narragansett and Canada, living side by side in the same township, upon different grants of lands, were greatly embarrassed in their civil policy, and it became necessary for the general court to make the two parties one corporate body. To this end an act of incorporation passed the house June 10, 1762, and received the approval of Governor Bernard the next day, June 11. The act reads as follows:—

" Whereas, the proprietors of the new plantation called New Hingham, are under such circumstances that they cannot carry on their public affairs without the aid of this court, they being originally two proprietors as to their property, and have never been united into one propriety as to their public affairs. Be it therefore enacted by the Governor, Council and House of Representatives, that the new plantation called New Hingham, lying in the county of Hampshire, bounded as follows: east on the township of Hatfield, south partly on Northampton and partly on land lately sold by the province, north partly on province lands and partly on a grant made to Narragansett Number Four, and extending west to make twenty-three thousand and forty acres, exclusive of Coleman's grant, which contains six hundred acres, be and hereby is incorporated into a town by the name of Chesterfield, with powers, privileges and immunities that towns within this government have or do enjoy."

According to the instructions contained in the last clause of the incorporation act, Samuel Mather, Esq., of Northampton, issued his warrant to Jeremiah Stockwell, calling a town meeting at the dwelling house of Elisha Warner, July 20, 1762.   At this meeting Eleazar King was chosen moderator and town clerk ; Joseph Burnell, Benjamin Bonney, and Everton Berwick, selectmen ; Benjamin Bryant, constable ; Elisha Warner, treasurer ; Everton Berwick and Benjamin Bonney, assessors.

Highways.—A vote was passed October 25, 1762, that " for every faithful day's work clearing and repairing highways," they would pay 3s. 4d., or about eighty-six cents.   The first town highway laid out by the selectmen and on record, is Ireland street, and it has held its original course till the present time.   It was laid out December 18, 1762, and is recorded as follows :—

" Beginning at a beach staddle which stands on ye south side of ye county road at ye east end of ye west row of lots in ye town of Chesterfield, extending south from ye staddle on ye line which divides ye west row of lots from that which adjoins it on ye east, extending so far south as ye lot No. 86— ye road forty feet wide till it comes within twenty rods of Mr. George Buck's well, then widening out till it comes to be sixty feet wide by ye well, then narrowing off till it goes twenty rods beyond ye well, then holding its first mentioned width to its aforesaid bounds."

The county road spoken of is the road known as the Pontoosuc road from Hatfield—Williamsburg—to Pittsfield, and was the first road through the town.   It was laid in 1760, and passed through the center of Chesterfield, crossing the Westfield river about midway between the old and new roads as they remain at present.   Indications of this road are still visible in the woods near Westfield river.   The site of George Buck's well is still visible near the roadside, and is probably one of the oldest wells in town.   To give some idea of the travel which crossed the town in the old staging days, it is only necessary to state that the town had ten hotels.

Almost every year several new roads were presented to the town for acceptance.   But few of the roads of an early date are now traveled.   Time and experience proved that it was not always the best way to go over the tops of hills, and they gradually learned that a kettle bail is as long standing as when lying down, and therefore experimental philosophy had somewhat to do in the changeableness of their roads.   One other road we will notice, however, which remains about as it was laid.   It was accepted March 6, 1769, and is as follows :—

" Beginning at a hemlock tree on ye county road about six rods east of ye Rev. Benjamin Mills' house, and thence straight by ye east end of his barn, and thence straight by ye east end of ye burying yard, thence straight to and between ye lowermost ledge and ye second ledge and Lieut. Abner Brown's lot, and thence between ye ledge to a convenient place to go down, thence straight to ye meeting-house, and ye road is four rods wide."

This, as it plainly appears, is the one from the hill to the north part of the town, and it remains almost precisely as it was formerly laid.

June 5, 1769, it was voted to clear the " new road across Westfield river," which is now the old River Hill road. At what time the bridge was built is uncertain, though perhaps not far from this time. March 9, 1797, the third Massachusetts turnpike corporation was established, and this road became a part of the turnpike from Northampton to Pittsfield. A toll-gate was kept just beyond the west end of the bridge. This neighborhood still goes by the name of "the Gate."

It seems that bridges were scarce in the early settlement of the town, and that streams were forded as they are in new countries at the present time. Streams evidently were larger then than they are now, and sometimes travelers were put to much inconvenience to cross them. To illustrate their ingenuity in discovering ways to cross under such circumstances, it is related of Jonathan Anderson, that he was coming from Northampton horseback with a load of provisions, he came to the river somewhere near Florence, which at the time was so high he could not ride on his load. So dismounting he headed his horse into the stream and applied the whip, catching the horse by the tail as it swam away, and was thus safely drawn across the river.

Early Schools.—The first notice of schools is under date of December 21, 1767, when the town voted to have a school or schools, and soon after voted not to raise any money to support them. September 28, 1768, it was voted to raise £9 to be expended in schooling. The town was to be divided into three districts. A line from east to west by the meeting-house would separate the north from the south district, and all over the river would form the west district. A committee of three was also appointed in each district, and "empowered to provide masters and dames for their respective districts and also places to keep at." The pay of a "dame" in those days the following fact will illustrate. Dea. Oliver Taylor records in his memorandum that he hired a "schoolmarm" for fifty cents a week, and she boarded herself. May 8, 1769, we find another vote to raise £12 for summer schools. The town was divided into five districts, and one man appointed in each district to act as a committee for the district. The men appointed were Dea. May, Benjamin Bonney, Joseph Burnell, Robert Hamilton and John Buck. The vote of instruction given them showed in what light they esteemed their schools. The committee "are hereby empowered to call their respective districts together at proper times and know their minds how and when the school should be kept, and make report to the selectmen who they have employed to keep school." December 11, 1769, they voted £18 for winter schools, and each district was authorized to build a school-house. December 22, 1772, they voted £24 for schools, and March 7, 1774, they had increased their appropriation to £30.

Military.—September 29, 1774, a special meeting was called to see whether a delegate should be sent to a provincial congress to be held at Concord on the second Tuesday of October following. They voted in the negative ; but December 21st they voted to comply strictly with the association of the continental congress, and a committee was chosen to carry out the mind of the association.   A committee chosen to look after those people who could not arm themselves, and voted to purchase 400 pounds of powder for a town stock.   Ezra May was chosen delegate to the provincial congress, and they agreed to indemnify all officers for all losses in not making returns to Harrison Gray, Esq., province treasurer.   Thus we see that a sudden change came over them within the space of three months, and now they took strong measures in the cause of their country.   January 16, 1775, the vote to purchase 400 pounds of powder was reconsidered, and another passed to buy 200 pounds as soon as possible, and 400 pounds of lead and 1,200 flints.   Affairs appeared more threatening in the country, and the people of Chesterfield were preparing to share in the dangers of the Revolution.   Capt. Webster of the minute men was ordered, if called into action before the March following, to procure guns enough to supply those men who could not purchase them for themselves, and in town meeting a subscription paper was drawn up for the benefit of the men.   April 21, 1775, Capt. Webster marched to Cambridge with forty-seven men, and mustered into Col. John Fellows's regiment.   July 10th, it was rated that fifteen men from each of the two companies in town should be enlisted and stand in readiness in case of alarm. April 1, 1776, Abner Brown's account was allowed "for a door, staple and hinges under the pulpit to secure the town stock of powder."   It was also "voted to run the town stock of lead into balls and buckshot of different sizes."   On June 19, 1776, it was voted "that should the Honorable Continental Congress for the safety of the United Colonies, declare themselves independent of the Kingdom of Great Britain, the inhabitants of the town of Chesterfield will, with our lives and fortunes, engage to defend them in the measure."

November 3, 1777, a consultation of the committee of safety was urged to determine what should be done with the German prisoners sent from Northampton ; but we have no report of their action.   These were some of the prisoners taken at Saratoga the October previous.   They were lodged in the barn of Jonathan Anderson.   Mrs. Anderson was a peculiar woman, ready to do what her sense of justice required, and it is related of her that some of the privates of the prisoners asked for some refreshments, and presently some of the officers made a like request, when they were told that they could have some when their turn came.

In brief, the town furnished about forty soldiers for the Revolutionary war, about twenty for the war of 1812, one for the Florida war, and one for the Mexican war.   In the late great war the town sent ninety-five men to the front, ten over its quota, two of whom were commissioned officers.   It appropriated and expended $14,662.00 for the cause, exclusive of $5,013.01 which was refunded by the state.

Biographical.—Of the families of the first settlers but little can be learned except that they came from such a place, settled at a certain spot marked by a pile of stones or a cellar hole, and that they died about such a time.   But a few family records are known to exist, and the memories and records of the old inhabitants are as unsatisfying as the traditions handed down from generation to generation. The family name in many cases is lost, even where there are descendants by other names. Added to this is the fact that many of the old families lived in what is now the town of Goshen, and will appear in the history of that town. Of a few of the pioneers whose names are among us we append the following, omitting generally, names of those removed or died without children, tracing the family name down to the present generation.

Of the original settlers, Joseph Burnell and David Stearns came from Dudley; Benjamin, Consider and Prince Bryant, Abiel Stetson, Abner, Nehemiah and Benjamin Bates, Benjamin, Thomas and Jonathan Pierce, Seth, Nehemiah and Luke Sylvester, Jacob Litchfield, Robert, Amos and Isaiah Damon, Joshua and John Rogers, John Pynchon, Joseph and Joshua Baily, Charles and Job Cudworth, from Scituate; Ichabod Damon, John Stephenson and Zebulon Willcutt, from Cohassett; Seth Taylor, Benjamin Bonney, Zebulon Robinson, Gideon and Jotham Bisbee, from Pembroke; Paul and Silas King, Elisha, Elijah and Joel Warner, Justus Wright, Paul and Amasa Clapp and Oliver Edwards, from Northampton; Daniel Littlefield, George and Matthew Buck, Abram Joslyn and Prince and Barnabus Cowing, from Bridgewater; Thomas Holbert and David Macomber, from Easton; Samuel and Joseph Rhodes, from Marblehead; Samuel, Elijah and Barney Higgins, from Cambridge, N. Y.; Abijah Whiting (or Whiton), from Hingham; Nathaniel Bryant, from Plymouth; Thomas Moore, from Brookfield; Gershom Collier, from Boston.

The first family that wintered in town, as we have stated, was that of George Buck, who, with his son Matthew, from Bridgewater, settled on what is known as "Ireland Street." In fact this street was limited on the north by George Buck's well, just south of C. P. Hathaway's house, on land of John W. Cowing. A son (Thomas) of Matthew was the father of Cyrus, who, with his son Franklin, lived where Otis now lives. Isaac Buck, a descendant of the same family settled on the "Mount." Isaac, Jr., also lived on the Mount, and was one of the soldiers of 1812. One of his sons died in the Florida war. One son, Thomas, lives in Goshen.

Dr. Robert Starkweather was the physician of the town for more than fifty years. He was from Stonington, Conn., and settled here in 1790. He built and occupied the house now occupied by Oliver Edwards. Of his children, Horace went to Michigan, Rodney lived many years in town, but late in life removed to Ohio. Mrs. Oliver Edwards (the mother of the present Oliver) and Mrs. Emmons Putney, of Goshen, were his daughters. Anecdotes of the "old doctor," who was somewhat of a joker and very particular and peculiar in his habits, might be related, enough to fill this volume.

Oliver Edwards (grandfather of the present Oliver) removed here 1775 to 1780, from Northampton, at Robert's Meadow, so-called, where Eli A. Sylvester now lives. He was a son of Nathaniel Edwards, long known as "Land-

lord Edwards." He settled on "Sugar Hill," on the place now owned by
Ebenezer Edwards. Of his children, Luther and Oliver settled in Chester-
field; Elisha, in Springfield; Mrs. William Pomeroy, at Williamsburg; Mrs.
Ambrose Stone, at Williamsburg; and Mrs. Joshua Bates, at Skaneateles,
N. Y.

Lieut. Robert Damon, with his brother Amos, came from Scituate in 1762.
Robert built the mill now known as Bisbee's, and Amos located in the north
part of the town, about half a mile north of Utley Corners, and near the Frederick Utley house. His children were Isaac, Jemima, Debby, James, Nathan,
David, Hannah and Caleb. Isaac's children were Isaac, Thomas, Lewis,
William, Cyrena, Rufus, Zenas, Salma, Rowena, Calvin, Sophronia and
Wealthy. Calvin owns the old homestead of his father, and Wealthy married Orin Bisbee, at Bisbee's Mills. Most of these settled in town and have
an extensive family connection.

Elisha Witherell, while a single man, removed from Scituate and located in
the southeastern part of the town, about 1770, and while that section of the
town was a wilderness, making his first domicile in a cabin built against a
huge rock on his premises. He married Mrs. Rebecca Studley, who bore
him three sons and three daughters, all of whom settled in this town. His
sons were Nathaniel, Joseph and Elijah. His daughter Rebecca married
Joshua Nichols, father of Albert Nichols. Nathaniel's children were Levi
and Mrs. John Hayden. Elisha's children were Edsel, Lewis, Hiram and
Ransom. Joseph's children were Henry, Mrs. Charles Cudworth, Lyman
and Electa.

The Bisbee family came from England, in 1634, and settled in Marshfield,
or Pembroke, where we find the record of John Bisbee. His son Gideon
came to this town about 1755, and spent one summer clearing a portion of
land near the "Kidd Lookout," in the eastern part of the town. Returning
to Pembroke in the fall for his family, he arrived just in season to join in the
French and Indian war, where he died of the small pox. Soon after this his
widow and two sons and daughters removed to this town and located just a
few rods south of the present homestead of Otis H. Buck. The widow died
there and was buried at "The Gate" cemetery. Of his children, Jotham
married Lydia, daughter of Luther Curtiss, and remained at Home. Gideon
married Betsey, daughter of Nathaniel Bryant, and settled on the Mount.
Lydia married Joseph Nichols and located on the farm still owned by Albert
Nichols, one of the grandchildren. The other daughter married Luther Curtiss, and removed to the eastern portion of the town, where descendants now
live. Of these four children, Jotham had ten children, among whom were
Jonathan, Elisha, Job and Asahel. Gideon had five children, but the family
has long been extinct in town. The record of the daughters will appear in
other places. Jonathan had seven children, among whom we find Capt.
James, of Worthington; Rev. John H., of Westfield, and Martha, who married Capt. James Kelly, of Worthington. Elisha had eleven children, among

whom were Orin, Osmon, Miranda, Joanna, Arvilla, Asenath and Ursula. Asahel had four children, Henry A., of Williamsburg, George, of Goshen, Celia, who married Edgar, son of Patrick Bryant, Jr., and lives in Westfield, and Harriet, who died young. Of the children of Elisha, Orin married Wealthy Damon, who bore him seven children, Wealthy, who married C. T. Macomber, Horatio, who married Louisa, daughter of Col. Lyman Rice, Mary, who married Allen Shaw, Lydia, who married Joseph B. Macomber, Jane, who married C. S. Vanslike, and Almarin, who married Martha, daughter of E. W. Tilden. Osmon married Sophia, daughter of Lewis Damon, who bore him five children, Melvin, J. Eliot, Melissa, Rockwell and Adelbert. Miranda married Royal Harrington, and had two children, Hellen and Ella, the latter of whom married Albert Abbott, of Easthampton. Joanna married Waterman Buck, and went West. Arvilla married James Robinson and went West. Asenath married Chauncey Witherell, who lives at the Center. Ursula married Elijah Tilden, and lives in California.

Jacob Thayer, from Bridgewater, located in the west part of the town quite early. Of his children, Luke and Joel located on the "Mount," Stephen near the river, on the farm now owned by Mrs. Edward Thayer, and later on the farm owned by the Thayer brothers. One son married the daughter of Elder Vining. Of the descendants, Luke's children went West. Joel had two sons, Orrin and Daniel. Daniel removed to Connecticut and Orrin located in South Worthington. Stephen's children, among whom were Alpha, Ansel and Susan, settled in town. Alpha married Anna Whiton, and located on the "Mount." One son, Luther, represents the family in town as the last of Alpha's family. Ansel married Elvira, daughter of Job Cowing, by whom he had three children, Dwight, Electa and Lewis. His second wife was Emeline Manley, by whom he had three children, Elwin, Ella and Edwin. Susan married Lyman Culver, and had six children, all of whom removed from town.

Jesse Willcutt lived in the town as early as 1775, and tradition says he heard the firing from the battle of Bunker Hill by putting his ear to the ground, and the identical spot where he stood at the time is pointed out to those curious in such matters. There were twenty-one children, of whom seventeen grew to mature age, and among them was Jesse, Jr., a son of whom was Joel (Capt. Joel), father of Martin, who occupies the old farm. A few years since, at a cattle show at Cummington, Capt. Joel appeared in the procession with five generations of the family by direct descent, on horseback. But few of the people of the vicinity that have not seen the captain officiating as marshal or officer of the day on many a patriotic or festive occasion, and in his latter years he sported a sash taken from a Confederate officer by C. T. Macomber, at the battle of Newbern, N. C. The future historian can only speak of the Willcutts as "the old men," as the name dies out with the present generation in spite of the offer of Capt. Joel of a yoke of oxen for a grandson by the name of Willcutt.

Timothy Engram came from Williamsburg in December, 1798, and settled on the Coleman tract. Of his children, Timothy and Benjamin lived in Westhampton; Joel, Nathaniel, Porter, Otis, Deborah and Mrs. Edwin Damon remained in town. Sons of Joel, Joel, Jr., and Newman, and Nathaniel and Ammiel, sons of Otis, are still in the town.

James Utley lived near where Edward Cobb now lives. His children were Frederick, William, Knowlton, Sally, Ralph, Samuel and Mrs. Gershom House. A son of Knowlton represents the family name at present in town

Joseph Rhodes, from Marblehead, had children, Jacob, Chapman, Thomas, Joseph, Stephen, Samuel, Benjamin, Amy, Polly, Hannah and Betsy. Chapman's children were John, Norman, Horace, Harvey, Joseph, Mary Ann, Sarah, Jane and Janette. Thomas's children were Eunice, Matilda, Thomas C., Dorus L., Elmira and Alden.

Elijah, Barney and Simeon Higgins were from Bridgewater. Simeon was among the Revolutionary soldiers. Barney settled in Worthington and Lewis in Chesterfield, where J. W. Cowing lives. He had three wives. By the first he had children, Jonathan, who removed to Ogdensburg, N. Y., Lewis, who settled in Chesterfield, Elijah and Luther in Worthington, Rebecca, Deliverance, who married Mr. Billings and removed to Canada, Sophronia, and William, who in middle life removed to Worthington, where he died; by his second wife, Ruth; by his third wife, Billings, who lived in Worthington. Lewis, who married Mary, daughter of Rev. Asa Todd, and had children, Jacob, who married Eliza Moore and Julia Prentice, and removed in middle life to Cummington. Almon married Lucy Clapp and removed to Westfield, Elzina married Chauncey Langdon, of Westhampton. Lucy E. married Madison Cudworth, of Chesterfield, Deliverance married John Cady, of Westfield, Elijah married Zilpah Collier and Elmira Prentice, and lives in Chesterfield, Catharine married James E. Westcott, of Westfield.

Nathaniel Bryant, grandson of Lieut. John Bryant, of Plymouth, removed from Plymouth in 1777 and located a little east of E. S. Kinne's present domicile. There is a pear tree now standing near the site of the house. He married Joanna, daughter of Ebenezer Cole, of Plymouth, by whom he had twelve children, two only of them born after their removal to this town. Of the two children who settled in this town, Betsey married Gideon Bisbee, Jr., and located on the "Mount," and Colonel Patrick, who married Anna, daughter of Capt. Thomas Halbert, and settled near the "Mount." Patrick had seven children, of whom Patrick, Jr., and Ann located in this town. Patrick, Jr., married Bricea Dumbleton, by whom he had five children who grew to maturity, viz.: Elizabeth, Royal, Orrin, Calvin and Edgar. They located and built the mills now owned by H. B. Smith & Son, and the father and sons were widely known in mechanical matters and also as forming "Bryants' Band." Ann married Obed Skiff, of Williamsburg, and lived many years on the old homestead. They had seven children, all living, but widely scattered.

The Baker family trace their genealogy back to Edward Baker, an Englishman, who, as one of Winthrop's colonists, settled in Saugus in 1630. The name is perpetuated in town by way of Elisha, who came from Northampton, married Alice Wilder and had nine children, of whom Elisha, Jr., who married Samantha Parker, of Peru, and lived where his son Levi now lives. Zeruah, who married Ralph Utley and located in Goshen ; Andrew K., who married Eveline, daughter of Luther Edwards ; Sarah, who married Darius Stephenson and Asahel Bisbee; Daniel C. who married Mary Ann Wilder, of Pittsfield, and Fanny, a daughter by a former wife, married Israel Graves, of Northampton. Joshua Healy lived in the northeast part of the town and was the father of Seth and Parley and grandfather of the present Seth A. Healy. Joshua was in the Revolutionary war and his sons in the war of 1812. In the Shays Rebellion Joshua made himself obnoxious to the neighbors, by taking sides with the government, to such a degree that his house was fired into, three balls lodging inside.

Zebulon Robinson located and lived to middle life where E. S. Kinne now lives. Later in life he purchased the old "Gate Tavern" of Daniel Littlefield and remained there till his decease. Of his children, Josiah settled in Worthington ; Asa located and kept store where Horace Cole now lives, just opposite the tavern kept by his father. He was also interested in the woolen manufacture and in the raising of silk. Eleazer occupied the old homestead till middle life, when he removed to Worthington, where he now resides. Silas carried on the tannery in the west part of the town several years, when he removed to Worthington and engaged in farming till the burden of years and bodily infirmities forced him to relinquish hard labor and tarry with some of his children. His present residence is Florence. His wife was Cynthia Potter, by whom he had twelve children, eleven of whom grew to mature age.

By old deeds in possession of the Nichols family, we learn that Job Nichols owned and occupied a homestead in Scituate, and that in 1752 he purchased of Joshua Oldham, of Scituate, an addition to the same. Job Nichols married Mehetabel Oldham, by whom he had two sons, Joseph, and one who was lost at sea, leaving no family. Job removed from Scituate to Pembroke and lived with his son Joseph till his decease in 1778. Joseph Nichols, son of Job, settled in Pembroke, in that portion now Hanson. He married Lydia, daughter of Gideon Bisbee, of Pembroke, by whom he had three children, two sons and one daughter. In the spring of 1794 he removed and located in Chesterfield, his mother accompanying him, where she deceased in 1804. His sons were Joseph and Jonathan B. The latter, about 1800, removed to Otisco, N. Y., where he settled as a farmer and general business man, reared a large family, and about 1830 removed to Pittsfield, Mich., where he deceased in 1834. Joshua remained at home, and in 1803, married Rebecca, daughter of Elisha Witherell. His family consisted of six sons and three daughters, two sons being the only representatives now (1886) left. Of these remaining sons, John is living in Columbus, Ohio, is a physician and druggist. Albert, to the manor born in 1812, still remains loyal, has resided here almost continuously from birth and still retains the old homestead of his ancestors. In 1838 he married Clarinda B. Johnson, of Williamsburg, by whom he had three sons, all .of them rendering service to the government in the land and naval forces. The youngest (John H.) still survives, resides in Haydenville, Mass. The others, Warner B. and William J., have been resting these many years among the multitude of their silent comrades in "God's silent acre," at Arlington, Va. This last representative of the Nichols family now residing here, has, we think, been favored with opportunities to enjoy a busy life. In addition to farming interests, engaged in school work, as a member of the school committee or teacher, or both since 1838, several years' service as selectman and assessor, etc., now rendering his twentieth year of service as town clerk and treasurer of the town, by the good will of his fellows occupying a seat in the legislature three sessions, then with a commission as a justice of the peace for twenty years, must, as we think, have furnished abundant opportunities for doing many little things, while leaving those of greater magnitude to more ambitious citizens.

Ezekiel Pierce. from Attleborough, married Wealthy, daughter of "Uncle" Solomon Livermore, who lived on the Clarke farm, and located at the foot of the "Mount" hill. He had one son and one daughter. His daughter married E. B. Taylor, of this town, and the son is still a bachelor of eighty-two, yet Asahel, "the Major," still blows his flute as satisfactorily to himself as in the old training days when he bore the commission of fife-major.

The Macomber family is of Scotch descent, tracing their family history back to the time of King Robert the Second of Scotland. They were among the first of the colonists bearing the honorable title of "Pilgrims," and located in Bridgewater and Easton, where David was born. On reaching his majority he left Easton in a company of emigrants to Chesterfield, where he located in 1773. After a short service in the Revolutionary war, and becoming unfit for further service in the field in 1776, he married Katharine, daughter of Daniel Littlefield, purchased the farm now occupied by a grandson, Joseph B., and settled there. Here he reared twelve children, of whom six removed to Westford, Vt., two to Ohio, and four passed their days in Chesterfield. Alvan, a son, married Mercy Noyes for his first wife, by whom he had one son, D. Wright. His second wife was Nancy, daughter of Joseph Burnell, by whom he had five children, Chandler T., James H., Sophronia, Joseph B. and Martha G. His third wife was Malinda (Bates) White.

From the most reliable sources at hand we find that Ebenezer and Consider Cole came to Ireland street among the earliest pioneers. Of the children of Ebenezer we find Joanna, who married Nathaniel Bryant, Rachel, who married Daniel Littlefield and lived opposite the present residence of Horace Cole; Ebenezer, Jr., and Elijah. Of the children of Consider we find Consider, Jr., and Amaziah. The children of Consider, Jr., were Consider, Samuel and Horace. The last named at present living in Pittsfield, at the age of eighty-seven. Of the children of Amaziah we find Amaziah, Jr., the father of John, Ephraim and Betsy (Mrs. Crozier). Most of these named had large families and their descendants are very numerous, but those named are the principal ones who preserve the family name in town. Of the children of Consider, Jr., Horace, Consider and Samuel, above mentioned, married sisters, daughters of Elijah Cole. Other children of Elijah were Nancy, wife of Lot Drake, Amos, of Worthington, Isaac, Elijah, Jr., Lydia and Sophia.

Prince and Barnabas Cowing, from places unknown, were among the pioneers and both were in the Revolutionary war. Of their descendants we find that John, a son of Prince, was the first child born in town. We also find Samuel, Calvin, Thompson, Thomas, Job and Gathelius. Job settled on the "Mount" and had a large family. Of the sons of Gathelius we find Job, the father of Lewis, and John, now living on Ireland street. One daughter married Elijah Cole, Jr.

Archelaus Anderson resided at the Center and afterwards where Dr. D. W. Streeter now lives. In 1805 he sold the Streeter place to Gershom Collier, just arrived from Boston, and bought the place where T. S. Ring now lives. Afterwards he sold this place to Elijah Graves and removed West.

Amasa Clapp settled where W. I. Rice now lives. Of his children are Ira (father of Ira, now living in town), and a daughter was Mrs. Alvin Rice.

Luther Curtiss's homestead in the east part of the town is now occupied by his descendants.

Samuel Reed settled on the "Mount." His children were Samuel, Daniel, Mrs. Joseph Nash, Mrs. Luther Tower, Simeon, Joseph, Mrs. Jacob Bates, Mrs. Thomas Stearns and Alanson.

Nehemiah Bates came to Chesterfield with his three brothers about 1771, and built the house which is now occupied by his great-granddaughter. He reared eleven children, of whom Solomon B. lived and died on the homestead. Hudson B., oldest son of Solomon B., was born September 11, 1802, married Judith Pynchon, February 7, 1825, and had born to him four children. One son died in the army, where he served as a corporal in the 52d vols. Mr. Bates was for many years captain of the old home militia, and was always known afterwards as Captain Bates. He served as town representative in 1850–51. He died October 3, 1884, aged eighty-two years, his wife having died ten years previous.

Dyar Bancroft, the fourth of the legal profession to settle in Chesterfield, and for more than half a century one of the most respected of the town's residents, was a grandson of Ephraim Bancroft, of East Windsor, and subsequently of Torrington, Conn., an officer of the Revolution. Ephraim married Esther Gleason, of East Windsor, Conn., who bore him six children, and lived to the great age of ninety-six years, dying in December, 1809, surviving her husband eighteen years, who died in 1791. Noadiah, the second of their children, married Jerusha Loomis, of Torrington. They both died in 1827, he surviving her from October 6th until November 28th of that year.

15*

Eight of their eleven children attained an adult age, viz.: Luman, Dyar, Erastus, Chester, Warren, Jerusha, Clarissa and Charlotte, only one of whom is living, Chester, a resident of Winsted, Conn.

Dyar, a brief sketch of whose life we trace, was born in Torrington, Conn., April 12, 1786. Prophetic of the erudition he in his future life was to possess, at the age of eleven years he began the study of Latin in the district school. He entered Yale college in September, 1805 ; but at the earnest solicitation of his friends he left in the following spring and entered Williams college. Among his classmates here were Samuel A. Talcott, of Hartford, Conn., afterwards attorney-general of New York, Samuel J. Mills and Darius O. Griswold, the latter of whom became the first settled minister of Saratoga Springs. Wholly uneclipsed by this array of talent, he graduated with high honors in September, 1809. He then went to West Brattleboro, Vt., where he engaged as a teacher in the academy which is still sustained there. In 1810 he made his first visit to New York, by the way of Hudson river from Albany, his journey from that point by sloop, the fastest transportation in those days, occupying six days. He soon after entered the law office of Hon. Daniel Dewey, of Williamstown, where he continued about one year, when he was appointed to a position as tutor in Williams college, which he successfully held for two years, and when he took his final leave was strongly urged by the trustees to remain as professor of languages. In the meantime he had continued his study with Judge Dewey, and continued so to do until December 13, 1813. On the 14th of February of the following year, 1814, at the sessions of the Berkshire county court held at Lenox, he was admitted to the bar, and immediately afterward settled in Chesterfield, where he remained until his death, September 13, 1866, aged eighty years.

Of the circumstances which induced Mr. Bancroft to locate here, and the sensations he experienced on his first arrival, we quote his own version : " This was the time of the last war," he used to relate, " and was rather a dull time generally throughout the country for my professional business, and it was a matter of great difficulty to find an opening of much promise ; and my friends thought this place had as many encouragements as any one I should be able to find, so I came on. I really believe it is written out in the great book of Heaven, how ardently and devotedly I prayed to God when coming up the everlasting hill, in four feet of untrodden snow, that I might never lay my bones in Chesterfield. Whereas, as I now feel (in 1858), if I could get at that great book, I should be tempted to make an erasure. I love the place —it is to me a perfect paradise—it is the birthplace of my children."

Three lawyers had preceded him here, the last being Benjamin Parsons. He purchased of Parsons an old arm-chair which had been in use by both the other lawyers, and which he used up to the day of his death, preferring it to a modern easy-chair. It was made a special bequest to his son William, who prizes it highly. He held many positions of trust and honor, was elected justice of the peace in 1814, which office he held to the time of his death;

was justice of the quorum, notary public for many years, and county commissioner ; through his old master, Judge Dewey, who was then a member of congress (1814), he established the first postoffice in the town, Phineas Parsons being the first postmaster, who accepted the office on condition that Mr. Bancroft should transact the chief business for him, he feeling incompetent for the task, though Mr. Bancroft was soon after appointed postmaster, and held the office more than a quarter of a century; he was first elected to the legislature in 1825, holding the office, with one exception, twelve consecutive years. He was very familiar with the general routine of legislative business, was always on some respectable committee, and very often its chairman. He was a prominent member of the Hampshire county bar, and was steadily advancing on the sure road to fame when, in 1834, he was sorely afflicted by the loss of his eyesight. In all of his earlier years in Chesterfield, his prospects, social, professional and political, were most promising, but after this affliction came upon him he was painfully handicapped, and lived in an eclipse.

May 25, 1815, Mr. Bancroft married Sally Hayes, daughter of Rutherford Hayes, of Brattleboro, Vt., granddaughter of Ezekiel Hayes, of Branford, Conn., and aunt to ex-president Hayes. They began housekeeping in Chesterfield, in the house now owned and occupied as a summer residence by the Rev. J. W. Chadwick, of Brooklyn. Their union was blessed with a family of four children, viz.: One daughter, Helen, who in 1834 married Hazelton Walkley, of Hartford, Conn., and shortly afterward moved to New York, where she spent most of her life, and where her husband died in 1864. She subsequently married Emmons Putney, of Goshen, Mass., where she died in 1868 ; Talcott and William, who still live on the homestead in Chesterfield ; and Edward, who died here in 1873. Mrs. Bancroft died August 31, 1882, in her ninetieth year.

"The Bailey Tavern building," which Mr. Bancroft bought early in his life in Chesterfield and made his family residence for forty years thereafter, was burned in December, 1859. His son William, then a merchant living in New York, came home and immediately re-built the present mansion, standing precisely upon the original site. In 1864 he replaced the old barns with a commodious new one, and with the other out-buildings the homestead makes one of the finest farm establishments in the county. William, with his family, have made this place their permanent home since 1864. His wife was Miss Julia A. Trowbridge, daughter of the late Henry Trowbridge, Esq., of New Haven, a distinguished West India merchant. They have three surviving children, Ellen J., Frederick H. and Eliza T. Talcott and William are the sole survivors of the only Bancroft family that ever lived in this town.

Physicians.— Dr. Robert Starkweather settled here in 1790, emigrating from Stonington, Conn. He studied with his brother Ezra at Worthington, and for fifty years was the only settled physician in town. His father and mother finally removed to Chesterfield and died here, the former in 1819, aged ninety-one, and the latter in 1824, aged ninety-three.   Dr. Robert died in 1858, aged nearly ninety-three.   Dr. Starkweather was succeeded by Drs. Ellis, Wilson, Perry, Richardson and D. W. Streeter.   The latter settled here in 1866, and has a wide range of practice in this and neighboring towns.

VILLAGES.

CHESTERFIELD is a fine post village located in the central part of the town, occupying a fine, sightly location, commanding a lovely view.   The village has a number of fine private residences, a town-hall, church, store, etc.   The first postmaster here was Benjamin Parsons, the present, William Baker.

WEST CHESTERFIELD village received its name when the postoffice was established here about 1850.   The postmasters have been Job Cudworth, James M. Angell, Ansel Thayer, Joseph W. Tirrell, Nelson A. Higgins and Dwight I. Stanton.   The postoffice occupies a building erected for the purpose of a store, postoffice and a public hall.   The latter is used for Sunday-schools, meetings, lectures, etc.

MANUFACTURES.

Ruins of mills and dams may be seen on most of the streams, but their history is lost in the treacherous memory of the oldest inhabitants and in the scarcely less trustworthy traditions handed down through the generations. Years ago large quantities of broom-handles were manufactured here ; but the tempting tobacco raising speculation has driven the raising of broom corn from the fertile valleys of the Connecticut river and ruined the broom business in this section.   The manufactures of the town are as follows:—

S. C. Damon's saw-mill bears the worthy distinction of being the oldest in town.   About 1760 Joseph Burnell emigrated from Dudley to this spot, and built a dam and grist-mill at what is known as the Narrows at the head of the present lower pond, and just below a beaver dam that existed at the time.   At the decease of Joseph Burnell the property passed into the hands of his son, Joseph, Jr., who built the dam now standing early in the century. For many years this dam served the purpose of a highway from Chesterfield to Goshen.   During the ownership of Joseph, Jr., a grist-mill, carpenter shop and blacksmith shop were erected and occupied by him, and after his decease by his son Francis, who inherited the mechanical genius as well as the property of the family.   At his death, in 1863, the property passed to William Baker, who had married one of the daughters, and from him the property went into the hands of the present owner.   " Burnell's Pond" is known far and near to fishermen, and a picnic ground on the shore of the pond is a favorite resort for Sunday School and Fourth of July festivities, and the immense quantities of blueberries in the vicinity help to make the place very attractive. The grist-mill has long since ceased its hum, and the carpenter shop has been converted into a dwelling house. The dwelling house has put on a more pretentious style of dress, but the old oaken bucket still hangs in the well as it has for more than a century, and children's children to the fifth generation have drank from its mossy brim.

Bisbee's mills.—The saw-mill on the east branch of the Westfield river was built prior to 1773, as it appears from the town records of that year that money was voted to build a bridge at that location. The mill afterwards passed to James Cox, and from him to Benjamin Pierce, who built a grist-mill on the east side of the stream. From Pierce the mills passed to Gershom Collier, who owned them till his death, when Elisha Bisbee purchased them, in 1819, of Collier's widow, and in 1823 erected the grist-mill on the west side of the stream. He also built a small shop in connection with this mill, using the dwelling house of Thomas Collier for that purpose. This shop was soon burned and the present shop was immediately erected. The present grist-mill was built in 1854. The present saw-mill was built by Orin and Osmon Bisbee, about 1840, and by them sold to Elisha and Andrew Baker, and by them to Orin Bisbee. The present owners are Orin Bisbee & Son, Horatio, the son, having purchased an interest in the property. The original dam stood near the mills, but for thirty years the water has been taken from the stream farther up.

H. B. Smith & Son's mill was originally built by Jonathan Burr, for a tannery. Chittenden, Job Cudworth, Silas Robinson, Alpha Thayer and P. H. Cudworth succeeded to the business, until about 1855, when the property passed into the hands of Patrick Bryant, who changed the business for the manufacture of seive-hoops, until February, 1866, when the mill was destoyed by fire, but was immediately re-built, a few rods below the original location, where it now stands. About 1877 the property passed into the hands of H. B. Smith, who, in company with his son, Thomas E., has continued the hoop business in connection with the lumber business, employing eight or ten hands usually.

S. A. Healy's mill, occupied by him in the manufacture of plane and saw-handles, and by Henry L. Eddy in the manufacture of gun nipples, and by Lyman Hitchcock in the general turning business, occupies the mill privilege originally constructed by William Williams, in 1839. The original dam was about 200 rods higher up the stream, and the mill about thirty rods above the present location. This property has had many owners. L. K. Baker and Rufus Hyde used it for a long time for a saw-mill, carding works, broom handle and button works, until about 1849, when G. W. Rhodes succeeded Baker and commenced the manufacture of plane handles in that year. In June, 1850, the dam was destroyed, and Rhodes substituted a steam engine in place of water-power, and in 1852 the present mill, which had formerly done good service at the Green Mountain academy, located at Worthington, was erected and run by steam till 1860, when Parsons & Healy became sole proprietors of the mill rights and erected the dam as it stands. About 1864

S. A. Healy became sole owner and continues the business, employing from three to six hands.   After the loss of the dam in 1850, Rufus Hyde conceived the idea and carried it into execution, of building a dam higher up the stream, bringing the water a part of the way on the opposite side of the river and thence across the river in a cylinder into the old canal.   This proved an expensive experiment, although temporarily successful.   Hyde and his wife were both drowned in a flood at Rowe, Mass., while trying to save his mill from destruction.

George S. Spencer's mill was originally built by Lyman Litchfield and Duandler Moore, for an iron foundry, and for many years the "Green Mountain" cook stove, made by Moore & Litchfield found a place in the kitchen of most farm houses in the vicinity.   Plows, cultivators and mop sticks were made in large quantities.   The business and mills were sold to Alpha Thayer & Son, about 1856, who carried on the same business several years.   In 1861 the foundry was burned, and immediately Edward Thayer re-built the mill as a grist-mill, and put in a new dam, where it now stands.   Several owners carried on the grist-mill till it came into the possession of George S. Spencer, the present owner, who exchanged the machinery for other kinds and has since carried on a business manufacturing factory supplies.

E. H. Higgins & Son's mill was originally built by Elisha Bisbee, about 1800, and the dam now standing includes the original dam.   Bisbee sold the mill to Capt. Joel Thayer, who occupied it till his decease, in 1832.   Reed & Tower owned it a long time, and through successive owners it has come down to the present.   The saw-mill was taken out many years ago, and the building is now used for the manufacture of gun tubes.

Hiram Higgins's saw-mill near the mouth of Dead branch, was erected about twenty years since, by Job Torrey and Dexter Damon, passing through the hands of several owners before coming to the present proprietor.   Just above this mill is a small establishment owned by Henry A. Weeks, and used for the manufacture of cutlery.

The Fiske saw-mill.—The saw-mill on Culver brook at present belonging to the estate of Rufus H. Fiske, was built about 1840, by Lyman Culver, passing at his decease to his son Horace and from his heirs to Rufus H. Fisk.   There is also a cider-mill connected with the saw-mill, where large quantities of apples meet a horrible death in the hope of an ignoble resurrection in the form of cider.

CHURCHES.

The Congregational church of Chesterfield.—There have existed a Baptist church and a Methodist church in Chesterfield, but as in most of New England towns the Congregational faith always was in the majority.   The Congregational society was formally organized, October 30, 1764, by Rev. Samuel Hopkins, of Hadley, and Rev. John Hooker, of Northampton.   There were seven members besides the Rev. Benjamin Mills, who had received a call from the town the preceding July, had accepted, and commenced his labors. He was installed as the first pastor of the newly formed church, November 22d, three weeks after the organization. The first members were Benjamin Mills, Joseph Burnell, Joshua Healey, David Stearns, Ezra May, Robert Hamilton, Benjamin Tupper and George Buck. The meeting-house was repaired in 1814–15, and stood till 1835. The new house was dedicated November 18, 1835. The society now has sixty-five members. Its pastors have been as follows :—

Rev. Benjamin Mills, 1764–74, continued to reside in town, and became prominent in public affairs during the Revolution ; Rev. Josiah Kilburn, 1780–81 ; Rev. Timothy Allen, 1784–96, remained in town and died in 1806, aged ninety-one ; Rev. Isaiah Waters, 1796–1831, died at Williamsburg, N.Y., 1851 ; Rev. Benjamin Holmes supplied the pulpit 1832–33 ; Rev. Israel G. Rose, 1835–42, he died while pastor, in 1842, aged forty-three ; Rev. Oliver Warner, ordained in 1844, services closed by reason of ill health, in 1846, but he, however, supplied the pulpit considerably before the settlement of another pastor ; Rev. Samuel W. Barnum, ordained in 1853, dismissed in 1855 ; Rev. John E. Corey, stated supply, 1856–59 ; Rev. J. W. Allen, 1859–62 ; Rev. William Rose, ordained in 1862, continued pastor till 1864 ; Rev. J. A. Wilkins, 1864–65 : Rev. Edward Clarke, 1865–72 ; Rev. I. P. Smith, 1872–73 ; Rev. William A. Fobes, 1873–81 ; Rev. Truman A. Merrill, 1882 –85 ; Rev. Elijah Loomis, 1885, now holds the position.

Baptist church.—By the records of the association, there existed a Baptist church in Chesterfield as early as 1780, but there is no record at hand dating farther back than 1789, at which date a meeting was held at the house of Zebulon Robertson (Robinson), where E. S. Kinne now lives, with Luke Bonney as clerk, and for a long time after the meetings were held at private houses. October 6, 1789, a committee consisting of Luke Bonney, Zebulon Robinson and Seth Taylor, was chosen to provide a "teacher." January 26, 1790, it was reported from this committee favoring and recommending the engagement of brother Vining as minister, and, the report having been accepted, it was voted to raise £45. 14s. 6d. by subscription, to defray the expenses of moving, ordaining, and furnishing a suit of clothes for him. June 15, 1790, Brother Vining was ordained pastor of the Baptist church in Chesterfield. In the following May it was voted to move the place of meetings to Mr. Stone's new barn, and in 1798 we find a meeting recorded at the meeting-house, with Dan Daniels, of Worthington, clerk, an office held by Daniels for thirty years, assisted in the latter years by his son, Ira Daniels. January 30, 1801, Samuel Kingman, of Worthington, and William Keene, of Chesterfield, were chosen deacons to wait on the church. In 1803 the name of Asa Todd, who had arrived from Whately, appears as the minister, and in 1805 Noah White was chosen deacon in the place of William Keene, who removed to the state of New York. January 31, 1807, Deacon Kingman was dismissed, and in March, 1808, David Macomber was chosen deacon, and in July 1815, Timothy Austin was chosen deacon in the place of Noah White, dismissed. In 1817 the name of Job Cudworth appears as one of the deacons. Deacon Macomber died in 1819, and subsequently the names of David Todd, Asa Robinson and Almon Higgins, appear as holding that office.

In 1817, by the death of one of the brethren, a fund was left to the church for the support of the communion table, and a committee, consisting of Deacon Macomber, Deacons Austin and Daniels, was chosen "to obtain the money left to the church by our brother Reuben Hitchcock, of Worthington." Previous to this time and, as tradition has it, long before the organization of the church in the west part of the town, there had been a small body of Baptists in the northwest part of the town, holding their meetings where Edgar Damon now lives, and in 1818 they erected a meeting-house in the east part of the town, a little East of Bisbee's mills, and from the records we infer that this was a part of the same church organization with the one in the west part of the town, with the same officers and minister.

November 2, 1820, Elder Todd was dismissed from the pastorate in consequence of a dissatisfaction among some of the members on account of his belonging to the Freemasons, a society not just then in very high repute, and added to this were difficulties of a more personal nature ; but he continued to reside in town till his death, in 1847, aged ninety-one. In June, 1822, Rev. Paul Hines was chosen pastor. At this date there appears 225 names on the church book as belonging to the church. Among them we find the names not yet extinct of Curtiss, Macomber, Hayden, Davis, Thayer, Torry, Bisbee, Litchfield, Bryant, Cole, Todd, Cudworth, Higgins, Stanton, Tower, Taylor, Cowing, Sampson, Angell, Bissell and Robinson.

From about 1822 the records are lost, and facts exist only as far as known in the memory of many now living, and although these facts exist, the precise dates may be lacking. About 1825 the meeting-house, a large rambling structure standing just above the present location of Asa Todd, where the road turns from Ireland street to Worthington, was taken down, condensed in its proportions and removed to the corner opposite the present house of Horace Cole. At about the same time the meetings in the east part of the town were discontinued, and Rev. Ambrose Day appears as pastor till about 1845. Some time during his pastorate it appears there were three deacons, Deacon Cudworth having removed from the east part of the town and located in the west part. But a difficulty having arisen in the church concerning the bequest of Reuben Hitchcock, previously mentioned, and which was left in trust to the senior deacon, Deacon Robinson, with about forty others, was expelled from the church. The main body of the church erected a new meeting-house at the center of the town in 1845, and Almon Higgins was chosen deacon.

This house was occupied about fifteen years, with Rev. William Smith, F. Bestor, Zalmon Richards and William Phillips as ministers or pastors, when, by the removal or death of many of the able and influential members, and the gradual depopulation common to these hill towns, the burden became too heavy for those remaining. The meetings were discontinued, and in 1874 the meeting-house was taken down. The church still (1886) keeps up its organization with about twenty-five members, who meet with other churches wherever they happen to be located, and the avails of the fund left the church by the late Dr. Robert Starkweather is used according to the terms of the will.

In 1825, in consequence of a change of views among some of the members living in the east part of the town, a portion, under the lead of Isaac King, Esq., withdrew and established a church known as the Free-will Baptist church, which occupied the meeting-house till 1845, when a new meeting-house at the Center was erected in connection with the Methodist church.

The Methodist church.—In 1843 several families of Methodist sentiment being resident in town, meetings were held in the town-hall, with Josiah Hayden and Mr. Morse, from Williamsburg, as leaders. In 1844 the conference sent Rev. Daniel K. Bannister, a native of this town, to conduct the meetings. In 1845, Rev. E. A. Manning was sent here, a church was formed and a house of worship erected. This house is the present town-hall, and is a neat and handsome building, founded literally " on a rock." In 1848 Rev. McClouth officiated for one year. In 1849 Rev. William Bardwell came here and remained two years. He was succeeded by Rev. I. B. Bigelow, who remained two years. In 1853 and 1855 Rev. John Smith was the preacher. E. B. Morgan succeeded him for one year. The last pastor was Rev. J. W. P. Jordan, who remained two years. The house was occupied several years by the Free-will Baptists and was finally sold to the town for a town-house. The church records were lost in the Mill river flood, May, 1874.

CUMMINGTON* is one of the western tier of the county's towns, and is bounded north by Plainfield, east by Goshen, south by Chesterfield and Worthington, and west by parts of Windsor and Peru in Berkshire county, having an area of 13,711 acres.

This town has been the birthplace of poets and statesmen, and has a record which compares favorably with many better known places. But the town has not yet awakened to a sense of her duty in having prepared a full and authentic history of the first century of her existence. Brief sketches to be sure have been prepared from time to time. It is the writer's purpose to add one more to this number, with the fond hope that it may enthuse its resident readers to search records and trace traditions, to learn more fully the pleasing story of the early life of their town—a story long, yet interesting, replete with pathos and humor. Limited space demands that our remarks

*Prepared by Miss Mary E. Dawes.

shall be a brief narration of facts.   Our authority in nearly every case are the records of the town or state.

Natural Features.—The surface of the town is broken, presenting charmingly diversified scenery.   Parallel ridges cross the town in a northeasterly direction and through the intervening valleys flow the several streams, though all are tributaries of the larger, the Westfield river.   The streams are locally known as Swift river, north branch of Swift river, Shaw brook, Roaring brook, Childs brook, Kearney brook and Whitemarsh brook.   A number of excellent mill sites are afforded.   There is good arable land with rich tillable soil, though stock growing facilities predominate.

Grant and Early Settlement.—On February 16, 1762, by an order of the general court, "Colonel Oliver Partridge and Mr. Tyler, with such as the honorable board may join" were appointed a committee to sell at public vendue ten townships included in Hampshire and Berkshire counties.   "Number 5," now Cummington, is desbribed as follows :—

"Also another township, to join west on the east line of said last mentioned township [number 4, afterwards Gageborough, now Windsor] and to extend east 20° south, and square off at right angles to make the contents of six miles square."

The committee reported the sale as having taken place on June 2, 1762, at the "Royal Exchange Tavern, in King street," Boston.   Number 5 was then sold to John Cummings for eighteen hundred pounds, he paying the required twenty pounds down and giving a bond for the remainder.   At a division of lots December 29, 1762, the names of twenty-seven other men are recorded as having become proprietors.

Tradition has uniformly fixed upon Samuel Brewer as the pioneer settler of the town.   We first find his name among those of the party sent here to survey one hundred lots in the summer of 1762.   Again, in the records of 1763, we find a deed from John Cummings to Samuel Brewer, transferring certain lots of land in "Plantation No. 5 ;" and we next see him climbing these rugged heights, hewing down the dense forest trees and making for himself a home near the old Indian trail from Northampton to Pittsfield.   He built his house near the south line of the farm now occupied by P. P. Lyman, and midway between the old Stephen Warner house and the Seth Porter place.   From here, unaided and alone, he opened a road nearly five miles through what is now Worthington to the place once occupied by Jonah Brewster, there striking the old military road from Chester to Bennington.   The time of Samuel Brewer's death and the place of his burial are not known, and diligent search has failed to discover even any reliable evidence in regard to the last years of his life.

Through the road which this pioneer had opened the settlers came rapidly into "Plantation No. 5," principally from Plymouth and Worcester counties.

But the story of these early times, as we have said, is vague and traditionary.   To be sure records are extant, but they have not, it seems, been thoroughly sifted.   The town was controlled by the proprietors, their names appear as settlers, when they were in reality non-residents; transients here to build mills or kindred work for the proprietors, are recorded as settlers; votes were passed for improvements, for public buildings, for organization—an array of facts that would naturally suggest a rapid and flourishing growth, when such was undoubtedly not the case. The settlement during those early years increased slowly. The population of the town in decades from 1790 appears as follows: 1790, 873; 1800, 985; 1810, 1,009; 1820, 1,060; 1830, 1,261; 1840, 1,237; 1850, 1,172; 1860, 1,085; 1870, 1,037; 1880, 881.

Changes in Boundaries.—In 1778 the general court was petitioned to set off one-third of the public lands of the town to "Gageborough," giving as a reason the difficulty of getting over the great hill which intervened between this third and the main portion of the town; also the difficulty of transacting town business, as this third lay in Berkshire county, while the other two-thirds were in Hampshire county. The petition was granted.

The State, for some public service performed, had given a certain tract of land to the town of Hatfield. This land was afterwards incorporated into the area of other towns, and a section further north and west was given to Hatfield in its stead. This latter was known as "Hatfield Grant" or "Equivalent." Plantation No. 5, when surveyed, was found to include nearly the whole of this "Equivalent."

In 1778 the inhabitants of No. 5 sent to the house of representatives a petition asking to be incorporated into a town, exclusive of this Equivalent. This petition was accompanied by one from the inhabitants of said tract, asking to be excluded from the act of incorporation, "because of the mountains and rivers that attend." It appears that this petition was not granted, for in the act of incorporation, in June, 1779, a part of the Hatfield Equivalent is included in the town of Cummington. This act made the west line of the town the same that it now is, the east line of Berkshire county. The east line of the town, however, begun at the lot of Joseph Warner, and running north, 19° east, crossed the East village near the Baptist church and extended in the same straight line to what is now the north line of Plainfield.

These boundaries, also, were soon changed, for in 1785 the district, then the town of Plainfield, was set off by the general court, by a line drawn east and west through the centre of the original town. In 1788 a considerable unincorporated territory lying between the then east line of Cummington and the towns of Ashfield, Goshen and Chesterfield was annexed to Cummington. In 1794 a small gore lying north of the southeast corner of Plainfield was set off to that town, and Cummington's present boundaries were established.

Organization.—The town was incorporated June 23, 1779, under the name it now bears, given in honor of one of its original proprietors, Col. John Cummings. The first town meeting was held at the house of Enos Packard, December 20, 1779, when William Ward, John Shaw and Ebenezer Snell were elected selectmen, and Barnabas Packard, clerk.

Educational.—The town has from the very first taken an unusual interest in educational advancement. As early as 1790 a building was erected for the purpose of opening a select school, or, as it was then called, an "Academy." It was situated on the road leading from the old Stephen Warner place to the house of Fordyce Packard. Col. William Ward took a great interest in this achievement, and it was largely through his liberality that the town was enabled to complete it. Some of the less sanguine ones christened it " Ward's Folly," and by that name it was long known. Many years later, when East Cummington had grown to be the business center, a large academy was built there and a flourishing school started into existence. Here the pupils were prepared for college, or armed themselves for the battle of life by a thorough practical education. During the reign of this school the number of college graduates from Cummington exceeded that of any other town of its size in the state. Since its abandonment there has been at various times a high school term during the winter. The large percentage of the inhabitants who have availed themselves of what educational advantages they could command, must account for the numbers that have been sent forth to occupy positions of trust throughout the land. Among those who have become illustrious or have achieved national reputation may be mentioned William Cullen Bryant, in the literary, and H. L. Dawes in the political world, as so well known that any remarks here would seem uncalled for. There is still another, John Howard Bryant, whose poetic genius and literary culture have given him a high place among the writers of our time. Others have shown large capacity in special research, viz.: Arthur Bryant, as a horticulturist and author of a standard work on forestry ; Cyrus Bryant, a chemist and geologist ; Dr. Oliver Everett, as a geologist and botanist ; Dr. Jacob Porter, whose discovery of that rare mineral Cummingtonite, procured for him a membership in the Northern Antiquarian Society of Copenhagan. Some of Cummington's sons have developed those sterling business qualities calculated to give pecuniary success in life, prominent among whom are the Shaw Brothers, the largest tanners in the world ; the Hayden family, whose mechanical skill gave them great wealth and high standing in the country. But these are only a few of the prominent men who have claimed the mountain town as a birthplace.

Lawyers.—Cummington has never proven a profitable location for lawyers. William Cullen Bryant, when a young man, tried one case here before his grandfather, Ebenezer Snell. A Mr. Cushing lived for some time here, but no records of cases tried by him are to be found. Horatio Byington, afterwards a judge of the court of common pleas, had an office in town for two years.

Physicians.—One physician or more the town has always had. Drs. Bradish, Mick and Fay were here before " Plantation No. 5 " became a town ; since then there have been the following : Drs. Peter Bryant, Howland Dawes, Ira Bryant, Samuel Shaw, Robert Robinson, Royal Joy, Abel Packard, Atherton Clark, Morris Dwight, Stephen Meekins, Beemis Brothers, William Richards, Thomas Gillfillain, Arthur Kimball and Walter A. Smith.

Biographical Notes —Dr. Peter Bryant, when a young man, came from Bridgewater to Cummington, where, in 1792, he married Sarah Snell. Their third son, William Cullen, born November 3, 1797, though never strong physically was always considered a precocious child. At nine years of age he began to write verses. At ten years he declaimed at school a poem of his own composition, describing a district school. At eleven, he was given as a task by his grandfather the first book of Job, to put in rhyme. At thirteen he wrote *The Embargo*, a satyrical poem which called forth much comment. During his sixteenth year he entered the sophomore class in Williams college; but finding some features of college life distasteful to his shy, sensitive nature, he obtained an honorable dismissal the next year. However, in due time he received a degree as member of the class of 1813. In 1817 the *North American Review* published his *Thanatopsis*, of which Professor Wilson said, " It alone was sufficient to establish the author's claims to the honors of genius." Mr. Bryant studied law with Judge Howe, of Worthington, and afterwards with William Baylies, of West Bridgewater ; was admitted to the bar at Plymouth, in 1815 ; practiced one year in Plainfield, then removed to Great Barrington, where he met Miss Frances Fairchilds, who became his wife in 1821. Several of his poems were addressed to her, and he once called her the "good angel of my life." In 1825 he went to New York, and abandoning the law determined to become a man of letters. He edited a monthly magazine for one year, before becoming connected with *The Evening Post*. He assumed editorial charge of that paper in 1836, a position he held until his death. Between the years 1834 and 1867, inclusive, he made six visits to Europe, and in 1872 a second voyage to Cuba and the city of Mexico. His *Letters of a Traveler* give interesting accounts of these journeys. He spent the winters in New York, and divided his time during the summers between "Cedar-mere" his place at Roslyn, Long Island, and " The Homestead," at Cummington, which he purchased and re-modeled in 1866. His last public utterances, the final sentences of his address at the unveiling of the statue of Mazzini, were a fitting close for a life which for purity and sweetness has not been excelled. At the close of these exercises Mr. Bryant walked about two miles under a burning sun. At the end of the walk he fainted, and in falling, struck his head, causing an injury of the brain which resulted in his death fourteen days later, and on June 12, 1878, he was laid to rest in the pretty cemetery at Roslyn, Long Island.

Howland Dawes, born in 1766, came with his father's family, from Abington, to Cummington in 1773. He studied medicine with Dr. Peter Bryant, and for about fifty years practiced his profession here. He never married, making his home with a brother. His genial, social nature made him many friends, and his kindly, urbane manners made him a welcome visitor at every fireside. And the name of Old Dr. Dawes still brings with it a smile and a pleasing anecdote from the older inhabitants of the towns in which he practiced. He died in 1844, and lies in the cemetery east of Mr. Charles Dawes.

Henry L. Dawes, born October 30, 1816, graduated at Yale in 1839, studied law at Greenfield, while acting editor of the *Greenfield Gazette* and afterwards in Albany with the firm of Cagger & Stevens, was admitted to the bar about 1842, practiced at North Adams and edited the *North Adams Transcript* for several years ; and had been a member of the Massachusetts legislature—serving in both houses—for six or eight years, when, in 1857, he was elected to the house of representatives, where he served eighteen years. He entered the senate in 1875, and served two terms, having, during this long period of public service, discharged all duties devolving upon him with conscientious fidelity, to the satisfaction of his constituents and honor to himself. Francis H. Dawes, born May 11, 1819, has always lived in Cummington. He has been fifteen years assistant assessor, thirty years a magistrate, and fifteen years a trial justice. He married Melissa Everett, in 1847. Has had charge of Bryant Homestead for over twenty years.

Peter Tower, a decendant of John, who came from Hingham, England, about 1838, was one of the early settlers of this town. His son Stephen married a Miss Bowker, and reared thirteen children. His son John was born in Cummington in 1781, married Ruth, daughter of Rev. Jesse Reed, and had born to him seven children, viz.: John M., Salome, Coleman, Dexter, Laura, Roswell and Russell. Of these, four are living, John M., Dexter, of Williamsburg, Laura (Mrs. Cephas Thayer), and Russell of Worthington. The last mentioned married Rebecca Granger, and has two children, Coleman E. and Mary E. Dexter married Irene Pierce, and has four children, namely, Clinton B., C. Belle, Lizzie J. and Pearly D.

Stephen Tower was born March 8, 1778, came to Cummington in 1781, married Milly Bartlett, of Bridgewater, Mass., December 15, 1803, and had born to him seven children, as follows : Wealthy, Pamelia, Calvin B., Parmelia, 2d, Zilpha, Anna and Luther. Wealthy and Luther are the only ones living. Luther was born December 13, 1819, married Sabrina Tower, November 25, 1841, and has four children living, namely, Mary A., Henry L., Charles W. and Adella A. He resides on the homestead on road 55. His father died June 7, 1856, and his mother died August 18, 1864.

Lorenzo Tower, a direct decendant in the seventh generation of John Tower who came from Hingham, England, resides in this town on road 31, and is librarian for the William Cullen Bryant library.

Daniel Nash was born in 1743, and came to this town in 1788. He married Susanna Richards, October 7, 1773, and had born to him twelve children, namely, Susanna, Daniel, David, Susanna, 2d, Sarah, David, 2d, Sally, Mary, Asa, Olive, Jairus and Iantha. David, 2d, was born August 4, 1784, married Ruth Colson, June 3, 1813, and lived on the homestead. He died April 30, 1856. His children were as follows: David, Sarah, Caroline, Daniel, Susan, Edwin, Mary and Webster. Of these Sarah and Mary are living. The latter lives on the homestead.

Asa Porter was born January 25, 1771, came to Cummington in 1795, and settled on road 45. He married Elizabeth Huntington in 1797, and reared eleven children, two of whom are living, Mary and Milton. The latter was born July 27, 1806, married twice, first, Miss L. Hume, who bore him three children, Harris H., Ralph M. and Julia H. The mother of these children died March 29, 1857, and Mr. Porter married for his second wife Clarissa K. Bisbee, who died February 8, 1886. Mr. Porter and his son Ralph reside on the homestead, on road 45.

Wareham Hitchcock was born February 29, 1796, married Olive Clough, of Belchertown, in 1815, and moved to Chesterfield in 1826. After living there two years, he moved to Cummington, locating on what is known as " the Mount." He finally moved to Swift River, first building a house and grist-mill on road 34, and in 1843, built a house and saw-mill on road 35. He reared eleven children, viz.: Dwight W., Julia A., Jane M., Levi L., Lewis F., Nancy J., Lyman H., Henry H. and Eliza, now living, and Olive L., who died December 31, 1879, and Lewis O., who died in 1825. Mr. Hitchcock died October 13, 1869, and his wife died April 19, 1867. Henry H. resides on the homestead at Swift River, is postmaster, and part of his house is used as the postoffice.

Arunah Bartlett was born March 30, 1797, and married Amanda Tower, March 13, 1824. Mr. Bartlett resides on road 56, where he has lived for fifty-two years.

Hiram Steele was born in Weathersfield, Vt., in 1799, married Rebecca Witherell, of Chesterfield, in 1834, and came to Cummington, in October, 1838, locating on road 48. He has had born to him three children, namely, Isaac H., Mary J. and Lucius. The last mentioned married Adelaide Clapp, of this town, and resides on the homestead with his father.

VILLAGES.

CUMMINGTON village is located just east of the central part of the town, in a narrow valley. In its vicinity the scenery is unusually picturesque and romantic. The village has a number of fine residences, and with its schools, churches, business interests and dwellings, presents a pleasant appearance. Thomas Tirrell was the first settler here. The postoffice was established about 1716, with Maj. Robert Dawes, postmaster. The present incumbent of the office is Theron O. Hamlin.

WEST CUMMINGTON is a pleasant little post village, located in the northwestern part of the town, on the Westfield river. It was mainly founded by William Hubbard, who established a tannery here in 1805, and Elisha Mitchell, who established a store here in 1823. About this time the postoffice was established, and Mr. Mitchell made postmaster. The present postmaster is Luke E. Bicknell.

SWIFT RIVER, the latest established of the town's three post villages, is pleasantly located in the southeastern part of the town, at the junction of the two branches of Swift river. The postoffice was established here in 1869, with William H. Guilford, postmaster. The present postmaster is Henry H. Hitchcock.

HOTELS.

The first hotel was owned by William Mitchell, and stood where C. C. Streeter now lives. Another early hotel was kept by Asa Streeter, on the farm now owned by H. A. Streeter. Adam Packard opened a public house on Cummington hill, and at a later date Seth Williams established a store and hotel at the village. In 1821 Levi Kingman opened a hotel here. The present hotel, known as the Valley House, was built by William White, in 1846. The later proprietors have been E. B. Bruce, C. M. Babbitt, R. W. Shattuck and F. L. Holmes, the present proprietor.

INDUSTRIES.

Cummington has always been a manufacturing as well as an agricultural town. During the first years of settlement measures were taken to induce parties to purchase and build here. In September, 1764, the owners of the town agreed to give Charles Prescott one hundred acres of land if he would "build a saw-mill on the north end of lot No. 45." The old foundation may still be seen on the land of O. B. Bartlett, near the dwelling of Jacob Higgins. This was the first mill in town; but set·back as it was on the hills, it soon gave way to the more substantial and easily accessible mills built on the river, which was then a much larger stream than at present. There were at one time two cotton and four or five woolen mills; but with the exception of one small woolen-mill these have all long since disappeared.

B. E. & C. M. Bradley's variety wood-work shop, on road 33, was established by them in 1877, where they manufacture all kinds of variety wood-work, the principal market for which being New York city. The site they occupy was formerly occupied by the cabinet shop of Ebenezer Gilbert. This shop was burned and re-built in 1846.

The L. L. Brown Paper Co. are engaged in the manufacture of bond and linen paper here, employing twenty-five hands. The present firm took possession in 1886. The officers are L. L. Brown, president; T. A. Mole, treasurer; and John Wiethuper, superintendent. The mill was erected in 1856, by J. D. Nelson.

Nathan S. Stevens & Son's mill, on road 32, was established in 1860. During that year N. S. Stevens purchased the factory of Alanson Bates, where he did quite a business in sawing and planing and the manufacture of pen-holders, and was also connected with A. Rhoades in the manufacture of scythe stones. The latter connection he severed in 1865, continuing the former till

1874, when he admitted his sons A. S. and A. V. as partners, and added the manufacture of brush blocks and handles. In February, 1883, the building was destroyed by fire and immediately re-built, and subsequently the manufacture of lead pencils was added. In 1884 A. S. Stevens died, since which time the firm name has been Nathan S. Stevens & Son. The firm imports its own leads for its pencils directly from Germany, in 10,000 gross lots, and its machinery is original with it and especially adapted for its own work.

H. F. Bradley is engaged in the manufacture of pencils, pen-holders and brush handles, and also does custom sawing. His mill is located on road 18.

CHURCHES.

In 1771 the proprietors located a "meeting-house spot" very nearly in the geographical center of the town, which was on the rocky ledge northwest of what is now known as the "Daniel Dawes place;" but when they found how unsuitable it was, a dispute arose as to the proper locality. This dispute lasted seven years and was only settled when, a part of the town having been set off to Gageborough (now Windsor), the center of Cummington was changed. Meantime a meeting-house had been built by private individuals near the "four corners," between the Adam Porter and Squire Snell farms. After the set off to Gageborough the town bought this meeting-house, and moving it about a mile east on to the old "Meeting-house Hill," enlarged it by putting a section in the middle. Services were held in this church till another was built, a few rods south of it, in 1839. The first act of the town as a corporate body was the installation of a minister of the gospel. Before this time Rev. Mr. Hooper, Jesse Reed, Mr. Porter, Mr. Billings and Mr. Hotchkiss had officiated at brief intervals, but no minister had been settled until on the 7th of July, 1779, the little church consisting of eight male members ordained Rev. James Briggs. According to the terms of purchase two lots were set off for the minister at the first division, and these were on the west side of Remington hill, a very unsuitable place to locate the people soon discovered, and Mr. Briggs was given land in another part of the town. He officiated for forty-six years. This first Congregational organization existed for eighty-nine years. When it became extinct, two organizations were formed and churches were built, at East and at West Cummington. A Baptist church was organized in 1821, and about 1837 a Methodist church was built at "Lightning Bug," midway between the two villages. This church as well as the one on the hill was removed several years ago. There are now four churches in town, two Congregational, one Baptist and one Universalist.

The Village church of Cummington was organized July 1, 1839, by forty-seven members dismissed from the First Congregational church, Rev. Royal Reed being their first pastor. The society now has one hundred and forty-three members, with Rev. Franklin G. Webster, pastor.

16*

The Congregational church of West Cummington was formally organized September 1, 1841, though the building was erected in 1839. The present pastor is Rev. Joseph B. Baldwin.

The Baptist church at Cummington village was organized in 1821, with fourteen members, the first pastor being Rev. Asa Todd. The church building was dedicated February 5, 1825. The present pastor is Rev. George E. Spaulding.

The Universalist Church of Cummington.—As early as 1835 occasional Universalist meetings were held here, and in 1839 a council of Universalist churches was held in Cummington. The present church building was erected in 1845–46.

———

E ASTHAMPTON* is, in point of area, the smallest town in the county; but in point of population, learning, wealth, manufactures, beauty and general thrift and prosperity the township ranks among the largest. Its area is 6,613 acres, lying in the southern part of the county, bounded north and east by Northampton and the Connecticut river, south by a small part of the county line and Southampton, and west by Southampton and Westhampton.

In surface, the little township is quite level, though having mountains on either side, lying nestled at the very base of the bold and rugged Mt. Tom range. No more delightful location could be opened to the summer resident, and not a few avail themselves of the fact. Here one may enjoy the blending of the beautiful, picturesque and even sublime in nature, charming drives and a healthful climate, without dispensing with any of the comforts of city life—a fine library, congenial society, banks, and stores of all kinds, while landlord Johnson of the Mansion House furnishes a *cusine* inferior to none. The soil of the township is deep, moist and fertile, and the farms well cultivated and remunerative.

Two branches of Manhan river, one flowing south from Westhampton, the other north from Southampton, unite upon the western border and flow eastward through the center of the town to the Connecticut, joining the lattter at the south part of the Oxbow. The tributaries of the Manhan from the north are Pomeroy brook, Saw-mill brook and several smaller rivulets. It has one tributary from the south of considerable importance, named Broad brook. This furnishes the power for most of the great manufactories. Broad brook has a small tributary in the south part of the town called Rum brook.

Settlement.—Originally and for many years Easthampton was a part of and subject to the jurisdiction of Northampton. Its Indian name was *Pascommuck.* The first white settler in Pascommuck, then, was John Webb. His land was

———

*For this brief sketch of Easthampton we acknowledge our indebtedness to the writings of Rev. Payson W. Lyman, of Belchertown.

granted to him December 13, 1664, and he soon after located upon it, near the present Henry Clapp residence. Of Webb's subsequent history little is known, and some authorities place his death in 1670; but be this as it may he had two sons, and his widow married Robert Danks, of Northampton. His descendants were residents of Easthampton for three quarters of a century or more.

In 1668 the the first bridge over the Manhan river was voted. This was located near Webb's home, not far from where the meadow road now crosses the stream. Just across the Manhan from Webb's home, also, was a beautiful plateau. This was the location of the next settlement, and which bore the Indian name of *Pascommuck*. The settlers here were Moses Hutchinson, John Searle, Benoni Jones, Samuel and Benjamin Janes, with their families. To these were home lots granted in 1699.

On the morning of May 24, 1704, there descended upon this hapless hamlet a marauding band of Indians. Nineteen of the settlers were killed, nine of the name of Janes, either here or shortly after capture. Benjamin Janes escaped, and rowing to Northampton across the flooded meadows, gave the alarm. A troop of cavalry, under Capt. John Taylor, started in pursuit, who encountered the Indians, but with no other result than the death of nearly all the captives, and of Capt. Taylor himself. More than ten years elapsed before this ruin was repaired, but at length others came in to take the places of the ill-fated ones, some of them being children of the slain.

Twenty-five years before the settlement at Pascommuck, or in 1674, Northampton gave "David Wilton, Medad Pumry and Joseph Taylor liberty to erect a saw-mill on the brook, on the right hand of the cart-way going over Manhan river." Twelve years later, 1686–87, they voted Samuel Bartlett liberty to set up a corn-mill " on the falls below the cart-way on the river." The cart-way was just above the covered bridge at the foot of Meeting-house hill. These mills were doubtless built soon after, though their owners did not effect a residence here. Samuel Bartlett gave the corn-mill to his son Joseph, in 1705, who made the first permanent settlement in the region of the present village, probably as early as 1725 or 1730. His house he kept open for the accommodation of travelers for twenty years. His nephew, Jonathan Clapp, ancestor of all the Clapps here, lived with him and succeeded to the greater portion of his estate, and to his business. About the same time at which landlord Joseph Bartlett built his house, his brother David settled some forty rods westerly from the Julius Pomeroy residence, and after him his son lived there till near or quite the time of the Revolution. Between the homes of the Bartlett brothers was the home of four brothers named Wait.

Twenty years later, May 28, 1745, Dea. Stephen Wright and Benjamin Lyman bought of Northampton the Upper School Meadow, a tract of eighty acres of land, lying on both sides of the river above the cart-way, which the town had set apart for the support of schools. They were the ancestors of the Wrights and Lymans of Easthampton, and, until recently, most of their lands have been held by descendants.

Not far from 1732, Samuel and Eldad Pomeroy settled upon what is now the Hannum homestead. In 1742 the Pomeroys entered a protest to the general court against being set off from Northampton with the then recent settlers in what is now Southampton, who were moving for a separation, and with whom they had had no connection. In their address, they state that they had improved their lands, and paid taxes on them for forty or fifty years. This would seem to show that their land came under cultivation not later than 1700. They were afterwards, at their own request, received into the new society at Southampton.

As early as 1750, Josiah Phelps established himself upon Park hill, upon the place for many years occupied by J. Rockwell Wright.

The first settler upon the plain upon which the village stands was Sergt. Ebenezer Corse, who built a house where Spencer Clapp formerly lived, and cut his road for a mile through the forest to this point. He was followed soon after by Stephen Wright, Jr., and Benjamin Lyman, Jr., sons of the purchasers of School Meadow, and also by Benjamin and Aaron Clapp. The first settlement in the southeastern part of the town was effected by Israel Hendrick.

The settlement gradually increased so that in 1790 the first government census gives the town a population of 457 souls. The steady increase from that down is given by the following figures, a record for each decade since : 1800, 586; 1810, 660; 1820, 712; 1830, 745; 1840, 717; 1850; 1,342; 1860, 1,916; 1870, 3,620; 1880, 4,206.

Organization.—Just before the Revolutionary war some steps were taken to establish a separate town. The people upon the territory now included in Easthampton expressed their views by petitions to Northampton and South-ampton in 1773. In the former town a committee reported favorably, and the report was adopted. Southampton opposed the proposition, and the troubles of the Revolutionary period delayed any further action until 1781–82. The project was then revived, but required several years of effort to secure the act of incorporation, which was passed by the general court in the summer of 1785.

Robert Breck, Esq., of Northampton, issued a warrant for the first meet-ing. It was directed to Benjamin Lyman, and the people met accordingly at the house of Capt. Joseph Clapp. The territory was set off as *a district*, having all the rights of a town except that of representation in the general court. This district feature was a remnant of colonial policy, intended to retain power in the hands of the royal authorities, by not allowing a rapid increase of the people's representatives in the legislature. The policy sur-vived the Revolution, districts continuing to be incorporated for a few years.

The name Easthampton was rather appropriate, not so much from its loca-tion, as from the fact that the three other Hamptons were already named, and it needed this to complete the natural series. And, though almost inclosed by the others, this town extends at one point to the *east* line of the original tract, and has so far a right to be called Easthampton.

The act incorporating Easthampton as a district was approved by Governor Bowdoin, June 17, 1785. The warrant was issued June 29, 1785. It was directed to Benjamin Lyman, who "truly and faithfully notified and warned the inhabitants."

The list of officers chosen at this meeting, Monday, July 4, 1785, was as follows: Robert Breck, moderator; David Lyman, clerk; Aaron Clapp, Jr., constable; Jonathan Clapp, Capt. Philip Clark and Enos Pomeroy, surveyors of highways; Stephen Wright, Capt. Philip Clark and Eleazer Hannum, selectmen and assessors; Joel Parsons and Benjamin Lyman, tithingmen; Obadiah Clark and Lemuel Lyman, Sabbath-wardens; Daniel Alexander, surveyor of shingles and lumber; Solomon Ferry and Elijah Wright, fence viewers; John Brown and Joel Hannum, howards; John Clapp, David Chapman, Jr., and Elisha Alvord, hog-reeves; Capt. Joseph Clapp, treasurer; David Chapman, clerk of the market; Zadock Danks, sealer of leather; and Benjamin Clapp, packer.

The first municipal meetings of the inhabitants were held at the " dwellinghouse of Capt. Joseph Clapp," down to July 13, 1785, when they were held at the church for nearly half a century. In 1833 a town-hall was built, and was superceded by a new structure in 1842. This in turn did service till 1868–69, when the present elegant building was erected, at a cost of $65,000.00.

Military.—Except the massacre at Pascommuck, no Indian troubles disturbed the peace of the settlement, except in one instance when Nathaniel Edwards, of Northampton, was shot and scalped here in 1724. Alarms there often were, but no serious results followed.

Several who resided within the present limits of the town were in the battle near Lake George, in 1755, in connection with the Hampshire regiment which suffered so severely on that occasion. Eliakim Wright, son of Stephen Wright, was among the slain. Lemuel Lyman, son of Benjamin Lyman, was saved from a fatal wound by his bullet pouch, which checked the bullet which struck him.

Among those who served in the Revolution were Capt. Joseph Clapp, Capt. David Lyman, Quarter-Master Benjamin Clapp, Dr. Stephen Wood and his sons Daniel and David, John Clapp, Jonathan Janes, Benjamin Lyman, Samuel Judd, Stephen Wright, Jr., David Chapman, David Clapp, Joel Parsons, Levi Clapp, Phinehas Clark, Eliakim Clark, Barzillai Brewer, Zadock Danks, Stephen Wright, —— Brooks, Daniel Braman and Willet Chapman. Dr. Wood died in service at West Point, David Clapp never returned from the war, and Messrs. Brewer and Chapman both died in the army. Moses Gouch, who was brought up in Easthampton, served through the war and was suddenly killed here in 1797.

In the war of 1812 the town sent out the following: John Alpress, Elisha Alvord, Worcester Avery, Levi Brown, George Clapp, James Clapp, Philip Clark, Gershom Danks, Stephen Hendrick, Moses Gouch, Luther Pomeroy, Spencer Pomeroy, Jesse Ring, Harris Wright, Collins Wood, Ebenezer Wood, Thaddeus Parsons and Jesse Coats.

For the late great war Easthampton furnished 200 men, a surplus of eighteen over all demands, five of whom were commissioned officers. The whole amount of aid paid solely by the town was $30,367.00, while the the amount of aid to families, subsequently refunded by the state, was $6,705.03.

Notes.—Lemuel Lyman was born August 28, 1735, married Lydia Clark, and died July 16, 1810, aged seventy-four years. His children were as follows: Lydia, Lemuel, Justus, Ahira, Sylvester, Daniel, Esther and Elihu. Ahira located on the plain, west of the Center, building for himself the house now occupied by Elijah A. Lyman. He died November 1, 1836. His son Quartus P. was born here December 28, 1809, married Tryphena Wright for his first wife, November 7, 1832, who bore him two children, a daughter, who died in infancy, and John W., born November 9, 1836. The latter married Lucy Matthews, has two children, Carrie T. and Quartus, and is engaged in the wholesale vegetable and fruit business in Northampton, where he resides. Quartus P. married for his second wife Amelia Smith, June 26, 1851, and resides on road 26, where he has lived fifty-four years.

Eliakim Clark, son of Dea. John Clark, came to Easthampton at a very early day. His sons, Obadiah, Asahel and Job settled near him. Job was born September 10, 1733, married Eunice Strong, and reared six children. His son Luther moved to Skaneateles, N. Y., but soon after returned. He married Deborah Robinson, January 28, 1802, and his children were as follows: Luther, Alanson, Jason, Horace, Rowland, Emeline, Maria, Harriet, Cornelia and Cordelia (twins), Elvira and Henry. Henry was born in this town October 17, 1824, married Climena T. Benton, March 23, 1854, and resides on the homestead which is located on road 17. Horace was born in Skaneateles, N. Y., November 16, 1808, and came here with his parents when eight years of age. He married Lois Janes in 1833, who bore him three children, Emily J., George and Flora L. Mrs. Clark died April 20, 1880. George was born February 27, 1842, and married Hattie Cooley, who died in 1875.

Franklin W. Janes, son of Luke, who was a native of this town, was born here November 13, 1828, married Harriet A. Clark, and has had born to him one son, Harry L., born in June, 1873, and died November 21, 1880.

Israel Hendrick was the first settler in the southeastern part of the town, locating there about 1774. His son James moved to the opposite side of the brook, reared eleven children, viz.: Jesse, Pearson, who died in early childhood, Huldah, James, Lovy, Reuben, Joseph, Stephen, Pearson, Jabez and Rachel. Joseph was born November 24, 1790, married Lovina Newhall, and reared five children, only one of whom is living, Joseph N. He was a very energetic man, and lived to be over eighty years of age, up to which time he was engaged in business. Joseph N. was born July 17, 1824, and married Miss R. J. Olds, October 7, 1846. He has always lived on the homestead with the exception of about seven years spent in Wisconsin. He deals largely in live stock, and is located on road 30.

Pearson Hendrick married twice, first, Mary Mosely, and second, Elisheba Newhall, who bore him ten children, as follows: Daniel N., Mary L., Sarah B., Martin V. B., Sarah L., Charles B., Mary V., Huldah J., Ellen M. and Pearson. Mr. Hendrick died February 22, 1870, and his widow died March 4, 1886. Charles B. was born July 5, 1841, married Abby C. Barnes, December 25, 1865, and has had born to him thirteen children, namely, Charles Alfred B., Martin V., who died in 1872, Jennie, who died in 1873, Leslie N., who died in 1876, Oseola, who died in 1876, Lester B., Abbie I., Mary B., Ella B., Arthur G., Frank H., who died in 1885, and Lucy.

Stephen Hendrick was born July 9, 1792, married Nancy Phelps, March 1, 1821, and had born to him seven sons and three daughters. He was a soldier in the war of 1812, and died August 8, 1871, and his widow died in 1883. James M., son of Stephen, was born March 28, 1833, married Cornelia Sperry, February 1, 1876, and has had born to him one son, Lewis S., December 22, 1878. Mr. Hendrick has been engaged in railroad contracting until within the last few years, and is now located on roads 32 and 26, engaged in farming.

Theodore H. Hendrick was born May 10, 1822, married twice, first, Parmelia Ashley, and second, Mary L. Wood, of Plainfield, N. Y.

Benjamin Strong, great-grandfather of Calvin L., was the first settler in the Strong settlement, located in the southeastern part of the town. He came here from East street with his wife and son, all on horseback. Benjamin, Jr., married Dolly Wood, and reared nine children. C. L. and Calvin S. Strong now live on the homestead. C. L. married Lida Upson, October 8, 1879, who died December 20, 1885.

Stephen Wood was born July 7, 1774, married twice, first, Jemima Clark, who bore him four children, and second, Sally Braman, September 4, 1821. By his second wife his children were as follows: Ezekiel, who died December 28, 1864, Enoch E., Spencer C., Newton and Sarah. Enoch E. was born July 15, 1825, married three times, first, Achsah E. Strong, who bore him two children, Hattie E. and Edward E.; second, Miss S. E. Tilden, and has had born to him one child, Charles A.; and third, Carrie A. Frary, October 3, 1883. Newton, son of Stephen, was born April 16, 1828, married Mary M. Stebbins, July 30, 1856, and has had born to him three children, namely, Arthur N., Wallace W. and Francis. Mr. Wood served in the late war, in Co. K, 52d Mass. Vols. He is a carpenter and lives on road 27.

John M. Clapp, son of John, was born in this town, August 2, 1814, married twice, first, Lucia M. Frost, May 14, 1837, who bore him two children, George M. and Frederick O. The former resides in Westfield, and the latter died in 1871. The mother died May 12, 1862, and Mr. Clapp married for his second wife, Sophia Chapman.

Edmund Parsons was born in Northampton, January 20, 1803, married Emeline E. Morgan, and reared four children, namely, Eliza S., Sarah J., Harriet and Lucius E. Mr. Parsons died May 27, 1867, and his widow died in April, 1877. Lucius E. was born in Easthampton, May 19, 1841, married twice, first, Emily W. Ferry, January 25, 1866, who bore him one child, Herbert S., and second, Clara M. Clark, December 31, 1867.

Joel L. Bassett was born January 13, 1825, and married three times, first, Phœbe Thompson, who bore him children as follows : Nancy L., Elizabeth and Justin H. He married for his second wife, Lucy A. Dudley, who bore him two children, Cynthia L. and Joel, both deceased. He married for his third wife, Fannie W. Rogers, July 2, 1886. Mr. Bassett came to Easthampton in 1854, has been engaged as a contractor in stone mason work, has built the foundations of most of the finest buildings in town, and also built the mill dam. He was one of the company of the Mt. Tom thread mill, which was incorporated in 1873. Previous to this the mill was used as a saw-mill, and was burned 1882.

Gerard Searle was born in Southampton, March 7, 1778, married Salome Burt, February 20, 1816, and reared six children, viz. : Rhoda, Sloan, Sophronia, Luther B., Charles H. and Alvin C. Charles was killed in the late war, at the battle of the Wilderness. He served in Co. F, 27th Mass. Vols. Gerard died July 29, 1869, and his wife died November 14, 1863. Luther B. was born in Southampton, May 10, 1825, married Eunice Ranger, October 16, 1850 and came to Easthampton in 1866. He has had born to him seven children, as follows : Lelia A., born August 2, 1852, married Edward H. Clark, and resides in town ; Emma E., born in 1856, died in 1858 ; Frank L., born in 1859 ; Hattie E., born in 1861 ; Emma E., 2d, born in 1863 ; a daughter who died in infancy ; and Lewis H., born in 1872, and died in 1873. Mr. Searle has served as selectman from 1879 to 1885.

Dr. Frank C. Bruce was born in Peterborough, N. H., was educated at the Peterborough high school, Phillips academy, Andover, Mass., and University of Vermont, Burlington, from which institution he received his degree of M. D. He then returned to Peterborough, where he resided until October 13, 1885, when he located in Easthampton, where he now resides.

VILLAGES.

EASTHAMPTON village impresses one at first sight as a bright, business-like, busy manufacturing place—and this impression is perfectly correct. The streets of the village are broad, shady and pleasant, and lined with good, substantial, often elegant residences. It has also acres of extensive manufactories, two banks, several churches, the well known Williston Seminary, an elegant library building, beautiful town hall, and rows of business blocks.

The history of the village begins almost with that of the settlement, at least with the incorporation of the district. It grew up near the old mill of the Bartlett's, authorized by the town of Northampton in 1675, which we have already alluded to. One of the first to open a store here was Joseph Clapp, opposite the present store of A. J. Lyman, on Main street, in 1792. The postoffice was established here in 1821.

MT. TOM is a hamlet in the northeastern part of the town, at the junction of the Mt. Tom railroad with the Connecticut River road. There is also a postoffice at this village.

GLENDALE is the name given to a hamlet that has grown up about the elastic fabric mill, located in the northwestern part of the town.

MANUFACTURES.

Williston & Knight Co.—This firm is extensively engaged in the manufacture of covered buttons. The business was established by Samuel Williston, who moved his factory here from Haydenville. In 1847–48 Horatio G. Knight entered into partnership with Mr. Williston, under the firm name of Samuel Williston & Co. A little later Seth Warner was admitted, and the firm name changed to Williston, Knight & Co. The business was carried on thus till December 1, 1865, when a stock company with a capital of $150,-000.00 was formed, under the name of the National Button Co. This name was changed by the legislature in 1880, to the Williston & Knight Co. Mr. H. G. Knight has thus been actively engaged in the business for forty years, a great part of the time as general manager. The present building was erected in 1861.

The Nashawannuck Manufacturing Co.—The company was established in a small way, as the Samuel Williston Co., in 1850. In 1852 they received their charter from the state and changed to the present corporation, with $100,000.00 paid up capital. Since increased to $300,000.00. In 1853 the amount of business was largely increased by the purchase of the right to use Goodyear vulcanized rubber in the manufacture of elastic fabrics. They were the first in the country to use vulcanized rubber with fibrous material in the production of elastic goods. The amount of their production has steadily increased until to-day they are the largest manufacturers of suspenders and narrow webs in this country, if not in the world, employing over 500 hands in weaving and finishing suspenders, garters and other narrow elastic fabrics. E. H. Sawyer, Esq., was their first treasurer and general manager, continuing in office until 1879, when the present treasurer, G. H. Newman, was elected. C. Myer, of New York, is president. All goods are sold from their selling house, 74 and 76 Worth street, New York.

The Glendale Elastic Fabrics Co.—In 1862 a company consisting of H. G. Knight and E. H. Sawyer, of Easthampton, and William and C. G. Judson, of New York, was organized under the title of the Glendale Vulcanized

Rubber Company, with a capital of $50,000.00. Their business was the manufacture of elastic cords, frills, and other similar goods. They located at the place now known as Glendale, in the western portion of the town. They enlarged and occupied a building that had been occupied as a manufactory of twine and batting by Gregory & Wells. In 1864 they rented the two upper stories of the large brick factory erected by the Rubber Thread Company, near the Easthampton depot. Their operations were transferred to the village. They bought out the Goodyear Company in June, 1865, and their business rapidly increased until they occupied four mills. In 1867 something of a re-organization took place, and the name was changed to its present form. The machinery was brought from England by Hon. E. H. Sawyer, as an agent for certain New York capitalists. At about the same time the company bought the elastic cord and braid business, originally started by Lieut.-Gov. Knight, and they have since successfully connected both the goring and braided goods, together with the weaving of narrow-loom or garter-web, and have brought the standard of their productions up to that of the best goods made in Europe. The line of work embraces a wide variety. The present officers are Samuel T. Seelye, president, and Joseph W. Green, Jr., treasurer and manager.

Easthampton Rubber Thread Co., manufacturers of rubber thread of all sizes from fine Para rubber. This company was formed in November, 1863, with a capital of $100,000.00, and immediately began active operations. The managers had had previous experience in the business, and were thoroughly acquainted with the needs of the elastic fabric manufacturing business, and were determined to supply them. With this end in view, they employed the latest and best mechanical aids and gathered a corps of skillful workmen. Their productions were at once received with great favor, and gave such satisfaction as to call for increased facilities. In 1869 the capital was increased to $150,000.00, and their business greatly extended. Their line of work is confined exclusively to the manufacture of rubber thread. They buy only the best quality of rubber, the "biscuits" being expressly selected for this company in Brazil. Every step of the conversion from "biscuits" to thread is taken within the company's works. The last processes are rolling the rubber into sheets of such thickness as may be necessary to make the size required, and then cutting the sheets into strips whose width equals the thickness. The present officers are Chistopher Meyer, president, and E. T. Sawyer, treasurer and general agent.

The Williston Mills, extensively engaged in the manufacture of fine cotton yarn, were established by Samuel Williston in 1859. The present company was incorporated in 1866, with a capital of $350,000.00. The president is John J. Haley, of Boston.

The Valley Machine Co., extensively engaged in the manufacture of steam pumps, was originally established in 1868, as the Easthampton Steam-pump and Engine Co. In 1870 the Valley Co. was formed, and purchased the business. This company at first received a charter, but surrendered it in 1873, and organized on a partnership basis, with John Mayher, treasurer and manager.

N. O. Dibble's suspender factory was established by him in 1870. He employs five hands in the manufacture of shoulder-braces and suspenders. Mr. Dibble came to Easthampton from Granby, Conn., in 1865.

Hannum & Bosworth's saw-mill, on road 20, was established by them in 1884. They employ six hands and manufacture 6,000 feet of lumber per day.

Martin Rich's brick yard, on Clark street, was established in 1864, and taken by Mr. Rich in 1867. When in full operation Mr. Rich employs thirty hands here.

BANKS.

First National Bank.—Early in the days of the National banking system the need of banking facilities was strongly felt by the business men of Easthampton. The nearest bank was four miles away, at Northampton, and Greenfield and Brattleboro institutions were utilized to some extent. On April 23, 1864, the organization of the First National Bank of Easthampton was completed in the old town-hall. Samuel Williston was the first subscriber, taking 400 shares of the stock. Officers were chosen as follows: president, Samuel Williston; directors, H. G. Knight, E. H. Sawyer, Ebenezer Ferry and Levi Parsons; cashier, Eli A. Hubbard. The capital was $100,000.00, which was increased the next year $50,000.00, and again in 1869 to $200,000.00. Office room was obtained in the second story of the Preston's block until, in 1871, their present banking house was completed at a cost of $18,000.00. The lot was purchased of the town, and is a part of the old first burial ground. Mr. Williston remained president until his death, in July, 1874, when vice-president H. G. Knight was chosen. Cashier E. A. Hubbard soon resigned to accept a position on the state board of education. C. E. Williams acted until 1877, and Albert D. Sanders served till 1883. The present officers are, president, Samuel T. Seelye; directors, John Mayher, E. R. Bosworth, G. H. Newman and William G. Bassett; cashier, C. H. Johnson. The bank was re-chartered in 1883, for twenty years. Forty-four dividends have been paid, aggregating $342,663.00. The present surplus is $50,000.00, with undivided profits $5,000.00.

The Easthampton Savings Bank was organized June 7, 1870, and is located in the same building as the National Bank. The officers are John Mayher, president; O. G. Webster, secretary, and S. T. Seelye, treasurer.

GAS WORKS.

The Easthampton Gas Co. was organized September 7, 1864, with a capital of $20,000.00, which was increased April 23, 1866, to $30,000.00. Ebenezer Ferry was the first president, and Horace L. Clark, treasurer. The present officers are E. T. Sawyer, president; H. L. Clark, treasurer; and G. L. Manchester, superintendent.

WILLISTON SEMINARY.

This school was founded in 1841. It owes its existence to the generosity of one man, Samuel Williston, to whose business sagacity the growth of the town is largely due. During his lifetime he gave the seminary more than a quarter of a million dollars. Four large brick buildings occupy the school campus, three boarding-houses are located in different parts of the village, and the Williston homestead is used as the residence of the principal. The expenditure for apparatus and laboratories has been large and unusual in schools of this grade. Thus, while the school has been a classical academy, especial prominence has also been given the scientific department. At his death, Mr. Williston left the school an additional endowment of $400,000.00. Half of this was paid to the trustees upon the settlement of the estate. The remainder, in the form of two trust funds of $50,000.00 and $150,000.00, is accumulating and will become available when they have doubled.

Every school which lives and grows receives another endowment from those who serve on its boards of trust and instruction. In this second endowment, which cannot be enumerated in cash and real estate and apparatus, the seminary has been grandly enriched. To Tyler, the Wrights, Clark, Henshaw, Hubbard, Hitchcock and their associates in the past, and to others, the naming of whom might seem invidious, in more recent years the institution is indebted for its intellectual and religious impress. They have kept it abreast of the thought and claims of our time and land. It began as a local school and the founder thought it might remain such, but these other founders have made it national.

Fortunate in its location and rich in its endowments, the school has also been prospered by its patronage. It began as a school for both sexes, hence the name seminary was adopted. The ladies' department was suspended in 1864, and the seminary has been an academy for boys since that date. About 7,000 pupils have been gathered during its history. One fifth of these have been prepared for admission to colleges and other higher institutions of learning. More than 600 of these have received college degrees, of whom one-third have entered the gospel ministry, another third have become lawyers, and the remainder have entered the professions of medicine, teaching or journalism.

The present principal is Rev. William Gallagher, A. M., and the president and treasurer of the board of trustees is A. Lyman Williston, Esq., of Northampton.

CHURCHES.

The First Congregational church of Easthampton was organized November 17, 1785, with seventy-two members, over whom Rev. Payson Williston was installed as pastor, August 13, 1789. He held the pastorate till 1833, and the pastors since have been Revs. William Bement, 1833-50; Rollin S. Stone, 1850-52; A. M. Colton, till the present pastor, William F. Bacon, succeeded him a few years since. The first church building, erected in the spring of 1785, occupied the present site of the park. The present building was erected in 1836-37, though it has been extensively re-modeled and repaired since. It is now valued, including grounds and other property, at $20,000.00. The society has 428 members.

The Payson Congregational church was organized July 8, 1852, with 100 members, over whom Rev. Rollin S. Stone was installed as pastor. Their church building, erected in 1852, was burned January 29, 1854, and another, partly finished, was destroyed by fire September 1st of the same year. The present building was erected in 1855. It is a brick structure capable of seating about 700 persons, and is valued, including grounds and other property, at about $30,000.00. The society now has 460 members, with Rev. Charles H. Hamlin pastor.

The Methodist Episcopal church was organized by its first pastor, Rev. S. Jackson, with fifty-three members, in April, 1863. The church building was dedicated December 12, 1866, and cost $16,396.36, including furniture. In 1882 they built a chapel at a cost of $4,000.00. Rev. James F. Mears is the present pastor. The society has 150 members.

St. Philips Mission Episcopal church was organized in 1871. The building was erected in 1885, at a cost of $4,000.00. The society now has sixty-four members, with Rev. Charles W. Ivie, rector.

The Immaculate Conception Roman Catholic church was organized by Rev Father Moyce, in 1872. The first pastor was Rev. Father Toomey. In 1872 a church building was erected, a wooden structure, which was superceded by the present brick edifice in 1884. It will comfortably accommodate 850 persons and is valued, including grounds and other property, at $60,000. The society now has 1,500 communicants, with Rev. R. F. Walshe pastor.

ENFIELD lies in the extreme eastern part of the county, and is bounded north by Pelham and Prescott, east by Greenwich, south by Ware, and west by Pelham and Belchertown.

The surface of the town is sufficiently diversified to present a pleasing, picturesque landscape, while it is not so broken as to retard cultivation of the soil to any considerable degree. Great Quabbin mountain is the principal elevation. It lies just south of the village and has an elevation of about 500 feet above Swift river. Mt. Ram, north of the village, attains an altitude of about 300 feet, while Little Quabbin, lying northeast of the village, is smaller. These constitute the principal elevations. In fact, ridges of high and wood land extend north and south throughout the township. The town is well watered by the east and west branches of Swift river, the latter of which separates Enfield from Belchertown. The east branch furnishes several fine mill privileges. Cadwell creek, a tributory of the west branch, waters the western section of the town, while several small brooks exist in other parts. The soil is productive, yielding average crops.

Settlement, Organization, etc.—Enfield originally formed a part of Narragansett Township No. 4, which included the present town of Greenwich and a part of the " Equivalent Lands " as described in the history of Belchertown, page 180. This whole tract was given the general name of Quabbin, after a celebrated Indian sachem, and is supposed to mean "many waters." For the facts which brought this early grant into existence we refer the reader to the sketches of Greenwich and Chesterfield.

On June 29, 1749, Quabbin was granted an act incorporating it into a parish, by which provision the inhabitants were empowered to call a minister and levy a tax for his support. This form was continued till April 20, 1754, when an act was passed making Quabbin parish a corporate township, under the name of Greenwich. As the settlement expanded, however, it became inconvenient for those living in the southern part of the town to go to Greenwich village to transact public business, or attend religious meetings. Accordingly, June 20, 1787, an act was passed incorporating the southern part of Greenwich into a separate parish, known as the South Parish of Greenwich. On February 15, 1816, this parish was incorporated as a separate township, under the name of Enfield, deriving its name from Robert Field, one of the early settlers. The boundaries of the new township are set forth in the act of incorporation, as follows :—

" That all the lands in the towns of Greenwich and Belchertown, which are comprised within the limits of the South Parish, of the town of Greenwich, as they are now settled and established according to the provisions of an act entitled ' An act to divide the town of Greenwich into two parishes, and for including the northeast corner of the town of Belchertown in the South Parish,' passed on the twentieth day of June, in the year of our Lord, one thousand, seven hundred and eighty-seven ; an act in addition thereto, passed on the twenty-second day of February, in the year of our Lord, one thousand, seven hundred and ninety-two, together with the farm of Robert Hathaway, in said Greenwich, with all the inhabitants dwelling thereon, be, and hereby are, incorporated into a town by the name of Enfield, and vested with all the powers, privileges, rights and immunities, and subject to all the duties and requirements of other towns in the common wealth."

An inscription on the tomb-stone of David Patterson, born in 1735, states that he was the first child born in Greenwich. He was a son of John Patterson, who is said to have been the first white settler to locate within the present limits of Enfield. He located about a mile south of the village, upon the Josiah W. Flint farm. He brought with him two sons, William and James, who soon after located in the southern part of the town, upon what is known as the McMillin farm. Among the other early settlers and families of prominence may be mentioned the following :—

John Patterson, with the Stevensons (of whom David was one), and the McMillins, who settled in the town soon after Patterson, about the year 1742, were Presbyterians, from the North of Ireland. The young Pattersons were " mighty hunters " and expert wrestlers. David Patterson had three sons—Robert, Oliver and John. He was a superior wrestler, and it is said that on one occasion a messenger came down from New Salem for him at midnight, to visit the latter place to wrestle with a man who had overthrown all competitors. He responded to the call, laid the champion on his back, and returned the same day. Of the Stevensons, there were four brothers, Edward and Isaac were hatters, and lived and worked in the Hooker house ; their shop for felting and dyeing hats was on the bank of the river below the house. John lived on the farm situated on the hill north of the Lamson place.

Another settler of the town was John Rea, who resided, in 1764, south of the village, near the Bondsville road. Several brothers lived in town about the same time. They were large land-owners, and built several houses. Some of them subsequently removed to Pittsford, N. Y.

A man by the name of Carver settled early in the town, and owned a large tract on the southern side of the Swift river, including the farms of S. Boynton and S. S. Pope, and a large strip of land on that side down to the Cabot place.

Other families who settled early in the town, all of them prior to 1793, were Sylvanus Howe, son of Lieut. Howe ; Daniel Howard, who located on the " old Howard place," where his father had preceded him ; David Newcomb, who lived in the eastern part of the town ; Capt. Joseph Hooker (grandfather of Gen. Joseph Hooker, prominent in the late war), who was a large tract-owner in the town, owning most of the land between the two villages, and who lived on the spot now occupied by the residence of Edward P. Smith ; Robert Field, also a large tract-owner, and a man of enterprise, public spirit, and great personal popularity, and who lived opposite the present residence of Charles Richards, Esq.; Benjamin Harwood, who early left Hardwick, where he was born, settling first in Greenwich, where he married a daughter of Rev. Robert Cutler, the first minister of that town, and who settled finally at the upper village of Enfield, where he passed the remainder of his life ; Nathan Hunting, who settled on the Cabot place, and early engaged in the business of a miller ; Caleb Keith, who settled in the western part of the town ; William Stone ; James Richard, who was born December 13, 1766, and who finally settled in the eastern part of the town ; Joseph Ruggles, who lived about four miles south of the village ; Abner Eddy, who resided where Washington Aldrich now lives ; Ebenezer and Barnabas Rich, the first of whom owned an early grist-mill in town, and lived where Benjamin Harwood now resides, and the latter of whom served in the Revolutionary war ; Joseph Fobes, who lived in the southern part of the town ; William Morton, who lived on the old Monson turnpike, where L. M. Morton now lives, and Nathaniel Lane, who lived about half a mile south of the village.

Other families were those of Oliver Kingsley, who lived in the southern part of the town; Phineas Howe, John Rich, father of William, who lived where the Thurston family now resides; Moses Colton, who occupied the house now the Swift River hotel; Simeon Stone, who lived in the old "Fleming House;" Paul Paine, who resided on the old Monson turnpike, near the Richards place, and was a sea captain; Rufus Powers, who resided at the upper village; Ichabod Randall, who came from Bridgewater and settled as early as 1775 in Enfield, in the southern part of the town, on the place now occupied by Alvin Randall, and whose descendants still live in town; and Simeon Waters, who settled early in the town and was a cloth-dresser and a wool-carder by trade, and who removed to Millbury about 1830.

Other early names are those of Rider, Caldwell, Clifford, Colburn, Drake, Collins, Wheeler, Mitchell, Lathrop, Ruggles, Swetland, Pratt, Underwood, Winslow, Bailey, Rice, Briggs, Gross, Gibbs, Clark, Torrance, Lyman, Osborne, Forbush, Messinger, Woodward, McIntosh, Adams, Chickering, Bartlett, Shearer, Newell, Gilbert, Hanks, Barton, Lamson, Kentfield, Weeks, Cary, Snow, Pope, Smith, Hawes, Woods and Jones.

Dea. Aaron Woods was born in New Braintree, Mass., in 1763. He was the only child of Aaron Woods, who, with a number of brothers, came to New Braintree from Marlboro, Mass., where the old Woods' house is still said to be standing. The Woods families are said to have settled in Marlboro when they came from England. Dea. Woods came to Enfield, with his newly married wife, Sarah Bridges, in 1785, and settled on Great Quabbin, buying his farm for £80. To the year of his death in 1845, he was a devout Christian. Faith had the first place in his heart, conscience ruled his life. To no man—certainly to no layman—does the church in Enfield owe more than to Deacon Woods. Dr. Robert McEwen, for twenty years pastor of the church, once said "the foundations of this church were laid on Great Quabbin Hill." So faithful was Deacon Woods to his spiritual office that he made an effort every year to meet every fellow church-member for converse on personal religion. The following anecdote illustrates his conscientiousness. On one occasion he sent his son Moses to buy a yoke of oxen for $80.00. Moses beat the seller down to $75.00. This so disturbed his father that the young man was obliged to carry the extra $5.00 back to Amherst and deliver it to the former owner of the oxen. Like Abraham, however, Dea. Woods ruled his house well. All his ten children are buried in Enfield. Anna, the youngest, died at the age of four, Jonathan Edwards died in early manhood, leaving his young wife, Caroline Mattoon, and his only child. Of the daughters, Sally and Catharine never married. Patty and Serene were married to Ichabod Pope, Esq., and the three surviving children of Serene—Mattie Woods, Charles F. and William H. Pope, live in Providence, R. I. Of the four remaining sons, Aaron, the oldest, spent much of his early life in Canada. He died in Enfield, in 1871, esteemed by all for his Christian intelligence and his courtly manner. Moses, second son of Deacon Woods, was a dyer. He is chiefly remembered as an imitable story-teller, full of humor and mimicry. He also distinguished himself when young, as a wrestler, but after he had been one night dragged out of bed, transported ten miles to meet a new rival, and broken his adversary's leg in the first trial, he abjured the sport. Leonard and Josiah B. were for a long time associated in the manufacturing business in Enfield, first making card clothing, afterwards woolen goods. Leonard had few equals as a business man. Josiah B., an excellent business man, was also a skillful mechanic. The invention of the machine for setting the teeth of card clothing is claimed for him. Aside from his constant devotion to the church, of which he was a member, Leonard gave his attention to little outside of the claims of his business. Josiah B., early in its history became interested in Amherst college, largely on account of his personal friendship for Dr. Edward Hitchcock. He was member of the Massachusetts senate in 1845–46, and of the constitutional convention in 1852–53. He married Francis C. Belcher, daughter of Joshua Belcher, of Boston. They had eight children, four of whom died young. Charlotte J., who married E. P. Smith, died in 1881; Fanny C., who married Capt. W. B. Kimball, lives in Enfield, on the old homestead; Mary P., wife of Prof. W. E. Chandler, of New Haven, Conn.; and Robert M., who graduated at Amherst college in 1869, and is now pastor of the Congregational church in Hatfield, Mass. The older sons of Deacon Woods all had large families, and his descendants are scattered from the field of the Nestorian Mission, in Persia, to California. Unfortunately comparatively few bear his name. The surviving descendants in Enfield are J. E. Woods, J. B. Woods and Miss Carrie M. Woods, children of Aaron Woods; Mrs. William B. Kimball, daughter of J. B. Woods; and Mrs. George C. Ewing, Jr., granddaughter of Leonard Woods and daughter of Hon. Rufus D. Woods. He was the oldest grandson of Dea. Aaron Woods, and was born in Enfield, May 1, 1818. He was graduated at Williams college in 1838, and afterwards devoted himself to business, for many years in Enfield, and for some time in Holyoke, where he was president of the Hadley Falls bank. He afterwards retired from business and was prominent in politics and served as representative and senator in Massachusetts, also as a member of the executive council with Governor Long. He traveled extensively, and died in Australia, in September, 1884.

Rev. Joshua Crosby, the first pastor of the church in Enfield, was installed in 1789, and retained the pastorate until his death, in 1838. He served in the Revolutionary war and was chaplain in the war of 1812. He was one of the first trustees of Amherst college, and after the death of the first president, filled that position until another could be chosen. He married Lydia Terry in 1790, and reared seven children, namely, Betsey R., Lydia T., Sophronia, Joshua K., Ansel, John and Austin. Mr. Crosby died September 24, 1838, aged seventy-seven years. Betsey R. married Nathan Hooker, of Hadley, and her children were Betsey, Austin, Luther, Lydia, Mary, Joshua and Jane. Lydia T. married Col. Thomas Ashley, and their

17*

children were Jonathan, John C., William, Mary and Joseph. Sophronia mar-. ried Timothy Brainerd, of Palmer, whose only son, John C., resides in Amherst.   Joshua K. married Minnie Sears, of Williamburg, and their two sons, Benjamin F. and Joshua, now reside in that town.   Ansel married Eveline Chamberlain, and their children were John Marshall, Jane E., George A., Luther and Lyman.   John married Rebecca Converse, who died in 1834, and in 1836 married Harriet Beers, and his children were Rebecca C., who married Charles E. Davis, M. D., of Greenwich, Lydia A., Mary D. F. and Nela.   Austin married Mary Beals, and had no children.   John M., son of Ansel, married Sarah Lodica Shaw, and has had born to him three children, namely, John M., who died in 1878, Luther, ho died in infancy, and Frank S., who is engaged in the merchantile trade in Ware.   Mr. Crosby is a member of the present legislature.

Abner Eddy, an early settler of this town, came here from Cape Cod, and settled on the farm now owned by Henry Squires.   He married twice, first, Elizabeth Cotton, and second, Dorcas Gross.   Abner, Jr., one of his fourteen children, was born April 15, 1788, married Mary Robbins, and reared eight children, viz.:   Maria, Henry, Eliza, Mary, Jane, John, Duran and William. John married Sarah, daughter of Michael Gross, and has six children, as follows: Emma, Mary, Stella, John M., Delia and Sadie.

Jonah Gross, an early settler of this town, came here from Truro, Mass., and first settled on the farm now owned by John Eddy, who married Sarah, daughter of Michael, and great-granddaughter of Jonah.

Solomon Howe was born September 14, 1750, graduated from Dartmouth college, was a Baptist minister, and lived in various places, residing for a time in this town, where he officiated as a minister.   He was also a teacher of subscription schools, married Polly Holmes, in 1778, and reared nine children, viz. :   Abigail H., Hannah, John, Nancy, Solomon, Jonah, Jedediah, Silas W. and John M.   John Howe was born in Brookfield, December 20, 1783, and in 1791, came to Enfield with his father who settled on the farm now owned by Samuel L. Howe.   He married Rhoda B. Babbet, and reared six children, as follows: John H., Myra M., Frances M., Henry C. M., Bolivar J. and Fenelon W.   Early in 1800 Mr. Howe learned the art of printing, and in 1804, printed the first number of the Howe genuine almanac, which he continued up to 1826, making his own calculations.   He also published hymn books and spelling books.   John H., the oldest son of John, was born in this town, October 24, 1816, married Melissa J. Lemon, and reared nine children, viz. :   Fannie, Mary, Carrie, Jennie, Emily, John H., Hattie A. and Samuel L.   Henry C. M., was born January 10, 1823, married Theodosia Johnson, July 20, 1848, and has had born to him four children, namely, Henry J., William F., Edwin H. and Lillian.   Edwin H. graduated from the Eastman Business college at Poughkeepsie, in 1882.   William F. married Hattie Hubbard, and is engaged in mercantile trade in this town.

Reuben Shearer, son of Reuben, was an early settler in this town, and had

·seven children, viz.: Reuben, James, Field, Pierce, Charles and two daughters. William, brother of Reuben, built a house in 1779 on the farm now owned by Lyman F. Shearer. He reared a family of four children, William, Reuben, Sophia and Fanny, and subsequently moved to Cortland, N. Y. William, the eldest son, married Rachel Haskell, and had born to him five children, namely, John, Fanny, Seth, William and Reuben. Charles married Ruth, daughter of Isaac Gleason, and had two children, Jane and Lyman F. The latter, who lives on the homestead, married Frances, daughter of William Shearer, of Cortland, N. Y.

David Newcomb, son of Ebenezer, came to this town about 1782, locating on the farm now owned by James McCort. He filled many town offices, and built the first Congregational church in Greenwich. He married Elizabeth Goss, and reared nine children. Nehemiah, son of David, was born in 1762, came to this town with his father, married Hannah Thayer, and reared six children. Foster, son of Nehemiah, was born in this town, on the farm now owned by his son Leander W., January 26, 1789, married twice, first, Hannah Latham, who bore him one child, Bethany, and second, Fanny Collins, and had born to him seven children, viz.: Jason G., Anson F., William P., Gamaliel C., Leander W., John H. and Fanny L.

Nathaniel Chickering, son of Nathaniel, was born in Dover, Mass., came to this town about 1800 and purchased the place now owned by his son Otis. He and his father built a grist-mill here, which he continued to run until 1819, when the dam was swept away by a freshet. He married Fannie Nelson, and reared six children, viz.: Darius S., Fanny E., Lucy, Nathaniel, Otis and Betsey T. Otis married Sarah Winter, and has one child, Darius O., who resides on the homestead with his father.

Ephraim Richards was born in Dedham, March 2, 1774, came to Enfield about 1810, and transacted business here as a merchant and a manufacturer, accumulating great wealth. He married Susannah Holden, and reared children as follows: Alona M., Fanny F., George L., Susan P., Charles, William H., Dexter N. and Isaac N. Richards held many offices of trust, and died January 20, 1862. Charles was born September 30, 1818, married twice, first, Caroline C. Clark, who bore him four children, viz.: Charles E., of Waltham ; Edward S., of Boston ; Joseph C., of Hartford ; and Frederick B., who graduated from Amherst college in 1885, and resides in Michigan. The mother of these children died January 5, 1872, and he married for his second wife Lorana S. Hunt, and has had born to him two children, Caroline C. and Raymond H.

James Richards came to this town from Bridgewater, was an early settler, married Sarah, daughter of Dea. Ebenezer Rich, and in 1800 moved on to the farm now owned by Arvilla Richards.

Benjamin F. Potter was born in North Brookfield, married Lydia Day, and came to Enfield in 1825. He had born to him five children, namely, Joseph

A., Nathan, both deceased, one who died in infancy, Henry M., of North-ampton, and Lyman D., of this town.

Dr. William Stone was an eminent physician, practiced here for many years, and reared a family of six children, viz.: William, Rufus, Clark, Sarah, Mary and Eliza L. He died here February 7, 1839, aged seventy-nine years. Clark was born March 30, 1788, married Mary Nichols, and had born to him six children, as follows: William P., Sumner, James, John H., Percy and Mary.

Benjamin Harwood, son of Abel, was born in Hardwick, married Eliza-beth Cutler, and reared seven children, viz.: Betsey, Abel, Ruggles, Harriet, Harlan, Ezra and Bernice. Abel married Polly, daughter of Benjamin Town-send, of Greenwich, and had born to him six children, as follows: two who died in infancy, Benjamin T., Ruel S., and Myron W., of this town, and Charles E., of Fairfield, Neb.

Asahel Blodgett came to this town when very young. His son David was born in Amherst, March 12, 1807, married Sarah Dickinson, and came to this town in 1832. He has had born to him two children, David H. and Sarah D., both deceased. He moved on to the place where he now resides in 1834.

Jonathan Towne was an early settler of Greenwich, locating on the farm now owned by George Kelley, and reared six children, viz.: Jonathan, Rufus, Orin, Freeman, Eliza and Sally. Jonathan married Abigail Gleason, and reared nine children, as follows: Joseph W., now in Florida, Loriston H., de-ceased, William B., Andrew J., Loriston H., Elmer E., Abbie E., who mar-ried Nehemiah Doubleday, Maria M., who married George W. Foster, and Theodosia. William B. married Elizabeth Curtis, and has six children, namely, Carrie L., Benjamin W., Ernest E., Ida Bell, Alice C. and Lewis W.

Edward Smith, son of Maj. David Smith, was born in Granby, March 13, 1805, moved to Holyoke about 1830, where he took charge of a cotton mill, and was a partner in a company known as the South Hadley Falls Company, for the manufacture of cotton cloths. They owned the entire water privilege on the Holyoke side at that time, and about 1848 they sold the entire prop-erty to the Holyoke Water Company. Mr. Smith then moved to Easthamp-ton, where he managed the suspender factory for Samuel Williston. He came to Enfield in 1852, and became associated with the Swift River Company, of which he is still president and treasurer. He married Eliza, daughter of Dr. Enos Smith, and has had born to him two children, Edward P. and Henry.

Daniel Gillett, a descendant of Cornelius Gillett, who came from England as one of the early settlers of this country, was born in Windsor, Mass., No-vember 25, 1781, moved to Granville, Mass., where he married Edith, daughter of Col. Jacob Bates, and reared six children, viz.: Catherine, Eliza-beth, Mary A., Edward B., Daniel B. and Edith B. He moved to South Hadley Falls, where he engaged in the mercantile trade. Daniel B. was born in South Hadley Falls, July 21, 1819, married Charlotte E. Woods, May 6,

1845, and came to this town in 1846, and became associated with Woods & Bro., in the manufacture of card clothing. He continued here about three years, and then became associated with the Minot Manufacturing Company. He has had born to him two children, Daniel B. and Rufus W. His wife died August 30, 1856, and he married for his second wife Persis Winslow, who died March 20, 1880.

The first census taken after the town was incorporated, in 1820, shows the population to have been 873. The population at different times since has been, in 1830, 1,056; 1840, 976; 1850, 1,036; 1855, 1,036; 1860, 1,025; 1865, 997; 1870, 1,023; 1875, 1,065; 1880, 1,043; 1885, 1,010.

First Town Meeting.—The first town meeting was warned by Elihu Lyman, and convened at the meeting-house Monday, March 4, 1816, when the following list of officers were elected : Benjamin Harwood, moderator ; Simeon Waters, clerk ; James Richards, Benjamin Harwood and Jesse Fobes, selectmen ; Ephraim Richards, treasurer ; and Capt. Sylvanus Howe, Alden Lathrop and Oliver Patterson, assessors. Several other minor officers were also elected. The following notes are from the town records :—

"One of the first subjects to receive the attention of the new town (a church being already established) was that of education, and April 1, 1816, $300 was appropriated for schools. On the same date provision was made for the ringing of the meeting-house bell at stated hours in the day. It was also 'voted that Ebenezer Winslow sweep the meeting-house for one dollar and fifty cents per year, to sweep it six times per year and after every town meeting.' The amount of money voted the year 1816 was $1,166.67.

"April 7, 1817, Hosea Hooker was allowed $2 for the use of his yard for a pound, and he continued to exercise the functions of pound-master for many years thereafter.

"April 3, 1820, Lieut. Joseph Keith presented a bell to the town, on condition that it should be forever kept and used for the accommodation of the town, and preserved in good repair and condition.

"October 16, 1820, Benjamin Harwood was chosen to represent the town in the constitutional convention, to be held at Boston, November 3, 1820. In April, 1822, the sum of $50 was appropriated to support church music. On December 11, 1826, $75 was appropriated to support a singing-school the ensuing winter. In the month of March, 1827, a committee was chosen to dispose of the old bell and buy a new one. In the following year the town was divided into eleven highway districts. In 1832 measures were taken to build a new bridge over the river on the road to Ware ; and in the following year like action was taken toward building a bridge over the west branch of the river, on the road leading to Amherst. In 1844 a committe purchased in behalf of the town the farm of Ezekiel Keith, called the "Dale farm," for the sum of $1,900, to be used as a poor farm.

"March 19, 1883, it was voted that a committee of three be appointed to report at an adjourned meeting to be held April 2, 1883, with reference to locating a site and building a hall for town purposes. At the adjourned meeting a committee of five was appointed to purchase land, or to locate a new town building, authorized to procure plans, purchase material, and make all necessary contracts to build such building, and to do all things necessary to be done in the matter, limited to the sum of $12,000.00. Henry M. Smith,

Solon R. Towne, Arthur J. W. Ward, Daniel B. Gillett, and William B. Downing was the committee. The building was constructed of brick, is 50x20 feet with two stories and a basement.''

Items.—The earliest taverns known were kept, one where Lyman D. Potter's barn now stands, and another where Daniel B. Gillett resides. Another was kept, at an early date, in the old Field residence.

One of the first stores was kept by Field & Canedy, where the Congregational parsonage stands. The first physician was Dr. William Stone. The first lawyer was Joshua N. Upham. The first record of a highway through the town was of one from the Pelham line to Chicopee, in 1754.

MILITARY.

Those citizens of the town who served in the Revolutionary war, were Joshua Crosby, Benjamin Rider, Giles Rider, Barnabas Rich, —— Pratt, —— Newcomb, and John Stevens. The latter was present at the battle of Bunker Hill, and only escaped being killed by the thrust of a British bayonet as he was leaving the fortifications, by having in his knapsack a loaf of bread that had been left in the oven too long before he left home, and had grown very hard. This checked the bayonet and saved his life.

In Shays Rebellion there were many active partisans in the town, but the only citizens who are known to have taken part were Benjamin Harwood, Joseph Fobes, Jr., and John Rea.

In the war of 1812, Ichabod Pope, Daniel Ford, Roswell Underwood Henry Fobes, Joshua Crosby, Samuel Rich, Ruggles Harwood, Samuel Barton, Packard Ford, Daniel Eddy, and Kingsley Underwood represented the town.

In the late great war Enfield furnished 107 men, a surplus of nine over all demands, two of whom were commissioned officers. It expended $13,801.04, and loaned the state $4,564.21.

VILLAGES.

ENFIELD VILLAGE, located in the central part of the town, on a branch of Swift river, and on the Athol railroad, contains the only postoffice in the town. The village is pleasantly located, in the midst of some very pleasing scenery, and is altogether a neat and prosperous little place. The postoffice was established here in 1820, and Elihu Lyman was the first postmaster.

The dam at the village was built about fifty feet above the present location, prior to the year 1770, by Ephraim Woodward, who erected a saw-mill thereon. He sold to Ebenezer Rich, who built a grist-mill, and Robert Field, about the year 1773, put up a clothier's shop. A blacksmith shop, with a tilt hammer, was soon after erected by Robert Field and others, who also operated an oil-mill. Reuben Colton had a fulling-mill and cloth-dressing shop just below Haskell's store. There were also other improvements at this point. Calvin and Charles Lawson made cut nails from plates by means of a machine, and headed them by hand. Under the bridge was a mill-stone for grinding whetstones, and about 1804 James Harrison, an Englishman, set up a carding-machine for making rolls from wool, it being the first of its kind in that part of the country.

SMITH'S STATION, or Enfield Upper Village, lies on the river just above Enfield village proper. It contains the woolen-mills, grist-mill, saw-mill and box-factory of the Swift River Co., a store, about thirty-eight dwellings and about 250 inhabitants.

The dam here was erected in 1812, and a cotton-yarn mill was built the year following by a company of neighbors, of which John Allen was superintendent and agent. It ran for a few years, when larger mills were erected, that made not only yarn, but wove it into cloth, which put a stop to domestic weaving. There were also a saw-mill, blacksmith shop, shingle-mill, and other works erected on this privilege at an early day.

MANUFACTURES.

The Swift River Co.—This company dates its origin back to 1821, when Alfred, David and Alvin Smith, under the firm name of D. & A. Smith, began in a small way the manufacture of cotton. In 1836 the factory was burned, and immediately re-built. They carried on the enterprise till 1852, when they were joined by Edward Smith, and the present company incorporated. The new company started the mill on satinets, but continued to make cotton warps. They added several sets of satinet machinery, and made other improvements. Finally, about the beginning of the war, or in 1862, the mill was increased to more than double its old size and capacity, the cotton and satinet machinery thrown out, and eight sets of machinery for the manufacture of fancy cassimeres put in, which business they have since continued. From time to time modern improvements have been added, and as the company only manufactures number one cassimeres, it has gained an enviable reputation. The mills are built of wood, are operated by both steam and water-power, give employment to one hundred hands, and turn out about 6,000 yards of goods per week. The company has a grist-mill, saw-mill, box factory and tenements for the accommodation of fifty families. The mills have been kept steadily at work through all the business depressions, furnishing steady employment to the hands, many of whom have been employed from fifteen to twenty years. Edward Smith is president and treasurer of the company, and H. H. Smith, general manager.

The Minot Manufacturing Co.—The first mill for making cloth at the lower dam was built by Elihu Lyman and Ichabod Pope about the year 1825. It was used in the manufacture of satinets, and run by Elihu Lyman, Ichabod Pope, Abner Hale and Moses Woods. The enterprise was not a profitable one, and was succeeded by the Swift River Manufacturing Company, which was organized by Marshall and Thomas Jones, Leonard and Josiah B. Woods, Ephraim Richards, George Howe and a few others. This company not only manufactured satinets, but also carried on the carding business, which Leonard Woods had established about 1820. Their factory was burned in 1830. A stone mill was then erected, but the inside with all its machinery was burned out in 1848. The walls were not injured, and the factory was again re-built and is still standing. The Swift River Manufacturing Company was short lived. The business was divided up. M. S. & T. Jones continued the manufacture of satinet, and the Woods, with Marshall Jones, carried on the carding business, under the name and style of Jones, Woods & Co. In 1837, M. S. & T. Jones failed, and the Minot Manufacturing Company was incorporated on April 7 of that year, having as incorporators Marshall Jones, Leonard Woods and Alvin Smith, with a capital stock of $75,000.00. The company, with an occasional change of members, has been running ever since, at first manufacturing satinets, but now Shaker flannels and light-weight cassimeres. They have two mills, with five sets of machinery, and employ about sixty persons.

A. J. N. Ward's steam saw-mill, located at Enfield, is operated by steam power, generated by a forty-five horse-power boiler and forty horse-power engine. He employs three men in the manufacture of lumber and shingles.

Gillett & Flint's portable saw-mill is of twenty horse-power, and cuts 1,500,000 feet of lumber per annum.

CHURCHES.

Congregational church.—A meeting-house on land presented by Capt. Joseph Hooker, was built in the parish in the years 1786 and '87, and accepted October 15, 1787. Movable benches were first placed in this church. Pews were substituted in 1793. In 1814 a belfry was erected, and a bell, the gift of Josiah Keith, afterward placed therein. In the year 1835 the pews were displaced by slips, and other alerations and improvements made. The House was repaired about 1855 and an organ added. In 1873 it was again repaired and a considerable addition was made to the rear of the church, and an elegant organ took the place of the old one, at a cost of about $2,500.00. The edifice now presents an attractive appearance, the steeple being graceful and unique in design, and containing a costly town-clock. The interior of the church is neat and appropriately embellished, and its acoustic properties are excellent. The first regular pastor of the church was Rev. Joshua Crosby, who was called May 12, 1789, and installed December 2d following. He was furnished with a farm bought of Barnabas Fay as settlement, and had a salary of £70 a year, his fire-wood being also furnished by the parish. The names of the first purchasers of pews in the meeting-house, in 1793, were Calvin Kingsley, Sylvanus Howe, Daniel Hayward, Simon Stone, David Newcomb, Joseph Hooker, Robert Field, John

Sawin, Benjamin Harwood, Benjamin Rider, Nathan Hunting, Caleb Keith, William Stone, Joseph Ruggles, Abner Eddy, Ebenezer Rich, Reuben Colton, Barnabas Rich, Nathaniel Boker, Joseph Fobes, David Swetland, William Morton, John Eaton, Moses Colton, Jonathan Hunting, Nathaniel Lane, John Bailey, William Patterson, John McIntosh and William McIntosh. Parochial affairs were conducted by parish officers from 1787 until 1816, when the town was incorporated; by the town from that date until 1831, when the parish was re-organized and still continues. The present pastor is Elbridge P. McElroy.

The Methodist Episcopal church was organized October 15, 1843, with sixteen members, and Rev. Samuel Tupper, pastor. The church building was erected in 1847-48.

GOSHEN* is one of the northern hill towns of the county, lying on the north line about midway between the Berkshire line and the Connecticut. It is bounded on the north by Ashfield, in Franklin county, east by a small part of Conway, in the same county, and Williamsburg; and as the town is triangular in form, the other bounds may be generally said to be Chesterfield and Cummington on the south, southwest and west. The town has an area of about 6,951 acres.

The outline of Goshen is extremely irregular, there being no less than twenty angles in the boundary lines, and some of them far from right angles. As we come to glance at the surface of the little town, here too are angles. But these latter could hardly be dispensed with, for they, the law of " no beauty in angles " to the contrary, diversify the township's area into a most charming bit of landscape. In the northeastern part of the town is the principal elevation, Moore's hill, rising to an altitude of 1,713 feet. The western and central portions of the town are drained by tributaries of Westfield river, supplying water-power of considerable value. In the northeastern and central part of the town are found tributaries of Mill river, and here large reservoirs have been built for the benefit of the manufacturing establishments below. The waters that contribute to Mill river, and those that flow into the Westfield, are in the northern part of the town almost interlocked with each other, the dividing ridge which separates the basins being narrow and low, so that a dyke has been constructed to turn them in the direction desired.

The town is rich in minerals, having a good granite quarry, and furnishing specimens more or less abundant of tin ore, galena, graphite, spodumene, blue and green tourmaline, smoky quartz, beryl, zoisite, mica, albite and columbite.

Grant and Settlement.—The territory which now makes up the township of Goshen was formerly part of the military tract granted to satisfy the

---

* For this sketch we are largely indebted to the writings of Hiram Barrus, of Boston.

claims of the heirs of the 840 soldiers in the Narragansett expedition in King Philip's war. But we have defined the conditions of these old grants in connection with the sketch of Chesterfield, and shall speak of them still further in the sketch of Greenwich, so it is only necessary to add at this point that "Narragansett Township" No. 4, located in New Hampshire, was reported unfit for settlement, and in lieu of it the territory of "Quabbin" (Greenwich and vicinity) was granted. But this grant proving less than the required "six miles square," 3,000 acres lying west of Williamsburg was granted, which took the name of "Quabbin," "Quabbin Proprietary," or "First Additional Grant." This failing to supply the deficiency, "The Second Additional Grant" was made, consisting of about 3,500 acres, lying between "Quabbin" and Huntstown (now Ashfield). This was also called "The Gore," and "Chesterfield Gore." The division line between Quabbin and the Gore extended from the northwest corner of Williamsburg westerly, passing just south of the present meeting-house, to the Cummington line.

In 1762 Chesterfield was incorporated, including the territory called New Hingham and "Quabbin," or the "First Additional Grant." This brought its north line as given above, with "The Gore" on the north.

In January, 1763, a petition was sent to the general court from the people of the Gore, asking to be annexed to Chesterfield. "This was so promptly done by the court that, no notice having been given, Chesterfield waked up one fine morning surprised to find its territory enlarged by the addition of 3,500 acres of land it had never asked for. It rubbed its eyes, saw that it meant the removal of the church location to some unknown point northward, and sent at once a counter petition for a speedy divorce, which was granted in June following."

The first settlers within the present limits of the town were David Stearns and Abijah Tucker, who came on from Dudley in 1761 and began a clearing on the farm now owned by Amos Hawks. In the fall they brought their families and passed the winter. Stearns finally settled upon what is known as the David Beals farm. These men the first winter were often absent, seeking work in Northampton, and the families met the hardships of pioneer settlement alone for several days at a time. It is told of them that they had a cow and a horse that were pastured at the "Great Meadow;" that in the deep snow of the following winter the cow wandered off to the same ground one day, and night came on before the absence was noticed. Then neither of the women could safely go after the cow alone, nor stay with the children alone, so one woman mounted the horse and took the five children on with her, the other woman led the horse, and so they went after the cow, two miles away and back, through the snow.

The influx of immigrants in the spring of 1762 must have been quite extensive all along the line of this town and Chesterfield. William White, of Charleton, was one of these. He received a deed of land here May 17, 1762, from Gad Lyman, then of Northampton, but later of Goshen.

Col. Ezra May, from Woodstock, Conn., with ten men to assist him in his labors, came about the same time, with "old Mr. Corbin and wife to do their cooking." The north bound of his farm was a few feet south of the present church. White took the third hundred acre lot south of May's, and boarded with May during the first year. The next lot, north of May's, on which the church now stands, was taken by Lieut. Lemuel Lyon, also from Woodstock, and probably the same year.

Capt. Robert Webster, from Dudley, with his wife and one child, also came this year. There may have been a few other arrivals upon our territory at this time, but probably not. Farther south, on land now included in Chesterfield, there was, doubtless, a greater number.

Other settlers upon our territory that came within a few years, were Asa Grant, from Wrentham, John James and Zebulon Willcutt, from Cohasset, Joseph Blake and Edward Orcutt, from Hingham, Reuben and Moses Dresser, and Ebenezer Putney, from Charleton, Thomas and Daniel Brown and the five Banister brothers—John, Lemuel, Christopher, Barzillai and William—and probably Artemas and Sylvanus Stone, from Brookfield, Joshua Abell, from Rehoboth, Capt. John Bigelow, Isaac Kingman, James and Joshua Packard, from Bridgewater, Dr. Benjamin Burgess and Samuel Mott, from Tisbury, John Smith, Timothy Lyman, Benjamin Parsons and his sons, Ebenezer, Justin, Solomon, Silas and Benjamin, from Northampton, Thomas Weeks and Ambrose Stone, from Greenwich, and William Hallock, from Long Island.

William White was a man efficient and prompt to act in every good cause. He was one of the first that went to the country's defence, on the alarm that followed the battle of Lexington. He drew up the petition for the incorporation of the town, was its town clerk for some thirty years, selectman for many terms, justice of the peace thirty-five years, representative to general court, and delegate to many important conventions.

Col. Ezra May, a man of such acknowledged ability that upon the incorporation of Chesterfield, which included his farm, he was, in the very first year of his residence here, chosen the moderator of the first town meeting in Chesterfield, and constable and chairman of the selectmen. He was first deacon of the church in that town, went early into the army, rose to the rank of colonel, was in the battle of Saratoga, and at the taking of Burgoyne, where he took a violent cold, which resulted in his death a few months later, at the early age of forty-six years. Two of his sons, Nehemiah and Dexter, were in the army with him.

Thomas Weeks, from Greenwich, went down to Lexington with a small company of men, and was with the army near Boston, in 1775-76. He was a man of more than usual education for his time, had been deputy sheriff in Worcester county for many years, and served as paymaster for the troops. He left many records and several journals of the scenes through which he passed, and from which it appears, that in 1777 he was at the surrender of Ticonderoga ; an event which he branded with the terms—"Shame, Infamy, Disgrace." He was an able surveyor, laid out many of the highways of the town, was often employed in running the boundaries of the land, and was the first town clerk of Goshen ; the first subscriber to the papers for the organization of the church, and a delegate to the convention that formed the constitution of the state.

Dr. Benjamin Burgess came during the Revolutionary war, and for a long period was one of the leading physicians of this vicinity. He was a man of sound judgment and strong common sense, and was often called to serve in town affairs. He came from Martha's Vineyard, bringing his wife with him. Before setting sail for the main land, his wife quilted what money they had—$1,000 in gold—into the skirts of her dress for greater security if they fell into the hands of the British, whose vessels were troubling our coasters. They were once fired upon, but escaped unharmed.

Dea. Oliver Taylor was another important man in the early affairs of the town and church. He was a man of great firmness of character, and seems to have had things pretty much in his own way. He was first deacon of the church, an office he held for nearly forty years ; was four times elected to represent the town in the legislature, and was justice of the peace for sixteen years. He enlisted in the army of the Revolution, but was sent home to work at his trade—that of a tanner—as his services for his country in supplying leather for shoes for the army were more important as a tanner, than they could be as a soldier.

John James, the moderator of the first town-meeting called by the selectmen, and the first merchant in town, was a man of much force of character, and a successful man of business. He died in 1804, leaving to the town a donation of $100, to be kept on interest for one hundred years. After that time the income is to be devoted to the support of schools and the gospel, and for such other purposes as may be desirable.

Reuben Dresser, from Charleton, was another of the sturdy yeomanry who was among the early settlers. He made large purchases of land, employed many workmen, set out extensive orchards, and built, it is said, on his own land fifteen miles of heavy stone wall, much of which stands to the present time. The farm is still in possession of his descendants.

Joshua Packard was an early settler, locating here about 1770. He had born to him three sons, one of whom Willard, always lived in town, married Bathsheba Smith, and nine children were born to them, viz.: William S., Cordelia, Edmund, Malesta, Julia, Willard, Emeline, Hiram and Freeman S. Hiram was born September 6, 1816, married Lurane A. Carpenter, and has had born to him three children, namely, Henry W., Edward C. and Charles S. Henry died in New Mexico. Mr. Packard resides on road 9.

To give some idea of the increase in the population we quote the following from the records, a list of those living in the several school districts of the town in October, 1781 : Samuel Old, John Hatch, Deborah Narramore,

James Packard, Isaac Kingman, Ezekiel Thomas, Wait Burk, Samuel Snell, Joshua Packard, James Orr, John Jepson, Moses Elwell, Ambrose Stone, Justin Parsons, Caleb Cushman, Barzillai Banister, Sylvanus Lyon, Nathan Bigelow and Thomas Hamilton, District No. 1; John James, Oliver Taylor, Lemuel Banister, Ebenezer Amadon, Joel Gustin, Barnabas Potter, David Stearns, Cyrel Leach, Jesse Willcutt, William Banister, Benjamin Bourn, Christopher Banister, Samuel Grimes, Isaac Tower, Cyrus Lyon and Thomas Weeks, District No. 2; John Smith, Ebenezer Parsons, John Williams, Lemuel Lyon, Nehemiah May, Benjamin Burger, Timothy Lyman, Artemas Stone, Widow Halbert, Reuben Lummis, Jedediah Buckingham, Stephen Grover, Thomas Brown, Daniel Brown, Dexter May, Edward Orcutt, Farnum White, Christopher Grant, Asa Grant, Adam Beal, William Hallock, Adam Beal, Jr., William Meader and Benjamin Abell, District No. 3; Joshua Abell, William White, Ebenezer Putney, Reuben Dresser, Richard Tower, Moses Dresser, John King, Daniel Wyman, Nathaniel Vinton, James Lull, Joseph Blake, Ebenezer Paine, Ezekiel White, Widow White, Noah White, District No. 4.

The population at the beginning of the several decades since then has been as follows: 1790, 681; 1800, 724; 1810, 652; 1820, 632; 1830, 617; 1840, 556; 1850, 512; 1860, 439; 1870, 368; 1880, 327.

Organization.—The "Gore" seemed to be, in some respects, unfortunately situated. Its early settlers, as already stated, had been at one time annexed to Chesterfield, but to restore peace, were again set off. Their necessities finally compelled them again to appeal to the general court, reciting their grievances, and asking to be incorporated as a town. Capt. Thomas Weeks presented the matter to the court in 1779, and again in 1781. In January of the latter year, moved by the "petition of Thomas Weeks, agent to the petitioners of a part of Chesterfield," also of the "Gore of land called Chesterfield Gore," a committee was appointed by the general court to repair to Chesterfield, hear the parties, and report at the next session of the court. The action of the committee may be inferred from a letter of which the following is a copy:—

"NORWICH, May 1, 1781.

"Sir: I have left the report of the committee appointed on the matters relating to the Gore, Narragansett No. 4, and Chesterfield, with landlord Elisha Lyman and all the papers except yours, left with me, which are here enclosed. If you go down this session, remember to carry down to Court the plan of that part of Narragansett No. 4, as Capt. White proposed to the committee when at Mr. May's representing those that were willing to be annexed to the Gore. Doct. Mather and Doct. Shepard propose not to go down this session, and I can't. You will do as you think best respecting going down this session or the next. We have closed our report, which if you send, you will have safely conveyed to the Secretary as directed.

"I am Sr. your most Humble Serv't
"JOHN KIRKLAND.

"*To Mr. Joshua Abell.*"

The act of incorporation finally passed May 14, 1781, and was approved by John Hancock, governor. The name given in the act is Goshan—probably a clerical error. The origin of the name, as given by Dea. Oliver Taylor to his daughter, Mrs. Catheart, is said by her daughter, Mrs. Polly Tilton, to have been this : Goshen of old was the best part of Egypt, so the name was considered appropriate for what was claimed to be the best part of Chesterfield. The town meeting, for organization, was held pursuant to a warrant issued by Jacob Sherwin, Esq., of Ashfield, May 23, at the house of John Williams, which then stood just above the burying-ground. Lieut. Thomas Weeks was chosen clerk; Joshua Abell, treasurer ; Capt. William White, Lieut. Lemuel Lyon, Maj. Christopher Banister, selectmen and assessors ; Thomas Brown and Ebenezer Parsons, constables ; Farnum White, Lemuel Banister, Ebenezer Putney, Lieut. Timothy Lyman, Thomas Weeks and Barzillai Banister, highway surveyors ; John Williams, sealer of weights and measures ; Lemuel Banister and Farnum White, tithingmen ; John Smith and Maj. Christopher Banister, fence viewers ; Samuel Olds, leather sealer ; Barzillai Banister, deer-reeve ; Nehemiah May, Daniel Brown, Barzillai Banister and Lemuel Banister, hog-reeves.

Education.—The earliest schools in the " Gore " or in "Quabbin " were kept in private houses. Capt. Thomas Weeks taught school in the house of John Williams, but names of other teachers of that date are unknown. The first shool-house in town was erected just west of the bridge, in the northwest district, near the former residence of Col. L. Stone. The first teacher in it was James Richards, of Plainfield. Another school-house was built near the meeting-house, and a third near the house of Ebenezer Putney. The town was divided in four school districts in 1781.

In 1799 the town passed a vote that the money raised by the tax on dogs should be used towards the support of the school. In 1869 the legislature passed a law making this rule throughout the state.

In 1805 the town seems to have originated another idea that the state put into more general practice. The town voted that the selectmen have the care and charge of the school-books belonging to the town, and distribute them among the schools as they judge proper, indicating beyond question that the town furnished the books for the scholars, so that none should fail through poverty, or other cause, of having the necessary books for use in their studies. The state, it will be remembered, recognized the same benevolent principle in the law passed in 1873, giving towns permission to authorize their school committees to purchase text-books for use of the schools, to be owned by the town and loaned to the pupils under proper regulations.

The town began to choose school committees a quarter of a century before the state required it by law. In 1799 William White, Reuben Howes, Justin Parsons, Ambrose Stone and Moses James were appointed to this office. In 1826 Rev. Joel Wright, Capt. Joseph White, Capt. John Grant, Dr. George Wright, David Carpenter, Jared Hawks, Jr., and Emmons Putney were chosen the first general school committee under the act of the legislature. This was the commencement of the new era in the history of Massachusetts schools, which, in a few years later, placed Horace Mann at their head as secretary of the board of education.

Another important factor in the education of the early residents of the town was a first-class town library. In Captain Grant's journal he speaks of attending a library meeting in 1796, and it was continued for many years after, but how long we are not informed. It contained valuable books, history, biography and travels, and we are told that the young men read them. Of one of them it was said that he was one of the most thorough students of history that could be found in his time.

First Highway.—The first highway through Goshen was the old military road from Boston to Albany, established in 1758. The soldiers in passing over this road made camps from time to time, where small clearings were made. The road passed over the farm of the late Captain Grant, where a log bridge was built which remained to his day. One of the old camping grounds was the spot where Col. L. Stone's "red house" was built. The remains of their bark huts were found here by Major Stone later than 1780. Joshua Packard once passed over the route with the troops, and on this camp-ground he lost his pocket-knife. After he became a resident of the town he searched for it and found it. John Williams, in 1786, owned the first wagon in the town.

Military.—A company of minute-men was early formed in Goshen, and when the news of the battle of Lexington, April 21, 1775, was received, this company started out for the scene, two days after the battle. There were forty-four men in this company, with Robert Webster, captain ; Christopher Banister, lieutenant ; William White, first sergeant ; Timothy Lyman, second sergeant, and Jonathan Nelson, corporal. Thirty-nine of these men continued in the service, joining Gen. Pomeroy's regiment, and fifteen returned home after terms of service, varying from seven to thirty-seven days. The men who returned received one cent per mile for expenses, and twenty-five cents per day as wages. The privates from what is now Goshen, were Tilly Burke, Benjamin Bourn, Caleb Cushman, Barzillai Banister, Nehemiah May, Cyrus Lyon, Oliver Taylor, Artemas Stone, Reuben Dresser, Samuel Thomas, Ebenezer Parsons, Samuel Olds, Christopher Grant, Adam Beals and Wait Burk.

In the war of 1812 it is probable that only one went out from Goshen into the regular service, John Manning. The following, however, went to the defense of Boston : Capt. Timothy Lyman, Asahel Billings, William Abell, William Tilton, Oliver T. Catheart, Enoch James, John Fuller, Robert Barrus, Abisha Williams, Arad Hasford and Moses Dresser.

In the late great war Goshen furnished forty-seven men, a surplus of six over all demands ; expended $5,374.50, and loaned the state, in aid to soldiers' families, etc., $2,178.42.

Notes.—Among the natives of Goshen who have achieved prominence in the world may be mentioned the following :—

Ezra Weeks, son of the first town clerk, removed to New York city, accumulated a large fortune, owning at one time seven acres of what is now the most fashionable portion of that city, became president of a bank, and an author of a popular pamphlet on the treatment of cholera.

William Lyman became a merchant, and was one of the leading citizens of Schenectady, N. Y.   He educated his nephew and namesake, Dr. William, son of his brother, Captain Francis, whose residence was here.   The young William became a physician of acknowledged skill, an orator of much eloquence, a member of the Illinois legislature, and in the civil war, was medical director on General Logan's staff.

Joseph H. White, grandson of the early settler, William, son of Joseph, was born on the White homestead in 1824.   He was for many years the leading member of the firm of White, Browne & Co., the senior member of the firm of White, Payson & Co., the selling agents of the Manchester mills, and a principal stockholder and director.   He soon accumulated a handsome fortune and assisted his brothers in starting in mercantile business, one of whom is R. H. White, the head of the house of R. H. White & Co., whose business is not exceeded by more than three or four establishments in this country. Another brother, Hon. James White, was formerly in business with Joseph H.

Dea. Benjamin Burgess, grandson and namesake of the long time physician, a prominent merchant and citizen for nearly half a century, and his brother Silas, a lawyer of Worcester.

Enoch and L. L. James, grandsons of the early settler, John James, became successful merchants in their day, and Luther James, of Ann Arbor, Mich., all prominent as business men and capitalists.

William Mayhew, the wealthy and generous Baltimore merchant, of national reputation, was a son of Freeborn Mayhew, for many years a resident of this town.

Mrs. Martha J. Lamb, whose literary ability has placed her name high upon the roll of honor.   Her *History of New York* is said to be the largest work of the kind ever accomplished by a woman.   It is not only the largest, but has received the endorsement of eminent literary authorities as worthy of rank with the best.

Lucretia Parsons, daughter of Rev. Justin, married Rev. D. O. Morton, and was the mother of Levi P. Morton, the New York millionaire, member of congress and United States minister to France.

Mercy Burgess, daughter of Dr. Benjamin, married Mitchell Dawes, and was the mother of Hon. Henry L. Dawes, one of the honored and worthy senators of this state.

This list might be largely extended.

GOSHEN is a pleasant little post-village, located in the central part of the town.   It lies principally on one street, has a store, hotel, two churches, and a number of substantial residences. The postoffice was established here in 1817, and John Williams was the first postmaster.

Early mills and manufactories.—Reuben Dresser built a saw-mill, one of the first in town, more than a hundred years since, below the Dresser pond. A broom-handle factory was added about forty years ago; and later, button moulds have been manufactured there. It now belongs to the heirs of C. C. Dresser. About two miles above, Emmons Putney built a saw-mill not far from 1835, which ran for twenty years or more, and was owned finally by William H. Webster.

Ezekiel Corbin had a grist-mill on Swift river, a little below Shaw's bridge, near Cummington line, as early as 1796. James Patrick had a saw and grist-mill two miles or so above, on Swift river, near Ashfield line, built about 1788. Daniel Williams, many years later, built a new mill and stone dam a few rods above the old mill, which has since been owned by Samuel Ranney and others, and later, for many years, by J. D. Shipman, who sold, in 1880, to Ansel Cole. Stone's saw-mill and broom-handle factory on Stone's brook, a branch of Swift river, were erected in 1828. It was the first factory for turning broom-handles by machinery in this vicinity. Planes were made here from 1854 to 1859, by Hiram Barrus & Brothers. At the present time the works comprise a saw-mill and brush-handle factory, owned by Amos H. Stone & Son. The second grist-mill in town stood about forty rods higher up the stream, built by Captain Bigelow. Maj. Ambrose Stone, in 1780, changed the works to a fulling-mill and clothier establishment, the first by nearly forty years for many miles around. Nearly a mile above, Willard and Hiram Packard had a saw-mill, which was abandoned more than twenty years ago. Still further up, on a branch of Stone's brook, at the outlet of Beaver Meadow, is Sear's saw-mill, formerly owned by Dea. Stephen Parsons. Beaver Meadow is connected by a small stream with the upper reservoir, which, in time of high water, discharged its waters in two directions—one, through Stone's brook into the Westfield river, the other through Mill river into the Connecticut. Near the south end of the upper reservoir, built in 1873, was another saw-mill erected by Francis and Thomas Lyman, about 60 years ago. At the lower reservoir, on the street east of the meeting-house, there was an ancient saw-mill, owned by John Williams—called "Carpenter John," to distinguish him from "Squire John," the postmaster. It was afterwards owned by Abner Moore, who added a small grist-mill with broom-handle and button-mould factory. A little below is the saw-mill of Rodney Hawks, on the site of another built some forty years ago.

Farther down Mill river is the remains of an old dam that marks the place where Nehemiah May and Ebenezer Putney about 1788 erected a mill for grinding sumac to be sent to Europe for tanning morocco. But it did not pay and was given up. Just below, Emmons Putney erected a saw-mill in 1839. He has made button moulds here for many years. He states that one girl turned off for him in one day 150 gross of moulds, equal to 21,600

18*

pieces. Below Putney's mill, was another, built about 1815 by Ebenezer White and Elias Lyon, and afterwards owned by Capt. Horace Packard & Sons. About a mile below, Nehemiah May built a grist-mill more than a century since, said to have been the first in town, which stood for fifty years. Not a vestage of the old timbers remain, but Maj. Hawks remembers going there to mill in his boyhood. On Harding's brook, a tributary of Mill river, coming down from the vicinity of Moore's hill, Asa White built a saw-mill nearly fifty years since, which run for only a few years.

Cider-mills, run by horse-power, belonged to Dresser, White, James, Gloyd, Lyman, Packard and Naramore. The Packard mill, owned by Joseph Beals, still exists ; and E. C. Packard has recently set up another.

In 1812 Major Stone & Sons furnished considerable quantities of cloth for our army. It was narrow in width, but sold for a high price. In 1780 he bought wool at an average price of twenty-five cents per pound, which in 1812 was worth $2.00. Other mills of the kind becoming inconveniently numerous, Stone finally gave up the business, having pursued it for nearly fifty years.

Levi Kingman, of Cummington, did a successful business here about 1812–14, in the manufacture of patent overshoes, called " Tuscarora socks." They had an extensive sale, and were long a popular article.

Solomon Parsons and John James engaged quite largely in the manufacture of potash, and continued in the business for many years.

There was formerly a tannery owned by Oliver Taylor where William H. Webster lived. It was in operation before the Revolutionary war. Taylor enlisted and went into the army, but it becoming known that he was a tanner, he was sent home to work at his trade, as he could be more useful in that department, laboring for the soldiers, than by serving in the field with them. Another tannery near where William Tilton lived was owned for many years by his brother, Benjamin Tilton.

CHURCHES.

The Congregational church of Goshen was organized December 21, 1780, the foundation, indeed, of the town itself, which was incorporated some months later. This, it will be remembered, was the usual order in these matters, the general court from the earliest period in the history of the state, never allowing the incorporation of a town till the formation, or " some good proceeding" was had toward the formation of a church within the limits of the proposed town.

For seven years no pastor was settled, though many were called. When a minister was needed for special occasions in the absence of a supply, as in cases of discipline, admitting new members, administering the ordinances, the pastors from the neighboring towns on invitation, kindly assisted. In one case this seems to have led to trouble as indicated by the following vote, passed November 2, 1786 :—

"Then attended to a remonstrance which the Rev. Timothy Allen of Chesterfield, sent in against this church, for desiring him to assist in admitting a person into our church which he supposes was not a fit member. Voted to choose a committee of two of the Brethren to answer in behalf of the church the above remonstrance."

Chose Oliver Taylor and Thomas Brown. There may have been two sides to the story, but how it was finally disposed of the records do not say. We suspect, however, that the Chesterfield pastor did not consider that turning out a bad member was equivalent to receiving a bad one, and so was not conciliated, for in the latter part of the same month, the church wanted his assistance in excommunicating a member whom they considered bad, but he declined, and Rev. Mr. Bascom was invited to take his place.

Rev. Samuel Whitman, of Ashley, a native of Bridgewater, was finally installed as the first pastor of the church, January 10, 1788. Rev. Mr. Allen was moderator of the council, offered prayer and preached the sermon. Rev. Joseph Strong, of Williamsburg, gave the charge and Rev. James Briggs, of Cummington, offered the closing prayer.

The church at this time had about fifty members. It had chosen one year previous two deacons, Oliver Taylor and Artemas. They were strong men and no church could have better material from which to select their leading officials. Among them were William Hallock and his two sons, Jeremiah and Moses, Nehemiah May, Ebenezer Putney, Joseph, Christopher and Lemuel Banister, Farnum White, Justin Parsons and Dr. Benjamin Burgess.

The church was early alive to the work of missions and a missionary society was formed for promoting the cause. One result of this is seen in the number of young men, natives, or sometime resident here, who engaged in missionary work. Among them was Rev. Levi Parsons, son of Deacon Justin, who was one of the first two missionaries from the United States to Palestine. Rev. Horatio Bardwell, D. D., missionary to Bombay and afterwards agent of the American board, of whom his biographer said, "The key to his entire life and character is found in his consecration to the work of missions." Rev. Ralph Cushman went to Kentucky as a home missionary, and was afterwards appointed general secretary of the American Home Mission Society for the Western States. Calvin Cushman, Elijah Bardwell, brother of Rev. Horatio, together with Mr. John Smith, went out as missionaries with their families, to the Choctaws in Mississippi in 1820. Miss Electa May, daughter of Nehemiah, married Rev. Cyrus Kingsbury, the missionary, and accompanied the Choctaws across the Mississippi to their new home. Sarah Bardwell, sister of Rev. Horatio, married Rev. James Richards and went as a missionary to Ceylon. Hannah, daughter of Ebenezer Putney, was the wife of John Smith, and went with him to the Choctaw mission. Alvan Stone, in the early history of Illinois, went out to that state and engaged in active work as a home missionary till removed by an early death. Jeremiah Hallock and his brother Moses, both long in the field and efficient laborers—Jeremiah forty years at Canton, Conn.; Moses a still longer term in Plainfield, father of Rev. William A. Hallock, the long time secretary of the American Tract Society in New York, and Girard Hallock, of the Journal of Commerce. It is said that Rev. Moses Hallock fitted more men for the ministry than any other man of his time, and that they were so well fitted for college that his own sons were educated by the college without charge. Then follows Rev. Justin Parsons, one of a large family that came from Northampton, a man of energy, good judgment, honored by the town and church with the highest offices in their gift, turning his attention to the ministry when more than fifty years of age, preaching more than forty years, building a church for his people at his own expense, helping Lane seminary in its early struggles for existence, giving a son to labor and die as a missionary in Palestine, having a daughter who married a clergyman—the parents of our new United States Minister to France, Hon. Levi Parsons Morton, of New York. Justin Parsons had also two brothers who lived here and finally became preachers—Rev. Silas and Rev. Benjamin Parsons. Silas also had a son Erastus, born here probably, became a preacher and labored with remarkable success during a short but active life. Rev. Rufus Cushman, brother of Rev. Ralph, was twenty two years pastor of a church in Fair Haven, Vt., was a man full of good words, faithful and beloved. His son, Rufus Cushman, D. D., thirty-four years in the ministry, died a few years since in Manchester, Vt.. And many others might be mentioned.

The pastors of the church who succeeded Mr. Whitman, many of whom like him had each their share in the work of fitting and inspiring some one or more of this large number of men and women for their noble work, were Rev. Joel Wright, Henry B. Holmes, John C. Thompson, Royal Reed, Robert Crossett, Thomas H. Rood, Sidney Holman, H. M. Rogers, Townsend Walker, George Juchan, D. B. Lord, and the present pastor, Rev. J. E. M. Wright, son of one of the worthy daughters of Goshen.

The society now has eighty-two members; their church building will comfortably accommodate 300 persons, and is valued, including grounds, at $3,000.00. The church has a fund of $5,000.00, known as the " Mrs. Mary Williams fund," which turns in an annual income of $250.00.

The Second Advent Society was organized by its first pastor, Elder Henry Pratt, in 1851. About forty members came into the society, some of them from adjoining towns. The church building was erected in 1878. It is a small affair, capable of accommodating 125 persons, and cost $600.00. The society now has thirty members.

GRANBY* is one of the smallest towns in the county. To one standing on Mt. Holyoke, looking northward, the old town of Hadley, lying on the east bank of the Connecticut river, presents a very beautiful picture, scenery as lovely as any to be found in the state ; fertile fields, luxuriant orchards, broad and productive farms, with fine buildings, indicative of thrift and comfort. Then, to the beholder looking southward and southeasterly, her two lovely daughters, South Hadley and Granby, present an equally comely appearance—beautiful farms, with acres of woodland interspersed, fruitful orchards, commodious barns, and comfortable houses, which are the homes of an intelligent, independent and cultured people.

The town of Granby lies east of South Hadley, west of Belchertown, south of Amherst, and is bounded on the south by Ludlow and Chicopee. It was incorporated as a separate town June 11, 1768, before which time it was reckoned a part of the precinct of South Hadley, which became a town in 1775. Efforts were made from time to time, though without success, to unite the two as one town.

Early Settlement.—The first grant of land south of the mountain by the mother town to Thomas Selden was made in 1675. Others were made soon after, some of which appear to have become void; for it was a half century later that the first permanent settlement was begun.

In 1727 twenty-one men settled south of the mountain, four of them in Granby. The latter were Ebenezer Taylor, John Smith, Ephraim Nash and John Lane. During the next four years their number was increased by five, the new neighbors being Timothy Nash, Joseph Nash, William Dickinson, Jr., Nehemiah Dickinson and Thomas Taylor. Six others were added during the next nine years, viz.: Stephen Warner, Sr., James Smith, Noah Ferry, Samuel Moody, John Moody and Hezekiah Smith. From 1740 to 1750 there were twelve additions, viz.: William Eastman, Aaron Nash, Phinehas Smith, 1st, Seth Clark, Noah Clark, John Preston, Experience Smith, Eleazar Nash, Martin Nash, Hezekiah Smith, Jr., Jonathan Selden and Samuel Dickinson. Of these, Seth and Noah Clark came from Northampton.

After 1750 the increase was much more rapid, and at the time Granby was incorporated as a town the population numbered about four hundred. This was forty years after the first settlement was made, and a hundred and nine after the settlement of the mother town. The population at different periods has been as follows: 1776, 491 ; 1790, 596 ; 1800, 786 ; 1810, 850 ; 1820, 1,066 ; 1830. 1,064 ; 1840, 971 ; 1850, 1,104 ; 1855, 1,001 ; 1860, 907 ; 1865, 908 ; 1870, 863 ; 1875, 812 ; 1880, 753.

Organization.—The Second Parish of South Hadley was incorporated as the township of Granby, June 11. 1768. The first town officers were Nathan Smith, clerk, who served until 1781, and was succeeded by Phinehas Smith,

---

* Prepared by Pliny S. Boyd.

Jr.; and selectmen, Aaron Nash, Samuel Moody, John Moody, Waitstill
Dickinson and Stephen Warner, Jr., who served one year and were succeeded
by an entirely new board, namely, Phinehas Smith, Eleazer Nash, Jacob
Taylor and Eleazer Warner. It was not thought best to change the entire
board the next year, for Aaron Nash appears again, the other members
being Benjamin Eastman, Thomas Hovey Moody, Asaph Stebbins and Samuel Vinton. The fourth year, Asahel Smith and Israel Clark were new members, the other three, Phinehas Smith, Eleazer Nash and John Moody, having
served before.

Not until the town was nine years old did it have again an entirely new board
of selectmen ; but in 1777 the records give, as having been chosen to this
office, Reuben Moody, Ebenezer Bartlett, Aaron Ayres, Joseph Lane and
Joseph Dickinson. But not another such complete revolution has occurred
since. In 1826 the board was reduced to three in number, but every year
one or more has been chosen who had served before.

It was the custom from the first, though not a uniform custom, to choose
three of the selectmen to serve as assessors. The person chosen town clerk
was elected to serve also as treasurer.

The other officers chosen at the first meeting were Asahel Smith, constable ; Samuel Warner, sealer of leather; Benjamin Eastman, sealer of measures, packer and clerk of the market, who was continued in this office twenty-
four years, and was succeeded by Perez Cook; Eleazer Warner, Seth Clark
and Joseph Montague, surveyors of highways ; Samuel Elmer and Reuben
Moody, wardens ; David Barton and Samuel Warner, tithingmen ; Israel
Clark and John Ayres, deer-reeves; and Jonathan Selden, James Preston
and William Negus, hog-reeves.

Deer-reeves were chosen up to the year 1793, and hog-reeves up to a much
later date. All the town officers were sworn to a faithful discharge of the
duties of their office. The town has, from the first, been highly favored in
being able to call to its service men of intelligence, ability and integrity, to
fill the various official trusts to be administered. A full list of all the town
officers would make a long chapter ; we venture only to mention a few names
prominent among them, some of whom have rendered signal service to the
town in various official positions. The order of mention is alphabetical,
rather than chronological: Aaron Ayres, John Ayres, Rodney Ayres, Samuel
Ayres, C. C. Aldrich, E. J. Aldrich, David Barton, James M. Barton, J. H.
Barton, William D. Barton, William Belcher, William Carver, Orlando Cha-
pin, Philo Chapin, Daniel Church, Samuel Clark, Noah Clark, Israel Clark,
Israel Clark, Jr., Jotham Clark, Charles F. Clark, Spencer Clark, Perez Cook,
Jr., S. M. Cook, Waitstill Dickinson, Eli Dickinson, Joseph Dickinson,
Henry A. Dickinson, Abner M. Dickinson, William B. Dickinson, Benjamin
Eastman, William Eastman, Reuben R. Eastman, Luther Ferry, Lucius
Ferry, Charles Ferry, Charles S. Ferry, W. W. Ferry, Harry W. Gridley,
Elijah Kent, Monroe Keith, Chester Kellogg, Samuel Moody, John Moody,

Simeon Moody, Reuben Moody, Enos Moody, Gideon, Moody, Augustus Moody, Eli Moody, Albert Moody, Aaron Nash, Lorenzo S. Nash, Asa Pease, John Preston, Jeriel Preston, Dexter Preston, William J. Patrick, Nathan Smith, Phinehas Smith, David Smith, Medad Smith, Enos Smith, Aaron Smith, Chester Smith, Samuel Smith, Dr. Cyrus B. Smith, S. C. Smith, William A. Smith, Simeon C. Stebbins, Levi Taylor, Willard Taylor, Francis E. Taylor, Frederick Taylor, Sylvester H. Taylor, Willard A. Taylor, John Tilley, Dr. Samuel Vinton, Stephen Warner, Jr., Eli Warner, Park Warner, E. D. Witt, Andrew White and A. S. White.

Educational.—In matters of educational interest Granby has held a place in the front ranks from the first. At the first town meeting after the organization it was voted to raise twenty pounds " for schooling," and that it be expended in " hiring schoolmasters." The amount was increased from time to time till it amounted to $1,500.00 annually, and more recently to $1,800.-00. For a great many years it was the custom of the town to make an appropriation for the encouragement of singing, and a committee was chosen at town-meeting to see that the money was judiciously expended.

In the early days the parents exercised large liberty with reference to what school they would patronize. And in 1789 it was " voted that any man shall have liberty to go to what District to a school he pleases, provided he shall make it appear to the committee that it is reasonable." It was then voted that the committee chosen should be elected to " divide the school money," although it appears that the duties of the committee were considerably more extensive. For a good many years it was customary to choose a general committee of the school, and then in addition a separate committee for each district. At present a committee of three has the entire charge of the schools of the town, one being elected each year. The present able and efficient committee consists of S. M. Cook, Willard A. Taylor and C. E. Hunt. The schools maintained are seven district schools, one conjointly with the town of Ludlow, and the high school.

Public Bequests—The town has received some valuable gifts, the first of which was a lot for the meeting-house, given by Samuel Moody in 1762, of which the deed was given by his sons in 1769. The same day James Smith gave a lot of one acre by deed, " in consideration of the respect and affection he bore for and towards the people of the town of Granby, for accommodating them with a convenient place for burying the dead."

In 1821 John Montague gave to the first parish "three acres of land to serve as the location of a meeting-house and a common." Twenty-four years later his son, Joseph Montague, gave for the purpose of enlarging the common an addition of two acres and a half. In 1886 Dexter Taylor gave to be maintained as a public park, or used for a public library building, the lot south of the common, opposite his home.

Military.—The history of the town in military affairs, like that in civil affairs, is such as to reflect great honor upon the people. It has been marked by great prudence, vigilance and determination, by genuine independence and patriotism. Nothing was undertaken through strife or vainglory, but for the liberties and rights of the people. It was voted in 1774 that the town should be represented by Mr. Phinehas Smith "at the Provincial Congress to be holden at Concord, on the second Tuesday of October, to hear, consider and determine, on all such matters and causes as shall then be thought necessary in this critical, dark and distressing day."

On May 20, 1776, it was voted that "the Selectmen purchase a drum and fife for the use of the Training Band of this town." And on the 20th of June, the same year, it was voted that "we of this town will support the independence of the American Colonies with our lives and fortunes, Provided the American Congress shall declare these Colonies Independent of the Kingdom of Great Brittain."

During the dark and bloody days of that period it was the custom to choose every year a committee of correspondence, direction and protection. At one meeting it was "voted to give Martin Nash 400 dolers to serve during the Present war for this town." And later it was " Voted to give Robert Owens the sum of two hundred Dolers for past services, and as an encouragement for him to serve for this Town during the present war."

In 1781 it was "voted to raise ten thousand pounds to procure beef for the continental army." It was voted that the pay of the soldiers should be in silver or gold, and Continental money or grain at certain specified rates. Great forethought was taken to secure to the people the liberties for which the war was carried on. A committee of nine men was chosen to examine the form of constitution proposed, and to report their opinion concerning the business contained therein ; and after their report the town voted to accept the constitution with such amendments as the committee suggested.

Town meetings were held with great frequency for the consideration of the public business. For the year 1781 the records report the doings of thirty-five meetings of the town.

The spirit of the people is shown in the vote that " The Town of Granby will use all means in their Power to render the intentions of the Gen'l Court of this State effectual Touching all things expressed in an act entitled an act to Prevent Monopoly and Oppression, &c."

The people did not hesitate to call their officers to account when they thought there was occasion for it ; nor to warn out of town any whose presence seemed likely to interfere with the general and public welfare. There independence was matched by their courage ; and their courage was tempered with prudence.

It is told of Levi Taylor, who at the age of sixteen joined the army of the Revolution, that when he left his home his mother said to him, " Levi, never let me hear of your being a coward." That determined spirit of the mother's found expression in the heroic services of noble sons, and is cherished and honored by an appreciative posterity.

Three generations later the same courage and patriotism were illustrated in the enlistment of a great-grandson, Joseph Knight Taylor, in the Union army in the war of the Rebellion, who, counting not his life too dear if only his country could live, gave himself a sacrifice, to die a patriot, and to live in memory a hero. He died in 1864, only 24 years of age. On his monument in the Granby cemetery, may be seen the expressive epitaph: "Sweet after battle is the tired soldier's rest."

The history of the town gathers luster also from the record of Capt. William B. Clark, in the war of the Rebellion. Of him it was said by one who knew him well, Surgeon Pease, also a son of Granby who served in the war, that "he was always perfectly cool and brave, and always led his men into action." "Few have had a better record; none could have had a more honorable death." It was said of him by a brother captain, "I have ever found him the same under all circumstances,—a kind, generous, noble-hearted, brave and Christian man. He combined the two qualities of bravery and prudence in a remarkable degree." In noble service he lost his life, struck down in battle, a hero and patriot, the true son of an honorable ancestry. Others, animated by the same spirit, shared their perils, but lived to enjoy the privileges and blessings they had saved to their country.

They went bravely to battle, some to sup with death and some to share the joys of victory. Their deeds have lent brightness to the annals of their country, and the muse of history has graven their names upon her enduring page. They were, George N. Fletcher, Samuel A. Chapin, Eliot P. Ferry, Lucien E. Robinson, Charles Bachelor, Frederick Bachelor, Edwin Smith, Andrew J. Converse, Danforth L. Converse, Lemuel Warner, Orlando Wilson, Cyrus B. Smith (surgeon), William Bartlett, William F. Pease, Robert M. Smith, Chapin Warner, Loren E. Goldthwait, Alexander P. Cook, William H. Cook, Michael O'Neil, George S Stebbins, Dwight A. Barrett, Frederick P. Converse, Charles A. Rhodes, Hiram Tilley, Charles W. Fletcher, John Warner, Malcolm Bridgman, Asaph P. Barton, Charles H. Bates, David Casey, Samuel B. Dickinson, Francis H. Gardner, Charles W. Hunter, Edwin N. Hunt, Dwight C. Morgan, Dwight Preston, Samuel C. Smith, William A. Smith, Charles Spooner, Sylvester H. Taylor, John Tilley, Frank H. Stearns, Charles H. Church.

While they were at the front, the home-guard of patriots sustained them honorably by vote, sympathy, material aid and kindly ministries. The record of the town during the war is a patriotic one. At the outset, "the sum of a thousand dollars was voted to pay the soldiers while drilling, and for the support for the space of a year thereafter, of the families of such as should lose their lives in the contest." And action in keeping with this beginning was maintained throughout the contest.

It may be added in a final word, that as in the war for independence and the war for union and liberty, the town can boast of an honorable record, so in all the great reformatory movements her people have shown a real devotion to the best interests of humanity. In wealth of character the town is as rich as in natural beauty and attractiveness. In this she is almost unrivaled, showing a great variety of hill and dale, mountain and meadow, upland and lowland, field and forest, rich in flowers and foliage, the fitting ornamentation of a land flowing with milk and honey, a land well suited to be the home of patriots and heroes, worthy citizens of a Paradise regained.

Notes Biographical.—David Church, son of Josiah, was born in South Hadley, and made the first settlement upon the farm now owned by Monroe Keith, and resided in Granby the larger part of his life. He married Rachel Moody, daughter of John Moody, one of the early settlers. She bore him five children, David, Jonathan, Nadoiah, Benjamin and Rachel. David married Lucy Scranton, who bore him nine children, namely, Lois, John, Rufus, Allen, Ruel, Augustin, Mary, David and Marilla, all of whom except Ruel and three daughters are living, and three, John, Rufus and Augustin, in Granby.

Noah Ferry was born 1712, and lived on the farm now owned by Charles Kellogg. He married Experience Allis, and both are buried in the cemetery at Granby. They reared four children, Noah, Charles, Daniel and Rebecca. Noah, Jr., was born in this town October 18, 1748, married Hannah, daughter of Joseph Montague, and reared ten children. Capt. Luther Ferry was born in Granby, and reared nine children, viz.: Lucius, Luther, Addison, Edwin, Alvin, Susannah, Lois, Azuba and Julia.

Elihu Clark, son of Israel, and a descendant of Lieut. William Clark, was born December 7, 1785, married Roxa Ayres, and had born to him six children, viz.: Clinton, who was a graduate of Amherst college, Climena, Sarah E., Spencer and Mercer. Spencer married Aurilla, adopted daughter of Alvan Davis, of Royalston, Mass., and lived on the farm now owned by Mrs. Clark, until his death, which occurred may 14, 1883, aged sixty-four years. He had born to him one son, William S., who is attending Yale college.

John Giddings was one of the early settlers of this town, and settled on the farm now owned by Angeline Kellogg. His son James was born in this town, and his children were as follows: Mary, Daniel, Sally, Patty, John, Joseph and Huldah. The last mentioned married Calvin Shaw, of Belchertown, who was a sea captain, and died at Savannah, June 10, 1812. They had one child, Calvin, who resides in this town.

Jonathan Burnet came to Granby, from Long Island, about 1770, and purchased the farm now owned by Nelson Smith. He married Mehetable Dickinson, and had born to him seven children. Bela, son of Jonathan, married twice, first Clarissa Warner, who bore him three children, all deceased, and second, Sally (Johnson) Alden, and had two children, only one of whom is living, Salena, the wife of Nelson Smith.

Dolphin D. Chapin, son of Dormer, who was a son of Capt. Phineas, and a lineal descendant of Dea. Samuel Chapin who came from Wales and settled in Roxbury about 1635, was born in 1810, married Achsah M., daughter of Amos Ferry of this town, and in 1842 moved on to the place where he now resides. His children are Edmund M., Dennison, Norman O., Dolmer F., Delia L. and Sarah E.

Israel Clark, Jr., was the sixth in lineal descent from Lieut. William Clark who came to this country from England, in 1630, and located in Northampton about 1659. Israel was the son of Israel and Sarah (Smith) Clark, was born in Granby, October 15, 1791, married Tibbel Clark in 1822, and had born to him two daughters. He was prominent in the building of the meeting-house, and served as an officer of the town for over twenty years. He was a clothier by trade, and owned a farm in the eastern part of the town. He had a saw-mill, a grist-mill and a satinet-mill on Forge pond. He also had a paper-mill on Swift river in Belchertown. He died March 20, 1865.

Phineas Smith was an early settler of this town, and was the first settler on the farm now owned by his grandson, Austin Smith. He married Mary White, of South Hadley, and reared eight children, viz.: Phineas, Irene, Medad, Adolphus, Giles, Calvin, Titus and Chester. Phineas, Jr., married Susan Ayres, and had born to him five children, namely, Cephas, Austin, Alva, Mary and Austin, 2d. Cephas, Mary and Austin all reside at the homestead. Austin married Mary S. Pease, and has had born to him five children, viz.: Susan, Charles A., Willis A., Edwin P. and Robert C. Adolphus, son of Phineas, was born in this town, married Susannah Ferry, and reared nine children, viz.: Emeline, Giles, Eliza, Finley, Julia, Edwin, Loman, Elliot and Susan. He made the first settlement on the farm now owned by his son, Elliot Smith, and built the house in which he now resides. Elliot married twice, first, Susan E. Hunt, who bore him one child, Edward H., and died in 1873, and second, Lucy Barrell, and has one child, George C.

VILLAGES.

GRANBY, the location approaching the dignity of a village, is located in the central part of the town. It has a store and a postoffice, Congregational church, town-house, high school, and twenty or thirty dwellings.

INDUSTRIES.

With regard to the industries of Granby, little need be said, except that they have been pursued, chiefly in the agricultural line, with patient and continuous application, and rewarded with honest and moderate gains. Thirty years ago, in his historical sketch, Dr. Holland, a resident of the town, remarked that "The manufacturing interest in Granby is limited." It has not grown in importance since that brief summary. Bachelor brook, in the north part of the town, has furnished power for the principal enterprises that have been undertaken. Fifty years ago a woolen factory was established and run successfully for a time, by Samuel Ayres, Jeriel Preston and Levi Taylor, under Mr. Taylor's superintendence. After Mr. Taylor's death in 1849, the business was continued by Ayres & Aldrich. Now, only a grist-mill is run in the same locality, by Mr. Aldrich. Near the outlet of Forge pond Israel Clark, long active and prominent in town affairs, was engaged in the manufacture of satinet. The power is now employed by Samuel C. Smith in running a grist-mill and saw-mill. In the early part of the present century an iron-forge was run there by Elijah Kent. About the middle of the present century Frederic Taylor and Anson Brown engaged in the manufacture of paper on Bachelor brook; their mill was burned and was never re-built. In the southeast part of the town, George Carver has a mill for manufacturing reeds, and Henry Carver runs a saw-mill and makes machines for manufacturing butter.

ECCLESIASTICAL.

The Church of Christ Congregational Society.—The long contest which existed between South Hadley and Granby at the time they formed the south or second precinct of Hadley, regarding the location of a meeting-house, which should equally accommodate each section, resulted in a division and the establishment of a separate church organization in Granby. The original church edifice was erected and the church organized in 1762, and in October of that year Rev. Simon Backus, of Norwich, Conn., and a graduate of Yale college, was settled as pastor. The church was influential and prosperous from the first, but owing to an unhappy difference in reference to the site of a new meeting-house in 1821, a division occurred, and two churches were maintained until 1836. Since the reunion, it has continued to prosper, as a strong and influential Christian body. The present church building was erected in 1822. The society now has 222 members.

The town has been served in the gospel ministry by Simon Backus, 1762–84; Benjamin Chapman, 1790–96; Elijah Gridley, 1797–1834; Chester Chapin, 1822–30; Joseph Knight, 1830–36; Eli Moody, as colleague with Mr. Gridley, 1530–34, then as pastor of the united churches until 1840; James Bates, 1840–51; Henry Mills, 1854–63; H. S. Kelsey, 1863–66; J. P. Cushman, 1867–70; Rufus Emerson, 1871–74; R. Henry Davis, 1875–78; F. R. Wait, 1879–81; and Fritz W. Baldwin, 1882–84. The present pastor, Pliny S. Boyd, was installed March 4, 1885.

GREENWICH lies in the extreme eastern part of the county, and is bounded north by Prescott, east by the county line, south by Ware, and west by Enfield and Prescott. It is a long, narrow township, nearly eight miles in length, and less than three in width, containing an area of about 14,000 acres.

The town has a pleasingly diversified surface and a fertile soil. It is decidedly a valley town, with skirting hills on either side, and drained by the east and west branches of Swift river, with their affluents, while several ponds lend a decided picturesqueness to the scenery. Into one of these, Moose pond, the east branch discharges its waters. The other ponds are Warner pond, in the north part of the town, Curtis pond, about a mile further south, and Davis pond, southwest of Greenwich Village. The principal elevation is Pomeroy mountain, just north of Greenwich Village, attaining an altitude of about 800 feet. Mt. Liz, south of the Village, attains about the same altitude. Cooley's hill, another elevation, is situated near the Enfield line. Added to attractive scenery, Greenwich has a decidedly healthful climate. Many from a distance make it their summer home on these accounts.

Grant, Settlement and Subsequent Growth.—In the well-known Narragansett expedition, during King Philip's war, the 840 soldiers who took part therein, were promised, "if they played the part of men, took the fort, and drove the enemy out of the country, they should have a gratuity in land besides their wages." Pursuant to this promise, the general court, on June 30, 1732, granted to their descendants seven townships, each six miles square, which thus gave one such township to each 120 soldiers.

These townships were located in Maine, New Hampshire and Massachusetts, and were designated as "Narragansett Township No. 1," etc., through the numerals to seven. Of these, Narragansett Township No. 4 was located in New Hampshire. It was subsequently reported that this New Hampshire land was unfit for settlement, and on November 17, 1735, a committee was appointed "to search out better land in exchange."

The land now included within the limits of Greenwich and Enfield was called "Quabbin," a name obtained, it is said, from "King Quabbin," an Indian sachem, who early dwelt with his tribe near the junction of the two branches of the river, in the southern part of the present town of Greenwich.

The committee appointed to look up another location for Township No. 4, selected Quabbin, which is described as bounded as follows :—

"North by Salem town; easterly by Lambstown [now Hardwick]; southerly by the Equivalent Land; and westerly by William Reed's land."

In 1737 this territory was surveyed, and found to lack considerable of the allotted six miles square, so additional grants were made, corresponding with the present towns of Chesterfield and Goshen, as we have detailed in the respective histories of those towns.

On January 14, 1736, the general court issued the grant of Quabbin to "Narragansett No. 4, especially granting 1,200 acres of it to James Patterson, Robert Fenton, Edward Miller, James Wheeler, John Patterson, Andrew Turner, Thomas Powers, Arthur Cary, Robert Evans, Robert Carlile, —— Thorp, and —— Holden, to each of them fifty acres for a house-lot, to be laid out by a committee of the general court, and the remaining fifty acres to be included in the general division." These twelve men are supposed to have been actual settlers on Quabbin's territory, and hence to them we look as the pioneers. They were from Brookfield, Connecticut and the North of

Ireland. The conditions of this grant were that they severally dwell thereon
with their families for four years, put ten acres under good cultivation, and
grant 300 acres to the first settled minister, the same to the second, and another for a school lot.

On May 12, 1737, a committee, consisting of John Foster, Shubael Conant, Samuel Childs, Samuel Tildake and Ebenezer Mun, was appointed to
lay out and allot the land of Quabbin, and were directed to lay out ten acres
of land for a meeting house and burying-ground, highways, and a lot of the
contents of sixty acres to each proprietor, besides ministry and school lots.

On June 20, 1787, the southern part of the town was incorporated as the
" South Parish " of Greenwich ; and on February 15, 1816, the town of Enfield was incorporated, reducing the area of Greenwich to its present limits.

Of the early settlement of Quabbin little is deffinitely known. Its first settler is supposed to have been John Patterson, as we have detailed in the
sketch of Enfield, where we have also given a long list of the early settlers.
Families by the name of Gibbs, Hinds, Powers, Rogers and Cooley have also
advanced claims to the honor of having furnished the first settler. The
records, however, do not seem to corroborate their claims. The name of
Thomas Gibbs first appears in the records in 1740. A little later Jeremiah
and David Powers appear, together with William Carpenter, Simon Davis,
John Rea, John Townsend, Nathan Fiske, Abraham Gibbs, John Harwood
and Timothy Ruggles. A little later is found the names of Hopestill Hinds,
Benjamin Cooley, James Nevins, James Wright, James Whitcombe, William
Rogers, Luke Hitchcock and ——- Holmes. These families were prominent
in the affairs of the town during the first thirty years of the town's history.

Later, families of prominence have been the Hales, Cutlers, Ayres, Blod-
getts, Walkers, Shumways, Davises, Marcys Trasks, Sprouts, Richards,
Sears, Blackmers, Vaughns, Roots, Fullers, Haskells, Hookers, Fields, Robin-
sons, Douglasses, Jordans, Stones, Warners, Snows, Doaks and Earles.

Elias Haskell was an early settler of this town, came here from Rochester,
Mass., and located on the place where his son, at the advanced age of ninety
years, now resides. The latter was born on the homestead, May 28, 1796,
married Mary Raymore and has reared four children, namely, Ira D., Elias,
who died at the age of two years, Mary, who married E. W. Sanderson, of
Northampton, and Harvey T., who died at the age of ten years. Ira D.
married Adeline E., daughter of Ezra Ayres of this town, and moved to Enfield in 1858, where he has since been engaged in mercantile trade. He has
one child, Charles D., who is engaged in the store with his father.

Peter Blackmer was born in Warren, moved to Greenwich at a very early
day, and settled on the place now owned by George Wheeler. He married
Esther Shepherd and reared ten children, viz.: Roland, who was a prominent man in town, having held the offices of treasurer, selectman and others ;
Mary, David, Peter, Susan, Esther, Thankful, Asa, Amos and Moses. Amos
married Margaret Gray in 1802, lived in the northern part of the town after

his marriage, and moved to Prescott in 1810. He died April 18, 1823, and his widow died March 7, 1853. His six children were as follows : Mary D., born in Greenwich in 1805 ; Daniel G., born in 1809 ; Peter, born in 1811 ; William H., born in 1814 ; Esther S. and Amos H. The last mentioned is the only surviving member of his father's family, and married Lydia Sanger in 1859. He met with an accident in 1835, which has since debarred him from hard labor. He moved to Greenwich Village in 1869.

James Richard, Jr., was born in Greenwich, South Parish, now Enfield, March 20, 1801, married Priscilla Newcomb, August 22, 1822, and reared nine children, namely, Maria F., Charles W., William W., George H., Sarah J., John W., Mary M., Louise F. A., and Marshall N. Maria F. married A. F. Newcomb, and has two children, Fannie and Charles. The latter married Azubah Powell. William W. married Alice Currier, and has had born to him three sons, all deceased. George H. married twice, first, Julia Stackney, and second, Lydia Newell, and has two sons, Edward N. and Louis H. Sarah J. married Erastus Marsh, and three of their four children are living, James E., George H. and Nellie. John W. married Ann Currier, and only one of their four children is living, namely, Harry. Mary M., born March 7, 1836, has always lived at home. Louise F. A. married Austin Shumway, and has had nine children. Marshall N. married Louise R. Munroe, and four of their six children are living, namely, Fannie L., Lottie M., Gracie and James R. James Richard, Jr., died February 16, 1886, aged eighty-four years, and his wife died November 1, 1881, aged eighty years.

Lorenzo Davis, son of Philip, was born in Stafford, Conn., September 2, 1808, and came with his father to Greenwich in 1811. He learned the carpenter's trade, and helped put up the first shafting in the first cotton-mill in Holyoke. He bought four acres of land in 1837, built the house where he now resides, and has continued to add to his farm, until he now has 290 acres. He married twice, first, Sophronia Shumway, who bore him four children, namely, Erasmus C., who served in the late war, in Co. I, Mass. V. I., died while there, Philip S., who died in infancy, Lucy S., who married Henry Pomeroy, and Ellen S. The mother of these children died in 1844, and Mr. Davis married for his second wife, Mary M. Esterbrook, in 1846.

Charles S. Record came to Greenwich Village in 1829, at the age of ten years, was apprenticed to Gen. John Warner, who was at that time engaged in the manufacture of scythes, and worked for him twenty-one consecutive years. He has held various offices of trust, has been town treasurer, road commissioner, and has been constable and collector for ten years. He has been chorister at the Congregational church for twenty-five years, and a member of the said choir for forty-seven years. He married Mary L., daughter of Cyrus Loud, in 1850, and has one daughter, Clara L., born in 1853. The latter married Ambrose E. Walker, of this town.

Mrs. Selina Morse, is the widow of Jeremiah M., and daughter of Ephraim Thayer, of Dana, Mass., and came to Greenwich Village with her husband, soon after marriage. Mr. Morse was a shoemaker, and died in this town in February, 1851, leaving four children, Oscar F., Charles P., Frances E. and Sarah L. Oscar F. was born in 1833, married Sarah J. White, in 1866, and has two children, Arthur L. and Mabel B. Charles P. married Clara Barns, and has two children. Frances married Daniel W. Parker, and has had born to her two children, Frank L. and Charles M. Mr. Parker died in 1875, and Mrs. Parker married for her second husband, Abel O. Parker, and has one child, Webster M. Sarah L. married Eugene Barrows, and died in 1872.

Ezra Alden, son of Festus, was born at Hardwick, Mass., in October, 1851, and came to this town with his parents while quite young. He married Mary Stevens, December 23, 1872, and has had born to him two children, Frederick E. B., born in 1873, and Sarah E., born in September, 1881.

The fluctuations in the town's population may be seen in the following figures: In 1776 it had 890; 1790, 1,045; 1800, 1,460; 1810, 1225; 1820, 778; 1830, 813; 1840, 824; 1850, 838; 1855, 803; 1860, 699; 1865, 648; 1870, 665; 1875, 606; 1880, 633.

Organizations.—On June 20, 1749, an act was passed by the general court incorporating Quabbin into a parish. On the 4th of November of the same year the first parish meeting was held, when the following officers were chosen: Thomas Gibbs, moderator; William Carpenter, clerk; Thomas Gibbs, Jeremiah Powers and David Powers, prudential committee; John Townsend, William Carpenter and Nathan Fiske, assessors; and Abraham Gibbs, collector.

On the 20th of April, 1754, the general court passed an act incorporating the parish into a township with all the privileges belonging thereto, though it included the present towns of Dana and Petersham, in Worcester county, and a large portion of Enfield. The name of the town was given in honor of General Greenwich.

The first meeting for the organization of the town under its new dispensation was held at the meeting-house on Thursday, August 15, 1754, when the following officers were elected: John Worthington, moderator; Nathan Fiske, clerk; Jeremiah Powers, James Nevins, Benjamin Cooley, John Rea and John Townsend, selectmen; Nathan Fiske, Abraham Gibbs and Benjamin Cooley, assessors; and several other minor officers.

Military.—In the war for independence, the records show that Greenwich performed well its part. Of those who entered the service were the following: David Blackmer, Charles Bruce, Roland Sears, Moses Robinson, Barnabas Rich, Giles Rider and —— Pratt.

In the war of 1812 the town sent out the following: Andrew Harwood, Luther Root, Ezra Sprout, Chester Hale, Daniel Tourtelott, Benjamin Rider, Henry Forbes, Samuel Barton, Daniel Eddy, Ichabod Pope and Kingsley Underwood.

In the late great war Greenwich furnished sixty-three men, a surplus of two over all demands, expended $6,893.29, and loaned the state $3,033.91.

VILLAGES.

GREENWICH VILLAGE is a thriving little post-village, located in the northeastern section of the town, on the east branch of Swift river. It is made of several stores, a hotel, the usual compliment of mechanics' shops, etc., and has some very pretty residences. The postoffice was established here about 1807, and Warren P. Wing was the first postmaster.

GREENWICH, or Greenwich Plain as it is locally known, is somewhat smaller than the "Village," but surely is as pleasantly located, near the geographical center of the town. About 1810 the postoffice was established here, and the present postmaster is Eugene G. Kellogg.

HOTELS.

The first hotel in the town is said to have been kept by Dr. Trask, on the " Marcy place." About the same time, however, Timothy Hinds kept one on the old Ayres place, and these two were for a long time the only ones in town. The next prominent place of public resort was kept for a great many years, beginning about the first part of the present century, by Col. Thomas

(RIVERSIDE HOTEL, H. M. BROWN, PROPRIETOR.)

Powers, on the old Powers place, at Greenwich Village. It was afterwards kept, either in the same place or on the site of the present hotel, by Edmund Raymore. The present house here, of which we give the accompanying en-

19*

graving, is called the "Riverside Hotel," with Henry M. Brown, proprietor. It is pleasantly situated on the main street, in the midst of a fine maple grove, and is a delightful summer home. It runs a free 'bus to the railroad station, and has a good livery connected.

At the "Plains" is the "Greenwich Hotel," with Edward O. Williams, proprietor. This, too, is pleasantly located, and in the midst of a region that is popular with summer boarders.

INDUSTRIES.

In the early part of the century a scythe factory was established at Greenwich Village, by Gen. John Warner. He was afterwards joined by his son-in-law, David Allen, who finally succeeded him in the business. The factory was destroyed by fire in 1858. About 1818, Ezra Ayres, at the old "Ayres place," engaged in the manufacture of pewter buttons. Nathan Powers had a woolen-mill, at an early date, and later Warren P. Wing engaged in the manufacture of "cards" at the village. The first saw and grist mill was built in 1745, by a Mr. Holmes, at Greenwich Village.

S. P. Bailey's lumber-mill, at Greenwich Village, is operated by water-power, gives employment to three hands, and turns out about 300,000 feet of lumber per year, and also furnishes considerable material for builders.

M. J. Wheeler's brush and broom factory at Greenwich Village, turns out about 2,500 dozen brooms and brushes per year.

Tourtellott & Walker's saw and grist-mill, on the east branch, has three runs of stones and the capacity for sawing 1,000,000 feet of lumber per year, while they also manufacture shingles and chair stock.

John Powers's saw-mill, located on the outlet of Brown's pond, in the northern part of the town, has the capacity for sawing about 8,000 feet of lumber per day.

The Congregational church.—The church in Greenwich is among the older ones in Hampshire county, established in 1849, and for 137 years has had an honorable record in its relation to Christ's kingdom upon earth. Its first minister for eleven years, was the Rev. Elijah Webster. In 1760 Rev. Robert Cutler became its pastor, and for twenty-six years continued to break to them the bread of life. In 1786 he was succeeded by the Rev. Joseph Blodgett, who for forty-three years continued in the pastoral office. The words on his monument : " He was a meek, faithful and holy minister," are without doubt a just tribute to his worth. The Rev. Joseph Patrick was installed his successor and colleague, and continued in faithful service until 1842. The present pastor is Rev. Edward P. Blodgett, who also is in the forty-fourth year of his ministry to this church, being ordained and installed in July, 1843. He has only one his senior in service as pastor of the same church in the Commonwealth connected with the evangelical ministry, the Rev. Edmund Douse, of Sherborn. He came a young man directly from his seminary life to this field, and is now past his three score years and ten. During his ministry he has officiated at funeral services among the people, and has followed to the grave more in number than the present population of the town. The organization of the church dates back farther than that of the town itself. Its record is worthy of note. Its children are scattered from Vermont to Florida and from Massachusetts to Kansas. The great wish of the pastor has been to fit young men and women for service elsewhere—to enrich churches in larger places. Thus it has sent away neary ten to help others, where it has received one from other churches. And although so many have been removed to the future world, and such drafts made upon it to enrich others, yet, through the grace of God, the names upon its record are more in number to-day than forty years ago. In its early formation and along its earlier history it was blessed with men and women of Puritan stock, who were rooted and grounded in the truth, who in storm and in sunshine held to the faith once delivered to the saints, and who in their lives as well as by their belief were ever ready to vindicate the truth and honor of God.

To what this worthy pastor has thus written we will add, the first church building was erected in 1744–45. The present structure at the "Plain" was built in 1824, and is now valued, including grounds, at $5,000.00. The society now has 132 members.

There is also a neat Spiritualist church here, built by Henry W. Smith; but those who we depended on for a sketch of the same failed to send in statistics.

HADLEY* lies in the central part of the county, and is bounded north by the county line, east by Amherst, south by South Hadley, from which it is separated by Mt. Holyoke, and east by the sinuous course of the Connecticut river, which separates it from Northampton and Hatfield. It has an area of about 17,000 acres.

The surface of Hadley is varied, or rather while it has considerable plain land, it has yet diversity enough to lend a pleasing picturesqueness to its scenery. Along the river the surface is nearly level, and at the village of Hadley spreads to the westward, forming an extensive peninsula, inclosed by the Connecticut on the north, west and south. South and east of Fort river is a considerable table-land, called "Lawrence Plain," whose general surface is from thirty to fifty feet above the river bottoms, and extends southward and eastward to the vicinity of the mountain range. Most of the eastern-central portion of the town consists of rolling land, whose connection with the lower surface to the westward is, for some distance, sharply defined by a low terrace or bluff. Mt. Warner rises from the central part of the northern half of the town. North of

*For much of this sketch we are indebted to the kindness of Bishop Huntington, now of Syracuse, N. Y.

Mill river the surface foams a low, undulating plain, except in the northeast corner of the town, where are still lower lands called the "Great Swamp." Another small tract of low land lies east of Mt. Warner, near the Amherst line, and is called "Partrigg Swamp."

In an agricultural point of view, the lands of Hadley are of the richest in the Connecticut valley. In the river-flats the soil is made up of a sandy alluvium. The uplands are principally of loam, with more or less sand. Intervals composed chiefly of light clay are also found.

The streams are Fort and Mill rivers. The former flows a westerly and southwesterly course through the southern half of the town, emptying into the Connecticut just above Hockanum. The latter flows in the same general direction across the northern half of the town, dropping into the Connecticut at North Hadley.

Grant and Settlement.—Of the general causes which led to the settlement of this section we have spoken, in the general county narrative, in the sketch of Northampton, and in other places in this work, so that to go over the ground again would be a needless repetition; while the same may be said of the scenery, description of Mt. Holyoke, and the geology. At this point, then, we will simply say that the settlement of Hadley was brought about by certain troubles existing in the churches of Hartford and Wethersfield, in Connecticut —troubles that had long been a subject of contention, but were more vigorously stirred up about two years before the grant of the plantation, which was given by the general court May 25, 1658.

As we have said, about two years before this town was planted, a church council, sitting in Boston, composed of delegates from the Massachusetts and Connecticut colonies, has so far innovated upon previous ecclesiastical usage as to declare that the rite of baptism might be administered to the children of non-communicants, if themselves baptized, and of a decent external life. Among the places where this rule of the half-way covenant introduced a division of sentiment, was Hartford. Perhaps there were other occasions of difference. Cotton Mather says that "from the fire of the altar" in Hartford, " there issued thunderings and lightenings and earthquakes through the colony," but that " the true original of the misunderstanding was about as obscure as the rise of the Connecticut river." Rev. Mr. Hooker, who had moved there from the First church in Cambridge, eminent and judicious, had died ten years before. His colleague and successor, Samuel Stone, leaned to the new way, was possibly a little disposed besides to extend the recognized conditions of church membership, and at the same time to favor some of the measures of the Presbyterians. A minority of the church opposed these tendencies, to the extent of a controversy, venerating the measures and the memory of Hooker, and standing firm on the Cambridge platform. That the origin of these difficulties, however, was earlier than the Boston synod, appears from the fact that special local councils had been previously held at Hartford, three years in succession. At last, an apparent agreement, called a " pacification," was reached ; but this was soon broken, and as several of the recusant minority, including Governor Webster, having been threatened with discipline, were on the point of withdrawing, for the purpose of joining the church under Rev. John Russell, at Wethersfield, the general court interfered and peremptorily laid an injunction on both parties, forbidding at once the excommunication and the secession—a characteristic illustration of the existing relations between the civil and ecclesiastical power. Just now the minority sagaciously bethought them of a less offensive expedient for getting rid of the obnoxious connection : that of moving up the river into the Massachusetts colony. A formal and pious petition to that effect was entered at Boston, by John Cullick and William Goodwin, expressing a hope that " through the grace of Christ," " the conversations " of the petitioners should " be without offence." A grant was secured for lands " East of Northampton," with a condition affixed that a new council should be called for an orderly composing of the Hartford troubles—a condition that shows how scrupulously the authorities guarded both the purity and the peace of their religious organization. They would not suffer a diplomacy which merely separated the antagonists without healing the discord. The upshot was a censure of both sides, acceptable terms of reconciliation, and a continued fellowship between the Hartford and Hadley churches. There had evidently sprung up a sympathy between these Hartford emigrants and a portion of the church at Wethersfield, including their minister, Mr. Russell, which resulted in a transfer of a majority of the latter, with Mr. Russell himself, to Norwottuck, or Hadley. Thus it appears that the founders of Hadley were strict and determined Congregationalists, as opposed to the half-way baptismal covenant on the one hand and to Presbyterianizing tendencies on the other.

The meeting at Hartford, at which the engagement to move was drawn up and signed, was held April 18, 1659, at the dwelling house of " Goodman " Ward. Among the names of signers which are still known in the living generation of the present town are Porter, Warner, Marsh, Russell, White, Field, Dickinson, Smith, Hooker, Hitchcock, Montague, Billings and Hubbard. The name of Partrigg also occurs, being undoubtedly the same from which the considerable district east of the mountain has been called " Patrick's," or Partrigg's "Swamp." The whole number of the withdrawers' names is sixty, more than half of which belonged to Hartford, the rest being divided between Wethersfield and Windsor ; but only forty-two men appear to have actually joined the expedition. It was stipulated that house-lots, embracing eight acres each, should be laid out on the east side of " the great river," leaving " a street twenty rods broad betwixt the two westermost rows of house-lots." To this wholesome provision at the outset is due the ample breadth of this avenue, unsurpassed in New England, which, with its two rows of sentinel elms, supplied by the taste of successive generations, has left an image of beauty in the memory of admiring travelers scattered in all lands.

On the part of the Northampton settlers it had been voted, in October of the previous year, to "give away Capawonk"—the Indian name of the lower meadow in Hatfield—provided the Hartford men should "settle two plantations, one on each side of the river;" provided they should "maintain a sufficient fence against hogs and cattle;" provided they should "pay ten pounds, in wheat and peas," and provided, fourthly, they should "inhabit here by next May."

An order was adopted by the general court, May 28, 1659, directing five persons, viz.: "Capt. Pinchon, Left. Holyhoke, Deacon Chapin, Wm. Holton and Richard Lyman,"—three being of Springfield and two of Northampton—to "lay out the bounds of the towne at Norwottocke"—"not only to carry on a towne but Church-worke also," "that this wilderness may be populated, and the maine ends of our coming into these parts may be promoted." By their report, the limits were defined; being fixed at "the head of the Falls" on the south, near "the hills called Petowamachu," our Holyoke; at the little brook called Nepasoaneag and Mount Kunckquachu, our "Toby," on the north; at a line nine miles from the Great River Quienecticott, eastward; together with a strip on the west side of the river north of Northampton, two miles wide, extending from a "little riverett" running by Capawonk up to "a great mountain called Wequamps." These two last boundaries are readily recognized now as Mill river in Hatfield and Sugar Loaf mountain. In the actual allotment, the town on the eastward never extended nine miles. Among those who settled on the west side we find the names of Dickinson, Graves, Belding, White, Warner and Billings, with Allis and Meekins, of Braintree, in the Massachusetts colony. The three sachems of Nolwotogg, or Norwottuck, of whom Pynchon procured the deed of this territory, were Chickwollop, Umpanchella and Quonquont. The price was about seven hundred feet of wampum and a few trinkets. In money the whole cost of the town territory was one hundred and fifty pounds, and this was thought to be a higher rate than was paid for any other plantation in New England. It serves to show the rapid increase of value, that only in 1664, seven hundred acres of the "Bradstreet farm" in Hatfield were bought for two hundred pounds in money—fifty pounds more than the original price of the whole settlement—besides a thousand acres in Whately and five hundred elsewhere given in exchange.

The name HADLEY—adopted for no very apparent reason, probably the early associations of some settlers from the Hadley of Suffolk county, in Old England—was applied by the general court in 1661. Commissioners were required to be appointed to sit as magistrates at the local courts in Northampton and Springfield; and Mr. William Westwood was "authorized to joine persons in marriage."

By the first plan of the village in 1663, it would appear that the general and unusually regular features remain essentially unchanged. Forty-seven house-lots were arranged on the two sides of the single street. There were three highways leading into the meadows, one at the north end, on ground since abraded by the river, another at the south end as now, and the third the same that still, as it did at first, conducts by the grave-yard. There were also, as now, North and South and Middle highways running eastward, toward Pine Woods, or the Pine Plain,—the middle one, since "Academy Lane," and later yet "Russell Street," ending with a gate. Of these house-lots a few seem to be, or to have been during the present generation, held by persons of the same name and blood as their original owners—as those of Montague, Porter, and White. The spot occupied by the "Russell church," or a little north of it, was reserved as town property, and was next north of the residence of Rev. Mr. Russell. After Mr. Russell, the settler that was found most frequently in public connections was Peter Tilton, a man of great energy and activity, sagacious and trusty; the ancestor of the Eastmans.

According to the general principle of the settlements, all settlers were assigned land, though not in the ratio of their previous possessions; and it does not appear that there was any case of serious discontent or breach of harmony, in what, judging by the common characteristics of human nature, and the Yankee human nature in particular, we should pronounce a very delicate and difficult undertaking. It was clearly the approved policy to make as many citizens as possible proprietors in the soil, thereby laying what has always proved one of the surest foundations not only of local prosperity, but of patriotism and civil stability. Consider the democratic equality. It is proved by the records, that the largest difference of ownership among the original assignments, was as the difference between one and four; that is, that the largest landholder owned only four times as much as the smallest.

The outlying portions of the township were ultimately distributed in a similar way to the inhabitants—"Forty acre Meadow," to the north, between the main village and "School Meadow,"—"Fort Meadow" to the southeast, —"Hockanum Meadow," so called from a similar district of land in East Hartford, on the south, and the "Great Meadow" occupying the body of the peninsula; including "Meadow Plain" next the home-lots, "Aquavitæ," or "Aquavitæ Bottle," from some resemblance to such a vessel, southward, "Maple Swamp" adjoining, and a region on the northwestern extremity, named 'Forlorn" or otherwise "Honey Pot," either from a deep place in the river, or, as some have supposed, from being the resort of wild bees, or as is less likely, from the richness of the soil. Besides these there were four meadows on the west or Hatfield side of the river, viz.: the "Great North," the "Little Meadow," the "South Meadow," or Wequettayag, including an Indian "reservation" called "Indian Bottom," or "Indian Hollow," and the "Southwest Meadow," toward Northampton, or "Capawonk," the two latter, separated by Mill river, being sometimes called Great and Little "Pansett."

It was only eight years after the laying out of the town that the people of the West-side, to the number of fourscore and ten, sent to the colonial governor and deputies a petition for a separate organization—setting forth the distressing and intolerable inconveniences of the ferry, especially as creating a violation of the Lord's day in the labor and time of crossing, in rough weather causing the women and children to "screech" and be made "unfit for ordinances," bringing the men into the water and through the ice, wetting them to the skin, and obliging them to leave many of their number at home, exposed as "a prey to the heathen." One house was already burnt to the ground while the men were gone to worship. The people of the East-side opposed this dismemberment, conceiving that their neighbors had "no call of God thereto." The matter was debated with spirit by both parties some three years, when in 1670, the incorporation was granted, and the territory set off was called Hatfield, or "Hattsfields," after an English town. By the terms of the separation, a large portion of the meadow land next the river, west of the ferry, was reserved to Hadley. In 1692 Hatfield moved for a transfer of this land to her own domain, which was not obtained till after a series of hard legal contests extending over forty-one years.

From time to time, on petition of the inhabitants, the general court extended the bounds of Hadley towards the east and south. The contents at the largest were eighty square miles. Oliver Partridge, of Hatfield, surveyed, in 1739, from a point six miles east of the old meeting-house, five miles north and four miles south, and from each extremity a line straight to the river—a very regular outline. A difficulty in settling with Sunderland the north line, which had formerly terminated at the mouth of Mohawk brook, led to the grant of an equivalent at "Deerfield Falls," above Sunderland, called Hadley Farm, sold in 1749. Middle Street was called "the hill over the low valley." In 1681 Isaac Warner had a grant of a house-lot on the river bank, extending from the main street up towards "Coleman's brook."

The vote for a tier of lots on what is now Middle Street was first passed in 1684; but very few lots were taken till the close of that century, on account of danger from savages. Swamp lands east of forty acres, between Coleman's brook and the upper mill, were fenced in 1699, and called "The Skirts of Forty Acres." Traces of the "old ditch" connected with this skirt fence are still visible. All this region above Coleman's brook, including the land which afterwards, as the "Phelps Farm," was enthusiastically described by President Dwight, in his *New England Travels*, was kept as a common field till after 1750, about which time Capt. Moses Porter built there. Two gates, on the highway, had to be opened and shut by all travelers. Lots were laid out north of Patrigg's swamp in 1714.

But there came a time when Hadley was called upon to part with a still larger part of her territory, viz.: South Hadley was made a separate precinct, also including the present town of Granby, in 1733, and Amherst was set off in 1734, as detailed in the respective sketches of those towns.

The settlement of the town was slow, owing to the danger attending frontier settlements, a bar that existed till well into the next century. The progress may be comparatively estimated from the following statement of Mr. Judd as to the condition in 1770, viz.:—

"The progress of the town was slow. There may have been in 1770 about 108 or 110 families, and 600 inhabitants. Only a small portion of the 13,000 acres of Inner Commons, distributed long before, had been cleared, and not more than six or eight houses had been built on the commons. Some of these were at North Hadley. A few began to build on the Boston road about this time. There were no inhabitants at Plainville, nor further south in the eastern part of Hadley, nor on the Sunderland road north of Caleb Bartlett, nor between Charles Phelps and the back street. Samuel Wright had settled in the northeastern part of Hadley, where his son Silas and his grandson Silas, the late Senator and Governor of New York, were born. Lieut. Enos Smith erected the house in which his son, Dea. Sylvester Smith now lives, and finished one room in 1770. Gideon Smith had a house northeast of him, Stephen Goodman had built a house beyond the mill, and Nathaniel White farther east, where he long kept a tavern. There was a house near the mill for the miller."

The population at various times since then has been as follows: In 1776, 681; 1790, 882; 1800, 1,073; 1810, 1,247; 1820, 1,461; 1830, 1,686; 1840, 1,814; 1850, 1,986; 1855, 1,928; 1860, 2,105; 1865, 2,240; 1870, 2,301; 1875, 2,125; 1880, 1,938.

Organization—The town was duly incorporated by the general court May 22, 1661. The first officers, elected from time to time as occasion required. The first selectmen chosen at a regular town meeting, December 14, 1660, were Andrew Bacon, Andrew Warner, Nathaniel Dickinson, Samuel Smith and William Lewis. Other officers were chosen as follows: Nathaniel Dickinson, recorder of orders or town clerk, December 17, 1660. He was succeeded by Peter Tilton, September 4, 1661, who was made also "to record lands," February 9, 1663, and who served more than thirty one years; Samuel Barnard, who followed in 1693, was "clerk"; Samuel Smith and Peter Tilton, measurers of land, 1660; Stephen Teery, constable, March 1662; Mr. William Westwood and Brother Standley, fence-viewers, "to view the meadow fences," April 24, 1661; Goodman Richard Montague, hayward or field-driver, May 11, 1661; Edward Church and Chileab Smith, east side of the river, and Nathaniel Dickinson, Jr., west side, surveyors of highways, January 27, 1663; John Barnard sealer of weights and measures, 1663; Richard Montague, grave-digger, March, 1663; Timothy Nash, Samuel Moody, Samuel Church, Chileab Smith, tithingmen, appointed by the selectmen, 1678; Samuel Partrigg, packer of meat and fish, 1679. Hog-reeves, hog-ringers, cow-keepers and shepherds were chosen at times in the early days.

First Things.—The first school-house was previously the dwelling of Nathaniel Ward, who gave it with a portion of his home lot for school purposes, and it was so used for many years. Mr. Ward died in 1664. The house was "ready to fall down" in 1710, and two years later the property was leased to Dr. John Barnard for ninety-seven years, at eighteen shillings per year. The

first building erected as a school-house was built in 1796, in the broad street
"in the middle of the town," and was twenty-five by eighteen feet in size,
and was seven feet between joints. The first meeting house stood in the
wide street, opposite Richard Montague's; was framed in 1665, but not finished until January 12, 1670. A house for meetings was hired in 1663 and
1664. The first inn or ordinary was kept by Richard Goodman in 1667, in
which year it is probably the first general training occurred, Mr. Goodman
entertaining the officers. The first marriage in Hadley was that of Aaron
Cooke, Jr., and Sarah Westwood, daughter of William Westwood, magistrate,
May 30, 1661. The ages of bride and groom were respectively seventeen and twenty-one years. She died March 24, 1730, aged eighty-six. He
died September 16, 1716, aged seventy six. The children of this marriage
were Sarah, who married Thomas Hovey, Aaron, of Hartford, Joanna, born
1665, married 1683, Samuel Porter, Jr., and died in 1713, Westwood born
1670 or '71, Samuel born 1672, Moses born 1675, Elizabeth, born 1677, married 1698, Ichabod Smith, Bridget born 1683, married first, 1701, John Barnard, second, Deacon Samuel Dickinson. The first, and it is believed, the
only couple, belonging to Hadley who were ever divorced were negroes.
Ralph Way obtained in January, 1752, a divorce from his wife, Lois, on the
ground of adultery with a negro named Boston. The first male child born
was Samuel Porter, son of Samuel, one of the first settlers. He died July
29, 1722. The first death was that of an infant without name, child of Philip
Smith, which was buried in Hadley cemetery, January 22, 1661. John Webster, who died April 5th the same year, an ancestor of Noah Webster, was
the second person buried there. The first minister was Mr. John Russell,
Jr., an Englishman by birth, who came with the first planters to Hadley and
remained until his death, 1692. Dr. John Westcart was the first physician
resident in Hadley. He came in 1666, and was the first Indian trader.
Richard Montague, baker; Asahel Wright, butcher; Oliver Warner, hatter;
Timothy Nash, blacksmith; John Russell, Sr., glazier; William Partrigg,
cooper; Samuel Gaylord, Jr., and Jonathan Smith, weavers; Hezekiah Porter, and possibly his father, Samuel, carpenters. John Barnard had a malt-
house in Hadley prior to 1664. Elijah Yeomans, goldsmith, was in Hadley
from 1771, for twelve years, and made clocks and articles of jewelry. Samuel Porter, who died in 1722, was probably the first merchant.

Highways.—Roads were laid out in Hadley while the land was common,
the lots upon them being appropriated afterwards. A cart-path was made
through "Forty Acres" to Mill Brook, now North Hadley, in 1667. Mend-
ing highways was then a somewhat extensive town practice. Communication
had to be kept up with Hartford; and in one instance it seems that the teams
of Hadley and Northampton were called out to repair the roads in Suffield,
Conn. Even so late as the close of that century, the records show that the
people had a difficulty in keeping down the bushes in the highways. The
Northampton ferry was long at the south end of Hadley street, and by that

the Northampton people went principally to Springfield. Towards Massachusetts bay the first settlement that offered a lodging—and that not till 1664
—was at Quaboug, or Brookfield. Beyond there, the Bay road branched into
three routes—one by Nashua, now Lancaster, another by Worcester, and a
third by Grafton. These, however, were little more than savage trails for
traveling "Indian file,"—paths for a single horse or man. No wheeled vehicle passed between Hadley and Boston till about the close of that century.
The first bridge in that direction, except for foot-passengers, crossed Fort river
near the south end of Spruce hill, was built in 1675, and was succeeded some
thirteen years later, by Lawrence's bridge, near the site of the one now in use.
Produce for Boston was carried around by water. It was carted to William-
ansett, below the Falls. Skillful boatmen navigated the Enfield rapids. The
grist-mill was at Hatfield; and the grist from the east side was carried over
by two ferrymen, on certain days of the week, for three pence a bushel, pay-
able, like other toll, in grain. In 1670, however, the east side farmers set up
a mill of their own, on the North Stream, now North Hadley. In Philip's
war this mill was turned into a military garrison, and shortly after was burnt
by the Indians; but it was re-built and became the nucleus of enterprise in
the upper village. Flour was sent down the river. Joseph Smith, the first
permanent settler there, was the miller, and brought up his sons to the craft.

Indian Depredations and Military.—As we have stated, Hadley was for
years exposed to Indian depredations, and the inhabitants lived constantly in
fear. A garrison of soldiers were quartered here, and in 1676 the settlement
was fortified with palisades. These were placed some distance in the rear of
the buildings, on both sides of the street, and extended across the street at
both ends, enclosing a space about a mile long and forty rods wide. Gates
were made wherever the palisades crossed any of the lateral highways, and at
the ends of the principal street, through which alone ingress and egress were
permitted.

The first attack was made in 1675, at which time the inhabitants, tradition
affirms, were led on to the repulse by Gen. William Goffe, the regicide, who
with his father-in-law, Gen. Edmund Whalley,* were living, under assumed
names, in the family of Rev. John Russell. Dr. Timothy Dwight has given
the following version of the affair; but there are several which contradict it,
and still others that pronounce the whole matter a myth:—

"In the course of Philip's war, which involved most all the Indian tribes
in New England, and among others, those in the neighborhood of Hadley,
the inhabitants thought it proper to observe the first of September, 1675, as
a day of fasting and prayer. While they were in the church and employed

---

* These judges of Charles I. arrived in Boston July, 1660; thence they went to New
Haven, in March, 1661. Here they secreted themselves at West Rock and at other places,
as well as they could, until October, 1664, when they came to the house of Rev. John Russell, of Hadley, where they resided in secrecy more than fifteen years. At one time they
were joined at Mr. Russell's house by Col. John Dixwell, another of the prescribed judges
of the unfortunate Charles I.

in their worship, they were surprised by a band of savages. The people instantly betook themselves to their arms,—which, according to the times, they had carried with them to the church,—and, rushing out of the house, attacked their invaders. The panic under which they began the conflict was, however, so great, and their number was so disproportioned to that of their enemies, that they fought doubtfully at first, and, in a short time, began evidently to give way.

"At this moment an ancient man with hoary locks, of a most venerable and dignified aspect, and in a dress widely differing from that of the inhabitants, appeared suddenly at their head, and with a firm voice, and an example of undaunted resolution, re-animated their spirits, led them again to the conflict, and totally routed the savages. When the battle was ended the stranger disappeared, and no person knew whence he had come, or whither he had gone. The relief was so timely, so sudden, so unexpected, and so providential, the appearance and the retreat of him who furnished it were so unaccountable, his person was so dignified and commanding, his resolution so superior, and his interference so decisive, that the inhabitants, without any uncommon exercise of credulity, readily believed him to be an angel sent by Heaven for their preservation. Nor was this opinion seriously controverted, until it was discovered several years afterward, that Goffe and Whalley had been lodged in the house of Mr. Russell. Then it was known that their deliverer was Goffe, Whalley having become superannuated some time before the event took place."

The first fatal attack occurred on the first of April, 1676. A number of the inhabitants had gone, under protection of a guard of soldiers, to Hockanum to work in the fields. Here they were ambushed by a party of Indians who killed Dea. Richard Goodman and two of the soldiers, and captured a third soldier named Thomas Reed. These unfortunate ones seem to have strayed away from the main body, and thus came to grief.

The next, and last attack attended with fatality to the inhabitants, was on the 12th of June of the same year, of which Rev. Increase Mather gives the following account :—

"June 12th the enemy assaulted Hadley. In the morning, the sun an hour high, three soldiers, going out of the town without their arms, were dissuaded therefrom by a sergeant who stood at the gate, but they, alleging that they intended not to go far, were suffered to pass ; within a while the sergeant apprehended that he heard some men running, and looking over the fortification he saw twenty indians pursuing those three men, who were so terrified that they could not cry out,—two of them were at last killed, and the other so mortally wounded that he lived not above two or three days,—wherefore the sergeant gave the alarm. God, in great mercy to these western plantations, had so ordered by his providence that the Connecticut army was come thither before this onset from the enemy. Besides English, there were near upon two hundred Indians in Hadley, who came to fight with and for the English against the common enemy, who was quickly driven off at the south end of the town. Whilst our men were pursuing of them here, on a sudden a great swarm of Indians issued out of the bushes and made their main assault at the north end of the town. They fired a barn which was without the fortification, and went into a house where the inhabitants discharged a great gun upon them, whereupon about fifty Indians were seen running out of the house in great haste, being terribly frightened by the report and slaughter made amongst them by the great gun. Ours followed the enemy (which they judged to be about five hundred, and, by Indian report since, it seems they were seven hundred) near upon two miles, and would fain have pursued them further, but they had no orders so to do. But few of ours lost their lives in this skirmish, nor is it yet known how many the enemy lost in this fight. The English could find but three dead Indians, yet some of them who have been informed by Indians, that when the Indian men were thus fighting against Hadley the Mowhawks came upon their headquarters, and smote their women and children with a great slaughter, and then returned with much plunder."

During all the period of the Indian wars, down as late as 1757, Hadley had furnished men to aid other localities, and the names of many who went out for this purpose are on record, but our limited space prevents their insertion in this sketch.

When the Revolutionary war came on, it found men here inured to hardships, practiced in border warfare, and of these the town made a generous contribution to the great cause.

In the late war Hadley furnished 224 men, a surplus of twenty-three over all demands, three of whom were commissioned officers. The town expended $27,700.00, and loaned the state $8,378.56.

Prominent Men and Biographical.—Charles P. Phelps, graduate of Harvard, 1791, Giles C. Kellogg, and Moses Porter each served several years in the legislature. Mr. Kellogg, a graduate of Yale, was admitted to the bar in 1804, was instructor in Hopkins academy a number of years, and became register of deeds for Hampshire county in 1833, and remained in office twelve or thirteen years. John Porter, son of William, graduate of Williams college, 1810, has served in both branches of the New York legislature, and has held the office of surrogate. Joseph Smith was senator, 1853–54. Worthington Smith, D. D., late president of Burlington university, who died February 30, 1856; Parsons Cooke, D. D., graduate of Williams college, 1822, founder of the *New England Puritan*; Rev. Jeremiah Porter, Gen. Joseph Hooker, distinguished in the Mexican war and in the late war of the Rebellion; William Porter. Charles P. Huntington, and Rev. Frederick Dan Huntington, sons of Rev. Dan Huntington,—all, many years since, went forth from Hadley, their native town, and have not failed to do her honor.

Hon. Charles Porter Phelps, only son of Dea. Charles Phelps and Elizabeth Porter, and grandson of Capt. Moses Porter, was born in Hadley, August 8, 1772, and died December 22, 1857. He was fitted for college by the Rev. Dr. Lyman, of Hatfield, entered Harvard college at the age of fifteen and was graduated in the class of 1791, giving the Latin salutatory at their commencement. He then entered the law office in Newburyport of the Hon. Theophilus Parsons, afterwards chief justice, whose niece, Sarah Davenport Parsons, he married in January, 1800, having commenced the practice of law in Boston. He remained about twenty-one years in that city, and was connected during a part of that time with mercantile life, holding the position at one time of cashier in the old Massachusetts bank. He was much interested in the formation of the celebrated old Hussar company of Boston, and became one of its officers. This company, of which Hon. Josiah Quincy was the first captain, was famous for its brilliant uniform of green, white and gold, and scarlet cape or cloak thrown over one shoulder, and was a conspicuous feature of the pageants of that day. At the end of the first year Captain Quincy resigned and Mr. Phelps was unanimously chosen his successor. In the war of 1812 the Boston Light Dragoons and the Hussars were united, and Captain Phelps was chosen their commander under the title of major. In 1816, his father having died, and his own health requiring a change, Major Phelps returned to settle in Hadley, where he had built a house on his share of the farm left by his father, his sister Elizabeth, wife of Rev. Dan. Huntington, occupying the old homestead. The new house was built on the east side of Central street, a little south of the old home and about one mile south of the village of North Hadley. Major Phelps's farm originally comprised over 200 acres of meadow and woodland, extending along the east bank of the Connecticut, and including a great part of Mt. Warner. The estate now comprises about fifty-eight acres, nearly square, lying directly south of Bishop Huntington's farm. The return of Major Phelps to Hadley was shadowed by the death of his wife, October, 1817, just before leaving Boston, and their family of six surviving children were left motherless. After a few years Major Phelps made a second marriage with his wife's cousin, Charlotte, born 1793, daughter of Chief Justice Parsons, by whom he had five children, and her death on July 11, 1830, left him again a widower. In August, 1833, he married an estimable widow, Mrs. Judkins, of Castine, Me., who was born October 8, 1787, and who survived him. During his residence in Hadley, where he passed his remaining years, Major Phelps was frequently chosen representative to the general court, and once as senator. He held the office of county commissioner for many years, besides holding numerous town offices of responsibility and trust. Continuing, to some extent, his legal practice, he was an authority on points of law and equity, and his advice was constantly sought by his fellow townsmen. A man of striking personality, he was eminent for his strict integrity and inflexible decision of character. His estate passed at his death to his children, and several of them now make it their home there. Charles Phelps, born 1801, died in 1882; Edward, born in 1803, died in 1807; Sarah, born in 1805, died in 1886; Francis, born in 1807, was graduated from Harvard college, and soon after became a teacher in the Boston Latin school, and was subsequently for many years, a private teacher in Boston, where he still resides; Elizabeth, born in 1808, died in 1809; Marianne, born in 1810, and married to Alfred Belden of Whately in 1849, now living at the Phelps' home; Louisa, born in 1812, died in 1813; Caroline, born in 1814, married Rev. S. G. Bulfinch, of Boston, in 1842, now left a widow, with one daughter, residing in Cambridge; Arthur Davenport, born in 1817, married Harriet N. Pratt,

of Boston, and after holding an office of trust in the United States sub-
treasury for more than twenty years, resigned on account of ill health,
and is now living on his father's estate in Hadley; Theophilus Parsons,
born in 1821, living at the home ; William Porter, born in 1823, died
in 1880 ; Charlotte Elizabeth, born in 1825, married P. M. Bartlett in 1869,
died in 1871 ; Frederick Ashley, born in 1826, lived one day ; Susan Davis,
born in 1827, died in 1865.

Rev. Dan Huntington, of Hadley, was born in Lebanon, Conn., October
11, 1774, and was the second son of William and Bethia (Throop). He was
graduated at Yale college in 1794, and was afterwards a tutor in the college.
He was successively pastor of the Congregational societies of Litchfield and
Middletown, in his native state. He had married, in 1801, Elizabeth Whiting, only daughter of Charles Phelps, of Hadley, and on the death of
the latter, he removed with his family (in 1816) to Hadley and took
charge of the estate. This consisted of three hundred acres of land and the
house, still standing on the road running south from North Hadley along
the river. It was built in 1753–54, by Mrs. Huntington's grandfather, Capt.
Moses Porter, who was killed in the French and Indian war at the "Bloody
morning Scout" at Lake George, September 8, 1755. On the death of
Charles Phelps, the farm was divided, and his son Charles Phelps built
a house farther south on the east of the main road, where several of his
children still reside. Another ancestor of Mrs. Huntington was Rev.
John Whiting, of Hartford, whose widow afterward married Rev. John Russell, of Hadley, in whose house the regicides Goffe and Whalley were concealed. After removing to Hadley, Rev. Mr. Huntington was for a time
the principal of Hopkins academy. He preached constantly in neighboring
towns. After 1820 he was connected with the Unitarian denomination.
Among his printed sermons are discourses delivered at the Connecticut
"Anniversary Election," in 1814, and before the Massachusetts legislature, in
1821. He died in 1864, at the age of ninety years, and was buried in the
family lot in Hadley. His children were Charles Phelps, Elizabeth Porter,
(married George Fisher, of Oswego, N. Y.), William Pitkin, Bethia Throop,
Edward Phelps, John Whiting, Theophilus Parsons, Theodore Gregson, Mary
Dwight, Catherine Cary, Frederick Dan.

Charles Huntington, born in 1802, and graduated at Harvard college, was
a lawyer, first in North Adams, and for many years in Northampton. After
his appointment to the bench of the superior court he resided in Boston.
His first wife was Helen Sophia, daughter of Hon. E. H. Mills. She died
in 1844, and he afterwards married Ellen, daughter of David Greenough, of
Cambridge. His widow and seven children are still living.

Rev. William P. Huntington, born in 1804, was graduated at Harvard college in 1824, and taught an academy many years in Kentucky. He married
Lucy, daughter of Luther Edwards, of Chesterfield. After practicing medicine in Hadley, he settled as a Unitarian minister in Wisconsin. He became

a farmer, and late in life was ordained to the ministry of the Episcopal church. His last years were spent in Amherst. His wife and eight children survived him.

Theophilus P. Huntington, born in 1811, took the northern portion of the original farm and built a house there. He was a farmer. He married Eliza Fitch, daughter of S. H. Lyon, of Abington, Conn. His wife and three children are living.

Theodore G. Huntington was a farmer, living for a time at the homestead. He took much interest in town and state affairs and was at one time a member of the state board of agriculture. He built two houses in different parts of Hadley, and afterwards built a house in Amherst where he lived many years. Latterly he resided in Eastford and died there. His widow, Elizabeth, daughter of Azel Sumner of that place, survives him. They had no children.

Frederick D. Huntington, S. T. D., bishop of the Episcopal diocese of Central New York, was born in this town May 28, 1819. He graduated at Amherst college, 1839, as valedictorian of his class, and at the Divinity school of Harvard University, in 1842. He was the minister of a Unitarian congregation in Boston for thirteen years; from 1855 to 1860 he was professor of Christian morals in Harvard college, and preacher to the university. He also served as chaplain and preacher to the Massachusetts state legislature. He married Hannah D. Sargent, of Boston, a sister of the poet Sargent. The bishop's two sons are priests in the Episcopal church. He received the degree of S. T. D. from Amherst, in 1856. His researches led him to renounce Unitarianism and apply for orders in the Episcopal church. He was ordered deacon September 12, 1860; ordained priest March 19, 1861. He organized Emmanuel parish, Boston, became its rector, and remained there until his elevation to the episcopate. He was consecrated first bishop of Central New York in Emmuanuel church, Boston, April 8, 1868. His writings which have been given to the public through the press are numerous, and many of them deservedly popular. They are chiefly of a religious character. He was also editor of the *Church Monthly* of Boston, and of two other religious periodicals. He was chosen by the house of bishops to write the "pastoral letter," and to read the same at the general convention of the Episcopal church in Philadelphia in 1883. Although the bishop has attained an age when most men look for rest from cares and arduous labors, he still works with an untiring energy for the social, moral and religious elevation of his fellow-men, for whom his love seems never to grow cold, nor his zeal to abate. The seat of his diocese is Syracuse, N. Y., where no man stands higher in the respect and estimation of his towns people than he. The schools and charitable institutions which he has founded within his diocese he has zealously fostered until they have attained that degree of usefulness that they have become indispensable to the towns and cities where they are located.

Franklin Bonney, M. D., was born in Hadley, Mass., February 2, 1822. He is the son of the late Oliver Bonney, who was born in Hanover, Mass., in 1790, sixth in descent from Thomas Bonney, who came from Sandwich, in Kent, England, in the ship " Hercules," in 1634 or '35, and settled in Duxbury, Mass. The ancestor of the family in England was named De Bon, who, according to one account, was a Huguenot driven from France. Another tradition is that he was a Knight of Normandy under William the Conqueror. His mother was Betsey F. Hayward, daughter of Elijah Hayward, of West Bridgewater, Mass. Dr. Bonney obtained his preliminary education principally at Hopkins academy, in Hadley. After a three years' course of study at the Dartmouth Medical school, and an attendance upon a course of lectures at the Bowdoin Medical college, he graduated from the former institution in 1847, and at once commenced the practice of his profession in his native town, which he still continues. He is a member of the Massachusetts Medical society, and of the Hampshire District Medical society. Of the latter organization, he has been vice-president and president for the period of three years, and he has held most of the minor offices of the same society. He is also a member of the American Social Science society. In 1869 he was given the honorary title of A. M., by Amherst college. During the war of the rebellion he was surgeon for the preliminary examination of recruits for the army from his vicinity. In 1864 he also did service for a time, as a volunteer surgeon at City Point, Va. He has been for many years, a trustee of the Hopkins academy fund, and is secretary of the board of trustees. For some years he was a member of the school committee of his town. In 1873 he served his district in the legislature. In addition to his ordinary professional labors, he has occasionally prepared papers for the District Medical society, and for the *Medical Magazine*, and he has made frequent contributions to agricultural and other journals. He has been twice married. His first wife, Priscilla P. Whipple, was a daughter of Hon. Thomas Whipple, of Wentworth, N. H. Of the two sons and two daughters born of this marriage, one son and the two daughters are living. His second marriage was to Emma W. Peck, daughter to the late Sherman Peck, Esq., of Honolulu, Sandwich Islands. Of this union there are three sons. As a citizen, Dr. Bonney has always felt a deep interest in the welfare of his native town, and has given a cheerful and helping hand to every enterprise that promised to add to her prosperity.

Elbridge Kingsley, the artist engraver, was born at Carthage, near Cincinnati, Ohio, September 17, 1842. His parents were Hatfield people, and when he was but a few months old they returned to their former home, where they are still living. Elbridge was the oldest of six children, all boys, and was brought up in the regulation manner on a farm. His school education was finished at the Hopkins academy, when, at sixteen years of age, he entered the office of the *Hampshire Gazette* as an apprentice. Here he worked till he was of age, often obliged to be up by four and five in the morning to start

20*

the office fires, and spending his spare time in making all sorts of imaginative drawings. He found many of his subjects in the Bible, one picture being an elaborate Belchazzer's Feast, in water colors. Indians, too, were possessed of a great fascination for him. When his apprenticeship ended he went to New York, and for a short time studied in the Cooper Institute. He next entered the *Tribune* office as a compositor, but soon left and presently became interested in wood engraving. To begin with, his work was the engraving of machinery, but finally, after changing employers two or three times, he became connected with a firm where he had an opportunity to do blocks for *Harper's Magazine.* While in New York he was for some time city correspondent of the *Hampshire Gazette.* The year 1871 finds him in Northampton once more, in the printing and engraving business with C. A. Snow and G. L. Harris. Here he became acquainted with two such artists as J. Wells Champney and the late C. A. Burleigh. He at this time began to work in oil colors, out of doors, and one winter walked daily to Amherst in order to draw from the casts in the college gallery. In 1874 the Northampton partnership was dissolved, and he drifted back to New York, where in time he engraved a block for *Scribner's Monthly.* They were pleased with the result and since that time his connection with the magazine (now the *Century*) has been continuous. His family in the meantime lived in Hadley. This brought him into the country every summer and led to the building of his famous car to facilitate his open air sketching. In the spring of 1882, while out with his car in the Hatfield woods, he engraved a block which gave him a distinctive place among engravers and made no small stir in the art world. This appeared as a full page cut, in the fall of the year in the *Century Magazine,* accompanied by a short article written by Mr. Kingsley himself, descrive of his methods. Ever since then these original engravings have appeared from time to time in the *Century* and *St. Nicholas,* most of them being made from, or suggested by the scenery of Hampshire county. In 1885 he illustrated *Poems of Nature,* by Whittier. Years ago Mr. Kingsley was ranked by Hammerton, perhaps the ablest of English art critics, in his *Graphic Arts,* as one of the best wood engravers in the world. Since then he has made a decided advance and the power, delicacy and refinement shown in his landscape work has never been excelled. Mr. Kingsley has written an entertaining lecture on wood engraving, historical and descriptive, which he has delivered a number of times about home and before art clubs in New York and Brooklyn. He is still a young man, and undoubtedly the most perfect results of his genius are yet in the future.

Caleb Dexter Dickinson was born on a farm in Amherst, May 23, 1806. He attended the common schools until fifteen, when desirous of earning his own living, he started out with his effects tied up in a handkerchief, and walked to Goshen, where he apprenticed himseif to Asahel Billings, blacksmith, with whom he remained until twenty. Returning to Amherst, he remained at home a few months and then went to Pittsfield, where he worked at his trade about a year. Returning again to Amherst he did business on his own account in the same building with Benoni Rust, nearly opposite where the first National Bank now stands. On January 13, 1830, he married Tryphena Russell, of Russellville, Hadley, and went to Greenfield, where he continued ordinary blacksmithing about two years, after which he formed a partnership with John Russell, of New York, and commenced the cutlery business, Mr. Russell furnishing the capital and Mr. Dickinson the mechanical skill, which had already become quite celebrated. He continued this business, which has since greatly developed and is now the John Russell Cutlery Co., of Turners Falls, until 1840, when to please family relatives he moved to North Hadley. There, in partnership with C. A. Lyman, until June 15, 1842, under the title of Dickinson & Lyman, he did general blacksmithing and made a few tools for the manufacture of brooms, of which this vicinity was then the center. His wife died March 29, 1848, and on October 10, 1848, he married Louisa W. Billings, of Shrewsbury, Vt., who died July 18, 1864. He married again December 27, 1867, Mrs. Harriet N. Moseley, of Albany, N. Y., who died October 27, 1880. He has been the father of fourteen children, three of whom, one son and two daughters, are now living. Mr. Dickinson has always been public spirited, well informed on general topics, and a devoted Christian. In 1847 he was a member of the board of selectmen of Hadley. During the winter of 1851–52, beside managing his business at home he worked at the U. S. armory at Springfield. He is now probably the oldest business man in town, and retains his energy and vigor to a surprising degree.

Francis Newton, son of Francis, was born in Hadley, married Abigail Dickinson, July 21, 1794, and his children were Theodosia, Obed and John. Obed was born in Hadley, November 29, 1800, learned the carpenter's trade, and married Eliza Walker, in October, 1822. He had born to him six children, namely, Jason W., Julia E., Sarah A., Francis L., Eliza A. and Mary N. The mother of these children died in 1835, and he married for his second wife, Catherine Bugbee, and had born to him three children, George, Charles and Elizabeth. Jason and Francis are farmers, residing in this town, and Eliza A. married Charles B. Armstrong, of Buffalo, N. Y.

Winthrop Cook, a descendant of Capt. Aaron Cook, the first of that name in town, was born in 1785, married twice, first, a daughter of Joel Smith, and second, Sophia, daughter of Erasmus Smith, and died in 1854. Horace, son of Winthrop, was born in 1824, married Cornelia Asenath, in 1855, and had born to him two children, Herbert S., who died in 1860, and Fannie A., born in 1863. Mr. Cook represented the town in 1862 and in 1876, has been selectman seventeen years, has been assessor, and has held other offices. His house was built previous to 1800.

Aaron Cook, son of Dan, was born April 21, 1800, married catherine Lyman in 1832, and his children were as follows: Julia, who married Amasa B. Davis, Henry L., who married Harriet A. Morton, and resides on road 40, and Rufus, who served in the late war, in Co. D, 27th Mass. Vols., and died in the hospital at Newburn, N. C.

Joseph Marsh was born in Worthington, in 1786, a son of Dr. Job Marsh, who came to Hadley when Joseph was about eight years of age, and died here soon after. Joseph subsequently, after a few years' residence at North Amherst, went to Hatfield, and learned the joiner's trade of Cotton White. He then came back to Hadley, located on the farm now owned by his son Henry M., and died here in 1871, aged eighty-five years. He was the husband of four wives, and reared five children, four of whom, Elvira, Mary, Charles C. and Henry M., are living.

Luther Barstow was born on the place now owned by him, on road 45, December 27, 1813. His father, Septimias, came here from Connecticut about 1805. Luther married Llizabeth C. Graves, May 5, 1847, who bore him seven children—Asaph S., Harriet E., John S., Susan S., Hannah, Sophia G. and Sarah O. Mrs. Barstow died December 24, 1881. All of the children are living, four of them residing in town.

Hiram Thayer located in Hadley about 1820, coming from Williamsburg, and located upon the farm now owned by E. and C. N. Thayer. He married Calista P. White, who bore him nine children, three of whom are living, Morris, Ezra and Eben. For his second wife he married Laura M. Stiles, who bore him three children, Charles S., Francis and Hiland H. Hiram died in 1854, aged fifty-three years. Mrs. Thayer died in 1850.

Elam Cutler was born in Leverett, Mass., in 1792, married twice, first, Judith Thayer, in 1816, who bore him one child, Judith O., and died about 1817. He married for his second wife, Mary M. Gaylord, of Amherst, in 1820, and had born to him eight children, viz.: Lizzie, Mary G., Elijah B., Elan B., Fanny M., George H., Charles H. and Jennie E. In 1829 he moved to North Hadley, and bought the place where he died in 1883, aged ninety years.

Zachariah Hadley was born in Amherst, married Anna Howard, and reared ten children, viz.: Roswell, Esther, Zachariah, Louis, Eli, Anna, Malinda, Gideon, Eliza and Clarrissa. He moved to Hadley, and died on the place now owned by Albert Hawley, in October, 1836. Zachariah, Jr., married twice, first, Malinda Belden, who bore him three children, two of whom are living, Allen and Emily. Mrs. Hawley died in 1862, and he married for his second wife, Maria A. Bancroft, in March, 1863, and has had born to him one son, Charles, who lives at home. Mr. Hawley is now nearly eighty years of age.

Edward Cunningham was born in September, 1816, married Honorah Dalton, about 1846, and came here from Ireland, in 1850. He has had born to him six children, four of whom are living, John, Edward P., William J. and Mary A. Edward P. and William J. reside at home and help carry on the farm with their father. This place is noted as having been at an early period the camping-ground for the Indians.

Wooster H. Tuttle and Albert Tuttle, brothers, came to Hadley from Holyoke, in 1850, and bought about fifty acres of land on Front street. Albert died about 1863. Wooster married Margaritha Helmsing, who bore him four sons and four daughters, viz.: Edward W., George A., Charles A., Franklin E., Anna, Clara, Maria and Eurania. Two of the sons are graduates of Amherst college, and a third is attending that college. The mother of these children died in 1872, and two years later Mr. Tuttle married Mrs. Caroline Smith, widow of Jacob Smith. The oldest daughter, Anna, married Dwight Morton, and resides about a half mile from the homestead. Clara has been twice married, but is now a widow. Maria L. married George Fenton, and resides in Nebraska.

Jesse L. Delano, of Hadley, is a native of Sunderland, the adjoining town north, having moved from there to Northampton in 1883, and from thence to Hadley in 1884. His ancestors came from France and settled in Marshfield, his great-grandfather, Lemuel, moving from there to Sunderland about 1779, and his son William held the office of postmaster there for thirty-six consecutive years. A part of the family still reside there on the old homestead that has been in the family for over 100 years, while other members of it have migrated far and wide, though very few have ever settled in Hampshire county. The late Charles Delano, who died in Northampton in 1883, belonged to the same family, the genealogy of which is easily traced back to Philip De La Noye, a French Protestant who joined the English at Leyden, when they were about to start for America, and was allowed to come with them in the second vessel, "The Fortune," which arrived at Plymouth Rock, November 9, 1621. He settled in Marshfield.

VILLAGES.

HADLEY, the largest of the two villages, settled in 1659, is situated chiefly on the neck of the large peninsula which projects westward—within a large bend of the Connecticut river—from the western border of the town, and is somewhat south of the town's central line of latitude. It contains upwards of one hundred and fifty dwellings, a postoffice, town-hall, two church edifices, and a high school building, besides four others for the minor schools ; also a grist and saw-mill. The ancient cemetery lies immediately west of the village. "West" and Middle streets, running north and south, contain the major portion of the dwellings, and are bordered with elms and maples of magnificent growth and graceful proportions, some of which have braved a century's storms. West street, with its generous breadth of nearly three hundred feet, its marginal elms and intervening meadow, fronted sparsely by dwellings, some quaint and olden, its charming vista southward, enriched, though interrupted, by stately Holyoke, has not a peer in all New England. Russell street, lying east and west,—the old "Middle highway to the woods," —is handsomely lined with forest-trees, chiefly maples.

NORTH HADLEY is a small village on Mill river, between two and three miles north of Hadley, and near the Connecticut. It contains from sixty to eighty dwellings, two stores, a postoffice, a public hall, connected with a grammar school building, one meeting-house, a grist and saw-mill, and a few other manufacturing establishments. The village has also a small park and cemetery.

Five other thickly settled neighborhoods are called, respectively, Russellville, Plainville, Fort River, Hart's Brook and Hockanum.

Stores of North Hadley.—The earliest account of a store in the north part of the town is that of Windsor Smith & Co., at North Hadley, Chester Smith being the junior partner. In January, 1818, they sold to John and Elias Hibbard, who sold on August 21st of the same year to Erastus Smith, 2d, Chester Smith and Cotton Smith, who then owned the grist-mill. The next we find is John Hibbard selling to Albert Jones, on August 12, 1822, who kept the store till 1829, when Edward Huntington took it, and on May 1, 1831, we find that Albert Jones sold the store building to Edward P. Huntington, probably the same man named just above. On the same day Mr. Huntington leased the land on which the store stood, of the mill owners, John Hibbard, Cotton Smith, Elias Hibbard and Albert Hibbard, at $2.00 per year. In 1834 Ebenezer W. Skerry took the store, Mr. Huntington going to Northampton. From 1835 to '37 it was run by Skerry, Hibbard & Co. On February 8, 1837, Elias Hibbard sold one-fourth of the store to Thaddeus Smith and Alonzo Dougherty, and two days later Mr. Skerry sold one-twelfth to the same parties, and on the 11th of the following July, Truman Hibbard sold one-fourth to Mr. Dougherty.

From 1837 to '40 the firm was known as Skerry, Smith & Co., and their assignees, Cotton Smith and Erastus Smith, Jr., sold on April 27, 1841, to Dexter M. Leonard, who took the store in 1840 and kept it till he went to Providence, in 1851, when Dexter S. Cooley, of Springfield, had it about a year, or until his death, when, in 1852, his brother Simon F. Cooley of the same place carried it on, and on April 10, 1855, bought the store of Mr. Leonard. Mr. Cooley owned it till it was burned, with the mills, in 1875.

In the spring of 1877 Geo. C. Smith, owning the land, rebuilt the store on the old site and business was conducted by G. C. & G. M. Smith, until the fall of 1885, when they sold out to their clerk, John H. Mordoff.

A store was once kept in the house just north of the old hotel and later owned by Hubbard Lawrence. Dwight Ben. Smith had charge of it for a time, and we think it was this one for which O. Marsh & Co. were taxed in 1836 and Skerry, Hibbard & Co. in 1838.

A new store lot was at one time sold by Albert Hibbard to D. M. Leonard.

Austin Lyman sold a few groceries in connection with a bar in the building which stood in the saw-mill yard and was later used as a carpenter shop by Darius Howe.

When the present school-house was built the old one at the north end of the street, opposite the parsonage, was converted into a store, which was conducted by Thaddeus Smith & Co., Francis Smith being the junior partner. G. Myron Smith succeeded Thaddeus Smith and the firm was known as F. Smith & Co. In a few years F. Smith conducted the business alone, excepting a year or two when Fred S. Smith was a partner.

In 1875 when Mr. Cooley's store was burned he moved his goods into this building, which had been vacant for a time, and kept it about two years, when it was given up.

Alvah Park opened a store in the first house south of the grist-mill, on the same side of the street, and in six months (1870) moved into the building he now occupies as a store and dwelling.

A Frenchman, Peter Parenteau, kept a store a short time, about 1875–76, in the second house south of the grist-mill on the east side of the street.

MANUFACTURING INDUSTRIES.

The history of North Hadley, which until about fifty years ago was called Hadley Upper Mills, begins with the establishing of a saw-mill on the east side of the stream, a little over a quarter of a mile above the point where it empties into the Connecticut river. The town granted on January 27, 1662, Thomas Meekins and Robert Boltwood the privilege of setting on this stream a saw-mill, which was probably built about three years later. The first dam, which was probably built in 1662, was located nearly thirty rods above the present one, and beside which the first grist-mill was probably located in 1671 or 1672. This mill was burned by Indians in September, 1677, and re-built by Robert Boltwood, encouraged by the town, about 1678; the grammar school obtained it again in 1683; Samuel Boltwood, by aid of the town, in 1685; and in 1689 it was delivered up to the Hopkins school, in whose possession it remained for years. It was probably in 1692 that the dam was removed to its present site, and the mill built by it. A new mill is recorded in 1706, and another in 1721. John Clary was the miller in 1683, and in 1687 Joseph Smith began a long service in that capacity, and is recorded as the first permanent settler at "Mill River," now North Hadley.

We are unable to find any records which give us a history of the events of interest concerning the mills for about a century, or until January 25, 1796, we find Isaiah Washburn deeding one-half of the grist-mill as a security. September 11, 1812, Lewis Jones, Jr., sold one-half the grist-mill to Isaac Abbercrombie, of Pelham, who, on October 24, 1818, sold to Charles and Calvin Lamson, of Greenwich, who bought the other half of Erastus Smith on the same date, when also they leased the stream and dam of the Hopkins academy for ninety-nine years, at $20.00 per year. On January 3, 1818, they sold to Erastus Smith, 2d, Chester Smith and Cotton Smith. The 12th of the following December Chester Smith disposed of his interest to John Hibbard,

who, on April 18, 1821, sold to Elias Hibbard, who probably sold one-half of
his interest to William Montague, Jr., a blacksmith. On December 25, 1824,
Erastus Smith, 2d, sold his third to John Hibbard and Albert Hibbard, the
latter of whom also bought one-twelfth of Elias Hibbard and William Montague, Jr., and on the same date Cotton Smith sold a twelfth to John Hibbard, thus making a new arrangement and division into quarters, with John
Hibbard, Albert Hibbard, Hibbard & Montague, and Cotton Smith, as the
owners.

We find up to this time in relation to the saw-mill, which had for years
been held in sevenths, that Daniel Bartlett sold, on September 23, 1808, three-
sevenths to John Hibbard and Chester Smith, the latter of whom sold to the
former January 2, 1810, one-fourteenth part. On March 8, 1822, Chester
Smith's administrator sold two-sevenths to John Hibbard " who owns the
other parts," thus making him the sole owner of the saw-mill, which, however,
he shared with Albert Hibbard on June 18, 1822. On December 25, 1824,
the day mentioned of the re-arrangement of ownership of the grist-mill, there
was a like exchange of the saw-mill property. Albert Hibbard sold one-half
of his interest to Elias Hibbard and William Montague, Jr., and John Hibbard sold a half of his part to Cotton Smith, thus making the saw-mill and
grist-mill owned alike by the same parties.

After William Montague, Jr., sold his interest in the mills to his special
partner, Elias Hibbard, on February 23, 1828, there was no change of ownership until February 11, 1835, when Elias Hibbard sold his quarter to Cotton
Smith. September 23, 1835, John Hibbard disposed of his quarter of the
saw-mill to Albert Hibbard, and soon after, on October 16, 1835, his quarter
of the grist-mill to Elias Hibbard and Albert Hibbard, the latter of whom
bought the former's eighth on April 9, 1836, thus making Cotton Smith and
Albert Hibbard the proprietors of the mills.

Albert Hibbard soon retired by selling, on August 7, 1837, to John Smith,
2d, and Lorenzo N. Granger. After the death of John Smith, 2d, August 13,
1843, his interest in the saw-mill was set off to Frederick D. Smith, and sold
by his guardian to L. N. Granger, on April 24, 1845. The quarter of the
grist-mill left by John Smith, 2d, was bought, as personal property, by L. N.
Granger. After the death of Cotton Smith, on June 25, 1860, his son,
George C. Smith, assumed title to his father's half of the mills and sold it to
L. N. Granger, on May 1, 1874, who bought of the trustees of Hopkins
academy, on August 24, 1875, the water and dam, thus terminating the
ninety-nine-year lease. Mr. Granger died March 27, 1876, and his widow,
Sophronia Granger, chose as part of her interest in his estate the mills, which
she sold on December 25, 1876, to George C. Smith, who conveyed them to
his mother-in-law, Martha Smith, on October 26, 1877. The trustees of
Hopkins Academy gave to Martha Smith, on March 30, 1881, a quit-claim
deed to the land on which the grist-mill stands. Upon the death of Martha
Smith, August 4, 1882, her will gave possession of the mills to Nancy B.

Smith, who sold them, on September 14, 1884, to the present proprietor, John C. Howe.

Most of the above named men have been of the foremost importance in the history of the village. John Hibbard was an innkeeper and a very influential man. It is said of Cotton Smith that he could count off lumber with surprising rapidity and converse fluently at the same time.

There was a flax carding machine in connection with the grist-mill for many years, but it is not spoken of after the disaster of the fall of 1847, which was the tipping of the grist-mill and wire-mill just south, into the water, caused by a sudden freshet in the night breaking away the flume during repairs.

From 1840 to 1850 the firm of C. and J. Smith and Co., afterwards Smith & Granger, had an extensive lumber trade down the river. They furnished Springfield and Hartford and even New Haven with quantites of lumber which they delivered in rafts. Besides drawing on the local timber supply to fill their bills, they floated down logs from Vermont and New Hampshire. Mr. Granger did a large contracting business from 1860 to 1874, building several of the Agricultural college buildings at Amherst ; Memorial hall, at Northampton ; and other important buildings in the vicinity.

The mills were destroyed by fire the 27th of June, 1875, and immediately rebuilt. Mr. Granger is remembered by those who knew him as a successful large-hearted business man.

Under the present ownership there have been extensive repairs and improvements made. In 1884 grinding plaster was discontinued, the machinery taken down and the mill turned into a store-house. Early this summer (1886) a new elevator and store-house was built as an addition to the grist-mill, which increases the storage capacity from six or eight to twenty or twenty-five car loads according to the feed or grain put in store.

The water privilege consists of a fall of about fourteen feet with a pond of about one hundred acres surface. In the grist-mill there is a flouring-mill with its cleaning and bolting machinery, and two corn mills, which are kept busy most of the year.

There have been three different wire-works started in connection with the grist-mill, which are now prosperous concerns in other places. The first one was that of Nathan Clark, of Spencer, who bought of the mill owners on April 28, 1834, the building standing just south of the grist-mill, and the privilege of a certain quantity of water, where he manufactured piano-string and other wire, until the disaster of 1847. On April 5, 1849, he re-sold his right to the mill owners, and continued his business in the second story of the new grist-mill, until either late in 1851 or early in 1852, when he moved his business to Holyoke, which is probably now that of Geo. W. Prentiss & Co. His place here was immediately fitted by Horace Lamb, of Worcester, who conducted the wire business over the grist-mill until late in 1859, or early in 1860, when he moved it to Northampton, where he still carries it on.

George C. Prouty was the next wire manufacturer over the mill. He went to Charleton in about 1868, where he continues the same business.

The manufacture of broom-tools here is the only one in America, and undoubtedly in the world. It was established in 1840, by C. D. Dickinson. For years the demand for tools was limited to this immediate vicinity, but it gradually spread with the migrations of the broom manufacturers, until now they go to Canada and Australia, and are scattered through most of the states and territories. Mr. Dickinson carried on the business at the black-smith's shop just east of the bridge and opposite the saw-mill, using what power he needed at the grist-mill for about twenty-five years. During the summer of 1848 his shop was burned and soon re-built. In 1865 the business had so increased that he had to abandon all other work and devote his entire attention to that, and on April 18th bought the water privilege formerly the seat of an oil-mill and later a saw-mill, just below the center of the village. Here he carried on the business until 1870, when it had so developed that he required an assistant manager and so admitted his son-in-law, John C. Howe, as an equal partner in the business, which has since been conducted under the firm name of C. D. Dickinson & Son. The company's buildings were burned in September, 1875, and re-built the same year. Additions were made in the fall of 1883, when they were just starting in the manufacture of razors and kitchen cutlery, and all burned again on January 10, 1884. Not discouraged, they had their new buildings up and were at work in them before the first of April. With the brick forging shop added during the fall of 1885, they are now model buildings for this limited but sure business.

G. M. Smith's broom factory is also located at North Hadley. He employs twenty hands, his goods being manufactured principally for the export trade.

Hadley grist-mill, on Fort river, operated by William Phillips, was built by Rodney Smith and his father, in 1852. The present proprietor leased it in 1879. It has three runs of stone, a cracker, bolt, etc. The mill is operated by water-power, and has the capacity for grinding 500 bushels of grain per day. Mr. Phillips does both custom and merchant grinding.

Alfred S. Willard's soap factory and cider-mill, at Hadley, was built by him in 1880. He manufactures about 2,500 barrels of cider, about six tons of hard soap, and 400 barrels of soft soap per year.

Hopkins Academy.—This well-known school came into existence as follows : Three years before the settlement of Hadley, Governor Edward Hopkins, then of England, died in London, and by his last will bequeathed a part of his property for the encouragement of learning in New England. He had been in earlier life a London merchant, but removed to New England in 1637, and established himself at Hartford, Conn., and was governor of that state every alternate year from 1640 to 1654. In his will he says : "And the residue of my estate there (in New England), I do hereby give and bequeath to my father, Theophilus Eaton, Esq., Mr. John Davenport Mr. John Cullick and Mr. William Goodwin, in full assurance, and trust, and faithfulness of disposing of it according to the true intent and purpose of me, the said Edwin Hopkins, which is to give some encouragement in those foreign plantations for the breeding up of hopeful youths, both in the grammar school and college, for the public service of the country in future times." He afterwards bequeathed "£500 to be made over to New England" for a like purpose. Mr. Davenport, one of the trustees, was a minister in New Haven, and Mr. Goodwin seems, at this time, to have resided in Hadley, though he had previously been an inhabitant of Hartford. These two gentlemen soon became the only survivors of the trustees, in whom was vested the power of disposing of the funds. They decided to "give to the town of Hartford the sum of £400,   *   *   *   for and towards the erecting and promoting of a grammar school at Hartford. We do further order and appoint that the rest of Dr. Hopkins' estate, both that which is in New England, and the £500 which is to come from Old England, when it shall become due to us after Mrs. Hopkins' decease, be equally divided between the towns of New Haven and Hadley, to be in each of the towns respectively managed and improved towards erecting and maintaining a grammar school in each of them." Mr. Goodwin, in a certain agreement with the town, desired that the "name of the school may be called the Hopkins school." Such was the foundation of this institution. Other donations were made by various individuals, and the income of the funds is between five and six hundred dollars per annum. It appears that but a small portion of the sum bequeated by Mr. Hopkins ever reached Hadley. Three hundred pounds were invested in building a "corn-mill," which was burnt by the Indians; and two hundred and fifty pounds, to be paid at the decease of Mrs. Hopkins, never came to Hadley. The corporation of Harvard college, hearing that such a legacy was left for the benefit of New England, took measures to secure it for that college, and appointed an agent in London, remitting forty pounds sterling to stimulate and aid him. He was successful. In 1840, according to president Quincy, these funds, "on a foundation of productive and well-secured capital, amounted to nearly thirty thousand dollars."

In 1816 the Hopkins school became an incorporated institution, under the name of Hopkins academy. The new building was dedicated December 9, 1817, a brick structure facing the south on Russell street, about fifty rods east of West street. In 1860 it was destroyed by fire, and never rebuilt. The trustees of the fund maintained an advanced high-school department in the present town's high-school building, erected in 1865. The trustees hold over $30,000.00.

CHURCHES.

The First church in Hadley, Trinitarian Congregational.—The church and town were planted at one and the same time in Hadley, as we have shown. Just at what time the formal organization took place is not known, owing to the loss of the church records in 1766, but it was doubtless in 1660, and certainly before 1661. Rev. John Russell was first pastor. The first church building was completed in 1670, and did services till 1714, and in 1808 the present building was erected, and removed to its present location on Middle street in 1841. It is a wooden structure capable of seating 500 persons and valued, including grounds, at $5,000.00. The present pastor (*emeritus*) is Rev. Rowland, Ayres, D. D., with Rev. George W. Stearns, acting pastor. The society has 194 members.

The Second Congregational church, located at North Hadley, was organized October 26, 1831, with twenty-four members, and the first settled pastor was Rev. Ebenezer Brown, installed in 1835. The church building was erected 1834, a wooden structure capable of seating 350 person, and valued, including grounds, at 8,000.00. The society now has 144 members, with Rev. John W. Lane, pastor.

The Russell Congregational church, located on West street, was organized in 1841, with eighty-seven members from the First church, and Rev. John Woodbridge, D. D., pastor. The church building, a wooden structure capable of seating 350 persons, was built during that year. The society now has ninety members, with Rev. Edward S. Dwight, D. D., pastor.

———

HATFIELD lies in the center of the county's northern tier of towns, upon the west bank of the Connecticut. In area one of the smallest towns of the county, yet one of the most important. Its earlier history, the causes which let to its settlement, etc., are given in connection with the history of Hadley, of which it formed a part till May 11, 1670.

Two years later, October 19, 1672, the town purchased of the widow of the Indian chief *Quonquont* a tract to the north comprising what is now the town of Whately and a portion of the north part of Hatfield. The Hatfield of then included within its geographical limits also the present towns of Williamsburg on the west and Whately, north. The town is finely situated, as we have said, upon the west bank of " ye Great River Quinnaticot," whose general course is north and south, and which by its great bend to the west on the southern border makes the river both the eastern and southern boundary of the town, separating it from the town of Hadley, which is located east and south. Its northern bound was Pocomptuck, the town line running west about nine miles, from where the Pocomptuck path crossed the Sugar Loaf brook. It was also bounded on the south by Northampton for a distance of six miles, abutting on the unclaimed wilderness west, comprising a territory of about sixty-five square miles. After its territory was shorn by the incorporation of the towns of Williamsburg and Whately, its area was reduced to about sixteen square miles. It is watered by the Capawonk (Mill river) and its tributaries, Beaver brook, Running gutter, West brook and several smaller brooks. On the westerly side of North Meadow was Great pond, which fed a brook running from it to the Connecticut.

The topography of the town is peculiar. Along the line of the Connecticut river lie fertile meadows, extending westerly in varying widths, from two hundred rods to two miles. Beyond this is a plain, elevated about fifty feet, which extends westerly one and one-half miles, including the mill swamp lands to the foot of "the Rocks." The highest ground within the town limits is Horse mountain, which is about eight hundred feet.

The territory described includes about two-thirds of the area of Hatfield, most of it very fertile, and much of it still occupied by the descendants of the first white settlers, who located the house lots on Main street in the year 1660 From the foot of the Rocks to the Williamsburg line at the summit of Horse mountain is a wild and desolate region abounding in gravel and rocks, better suited for the growth of wood and timber than for agricultural purposes. This territory of six square miles does not contain a single human habitation, and is but little changed from what it was when first seen by the English settlers. Running gutter starts from an immense spring near the north line of the town in this region, and runs southerly a sparkling trout brook of clear cold water about two miles to its junction with Beaver brook. Its waters were first utilized by Ebenezer Fitch, who built his linseed oil mill about a half-mile north of the junction, more than one hundred years ago— and the greater part of this section has since been known as Linseed woods. It was laid out into lots running west to the town limits by the early settlers and called the "Third Division of Commons." The tillage land for the first century after the settlement of Hatfield was with the exception of the house lots on Elm street, in the meadows. The top of the hill which separates the meadows from the plain was marked by a ditch and at its top was erected a strong post and rail fence, which extended from the Great river at the southwest point of Capawonk meadow (Little Ponsett) to the north line of the town and thence east to the Great river. All of the territory outside of this line of fence was the "Commons," or the common pasture where the farmers summered their cattle. A system of brand and ear marks was adopted and recorded on the town records. These marks settled all disputes among the proprietors about the ownership of cattle after the grand "round up" in the fall. As each farmer had his special and distinctive brand recorded, no questions could be raised. Each year after the corn was gathered into the barns, the cattle and sheep were turned into the meadows until the snow came.

The whole territory of the town was divided up among the original settlers and their children during the first fifty years after the incorporation of the town. It consisted of eight grand divisions, viz.: First, the forty-four home lots on Main street, containing from four to eight acres each; Second, the Meadows; Third, the Mill Swamp, which extended from the grist-mill built by Thomas Meekins in 1661, northwesterly to the Deerfield line, and on the higher ground at the edge of the swamp east and west two highways were laid out ten rods in width ; Fourth, the First Division of Commons, which extends from the Meekins mill northerly to a point within the present town of Whately, and bounded east by the top of the hill adjacent to Great pond, the home lots and the North Meadows and west by the East Mill Swamp highway; Fifth, the Second Division of Commons, which extends from the First Division to the Deerfield line, the whole Division being now within the town of Whately in Franklin county ; Sixth, the Third Division of Commons, now partly in Hatfield, but including Haydenville and the center of the town of Williamsburg, bounded on the south by Northampton and east by the West Mill Swamp highway ; Seventh, the Fourth Division of Commons located north of the Third Division now wholly within the towns of Williamsburg and Whately, including about one-half of the territory of each town ; Eighth, the Dennison and Bradstreet grants—1,000 acres located north of the North Meadows, now lying partly in Hatfield and partly in Whately.

These grants were early purchased by the town of Hatfield. The Meadow lots were small, and the land of the First and Third Divisions of Commons were divided into long, narrow strips by parallel lines running west through each division and numbered from the Northampton line northerly to the lines of the second and fourth divisions, which are similarly run and numbered.

The Meadows were sub-divided. Capawonk Meadow (Little Ponsett) 157 acres was purchased of Northampton. It is separated from the other South Meadow by Capawonk river (Mill river) and Great Ponsett Meadow, is bounded west and north by this river. East Division, Middle Division, Indian Hollow and Indian Field form the eastern divisions of South Meadow. Lower Plain is situated south of the home lots on the Hill, and is bounded south and east by the Capawonk river.

Little Meadow is at the north end of Main street, and separated from North Meadow by a high ridge extending from King's Hill to the Connecticut. The other divisions of the North Meadow were Cow bridge, Long lots, Fifty pound lots, Bashan, Old Farms and Great Pond.

Settlement and Growth.—At the first town meeting held in Hadley, October 8, 1660, the following vote was passed :—

" Voted that all who sit down on the west side of the river (Hatfield) shall be one with those on the east side in both ecclesiastical and civil matters that are common to the whole, they paying all charges from their engagement and all purchase charges from the beginning. Those admitted for inhabitants on the west side of the river are to be inhabiting there in houses of their own by next Michaelmas (Sept 29, 1661), and to sign an engagement by themselves or some others for them."

Most of those who wished to settle on the west side of the river signed an engagement for themselves or their friends to be dwellers there before September 29, 1661. Some signed at the meeting October 8th, others November 1st, and some in January, February, or March, 1661. Twenty-five per-

sons " manifested an intention " before March 25, 1661, to establish them-
selves on that side of the river in the new town, viz : Aaron Cook, Thos.
Meekins, Wm. Allis, Nathaniel Dickinson, Jr., John Coleman, Isaac Graves
(with his father, Thos. Graves), John Graves, Samuel Belden, Stephen Taylor,
John White, Jr., Daniel Warner, Richard Fellows, Richard Billings, Edward
Benton, Mr. Ritchell (with his son), Ozias Goodwin, Zechariah Field, Lieut.
Thomas Bull, Gregory Wilterton, Nathaniel Porter, Daniel White, William
Pitkin, John Cole, Samuel Church, Samuel Dickinson.   Of these twenty-
seven persons, Aaron Cook and Samuel Church did not remove to the west
side of the river.   Ozias Goodwin, Lieut. Bull, Gregory Wilterton, and William Pitkin continued to reside at Hartford ; Nathaniel Porter at Windsor ;
Mr. Ritchell (and son) and Edward Benton at Wethersfield.   Seventeen appear to have become permanent residents on the west side, and thus constituted the first settlers of Hatfield.   They were from Hartford, Windsor, and
Wethersfield, Conn., except Thomas Meekins and William Allis, who belonged
to Braintree, Mass.   Several families, whose names were afterward very
prominent in all the public business of Hatfield, as Hastings, Partridge, Williams, Smith and others, settled a few years later.

"The home-lots in Hatfield village were assigned so that they were owned
from 1668 to 1672 about as follows, commencing at the north end, east side
of the street, at the old highway to the river [present Bliss Hotel corner] :
Thomas Bracy ; Hezekiah Dickinson, twenty rods wide ; William Scott,
twenty rods wide ; Daniel Belden, sixteen rods wide ; Samuel Allis, sixteen
rods wide ; Samuel Marsh, sixteen rods wide ; Nathaniel Foote, sixteen rods
wide ; a space left for a street ; Philip Russell, four acres ; Samuel Gil-
ett, four acres ; John Wells, four and one half acres ; John Coleman, sixteen
rods wide ; Samuel Belden, eight acres ; William Gull, eight acres ; Samuel
Dickinson, eight acres ; Edward Benton, Nathaniel Dickinson, Sr., six acres ;
John White, Jr., Nicholas Worthington, eight acres ; Nathaniel Dickinson, Jr., eight acres ; Richard Billings, Samuel Billings, eight acres ;
Daniel Warner, eight acres ; Thomas Bull, by the town to Mr. Atherton,
eight acres.   Returning to the north end, and beginning on the west
side of the street, opposite the Bliss Hotel, the proprietors were William King, afterward Samuel Field, sixteen rods wide ; Benjamin Wait,
sixteen rods wide ; John Graves, Jr., sixteen rods wide ; Samuel Foote,
sixteen rods wide ; Robert Danks, sixteen rods wide ; space for Deerfield
lane ; Isaac Graves, Jr., sixteen rods wide ; Samuel Northam, sixteen rods
wide ; Richard Morton, twenty rods wide ; a town-lot sixteen rods wide ;
space reserved for street ; John Hawks, four acres ; Mill lane ; Samuel Kellogg four acres ; Obadiah Dickinson, four acres ; John Allis, eight acres ;
Daniel White, eight acres ; Wm. Allis, eight acres ; Thomas Meekins, Thomas
Meekins, Jr., eight acres ; Eleazer Frary, eight acres ; John Graves, eight
acres, Isaac Graves, eight acres ; Stephen Taylor, Barnabas Hinsdale, eight
acres ; Ozias Goodwin, Mr. Hope Atherton, eight acres ; Zechariah Field,
John Field, eight acres ; highway to Northampton ; John Cowles & Son, eight
acres ; Richard Fellows, Widow Fellows, eight acres.

This plot or survey seems to have been made as early as 1661, for in the
Hadley records it appears that a committee was appointed for that purpose
January 21st of that year.

The Hill, so-called, west of Mill river, was not settled until after King Philip's war. But the mill is of very early date, and by the time the oath of allegiance was administered, 1678, there were doubtless some living out there.

The comparative growth of the town may be seen by the following figures placed after the respective years: 1776, 582; 1790, 703; 1800, 809; 1810, 805; 1820, 823; 1830, 893; 1840, 933; 1850, 1,073; 1855, 1,162; 1860, 1,337; 1865, 1,405; 1870, 1,594; 1875, 1,600; 1880, 1,495.

Among the prominent Hatfield residents may be mentioned Jonathan Dickinson (1688–1747), clergyman and author; Elisha Williams (1694–1755), president of Yale college from 1726 to 1739; Oliver Partridge (1712–1792), member of the first colonial congress; Col. Samuel Partridge (1645–1740), representative to the general court, judge of probate, one of his Majesty's council, "and the most important man after the death of Col. Pynchon, in 1703, in all the western part of the province;" Col. Israel Williams (1709–1788), prominent as a military officer; Col. Ephraim Williams (———1755), founder of Williams college; Hon. John Hastings, member of the state government for thirty years; Dr. Joseph Lyman, pastor of the church fifty-six years; Oliver Smith, (1766–1845), founder of Smith Charities, of Northampton, and Sophia Smith, founder of Smith college, of Northampton, and of Smith academy, and this list might be largely extended.

Nathaniel Dickinson, the ancestor of most of the family of this name now residing in Hatfield, Hadley and vicinity, came from Weathersfield, Conn., to Hadley in 1659, and died there June 16, 1676. William, a descendant in the sixth generation from Nathaniel, was born in Hatfield, June 13, 1783. He married Fannie Smith, and reared three children, of whom William H. is the only one now living. The latter was born March 4, 1820. He married Angelina Waite, a descendant in the sixth generation of Benjamin Waite, November 30, 1842. Their children were James W., Mary S., Sarah E. and William Cooley, the latter of whom is the only one now living, at home with his parents. J. D. Bardwell, son of Sarah, also resides with Mr. Dickinson, and a granddaughter, Mary J., resides in New York city.

Samuel H. Dickinson is a son of Solomon, and a grandson of Daniel, and came here as one of the early settlers, and located on the place now owned by John Brown, a descendant of the family.

John Cowles, the ancestor of the family of that name now residing in this town, was one of the early settlers here, and lived on the place now owned by Rufus Cowles, Jr. Rufus, Sr., was born in 1783, married Lucy Osborne in 1804, and had born to him six children, namely, Rufus, Alpheus, Augustus, Erastus, Orsamus and Elizabeth. Erastus was born in 1805, married Olive Dickinson, and reared seven children, four of whom are living, Elizabeth (Mrs. Billings), of Deerfield, Edward C., of Deerfield, Charles L. and Rufus H., who resides on Meadow street. Rufus, Jr., married Fanny P. Moody, and has one daughter, Lucy O., who resides with her father on Maple street.

Alpheus married Sophia Wells, and has had born to him one child, Henry, deceased.

Capt. Silas Billings, son of Col. Erastus, and a descendant of one of the early settlers of this town, was born October 30, 1800, married Mary Smith Graves, daughter of Lewis Graves, and had born to him eight children, viz.: Samuel F., Abbie F., Samuel F., 2d, Abbie A., Mary C., Jane M., Cornelia, and Sarah A. Of these, four are living, Samuel F., Abbie A., Mary C. and Cornelia A. Abbie A. married Lyman Clapp, and has one child. Samuel F. married Elizabeth H. Allis, and has had born to him six children, four of whom are living.

John Fitch was one of the early settlers of this town, and is supposed to have located on the farm now owned by Mrs. B. M. Warner. Ebenezer, son of John, was for many years a surveyor here.

Dea. John Brown lived in Heath, Mass., and reared thirteen children. His son Jonas was for many years a physician in Cazenovia, N. Y. Aaron, son of Dea. John, married Rebecca Dickinson, daughter of Daniel, and moved to this town about 1826, located on the farm now owned by John.

The Morton family traces its establishment in Hatfield to Richard Morton, who moved from Hartford, Conn., to Hadley, and thence to Hatfield about 1668. His wife's name was Ruth, and she bore him nine cnildren. From these have descended the Hatfield Mortons of to-day, in the sixth and seventh generations. Richard died April 3, 1710, and his wife survived him till December 31, 1714.

Jonathan Porter, a descendant of Ichabod Porter, an early settler of this town, married Electa Allis, and reared five children, viz.: Moses C., of South Amherst, Henry S., of Griswold, Conn., Sophia, of Sunderland, Mass., and Jonathan and James who still live in Hatfield.

Jacob, Fred and Philip Carl, sons of Christian Carl, came to America from Germany, Jacob in 1857, and Fred and Philip in 1858. Jacob married Abbie Pardenhiner, and has three children, Nellie A., Henry W. and Emma L. Fred married Mary Pardenhiner, and has two children, Hattie A. and Lillie A. Philip married Minnie Smith, and has two children, John S. and Ella M. All at present are living in Hatfield.

Eli A. Hubbard was born in Hinsdale, Mass., December 11, 1814, graduated from Williams college with the class of 1842, was tutor there till 1844 teacher in Williston seminary in 1848, and for twelve years thereafter was superintendent of schools in Springfield, from 1865 to 1873; agent of the Massachusetts board of education, from 1875 to 1883. His grandfather and grandmother were both descendants of John Hubbard, the first one of the name in Hatfield, the grandmother being the great-granddaughter, and the grandfather being the great-great-grandson of said John, of Hatfield.

Organization.—Meetings were held in the " West Side," as Hatfield was known from the very first, on account of the difficulty in crossing into Hadley to attend town gatherings. For this reason when the town was legally set off

21*

its municipal machinery was already in motion. The selectmen for 1670–71 were Nathaniel Dickinson, Sr., William Allis, John Cowles, Sr., Isaac Graves and John Coleman. John Allis was the first town clerk, and Samuel Partridge was the first representative to the general court.

Military.—The sufferings of Hatfield in the Indian wars are well-known facts of general history, and anything more than the following brief recapitulation would be out of place in a gazetteer sketch. On the 19th of October, 1675, a band of about 800 savages burst upon the town. They were expected, however, for this was only two days after the terrible affair of Bloody Brook, only fifteen miles distant, and the people here had prepared for an attack. Capt. Appleton's company, from Hadley, held the left, Capt. Mosely the center, and Capt. Poole the right. A regular battle ensued ; but the Indians were repulsed at every point. The whites killed were Thomas Meekins, Nathaniel Collns, Richard Stone, Samuel Clarke, John Pocock, Thomas Warner, Abram Quiddington, William Olverton and John Petts, mostly from Hadley.

On May 30, 1676, about 700 Indians again attacked Hatfield, this time succeeding in destroying many buildings. The flames were seen in Hadley, and twenty-five young men came to the rescue and the Indians were driven off. Of the five whites killed, John Smith was from Hadley, two others were from Connecticut, and two from the garrison at Hadley.

The greatest loss, however, was effected by only about fifty Indians, who fell upon the settlement about eleven o'clock on the morning of September 19, 1677. The killed were Isaac Graves, Sr., John Graves, Sr., John Atchinson, John Cooper, Elizabeth, the wife, and Stephen, son of Philip Russell, Hannah, the wife, and Bethia, daughter of John Coleman, Sarah, the wife of Samuel Kellogg, and their son, Joseph Kellogg, Mary, the wife of Samuel Belding, Elizabeth, the daughter of John Wells, and Thomas Meekins, thirteen in all. The captives were two children of John Coleman, Goodwife Wait and three children, Mrs. Foote and two children, Mrs. Jennings and two children, Obadiah Dickinson and one child, a child of Samuel Kellogg, a child of William Bartholomew, and a child of John Allis, seventeen in all. Six or seven others were wounded and not carried off by the Indians. One of Mrs. Foote's children was killed by the Indians afterwards, and one of Mrs. Jennings's. "A child was born to Mrs. Wait in Canada. The prisoners, with others from Wachuset, were all taken, a sad and weary company, to Sorel, Canada. Efforts to rescue them were immediately made. Benjamin Wait and Stephen Jennings obtaining a commission from the Governor of Massachusetts, proceeded by way of Albany, the Hudson River, and Lake Champlain to Chamblee, in Canada, arriving there late in December. The negotiation was long and tedious ; by the aid of the French authorities and the payment of £200 ransom, the captives that survived were finally gathered. The homeward route could not be taken till spring ; the captives were at Albany May 22d. The almost triumphal procession home, the re-uniting of families, the tearful memories of the dead mingling with the joy of the saved, —all this must be left for the imagination to paint."

The following rough diagram will give one an idea of the holders of house-lots on each side of Main street in 1677, those at the north end of the street being mentioned first :—

William King,[1]
Samuel Field.
Benjamin Wait.[2]
John Graves.
Samuel Foote,[3]
Robert Danks,
Stephen Jennings,[3]
Deerfield Lane.
Isaac Graves. Jr.,
Samuel Northam,
Richard Morton,
Mill Lane.
S. Kellogg,[4]
O. Dickinson,[5]
John Allis,[6]
D. White,
William Allis.
Thomas Meekins,
E. Frary,
John Graves,[7]
Isaac Graves,[10]
S. Taylor,
B. Hinsdale,
O. Goodwin,
Hope Atherton,
Z. Field,
John Field,
Highway to Northampton.
John Cowles,
John Cowles, Jr.,
Richard Fellows,

Bracy,
H. Dickinson,
William Scott,
Dan. Belden,
Samuel Allis,
Samuel Marsh,
Nathaniel Foote,
Philip Russell,[8]
Samuel Gillett,
John Wells,[7]
John Coleman,[9]
Samuel Belden,[7]
William Gull,
Samuel Dickinson,
Edward Benton,
Nathaniel Dickinson,
John White,
N. Worthington,
N. Dickinson, Jr.,
Richard Billings,
Samuel Billings,
Daniel Warner,
Thomas Bull,
M. Atherton.

Apropos of this sketch, we print the following extract from a communication from Mr. S. G. Hubbard of Hatfield :—

"The rough sketch herewith of Hatfield street with home lots and occupants is substantially correct. It proves that the published accounts of the Indian attack of 1677 are incorrect, in stating that the attack was made at the north end of the street. There is a tradition in the Graves family that

1. Three persons killed.
2. Four captives taken and two buildings burned.
3. Three captives taken.
4. One captive taken, two killed, and two buildings burned.
5. Two captives taken and a building burned.
6. A captive taken and a building burned.
7. One killed.
8. Two killed.
9. Two killed, two captives taken and building burned.
10. One killed and a captive taken.

John and Isaac Graves were shot from their barn which they were roof-
ing, near the south end of the street, as seen on the plan. The Indians
coming in from the western woods first went down Mill Lane and struck the
street at the center, where they burned five buildings and killed eight
persons, while only three persons were killed at the north end and two
buildings, the house and barn of Benjamin Wait, were burned. It is evident
that the center was the safest point for them to attack, as most of the men
were at work in the Meadows adjacent to both the north and south ends of
the street—the river being on the east and the plain woods on the west,
which was the natural point of retreat, where they would not be likely to
meet any men from the Meadows or re-inforcements from Hadley or Northampton.

"Samuel Kellogg lived where the Academy now stands. His wife and babe
were killed and his house burned. The Coleman place was opposite Mill
Lane, now School street, at present the home of J. H. Howard. Coleman's
wife and babe were killed and two children taken captive. Capt. John Allis's
house was on the spot where I live. His barn was burned and his little daughter taken captive. Within thirty rods on, four homesteads five buildings were
burned by the foe. Eight persons, consisting of mothers and infant children,
were killed within a space of fifty rods on Main street at the center. Three
men were killed at the north end, and two at the south end of the street.

"Samuel Belden, whose wife was killed, was one of the selectmen of the town
that year. It was no fight—simply a massacre of helpless women and
children, the men being at work in the Meadows. Of the seven buildings
burned, five were at the center and two at the north end, all within the line
of the palisades. It is a wonder that Judd, author of the Hadley history, who
visited Hatfield frequently, did not put these facts together and give a reasonable account of the affair, rather than copy accounts of men who probably
never visited the town and knew nothing of its topography.

"The plan shows all of the inhabited portion of the town in 1677, and
that the attack was probably made at three points—the main body at the
center, with detached parties both at the north and south ends, and that the
Indan retreat was up the Deerfield Lane, which run northwesterly—the
Great Pond separating it from North Meadow, preventing any attack upon
them from that direction.

"Taken in connection with the rescue of the captives by that heroic old
Indian fighter, Benj. Wait, makes this one of the most thrilling stories of that
early period. If there was *a hero par excellence* in the Connecticut Valley
in the first period, it was Benjamin Wait, who was at last killed by the Indians
in the fight at Deerfield in 1704, when the settlement was burned and most
of the people were taken captives to Canada. The Indians knew and feared
Benj. Wait—he was a scout and guide with Capt. Turner in the two days
Falls fight, and it was 'refinement of their revenge to go out of their way to
burn his buildings—take his young wife and three little children into captivity and leave him desolate.'"

Although in Hatfield defenses were kept up, many alarms sounded, and
the people kept in almost a continual state of suspense for years, no more
Indian depredations were visited on the town. A number of the citizens,
however, were sacrificed while assisting at the defense of other places, and
among them, as we have noted, the old hero Benjamin Wait, who was killed
at the Deerfield massacre in 1704.

In the Revolutionary war Hatfield was early and late earnest in the cause, and generous in her contrbution of men and means. In the wake of this came the Shay's Rebellion, as detailed on page 100 and following. In the second war with England, 1812–15, the town took a stand with its neighbors, a willingness to uphold the government, but with regret that other means were not adopted to effect the same result.

In the late great war Hatfield furnished 146 men, a surplus of seven over all demand, two of whom were commissioned officers. The whole amount of money expended was $14,994.71, exclusive of $6,678.64, as a municipal loan, afterwards repaid by the state.

VILLAGES.

HATFIELD VILLAGE, often called "Hatfield Street," is the site of the early settlement we have described. It l'es near the river in the eastern part of the town, a broad, shaded, elegant avenue, lined with fine residences. The postoffice was established here early in the present century, with John Hastings, Jr., postmaster. The present postmaster is Erastus F. Billings.

NORTH HATFIELD is a small post village and station on the Connecticut River railroad, near the north line of the town. The postoffice was established here in 1868.

HATFIELD STATION is a hamlet that has gathered about the railroad station in the southern part of the town.

MANUFACTURES.

C. S. Shattuck's gun factory.—C. S. Shattuck, the fire-arms manufacturer, purchased of J. E. Porter all the mill property and real estate on the north side at the Hatfield mills, which includes the old mill site, eight acres of land and one-half the water power. The sale was completed in March, 1881, and Mr. Shattuck proceeded at once to erect the present buildings. It is certainly a compliment to the people and the town that Mr. Shattuck, after having so many flattering offers to induce him to locate his business elsewhere, should decide, after carefully looking over the field, to rebuild in Hatfield, this being the only manufacturing enterprise of any magnitude in the town. This old mill-site has an interesting history. Its importance as a water-power was early discovered by the first settlers of Hadley, and Thomas Meekins, the only millwright there, was voted the mill site and twenty acres of land adjoining, and further voted that "they would have all their grain ground at his mill, provided he would make good meal," so that Hatfield had the first mill and furnished the meal, while Hadley had the first meeting-house and furnished the preaching.

Thomas Meekins built his first grist-mill on the north side of the river, and his saw-mill, adjacent thereto, eight years aftcr. The two mills, afterwards

rebuilt, were continued on the same spot for nearly two hundred years, until the Hatfield mills property came into the possession of Harvey Moore, now of West Whately. He removed the old buildings, built the present grist-mill on the south side, and the saw-mill on the old site on the north side. This latter was afterwards changed into a factory, where vegetable ivory buttons were made. Subsequently, when it became the property of the Messrs. Porter, it was enlarged, extended and fitted up for the manufacture of firearms, which business has since been carried on there by different parties. The mills were destroyed by fire in 1881 and immediately rebuilt. Mr. Shattuck employs thirty men and manufactures about 4,500 guns per year.

The Porter Machine Works, Jonathan E. Porter, proprietor, manufactures machine lathes on the south side, where Mr. Porter is owner of the privilege.

SCHOOLS.

As early as 1681, Hatfield had a school-house, and has always kept up a high standard of education. The present Smith academy, of which we give an illustration, was founded by Miss Sophia Smith, of Hatfield, in 1870, endowed with $75,000.00. Of these funds $20,000.00 was appropriated for purchasing grounds and erecting a building; $30,000.00 as a fund the income of which is to meet current expenses; $15,000.00 for the erection of new buildings when needed ; and $10,000.00 for a fund the income of which is devoted to the maintenance of indigent students of the school. The school was opened December 4, 1872.

CHURCH.

The Congregational church of Hatfield was organized by its first pastor, Rev. Hope Atherton, and others, in 1670. A church building was erected that year. The present building was built in 1849, a wooden structure capable of seating 450 persons, and now valued, including grounds and other property, at $15,000.00. The society has 309 members, and a flourishing Sabbath-school with 160 members, and a branch at North Hatfield. The pastor is Rev. Robert M. Woods.

HUNTINGTON lies in the southwestern part of the county, and is bounded north by Chesterfield, east by Westhampton and small parts of Chesterfield and Southampton, south and west by the county line. The surface of the town is varied by mountain, hill, valley, lakelet and stream, so that an extremely pleasing and picturesque view is presented from almost any point. Add to this, then, the delight of a healthful climate, and it will not seem strange that so many from less favored localities linger here during the summer months. The east branch of Westfield river is the principal stream, which flows in a sinuous course through a beautiful valley the whole length of the town from north to south. In the southern part of the town, just above the village of Norwich Bridge, it receives the Middle branch from the west. Their united waters continue on to a point just below Huntington village, where they are joined by the West branch, making up the volume of Westfield river proper. Several smaller tributaries add to the waters of the East branch, the largest of which are Pond brook, from the east, and Little river from the west. In the southeastern part of the town, Roaring brook and a branch of Manhan river drain the country. In the western-central part of the town lies Massasoit pond, a pleasant little sheet of water which serves as a reservoir for the mills below. Among the more prominent elevations are Mt. Pisgah and Walnut hill, in the northern part, Goss hill in the western part, and Deer and Horse hills in the southern part. The town has also 13,334 acres of good farming land.

Grant, Settlement and Subsequent Growth.—A large part of the present territory of the town was originally embraced in what was called " Plantation No. 9." On June 2, 1762, this plantation, in common with several others in the vicinity, was sold at auction by the general court, and was purchased by William Williams, for £1,500. Three years later, October 31, 1765, the new township was incorporated under the name of Murrayfield.

On June 29, 1773, the eastern part of Murrayfield was set off and incorporated as the " District of Norwich," with " all the powers, privileges and immunities of a town, that of sending a representative to the general court, alone excepted." But on March 23, 1786, an act was passed providing that all districts incorporated before January 1, 1777, should be considered towns and have the rights of representation.

On February 21, 1783, the western part of the old territory of Murrayfield was given the name of Chester. As time passed on a thriving village sprang up on the corners of the towns of Blandford, Chester and Norwich, and which, thus lying in three towns and two counties, rendered police regulations very difficult to enforce. Accordingly, through agitation of a means to remedy this evil, a portion of the towns of Blandford and Chester were annexed to Norwich, in 1853, thus bringing the village (now Huntington village) entirely within the limits of that town. The Hon. Charles P. Huntington, of Northampton, was actively engaged in securing this change, and in 1855 the legislature passed an act changing the name of Norwich to that of Huntington, which it still bears.

The exact date of the first settlement cannot be given ; but it was probably in the spring of 1769, and it is also probable that Daniel Kirkland and Samuel Knight and their families were here in the spring or summer of 1769. These are known to have been here, and there were doubtless others, for quite a group of families came on from Norwich, Conn., about that time. Among them, aside from those already mentioned, were Caleb Forbes, William Miller, David Scott, Isaac Mixer and John Rude. John Kirkland located upon the place now owned by C. H. Kirkland, which has always remained in the possession of the family. Isaac Mixer located near Norwich Bridge. Caleb Forbes located a little further up the river. William Miller and John Rude located still further up the stream, near the north line of the town. This section was long known as Norwich Hollow.

The settlement of the new town increased with moderate rapidity, for in 1773 the following were here, many of them with families : Christian Angell, Solomon Blair, Thomas Crow, James Crow, David Crow, William Carter, Asa Carter, John Crow, Caleb Forbes, William Forbes, Elijah Forbes, Zebulon Fuller, James Fairman, Samuel Fairman, William French, John Griswold, James Gilmore, David Halbard, Jabez Holmes, Nathaniel Bennett, John Barnard, Solomon Holiday, Daniel Dana, John Crossett, Ebenezer Freeman, Solomon Holiday, Jr., Patrick Buckle, John Kirkland, Ebenezer King, Samuel Knight, Daniel Kirkland, Isaac Mixer, Isaac Mixer, Jr., Ebenezer Meacham, William Miller, David Palmer, John D. Palmer, David Palmer, Jr., Capt. E. Geer, Elijah Geer, Mace Cook, Zeb. Ross, John Rude, David Scott, Joseph Stanton, John Tiffany, Miles Washburn, Peter Williams, Daniel Williams, Isaac Williams, Jr., Charles Williams, Jabez Story, James Clark, Jehiel Eggleston, Jonathan Ware and Peter Bunda.

The subsequent growth and fluctuation in the town's population may be seen in the following figures : In 1776 its population was 742; 1790, 742; 1800, 959; 1810, 968; 1820, 849; 1830, 795; 1840, 750; 1850, 756; 1855, 1,172; 1860, 1,216; 1865, 1,163; 1870, 1,156; 1875, 1,095; 1880, 1,236.

John Kirkland was a son of Rev. Daniel Kirkland, was born November 15, 1735. He bought in 1768 seven hundred acres of land, and built a log cabin on Norwich hill, as we have said, his nearest neighbor being at that time twelve miles distant. He was one of the first deacons of the church, and married Anna Palmer, who was a descendant of Thomas Palmer. His son Samuel was, in his younger days, surveyor on the Phelps tract near Canandaigua, N. Y., was representative to the general court in 1828 and 1830, for many years was justice of the peace, town treasurer, etc. He was taken prisoner in the Shays Rebellion, but was soon released. He married Dorcas Maxwell, daughter of Col. Hugh Maxwell, who was an officer in the Revotion, and died December 1, 1852, aged eighty seven years. His son Joseph was an officer of the church, and served the town in various ways, as a justice of the peace, etc. Edward, second son of Samuel, was a graduate of Amherst college, resided for many years in Louisville, Ky., but afterwards practiced law in Brattleboro, Vt., and died in January, 1866, aged fifty-nine years. The old homestead is now in possession of Charles H. Kirkland, son of Joseph, and has thus been in possession of the family for nearly one hundred and twenty years. He has served the town as selectman and school committee, and represented the Second Hampshire district in the legislature of 1860 and 1864. He served in the late war as lieutenant in Co. F, 46th Mass. Vols.

William Miller was one of the early settlers of Huntington, and made the first settlement on the farm now owned by William P. Miller, in 1763. The first night he spent in the town, he climbed into a scrubby hemlock tree, which is still standing, to avoid the wolves. He was a saddler by trade, married Elizabeth Perkins, and reared three children, Nathaniel, William and Rachel. William had born to him three children, namely, Electa, wife of William Gardner, Rachel, deceased, who married David Blair, and William P., who resides on the homestead.

Joel Searle came to this town, from Southampton, about 1795, and settled on the farm now owned by A. S. Searle. He married Sophia Sheldon, and reared nine children. Spencer, son of Joel, was born in 1804, married Philomelia Gaylord, and had born to him three children, Charles A., Albert S. and Clarissa P. Albert S., the only one now living, married Ellen M., daughter of John Peck, of Shelburne, Mass., and has three children, Clarissa B., John S. and Anthony C. On this farm is a ledge, which consists of mica, feldspar and quartz, which is considered valuable for the manufacture of crockery.

John Rude, son of Jacob, came to this town from Norwich, Conn., and made the first settlement on the farm now owned by Elias Rude, 2d, in 1770. His son John married Deborah Dunbar, and reared six children, namely, Zara, Clarissa, Alvin, Relief, Harvey and Elias. The last mentioned is the only one now living. Zara married Elizabeth Patch, and reared ten children, two of whom are living, Elias and John. The former married Ruth, widow of John Cole, and has had born to him two children, one of whom, Norman, resides in Syracuse, N. Y. Alvin married Mary, daughter of Jonathan Bisbee, and had six children.

Francis and Richard Cook came from England, and settled in the state of Massachusetts at a very early period in its history. John, a descendant of one of these brothers, married a Miss Tracy, and reared seven sons and four daughters. About 1770 he purchased a tract of land then in Chester, being the third lot surveyed in the town, and being a part of the farm now owned in Huntington by his grandson, John J. Cook. Perly, the third son of John, was born in 1764, came to Huntington about 1790, locating on the Cook farm, and married Lovina Burt, who bore him five sons and four daughters. Of these only four are at present living, viz., Pearly B., of Cohoes, N. Y., Edward W., of Hartford, Conn., Clarissa M. Clark, widow of Edward A. Clark, of Easthampton, and John J., of this town. The last mentioned was born July 13, 1806, married Lucy S. Taylor, and has two children, Franklin B., of Hinsdale, Mass., and Marion L., who resides with her father. Mr. Cook became interested in the manufacture of window shades, in 1833, in company with Thomas F. Plunkett; in 1836, bought the entire interest in the blind business, and a half interest in the cotton business, and in 1842, purchased the entire interest of Mr. Plunkett, carrying on the business until 1855, when through failing health he was compelled to retire.

Abel Stanton, son of Jabez, was born about 1748, and married Olive Reed in 1769. His son Joseph was born in July, 1783, married Grace Winchell, August 16, 1804, and reared a large family of children as follows: Luke W., born September 17, 1806, Jabez, born July 16, 1808, Hannon, born December 4, 1810, Fanny M., born February 12, 1813, Henry, born April 5, 1815, Joseph, born February 12, 1818, Adeline, born Februry 20, 1820, and Catherine, born April 19, 1822. Mr. Stanton was a prominent man in his day, held various town offices, was deacon of the church, and died March 12, 1870. Luke W. was a successful physician, and died in 1869. Jabez lived in Ohio, for a time, and at the time of his death, in 1872, was station agent of the Boston and Albany railroad at Huntington. He had born to him two children, A. J. and Mrs. H. W. Munson, the latter residing in this town. Hannon lives in the West. Fanny M. married twice, first Hiram Chapman, and second Moses Fisk, and died in 1879. She had three children, Emerson, who died in the late war, Henry S. and Irving. Henry reared nine children, seven of whom survive him. He died in 1874. Four of his sons reside in town, Henry E., Fred P., George K. and Edward W. His daughter Flora L. also resides in town, living at home with her mother. Adeline married Haverton Collins, a farmer at Huntington, and her children are Ella, who married A. J. Stanton, Carrie, who married Alex McDougall, Arthur and Isabel, the last two residing at home. Catherine has married twice, first, Dr. Homer Holland, and second John J. Bowles. They reside in Huntington.

Joseph Lindsey moved to Blandford about 1790, and purchased a tract of land extending from near Russell to what is now the village of Huntington. Joseph married Salvina Gere, and reared seven children, only one of whom, S. I. Lindsey, is now living. The latter married twice, first, Electa Lindsey, who bore him two children, Charles M., of this town, and Eunice A. Gilmore, of Springfield. He married for his second wife, Mary A., widow of Emmons Griffin, and has one son Frank H., who also resides in this town.

Ebenezer Williams moved from Canterbury, Conn., to Worthington, as an early settler. His oldest son, Leonard, was born in 1774, studied medicine with Dr. James Holland, of Huntington, and succeeded to his practice. He married Olive Wadsworth, March 7, 1799, and reared three children. Jabin B., son of Leonard, was for many years a merchant in this town, married Lydia Wilson, and had born to him six children. Of these L. B., Henry F. and Charles are engaged in the manufacture of baskets at Northampton, and Cynthia A. is the widow of Israel D. Clark. James H. was born in this town, June 20, 1805, married Mary Prentiss, and had born to him three children, only one of whom is living, Whitman P., who lives in Huntington, and is engaged in milling and is a dealer in flour and feed.

The first legal district meeting was held July 14 1773, when David Scott was chosen moderator; John Kirkland, clerk; John Kirkland, Caleb Fobes and David Scott, selectmen and assessors; David Scott, treasurer; Miles Washburn, constable. District meetings were first held at the dwelling-house of Caleb Fobes, afterwards at Isaac Mixer's hotel. The constable was di-

rected to warn such meeting by posting up a copy of the warrant at Isaac
Mixer's grist-mill, which appears to have been located about half a mile, more
or less, above Norwich Bridge.   From 1781 to 1841, they were held at the
meeting-house.   A town-house was then built near Knightville, which did
service till after Chester village was brought into the town.   A hall was hired
here, which burned in 1862, and the town then built their present town-hall.

The first town officers elected after the reconstruction of the township,
March 11, 1854, were Lyman Dimock, clerk ; E. B. Tinker, Edward Williams and Jabez Stanton, selectmen ; Whitman Knight, treasurer ; Rev.
Townsend Walker, Dr. N. S. Bartlett and Charles M. Kirkland, school com-
mittee ; John Parks, constable ; Washington Stevens, E. B. Tinker and Ed-
ward Williams, overseers of the poor ; G. S. Lewis, collector; Salmon
Thomas, F. H. Axtell, Homer Clark, Horace Taylor, Elias Rude and C. H.
Stickney, field-drivers ; Garry Munson, H. B. Dimock and William T. Miller,
fence viewers ; Daniel Granger, Jabez Stanton, G. S. Lewis, Whitman
Knight and A. S. Rollins, surveyors of lumber ; Seth Porter, sealer of leather ;
C. H. Stickney, E. S. Ellis, William T. Miller and Joseph Stanton, sextons ;
Garry Munson and H. B. Dimock, pound keepers ; Daniel Granger, James
Jones, Jabez Stanton, George Merritt and Whitman Knight, measures of
wood and bark.

Military.—In 1774, the district voted to provide powder, lead, flints and a
drum for the use of the district.   The same year Ebenezer Meacham was
chosen to attend the congress at Concord.   September 23, 1774, at a legal
district meeting, the resolves of a county congress held at Northampton were
read and considered satisfactory.   A committee was appointed to send to the
provincial congress the sentiment of this district respecting the public dis-
tresses of this province.   It was also " Voted, that it was proper at this critical day, to form into a military company for learning the art of military,"
and that Capt. Ebenezer Geer be requested to lead in the choice of officers.
A military company was accordingly organized October 6, 1774, by the choice
of the following officers :   John Kirkland, captain; David Scott, lieutenant;
Ebenezer King, ensign.   As a precautionary measure, to guard against dangerous persons and paupers, certain individuals were voted out of the district,
with the refusal to admit them as inhabitants.   In 1775, it was

" Voted to choose a committee in compliance with the method adopted by
the provincial congress, and also the same to be a committee of correspondence, and said committee are further enjoined by this body to take all possible
methods to suppress disorder, and that every person shall be fairly heard before he is condemned, that we may enjoy our interest and prosperity peaceably, and live as Christians."

When the war of the Revolution was fairly commenced, Norwich furnished,
it is believed, its full quota of men.   Though the town records are on this
point very imperfect, yet from various sources the following names of Revolutionary soldiers are obtained :   Halsey Sandford, Stephen Angel, Isaac
Coit.

In the war of 1812, the town took the usual stand of its neighbors, a willingness to fight if need be, but believing that the war was unnecesary. The following men went out to the defence of Boston under the call of Governor Strong: Samuel Lyman, Enos Wait, John Ladd, Solomon Belden, Samuel Henry, Samuel Sanderson, Harvey Stone, Russell Smith, and Perkins S. Pitcher.

In the late civil war the town furnished 137 men, a surplus of eight over all demands, five of whom were commissioned officers. The total amount of money furnished was $12,000.00, and $10,368.51 as a war loan.

VILLAGES.

HUNTINGTON VILLAGE lies in the southwestern section of the town, on the west branch of Westfield river and on the Boston and Albany railroad. The village is beautifully located in the midst of surrounding hills and being the business center of quite a large section of country, is a bright, flourishing place. A postoffice was established here early in the present century, and Daniel Falley was the first postmaster, whence the village took the name of Falley's X-roads. Thus it was known until the advent of the railroad, when the name was changed to Chester, the station having been located in a part of the village then lying within the limits of that town. But finally came the changes of 1853–55 we have already detailed, since which time the village has borne its present name.

NORWICH VILLAGE containing the town's only other past postoffice, lies nearly in the geographical center of the township. It is locally known as " The Hill." Here it was that the Kirklands, the Knights, the Hannums, and, not far away, the Fairmans, Fobes, and others located in 1773. The village is divided into two sections, the northern part, where are mills, shops, schoolhouse and postoffice ; and the southern part, where are the church, a schoolhouse and dwellings.

NORWICH BRIDGE is a hamlet just above Huntington village.

KNIGHTSVILLE is a hamlet still farther up the valley, opposite " The Hill," taking its name from the Knight family.

MANUFACTURES.

The Highland Mills.—Atherton J. Stanton, of Pittston, Pa., son of Jabez, was one of the early manufacturers at the village. In company with William Little, son of Benjamin Little, he built on the site now occupied by the Highland Mills. They manufactured bed-spreads, and claimed to be one of the first to make these goods, at least by power looms, in the country. They also made flannel. Little & Stanton's mill was burned, and the Hampshire Manufacturing Company was formed and built the present mill. A number of local parties were induced to invest in the stock of the company, and A. J.

Stanton was the agent.   The company failed.   In 1873 the mills came into the possession of the present company, of which R. S. Frost, of Chelsea, Mass., is president ; R. F. Greeley, treasurer, and H. J. Brown, superintendent.   The mills are operated by both water and steam-power, and are at present used in the manufacture of fancy cassimeres, employing about one hundred hands.

The Chester Paper Co.—This mill was erected in 1853, by the Greenleaf & Taylor Manfg. Co., and began the manufacture of book and news paper in the spring of 1854, making about 1,800 lbs. per day, which was considered a large product for the times.   After running several years on this class of goods, the company decided, in 1855, to change the mill on to fine writing papers, and immediately took steps to put in the necessary machinery, and in 1856 the first fine writing papers were made.   For years the mill has been famous for the uniformly fine quality of its goods, and has run with but little or no interruption (except for the necessary repairs incident to a paper-mill) for more than thirty years, during which time its capacity has been more than doubled.   The present company was organized in 1882, with a capital of $75,000.00, the property having been owned by the original founders up to that date.   The mill is probably the oldest in Western Massachusetts now in successul operation.   The property has a fine water-power ample for its needs during nine or ten months of the year.   During low water in the river the power is supplemented by a 150 horse-power steam engine, which is capable of driving the whole works if necessary.   The number of hands employed averages seventy-five, and the annual product of the mill amounts to about 500 tons of fine papers.

W. P. Williams's grist-mill, on road 27, has one run of stones and grinds about 16,000 bushels of grain per year.

M. R. Fisk's saw and grist mill, located at Huntington, is operated by a thirty horse-power engine, is equipped with circular, lumber and lathe-slitting saws, etc., employs five men and cuts annually 500,000 feet of lumber.   The grist-mill has one run of stones and grinds annually about 25,000 bushels of grain.

H. E. Stanton's saw-mill, located at Huntington, is operated by water-power and gives employment to ten men in the manufacture of lumber, whip-butts, basket-rims and handles, lath, shingles, etc.

CHURCHES.

Christ's Congregational church, located at Norwich village, was organized by Rev. Jonathan Judd, of Southampton, Jonathan Huntington, of Worthington, and Aaron Bascomb, of Chester, with twenty-five members, in July, 1778, and Rev. Stephen Tracy, of Norwich, Conn., was the first pastor.   Services were held in the school-house till 1796, when the first church building was erected.   The present building was erected in 1842.   It is a wooden structure capable of seating 225 persons, and valued at $2,500.00. The society now has seventy-three members, with Rev. Ernest F. Bochers, pastor.

The Second Congregational churh, located at Huntington village, was organized by the Hampden Association of Ministers, with twenty-eight members, August 26, 1846. Rev. Perkins K. Clark was the first pastor. In 1847 the society built a church, which was destroyed by fire in January, 1862, and in 1863 the present edifice was erected. It is of wood, capable of comfortably accommodating 300 persons, and is valued at $5,000.00. The society now has seventy members, with Rev. William F. Avery, pastor.

The Huntington Baptist church, located at the village, was organized by its first pastor, Rev. John Green, and others, with ten members, October 7, 1852. Their church building was erected in 1836, by the Methodist society that formerly flourished here. The society now has 111 members, with Rev. Howard R Mitchell, pastor.

St. Thomas' Catholic church, located at the village, was organized by the Rt. Rev. P. T. O'Reilly, April 4, 1886, and Rev. Lawrence J. Dervin was appointed its pastor. The church building was erected in 1880, at a cost of $6,000.00, and is now valued, including grounds, at $14,000.00. The parish includes the organizations in Russell, Blandford and Montgomery. Among other good works, Rev. Father Dervin immediately instituted a temperance society when he came here in April, now known as the St. Thomas Total Abstinence Society, which has eighty-five members, with the interest steadily increasing.

MIDDLEFIELD* lies in the southwestern part of the county, between the Middle branch of Westfield river, and the Western branch, having the former for its eastern border, and the latter for its southwestern, with Peru on the north, Worthington on the north and east, Chester on the southeast, Becket on the southwest, and Washington on the west. It was incorporated March 12, 1783, including within its boundaries what had been the southwest corner of Worthington, the northwest corner of Chester, the northeast corner of Becket, the south side of Peru, and a part of Washington, together with "Prescott's Grant," a considerable tract of land lying outside the limits of any corporate town. The reason given in the act of incorporation for granting the request of the petitioners was "the great difficulties and inconveniences" the inhabitants labored under "in their present situation."

The surface of the town is broken. Bold highlands in continuous ranges extend through the territory from northwest to southeast, interlaced by streams and valleys, and covered, during the summer months, with abundant foliage

----

*Prepared by Rev. Joseph M. Rockwood.

and luxuriant vegetation. Between the two branches of Westfield river which enclose the town, and emptying into these, are several considerable streams — the Den stream, the Factory stream, Cole's brook and some others. In the earlier days of the town the saw mill and the grist-mill and other establishments devised by a thrifty community were planted upon these streams ; and so they have contributed largely—especially the Factory stream—to the prosperity of the town.

Agriculture, particularly in the department of stock-raising, fattening cattle and dairying, has been the leading pursuit in the town. The organization of the Highland Agricultural society, in 1857, contributed much to the farming enterprise of this and the neighboring towns. Of this society, Matthew Smith was the first president. It has held its annual meetings for thirty years, with a creditable exhibition of stock and farm products, and furnished in its series of annual addresses much to awaken an enlightened zeal and a becoming self-respect in the farming fraternity. The ten leading articles of farm produce and their value, for the year ending May 1, 1885, are reported as follows : Butter, $6,034 ; beef, $6,502 ; hay, $18,018 ; milk, $5,667 ; potatoes, $3,749 ; firewood, $5,431 ; manure, $3,540 ; maple sugar, $3,396 ; pork, $1,741 ; wool, $1,552. At one time sheep-husbandry was prosecuted extensively. In Haywood's Massachusetts Gazetteer it is said that "in one year there were sheared in the town nine thousand seven hundred and twenty-five fleeces of Saxony wool, which weighed twenty-six thousand, seven hundred and forty-one pounds, and sold for seventeen thousand, three hundred and eighty-two dollars."

Early Settlers.—Three of the earliest settlers, Rhodes, Taggart and Taylor, were on the ground as early as 1773. Which came first is not perfectly clear ; let each enjoy the distinction of being " perhaps" the first. Rhodes settled on land now owned by Clark B. Wright ; he is said to have built the first grist-mill in town. John Taggart occupied a part of the flat now covered by the reservoir. Samuel Taylor built on land a little east from the grounds of the Highland Agricultural society, and erected the first frame building in town. He came from Pittsfield, where he first settled in 1752.

Two years later, in 1775, there were eight families in the town. David Mack became a resident, with his family, this year, who was so prominent in all the enterprises of the town. It was through his influence that the town came to be organized and incorporated. By his energy, persistency and large-hearted generosity the material and moral interests of the community were greatly furthered. He came to town with little else than his own capacity and indomitable purpose ; he amassed wealth, and distributed it wisely and with a princely bounty.

At the date of the incorporation of the town, 1783, there were said to be sixty-eight resident families. Some of these did not long remain. The following names appear upon the records at an early date : John Ford, Malachi Loveland, Amasa Graves, Thomas Blossom, Enos Blossom, Solomon Ingham, Thomas Bolton, James Dickson, Eliakim Wardwell, Samuel Jones, John

Jones, John Newton, Daniel Chapman, Job Robbins, Benjamin Eggleston, Anson Cheeseman, Abel Cheeseman, Benajah Jones, Timothy McElwain, Benjamin Blish (or Blush), Joseph Blish (or Blush), David Carrier, Israel Bissell, Justice Bissell, Matthew Smith, Timothy Allen, Erastus Ingham, Bissell Phelps, John Spencer, Ebenezer Emmons, Josiah Leonard, Nathan Wright, Thomas Durant, Uriah Church, William Church, Elisha Mack, Dan Pease, Thomas Root, Solomon Root, Daniel Root, Elijah Churchill and Calvin Smith.

Much the larger part of the early settlers came from Connecticut; and they were generally of the religious body that prevailed in New England. They had no ideals for the future of their community which did not require for their realization intelligence and general morality, industry and thrift; and they believed that the fear and worship of God were essential to the real interest and the true happiness of men.

Hiram Taylor was born in Middlefield, December 16, 1819, on the place where he now resides, on road 10. His ancestors are admitted to be the first settlers in Middlefield. He has always been a farmer, has filled the various offices of selectman, assessor, overseer of the poor, and constable and collector, for many years. He has a farm of 650 acres, pays attention to breeding Short-horns, and fattens large numbers of beef cattle yearly. He is chairman of the board of directors of the Highland Agricultural society, and is deacon of the Congregational church.

Timothy McElwain, one of the early settlers of this town, married Jane Brown, of East Windsor, Conn., and reared six sons and six daughters. His son Jonathan was born on the place now occupied by Jonathan, Jr., on road 9, married Lucy, daughter of John Smith, and reared five children. Jonathan, Jr., married Mary Smith, and has three children, viz.: Edwin S., married Maria L. Graves, and is a farmer on road 9. Mary J. married Capt. Fitz J. Babson, of Gloucester, Mass., and Lura V. is at home. Mrs. McElwain died March 7, 1886. Jonathan has always pursued farming as a business, has held various town offices, is at present town clerk, and is secretary of the Highland Agricultural society. Oliver is a resident of West Springfield. John S. is a paper manufacturer at Holyoke, having an interest in three paper companies in that city. Edwin is a member of Kibbe Bros. & Co., of Springfield.

Jacob Robbins was born in the house where he now resides, on road 2, October 8, 1817. His father, Job, was among the early settlers of the town. He married Mary J., daughter of John S. Scofield, of Pittsfield, and has five children, viz.: William E., who resides in Russell, Mass., Edward C., who died at the age of twenty-four years, Sarah A., Edson D., of Russell, and Myron L., who is proprietor of the mail and express route from Middlefield station on the Boston & Albany railroad to the postoffice at the Center. Mr. Robbins has also an adopted daughter, Florence.

Erastus Ingham was one of the early settlers of this town, locating in the

22*

forest in the western part of the town, and afterwards removing to a place on road 6. He was a prominent man in the affairs of the town, holding the office of selectman for several years, and was succeeded on the farm by his son Erastus John. The latter married Vesta, daughter of John Dickson, and reared a family of six children, only one of whom is living in Middlefield, Erastus J. The latter was born in 1828, and carries on the farm occupied by his father and grandfather. He married Julia Pease, February 4, 1851, and has had born to him four children, two of whom are living, Lillie C., who married Wayland F. Smith, of West Springfield, and Nora V., who married John T. Bryan, general merchant and postmaster at the Center.

Luther Granger came to this town about 1786, was a blacksmith by trade, and married twice, first, Miriam Waite, who bore him four children, and second Ruth Goodwell, who bore him eight children. Abraham, son of Luther, was born in this town, married Jane Adams, and located in Worthington. His children are Rebecca, wife of Russell Tower, Paul, Ruth, wife of E. J. Robinson, and Abraham.

Howard Smith, son of Ebenezer, and grandson of Calvin, who was one of the early settlers of Middlefield, was born in town November 4, 1838, married Maggie Ford, in May, 1871, and has three children. Mr. Smith resides on road 4, on the farm once occupied by his father, and adjoining the farm owned by his grandfather. He is perhaps the largest owner of fine-wool sheep in the town, for which industry the town was formerly noted.

Metcalf J. Smith was born in Middlefield, in September, 1830, was educated at Cortland, N. Y., graduating in 1855, and taught school ten years in Pennsylvania, Indiana and Connecticut. He held a professorship of mixed mathematics and natural science in Central college, and in 1857 accepted the same chair in a Lutheran college in Indiana. He returned to the homestead in 1864, and still resides there on road 2. He married Harriet L., daughter of Lyman Eldredge, of Cincinnatus, N. Y., and has had born to him seven children, viz.: Sophia S., Theodore W., who died in 1865, Gerald B., Louis C., Kate W., Edward C. and Samuel E.

Nathan Wright came to this town from Chester in 1799, locating on road 25, married Asenath, daughter of Daniel Cone, and reared eleven children, only four of whom are living, namely, Clark, Charles, Louisa and Amos. Clark married Anna L., daughter of Sylvester Prentice, occupies the homestead, which is called "Glendale Farm," has 500 acres, and is a breeder of Durham cattle. Charles married Sarah, daughter of Matthew Smith, and is a farmer on road 1. Louisa married Lawrence Smith, and lives in Chester. Amos is a bridge builder, and lives in Athens, Pa.

Milton Combs was a native of this town, married Laura Meacham, and reared a family of six children, viz.: Louisa, who married Charles Smith, and resides at Smith Hollow; Almira, who married Austin Rude, of Huntington; E. Stacy married Jane Hazelton, and resides in Russell; Andrew, who was a commission merchant at Albany, N. Y., and died there in 1885;

Charles M., who was born in April, 1830, married Sophronia Haskell, has seven children, and resides on the homestead, on road 39 ; and John, who was killed at the battle of Gaines Mills during the late rebellion. Milton died in 1855.

Lyman Meacham was born in Peru, Mass., October 2, 1825, spent his early life in that town, went to Brooklyn at the age of twenty years, engaged in the manufacture and sale of soda water, in which business he remained eight years, and afterwards carried on the business at Grand Rapids, Mich., two years. He engaged in the lumber business, having a mill at Blendon, on Grand river, Michigan, for a number of years. In 1864 he returned to Peru, carried on his father's farm, and about 1871 purchased the farm where he now resides, on road 1. He married Viola, daughter of Jesse Tarbell, and has had born to him nine children, three sons and six daughters.

Rev. Joseph M. Rockwood was born in Bellingham, Mass., July 1, 1818, attended Milford academy, Waterville college, graduated from Dartmouth college in 1837, and from the theological seminary at Newton in 1841. He commenced preaching in Rutland, Vt., in 1841, where he was pastor of the Baptist church for eight years, preached at the Baptist church in Belchertown six years, at the Second Baptist church at Grafton seven years, and in 1865 was settled over the Baptist church in this town, where he has since remained. In the fall of 1864 he was in the service of the Christian commission at City Point, Va. He married Elizabeth H., daughter of Jonathan Bixby, and has four childen living, two sons at Worcester, and two daughters at home. His fourth daughter, Mary Agnes, was a missionary to the Shans, under the auspices of the American Baptist Missionary union. She died at Toungoo, Burmah, August 4, 1882, after a service of two years.

George W. Cottrell was born in Worthington, August 31, 1830, was a carpenter by trade, married Angeline M. Dyer, in 1854, and located in this town in 1863, on road 24. He served in the late war, in Co. F, 46th Mass. Vols., and died June 23, 1883, leaving a family of four children, as follows : George W., who married Elsie A. Wright, and lives on road 24, Mary V., who married Herbert Prentice, and resides in this town, Carrie H., who married King C. Phillips, of Peru, and John B., who lives on the farm with his mother.

Henry Ferris was born in New Milford, Conn., June 1, 1818, learned the trade of a stone mason, and came to this town in March, 1866, locating at his present home, on road 14½. He married Selina Hall, August 22, 1841, and has four children living, and one adopted daughter. Mary J. married Willard Smith, of this town, who died in 1883. Clara L. married W. B. Graves, a farmer in this town. Katie A. and Charles live at home. Mr. Ferris has a farm of 400 acres, and makes a specialty of raising grade Durham cattle for market.

John T. Bryan was born in Worthington, February 17, 1808, spent his early life on his father's farm, and on attaining his majority commenced trade at the center of the town, keeping a general country store. He has

been often entrusted with public business, is now chairman of the school committee, and has been director of the Highland Agricultural society.   He has
been postmaster three years, and holds the office at the present time.   He
married Nora V., daughter of James Ingham, in April, 1885.

The growth and fluctuations in the town's population may be seen by the
following :   In 1790 its population was 608; 1800, 877; 1810, 822 ; 1820,
755 ;   1830, 720 ;   1840, 717 ;   1850, 737 ;   1855, 677 ;   1860, 748 ;   1865,
727 ;   1870, 728 ;   1875, 603 ;   1880, 648.

Organization.—After its organization the town prosecuted its work of local government, not unmindful of its relation to the interests of the state and
nation.   At the first town meeting Solomon Ingham was chosen town clerk.
Other persons who have held the office are Timothy Allen, John Dickson,
David Mack, Jr., Matthew Smith, Jr., George W. Lyman, John Smith, Solomon F. Root and Jonathan McElwain.   At the same meeting, Samuel Jones,
David Mack and Job Robbins were chosen selectmen and assessors.   Their
successors in office have included most of the business talent of the town.
Daniel Chapman was chosen town treasurer.   The first school committee,
chosen April 24, 1783, were Joseph Blush, Benjamin Blush, Timothy McElwain and John Jones.   In the list of their successors appear the names of the
town's most successful teachers, and business and professional men.   The
first representative to the general court was Uriah Church.   His successors
have been Erastus Ingham, David Mack, John Dickson, Daniel Root, Ebenezer Emmons, David Mack, Jr., George W. McElwain, Matthew Smith, Jr.,
Solomon Root, Daniel Root, Green H. Church, Samuel Smith, Oliver
Smith, James Church, Ambrose Newton, Alexander Ingham, Matthew
Smith, Uriah Church, Jonathan McElwain, Amos Cone, Harry Meacham,
Almon Barnes, Eliakim Root, Oliver Smith, 2d, Milton Combs, W. L.
Church, Arnold Pease, S. U. Church, Matthew Smith and Metcalf J. Smith.

Educational.—The schools of the town have received much of its care, and
have richly repaid the attention given them.   At the first meeting that occurred
after the organization of the town, April 24, 1783, it was voted to "raise ten
pounds for the support of schools for the year ensuing."   Twenty pounds
were voted on each of the two following years ; and the sum was increased
with the increasing needs of the rising community.   It is interesting to notice
that in 1843 the town appropriated $2.72 for each child of school age, and
contributed as much more for board and fuel.   It ranked third in the county
in the amount appropriated for scholars.   In 1857 it had increased the
amount per scholar to $3.55, yet not enough to retain its relative position
among neighboring towns.   In 1874 it appropriated an amount equal to
$7.31 per scholar.

Besides the system of schools maintained in the several neighborhoods, it
has been usual by voluntary effort to secure the services of a competent
teacher during the winter of each year to give instruction in advanced studies,
including the languages and higher mathematics.

The select school has attracted the youth of the town, and many from neighboring towns, numbers of whom have been prepared for the college and the seminary, or have qualified themselves for teaching in the public school. The select school has done much to elevate the standard of scholarship throughout the town. For some twenty years the school has been under the very competent management of M. J. Smith, Esq., a native of the town and a graduate of New York Central college. A considerable list of young men who obtained the rudiments of education in Middlefield have completed full courses of study in the college and professional school; and as many young women have graduated from the higher seminaries. The several professions have had their representatives from Middlefield; minister and missionary, college and theological professor, have dwelt tenderly upon the school-days of their early home. Prominent among the educated youth of Middlefield may be named, Rev. Alvan Nash, Ebenezer Emmons, LL. D., Rev. Lyman Coleman, D. D., Elisha Mack, LL. D., Rev. William Crowell, D. D , David Mack, Esq., Edward King, and the four Smith brothers, M. J. Smith, Azariah Smith, Rev. Judson Smith. D. D., and Prof. Edward P. Smith.

Physicians.—The earliest physician was Dr. Wright, brother of Nathan Wright, who lived where Arnold Pease now resides. The next was Dr. William Coleman, who lived where Mr. Friend now resides. Here his distinguished son, Lyman Coleman, was born. Dr. Coleman practiced in town for twenty-five or thirty years. After him came Dr. Warren, Dr. Underwood, and Dr. James U. Church. Dr. Edwin Bidwell was here in practice when the late war commenced, and for a short time after its close. He served with distinction as army surgeon. Latterly Dr. Elbridge G. Wheeler has rendered occasional service.

Military.—Of those who became residents of Middlefield, the following persons it is pretty certain had served in the army of the Revolution: Timothy McElwain, Lewis Taylor, John Smith, Elijah Churchill, Solomon Ingham, Erastus Ingham, Amasa Graves, Sr., and Thomas Durant, Sr. The story of want and suffering that prevailed at the close of the Revolutionary war, and the sympathy felt for the sufferers, culminating in Shays Rebellion, has often been told. The town sympathized largely with the sufferers, and was the theatre on which some of the revolutionary proceedings of the Shays men took place. One of the companies of these men that had bled to this place before its pursuers was captured here. This was in January, 1787. Soon after this an oath of allegiance to the commonwealth and to the congress was administered to twenty of the inhabitants of the town—and silence held undisputed sway.

The war of 1812 was distasteful to the town, as it was to the dominant political party in New England. The town by vote declared the war inexpedient. Against this vote the following persons entered their protest: Matthew Smith, Esq., William Skinner, William Church, Green H. Church, Warren Church, Lieut. Alexander Dickson and Dea. John Newton. Later, in

1814, when Governor Strong called for troops, Major Mack (son of the early settler, and afterwards known as General Mack), Lieut. Matthew Smith, Capt. Solomon Root, Abel Cheeseman and Abraham Moffett went to the defence of Boston.

In the war to maintain the Union, Middlefield did well. The town was deeply in sympathy with the general sentiment of the North, and promptly responded to every demand of patriotism. Eighty-six men went forth at the summons of the town, to maintain on the battlefield the cause of the Union, —seven more than the aggregate of all requisitions. The war expenses paid by the town were at the rate of more than nineteen dollars for every inhabitant. And this does not include private contributions and the generous and thoughtful endeavors of the ladies to cheer on by their aid and friendly tokens their sons and brothers in the field. Two of those who went forth for military service were commissioned officers; fifteen yielded up their lives in the service. Their names were Daniel Atwood, Charles W. Buck, Robert Burns, Howard Collier, Henry Dickson, Thomas Dooley, Calvin Noble, Henry Noble, Levi J. Olds, Charles W. Robbins, George K. Robbins, Michael Stanley, Seth Wait, John Waters, Thomas A. Wilson.

VILLAGES.

MIDDLEFIELD, or the " Center,"as it is locally designated, occupies about the geographical center of the town, and from the earliest times served as the town's metropolis. It was here the town-meetings were held, the church planted. The village has a delightful location, and is a pleasant summer resort. The postoffice was established here about 1811, and Edmund Kelso was the first postmaster. The present incumbent of the office is John T. Bryan.

BANCROFT, or Middlefield Station, as it is locally known, is a small village about the Boston & Albany railroad station, in the southern part of the town. Charles H. Fleming is the postmaster.

FACTORY VILLAGE, as its name indicates, is the small village that has gathered about the factories we mention below. It is located on Factory brook, in the western part of the town. It depends on the Center village for church and postal facilities.

MANUFACTURES.

The saw and the grist-mill and the tannery sprang up when everything was new, and considerable establishments for the manufacture of woolen cloths have existed from the beginning of the century. John Ford is said to have built the first saw-mill, in 1780, on the stream a mile below the Factory Village, where Leach's mill stood in later years. The Blushes, Amasa, succeeded by his sons Oliver Blush and William D. Blush, and the Churches, Uriah, succeeded by the four Church brothers, have been the principal manufacturers in town.

Church Brothers & Co. are manufacturers of woolen goods at Factory Village. They have two mills. Their power is furnished by water from Factory brook. A reservoir for holding water was washed out in 1874, causing great damage, carrying away and damaging many buildings, and causing a loss of many thousands of dollars. The reservoir has been re-built in a substantial manner. Uriah Church started business with carding machinery on the present site more than seventy years ago, and it has been carried on by his sons since that date, always manufacturing goods from wool. The present firm consists of Oliver Church and George W. Wilcox.

Buckley, Dunton & Co., r 37, manufacture paper with both water and steam power, employing twenty-five hands.

MORAL AND RELIGIOUS INTERESTS.

First Congregational Church of Middlefield.—The moral and religious interests of the town have been cared for by three religious societies. The first was coeval with the town—the Congregational. Of this society Rev. Jonathan Nash became the first pastor. The pastor's ordination, October 31, 1792, and the erection of the house of worship took place the same year. Mr. Nash's labors proved acceptable, and they extended over a period of forty years. He was a native of South Hadley, and a graduate of Dartmouth college, in the class of 1789. He died August 31, 1834, aged seventy-four years. His successors in the pastorate have been Revs. Samuel Parker, who served but a single year; John H. Bisbee, who was dismissed after some five years to accept a call to Worthington; Edward Clark, who served the church thirteen years; Moody Harrington, whose term of service was somewhat over three years; Lewis Bridgman, who served four years; John Dodge, who served two years; Charles M. Peirce, who served thirteen years, and resigned on account of failing health; Samuel E. Evans, who served one year; A. G. Beebe, who served two years; John A. Woodhull, the present pastor, who commenced his labors in September of the present year, 1886. The first deacons were Malachi Loveland and Daniel Chapman. Others who served in this capacity are David Mack, Job Robbins, Zachariah Field, William W. Leonard, George W. McElwain, Abner Wing, Alexander Ingham, Erastus J. Ingham, Amasa Graves, Ambrose Meacham, Harry Meacham, Hiram Taylor and Jonathan McElwain. The church and society have been prosperous, and many seasons of religious awakening and enlargement have marked the church's history. One of these seasons was during 1801–02; another in 1820–21. The period from 1826 to 1832 seems to have been one of more than usual prosperity. Another season of much interest mentioned is 1842–43. The same of 1857–58, and of 1866 and 1877. Not less than three hundred members were received into the church in connection with these seasons of special interest. The present house of worship is the first meeting-house, erected in 1790, but re-modeled and tastefully fitted up with modern appointments.

Baptist church.—The first house of worship erected by the Baptists in Middlefield stood east of the Center, not far from the residence of Mr. Friend. It was built in 1818. The church was constituted in 1817, consisting of twenty-nine members. To those, thirty were added during the next two years. There had been Baptists in Middlefield almost from the beginning. For many years they were connected with the Baptist church in Hinsdale, the Hinsdale pastor holding regular services in Middlefield a definite portion of the time until the erection of the meeting-house in Hinsdale in 1816. Then by mutual agreement the members in Middlefield became an independent church, and were recognized by a council July 21, 1817. Rev. Isaac Child was the first pastor, and continued in service ten years. He died at Goshen in 1842. The second minister settled was Erastus Andrews. The next was Cullen Townsend. Other ministers have been Thomas Archibald, Orson Spencer, Foronda Bestor, Volney Church, Homer Clark, Orlando Cunningham, John B. Burke, Lewis Holmes and Joseph M. Rockwood, the present pastor. Mr. Spencer and Mr. Clark did not long retain their connection with the denomination. The ministry of Mr. Andrews, though brief, was fruitful, as was that of Mr. Townsend and Mr. Archibald. Messrs. Bestor, Cunningham and Holmes continued their pastoral work some five or six years each, and were much blessed in their labors. The present pastor commenced his services in May, 1865. Years noted as seasons of religious awakening and increase in the history of the church have been 1818, '29, '31, '33, '38, '42, '50, '58, '70, '76. The first deacon was John Newton, who died at the advanced age of ninety-five. The names of those who have succeeded him are Clark Martin, David Ballou, Moses Gamwell, William W. Leonard, Solomon Root, Oliver Smith, Ebenezer Smith, Eldridge Pease, Solomon F. Root, Morgan Pease and Harlow Loveland. The present house of worship was built in 1846, succeeding the first, built in 1818.

Methodist church.—A Methodist class was formed in town as early as 1802. This was in the southeastern part of the town. It is thought to have consisted of Thomas Ward and wife, Daniel Falley and wife, David Cross and wife, Samuel Brown and wife, Jesse Brown and wife, the Gilberts, Rhodeses, Talcotts, Mrs. Elijah Churchill, and others. Thomas Ward was the class-leader. A few years later a church was organized and constituted a part of Pittsfield circuit. Subsequently it was connected respectively with the Dalton, the Hinsdale, and the Middlefield and Washington circuit. In 1827 a house of worship was erected, near the present residence of George W. Howe. There was wide-spread religious interest in connection with this church, extending through a number of years. The audiences that assembled were said to be as large as those of any society in town. Among the preachers whose labors were most effective appear the names of Peter C. Oakley, Bradley Selleck and Cyrus Prindle. In 1853 the society removed its house of worship to the center of the town; but the result of the change was not as favorable as had been hoped. In 1861-62 the society was very much weakened by a large number of deaths and removals occurring not far from the same time. The members left were too few to continue the services successfully; the society was dissolved and the house of worship sold to the Congregational church for a chapel, the families remaining finding in the growing liberality of modern times pleasant association with other churches.

Temperance.—There have been several temperance organizations in town which have contributed to the increase and prevalence of the temperance sentiment. Among these may be mentioned that of the Good Templars, which commenced its work in 1871. The Woman's Christian Temperance Union has also exerted useful influence for a number of years.

NORTHAMPTON occupies a location in the geographical center of the county, and is bounded north by Williamsburg and Hatfield, east by the Connecticut river, south by Easthampton and a small section of the county line, west by Westhampton. Within the bounds thus roughly stated is enclosed a small inland city, which presents a striking example of what may be accomplished by the full and free exercise of moral and mental agencies in attaining a high degree of civilization, intelligence, refinement and comfort; affluent in charitable, benevolent and educational institutions, possessing an unequaled natural beauty and satisfactory material prosperity, the "Meadow City" has secured an enviable reputation. Her sons and daughters may be found throughout the republic, diffusing in society a benign and salutary influence, seeming ever to bear before them the legend of the city's great seal: "*Charitas, Justitia, Educatio.*"

In the opening chapters of this work, devoted to the general history of the county, we have detailed the causes which led to the petition for and grant of the fertile *Nonotuck* in 1653-54; told of the settlement begun thereon at the present city in 1654, the establishment of the new settlement as a half-shire town and subsequent county seat; detailed the history of its county buildings and the courts of justice which are held therein, its railroads and its press. At this point, then, it is our purpose only to briefly sketch the subsequent growth of that early settlement, record its final erection into one of the municipalities of the commonwealth, and record its appearance and resources of to-day. For over two hundred years the city constituted one of the townships of Hampshire county, when it was incorporated, September 5, 1883, and organized, January 7, 1884,* as the county's only incorporated city or village.†

------

* At its organization Benjamin E. Cook, Jr., was elected mayor, who held the office until Arthur G. Hill was elected as his successor, in December, 1886. The city is divided into seven wards. A list of its officers is given on another page.

† In the Directory portion of the work we shall consider the "City" as the "Township of Northampton," in order that our system of road-numbering and the references to the several postoffices within the city's limits may not prove perplexing to the stranger who seeks its aid.

The city, comprising the old township of Northampton, consists of two disjointed tracts of land. When Easthampton was incorporated her territory was inserted like a wedge to the river, completely severing the former into two unequal portions. The smallest, a long, narrow strip of land, bearing the local name of South Farms, extends from the crest of Mount Nonotuck to the river, and from Easthampton on the north to Holyoke on the south. Easthampton was one of the three towns that have been lopped off from the old one. Southampton was organized as a town by the general court in 1753; Westhampton in 1778; and Easthampton as a *district* in 1785, with all the rights and privileges of a town with the exception of sending a representative to the general court.

PHYSICAL FEATURES.

The city seems to nestle quietly in a deep depression among the hills and mountains which surround it in every direction, on the margin of the fairest river in New England. In fact it occupies a central portion in what President Dwight, of Yale college, whose familiarity with the valley excelled that of any other man in his time, was in the habit of terming in his writings the valley's third great expansion. At this point the valley is probably not less than twenty miles in width, and abounds in the richest and most gorgeous natural beauty. Mountains, some of them attaining an altitude of nearly fifteen hundred feet above the level of the sea, encircle this expansion. On the east, beyond Amherst, which clusters upon the summit and along the gentle slopes of a beautifully rounded eminence, are seen the dark and lofty Pelham hills; in the foreground is Mount Holyoke, unique and picturesque, from whose top a picture of rural loveliness meets the vision, unsurpassed even in a region where the choicest gifts of nature have been scattered with a lavish hand. On the north are the Montague mountains and the conical outline of Sugar Loaf, on the west the outlying spurs of the Green Mountain range, and on the southwest and south the elevations known as Pomeroy and Mt. Tom range.

The surface of the whilom township is uneven and undulating. Between the compact part of the city and the river, which here flows in the form of a semicircle, are the intervals or meadows, comprising several thousand acres of level and fertile land. A succession of terraces of a few feet in height lead from the meadows to the uneven and more elevated parts of the city on the west, where plains, knolls and hills are curiously and irregularly mingled. Round Hill has obtained a wide celebrity for its unrivaled beauty. Its slope is so gentle that nearly every part of it can be utilized for the erection of residences for citizens of taste and wealth, while the view from its sides and summit is simply magnificent. It was on Round Hill that George Bancroft, the historian, and Joseph G. Coggeshall established their famous school which attained such an enviable reputation that it found patrons in the most distant states of the Union. This institution was at the zenith of its prosperity some half century ago. But Mr. Bancroft had a natural aptitude for the discussion of political questions, and an irrepressible desire to participate in the political movements of the day. The school was eventually closed. Mr. Bancroft's career is well known to the school children of the land. His associate, Mr. Coggeshall retired to the tranquility and repose of literary pursuits. Since that event Round Hill has been devoted mostly to private residences. Occasionally it has been honored with a water-cure establishment and a hotel. But these are things of the past, and such public institutions as shall hereafter grace its picturesque declivities will probably be of a benevolent and charitable character, and designed to alleviate human suffering.

In saying this of that charming locality, it must not be supposed that other parts of the old town are devoid of attractions as homes for the people. The inequalities of the township are such that the varying fancy of individuals finds ample resources for the selection of eligible sites for the erection of homes combining the elements of taste and elegance. Gentlemen of culture and refinement have discovered that the landscape of Northampton possesses many pleasing features, and are now embellishing the terraces and the miniature hills and vales with edifices of which any town or city may well be proud. Especially do the educational facilities of the city tend to this result, as they allure to it the best elements in American society, who hasten to avail themselves of the benefits conferred by the superior excellence of its schools and other institutions of learning. As an example of this the case of the eminent Southern writer, George W. Cable, whose brilliant imagination is equaled by his conspicuous philanthropy, may be cited as worthy of imitation, who finds a delightful home within the romantic precincts of "Paradise."

The principal inland stream is Mill river, which enters the town from Williamsburg in the extreme northwest corner, and flows into the Connecticut in the southeast. Its waters are utilized for manufacturing purposes, and several flourishing villages—Leeds, Florence and Bay State—have arisen upon its banks. Roberts Meadow brook is the source of the city's water supply, and a branch of Manhan river, which crosses the southwestern boundary at Loudville, affording some motive power.

Geologically, new red sandstone is the prominent feature in the eastern part of the city, and the primary or granitic rock in the western, where boulders of varying sizes are thickly strewn by elementary actions upon the surface. In many sections of the town these stones and rocks are being removed and the land fitted for cultivation.

SOIL AND AGRICULTURE.

The soil varies greatly in character and quality. There are several thousand acres of interval or meadow land of unsurpassed beauty and fertility, the stony, loamy uplands, and some level tracts of a sandy nature. Interspersed with these are fields in which clay predominates. A large proportion is cultivable.   At the first settlement of the town, and for a long period thereafter, cultivation seems to have been mostly confined to the intervals, and with some unimportant alterations and modifications they remain very much as when Holyoke and Pynchon were fascinated with their dense and prolific vegetation.   There has been much speculation as to the origin of these bottom lands, and the opinion has been expressed by those who have investigated the matter, that originally they were mounds or islands in the body of the stream, which by the constant accretion of fine, silty particles borne by the waters of the river from the regions far to the north, gradually expanded until the mass became consolidated and attached to the adjacent upland.   But whatever may have been their origin they constitute a large tract of valuable land in Northampton.   The soil is a fine, deep, rich, unctuous mold, and when first cultivated must have been surpassingly fertile.   Much of its inherent productiveness is maintained by the abundant sediment deposited on the surface by the annual overflow of the river, though other enriching matters are used, and perhaps required, in the growing of maximum crops.   When it is considered that these lands have been in cultivation for more than two hundred years, in each one of which they have produced prolific harvests, the inference is conclusive as to their great strength and durability.   It is an indisputable fact that in the first years of the settlement and for a century afterwards, the meadows were found well adapted to the growth of wheat and produced luxuriant crops of that invaluable cereal.   The province tax was paid in wheat in Boston, and the transportation of the grain, which was invested with all the properties of a circulating medium, was a matter of no small importance.   To accomplish this object a road was constructed, with infinite labor and expense, through the forest to the settlements in Connecticut, and the golden grain was conveyed in ox carts to Hartford, and loaded on sloops that made the perilous voyage round Cape Cod to the capital of the Province.

About a century ago there were indications that something was the matter with the meadows ; the wheat crop frequently failed, and its cultivation was reluctantly relinquished.   A writer of that era, and a native of the town, investigated the causes of the failure, and came to the conclusion that it was owing to the exhaustion of the fine vegetable mold or humas in the soil ; and he reasoned that wheat would again grow if the original conditions were restored.   And to do this he argued that it would be necessary to grow such crops as would fill the surface soil with an abundance of vegetable fibres.   He had ascertained in the course of his investigations that lands in the Middle States which had manifested the same symptoms as the meadows, had been restored to their prestine fertility by plowing down a rank growth of clover, and again produced good crops of wheat.   This, it should be remembered, was one hundred years ago.   It is not known that his recommendation was tested to such an extent as to establish its utility.   At all events the meadows were generally devoted to other crops, and new land was cleared for wheat, which struggled for a few years to maintain a precarious existence until compelled to yield to the assaults of the midge, smut and rust.   In late years there have been occasional instances of immense crops of wheat on this discription of land after a crop of tobacco.   For the last half century the meadows have been devoted to the growth of broom corn, oats, corn, grass and tobacco.

RENOVATING THE SOIL.

The Hon. William Clark was an intelligent agriculturist of Northampton during the first half of the present century.   Besides a due proportion of meadow land, he was the proprietor of an extensive tract of plain land of a light, sandy soil.   Mr. Clark undertook the improvement of this light land with commendable enthusiasm, and was measurably successful in his efforts. It was his principal object to obtain a good, thick sod ; this accomplished, a satisfactory grain crop was certain to follow.   In his experiments no animal manure was used, his entire dependence being upon sod and gypsum, or plaster.   It was his practice to sow red-top and clover seed, and fill the soil as frequently as possible with grass and clover roots.   By this system there was a gradual and perceptible improvement in the producing capacity of the land, and Mr. Clark became fully sensible of the enriching properties of sod or turf, which has been found so efficacious in other sections of the country in preserving the fertility of the soil.   Another method in the treatment of sandy land has been practiced to some extent in Northampton, and measuredly results are worthy of imitation elsewhere.   It is to mingle clay with the surface soil.   The adhesive properties of the clay impart adhesion to the mass, improves its texture and converts it into a friable loam.   In most clays there is a considerable amount of fertilizing matter, and it has been found by experience that clayed lands are tolerably retentive of animal manures.

Contemporary with Mr. Clark was David Lee Child, better known, perhaps, as the husband of that charming writer, Lydia Maria Child.   Mr. Child was originally a Boston lawyer.   He filled the office of consul in one of the cities of Europe for several years, and became deeply interested in the cultivation of the sugar beet.   On his return to this country he located in Northampton near the village of Florence, and essayed to turn his knowledge of beet culture to practical account.   But he appears to have been unfortunate in the selection of a suitable and congenial soil in which to pursue his experiments.   Some of it was a deep, black muck, probably imperfectly drained, better adapted to the grass than the root crop, and incapable of producing other than stinted vegetables of inferior quality, while other portions were too thin and light to pay the expense of cultivation.   It was not from lack of zeal, but from lack of judgment that Mr. Child failed in his undertaking, and the practicability of the beet culture is still an unsolved problem in Northampton, at least so far as its conversion into sugar is concerned.

EARLY PRICES.

During the first hundred and fifty years of the town's existence, in a financial point of view, the inhabitants had most emphatically a dreary experience. They rested literally on hardpan.   There was no coinage of money in the province, and consequently it was very scarce and dear.   It required a large amount of agricultural products to purchase a very small sum of the precious metals, and they, except at intervals, constituted the only circulating medium. As an illustration of the hardness of the times some of the prices then prevailing may be mentioned.   Butter was worth six cents per pound, beef and mutton two cents, wheat and peas about two shillings, and corn and oats one shilling and sixpence each per bushel.   A good horse might possibly bring twenty dollars in the market, provided a purchaser could be found, and a pair of working cattle would command the same price.   It was a first-class cow that would bring eight dollars.   No buyers then for fancy Jerseys, Ayrshires and Holsteins at fabulous prices.   But as some compensation for these low prices, luxurious living did not involve a large expenditure.   Eggs were three pence per dozen, wild turkeys one shilling, and fowls four pence each. Good, juicy, fat, luscious shad from one to two pence each, and salmon one penny per pound.   Land was cheap, but the population being scanty, purchasers were few in number.   Choice land was valued at one dollar an acre, and this, for ought that is known to the contrary, included the fertile river bottoms, and out-lots twenty-five cents.   The salaries of ministers ranged from one hundred and fifty to two hundred dollars per annum, with a fair allotment of land by way of settlement.   The settlement of a clergyman implied a location for life unless irreconcilable differences should arise between pastor and people.   Differences did sometimes arise, and a notable one did in Northampton, as will be observed in the course of this narrative.   When young men and maidens wished to be united in wedlock—that state of happiness to some, of misery to others—the parson exacted three shillings for securely fastening the nuptial shackles.

STREETS.

The older streets of the city are somewhat winding and irregular.   Two reasons have been assigned for this divergance from straight lines.   One is that the early settlers consulted convenience and economy in the construction of roads; the other that they adopted the paths made by the cows in going to and returning from their grazing grounds, the bovine race instinctively selecting such routes, and adhering to them, as were the easiest to travel.   Either reason is sufficient to account for the peculiar character of the old highways now transformed into streets.   Whatever may be said against such streets in a busy, commercial city, the objection will not be regarded as valid in a rural one like Northampton, where they may be considered as an attribute of beauty. At least, this may be said that, had the surveyor with his compass and chain laid out the original highways at right angles one with another, every person of taste would have been forced to admit that art had marred the symmetry of nature. The principal streets of the old town, following the sinuous paths made by the cows more than two hundred years ago, extend in all directions from the center or Merchants' Row. Fancy Pleasant street extending as a wide avenue in a direct line over Round Hill, in one place obliterating a charming plateau, in another destroying a delightful terrace, and the people of this model city will realize their great obligations to the brute creation in deviating in their daily walks from right angles.

SETTLEMENT AND GROWTH.

Previous to the settlement of Northampton, civilization in Western Massachusetts was confined to Springfield. But the residents of the latter place were familiar with the adaptability of the location for purposes of improvement, and in 1653 a petition was presented to the general court for liberty to plant in Nonotuck, and the request was granted. Nonotuck, however, already contained a small aboriginal population with whom resided all proprietary rights, and before occupation and planting could begin on the part of the petitioners or their representatives, justice required that these rights should be equitably extinguished. To the honor of the founders of Nonotuck it should be stated that they dealt uprightly with the native and original owners of the soil. The price paid for this magnificent domain was, indeed, insignificant, but to the Indian mind it seemed an ample equivalent for the territory they surrendered to the whites, and, it may be remarked, they never afterwards complained that they had been overreached in the bargain. It may be mentioned that, among others who held vested rights in the property thus transferred, was Awonusk, the wife of Wulluther. The deed was given to John Pynchon, of Springfield, for the planters, and some of them immediately removed to the new plantation. Of the twenty-four persons who petitioned the general court for liberty to plant in Nonotuck, for reasons which do not appear, only eight availed themselves of the privilege. These were Edward Elmore, William Miller, William Clark, Thomas Root, Robert Bartlett, John Webb, William Holton and William Janes.

Among those who settled and erected houses within the first four years, that is, previous to 1658, these names occur: Robert Bartlett, Richard Lyman, James Bridgman, John Lyman, Thomas Bascom, Thomas Root, Alexander Edwards, Samuel Wright, William Miller, John King, Isaac Sheldon, Samuel Allen, Joseph Parsons, William Hannum, William Hulburt, Nathaniel Phelps and John Stebbins. In the next four years they were followed by Edward Baker, Alexander Alvord, Rev. Eleazer Mather, William Clark, Henry Woodward, Enos Kingsley,

Aaron Cook, John Strong, Medad Pomeroy, Jonathan Hunt and John Searle. And shortly afterwards came Mark Warner, Samuel Judd, Robert Danks, Thomas Judd, Israel Rust, Rev. Solomon Stoddard and Preserved Clapp. Most of these names still survive in the city, or did until a very recent period, in the persons of their descendants. Subsequently the increase of population was greatly accelerated by the arrival of new settlers.

It may be interesting to know how the first plantation was defined by the commissioners appointed by the " honored General Court " to perform this duty, namely, John Pynchon, Elizur Holyoke and Samuel Chapin. If the description lacks clearness it is not deficient in quaintness. " We," the commissioners say, "allow the great Meadow on the west side of Conecticote River, as also a little meadow, called by the Indians (Capawonke), which lieth about two miles above the great Meadow, the bounds of which plantation is to extend from the (south side) of the little meadow, called Capawonke, to the great falls, to Springfield ward ; and westward is to extend nine miles into the woods, from the river of Conecticote, lying east of the foresaid meadows."

The settlements in point of time were made, first, about Pleasant, King, Hawley and Market streets ; then west from the Old Church, and still later on the south side of Mill river. The growth and fluctuations in the population since 1776 is represented by the following figures : 1776, 1,799, 1790, 1,628; 1800, 2,190 ; 1810, 2,631 ; 1820, 2,854 ; 1830, 3,613 ; 1840, 3,750; 1850, 5,278 ; 1855, 5,819 ; 1860, 6,788 ; 1865, 7,925 ; 1870, 10,160 ; 1875, 11,108; 1880, 12,176.

INDIAN TROUBLES.

It may be noted as a significant fact of the terror created by French and Indian forays upon the outlying settlements of New England, that more than a century elapsed after the settlement of Northampton before any improvements were made or dwellings erected in Westhampton, although it was only a few miles distant from the center of the town. It virtually remained an unbroken wilderness until the subjugation of Canada by the English, when the incursions of the savages ceased. Indeed, many tracts that had been cleared at a short distance from the town at an interval of peace, were abandoned for a long series of years, and in most instances reverted to a state of nature. President Dwight, whose statements in regard to everything which relates to Northampton may be implicitly relied on, mentions, as illustrating the insecurity of the times, that his father or grandfather cleared and grew crops upon several acres of land two or three miles from the village ; but the cultivation was discontinued owing to the almost uninterrupted prevalence of hostilities, and after the lapse of half a century it was covered with a dense and heavy growth of pines.

The relations existing between the people of Northampton and the In-

Eng'd by H B Hall's Sons, New York.

E. B. Nims

dians of this vicinity were of an amicable nature for nearly twenty years. The former red proprietors were permitted to build a fort on the south side of Mill river as a protection against the assaults of their less peaceably disposed brethren. This fort occupied a site near the residence of E. H. R. Lyman, Esq., and in close proximity to the most populous part of the town. There seems to have been some solicitude on the part of the inhabitants for the welfare of these poor, ignorant creatures, as a few regulations were adopted at a town meeting (1664) for their guidance, the "town's mind" being delivered to them by John Lyman, David Wilton and Joseph Parsons. On the following points the "town's mind" was clear and decisive:

(1) "They shall not break the Sabbath by working or gaming, or carrying burdens or the like. (2) They shall not Pow-wow on that place or any where else among us. (3) They shall not get Liquors or Cider and drink themselves drunk as so kill one another as they have done. (4) They shall not take in other Indians of other places to seat amongst them, we allow Nowutague Indians that were the inhabitants of the place. (5) They shall not break down our fences and let in cattle and swine, but shall go over a stile at one place. (6) The murderers, Callawane and Wuttowhan and Pacquollant, shall not seat amongst them. (7) They shall not hunt or kill our cattle or sheep or swine with their dogs; if they do they shall pay for them."

At the beginning of King Philip's war the village was fortified by palisades —stakes driven into the ground—the whole place being thus enclosed. On the 14th of March, 1676, the Indians suddenly assaulted this barrier and succeeded in breaking through it; but were forced back by the inhabitants, not, however, until they had killed six persons and burned several dwellings. The town was not again disturbed, but at the Deerfield fight in the following May, fifteen residents of Northampton lost their lives. In the meantime the Nonotuck Indians had decamped and joined Philip.

As Northampton men participated in the Falls fight, so-called, that expedition may be briefly alluded to. In May, 1676, it was ascertained that the Indians had gathered in considerable numbers at Pasquamscut, now known as Turner's Falls, and preparatory to taking the war-path, were indulging in a prolonged feast. Ample supplies for a sumptuous entertainment were at hand, consisting of cattle which they had secured in their raids upon the settlements, venison and shad. Shad, in the proper season, were then plentiful in the Connecticut river. The Indian palate is never exacting as to quality though it is as to quantity. It was not simply a matter of eating, but of thorough and complete gormandizing. With intervals of sleep both day and night were spent in stuffing themselves to repletion with beef, venison and shad. Imagine the condition of these dusky children of the forest when the thunderbolt burst upon them in the morning. No wonder they were dazed and bewildered, and incapable of making any effective resistance.

While the feasting and gorging were going on at the Falls, the settlers were in motion. One hundred and sixty men had been silently mustered and organized for the expedition. They were from Springfield, Hatfield, North-

ampton and Hadley.   Those from Northampton were under the command
of Lieutenant John Lyman, a wary and valiant Indian fighter.   The chief
command was vested in Captain Turner, an unfortunate selection, as he was
so ill at the time as to render him somewhat inefficient.   All were mounted.
They started from Hatfield on the afternoon of the 16th of May.   Following
the usually traveled path, they crossed Muddy brook, the scene of the fearful tragedy of the previous year.   Darkness had closed upon them as they
passed through silent and deserted Deerfield.   Presently they reached the
Deerfield river, but by the mistake of the guide, and a fortunate mistake it
was for the party, a short distance above the usual fording place.   Up to
this time there had been no indications of the presence of Indians on the
line of their route to the Falls.   Just as they entered the river the agitation
of the water by the horses' feet aroused a red-skin sentinel who was dozing
on the opposite bank at the ford below.   A halt ensued, and the scout, probably thinking the noise was occasioned by some deer sporting in the stream,
either joined his companions in the vicinity or resumed his slumbers, and the
alarm subsided.   Passing up the banks of Green river to the northern part
of the present town of Greenfield, they turned abruptly to the east and
reached a point within a mile or a little more of the Falls.   Here their
progress was much obstructed by the fallen timber, and they were obliged to
secure their horses and proceed on foot.   Leaving a few men to guard the
animals, the others pressed on as rapidly as possible.   In the gray dawn of
that May morning they fell suddenly upon the gorged and sleeping Indians.
The surprise was complete, and the English applied themselves vigorously to
the work of shooting and knocking on the head the unresisting enemy.   Some
plunged into the water and swam to the small island midway in the Falls,
where, as they climbed up the rock, they were deliberately shot.   Others
rushed to the canoes, and, in the excitement of the moment, forgetting to
take their paddles with them, helplessly drifted over the cataract and were
drowned.   A few succeeded in gaining the covert of the woods.

Thus far the slaughter had been entirely on one side.   But several hundred Indians were encamped a short distance up the river.   Their attention
was first attracted by the firing; then the arrival of some of the fugitives
gave them information of the fearful disaster that had befallen their brethren.
They were soon in motion, and made an effort to gain the rear of the English.   The latter, fortunately and opportunely learning of this movement,
fell back at once, standing very little upon the order of their going, to the
fallen timber where they had left their horses, and retreated down the grassy
margin of Green river much faster than they had ascended it the previous
evening.   It was a continued and desperate struggle all the way to Hatfield;
sometimes a hand to hand fight, as the colonists charged back upon their
pursuers and drove them to the shelter of the forest.   The most bloody en-
counters were in the low grounds and thickets south of Muddy brook, in
what is now known as Whately.   For several miles the infuriated savages

pressed upon the retiring soldiers as they slowly, rod by rod, relinquished the ground to their adversaries, and it was here that they suffered the greatest loss. It was night when the survivors of this raid found themselves in safety in the village of Hatfield. The result may be briefly summed up : Three hundred Indians had been suddenly hurled into the eternal world, and thirty-seven Englishmen, nearly one-quarter of the attacking force, had accompanied them on the journey.

Nearly thirty years afterwards, in what is known as King Williams's war, the hamlet of Pascommuck, not far from Mount Tom station, in the present town of Easthampton, was attacked, and the inhabitants either killed or taken prisoners. During the French and Indian wars the savages constantly prowled about the settlement, but never attacked the village itself which was vigilantly guarded.

THE REVOLUTIONARY WAR.

Northampton took an active part in the struggle with Great Britain which resulted in the independence of the colonies, appointing committees of correspondence, raising four companies of troops, voting bounties for soldiers, and furnishing a brigadier-general of the Continental army in the person of General Seth Pomeroy, an ardent and unflinching patriot.

THE REBELLION.

During the war of the Rebellion Northampton furnished 751 men for the Union army, and raised for bounties a little over $71,000.00.

INCIDENTS OF THE OLDEN TIME.

This queer entry is found in the ancient records under the following date: "17th day, 9th mo., 1663. At a legal town-meeting there was then granted to Cornelius, the Irishman, three acres of land, upon condition he build upon it and make improvements of it within one year ; yet not so as to make him capable of acting in any town affairs no more than he had before it was granted to him."

It seems that in 1660, and previously, town-meetings were sometimes tumultuous, many speaking at one time, and the selectmen in a formal order declare that the practice "is dishonorable to God and grievous to many persons." So they decree that there shall not be "more speakers than one at a time, lovingly and moderately, upon the'penalty of 12d. for every such offence, to be levied by distress." They did not intend to obstruct debate, nor "hinder any man to give his advice in any matter one at a time."

Horse racing was not regarded favorably, and it was provided "that if any shall run races with their horses or mares in any street in this town shall for every such offence pay 2s. 6d., the one-half to the town and the other half to its informer."

In 1660 "it was voted and agreed that the town rates for this present year wheat shall go for 3s. 6d. per bushel." Not much chance for grain syndicates and grain gambling then.

The good people of Northampton in 1672 were not over friendly to strangers and foreigners, as the selectmen ordered that "whosoever in this town shall bring into it or receive into his family a foreigner or stranger, or any man from abroad, or entertain him in his house above ten days without liberty from the selectmen, shall forfeit to the town ten shillings for every week so entertaining him."

Voting was rendered imperative. Absentees were fined 12d. each. And if not present "at the beginning of the meeting when it is orderly begun," 1d. was forfeited. This in 1658.

Northampton happily escaped the lamentable consequences of the witchcraft delusion towards the close of the seventeenth century. One Northampton man did, indeed, appear before Colonel Partridge, a prominent Hampshire county magistrate residing in Hatfield, and made complaint against one of his neighbors for bewitching him. Colonel Partridge listened to his story, and remarking that complainants in witchcraft cases were in certain instances entitled to one-half the mulcts, he ordered the accuser to receive his share then and there, which consisted of twenty or thirty lashes well laid on. President Dwight, writing a century afterwards, said that strong doses of ipecacuanha administered to complainants and accusers would have effectually dispelled the witchcraft delusion from their brains.

They had sumptuary laws, too, in those primitive times and regulated dress by statute or by-laws. It might prove beneficial to society to revive some of these obsolete enactments, and return to the era of plain raiment and simple fashions. Fancy the feelings of these stern old puritans if they could only revisit Merchants' Row, and gaze upon the stunning pull-backs or tie-backs, or whatever else they are called, which envelop the bodies of the angels of this lower sphere. They would stand aghast with astonishment, and wonder why the grand jury did not indict them, as were sixty-five persons about two hundred years ago from five towns in Hampshire county, thirty-five "wives and maids," as the ancient record affirms "and thirty young men, some for wearing silk, and that in a flaunting manner, and others for long hair, and other extravagances to the offence of sober people." One case will suffice as a sample of the rest. Hannah Lyman, a vivacious damsel of sixteen, and granddaughter of Richard Lyman, one of the first selectmen of the town, was a conspicuous offender against Puritanic notions of propriety. This young lady, occupying a position of the highest respectability in society, appears to have possessed much independence and resolution, and when arraigned before the court was attired in the identical silk dress which had given such umbrage to "sober people." If the court of his majesty's county of Hampshire in the Province of Massachusetts Bay, did not understand from her language and demeanor on that occasion that she considered this legal interference with her taste in matters of dress an act of intolerable impertenence, it must have been because the occupants of the bench were exceedingly stupid and obtuse. The august tribunal, however, took sweet revenge by fining Miss Hannah ten shillings for flaunting her silk " not only in ordinary but in extraordinary times." This language of the court was, no doubt, a foul libel on youth, innocence and beauty. Miss Hannah subsequently married Job Pomeroy.

BIOGRAPHICAL.

Rev. Solomon Stoddard, the second pastor of the " Old Church," was born in Boston in 1643, and graduated at Harvard college. When about to sail for Europe he received a call to settle in the ministry at Northampton as the successor of Rev. Eleazer Mather, which invitation he accepted, and married the widow of his predecessor, a lady somewhat noted in her time, Esther Warham Mather. His labors extended over a period of nearly sixty years, and he could say at the close of his life that his ministry had been blessed with five great harvests of souls. With him and his church originated the Stoddardean or half-way covenent system of church membership, which involved him in a controversy with Doctors Increase Mather and Cotton Mather, of Boston, in which his clerical opponents were clearly discomfitted. He was a man of profound learning, a powerful preacher, and was held in great reverence throughout the colony. Tradition says that he passed an ambush of French and Indians at Dewey's Hole while on a visit to his daughter at Hatfield. A Frenchman leveled his gun to shoot him. The act was arrested by an Indian who recognized him, and laying his hand upon the weapon impressively remarked: " Don't shoot. That man is the Englishman's God !" His house was on Prospect street.

John Stoddard, known in colonial history as Colonel Stoddard, was, morally and intellectually, one of the greatest men that New England ever produced, and in the statesmanlike qualities of his mind he had no equal among his contemporaries. His nephew, Jonathan Edwards, who preached his funeral sermon, said: "Upon the whole, everything in him was great, and, perhaps, there never was a man in New England to whom the denomination of a great man did more plainly belong." He inherited the paternal homestead, and his estate at one time included Round hill. One of his sons, Solomon Stoddard, was high sheriff of Hampshire county, and another, Israel Stoddard, filled the same office in Berkshire county. This story is told of Mary Stoddard, daughter of Rev. Mr. Stoddard. Rev. Stephen Mix, of Connecticut, visited her and proposed marriage. Requiring time for deliberation, in a few weeks she sent him the following answer : " Rev. Stephen Mix : Yes. Mary Stoddard." The Stoddard family has always occupied a prominent place in the annals of Northampton.

Rev. Jonathan Edwards was the grandson and successor of Mr. Stoddard, his mother being Esther, second daughter of the Northampton divine, who married Rev. Timothy Edwards, of East Windsor, Conn. Mrs. Edwards was a lady of superior mental endowments. Jonathan Edwards graduated at Yale college in 1720, and became pastor of the Northampton church in 1727. Mr. Edwards gave great prominence to the distinctive doctrines of Calvinism, and declared that he could not see how any person who rejected them could " stop short of deism or atheism itself." He was conspicuous in the great revival in New England in the middle of the eighteenth century, and he was held in high estimation by the dissenting clergymen of the mother country. George Whitefield, the celebrated evangelist, visited him at Northampton and preached in the old church. Whitefield, though a minister of the Church of England, a church of whom it has been said that while its creed is Calvinistic it has an Arminian clergy, sympathized with the views of the great theologian, and under his glowing and splendid oratory, Jonathan Edwards, cold, austere and stern, actually wept. His influence over the church was very great, until he attacked the half-way covenant system of his grandfather. This and his proceedings in regard to books of a questionable character, which were said to be circulating among the young people, utterly destroyed his capacity for usefulness in the town and engendered sentiments of bitter hostility to the pastor himself. The church refused to hear him preach upon the controverted subject. Finally the society voted, with few dissenting voices, to dismiss him, and he was dismissed. He continued to reside in the town for some months, but the inhabitants would not suffer him to enter the pulpit. Probably no church controversy in Massachusetts elicited such acrimonious and embittered feelings as those which unhappily existed between Mr. Edwards and his people. After some missionary labors at Stockbridge among the Indians, he was elected to the presidency of Princeton college in New Jersey, but died of confluent small-pox in the same year. His mortal remains now repose in the ancient burial ground in Northampton. Intellectually he was a great man ; as a theologian he was unsurpassed ; as an individual opinionated, inflexible and unyielding. Had he been less obstinate and uncomplying in non-essentials, he might have lived and died as the esteemed and beloved pastor of the Old Church. There is nothing on record to show that he ever thought his opinions other than infallible. His son, Jonathan Edwards, Jr., was a voluminous writer, a distinguished preacher, and a clear thinker. He was elected to the presidency of Union college, Schenectady, but died soon after. Timothy Edwards, the eldest son, became a respected citizen of Stockbridge ; was a member of the state council and judge of probate for Bershire county. The youngest son, Pierpont Edwards, graduated at Princeton, read law in Northampton, settled in New Haven, became eminent in his profession, was a member of the continental congress and judge of the United States district court of Connecticut. Three of his sons filled prominent positions. One was elected to congress ; another was a lawyer and judge in New York ; and the third was United States senator and governor of Connecticut. Esther Edwards, daughter of the eminent theologian, married Aaron Burr, president of Princeton college, and was the mother of Aaron Burr, vice-president of the United States during Mr. Jefferson's first term as president. Mr. Burr possessed much of the clearness of analysis and power of generalization, but was entirely deficient in those moral qualities which distinguished his celebrated ancestor.

Major Joseph Hawley was the son of Lieut. Joseph Hawley, whose wife was Rebecca Stoddard, daughter of the first minister. Joseph Hawley, after his graduation at Yale college, in 1742, at the age of eighteen, devoted sometime to the study of theology, and preached occasionally. He accompanied the expedition for the reduction of Louisburg, on the island of Cape Breton, under Gen. Pepperell, as chaplain of one of the regiments, but eventually embraced the profession of the law, in which he became eminent. He was noted as a vigorous and forcible public speaker. In the unhappy troubles in the Northampton church, he took a prominent part, strongly opposing the course of his cousin, Mr. Edward's conduct, for which he afterwards expressed great contrition in an elaborate written apology. Major Hawley was honored for many years with a seat in the general court, and did much to promote and cultivate the patriotic sentiments which culminated in the Revolution. Able, pure nnd incorruptible, he must be classed among Northampton's worthiest sons.

Hon. Caleb Strong, like Major Hawley, was descended from one of the old families of the town, and a graduate of Harvard college, where he received the highest honors. He read law with Mr. Hawley, was admitted to the bar, and was county attorney for twenty-four years ; was a member of the legislature, house and senate, about fourteen years ; was a member of the convention that framed the constitution of Massachusetts, in 1779, and also of the United States, in 1787 ; also served in the United States senate two terms. He was elected governor of the commonwealth eleven times in the most exciting period of our early political history as a nation, and narrowly escaped, by his official action, in bringing the state authorites in collision with the general government, by refusing to send any troops beyond the limits of the state in the war of 1812, on the requisition of the president, a precedent which was followed by two or three recusant governors in the war of the Rebellion. Governor Strong was a man of great ability, bnt opinionated and obstinate. He was a powerful advocate before juries, and was especially dreaded by attorneys all over the state in closing arguments. Lewis Strong, son of the governor, graduated at Harvard college, entered the legal profession and practiced about thirty years, and was regarded as one of the ablest lawyers in the western counties. Some one who knew him well has remarked that he was " an upright, accomplished Christian gentleman, lawyer, citizen, neighbor and friend." Several of his sons entered the different professions.

Rev. Thomas Allen was a native of Northampton, and graduated at Harvard college in 1762. He was the first minister of Pittsfield, an inflexible

patriot, and was with General Stark at the battle of Bennington, where as he
said, " observing a flash often repeated from a certain bush, that was generally followed by the fall of one of Stark's men, he fired that way and put the
flash out." William Allen, son of the preceding, succeeded his father in the
Pittsfield pulpit, but was soon chosen professor of Dartmouth college, and
afterwards of Bowdoin. Removed to Northampton in 1839. His son William Allen commenced the practice of law in 1848, having previously graduated at Amherst college and the New Haven law school. He was in partnership at different periods with Hon. C. P. Huntington and Messrs. W. & H. H.
Bond. Received the appointment of judge of the supreme court in 1872,
and in 1881 was transferred to the supreme court of the commonwealth.

Rev. Timothy Dwight, son of Major Timothy Dwight. His mother was
Mary, daughter of Rev. Jonathan Edwards. He was a tutor in Yale college
six years, chaplain in the Revolutionary army, a teacher in his native town,
pastor of the church at Greenfield Hill, Conn., and then president of Yale
college. He was an excellent scholar, an eloquent preacher, and his poems,
of which he wrote several, were reputable performances. His travels in
New England and New York fill several volumes. His father, who was at
different times selectman, register of probate and judge of the court of common pleas, possessed, so tradition says, great muscular strength, and once
threw a stone across the Connecticut river and thirty rods beyond, seventy
rods in all. The Dwights comprised a numerous family, most of whom were
conspicious in the various walks of life. One of them, Theodore Dwight,
was a member of congress and editor of the New York *Commercial Advertiser.*

The Tappan family one hundred years ago was prominent in Northampton. Benjamin Tappan was an ardent and zealous patriot and fought man-
fully at Saratoga. Benjamin Tappan, his oldest son, was bred to the law,
and settled at Steubenville, Ohio. He filled the office of judge in his adopted state, and was elected to the senate of the United States. When Mr.
Calhoun, as Secretary of State under President Tyler, negotiated his secret
treaty for the admission of Texas to the Union without submitting the question to the people, Senator Tappan, in violation of the conventional rules of
the body of which he was a member, gave the text of the treaty to the public, and succeeded in temporarily defeating the schemes of the conspirators.
In politics he was a democrat of the Jeffersonian stripe, pure and incorruptible.
Another son, Arthur Tappan, was a noted merchant in New York, and distinguished for his philanthropy. An opponent of slavery, his property suffered at the hands of an infuriated mob. Oberlin college was indebted to him
for large benefactions.

Samuel Howe was the son of Dr. Estes Howe, of Belchertown. After a
thorough course of literary and legal studies, the latter in the celebrated law
school of Judge Tapping Reeve at Litchfield, Conn., he settled at Worthington, where he remained twelve years. Appointed a judge of the court of

Pliny Earle.

common pleas he removed to Northampton and opened a law school in imita-- tion of that of Judge Reeve's. Nearly all the lawyers of the past generation in Western Massachusetts received their legal training at this institution. An able, learned and upright judge, he died at the early age of forty-three.

Hon. Elijah Hunt Mills, a man of eminent ability, resided in Norhampton in the first quarter of the present century. His father was the first minister in Chesterfield, and his mother was Mary Hunt, daughter of Captain Jona- than Hunt. He was adopted by his uncle, Elijah Hunt, and trained for the profession of the law. As an ornate, chaste and elegant pleader he was un- surpassed in the commonwealth. He was connected with Judge Howe as an instructor in the Northampton law school, and was elected to the senate of the United States. He died in 1829, at the age of fifty-three.

Isaac Chapman Bates was a native of Granville, and a graduate at Yale college in 1802, read law, settled in Northampton, and at once secured a large and lucrative practice. He was elected to congress in 1817, and was continued a member of that body for eight years; was a member of the Governor's council two years, and in 1841 was elected to the senate of the Uuited States. As an orator, Mr. Bates was not surpassed by any individ- ual in Western Massachusetts. His manner was graceful and fascinating, and he was a master in the use of language. While in congress he became acquainted with Mr. Clay, who entertained for him a strong and enduring friendship, and when the great Kentuckian came to New England he visited his friend at Northampton. People who remember that event also recollect with pleasure that the speech of Mr. Bates in welcoming his distinguished guest, in felicity of expression and rhetorical beauty, fully equalled the response of Mr. Clay. Both were ardent friends of the protective system.

Charles E. Forbes was a native of Bridgewater, and settled as a lawyer in Northampton in 1818. At various times he filled the positions of representa- tive in the legislature, county commissioner, district attorney, judge of the court of common pleas and of the supreme judicial court, and a presidential elector in 1856. By his will he gave the town of Northampton the bulk of his property, amounting to about three hundred thousand dollars, for a free library. Mr. Forbes was an able and pains-taking lawyer. He was an admirer of the forensic ability of his contemporary, Mr. Bates, and often re- marked that Mr. Bates would come into court directly from his farm and argue a case in an exhaustive manner, which had taken him several days to master.

Eli P. Ashman was a native of Blandford, read law with Judge Sedgwick, of Stockbridge, and settled in Northampton in 1807. In 1816 he was elected a senator of the United States. His wife was the youngest daughter of Rev. John Hooker. John Hooker Ashman, son of Eli P., was bred to the law, and received the appointment of professor of law at Harvard college. He died at the early age of thirty-three. George Ashman, another son of Sena- tor Ashman, studied in Judge Howe's law school and settled in Springfield. Mr. Ashman served three terms in congress as the representative of the Valley district, and adhered to the political fortunes of Mr. Webster until the death of that distinguished statesman. He became a Republican on the organization of that party and presided over the National Republican Convention that nominated Abraham Lincoln for president, at Chicago in 1860.

Erastus Hopkins, born in Hadley in 1810, was by profession a clergyman. After preaching in several places he settled in Northampton and engaged in secular pursuits. He was a member of the legislature nine or ten terms, and also president of the Connecticut River railroad. An accomplished scholar and a superb orator.

Ebenezer Lane, son of Captain Ebenezer Lane, who lived on Bridge street, graduated at Harvard college in 1811, studied law and settled at Elyria, Ohio. He was first a judge of the court of common pleas, and then chief justice of the supreme court.

Joseph Lyman, a descendant of one of the first settlers, was educated at Yale college and studied law; was successively clerk of the courts, judge of the court of common pleas and of probate, president of the old Hampshire Bank, and sheriff of the county. His son, Samuel F. Lyman, graduated at Harvard college, read law with Judge Reeve, at Litchfield, was register of probate nearly thirty years, and then judge of probate.

Oliver Warner was born in 1818, and graduated at Williams college in 1842. He studied theology and was settled at Chesterfield. Afterward was a teacher in Williston seminary, and a member of both branches of the legislature. He was secretary of state of Massachusetts for nearly a score of years, and for some time was state librarian and clerk of the board of education. A genial and accomplished gentleman in all the relations of life.

Aaron Warner was a graduate of Williams college and Andover Theological seminary. He preached at Charleston, S. C., and at Medford, Mass.; was professor of sacred rhetoric in the Gilmanton Theological seminary, and professor of rhetoric in Amherst college.

Josiah D. Whitney, son of Josiah D. Whitney at one time president of the Northampton bank. He studied at Yale college and in Europe ; was engaged two years in surveying the western lake region, and has written a valuable work on the metallic resources of the United States as compared with other countries; has been professor in the Iowa State university, state geologist of California, professor of geology in Harvard college, in the school of metallurgy and practical geology.

William D. Whitney, brother of the preceding, received a collegiate education, studied Sanskrit, spending three years in Germany. A professor in Yale college. Five years ago the order of merit made vacant by the death of Thomas Carlyle, was bestowed on him by the Emperor of Germany.

Pliny Earle, A. M., M. D., late Superintendent of the State Lunatic Hospital at Northampton, was born in Leicester, Mass., December 31, 1809. He is a descendant of Ralph Earle, who, with nineteen others, successfully petitioned Charles the First, in 1638, for permission to form themselves into a body politic of the island of Rhode Island, and son of Pliny Earle, who made, for Samuel Slater, the cards for the first cotton-carding machine moved by water-power in America.

Dr. Earle received his literary and classical education in the academy at Leicester, Mass., and at the Friends' School, in Providence, R. I. He pursued his medical studies in the University of Pennsylvania, whence he graduated in March, 1837. Immediately afterwards he left for Europe, where he remained two years,—one in the medical school and hospitals of Paris, and the other in a tour of both professional and general observation, in which he visited various institutions for the insane, from England to Turkey. Upon his return, in 1839, he opened an office in Philadelphia, Pa., but shortly afterward became resident physician to the Friends' Asylum for the Insane, near Frankford, now a part of the aforesaid city. In 1844 he was appointed medical superintendent of the Bloomingdale Asylum for the Insane, in New York city. In 1849 he again went to Europe, and visited thirty-four institutions for the insane in England, Belgium, France and Germany; and in 1871 he went a third time, and visited forty-six similar institutions, in Ireland, Austria, Italy and the intervening countries. More than one hundred and forty hospitals and asylums for the care of the insane, in America and Europe, have come under his personal observation. In the course of these several journeys he also visited the schools for idiots in England, Paris and Berlin, and the then celebrated and popular monitorial public schools of London and Edinburgh.

In February, 1853, he was elected as one of the visiting physicians of the New York City Lunatic Asylum, on Blackwell's Island; and on the 2d of July, 1864, the trustees of the State Lunatic Hospital at Northampton appointed him to the office of superintendent of that institution. This latter position he held until October 1, 1885, when he withdrew, in accordance with his resignation tendered some months prior to that date. Relative to his resignation we find the following resolutions recorded in the thirtieth annual report of the trustees of the hospital :—

"*Resolved*, That, in accepting the resignation of Dr. Pliny Earle, Superintendent of this hospital, the Trustees have reluctantly yielded to the conviction that his advancing years and impaired health demand rest, and relief from the responsibilities and labors of his position.

"Dr. Earle has been at the head of this institution twenty-one years, and during nearly all of that period has also been its Treasurer. In its management he has combined the highest professional skill and acquirement with rare executive ability. By his professional knowledge, his long experience, his patient attention to details ; by his wisdom and firmness, his absolute fidelity to duty, and devotion to the interests of the hospital, he has rendered invaluable services to the institution, and to the community which it serves.

"The Trustees are deeply sensible of the assistance which he has given them in the discharge of their duties, and follow him, in his retirement, with the assurance of their highest respect and esteem.

"*Resolved*, That the Trustees indulge the hope that Dr. Earle will continue to make his home in this institution, that they may continue to profit by his counsels; and they will provide that his rooms shall always be open and ready for his use."

Consequently, the doctor remains, for the present, at the hospital, and is succeeded in his official position by Dr. Edward Beecher Nims.

In the winter of 1840–41, while at the Friends' asylum, Dr. Earle delivered before the patients a course of lectures upon natural philosophy, illustrated by experiments in pneumatics and electricity. This was the first known attempt to address an audience of the insane in any discourse other than a sermon. The following account of another previously untried experiment, is extracted from the doctor's annual report, for the official year 1866–67, of the Northampton hospital. In describing the lectures which he had given the inmates of the hospital during the winter of that year, he says:—

" No less than six of the discourses were upon diseases of the brain which are accompanied by mental disorder. This is the first time that an audience of insane persons ever listened to a course of lectures upon their own malady. When we remember how cautiously any allusion to the insanity of a person is generally avoided while in conversation with him; and, further still, in view of the prevalent fear of the insane in the popular mind, the attempt to entertain a gathering of more than two hundred and fifty mental aliens by discourses upon their disorder, may, by some persons, be regarded as hazardous. It must be confessed that, notwithstanding my long experience with this class of persons, the attempt was approached with some doubts and misgivings. It was considered possible both that offense might be given, and that some of the most excitable patients might become noisy by speech and turbulent in action, and that the tumult might extend until the only recourse would be an adjournment to home quarters.

" The event demonstrated the folly of any fears on those grounds, and triumphantly vindicated any claims which might have been advanced by the patients of being *reasonable*, if not wholly rational. No public speaker need desire a more quite audience than that at each of the six lectures in question. By the more intelligent of the patients they were considered the most interesting lectures of the course ; and, to a large extent, they were the subject of daily discussion among them.

" To what extent the hearers severally applied to themselves that part of the lecture which was properly applicable, cannot well be estimated ; but there is good reason for the belief that many of them applied much that was said, as scandal will have it that men generally apply the pith of sermons,— *to their neighbors*."

Doctor Earle was one of the original members and founders of the American Medical Association, as well as of the Association of Medical Superintendents of American Institutions for the Insane, the New York Academy of Medicine, and the New England Psychological Society. Of the association last mentioned he was the first president ; and he now holds that office upon his third term. He was vice-president of the American Association of Medical Superintendents during the official year 1883–84 ; and president of the same association in 1884–85. He was elected a member of the Philadelphia Medical Society in 1837 ; of the New York Medical and Surgical Society in 1845 ; of the Massachusetts Medical Society in 1868 ; of the American Philosophical Society in 1866; fellow of the New York College of Physicians and Surgeons in 1846; councilor of the Massachusetts Medical Society in 1876, and corresponding member of the Medical Society of Athens, Greece, in 1839. He is also a member of the American Social Science Association, honorary member of the British Medico-Psychological Association, and corresponding member of the New York Medico-Legal Society. Among his contributions to medical literature which have been published in book or pamphlet form are: "A Visit to Thirteen Asylums for the Insane in Europe," 1841; "History, Description and Statistics of Bloomingdale Asylum for the Insane," 1848; "Blood-Letting in Mental Disorders," 1854; "Institutions for the Insane in Prussia, Austria and Germany," 1854; "Psychologic Medicine, its importance as a part of the Medical Curriculum," 1867; "The Psychopathic Hospital of the Future," 1867; Prospective Provision for the Insane," 1868; "The Curability of Insanity," 1877; and "A Glance at Insanity and the Management of the Insane in the American States," in 1879. To these may be added five annual reports of the Bloomingdale Asylum for the Insane, and twenty-two annual reports of the State Lunatic Hospital at Northampton.

Among his papers published in medical journals are: "Climate, Population, and Diseases of Malta;" "Medical Institutions, Diseases, &c., at Athens and Constantinople;" "The Royal College of Surgeons in London;" "The Inability to distinguish Colors;" "Experiments to Discover the Psychological Effects of Conium Maculatum;" "The pulse of the Insane;" "Paralysis Peculiar to the Insane;" "Insanity in its Coincidence with Age;" "A Description of Gheel," the Belgian Colony of the Insane; "European Institutions for Idiots;" and "The Lunatic Hospital at Havanna, Cuba."

In 1863 Dr. Earle was appointed Professor of Materia Medica and Psychology in the Berkshire Medical Institute at Pittsfield, Mass.; but in consequence of his appointment, in 1864, to the Superintendence of the hospital at Northampton, his lectures at that college were limited to the course for 1864. He was for several years a member of the Board of Health for Northampton. The doctor has never married.

Edward Beecher Nims, A. M., M. D., the present superintendent of the State Lunatic Hospital in Northampton, was born in Sullivan, Cheshire County, N. H., April 20, 1838. He is a descendant of Godfrey Nims, who, according to the oldest records of the family now extant, was married in Northampton, Mass., on November 28, 1677. Ebenezer Nims, a son of Godfrey, removed to Deerfield a short time previous to 1702, and when that town was destroyed by the Indians on February 29, 1703–04, O. S., he and Sarah Hoit were taken captives and removed, with others, to Canada, where they were detained as prisoners ten years. In the course of this captivity an Indian chief proposed to take Sarah in marriage; but she declined the alliance, promising, however, to marry one of her fellow captives. She subsequently became the wife of Ebenezer Nims.

David Nims, one of the five sons who sprung from this union, was the first town clerk and treasurer of Keene, N. H., to which offices he was elected May 2, 1753. Dr. Edward B. Nims, in the line of descent, is his great-great-grandson.

Dr. Nims studied at Kimball Union Academy, in Meriden, N. H., and graduated in 1862, at Williams College, Mass., which afterwards, in 1882, conferred upon him the degree of Master of Arts. His professional studies were in the Medical Department of the University of Vermont, from which he received the degree of M. D., in the spring of 1864. He then immediately entered the army as assistant surgeon in the first regiment of Vermont cavalry, a post which he held until the close of the civil war.

During the medical term of 1865–66, he prosecuted his professional studies at the College of Physicians and Surgeons, in New York, and in the latter year was appointed assistant physician at the Vermont Insane Asylum, at Brattleboro. After an experience of nearly three years in that institution, he was appointed assistant physician to the State Lunatic Asylum at Northampton. He entered upon his duties here on December 14, 1868, and, having performed them satisfactorily nearly seventeen years, until the resignation of Dr. Earle, he was promoted to the office of superintendent on the 1st of October, 1885. Prior to that date, and principally for the purpose of learning the recent improvements in European institutions, he went abroad, extending his journey to Rome, but passing most of the time in Great Britain, where he visited twenty asylums for the insane.

Dr. Nims is a member of the Massachusetts State Medical Society, of the New England Psychological Society, and of the Association of Medical Superintendents of American Institutions for the Insane. He is, also, one of the corporators of the Clarke Institution for Deaf Mutes, in Northampton.

Dr. Nims married Elizabeth E. Delano, of Ticonderoga, N. Y., on September 5, 1867.

Samuel Lapham Hill was born in Smithfield, R. I., July 30, 1806. His parents were Friends or Quakers. He learned the carpenter's trade and for several years worked at the bench. After a limited experience as teacher, he became superintendent and general manager of a cotton cloth factory in Williamantic. In the spring of 1841 he removed to Northampton and assisted in the organization of an attempt at co operation known as the Northampton Association for Education and Industry. He was the treasurer and one of the directors af this association until its dissolution in 1845. Soon after, with Samuel L. Hinckley, of Northampton, he formed the partnership of Hill & Hinckley, for the manufacture of sewing-silk and for other industrial purposes. He was also a prominent partner in the following manufacturing and mercantile enterprises: H. Wells & Co., manufacturers of saw-mills, pumps and wrenches; Wells & Littlefield, and Florence Sewing Machine Co., manufacturers of sewing machines; I. S. Parsons & Co., general merchants; Littlefield, Parsons & Co., manufacturers of buttons and daguerreotype cases; Florence, Manufacturing Co., manufacturers of hair brushes and hand mirrors; Northampton Emery Wheel Co., and Florence Furniture Co. The firm of Hill & Hinckley merged into the Nonotuck Silk Co., and until the failure of his health he filled the position of treasurer and general manager. Born a Quaker, he afterwards joined the Baptist church, acting for some time as one of its deacons. He early joined the anti-slavery movement, and finding the church not in harmony with its doctrines, he preferred practical christianity to the theoretical, and dissolved his church relationship. His religious ideas gradually grew broader until he became an active worker in the free religious ranks, discarding all dogmas and believing that earnest, true, conscientious lives can be lived, even though bound by no creed. He was one of the founders, in 1863, of the Free Congregational Society of Florence, and was its president for the remainder of his life. He was a large contributor towards the building of Cosmian Hall, which since 1874 has been the headquarters and place of meeting of the Free Congregational Society of Florence. He always took a great interest in all educational matters and made large contributions of money and personal effort to increase educational facilities. He organized before his death the Florence Kindergarten, endowing it with a large fund and selecting its managers, as he was desirous of seeing its success before leaving his earthly life. He died in Citronelle, Alabama, where he had gone for his health, on December 13, 1882, leaving a good record as one anxious to benefit his neighbors.

Dr. Austin White Thompson was born in Hampshire county in 1834. Dr. Thompson was brought to Northampton on the death of his father, Peleg Pierce Thompson, and adopted by his paternal uncle, Dr. Daniel Thompson, at so tender an age that the county seat may almost be said to have been the place of his nativity, as it was of his nurture. The name of his father indicates his descent, through his paternal grandmother, Matilda Pierce Thompson, from the Pierces; a family whose founder in America was a member of the Pilgrim crew of the Mayflower. From the same ancestor descended, in recent times, Franklin Pierce, president of the United States, and Dr. David P. Smith, of Springfield.

Among the instructors of his childhood and adolescence were Principals Sheldon, Adams, E. A. Hubbard and L. J. Dudley, and he was finally fitted for college under the private tutorship of Rev. Dr. Rufus Ellis, of Boston, who was then pastor of the Second Congregational church in Northampton. He was graduated at Harvard college, a member of the class of 1854, achieving the commencement honor of the salutatory oration.

He was, thereupon, cordially advised by Dr. Ellis to adopt the clerical profession in view of his fondness and success in philosophical studies and composition while in college; but then, as now, he was strenuously given to free thought, agnosticism, or scientific religion; and he held it not to be honorable to preach what he did not believe. Preferring the law, he pursued legal studies for a time in the office of Judge C. P. Huntington; but finally, in deference to the evident wishes of his uncle, to whom he was so much indebted, he entered upon the study of medicine, and was educated at the Medical school of Harvard university, graduating M. D. in 1857. A pleasant acquaintance with J. G. Holland and Samuel Bowles, while both of those journalists were in charge of the Springfield *Republican*, led to his employment as special writer and correspondent for that paper at times during a number of years; and he contributed editorials and articles in prose and verse, as well as news items from Hampshire county. He has done literary work for other journals as well.

Having acquired his profession and begun its practice, he followed his predilection and bent for the science of the mind, and accepted the position of second medical officer in the State Lunatic Hospital at Northampton when that institution was completed. As a preparation for the duties of the position, he resided a few months at the Taunton and Worcester state hospitals that he might thoroughly study their patients, a portion of whom were to be transferred to the new institution. This was in the time of Dr. Choate at Taunton and of Dr. Bemis at Worcester. Upon the death of his uncle, Dr. James Thompson, a brilliant physician, who, although a generation has gone by since his decease, is still gratefully remembered by many in Hampshire county—the subject of our sketch resigned from the hospital and resumed the general practice. He found at once an extensive business in medicine and surgery, which increased until he entered upon the enterprise with which he has been occupied for the past twelve years. While in general practice, however, he paid especial attention to the departments of his science to which Shady Lawn hospital is devoted. During the entire war of the rebellion he was on duty here as inspecting surgeon of United States volunteers, holding a commission for that service. He was also examiner of such drafted men as claimed to have disabilities precluding military service. There was no other inspecting surgeon at this point.

Samuel Bowles was once solicited by the historian of a work like ours for the facts of his career that would serve in preparing a sketch of his life. "Oh!" said Mr. Bowles, "Tell 'em I am so many years old; I have so many young ones; *and I created the Springfield Republican*! That's the size of it." We are in debt to Dr. Thompson for this very interesting anecdote. And, in all respects, we may apply it to him. For notwithstanding his long and successful career as a general practitioner of his most useful profession, with all its hardships, competition and self-denial, we are well aware that he will in the future be remembered quite solely as the creator of Shady Lawn. And justly. For in this crowning work he has given proof of those tastes and abilities that are his own for use and for output; and he has been of signal and exceptional use in his day and generation. Originality, self-reliance and staying power have been abundantly shown; and an ineffaceable success, greatly to his credit, has been tallied and recorded in the history of his time.

In its appropriate place elsewhere we give some account of Dr. Thompson's sanitarium, which we are glad to state was never so well and widely patronized as this year of our publication. In taking personal leave of its superintendent, we set down the hope that he will enjoy the strength and the length of days to develope and perpetuate it in accordance with his ardent and honorable ambition and energy of character.

Samuel Wright was one of the early settlers of this town, having come to this country from England in 1636, settled in Springfield, and removed to this town in 1656. His father's and grandfather's names were both John, and lived at Wright's Bridge, in Essex, forty miles from London, England. Samuel's sons were three, Samuel, Judah and James, who also settled in Northampton. James' son Preserved had a son Ephraim, he a son Ephraim, born 1747. His son, Martin, was the father of Dea. George L. Wright, who is a farmer at 42 South street. Martin Wright married Sarah, daughter of Josiah Parsons, June 18, 1818. They had a family of eight children, of whom four lived to manhood and womanhood. Isaac L. married Lydia A. Cobb, of Abington; Sarah L. married Hervey Miller, of Williamsburg, and died in 1855, one year after her marriage; Mary married Othinel M. Clark, who lives in Illinois; George B. married Elizabeth Cobb, of Abington, sister of the wife of Isaac L., and has four children, Sarah, who married Silas R. Cooley, of this town, Henry, who married Harriet M., daughter of Enos Clark, now resident of Florida, Charles M. and Elizabeth A., the two latter living with their parents. George L. Wright was elected deacon of the First Congregational church in 1878, for three years, re-elected in 1881 and 1884.

Joseph Parsons is the ancestor of that name in New England. He was supposed to have been born in England, and was first known in New England in 1636, in Springfield, then a boy. He married Mary Bliss in 1646, who died in 1712. Isaac Parsons, a descendant of the above, married Mindwell King, April 30, 1774. Josiah Parsons, a son of Isaac, owned and resided in the house now occupied by Mrs. Letitia D., widow of Lyman Parsons, a son of Josiah mentioned above. The house is probably the oldest in Northampton now inhabited. It was built as early as 1743, is in a good state of preservation and a very comfortable dwelling. When built, inside shutters were a necessity to prevent the incursions of unfriendly savages, and grooves were made in the window sills for holding them. The house was of two stories with the large chimney in the center, customary in those early times, and is so much of a relic that Mr. Sheldon, an antiquarian of Deerfield, has recently taken a photograph of it for the museum at Greenfield. Josiah Parsons married Sarah Strong of Southampton, December 28, 1791, and reared thirteen children. Lyman, the oldest son, succeeded to his father on the farm, and was born June 28, 1801. He married first, September 30, 1835, Olivia Wright, of Granville, O., who died October 6, 1842. His second marriage occurred April 24, 1846, with Letitia D., widow of Chauncey E. Parsons, of Rootstown, O., and has a family of four children. Chauncey E., the eldest son, married Annie A. Spaulding, of Saxton's River, Vt., is a resident of the
24*

old homestead, and is a member of the common council of the City of Northampton from the third ward. Josiah died at the age of fifteen years. Almira
E. married Henry Moore, of Hatfield. Lyman, Jr., died September 12, 1855,
at the age of six. Mrs. Parsons had two daughters by her first husband, Sarah
D., now resident with her mother, and Diantha, who married Josiah H.
Graves. The children of Chauncey E. Parsons are the fifth generation who
have resided in the house described above.

Joseph B. Parsons, a son of Capt. Samuel and Caroline (Russell) Parsons,
was born April 10, 1828, was educated in the public schools of his native
town, and spent his early life as a farmer. For ten years before the breaking
out of the late rebellion, he served in the Massachusetts volunteer militia.
At the commencement of the war, the 10th regiment, state militia, to which
he was attached, tendered its services to the government, which tender was
accepted, and they were mustered into the United States service June 21,
1861, as the 10th Mass. Vols. They participated in all the battles of the
army of the Potomac. Mr. Parsons was made captain of Co. C, when first
mustered into the United States service, and rose by promotion through the
several grades to colonel of the regiment, which office he held for the last
eighteen months of the service. After the return of his regiment, at a call
from Gov. John A. Andrew, he went to Fortress Monroe under a general
order from the war department allowing states to recruit in rebel territory,
where he recruited two regiments of rebel deserters and a regiment of contra-
bands. After peace was declared he commanded the 2d Regiment Mass
Militia, composed of veterans of the late war, for five years. At present
Colonel Parsons is Chief of Police of the city of Northampton, and is also
engaged in farming. He married November 20, 1849, Caroline, daughter of
Jonathan D. Kellogg, and has had four children, of whom only the youngest
is now living, Frank Bailey, engaged with the United Brass Co., being their
Chicago agent. Ida married Joel Hayden and died in 1883. J. Dwight, after
a few years in the Northampton Bank, went to California, and engaged in the
same business. He died about six years ago. Carrie E. died at eighteen
years of age.

Francis M. Cook was born in this town, April 29, 1834, and has always
resided here, engaged in farming and at the mason's trade. His residence
is on Massasoit street, and he has farming lands of 200 acres. He married in
1857, Mrs. Lucy Munwan, from Middletown, Conn., and has three children,
now living. Mr. Cook's father, Horace, and grandfather, Enos, were born in
this town, and in the same house in which he was born. The house in
which they were born was in West street, on the ground occupied by Music
Hall, and was built in 1754.

Charles C. Clapp is a descendent of Capt. Roger Clapp, who came to this
country from England 250 years ago, and settled in Dorchester, Mass. His
son, Elder Preserved Clapp, was one of the early settlers of Northampton.
His son, Samuel, married Mary Shelden, who was taken captive by the

Indians at Deerfield, in the time of the French and Indian war, carried to Canada, and afterwards redeemed and returned to her native town. His son, Ebenezer, was a resident on South street, in Northampton. His son, Sylvanus, married Charity Pierce, of Chesterfield, settled in Westhampton, and had two children, Bela P. and Ralph. Sylvanus, eldest son of Bela P., was an eminent physician, commencing practice in Chesterfield, and removed from there to Pawtucket, R. I., where he was president of the State Medical Society of Rhode Island. Mary, a sister of Sylvanus, married Elnathan Graves, a county commissioner for Hampshire county nine years. Franklin Clapp is a farmer in Williamsburg. Ralph was a farmer in the northern part of Westhampton, married Fanny, daughter of Cornelius Bartlett, of Westhampton, who was a Revolutionary pensioner, and had three children, Dexter, Esther and Charles C. Dexter, born July 15, 1816, married September 1, 1845. He graduated from Amherst college in 1839, studied theology at Cambridge Divinity school, and preached at Deerfield and at Savannah, Ga. He was installed in 1846 over the church in West Roxbury, Mass., from which Rev. Theodore Parker had lately removed to Boston. In 1851 he became colleague with Rev. Dr. Flint, in Salem, and remained at this post ten years, when he was obliged to retire on account of failing health. He died July 27, 1868. Esther, born January 6, 1820, died July 30, 1857. Charles C. married Sarah M., daughter of Asahel Bryant, of Chesterfield, and was a farmer in Westhampton on his father's homestead until 1868, when he removed to Bay State, still carrying on extensive farm operations. He has had born to him five children—Charles R., born October 6, 1863, Frederick D., born April 13, 1867, Ellery C., born October 2, 1871, Esther Fanny, born February 18, 1876, and Ellery C., born December 30, 1879. Of these, Freddie D. died February 28, 1882, and Ellery C. was drowned November 10, 1874.

Theodore Clapp was a native of this town, born in 1785, married in 1813, Betsey Newton of Northboro, Mass., and had born to him four children, one dying in childhood. Mary J., born in 1823, married Henry B. Graves, and died November, 1884. Elizabeth M. and Theodore, unmarried, and living at the old homestead, 47 South street. Theodore remembers making trips to Boston with his father driving cattle, when there was no railroad to Northampton, and the Boston and Albany railroad extended only from Boston to Worcester.

Elijah Clapp married Jane Munroe of Northboro, had a family of two children, Harriet, who married D. W. Willard, and lived in Springfield, and Munroe, who married Lydia F. Rice, of Northboro, and occupied the home of his father as a farmer, until his death in 1875. His children were Jane B., Frederic C. and Harriet L. The two daughters are still living. Frederic died at home in 1883. He enlisted in Co. C, 52d Mass. Vol. Inf'try, and was engaged in the first and second assault on Port Hudson, and the battle at Jackson.

Lyman Kingsley was a native of this town, born in 1800, was a carpenter and bridge builder. He built a bridge across Connecticut river between this town and Hadley, which was carried away by a flood, and afterward he rebuilt it. The latter was blown down about five years ago. He married Caroline, daughter of Capt. David Strong, who was a boatman on Connecticut river, reared a family of eight children, all living, with the exception of Francis. Henry married L. Maria Clark, and is a carpenter and joiner, residing at 74 South street. Edward married Susan Shepherd for his second wife. William F. married Elizabeth H. Clark. George L. married Lizzie Jones, and lives at La Crosse, Wis. Robert M. lives in Black Hawk county, Ia., proprietor of a hotel. Albert H. is a dry goods clerk at J. E. Lambie & Co.'s. Calvin B. married Harriet Arno, and is employed in the freight department N. H. & N. R. R. Co. Lyman Kingsley also built the fine bridge at Chicopee some thirty-seven years ago. While in process of building one-half of the bridge was carried away, incurring a severe loss. He also built the bridge at Bellows Falls, Vt., and some others across Connecticut river.

Lewis Smith was born in Great Barrington, and at the close of the Revolutionary war settled at Smith's Ferry. He married Eunice Judd, of South Hadley and raised a family of eleven children, who lived to manhood and womanhood. There were seven sons and four daughters. Five of the sons settled in the Smith's Ferry locality in five consecutive houses, and were all thrifty farmers. Of the eleven children only two now survive, Charles H., who, about five years ago, removed to Holyoke, and Eunice, who married Hiram Bagg, of West Springfield, is now his widow, and lives at Erie, Penn. Milo J., one of the five brothers mentioned above, born July 27, 1808, married Sally J. Street, of West Springfield, had a family of three children. Lurene S. married Solon N. Gould, of Charleston, N. H., who died October, 1874. Mrs. Gould now resides at Smith's Ferry. Josephine died in 1876, unmarried. Milo L. now resides on his father's homestead, carrying on a farm of over 300 acres, and also has a stock farm at West Liberty, Ia., where he keeps on an average one hundred head of pure blood Short-horns. He also carries on the manufacture of pure cider vinegar. He married first, Luthera Meekins, of Greenfield, who died July 20, 1882, leaving two children, a son and a daughter. The son, M. Wilbur, married Emily Nash, of Williamsburg. The daughter, Luthera J., is a student at the Northampton High school. Two children died before their mother. His second marriage was with J. Maria Avery, of Easthampton, by whom he has had one child, now dead. Milo J. Smith was often entrusted with offices of honor and responsibility, and was representative of his town in 1844, in the state legislature. He was, for a number of years, on the board of selectmen. For two years he was president of the Hampshire and Franklin County Agricultural society, was a member of the State Board of Agriculture for three years, and was often called upon to administer the estates of his neighbors.

Abner Barnard, probably from Connecticut, located in Northampton at an early date, and was buried in the old cemetery at Northampton. His grandson, William M., son of Israel, was born in the house now occupied by Mrs. Azariah Clapp, on South street. Here also Israel carried on a large clothier's business for those times. William married Maria Elizabeth Benson, who bore him seven children, of whom four are now living, Martha, Abner, Eliza and William. The two former now reside at West Farms, where Abner is postmaster.

Nelson Loud was born in Northampton in 1815, where he lived until twenty-three years of age, when he removed to Ohio. Here he worked at the trade of a carpenter and joiner in Geauga county a number of years, and afterwards removed to Cuyahoga county, where he, in company with Edmund Clark, built a saw-mill and carried on the lumber business for four years. In 1862 he returned to this town. In 1846 he married Martha Clark, a native of Huntsburg, O. They raised a family of three children, Frank W., who died in infancy, Caleb E., engaged with the American Organ Company in Boston, and Lucy J., who carries on a large dressmaking business on South street. Mrs. Loud died September 19, 1884.

Jonathan Munyan came to this town from Thomson, Conn., in 1817, and settled at West Farms, where he resided until his death in 1846. He was married before he left Connecticut to Olive Stockwell, reared a family of thirteen children, of whom only two are now living, Mary, who married Robert H. Aldrich, and James L., who resides on Bridge street. James L. married Nancy E. Church, of Middlefield, who bore him six children, three of whom are now living, Julia E., who married Milo L. Morgan, and resides in New York city, Fanny, who married Silas M. Wright, a farmer of Fruit street, and James C., who resides with his father. Mr. Munyan's second wife was Susan W. Williams, of Williamsburg.

James Collins came to South Hadley from England about 1775. He married and raised a family of four sons and one daughter. His son Horace married Lydia Ware, of Wilmington, Vt., and resided in Granby. They had a family of seven, of whom three are now living. Nathan G. who is a Baptist minister at Dodge City, Kas., has been influential in building a large number of churches in a number of different states, and was a chaplain in the army of the rebellion. Clark lives at Wolfsboro, N. H. Horace A. was born in Granby, December 9, 1813. When ten years of age he came to this town and resided with Chester Smith near where the railroad station is now located at Smith's Ferry. He made his home with Mr. Smith's family until 1832. In 1833 he married Mary A., daughter of the late Jonathan and Submit (Clark) Parsons. Mr. Parsons being in poor health, Mr. Collins took the management of affairs on the farm, and with abundant success. He remained on the same farm until 1854, when he removed to the present location at Smith's Ferry. Mr. Collins has been a successful grower of all kinds of fruit and a heavy grower of tobacco for twenty-two years past. They have had two sons and two daughters, one son died at the age of three years.

Cornelia, born January 29, 1837, married William W. Ward, station agent of the Connecticut River railroad at Holyoke, Jonathan E., born September 29, 1840, and Laura P., who married Clarence C. Cogswell, station agent of Connecticut River railroad at Smith's Ferry.

Frederick G. Richards was born in Stoddard, N. H., February 5, 1821. At the age of four years he, with his parents, removed to Gill, Franklin county, and shortly after went to Cummington. At the latter place his father carried on a general foundry business at the east village, where Frederick G. learned the trade of a moulder. Thirty years ago he removed to this town and worked for W. R. Clapp in his foundry fifteen years. The past fourteen years he has been on the police force of this town, and since it became a city has been janitor of city hall and lock-up. He married, in 1852, Emily Sherman, of Worthington, and has three sons and one daughter. The daughter, Nellie E., is the wife of George H. Smith.

Rev. Albert C. Hussey, A. M., was born in Fairfield, Me., August 17, 1836. Although enjoying but limited advantages for obtaining an education, living a long way from a school-house, at the early age of seventeen he had qualified himself to teach a large and quite advanced district school. In the fall of 1857, he entered Waterville college, now Colby university, Waterville, Me. Here he remained only a year, but made such a record that by this institution, at its annual commencement in 1876, was conferred upon him the honorary degree of Master of Arts. In 1866 he began to preach, supplying the pulpits of the Baptist churches in Starks, Anson and Industry, Me. In the spring of 1868, he accepted a call to the management of Baptist missions in Washington county, Me., was ordained pastor of the Baptist church at Princeton, February 18, 1869. He graduated from the Theological seminary at Newton, Mass., June 12, 1872. He became the pastor of the First Baptist church in Grafton, Mass , August 1, 1872, and in 1879 became pastor of the Baptist church in this city. The society under his administration have remodeled a handsome church edifice, built a new parsonage and greatly increased in social and religious influence.

Albert Waters was born at Oxford, Conn., February 22, 1831, and when sixteen years of age he went to Springfield, where he was employed in the Massasoit House and Union hotel. When twenty-one years of age he removed to Holyoke where he kept a restaurant. At Holyoke he married Mary Van Hoesen in July, 1854, whose ancestors were, on her father's side, of the Knickerbockers, of New York, and on her mother's side, the Jepsons, who were early settlers of Chesterfield and Ashfield. In 1857 he removed to Tioga county, Penn. In the first year of the rebellion he enlisted in Co. I, 45th Penn. Vol. Infty., and afterwards re-enlisted in the same regiment, serving in the army until the close of the war. After the war he returned to Holyoke, and soon after settled in this town, on road 48, where he now resides.

B. DeForrest Sheedy was born in Norwalk, Conn., October 17, 1857, where he remained on the farm with his father, and attending district school until sixteen years of age. He then went to study medicine with Dr. C. G. Bohannan in his native town, where he remained two years. At that time he went to study with Dr. W. G. Hoyt, of New York city, who was house physician to the Charity hospital at Blackwell's Island, where he remained summers, until the spring of 1883, at the same time spending the winters at New York university, from which he graduated in the spring of 1885. He then commenced the practice of medicine in company with Dr. Bohannan, of Norwalk, remaining with him till May, 1885, when he removed to Northampton and commenced the practice of his profession at 114 Main street, where he has acquired a lucrative and increasing patronage.

George Q. Terrill was born in New York city, September 28, 1865. His parents having both died, he removed to Northampton, Mass., when three years of age, to the residence of his uncle, James Quirk. He attended the public schools, graduated from the high school and subsequently entered Holy Cross college, Worcester, Mass., to finish his classical education. He began the study of medicine with his cousin, Dr. Quirk, at Ware, Mass., and afterwards pursued it with Dr. Sheedy, of this city, graduating from the University of New York in 1886. He is now assistant to Dr. Sheedy.

Orson E. Train was born in Whately, September 24, 1820; was educated in the common schools of his native town, and, at seventeen, learned the carpenter and joiner's trade. He enlisted in 1862, in Co. G, 37th Mass. Vols., and served in the Sixth corps, army of the Potomac. He received a serious wound in 1864, in front of Petersburg. He is a United States pensioner; married Eliza G. Bailey, of Lunenburg, in 1847, and has two children, Edgar R., at Holyoke, and Elva, who resides at home.

Charles H. Dickinson was born in this town, May 28, 1855, where most of his life has been spent, received his education here, graduating from the high school in June, 1874. He was graduated from the Columbia Medical college, New York city, March 1, 1878. He commenced the practice of his profession here in 1879, and was that year town physician. In 1880 he removed to Faribault, Minn., where he remained about two years, when he located at South Deerfield. In February, 1886, he resumed his practice in this town, with his office over Cook's jewelry store, Main street. In 1881 he married Clara C. Maynard, a native of Barre, in this state.

L. B. Parkhurst was born in Milford, in October, 1844, son of Ithiel Parkhurst. He received his early education at the schools of his native town, Worcester and Boston, and graduated from Boston University School of Medicine in the class of 1877. He settled at Northampton in 1879 as successor to the late Dr. E. B. Harding.

Amos Sawyer was born in Bradford, N. H., December 9, 1830. His father, William Sawyer, was a drover in the days when cattle and sheep were bought up and driven to Brighton market, before any railroads were built in New England. Amos was engaged in this business with his father until twenty-two years of age, when he went to Cambridge, Mass., and engaged in the manufacture of soap one year, when he removed to this, then town of Northampton, and engaged in the same business on the same location where he now carries on the trade. He married, in 1856, Cordelia R., daughter of James Tandy, of Cambridge, formerly from Newport, N. H. They have three daughters.

Willard M. Nichols was born in Halifax, Vt., July 30, 1820. When he went into business he engaged first in farming and afterwards in moving buildings two years. For three years he manufactured wooden pumps at Waltham, Mass., and at Halifax, Vt. Afterwards for a number of years he carried on house building in Ware, Mass. He worked for H. L. James of Williamsburg, fifteen years, making planes. Mr. James's shop burned while he was in his employ, and burned more than a hundred dollars worth of tools. Since 1870 he has engaged in keeping boarding-houses at Williamsburg and Bay State. He married Caroline Wicks, of Halifax, Vt., December 9, 1843, and has had three children, two sons deceased, and a daughter, Alice T., who married Edgar G. Towne, a merchant on Main street, in this city.

Dr. Payson J. Flagg was born in Coleraine, January 22, 1858. His early life was spent in gaining an education, and in teaching in the public schools in Franklin county, in the town of Coleraine, Bernardston, Charlemont and Heath. He attended the Jefferson Medical college of Philadelphia, graduating in April, 1885. He commenced practice with his brother H. H. Flagg, at Shelburn Falls, and in June, 1886, he located at Florence, with an office in Stone's block. For three years he was a student of Powers' Institute, at Bernardston, fitting for college. He has two brothers, physicians.

E. Brownell Coon was born in Cambridge, N. Y., May 8, 1841, where his early life was spent until the age of twenty-one. He at that time moved to Windsor Locks, Conn., where he remained one year, afterwards served an apprenticeship to the trade of a machinist with the Ames Manufacturing Co., at Chicopee, Mass., between four and five years. He worked at his trade as machinist and tool-maker in Boston the next three years. He pursued the same business at Springfield, Chicopee Falls, Florence, Hartford, Conn., Philadelphia and Illion, N. Y. In 1881 he removed to Leeds and engaged as mechanical superintendent of the Mill River Button Company, and has served in that capacity since that date. In December, 1877, he married Hattie A., daughter of Julius Phelps, of Florence, and has one son. Their residence is on a fine elevation on Chestnut street, in Leeds.

Dr. Edward E. Denniston was born near Londonderry, Ireland, and was educated in Dublin and Edinburgh. For five years before coming to this country he was surgeon and physician to a hospital located on the estate of the Marquis of Abercorn, in the county of Tyrone, Ireland, town of Strabane. He immigrated to this country with his wife in 1833, locating in this town, where for twelve years he engaged a large practice, where he has remained since that date. In 1847 he opened a water cure and home for invalids under the aspices of the professional gentlemen of Boston, New York, Philadelphia, St. Louis and Cincinnati, which he carried on for thirty-three years. This was very successful. Since 1880 he has been practicing his profession in Boston and along the seashore. The past three years he has spent in his farm home in this town. His first wife died in 1873. In 1883 he married Mary S. Dana, of Boston. By his first wife he had two children, a son and a daughter. Evans E. married Miss Helen Clark, daughter of E. W. Clark, of the firm of E. W. Clark & Co., bankers of Philadelphia. He died about 1862. His son, Edward E., is one of the banking firm of E. W. Clark & Co. at the present time. The daughter, Anna H., has a fashionable boarding-house in Providence, R. I.

Henry St. Lawrence was born in Canada, of French parentage, came to this town from Wallingford, Vt., in 1883, and engaged as foreman of Charles H. Maynard's hoe shop. Mr. St. Lawrence has made many improvements in the machinery at the works. He is inventor and patentee of St. Lawrence's power hammers and the H. St. Lawrence's forging machine, both of which have been introduced into the shop where he is foreman.

Erastus V. Lilly was born in Ashfield, April 22, 1834, where most of his life was spent until twenty-five years of age. In the meantime he learned the carpenter's trade, which he pursued for a number of years, and in 1858 he built the Parks House at Huntington village. He built a number of houses in Worthington, Ashfield and other towns. In 1862 he enlisted for three years in the civil war, where he remained until June, 1865. He was commissioned captain in Co. B, 34th Mass. Vols. In July, 1862, he married H. Lizzie, daughter of Horace Smith, of Huntington, and had born to him one son, Charles A., now a resident of Northampton. Mr. Lilly died March 13, 1878. He was selectman of Huntington for three years, chairman one year, receiving every vote for the office but two, was deputy sheriff in Hampden and Berkshire counties before his removal to Northampton. While here he was deputy sheriff for the counties of Hampshire, Franklin, Berkshire and Hampden, at the same time.

Lewis L. Draper was born March 28, 1801, in Attleboro, and when he was five years of age his father removed to Pelham, where he remained on a farm till twenty-one years old. At majority he went to Quincy and learned the stone cutter's trade, and remained there three years. He then set up in the mercantile business at Pelham, where he remained seven years, and at Shutesbury for three years. From there he went to Amherst and engaged in trade for the long period of forty-two years, and afterwards sold merchandise and engaged in farming for three years in this city. He has always been more or less of a farmer in connection with his mercantile business. His business has been a successful one, and for the past few years he has retired from active business pursuits. His first marriage was with Margaret, daughter of Luther Henry, a noted merchant of Shutesbury, July 4, 1827. She died June 12, 1838, leaving a family of five children. November 28, 1839, he married

Eliza, daughter of Martin Kellogg, of Hadley, who bore him one child, and died May 20, 1872, at the age of fifty-four years. Of his six children three are now living, Emerson H., who resides in California, Mary, who married William Gray, now living in Hadley, and John L., who is engaged in the livery business in this city.

Rev. Herbert W. Lathe was born at Worcester, graduated from Yale college in the class of 1873, and from Andover Theological seminary, class of 1877. He located in Portland, Me., in September, 1877, where he remained until January, 1831. In April, 1882, he became settled pastor of the First Congregational church in this town.

Curtis W. Braman was born at Brighton, May 18, 1819. At fourteen years of age he came to this then town of Northampton, living with Samuel Whitmarsh, and engaged in the mulberry and silk-worm business for seven years. In 1840 he took up the trade of mason, which has occupied his attention to the present time. In 1839 he married Martha A., daughter of Jonas Clapp, of Northampton, and has had born to him a family of ten children, of whom five are now living. One died in infancy, and one at the age of seven years. James Henry enlisted in 1861, in Co. C, 10th Mass. Vols., became surgeant, and was killed at the battle of Fair Oaks, Va., May 30, 1862. His remains were buried in the cemetery in this city. Carrie married Freeman Taylor, and died in 1869. Mattie L. died in 1881. Maria married Louis Duplessis, and resides at Wallingford, Conn. Sarah married George Spencer, of Meriden, Conn. Hattie L. married Willard E. Lacom, of this city, and now resides at Willimansett. William W. married Mrs. Ellen Waite, and resides in this city. George A. married Mina Mann, and also resides in the city.

John B. Clark was born in Providence, R. I., January 26, 1847. He was for two years a student at Brown university, Providence, and graduated from Amherst college in class of 1872. He also pursued special studies at the universities of Zurich, Switzerland, and Heidelberg, Germany, from 1877 to 1881 ; he was professor of history and political science in Carleton college, Minnesota, and, since 1881, has been connected with Smith college in a similar capacity. He is the author of a work on political economy and a number of review articles on the same subject. He married in 1875 Miss Myra A., daughter of J. G. Smith, Esq., of Minneapolis, Minn.

Charles M. Kinney was born at Sunderland, Vt., July 7, 1818, and remained with his father until he was sixteen years of age. The latter was a farmer, held the office of trial justice forty-five years, was twice representative of his town, and held various other town offices. Charles M. came to Northampton forty-one years ago, and established the business of a manufacturer of marble cemetery work. The business is still carried on by his son Charles W. He married, June 1, 1842, Submit, daughter of Benjamin Walker, and has a family of five children, four sons and one daughter, Albert C., Charles W., Ella, Fred and Edward. Ella married W. H. Abbott and resides in Holyoke. Albert married Mrs. Haskins, of this city, and carries on monumental, marble and granite work at Milford. The other three sons are residents of this city. Anna married T. L. Erwin of Natick, and died in 1883.

Rev. C. E. St. John was born at Prairie Du Chien, Wis., December 19, 1856, was educated at Harvard university, taking the degree of A. B. in 1879, and of B. D. and A. M. in 1883. He was ordained and settled as pastor of the Unitarian church in Northampton, November 1, 1883.

The Smith family of Northampton trace their genealogy to the sixteenth century. At the time of the breaking out of the Revolution the father of five brothers marched with his little band to Lexington and Bunker Hill. The family first settled on land here between Leeds and the river. Frank H. Smith, clerk of the common council, was born here November 24, 1859, was educated in the public schools and graduated from the high school at the age of eighteen years. He studied for the profession of dentistry, but ill health obliged him to relinquish it. He is engaged in the real estate and insurance business and the sale of foreign tickets.

Among others of the past and present residents of Northampton who are worthy of special mention, yet whom space precludes an extended notice are the following : Osmyn Baker, a descendant of one of the first settlers, a member of congress and president of the Smith Charities for several years ; conspicuous for force of character and sterling integrity ; his son William Lawrence Baker, a lieutenant in the regular army, was killed at the battle of Antietam, at the age of twenty-three ; Benjamin Barrett, M. D., a member of both branches of the legislature, county commissioner and treasurer of Northampton Institution for Savings ; Henry H. Bond, a lawyer and treasurer of the Florence Savings Bank ; Haynes H. Chilson, attorney at law, county commissioner, commissioner of insolvency, postmaster and chairman of the school committee; married a daughter of Hon. Isaac C. Bates ; Josiah Clark, Jr., principal of Williston seminary, and professor in Smith college ; Charles Delano, member of congress and county treasurer, and an excellent lawyer and advocate ; Charles A. Dewey, district attorney and judge of the supreme judicial court ; Samuel A. Fisk, president of the Massachusetts Medical Society and lecturer on physiology and hygiene at Smith college ; Samuel Henshaw, judge of probate and also of the court of common pleas ; George S. Hilliard, teacher in the Round Hill school, and United States district attorney for Massachusetts, married a daughter of Judge Samuel Howe ; Samuel Hinckley, register of probate nearly thirty years, and judge of probate seventeen years; Charles P. Huntington, law partner of Isaac C. Bates, represented the town several years in the legislature, and was a judge of one of the Boston courts; William Lyman, a soldier of the Revolution, member of congress and consul to London during Mr. Jefferson's administration ; Jonathan H. Lyman, a member of both branches of the legislature, district attorney, and chief justice of the court of sessions ; Benjamin S. Lyman, a geologist, and for some time in the service of the British government in exploring the mineral resources of Hindoostan ; Lafayette Maltby, an able financier, and treasurer of the Northampton Institution for Savings; Charles L. Seeger, a fine classical scholar and a skillful physician; Samuel T. Spaulding, district attorney and judge of probate; Daniel Stebbins, a physician, and county treasurer for thirty-five years, and greatly interested in the culture and manufacture of silk; William P. Strickland, clerk of the courts and judge of the Hampshire district court; Isaac Stone, United States consul at Singapore, representative in the legislature, and for a time superintendent of the Northampton Cutlery Company; Oliver Warner, proprietor of the Warner House, a member of the state senate, and an influential citizen; Samuel Wells, for thirty years clerk of the courts in Hampshire county; John P. Williston, a successful manufacturer; John F. Warner, a prominent citizen and member of the legislature; General John L. Otis, a soldier in the war of the rebellion, a member of both branches of the legislature, and a manufacturer; William M. Gaylord, largely interested in the iron business, and representative and state senator; Oscar Edwards, member of the governor's council and president of the Northampton bank; George W. Hubbard, formerly state senator and president of the Smith Charities; Lucien B. Williams, a successful business man; Luther Bodman, president of the Hampshire county bank, and recently president of the Smith Charities; Lewis J. Dudley, for many years the conductor of a classical school, a representative and a senator, and a legislator of ability; Enos Parsons, a lawyer, a man of practical talent, and a useful citizen; William F. Arnold, often elected to the legislature, and a merchant; Henry A. Longly, for a long term of years high sheriff of Hampshire county; Luke Lyman, a descendant of one of the first settlers, a colonel in the Union army, and register of probate; Harvey Kirkland, register of deeds; Daniel W. Bond, one of the leading lawyers of Western Massachusetts, and district attorney for the northwestern district; General Benjamin E. Cook, a merchant of fifty years standing; Mark H. Spaulding, a captain in the army, selectman and representative in the legislature; and Benjamin E. Clark, Jr., mayor of the city. This list might be extended indefinitely, but lack of space forbids a further enumeration.

About one hundred and sixty natives of Northampton have been graduates of colleges.

SUBURBS.

In several parts of the city's territory are located suburban villages and hamlets, giving it five postal stations outside the main office, as follows: Florence, Leeds, Loudville, Smith's Ferry and West Farms.

FLORENCE is located about three miles northwest of the main or business portion of the city, with which it is connected by a street railway. It has a somewhat remarkable history. It was known in the early part of the present century as the "Warner District," and contained some six or seven houses. It has, at different periods, been locally distinguished as the "Community,"

" Bensonville" and "Greenville." In 1835 the late Samuel Whitmarsh, in connection with two or three other gentlemen, engaged in the manufacture of silk. The enterprise was unsuccessful from causes now unimportant to the public, and was eventually relinquished. In 1840 the property was purchased by Joseph Conant, of Mansfield, Conn., who in turn sold it to the Community Association, which was composed of one hundred and fifty members, whose avowed object was to "progress towards a better state of society and the development of a true social and moral life." The estate possessed by the association comprised 500 acres of land, a silk factory, a saw-mill and gristmill and several houses. This association, composed mainly of earnest, sincere and intelligent men, was dissolved after an existence of five years. But it had existed long enough to assure the future growth and prosperity of the village. The Nonotuck Silk Company is an outgrowth of this enterprise of the "Community Association." In December, 1852, a postoffice was established here and the village given the name it now bears, taken from the famous silk producing city of Italy. The village subsequently became largely known through the extensive manufacture of the Florence sewing machine here.

LEEDS is a bright manufacturing village lying about a mile and a half northwest of Florence, in a deep and narrow gorge, on the banks of Mill river. It embraces a part of what was formerly known as the Rail Hill School District. Its present name was given after the city of Leeds, England, because of its large woolen manufacture, it having formerly borne the name of Shebard's Factory, till 1849, when the postoffice was established here. The village was almost entirely destroyed by the great Mill river disaster of 1874, an account of which is given on another page.

LOUDVILLE is a small village, noted for its paper-mills, lying in the southwestern part of the city's territory, partly in Westhampton.

WEST FARMS is the name of a postoffice about a mile and a half north, located for the convenience of the farming community in that vicinity.

SMITH'S FERRY is a hamlet in the southern part of the town, on the Connecticut River railroad. It originally bore the name of "Lyman's Farms," then "South Farms," later "South Harbor," and in 1835 or '36 was given its present name.

BAY STATE AND PAPER MILL VILLAGE are now localities in the city, but formerly villages in the old township.

MANUFACTURES.

Williams Manufacturing Co.—In 1850 Messrs. Bartlett & Williams started in business as basket manufacturers at Huntington, and continued in business at that place until 1862, when they removed to Northampton, where the style of the firm was changed to L. B. Williams & Co. The latter firm continued in business until 1867, when there was another change, and the present corporation of the Williams Manufacturing Company was organized. Starting in moderately, the business has increased and expanded until at the present time they own and operate the largest manufacturing establishment of this kind in the world, the works covering an area of more than 100,000 square feet, and have a capacity of upwards of 10,000 baskets per day. The dimensions of the main building of the manufacturing establishment is 40x250 feet, with an extension of 30x100 feet, all four stories in height, fitted throughout with the latest and most improved machinery and facilities for doing the best of work. For storing the goods large store-houses have been constructed, each 50x200 feet, and these are now filled with manufactured goods. The capital invested in this company is over $150,000.00. The firm is known in almost every state and territory in the Union. To endeavor to enumerate the different styles and various uses for which their goods are used would require more space than we can give. We only mention a few of the well-known specialties and more noted of their goods. Perhaps the most prominent of all is their fruit basket, which is known to every large dealer and jobber; next to this style, and hardly less prominent, are the truck, market, laundry and corn baskets, which they manufacture. Their clothes baskets have a national reputation, while their satchel and covered baskets can be found in every store in the United States or Canada that make any pretentions of keeping first-class goods in this line. The extra heavy coal baskets are the best of the kind in the market. At times they employ 200 hands, and even in the dull seasons 150 skilled workmen find employment beneath the roof of this great factory.

Nonotuck Silk Co.—This great enterprise had its beginning in the early days of Florence, in 1838, a sketch of whose history we give above. The establishment took its present name in 1844, and in 1865 was incorporated under the laws of the state with a capital of $360,000.00, Ira Dimock, of Hartford, Conn., president, and Alfred T. Lilly, treasurer. When sewing machines were first introduced it was found that the sewing-silk then made was not in all respects suitable for its use. After spending much time in experiment, the Nonotuck Silk Co. succeeded in producing a machine twist which was found to be exactly the thing needed. The first lot of this new industrial product was made and spooled in February, 1852, and being tried by the Singer Sewing Machine Co., was found to be just what they had long desired. The company now have mills at Leeds, Florence and Haydenville, and give employment to 800 hands. Mr. Lilly has been treasurer of the company since 1853, when they only employed thirty hands. At Leeds the company have a custom saw-mill, where they also purchase and saw large amounts of lumber for their own use and for sale. They also have in connection with this a planing-mill, and manufacture boxes for the shipping of silk, using for that purpose alone 200,000 feet of pine and basswood annually. It gives employment to a dozen men. L. B. Field is superintendent of the lumber department. They also employ fifteen hands at making spools for their silk.

Belding Brothers & Co.—This large silk manufactory was established here in 1874, in the building formerly used by the Arms Manufacturing Co. The company was incorporated July 1, 1882, with a capital stock of $650,000.00. The officers of the company are all non-resident, and Edgar F. Crooks is local manager.

The Northampton Paper Co., at Bay State, Vernon Brothers & Co., proprietors, have a large mill, where they manufacture a ton of colored paper daily, employing twenty men. On the site of their mill one owned by them was burned August 8, 1878. It was re-built in 1880–81. It is a brick structure run by both water and steam power, the latter one hundred and fifty horse-power, and the former fifty horse-power. Their engine is of the Harris-Corliss make.

The Florence Manufacturing Co. was incorporated in 1866, with a capital of $100,000.00, at Florence, for the manufacture of brushes and toilet sets. They succeeded the firm of Littlefield, Parsons & Co. Their works are located on Nonotuck street, and give employment to one hundred and twenty hands. They employ steam-power, which is supplied by a thirty horse-power engine.

The Florence Furniture Co. was incorporated in 1873, with a capital of $20,000.00, for the manufacture of caskets and coffins. On Myrtle street, Florence, they have a three-story brick building, 170 feet in length by 32 feet in width, besides engine, boiler and dry-house, their power being furnished by a forty horse-power engine. They employ twenty-five hands, principally males. Their trade is exclusively in the New England states.

The Northampton Cutlery Co. was incorporated in 1871, with a capital of $100,000.00, for the manufacture of table, butcher's, hunting and carving knives. Their works are located at the head of Main street, Bay State. The buildings are of brick, two-stories high, and four in number. They employ both steam and water-power. Their engine is of one hundred and fifty horse-power. Their water-power is one of the best on Mill river. They employ on an average two hundred and twenty-five men, and produce $160,000.00 worth of cutlery annually.

The Clement Manufacturing Co., incorporated in July, 1882, with a capital of $32,000.00, are manufacturers of cutlery at Bay State. The company was formed in 1880. In 1882 William W. Lee became manager of the concern. They employ one hundred and twenty-five men.

The Florence Tack Co. was organized in 1874, under the superintendence and management of George W. Bond, of Florence, who made the original drawings for the machines, which were made at Florence under his directions. The company was fairly under way when the factory and machinery was destroyed by an incendiary fire in March, 1876. The company rebuilt and repaired its works and machinery, and commenced running again in 1877. It is now manufacturing about forty tons of goods per month. This company manufactures all kinds of tacks, brads, finishing, Hungarian, trunk, chair and other small nails, between three and four hundred different sizes.

The Florence Machine Co., incorporated in 1877, capital stock $175,-000.00 manufacture sewing machines, oil stoves and cabinet work at Florence.

The Damon Narrow Fabric Co., incorporated January 1, 1882, with capital of $35,000 00, manufacture cotton tape.

The Riverside Lumber Co., John M. Turner, president, and Henry W. Clapp, treasurer, has a mill off from South street and near Mill river, on the line of the N. H. & N. H. R. R., for the manufacture of lumber, lath, doors, sash, blinds and mouldings. Their works are run by steam-power. The company was formed in 1884, and succeeded to the business established by Henry W. Clapp eight years previous to that date. They employ twenty men. Their business amounts yearly to $42,000.00. They have a capital of $20,000.00.

The Mill River Button Co.'s factory is established at Leeds. The present company was organized November 1, 1874, with a capital stock of $60,-000.00. After the great flood which swept away their factory and entailed a loss of $100,000.00, the present mill was built. It is of brick, two stories high, 40x125 feet. The mill employs 175 hands, producing 600 gross of finished buttons per day, using 600 to 700 tons of vegetable ivory nuts annually.

The Connecticut River Lumber Co., mills located in the southeastern part of the city, was incorporated in 1878. They have the largest lumber mills in this section of the country.

The Crystal Emery Wheel Co.'s works are located on Hawley street, near the Connecticut River Railroad station. The business was first started at Easthampton, in 1879, by Charles E. Stevens, and the present company was incorporated in 1880 with a capital of $15,000.00, and business commenced at their present location. The company's specialty is corundum and emery wheels of all sizes and for all purposes. They employ a dozen hands.

The Northampton Emery Wheel Co.'s works are located at Leeds. The company was incorporated in May, 1879, with a capital of $100,000.00. They manufacture emery wheels and machinery.

Horace Lamb Co., on Clarks avenue, have a large establishment for the manufacture of all kinds of wire. Their power is water from Mill river. They employ twenty hands. Mr. Lamb first started the business at North Hadley nearly twenty years ago, and fifteen years ago removed to this town, where the work has been constantly increasing. Theirs is the only factory of its kind in Hampshire county. They manufacture three hundred tons annually.

John G. Clapp's foundry and machine shop is located at the corner of Pleasant and Holyoke streets. He succeeded his father, William R. Clapp, in the business in the autumn of 1880. In 1848 William purchased a small foundry on the present location, of a Mr. Brown. A few years subsequent the old foundry was destroyed by fire, and Mr. Clapp then built the one now in use, and about twenty years later put up the building now used as a machine shop.

Stephen Rust's saw and planing-mill, at Loudville, was built by Zenas Kingsley about forty years ago, and was purchased by Mr. Rust in 1866. He does all kinds of sawing, planing and box-making, employing about three men.

Caleb Loud's paper-mill, at Loudville, was built by him in 1879–80, upon the site of one burned in 1878, which was built about forty years previous. He employs seven hands and turns out about 1,000 pounds of paper per day, mostly colored tissue paper.

John Watson's paper-mill, at Loudville, was built by him in 1867, upon the site of the old Fish mill, built by Fish & Lyman about forty years previous, and which was carried off by a freshet in 1867. Mr. Watson now employs eleven hands, and turns out about three tons of tissue paper per week.

The Easthampton Paper Co.'s mill, at Loudville, was built by John Watson, about 1865. This mill, a wood structure, was burned about 1874, and a brick building was immediately erected upon its site, which was in turn destroyed by fire in 1879, when the present brick structure was erected. Mr. Watson took Albert Chamberlain in partnership with him in 1867, and they sold the mill to the Easthampton Paper Co., in 1883. They failed, and the property went into the hands of a receiver in 1884, and the mill has been idle since.

E. N. Foote & Co. have the only manufactory for fancy metal buttons in the county. It is located on Masonic street. The works were established in 1860. They employ seventy-five hands and turn out seventy-five thousand dollars worth of buttons annually.

Clarence E. Brown, at 41 Center street, has a large establishment for silver and nickel plating. The business was started September 20, 1881, in a little room in the building now occupied by the Crystal Emery Wheel Company. Subsequently he removed to his present location, built a shop and put in a five horse-power engine. His work comes largely from abroad. Two men are constantly employed.

Luther J. Warner, at the terminus of Elm street, has a factory for the manufacture of silk.

Rodolphus Smith manufactures brooms and brushes at 22 Washington avenue. He has carried on the business in this town and city for thirty-one years. In October, 1878, he set up in his present location, doing most of the work himself.

The Manufacture of Nitrate of Iron is carried on under the firm name of A. King & Co., at Florence, Luther H. Bosworth, manager. It was established in 1876, by Albert King, and carried on by him until his death, in January, 1886. The product is used principally in coloring silk.

W. C. Goodwin, at 48 North Maple street, Florence, manufactures all

25*

kinds of wood packing-boxes. The business was established by him in 1877. He employs steam power, and on an average five hands.

William Pollard has an establishment for the manufacture of soft soap, off South street, Florence, and deals in ashes, bones, etc. He commenced business September, 1885.

A. L. Williston manufactures Payson's Indellible Ink. The business was established in 1834, by the father of the present proprietor, J. Payson Williston.

W. W. Boynton has a bottling establishment on River street, where he manufactures soda water of different flavors, and also charges syphons and fountains.

Milo L. Smith, at Smith's Ferry, has a manufactory for vinegar. The business was first started by Charles H. Smith, forty years ago, who carried it on for a number of years, when Milo J. Smith, his brother, went into company with him, which partnership continued fifteen years, and as Milo J. Smith & Son until the death of Milo J., in 1884. At present Milo L. carries on the business alone, and Charles H. has also a manufactory by himself. Milo L. produces from 500 to 800 barrels annually of pure cider vinegar. Of the former's business Lyman H. Briggs is manager and half owner. They make about 1,000 barrels of vinegar per year.

Day Brothers, in 1875, established the manufacture of brick on South street. They employ in the business an average of twenty-five hands through the brick-making season, turning out 2,500,000 bricks. They have also on South street a steam saw-mill, started in 1883. It gives employment to four men, and furnishes a large quantity of wood for their brick yard, and produces a half-million feet of lumber annually.

C. W. Kinney, on King street, has granite and marble works. It was established by A. Rankin at an early date, and has been carried on by C. W. Kinney and his father since 1845. He employs four hands and turns out ten thousand dollars worth of work annually.

E. P. Root carries on a manufacturing business in carriages, wagons and sleighs, on Fruit street, Florence.

Edson P. Clark has works on Strong avenue for the manufacture of Clark's indelible pencil, lead pencils and penholders. The business was established by him in 1859, and been continuously carried on since that date. He uses a ten horse-power steam engine, which furnishes the working power. In connection with the above named business he also does job printing.

R. B. Davis & Son carry on the manufacture of carriages on South street. The business was established on the same location of Luther Davis, in 1809. After his death, in 1861, Richard B. and George Davis, his sons, formed a co-partnership and continued until the death of George, May, 1884, when the present firm was formed. They manufacture carriages, wagons, sleighs and anything in that line, employing seven men.

Richard P. Smith started a grist-mill on Clark's avenue in February, 1885,

Elijah H. Bartlett having carried on the business at the same location one year previous to that time. Water from Mill river furnishes the power. He uses three runs of stones, doing custom and sale grinding. He employs three men.

Porter Nutting has a brick yard on Elm street. He established the business forty years ago, and has continued it at the same place since. He gives employment to twelve or fifteen men. His annual product is one million bricks.

Martin & Hill established the manufacture of Martin & Hill cash carriers at Florence, in 1882. Joseph C. Martin is the inventor of the carrier. They have a large building near the N. H. & N. R. R. station, and employ twenty-five men. Their system of cash carrying is adapted to the use of the largest establishments.

Amos Sawyer began the manufacture of soap at the location of his present factory on Locust street, in 1853. He employs ten men.

Mrs. Susan P. Temple, at 13 Market street, manufactures all kinds of human hair goods, artificial flowers, hair wreaths, watch chains, etc. The business was established in February, 1885.

H. B. Bartlett's steam saw-mill, on road 28, was built by him in 1885, to take the place of one destroyed by fire in September of that year, and which was built by him in 1880. Mr. Bartlett employs two men and turns out about 25,000 feet of lumber per week, doing custom work.

C. H. Brewster, florist and seedsman, located on South street, began business at this location in 1881, removing from Pleasant street, where he had been in business about ten years. He has on South street two acres. He has about 8,000 feet of green-house under glass. He makes a specialty of plants, shrubs and cut-flowers. Employs four hands.

A. M. Ewing's steam laundry, on road 41, was established by him in 1879, though the business had been conducted in a smaller way by him and his father for the past thirty years. He has lately added new machinery, which enables him to do all classes of work, including carpets, spreads, blankets, comfortables, etc. His machinery has the capacity for turning out 500 pieces per day.

PUBLIC INSTITUTIONS.

The State Lunatic Hospital.—In 1854 the movement was begun which resulted in the establishment of this important charity. This initiatory step was the appointment, under the authority of a resolve of the legislature, of a committee to inquire into the number and the condition of insane persons in the state. This committee, which consisted of ex-Gov. Levi Lincoln, Dr. Edward Jarvis and the Hon. Increase Sumner, completed their labors and recommended that a hospital be established in the western part of the commonwealth. Their suggestion was favorably entertained by the legislature, and Northampton was decided upon as the location for the institution.

Land was purchased in a beautiful part of the suburbs of what was then the village, and in March, 1856, the erection of the main building was begun. On the following 4th of July the corner-stone was laid, the ceremony being conducted by the Masonic Fraternity, and on July 1, 1858, the institution was opened for patients. It stands upon a commanding elevation at the distance, in a straight line, of about a mile, nearly due west of the station of the Connecticut River Railroad. The building (see frontispiece) is of brick, the central block being four stories in height, above the basement, with sectional wings on the two sides, three stories high above the basement. This block extends, in the rear, to a depth originally of 190 feet, but now, by additions, about 270 feet ; and the fartherest section of each wing has a corresponding rear extension of 85 feet. The front line of the building is 512 feet in length, and the area of all the floors is about four acres. The central block is surmounted by an observatory, which affords one of the finest landscape views in the Connecticut valley. There is a smaller cupola upon the central section of each wing.

The original cost of farm, buildings and furniture was $343,000.00. Since the erection of the hospital, however, various improvements and additions have been made. A large proportion of the floors have been relaid, a laundry has been added to the main building, and store-houses. carpenter-shop, etc., erected. In the four years next following its opening, the state appropriated for lands and outbuildings, $15,550.00. Since 1867 the institution has not only been self-supporting, but has purchased land and dwellings, erected buildings, and made other extensive improvements, at a pecuniary cost stated further on.

The hospital was opened by William H. Prince, M. D., as superintendent, who remained until 1864, when Dr. Pliny Earle was appointed to the position, and held it until October 1, 1885. He was succeeded by the present incumbent, Dr. Edward Beecher Nims. Dr. Earle was thus at the head of the institution a period of twenty-one years, and largely to his great executive power, and his ability as a financier does the hospital owe its exceptional financial success. In illustration of this, we quote the following paragraphs from the institution's report for the official year 1884–85 :—

" In april, 1865, the hospital was free from debt, and the financial statement at the close of that month showed a balance of $302.04 in its favor. Between that time and the first of June, 1867, it received a direct bond from the state of $5,000 00 in two appropriations, for specific purposes,—one of $2,000.00 and the other of $3,000.00,

" As an offset to the $5,000.00 bonds, the hospital has purchased and paid for several lots of land, amounting to nearly one hundred and seventy-five acres. together with four dwelling houses. The total cast of this real estate was $30,883.92. The state, then, has, in this way alone, been overpaid for its bonds, in the sum of $25,883.92.

" The amount paid by the hospital for repairs and improvements in the course of the twenty years, from September 30, 1865, is $233,702.44.

"The surplus of cash assets now on hand, including the reserve fund, is $31,819.27, or $31,517.23 larger than it was on the 30th of April, 1865.

"The purchased provisions and supplies, including fuel and stored clothing now on hand, are estimated to have cost $14,762.87. The estimated value of similar supplies on the 30th of April, 1865, was $2,500.00. The increase of assets under this head is, therefore, $12,262.87.

"The value of household furniture in the hospital is, at a low estimate, at least $10,000.00 greater than it was on the 30th of April, 1865, at the same rate or standard of appraisal. To be certain, however, of no exaggeration, let it be called $8,000.00. Collecting these several sums, the account of debit of the commonwealth to the hospital appears to be as follows:—

Excess of cost of land over direct bonus.................... $ 25,883.92
Repairs and improvements...............................   233,702.44
Excess of present cash asset............................   31,517.23
Increase of provisions and supplies..................... .. 12,262.87
Increase of furniture.....................................   8,000.00

Total...$311,366.46

"The necessary current repairs of the buildings may be estimated at $3,000.00 annually. Deducting this sum for each of the twenty years since September 30, 1865, a total of $60,000.00, there is a remainder of $251,366.-46. To this amount, then, has the hospital assisted itself to things, for most of which it is generally expected that such institutions will rely upon direct appropriations from the treasury of the commonwealth.

"In the preparation of this summary, we have taken into account only the actual disbursements of money by the hospital, in contributing to its own improvements. But aside from this, a large amount of work, in effecting those improvements, was performed by the teams of horses and cattle belonging to the institution, and by the regular corps of its employees. Agreeably to all correct business principles, as well as to the custom at some similar institutions, the hospital should be credited with the amount of the value of this labor. But no credit has ever been given for it. Many thousands of dollars might, in this direction, be justly added to the sum above mentioned, as the products of the efforts of the hospital in the promotion of its own material progress.

"In connection with the above exposition, it may be interesting to know to what extent the tax-payers of the state have contributed to the institution. From a list, furnished by the state treasurer, of all the appropriations made either for the construction, the repairs, or the improvements of the hospital, I find that, from the time of the passage of the act authorizing its erection, down to the present day, it has cost the people of the commonwealth only three hundred and seventy-five thousand five hundred and fifty dollars."

The hospital-farm has been increased by the various purchases mentioned to about 365 acres, and is now sufficiently large for the necessities of the institution. The site is admirably adapted to the purpose to which it is devoted, and a large proportion of the soil is available for tillage and pasturage. Somewhat more than 300 acres of the land is in one tract, nearly a mile in length from east to west, and varying from a quarter to half a mile in width from north to south. It is bounded on the north, for a distance of a little more than a mile and one-fifth, by Mill river; and on the south, through its whole length (a distance, including curves, of 6,084 feet, or a fraction over a mile and forty-eight rods), by a public highway. Thus its situation is such that, although in the immediate vicinity of a pretty large town, it can be subjected to that seclusion and isolation which are important to the treatment of the insane, with but comparatively little inconvenience to the surrounding inhabitants. Its position, and the irregularities of its surface, combine to invest it with the possibility of becoming one of the most beautiful of estates. Nature has done her share of the work ; and it now awaits the full share of art, a portion of which it is from year to year receiving.

The present trustees and resident officers are as follows : Lyman D. James, of Williamsburg, Hon. Christopher C. Merritt, of Springfield, Silas M. Smith, Esq , and Mrs. Sarah M. Butler, of Northampton, Mrs. Sarah A. Woodworth, of Chicopee, and Adams C. Deane, M. D., of Greenfield, trustees ; Edward B. Nims, A. M., M. D., superintendent and treasurer ; Daniel Pickard, M. D., first assistant physician ; David G. Hall, M. D., second assistant physician ; Emily F. Wells, M. D., third assistant physician ; Walter B. Welton, clerk ; John Mercier, farmer ; Danford Morse, engineer.

The Smith Female College was founded and endowed by Miss Sophia Smith, of Hatfield, who died in 1870, bequeathing for that purpose an estate valued at $386,000 00, to which, by the terms of the will, the town added $25,000.00. The property is now valued at more than $500,000.00. The college was dedicated July 14, 1875. It stands on the site of the Judge Lyman homestead, on Elm street, facing Main. An art gallery has recently been added, and Winthrop Hillyer, of this city, donated the handsome sum of $30,000.00 for the erection of an art building, which stands on the college grounds. Mr. Hillyer also left a bequest of $50,000.00 for a permanent endowment.

Northampton Free Public Library was established in 1860. The whole number of volumes is 17,161. The lot on which the building is located was purchased in 1868, and in 1872–73 the building was erected, at a total cost of $77,249.00. The library was opened to the public March 30, 1874. Chairman, W. P. Strickland ; secretary, J. R. Trumbull ; librarian, main library, Miss Caroline Laidley. Library hours every week day, except holidays, from 9 o'clock A. M., to 8 P. M. Librarian, Florence branch, Miss Mary Fuller.

Clarke Institution for Deaf Mutes is located on Round hill. It was founded by John Clarke, who donated $50,000.00 for its establishment during his life time, and bequeathed $223,500 00 additional in his will, making an endowment of $273,500.00. The school was established in 1867, the Round Hill property purchased in 1870, and new buildings erected, and the old ones enlarged. Additional buildings have since been erected.

Florence Kindergarten, founded by Samuel L. Hill, who left by will, an endowment of property sufficient to make it free for ever. Incorporated in 1884. President, A. T. Lilly, and secretary, H. B. Haven.

Smith Charities was founded by Oliver Smith, of Hatfield, who died December 22, 1845, leaving an estate valued at $370,000.00. In his will he directed that a board of trustees should be constituted in the following man-

ner: The towns of Northampton, Hadley, Hatfield, Amherst and Williamsburg, in Hampshire county, and Deerfield, Greenfield and Whately, in Franklin county, shall choose at each annual meeting a person who shall be called
an elector. The electors were to choose three persons who should constitute a board of trustees, who were to have control and management of all the
funds. He then set apart the sum of $200,000.00, which was to be managed
by the trustees as an accumulating fund, till it should amount to the sum of
$400,000.00. This accumulated fund was then to be divided into three dis-
tinct funds: One, of $30,000.00, to found the "Smith Agricultural School,"
at Northampton; second, $10,000.00, the income to be paid to the American
Colonization Society, under certain restrictions. The society failing to comply with the terms of the will, this fund was incorporated with the Agricultural fund. The third, of $360,000.00, for indigent boys, indigent female
children, indigent young women and indigent widows. The remaining portion
of his property was constituted a contingent fund to defray expenses and keep
the principal funds entire.

PRIVATE INSTITUTIONS.

The *Cooley Dickinson Hospital* was built in 1885, and was formally opened
January 1, 1886. Its object as stated in the bequest by its founder, the
late Caleb C. Dickinson, of Hatfield, is "to establish and put in operation in
the town of Northampton a hospital for the sick poor of the towns of Hatfield, Whately and Northampton, where they may receive such care, nursing
and medical attendance as their diseases and sicknesses may require, either
gratuitously or at a moderate charge according to the circumstances of each."
Mr. Dickinson in his will further says, "It is my design with the property
which a kind Providence has given me to found a hospital where the sick
among the poor of said towns shall be tenderly and kindly provided with
such care and treatment as their condition needs, and which in numerous
cases it is impossible for them to receive in their homes, and the same to be
wholly or in part free of charge." The building is a handsome wooden
structure, situated on the tract formerly occupied by Dr. Denniston's water
cure, on North Elm corner of Locust street. The lot embraces sixteen acres,
ten acres of which was given by the city of Northampton. The grounds are
being improved and put in order rapidly. George W. Hubbard and John
Whittelsey of Northampton, and William H. Dickinson of Hatfield, are
trustees of the institution; Miss Eva A. Castle is matron and superintendent.

Northampton City Alms House.—The city furnishes support for its aged,
insane and otherwise helpless poor, at an alms house situated on North
Prospect street. It embraces a two-story brick house with two extensions of
wood, also of two stories, and thirty-seven acres of land. It is under the
supervision of Oscar J. Damon, as warden, and Mrs. Damon as matron, with
a requisite number of assistants. The average number of inmates is fourteen.

Shady Lawn Sanitarium.—The character, peculiarities or usefulness of institutions, as of men, may differ with the point of view from which they are regarded. For their abilities may lie in more lines and fields than one, and their services may be multiple.

Thus Shady Lawn, an institution which its locality and the state owe entirely to Dr. Austin White Thompson, as elsewhere stated in this work, may be viewed on its public or its private side, with reference to its work in treating insanity and the various inebrieties, or with reference to its, perhaps, more conspicuous achievements in general surgery and in the surgical and other treatment of diseases peculiar to women ; or still again as a health resort for troubles of the nervous system and other ailments that can be better managed and cured away from the sufferer's home, and with the equipment, organization, discipline and method of a hospital competently governed, and liberally and conscientiously supplied and overseen.

It has its public side. This is turned towards the state authorities. By them its proprietor is officially addressed as " Superintendent of the Shady Lawn Lunatic Hospital," and in virtue of this official position he, no more than the superintendents of the state lunatic hospitals, can retain and treat lunatics and inebriates, *as such*, unless they have been committed to his hospital by a court of jurisdiction according to law. Precisely like the state superintendents, he has full sanction and authority to retain such patients as have been thus committed ; but quite differently, on the other hand, by reason of the private character of his asylum, Dr. Thompson may decline any case, thus excluding such as would be undesirable companions for cases already grouped together. For the state hospitals must admit all cases that are sent to them by the courts, no matter what the nature or severity of their insanity. It should not, however, be inferred that acute cases, with trying features that compel the removal of the lunatic from home and family, can not be cared for at Shady Lawn. Many persons, violently seized with mania, have been successfully treated there and have been restored and returned to their friends. It need hardly be said that in a private hospital special care can be given to cases whose means permit, and whose nurture and tastes require comforts or luxuries ; and that the most scientific treatment, thus individuated, is for that reason actually more effective and hopeful, especially in acute cases early committed. With veteran and agreeable attendants and a limitation of the number of inmates, a special environment and mental atmosphere can be commanded for insane cases in a private hospital ; and then, in this one, the insane come in social contact with other patients who are not mentally afflicted, to the great advantage of the former class.

Another important particular, wherein Shady Lawn differs from the state institutions for the insane and inebriates, relates to the law forbidding the public hospitals to admit patients who do not belong in the commonwealth. Shady Lawn is under no such restriction ; but has received the greater share of its cases from beyond the borders of Massachusetts. All parts of the

AUSTIN WHITE THOMPSON.

Union, including the West and California, and Cuba and Canada, have contributed inmates. An interesting and impressive illustration and result of the polyglot blending of nationalities in Dr. Thompson's establishment was the decoration of his grounds for a Fourth of July celebration, some years ago, with the flags of Germany, Spain and Great Britain, intertwined with the stars and stripes, subjects of all those powers, being then members of his resident *clientele*.

To no class of its residents, we judge, has Shady Lawn been more truly a home, or better than home, than to the aged *demens*, with decrepit health, whose broken and confused minds have made them an impossible feature in their own families. They must have, for their best comfort, the constant ministrations of both nurse and physician in a way requiring method and discipline quite foreign to domestic life. They must be controlled. They can be amused. So their life becomes more bright and orderly, and much suffering is spared them; while the relief to their relatives at home is unspeakable. Quite a number of aged persons thus necessarily, but pleasantly exiled from their homes have passed in this retreat the last few years of their lives. They have represented prominent families in many parts of the country.

Thus far the history of this sanitarium in its relations to the insane and inebriates, who have made up the larger part of its constituency. And here in passing we may appropriately mention that it is the only private lunacy and inebriate hospital in Western Massachusetts; and it is due Dr. Thompson to say that it is conducted upon the principles of regular medical science and the ethics of quiet self-respect—without 'ism or 'pathy, or the assumption of mystery, cant or quackish arts.

It remains to speak of the surgical side of his work. And this has been probably more brilliant, because more original, and because the performance and results of surgery are more visible and demonstrable than are the delicate labors that must be done for, and with the darkened minds under treatment for lunacy as the prime disorder.

In surgery, as in medicine, there are specialties that naturally arise in the practice; and one class of surgical cases that separate themselves from the generality in experience are such as are more safely attempted under hospital means, facilities and safeguards, where, during convalescence from operations, the surgeon can be constantly under the same roof with the patient. This division of surgical cases includes a good part of operations deliberately attempted for the restoration of health, when possible through surgical means, such as the removal of tumors, for example; and is distinguished from cases of accident and emergency that must be cared for wherever the accident befell. Shady Lawn receives for operation and care such cases as the former; and the test of experience has shown that its large grounds, its retirement from business streets and its equipment have given the very best results, even in midsummer.   Conservative surgery may, therefore, be said to have been, and to be, one of its features.

But it is with a surgical specialty, more strictly speaking, that this institution has been chiefly and prominently concerned, viz.: with that of the diseases peculiar to women.   Gynaecology is the name given to this branch of the science.   It is cultivated in the larger cities of the world, whither cases are commonly sent for operation, as are cases requiring delicate attentions to the eye or the ear.   In this very interesting and important field of Gynaecology Shady Lawn has been doing notable work ; indeed, in one particular it has made an epoch and won a distinction for Northampton that we are the first to record for permanent history.

In May, 1879, Dr. Thompson performed what is known as " Battey's operation," from the name of the surgeon who first propounded it, its first performance in the New England states.   This operation is the removal of the ovaries from the abdomen, for the sake of relieving some disease that seems to be ascribable to those organs.   He has since done this operation a number of times, with complete success : and in every instance but one for the care of mental disorder.   Lacerations of the bladder and of the womb have been repaired, and other surgical work falling within the same specialty has been a regular and constant element in the business of the hospital.   But Dr. Thompson's priority in this part of the country in the difficult and important operation in question, and his altogether successful repetitions of it, deserve to be put on record for his credit and that of the city and county wherein it was done.   In this particular Northampton has the start of all New England, its " love of proud cities," and even its " Hub."   We hope that long usefulness and many triumphs await Shady Lawn in the future ; but in the achievement we have just recorded " its past at least is secure."

In concluding our sketch, our historian would beg to express his thanks to Dr. Thompson for a courteous and considerate reception and treatment.

The Mary A. Burnham Classical School.—It was not long after the establishment of Smith college when President Seelye saw the need of a preparatory school.   At this time Miss Bessie T. Capen held the chair of chemistry at the college, and was consulted by the president with reference to the matter.   Miss Capen, at his suggestion, wrote to Miss Mary A. Burnham, then in Vermont ; she came on here, and after a brief consultation plans were formulated, and in September, 1877, Miss Burnham started the school on the Lyman estate on Elm street.   The success of the venture was assured almost from the start.   In about two years the ell addition to the old Lyman house was put up, and in June, 1880, Miss Capen retired from the department of chemistry at the college, joined Miss Burnham's enterprise and took the late Rev. Gordon Hall's house on Elm street, for additional study room.   In 1882 the Talbot place on Prospect street was taken by Miss Capen, Miss Burnham continuing with the school on Elm street, the two of course being identical in interests. Miss Burnham died in 1884, and the school with an efficient corps of teachers, is conducted by Miss Capen.

BANKS.

Early Institutions.—The first bank established here was the "Northampton Bank," which was organized March 31, 1803. At its first meeting the following persons were chosen directors: Ebenezer Hunt, Jonathan Dwight, Samuel Porter, Oliver Smith, Benj. Prescott and Erastus Lyman. The directors subsequently made choice of Levi Shepherd as president, and Levi Lyman, cashier. They also voted to build a banking house, and that the bank should go into operation September 1, 1803. In October of the same year a new board of directors was chosen. Hon. Samuel Henshaw was elected president, and Mr. Lyman continued as cashier. The first half-yearly dividend was declared the second Monday of April, 1804. Whether the vote of the directors to erect a banking house was carried out, is not known. The bank was continued for ten or fifteen years, and its affairs were wound up soon after the establishment of the Hampshire bank.

On the 15th of August, 1813, the "Hampshire Bank" was organized, and the following directors chosen: Joseph Lyman, Ebenezer Mattoon, Seth Wright, Oliver Smith and Ebenezer Hunt, Jr. Joseph Lyman was chosen president, and Thomas Swan, cashier. The capital stock was $100,000. The banking house was on the site of the store now occupied by Merritt Clark, and a portion of the wall of the original building is still standing. This institution continued to do business for about twenty years, its only president being Hon. Joseph Lyman. The affairs of the bank were closed up soon after the establishment of the present Northampton bank, the stock-holders having the privilege of taking stock in the new bank. A few only availed themselves of the opportunity.

Northampton National Bank.—April 13, 1833, the Northampton bank was organized with a capital of $100,000.00, which in 1837 was increased to $200,000.00. Eliphlet Williams was chosen president, and J. D. Whitney, cashier. In 1865 the bank was re-organized under the national currency act, with the name it now bears, and the capital increased to $400,000.00. On the night of Tuesday, January 25, 1876, the bank was robbed of nearly a million dollars, which disaster has since been known as "the great Northampton bank robbery." The facts in relation to this robbery are too well known to require recapitulation here. The present officers are Oscar Edwards, president; J. L. Warriner, vice-president; and J. Whittelsey, cashier.

Northampton Institution for Savings.—This bank was incorporated March 1, 1842, and on the 1st of the following October the first meeting of the corporators was held, when C. P. Huntington was elected president, and S. L. Hinckley, secretary and treasurer. The incorporators of the bank were J. H. Butler, Samuel L. Hinckley and Stephen Brewer, and it owes its existence to the first mentioned of these gentlemen.   The present officers are H. G. Knight, president; L. Maltby, treasurer; and T. G. Spaulding, secretary.

First National Bank of Northampton.—The Holyoke bank was chartered in the spring of 1848, with a capital of $100,000.00.   At its organization John Clarke was chosen president, and Thomas Green, cashier.   In 1849 the capital of the institution was increased to $150,000.00, and in 1850, to $200,000.00.   On May 2, 1864, it was re-organized and took the name it now bears, and the capital increased to $300,000.00.   In 1865 it was again increased to $400,000.00, and in 1869 to $500,000.00.   The present officers are William B. Hale, president; H. F. Williams, vice-president; and Frederick N. Kneeland, cashier.

Hampshire County National Bank.—This institution was chartered in May, 1864, with a capital of $100,000.00, and commenced business in August of that year.   The prime mover in the enterprise was Luther Bodman, who was elected its first president and who still holds that position.   W. C. Robinson was the first cashier.   In December, 1864, the capital was increased to $200,000.00, and in 1865 to $250,000.00.   Lewis Warner is the present cashier.

The Hampshire Savings Bank.—This bank was organized in May, 1869, with J. C. Arms, president; Lewis Warner, treasurer, and Luther Bodman, secretary.   In 1873 Luther Bodman was chosen president, and still holds the position, with Lewis Warner, treasurer.

The Florence Savings Bank.—This institution was organized April 5, 1873, and began business May 6th of the same year.   A. T. Lilly was chosen president, and H. H. Bond, secretary and treasurer.   The former still holds the office, and M. W. Bond is treasurer.

HOTELS.

The Hotel Norwoood, on Bridge street; a cut of which appears herewith, is one of the most elegant, home-like and hospitable public houses to be found. Late in the last century there stood upon its site the famous "Tontine" buildings, which were destroyed by fire about 1815.   John Clarke, father of Christopher Clarke, bought the land, and, in 1827, built the present building for a private residence.   After his death it was purchased of his executors by the late ex-Lieut. Gov. Hayden, and was long known as the Hayden place. In the spring of 1886 it was taken by George W. Forbes, it having been recently remodeled, and was elegantly furnished and opened as a first-class hotel.   Its fine appearance is shown by the engraving.   Mr. Forbes is a hotel man of experience, popular and genial, and we predict for the young "Norwood" many years of prosperity.

The Mansion House, Rodney Brown, proprietor, is located on Main street. It is a well-kept, popular hotel.

The Hampshire House is located on Main street, corner of Strong avenue. *The City Hotel* is located on the corner of Pleasant and Pearl streets.

HOTEL NORWOOD, GEORGE W. FORBES, PROPRIETOR.

WATER WORKS.

The construction of the Northampton water works was commenced in May, 1871. The water is taken from Roberts's Meadow brook, one and one-half miles west of Leeds. There is a fall of ninety feet in Florence, and 244 feet at the railroad crossing in Bridge street. There are now laid twenty-six and two-thirds miles of pipe. The number of families taking water January 1, 1884, was 1,647, and the supply proving inadequate, a second reservoir was constructed, with a capacity of 16,500,000 gallons. The cost of the entire works, including the second reservoir, was $240,620.00. The water commissioners are D. W. Bond, president; Oscar Edwards, treasurer; H. F. Williams, clerk; Lucius Dimock, Josephus Crafts, J. S. Lathrop and Jonas M. Clark, superintendents.

GAS WORKS.

The original charter of the Northampton Gas Light Co. was issued in 1853, to William H. Stoddard, Samuel A. Fisk and Daniel Kingsley. The company was empowered to hold real estate to the amount of $50,000.00. The company was organized in 1855, and the works were completed in 1856, at a cost of $35,000.00. The capital was increased to $100,000.00. The present officers are M. M. French, president, and William B. Hale, secretary and treasurer.

CHURCHES.

The First Church of Christ, Congregational.—The organization of a church was always a primary object in the settlement of new towns and plantations in the Province of Massachusetts Bay. So it is not strange that the petitioners to the general court for liberty to plant in Nonotuck, should adduce as a principal reason that it was suitably located for "propagating the gospel," as it seemed desirable to them that "they might live and attend upon God in his holy ordinances without distraction." The next year after the arrival of the settlers a contract was made with five of the planters for the erection of a house of worship, the materials and dimensions of which are thus described:

"A house for the town of Norhampton, of sawen timber, twenty-six foot long and eighteen foot wide, nine foot high from the lower part of the cell to the upper part of the roisens."

Other specifications of minor importance followed. This edifice was undoubtedly used both for civil and religious purposes. In 1658 the town unanimously extended an invitation to Mr. Eleazer Mather "to be minister to them in the way of trial in dispensing his gifts." Mr. Mather came at once, and it was agreed that he should have for half a year £25 in "good merchantable wheat." And soon after it was voted to raise £100 to build a minister's house. A home-lot of four acres was also donated to Mr. Mather in case he remained with them four years. This lot was bounded by Main and Pleasant streets. Seven years after the settlement and three years after the call to Mr. Mather, a church organization was effected. This singular vote appears in 1663: "Each person will contribute towards defraying the charge of the sacrament three pecks and half of wheat for a year," to be paid "to the deacon when he shall call for it."

Mr. Mather died after ministering to the church about eleven years. Rev. Solomon Stoddard succeeded Mr. Mather in 1672. The terms of his settlement were: Meadow land of the value of £100 and £100 a year for his support, £100 to build a house, the use of £100 worth of sequestered land for an indefinite period, and a home lot of four acres, upon the condition that Mr. Stoddard " doth settle and abide amongst us." On the fifth of November, 1672, the following significant note was passed by the church. It was the entering wedge, if not the very marrow of the "half-way covenant" doctrine which was destined nearly three-quarters of a century afterwards to exert a momentous influence upon the internal peace and harmony of the church in Northampton, and is inserted exactly as it appears upon the records :—

" Voted & consented unto by the Elders & Brethren of this church, that from year to year such as grow up to adult age in the church shall present themselves to the Elders, & if they be found to understand & assent unto the doctrine of faith not to be scandalous in life, & willing to submit themselves to the government of Christ in this church, shall publicly own the covenant & be acknowledged members of this church."

It may be remarked in this connection that, as will be seen by the preceding paragraph, the constitution of the " Half-way covenant" system was the work of the church itself, and not of the pastor, although accepted and defended by the latter. This departure from established usages was first assailed by Dr. Increase Mather, of Boston, in a sermon entitled "The Order of the Gospel." To this Mr. Stoddard replied with rare ability, and seemingly had the best of the argument, as his opponent gradually suffered the controversy to subside. It was only renewed when his grandson and successor, Jonathan Edwards, re-opened the whole question. During Mr. Stoddard's ministry, nearly the whole adult population was embraced within the pale of the church. On one occasion about fourteen hundred persons were ascertained by actual count, to be listening to one of his admirable discourses. His active pastorate extended through the long period of fifty-seven years. From such accounts as have come down to the present time, it appears that he was frequently, if not generally, an extemporaneous preacher.

The first meeting-house was converted into a school-house, and the second edifice was erected in 1663. A committee was appointed to assign seats to individuals and families, with directions to regard " age, estate, qualifications, only respecting commissioned officers and impartiality." This was somewhat vague. The new house was forty-two feet square. It was not until 1682 that steps were taken to procure a bell. Up to that time the people had been called together for public worship by the beating of a drum or the blowing of a trumpet. Jedediah Strong received 18s. per year for several years for blowing the trumpet on the Sabbath.

An accident occured in this meeting-house on the 13th of March, 1737, which may be briefly alluded to. While Mr. Edwards was conducting divine service, the gallery, full of people of all ages, fell upon those who were seated below. Of the hundreds who were involved in the ruins some were severely bruised, but fortunately, no bones were broken.

The third pastor of the church was Rev. Jonathan Edwards. Mr. Edwards was emphatically a great man, a profound thinker, and the most logical reasoner of his time. But he became involved in a little controversy with his people and his pastorate terminated in 1750. The third meeting-house was erected in 1738.

The fourth pastor was Rev. John Hooker, a grandson of Rev. Thomas Hooker, one of the founders of the Connecticut colony and the first minister of Hartford. He married Sarah Worthington, sister of Colonel John Worthington, of Springfield, an eminent lawyer, but favorable to the growing incroachments of the English crown upon the rights and privileges of the colonies, wherein he differed from nearly all his contemporaries in Western Massachusetts. Mr. Hooker was installed in 1753, and died in 1777, of small-pox after a pastorate of twenty-three years. It is stated that his style of preaching was simple and unaffected, direct and earnest.

His successor, Rev. Soloman Williams, was a native of East Hartford, Conn. It is said that at his ordination dinner the town furnished "one hundred and six pounds of beef, pork and veal," but declined to pay for any liquors. He married the daughter of his predecessor, Mr. Hooker. His success as a preacher was somewhat remarkable. During his ministry nearly one thousand persons were added to the church. He died in 1834 at the great age of eighty-two.

Those who succeeded Mr. Williams were : Mark Tucker, 1824–27 ; Ichabod S. Spencer, 1828–32 ; Joseph Penny, 1833–35 ; Charles Wiley, 1837–45 ; E. Y. Swift, 1845–51 ; John P. Cleveland, 1853–55 ; Zachary Eddy, 1858–67, and William S. Leavitt succeeded Mr. Eddy in 1867, and was followed by the present pastor, Rev. Herbert W. Lathe.

It was a common remark in the first half of the present century, that to be a member of the "Old Church" and own meadow-land assured the social position of any citizen of Northampton. Probably no inland town or city in New England can show such an imposing array of learned, able and eloquent ministers as the First Congregational society of this city. Every one of them was superior to the average preachers of his time.

The fourth meeting-house was a spacious edifice, erected in 1812. It was one hundred feet in length and seventy-five in width ; and the spire reached an elevation of one hundred and forty feet. One thousand persons could be comfortably seated in its pews. It was destroyed by fire, June 27, 1876. The present church, erected on the site of the former one in 1878, is a large and imposing structure of stone.

The Second Congregational church, Unitarian.—In the beginning of the present century a liberal element was manifesting itself in the Congregational churches of New England. This gradually assumed the form of Unitarianism, and was irreconcilably adverse to the opinions and views of the conservative or Calvinistic party. Unitarianism had made some inroads upon the Old Church. One-third of the taxable property of the society belonged to men of liberal sentiments, and among their number was a large proportion of the leading men of the town. They had remained quiet under the expectation that when a new pastor was settled some respect would be paid to their peculiar opinions in the way of ministerial exchanges. Space will not permit a statement of the details of the controversy that ensued on the settlement of Mr. Tucker as the colleague of Mr. Williams. It is sufficient to say that all attempts to harmonize the differences of the two parties utterly failed. The liberals were voted down on every proposition they made to the majority, and no alternative remained but to secede and form a new church society. This was done on the 22d of February, 1825, by the organization of the "Second Congregational chnrch and society of Northampton." The church edifice was completed and dedicated the same year, on which occasion a sermon was delivered by Rev. Henry Ware, Jr., of Boston. Many families of wealth, refinement and culture united in the formation of this religious society. The ministers have been Edward B. Hall, Oliver Stearns, subsequently professor of systematic theology in Harvard university; John S. Dwight, now, or recently conducting Dwight's *Journal of Music;* Rufus Ellis, later a popular preacher in Boston ; William Sillsbee, William L. Jenkins, William H. Fisk and Charles B. Ferry. The church building erected in 1825 is still in use. The present pastor is Rev. C. E. St. John.

The Edwards Congregational church.—This society is an offshoot of the Old Church, and was organized in 1833. It received its distinctive appellation in remembrance of Jonathan Edwards. The first pastor was Rev. John Todd, well known as the minister of the First church in Pittsfield. Other pastors were John Mitchell, E. P. Rogers, George E. Day, who was professor of Biblical literature in Yale Theological seminary, Gordon Hall and Isaac Clark. Their church building, erected in 1833, did service till 1872, when the present structure was built. The society now has 355 members.

The First Baptist church.—The Baptist church owes its existence mainly to the missionary labors of Elder Rand, who resided in that part of West Springfield now included within the limits of the city of Holyoke. Other clergymen of this denomination occasionally preached here. Subsequently, Benjamin Willard labored under the direction of the Baptist Missionary Society, performing much neighborhood work, and some conversions occurred. Mr. Willard encountered much opposition and many discouragements. It is

26*

said that when the rite of baptism was administered a great concourse of people assembled on the bank of the river to witness the immersion of the candidates.   A Baptist society consisting of eleven persons was organized in 1824,
and a church two years afterward.   By slow but constant accretion it now
numbers nearly three hundred.   The pastors have been Benjamin Willard,
Abel Brown, Jr., noted for his zeal in the anti-slavery cause, W. M. Dootittle,
H. D. Doolittle, D. M. Crane, D. Burrows, E. Jerome, I. D. Clark, G. L.
Hunt, C. Y. Swan, E. T. Hiscox, A. W. Jefferson.

First Methodist Episcopal church.—There was preaching in Northampton
by clergymen of the Methodist denomination in 1830, but the church was not
organized until twelve years afterwards.   The pastors have been numerous,
as frequent changes is the established usage of the Methodist church, and
may not be enumerated.   The present pastor is Rev. Wellen N. Richardson.

St. John's Protestant Episcopal church.—It was not until 1826 that any
movement was made for the organization of a Protestant Episcopal church
here.   The idea appears to have originated with Mr. Joseph G. Coggeshall,
who, in connection with the famous historian, George Bancroft, was conducting a school for boys on Round Hill.   But it was not until 1829 that the
building was opened for religious worship.   The consecration services were
performed by Bishop Griswold, of the diocese of Massachusetts.   Numerous
changes have occurred in the rectorship of the church, but it seems to be in
a prosperous condition, ninety communicants, and Rev. William P. Brush,
rector.   The first rector was Rev. Joseph Muenscher.

St. Mary's Roman Catholic church.—Strange as it may seem, the imposing
ritual of the Roman Catholic church was first chanted in the Old Church,
celebrated for its Calvinistic creed and Puritanic usages.   The occasion
was the religious services preparatory to the execution of James Holligan
and Patrick Daly for the murder of a man named Lyon, at Wilbraham, in
the old county of Hampshire, in the beginning of the present century.   The
trial of the alleged perpetrators of the crime was conducted in the meeting-
house, the primitive court-house being found inadequate to contain the multitude that assembled to witness the proceedings.   Jonathan Edwards Porter,
a grandson of the great Northampton pastor, defended the criminals, and
James Sullivan, afterwards governor of the commonwealth, conducted the
prosecution.   Both of these gentlemen won much distinction by the ability
they displayed during the trial.   It is yet an open question, in view of all the
known facts of the case, and the very slight evidence adduced on the trial, which
was purely of a circumstantial nature, whether these miserable men were actually
guilty of the horrible crime with which they were charged.   The masterly sum-
ming up of Porter and Sullivan probably excelled any intellectual effort within
the walls of the old building.   The celebrant of the mass was Father Cheverus,
of Boston.   He afterward returned to France, of which country he was a
native, and became a bishop of the Catholic church.   But it was at a comparatively recent period that the regular services of the church were estab-

lished. Religious worship was first conducted in the house of a man named Foley at Straw Hollow, now Leeds. In 1834 a lot on King street was secured for a church, but the building was not erected until ten years later. It has been enlarged several times. Recently the site of the old Mansion House was purchased, and a beautiful church has been erected. At first Northampton was attached to the Chicopee parish, and so remained until 1866, when it was detached and Rev. P. V. Moyce appointed pastor. The present resident pastor is Rev. M. E. Barry, a native of South Boston. This church has expanded in a marvellous manner and now constitutes a numerous congregation.

Florence Congregational church.—This church was organized in 1861, the first pastor being Rev. H. C. Hovey. He was succeeded in 1866 by Rev. E. G. Cobb, the present resident minister. Their church building, a fine wooden structure, was built in 1861.

The Florence Methodist Episcopal church.—This church was organized in 1871, and, in accordance with the custom of the church, has had several pastors whose term of service has been of limited duration. The first pastor was Rev. T. W. Bishop. The society now has 150 members, with Rev. James F. Allen, pastor. Their church building was completed in 1884.

The Free Congregational Society of Florence.—This is an institution somewhat peculiar in its character. It has no formulated creed, but seeks the truth and professes to make it the rule of life. "The brotherhood of the human race and the equality of human rights" are recognized, and "no distinction as to the conditions and rights of membership" are made "on account of sex, color, or nationality." The congregation occupy an elegant building erected at a cost of $40,000.00. A free platform is maintained by the society, and at various times it has been occupied by some of the most profound thinkers and orators in the country. The resident speakers have been Charles C. Burleigh, Mrs. Elizabeth Powell Bond, Rowland Connor and David H. Clark.

Church of the Immaculate Conception of Florence.—This society was organized by the Rt. Rev. P. T. O'Reilly, D. D., of Springfield, in 1877, and Rev. C. M. Foley was the first pastor. The church building was erected in 1880. The present pastor is Rev. John J. McMahon.

A Catholic church has been lately organized in the city by the Canadian French portion of the population.

———

PELHAM lies in the northeastern part of the county, and is bounded north by the county line, east by Prescott and Enfield, south by Enfield and Belchertown, and west by Amherst. Its average length, from east to west, is five and one-quarter miles, and its average width three and one-half miles, thus giving it an area of about 15,207 acres.

The surface of the town is rough and mountainous, presenting a wild and picturesque contour. Mt. Orient, the principal elevation, lies in the north-western part of the town, affording a grand view from its summit, about 1,000 feet above tide water. Mt. Lincoln, in the southern part of the town, and Pine hill, in the central part, are also prominent elevations. Though the country is so rough, rendering agriculture difficult, the soil is fertile and pro-ductive. Springs and streams are abundant. The principal of the latter is Fort river, which rises near the northern boundary of the town and flows a southwesterly course into Amherst, and thence on into the Connecticut. A branch of Swift river makes up the eastern boundary of the town. Both of these streams have several affluents.

Grant and Settlement.—Pelham originally formed a part of the "Equiva-lent Lands," whose history we have given in connection with the history of Belchertown. It only remains to say then, that this section of the "Equiv-alent Lands" was purchased by Col. John Stoddard and others, of North-ampton, whence it took the name of "Stoddard's Town," and remained in a wild and unsettled state with no effort made towards its settlement down to the year 1739.

On the 26th of September, of that year, Robert Peibles and James Thorn-ton, of Worcester, entered into a contract with Stoddard for the purchase of the land, with the purpose in view of taking thereto a colony of settlers. This project so far met with success that on January 31st the following deed was given to a company of persons, viz :—

"To all to whom these presents shall come, Greeting: Know yee that John Stoddard, of North Hampton, in ye County of Hampshire, in the Province of the Massachusetts Bay, in New England, for and in Considera-tion of the sum of seven thousand three hundred pounds, in bills of Public Creditt of ye old Tennor in hand already Received of the Persons herein-after named, the Receipt whereof he doth hereby acknowledge, and himself thereby fully satisfied and Contented, hath given, granted, bargained, and sold, and by these presents doth fully, freely, clearly, and absolutely Give, grant, Bargain, Sell, Release, convey, and confirm unto them, their heirs, and assigns forever, one-half (excepting eight hundred acres) of that Tract of Equivalent Land, lying and being in ye County of Hampshire, bounded Westerly on Hadley, Southwardly on another Tract of Equivalent land, commonly called Cold Spring Township, Eastwardly on land called Quobbin, North on land now called Well's Town, which Tract of land was laid out by Mathew Allin, Roger Woolcott, and Ebenezer Pomroy, Esq^s ., for Twenty-nine Thousand Eight Hundred and Seventy-four acres, a more particular Description of which land does appear by their Return, entered in ye Secre-tary's office at Boston, wch half part (excepting Eight hundred acres, as aforesaid), by a Division lately made by the owners or proprietors of said Equivalent land, is laid in severalty, and contained in ye first lott. and does contain ye whole of said Lott (excepting Thirty-eight acres Two Roods and thirty-three perch, which belongs to Mr. Elisha Williams Doct., of Yale Col-ledge), which Lott Lyeth on the north part of said Equivalent Land, and is bounded north by ye north Line of said Equivalent Land, and from said Line Extends south one Thousand and Eleven Rods and Eleven feet, to monuments Raised at Each end, and does extend from Hadley bounds on the West to the east bounds of said Equivalent land, a more particular description of which lott may be seen in ye Deed of partition, bearing Date ye seventh day of September, 1738, which said half (excepting as aforesaid) The said John Stoddard doeth hereby sell and Confirm, as aforesaid, to the following persons, and in ye following proportion (viz't): To Robert Peibles, five-sixfieth parts; To Patrick Peibles, one-sixtieth part; To Andrew Mc-Farland & Mathew Gray, Junr, Three-sixtieth parts; To Robert Lothridge, Two-sixtieth parts; To Robert Barber and William Johnson, Three-sixtieth parts; To William Gray, Jun., one-sixtieth part; To John McConkey, one-sixtieth part; To James McConkey, one-sixtieth part; To Alexander Mc-Conkey, one-sixtieth part; To Alexander Turner, one-sixtieth part; To John Stinson, one-sixtieth; To James Wood, one-sixtieth part; To Adam Johnson, Two-sixtieth parts; To Ephraim Cowon, one-sixtieth part; To George Cowon, one-sixtieth part; To Samuel Gray, two-sixtieth parts; To John Gray, Jr., three-sixtieth parts; To Thomas Dick, one-sixtieth part; To John Dick, one-sixtieth part; To John Alexander, one-sixtieth part; To James Alexander, one-sixtieth part; To James McAllach, one-sixtieth part; To Samuel Thomas, one-sixtieth part; To James Taylor, two-sixtieth parts (all the above-named persons are of Worcester, In the County of Worcester, except George Cowon, who is of Concord, in the County of Middlesex); To John Forguson, of Grafton, one-sixtieth part; To James Gilmore, of Boston, two-sixtieth parts; To Adam Patterson, of Leicester, in ye County of Worcester, one-sixtieth part; To Thomas Lowdon, of Leicester, one-sixtieth part; To John Chandler, of Worcester, Esq., one-sixtieth part; To John Johnson, of Shrowsbury, one-sixtieth part; To Adam Clark, of Worcester, one-sixtieth part; To James Thornton, of Worcester, fourteen-sixtieth parts.

"To have and to hold the aforesaid half part of said Equivalent Land (except the Eight hundred acres, as before excepted), and in that part Thereof above described, with ye appurtenances and priviledges thereto belonging to them, the above-named persons, their heirs and assigns, forever, according to their several and Respective proportions as before expressed, To their severall and Respective proper use, benefitt and behoofe for evermore. And the said John Stoddard for himself, his heirs, &c., doth covenant and engage to and with the before-named persons, their Respective heirs and assigns, that before and untill the ensealing hereof he was ye true, sole, and lawfull owner of the premises, and stood seized thereof in his own right, in Fee Simple, and had in himself good right, full power, and lawfull authority to grant, bargain, sell, alien, release, convey, and confirm the same, as aforesaid, and that free and clear and clearly executed, acquitted and discharged of and from all former and other Guifts, grants, Bargains, sales, leases, mortgages, wills, entails, Joyntures, Thirds, Executions, and In cumbrances whatsoever; and the said John Stoddard doth hereby further covenant and engage the before-granted premises with ye appurtenances to them the before-named persons and their Respective heirs and Assigns forever, to warrant same and defend against the Lawfull Claims and demands of any and every person and persons whatsoever.

"In Witness whereof, he hath hereunto set his hand seal this thirty-first day of January, in the twelfth year of the Reign of our Sovereign Lord George of Great Britain, &c., King Annoq. Dom. 1738–39.

"JOHN STODDARD."

On June 28, 1786, the eastern part of the town, with a part of New Salem, was incorporated as the East Parish of Pelham, and on January 28, 1822, this was set off to form the present township of Prescott.

Those named in the above deed and a few others became the first settlers of the town, about 1740. The territory took on the name of "Lishburne," or "New Lishburne," by which it was known down to the time of its organization, in 1743. The first proprietor's meeting held in the new township was August 6, 1740, at the house of John Ferguson. The growth of the township's population may be seen from the following figures : In 1776, its population was 729; 1790, 1,040; 1800, 1,144; 1810, 1,185; 1820, 1,278; 1830, 904; 1840, 956; 1850, 983; 1855, 789; 1860, 748; 1865, 737; 1870, 673; 1875, 633; 1880, 614.

It is possible that some of those who drew the original lots, never actually settled in Pelham. Among those who are positively known to have taken up their land, and established themselves thereon, may be mentioned Alexander Conkey, Robert Peibles, John Alexander, John Gray, James Taylor, Robert Lothridge, James McCulloch, Thomas Dick, Adam Petteson, Ephraim and George Cowen, James Hood, James Thornton, William Gray, John Ferguson, Adam and John Johnson, Samuel Thomas, Alexander Turner, and others. Other families of influence came in a little later. John Hunter appears to have been there in 1749, and John Clark and John Stinson some time before. The Crossett family came in about 1750. In 1752 appear John Savage, Patrick Peibles and John Blair. The Hamilton family, afterward one of the most prominent in town, appeared in the person of Thomas Hamilton, about the same time. A little later came David Thomas and James Harkness. The Berry family put in an appearance about 1755, along with John Crawford, David Houston and David Cowdan. Then appear in rapid succession the Mecklams (some of whom lived in Prescott), the McMullens, Halberts, Hollands, Thompsons, Livermores and others. The Kingman family, who were identified with the growth and development of the town for several generations, came in at the opening of the present century. Nathaniel Gray settled in Pelham at an early day. Oliver came from Walpole, and settled on the "Old Smith place." The Fales family, living in the western part of the town, is also one of the oldest now living in the town, having settled there the first part of the present century. The Newell, Jewett, Ward, Cook and Brewer families are also among the oldest and most influential now living in the town. Benjamin Randall was born in Belchertown, and settled in Pelham about 1830.

Isaac Presho, son of Zadok, was born in Raynham, Mass., in 1766, married Sarah Joslyn, and had born to him three children, William, Zadok and Lyman. Mr. Presho died April 25, 1808. William was born in 1792, married Melissa Crawford, had born to him two children, Anna and Merrick, and died in 1870. Zadok was born in 1795, married Betsey Robinson in 1817, and came to this town in 1820, locating on the farm now owned by his son Dwight. He reared nine children, viz.: Sarah A., Jane, Susan, Lurana, Rosina, Lyman, Betsey, Dwight and Julia. Mr. Presho died in 1869, aged seventy-four years. His widow is ninety-two years of age and lives on the homestead with her son Dwight. The latter was born in 1836, married Arvilla Phelps in 1861, and has three children, Fred D., Charles H. and J. Gertrude.

Seth Chapin married Mary Wood, in 1804, and reared six children, as follows: Emma, Cynthia, Sally, Seth, William and Calvin. The last mentioned was born in Dedham, Mass., July 14, 1816, came to Pelham to live with his uncle at the age of seven years, where he remained fourteen years. He married Amy Wedge, and has three children, Frances A., Mary A. and Frank W. Frances A. was born in 1843, married George W. Shaw, and has three children, Amy M., Hattie F. and Carl S. They live in Prescott. Mary A. was born in 1844, has married twice, first, Emory S. King, who died in 1876, leaving two children, Jennie A. and Jessie M., and second, Arthur O. Alden, and has two children, Ida A. and Sidney.

Sylvester Jewett was born in Northampton, August 18, 1824, married Maria, daughter of Cecil Jewett, in 1849, and has had born to him six children, viz.: Arthur C., Frank I., Charles P., Fred S., Maria and Martha A. (twins). Mr. Jewett came to this town in 1854, and is chairman of selectmen, which office he has held fourteen years.

The town of Pelham was legally incorporated by the general court, January 15, 1743, and was duly organized April 19, of the same year, at which meeting the following list of officers were elected: John Stoddard, moderator; Alexander Conkey, Robert Peibles, John Alexander, John Gray and Robert Lothridge, selectmen; William Gray, clerk; John Stinson, treasurer; James Taylor, John Conkey, John Johnson and Ephraim Cowan, surveyors. There were also some other minor offices filled.

The military history of the town is an honorable one. In the war of the Revolution it is said that nearly all the male residents took part in it. Just after the war, too, the town came into prominence as the dwelling-place of Daniel Shays, whose rebellion we have detailed on page 100. In 1812–15 the town furnished among others the following: Capt. John Taylor, John T. Conkey, Grove Hannum, Luther Thompson, Sydney Hannum, Henry Hannum, Luther Lincoln, James Smith, Amasa Jillson and Leonard Blue. In the late great war the town furnished seventy-eight men, being five over all calls. Of her wealth she gave $7,501.00, exclusive of the $4,125.96 which was subsequently reimbursed by the state.

VILLAGES.

There are really no villages in Pelham, though there are three quite considerable hamlets. The one containing the Pelham postoffice is located in the eastern part of the town, at what is known as "Pelham Heights." In the western part of the town, on the same street, is the "West End," another hamlet. In the extreme southeastern part of the town is the hamlet of Packardsville.

Eugene P. Bartlett's fishing-rod factory, located on what is called Amethyst brook, off road 11, was established by Horace Gray & Son, in 1860. They sold to Ward & Latham, in 1874, and they in turn to Bartlett Bros., in 1880 Eugene P. became sole proprietor in 1883, and has since largely increased the business. He employs about twenty hands, uses about 30,000 feet of native wood and $800.00 worth of lance-wood per year, making about 3,000 dozens rods, in 250 different styles.

L. W. Allen's saw-mill, located in the western part of the town, on Amethyst brook, gives employment to four men, cutting 250,000 feet of lumber. Mr. Allen also manufactures boxes here.

David Shores's saw-mill, on Purge brook, has a capacity for cutting 5,000 feet of lumber and 10,000 shingles per day.

W. J. Harris's turning and repair shop is located on road 26.

The Congregational church, located at the "Center," was coincident with the settlement of the town, though it was originally Presbyterian in form. As early as 1740 it was voted by the proprietors to "build a meeting-house," though it was several years before the building was completed. The first pastor, Rev. Robert Abercrombie, was ordained August 30, 1742. The present church building was erected in 1838.

The Union Congregational church of Packardsville was organized November 29, 1868, with nineteen male and fourteen female members, and Rev. W. K. Vaill was the first pastor, who still holds the office. The church building was erected in 1869. It will seat about 200 persons and is valued at about $4,000.00. The society now has about twenty members. Mr. Vaill also acts as pastor of the church at the "Center."

The Methodist Episcopal church.—The beginning of permanent Methodist worship in Pelham was in the spring of 1831, when Rev. Isaac Stoddard was invited to preach. Previous to that, meetings of a general character had been held in town. Mr. Stoddard was formally settled as pastor by the conference of 1831. In 1832 the society had grown to a membership of 125. In 1834, Pelham and Greenwich were connected together under the same pastoral charge. In 1836 the society occupied the old meeting-house on Pelham Heights, near the town-house. Between 1838 and 1843 the Methodist meeting-house in the west end of the town was erected. The deed for the original parsonage at the west end was made by Emory Ballou, July 5, 1847, "for the benefit of such men as shall be employed by the Methodist

Episcopal church to preach in the western part of Pelham," to the following trustees: Rufus Grout, David Newell, Lemuel C. Wedge, Horace Gray, Zadoc Preston, Ansel A. Rankin and John Sisson. This parsonage was used by the various ministers who have been in charge, until August 11, 1875, when it was sold and a new one erected, at a cost of $1,050.00, on land given for that purpose by Russell Whipple. The present pastor is Rev. Henry A. Jones.

———

PLAINFIELD* lies in the extreme northwestern corner of the county, has an area of about twenty square miles, being five miles in length from north to south and four miles in width from east to west, and is bounded north by Hawley and east by Ashfield, both in Franklin county, south by Cummington, and west by Savoy and Windsor, in Berkshire county.

The surface of the town is rough and mountainous, as it lies upon the eastern slope of the Green Mountain range of Massachusetts, and presents an almost endless variety of beautiful scenery. From Deer hill, in the southwestern part of the town, a magnificent view may be obtained. While the township is thus diversified and broken, there yet remains a large percentage of good arable land, with a strong, moist, fertile soil. Copious springs abound and many streams dance through the many valleys. Mill brook, a branch of Westfield river is the principal stream. This may also be said of the other streams and brooks, they flow a southerly course and help to swell the current of the Westfield river. North pond, in the northwestern corner of the town, is quite a romantic little body of water, surrounded by wild and picturesque scenery. Among the minerals found are two ores of manganese—rhodonite and pyrolusite—and the rare variety of hornblende, cummingtonite.

Grant, Settlement and Growth.—The original grant of this section, as " Township No. 5," its subsequent sale at public vendue at Boston, February 16, 1762, and its final erection into the township of Cummington, has all been detailed in the sketch of that town, on page 222. A repetition of all this is unnecessary. On March 16, 1785, the northern part of Cummington was incorporated as a district, and on June 15, 1807, this district was made a township—the Plainfield of to-day. Additions to the original territory have twice been made. February 4, 1794, when a portion of Ashfield, with the families of Joseph Clarke and Joseph Beals was added, and June 21, 1803, when a tract of one mile in width from the southerly portion of Hawley was annexed. A tract in the northeastern part of the town, comprising 600 acres, was early granted to Mr. Mahew, for missionary and legal services among the Indians, and was soon after transferred to one Wainwright, whose name it subsequently bore.

*For this sketch we are largely indebted to Rev. Solomon Clark.

Of the early settlement of the town nothing more of importance may be said than what has already been said in connection with the Cummington sketch. Most of the settlers were from Bridgewater and Abington, Conn. The first settler in this part of the old town of Cummington was doubtless a Mr. McIntyre, who located about where Mrs. Mary A. Dunning now lives, not far from 1770. Drs. Fay, Bradish and others were located here previous to 1774, and between that time and 1880 we know that the following were here, and doubtless a number of others, viz.: Lieut. Joshua Shaw, Andrew Cook, Isaac Joy, Caleb White, Lieut. Colson, Lieut. Samuel Noyes, Ebenezer Bisbee, Abram Beals, John Streeter, William Robbins, Jonathan Munroe and Noah Packard. The first birth was that of John Cook, October 27, 1778.

The growth of the town may be seen from the following figures, which show the population for the several years mentioned: 1790, 458; 1800, 797; 1810, 977; 1820, 936; 1830, 984; 1840, 910; 1850, 814; 1855, 652; 1860, 639; 1865, 579; 1870, 521; 1875, 481; 1880, 457.

Organization.—After the incorporation of the district, in 1785, the first legal meeting was held at the house of Simon Burroughs, July 25, 1786, when Lieut. Ebenezer Colson was chosen moderator; Lieut. Joshua Shaw, clerk; Lieut. Ebenezer Colson, Lieut. John Packard and Lieut. John Cunningham, selectmen; Lieut. John Shaw, treasurer; Simon Burroughs, constable; Isaac Joy, Lieut. John Packard, tithingmen; Josiah Torry, Solomon Nash, Nathan Fay, William Daniels, Jacob Clark, Abijah Pool, Jonathan Munroe, David White and Daniel Streeter, surveyors of highways; Lieut. Samuel Noyes, surveyor of lumber; Daniel Streeter, sealer of leather; John Streeter, fence viewer; Asa Joy and Azariah Beals, hog-reeves; David White, field-driver, and John Streeter, deer-reeve.

Notes.—Dr. Marcus Whitman, noted as a missionary, physician and surgeon for over ten years in Oregon, also for the long, tedious journey which he made across the Rocky mountains in mid-winter to Washington, D. C., when Mr. Webster was secretary of state, a journey requiring heroic bravery and uncommon physical endurance, spent many of his boyhood days up to early manhood in Plainfield, living with Col. John Packard. He is remembered by some, then his associates, as an energetic youth, possessing a good mind and good principles. By his daring, promptness and skill when a large boy, he saved another boy on the point of drowning, from a watery grave. He attended the school of Rev. Moses Hallock, in this town, which was probably the means of shaping his subsequent career. His acquaintance, more or less, with several connected with the same school, who afterwards became foreign missionaries, probably contributed to the same result. It is understood that on leaving Plainfield, having decided on his profession, he entered the Pittsfield medical school. Time passes on; in 1835 he became an accepted missionary of the American board, his future field being some of the Indian tribes in Oregon. The next year, 1836, associated with Rev. Henry

H. Spaulding, they and their wives crossed the Rocky mountains and became located at two stations, one on the Walla Walla river, the other on the Clear Water. These missionary ladies were the first white women who ever crossed those mountains. Their courage and patience in meeting and overcoming the many hardships and perils of the journey astonished both hunters and traders. Visiting as physician and surgeon the various forts and agencies of the Hudson Bay Company, Dr. Whitman at length became satisfied that the plan was formed by that company to secure that vast territory, with all its unknown wealth and resources for Great Britain. He felt certain that American immigration must be brought over the Rocky mountains or the entire region would be lost to the United States. Sitting at table one day at Fort Walla Walla, in the autumn of 1842, a messenger came in, announcing the arrival of British immigrants from Red river, this side of the mountains. Toasts were drank, and one of the company said, " Now the Americans may whistle, the country is ours." Dr. Whitman soon excused himself and left, rode that night twenty-four miles to his home, sent his wife to the family of a Methodist missionary, made preparations, and started off to cross the continent in mid-winter, risking cold, starvation and hostile Indians, to save Oregon for his country. Reaching Missouri in February, 1843, frost-bitten and exhausted, with all earnestness he told the people that the Pacific coast must be rescued from the Hudson Bay company. Contradicting the reports that wagons could cross the mountains, he engaged to pilot a colony in the spring to the Columbia river. At Washington he called on Daniel Webster, then secretary of State, and told his story. The secretary replied, " Wagons cannot cross the mountains. So says Sir G. Simpson. So say all his correspondents in that distant region. Besides, I am about trading that worthless territory for some valuable concessions in relation to the Newfoundland codfisheries." With earnestness in his looks and tones, Dr. Whitman replied, " I hope you will not do it, sir. We want that valuable territory ourselves." He emphasized the word valuable. The long head and profound intellect of Mr. Webster did not then penetrate the design of the agents of Great Britain. But he saw it afterwards. Saw how near he came towards committing a fundamental mistake. Those " valuable concessions " pertaining to Newfoundland codfisheries were trifles compared with Oregon in its vast extent and wealth. Leaving the secretary, Dr. Whitman next went to President Tyler and said 'the same things, affirming that wagons and emigrants could cross the mountains. The president replied, " Dr. Whitman, since you are a missionary I will believe you, and if you take your emigrants over there on your return as you propose, the treaty will not be ratified." In March, after a hurried visit to Boston, he was back in Missouri, and led a thousand emigrants to Fort Hall. Captain Grant who commanded it, in the service and interest of the Hudson Bay Company, asked where they were going, and pronouncing the rest of the way impassible for wagons, offered to change them for pack horses, as he had done for others. The men were in great trouble when they heard this. Dr. Whitman rose up and said : "Friends, you have trusted me so far, have I deceived you? Continue to trust me, and I will take you, wagons and all to Oregon." They trusted him, he went before, marking the road with stakes and bits of paper with written directions, till they reached his home, and, at length, the Willimette valley. It was a long and successfnl journey. September 4, 1843, he and his 800 emigrants emerged on the plains of the Columbia river. Those who a few months before, in sanguine tones had said " Now the Americans may whistle, the country is ours," were mortified andlsilenced. The treaty was not signed. Oregon and the Northern Pacific coast were saved by the heroism, the energy and Christian zeal of one individual, a missionary physician of the American board, many of whose boyhood days up to early manhood were spent in the remote, quiet town of Plainfield. Joseph Beals, known as the "mountain miller," united with the Plainfield church in 1792. Came from Bridgewater, and settled here in 1779, with his wife and several young children. For the first ten years of his residence in town he considered the mere externals of morality enough for his safety here and hereafter. He experienced a severe reverse in 1789. A scarcity of provisions prevailed in the community that year. In the absence of himself and wife from home one evening his cottage took fire, and with it, in one short hour, was consumed the fruits and avails of several years. It was a severe lesson, but one which a wise Providence appointed to make him acquainted with himself. He became an altered man, one of the most humble, useful Christians the town ever had. The year 1798 marks an important date in his career. He purchased a corn-mill, so-called, a mile south of the meeting-house—not the one that now stands on the same spot. Many the incidents connected with that mill, covering fifteen years. Numbers resorted thither for special conversation. It became a noted spot. Troubled ones there found help. The church elected him one of the deacons in 1803. He died ten years after at the age of sixty-one. For more than half a century, people in various countries have read the story of his life. In 1831 the American Tract Society published the " Mountain Miller," a popular and useful tract. Within a year 140,000 copies were circulated. Soon a larger edition was issued. Societies in other lands published the same. How many editions have been given to the world we cannot say. It has gone to the ends of the earth. The instances of its usefulness would fill a volume. This example shows that a quiet community on the hills, not rich as judged by a material standard, may send out an influence for good that shall bless multitudes in distant parts of the earth.

Jacob Nash came to Plainfield directly after the close of the Revolutionary war, and settled on the farm now owned by Stephen Parsons, on road 8. His son Arvin was born in 1790, and married three times, first, Lucinda Vinton in 1813, who bore him four children, namely, Eunice V., Martha J., Spencer and Maria S. He married for his second wife Mrs. Dorothy Covell, in 1834, and had born to him two children, James A. and Mary L. The mother of these children died in 1841, and he married for his third wife Lucretia Pixley. Mr. Nash died in July, 1869, aged seventy-nine years. His son James was born in December, 1836, married Mary A. Torrey in 1860, and has had born to him four children, Elmer E., Frank E., Charles A. and Lewis S. He lives on road 34, on the west bank of Mill river, and is proprietor of a grist-mill there.

Jacob Clark was born in Abington, Mass., in 1756, served in the Revolutionary war, and came to Plainfield in 1783. He married Susanna Jones, had born to him eleven children, and died in 1832. His son Chester was born in this town in 1805, married Minerva Jones in 1831, and had born to him two children, Seth W. and Elizabeth S. Mr. Clark and his wife both died in 1885. Seth W. was born in 1838, married Nancy W. Jones, and had born to him six children, five of whom are living. He now resides on road 44.

John Hamlen was born in Bridgewater, Mass., October 22, 1762, moved with his parents to Cummington in 1776, and began service in the Revolutionary war at the age of sixteen years. He married when he was twenty-eight years old, about the year 1790, Sally Town, who bore him ten children, and with whom he lived twenty-eight years. He married for his second wife Dorothy Gove, who died in 1847. He served his town in many public offices, serving as selectman nineteen years, justice of the peace, etc. He died April 15, 1852, in the ninetieth year of his age. His son Freeman was born May 8, 1805, married for his first wife Clarissa Whiting, June 4, 1829, who bore him one son, Edward F., and died October 13, 1847. He married for his second wife Martha Taylor, November 30, 1848. Mr. Taylor served the town as selectman six years, and was town clerk twenty-three years.

Samuel Thayer was an early settler of this town, locating here about ninety years ago, at which time he cleared 100 acres, and built a log cabin. He lived many years on the farm now owned by Lemuel Mason.

Sumner Martin was born March 2, 1801, came to this town about 1821, and married twice, first, Temperance Taylor, July 4, 1822, who bore him seven children. He married for his second wife Mrs. Abigail Taylor. Mr. Barton died October 7, 1880. His son Nathan was born May 27, 1835, married Louisa E. Gardner, in 1860, has four children, and lives on road 5.

Leonard Campbell was born in this town in 1811, married Louisa Bisbee, in 1835, and has had born to him one child, Fred E. He served as deputy sheriff twenty-eight years, and was appointed postmaster in 1850, which office he still holds. The postoffice occupies a part of the store in which he has been engaged for forty years.

Jerijah Barber was born in Windsor, Conn., in 1804, came to this town about 1827, and married Dorothy Morton, in 1834. He has had born to him three children, two of whom are living, a son, who resides in Pittsfield, and a daughter, who is a widow, and resides at home with her father. Mrs. Barber died June 23, 1882.

Professional Men.—Among the professional men who have originated in Plainfield may be mentioned the following :—

First, lawyers—Cyrus Joy, son of Jacob, graduated at Williams college in 1811, studied law and practiced at Northampton, afterwards in his native town.   Hosea F. Stockwell, lived forty years at the West, a lawyer, having an extensive practice in New Philadelphia, Ohio.   Elisha Bassett, son of Thomas, studied law, for forty-seven years connected with the United States district court, Boston.   Alden B. Vining graduated at Williams college in 1843, a lawyer, located in Bridgeport, Conn.   Erastus N. Bates graduated at Williams college in 1853, studied law, his health did not allow him to pursue its practice, and in the last war rose to the rank of major, and has been twice state treasurer of Illinois.   Ephraim L. Lincoln graduated at Williams college in 1855, studied law, was admitted to the Hampshire bar in 1858, and died at Westfield in 1859.   Almon Warner, son of James, now a lawyer in Cincinnati, Ohio.

Second, editors and literary persons—Gerard Hallock graduated at Williams college in 1819, started the *Boston Telegraph*, united it with the *Boston Recorder* in 1826, then removed to New York, became one of the editors and proprietors of the *New York Observer*, and in 1829 established the *Journal of Commerce*, a first-class paper.   Charles Dudley Warner graduated at Hamilton college in 1851, has published extensively, now edits one of the Hartford daily papers.   Mrs. Fidelia Cook for some time superintended the literary department of the *Springfield Republican*.   Mrs. Martha J. Lamb has published in two magnificent volumes, the *History of New York City*.   A work of hers, *Coast Survey*, has become a text-book in some colleges.

Third, professors and classical teachers—James Hayward, graduated at Harvard college in 1819, tutor there; also professor of mathematics and natural philosophy; published *Elements of Geometry*.   Isaac Newton Lincoln, graduated at Williams college in 1847 ; professor of Latin and French at that college nine years.   Tilly Brown Hayward, brother of Professor James, graduated at Harvard; born in 1820 ; a teacher for many years. Alden Porter Beals, graduated at Williams college in 1849; high school teacher for over thirty years.   Francis Torrey, superintendent of schools in Newark, N. J.   Charles Shaw, graduated at Williams college in 1864 ; taught a classical school for many years in Astoria, N. Y.   Fordyce A. Dyer, son of Albert, graduated at Williams college in 1865.   Capt. Edward Hanlin, clerk of the executive department, state house, Boston.

Fourth, physicians—Samuel Shaw, M. D., had an extensive ride in his native town for thirty years, a man of great endurance, never lost a meal through sickness for forty-seven years.   Dana Shaw, M. D., brother of the foregoing, for over twenty-five years was a physician in Barre, N. Y.   G. Washington Shaw, nephew of the foregoing, settled in Williamsburg, Mass., highly esteemed.   Joseph Richards, a brother of the missionaries, long a physician in Hillsdale, N. Y.   Chilion Packard, M. D., in early life went South.   Seth H.

Pratt, M. D., went West many years ago. Newell White, M. D., is still living in Pennsylvania. James F. Richards, a physician in Andover, Mass. Royal Joy, studied with Dr. Samuel Shaw and settled in Cummington. Francis Pratt is a physician in Ohio. Newton Robinson resides as a physician in the same state. Francis Shaw, surgeon in United States navy. Lewis Whiting, deceased, resided in Saratoga, N. Y. Emerson Warner, a physician in Virginia. Daniel Thayer, a physician in Cheshire. Dr. Shepherd L. Hamlin, was a dentist in Cincinnati, Ohio. Dr. Joseph Beals is a dentist in Greenfield.

Fifth, ministers—Rev. Jephthah Pool, many years ago a pastor in Windsor, Mass. Rev. James Richards, a foreign missionary. Rev. William Richards, missionary to the Sandwich Islands. Rev. William A. Hallock, corresponding secretary of the American Tract society. Erastus Dickinson, settled in several places. Rev. Austin Richards, D. D., settled in Francestown, N. H. ; also in Nashua, N. H. Rev. David Rood, missionary to South Africa. Isaac Newton Lincoln, professor in Williams college. Rev. Stephen C. Pixley, missionary in South Africa. Rev. Spencer Dyer, minister in the Methodist denomination. Elder James Clark and Elder Thomas Thayer, both ministers in the Baptist denomination. Rev. William A. Hallock, settled in Bloomfield, Conn. Rev. Leavitt Hallock, settled in Portland, Me. William Austin Richards, son of Col. Jason, graduated at Amherst college, had the ministry in view, died suddenly in 1863.

Military.—The settlement of Plainfield was effected about the time of the Revolutionary war, and then as a part of Cummington, hence as a town it could take no action in those stirring times. Many of the settlers though took part in the struggle, and many veterans subsequently became residents of the town. In 1834 the following pensioners were here : Lemuel Allis, Joseph Barnard, Ebenezer Bisbee, John Campbell, Vinson Curtis, Ebenezer Dickinson, James Dyer, Joseph Gloyd, Rev. Moses Hallock, Jacob Nash, Philip Packard, Whitcomb Pratt, James Richards, Josiah Shaw, Samuel Streeter, Josiah Torrey and Caleb White.

In the late great war the town furnished sixty-one men, an excess of seven over all calls, and three of whom were commissioned officers. The town also furnished $4,505.00 in money, besides $1,622.02 in aid to soldiers' families, etc., which was subsequently reimbursed by the state.

VILLAGE.

The only village, Plainfield, is located at the center of the town. It consists principally of one street, nearly three-quarters of a mile long, extending east and west. This is intersected by two roads from the south, which unite in one north of the village. The postoffice was established here in 1816, and John Mack was the first postmaster. The present incumbent of the office is Foster W. Gilbert, to whom we are indebted for the following sketch of the

MANUFACTURES.

On the brook in the northwest part of the town is situated Campbell's saw-mill. It was built by Levi Campbell and was for many years conducted by his son, Levi N. Campbell. It is now managed by George Billings. A limited amount of custom work is done.

The small stream which flows from the northeast to the south part of the town has been from the first the scene of many attemps at manufacture. Probably the first enterprise of this sort was the grist-mill of Thomas Shaw. This was situated several rods above the present residence of W. H. Dyer. Evidence exists that places the date of its erection before 1800. The mill was abandoned about 1830, and no trace of it now remains.

On the stream below the grist-mill, in the earlier years of the present century, was the cloth factory of Jacob Clark. In 1825 or 1830, on the same site, Randall Whiting, James Warner and Jacob Clark, under the firm name of Whiting, Warner & Co., built a factory for the manufacture of satinets and for general custom work. They employed about a dozen hands at their looms. The above firm conducted the business for about twelve years, and afterwards it was managed by Jacob Clark alone. Subsequently, one Gurney made an attempt to revive the business, but it soon died away and the buildings were removed about 1857. Remnants of the dam and raceway are yet discerned.

Still lower on the stream John White established a mill for the manufacture of broom-handles, about 1836. This was in operation for eight or ten years, and the buildings were then removed. A saw-mill on the same site was continued a few years longer.

Further down was the ancient saw-mill of Ziba White. This mill was supposed to have been erected near the beginning of the century. After forty years of service it fell into disuse.

A mill-privilege below was improved by Warner & Lloyd about 1845. They erected a saw-mill and afterwards a cider-mill. Both have long since become untraceable.

The small stream emptying from the sluice directly below the store of Leonard Campbell seems hardly sufficient to turn a boy's water-wheel, yet on this rivulet, about one hundred years ago, a pretentious tannery was erected by Messrs. Dorn & Remington. Their water-wheel was an overshot wheel, eighteen feet in diameter, and their buildings were of unusual size. The preparations were for some reason unavailable and they went down the valley and settled on Mill brook. On this brooklet also were, at about the same time, the potash works of Iram Packard.

Going west from the village we come upon the busiest stream of water in town. It is called Mill brook, and empties into the Westfield at Cummington.

The upper water privilege was made efficient by Josiah Stetson, in 1817. He built a saw-mill and managed it for several years. Afterwards David Stowell purchased it and continued the business until 1854, at which date it passed into the hands of W. C. Gilbert. In 1855 George W. King bought the property, and still owns it. Mr. King turns out yearly from forty to sixty thousand broom and brush-handles, besides custom sawing and planing.

Following the stream a few rods further we come upon the ruins of a saw-mill built in the latter part of the last century. Adjoining this saw-mill were the old clothier works conducted successively by Daniel Richards, Mr. Gleason, Mr. Shattuck and others. In 1820, Arnold and Nahum Streeter built on the site of the clothing-mill a factory for the manufacture of satinet, flannel and other woolen goods. This mill was burned in 1825, It was rebuilt and managed by the family of Streeters until 1876, when it was again destroyed by fire. No attempt has been made to rebuild it.

Lower on this stream, nearly opposite the present residence of Lester Streeter, Messrs. Dorn & Remington, in 1830, built a large tannery, 100 x 30 feet, covering eighty vats. Here a large business was done. Mr. Dorn sold his share to a Mr. Parsons, and later the new firm disposed of the property to Giddons & Latham. In 1851 the business was discontinued. A small saw and broom-handle-mill was for a time continued by Nelson Clapp, and after him by Sebert Whitmarsh.

On the other side of the road from the present Wilcutt mill, in 1810, was a flax-dressing-mill owned and run by Noah and Iram Packard. About the year 1816 Reuben Hamlin and Otis Pratt built on the same site a factory for the manufacture of satinet and woolen goods, The building was removed in 1820 to its present location. Mr. Pratt sold his share to Erastus Bates. Mr. Bates moved West in 1834, and for a time Mr. Hamlin managed the mill alone. After his retirement, different individuals endeavored to make use of the buildings and water privilege. Jason Noyes used the mill for a chair factory. Elbridge King rented it for a time. Capt. James Cook finally bought the property and gave it to his sons Andrew and Nelson Cook. The Cooks sold to Daniel Ingraham, who manufactured baskets. William Wilcutt bought the plant from Mr. Ingraham, repaired it thoroughly and put in entirely new machinery. At the present time he uses annually from thirty to fifty thousand feet of hard lumber for the manufacture of whip-stocks, and broom and brush handles. There is also a lumber yard attached, and custom sawing is done.

Half a mile further down the stream the earliest tradition places the grist-mill, owned at first by the Cooks. From them it passed into the hands of Jeremiah Robinson. In 1798, Joseph Beals, the celebrated "Mountain Miller," purchased the property and managed the business until his death, in 1813. His son, Joseph Beals, Jr., then conducted it for a number of years. Dea. Jared Bisbee, Joel Lyon, Loren White and Edwin Torrey succeeded

in turn to the management.   In 1861, James A. Nash came into possession
of the property and he is the present miller.

In 1852 William Shattuck built a saw-mill on the branch of Mill brook running from the west part of the town.   After a few years he sold it to W. M.
Cleveland, who continued the mill and also manufactured broom handles.
The quantity of water proving insufficient the buildings were removed
in 1884.

There is at present a saw-mill at the outlet of Crooked pond, in the extreme
northwestern portion of the township.

Many manufactures of minor importance have from time to time been undertaken by the inhabitants.   During the earlier settlements distilleries for
making cider brandy were not uncommon.   Later spruce tar and spruce oil
were made in limited quantities in the west part of the town.   Brickmaking,
begun by Thomas Shaw about 1800, has been revived at intervals by different
persons and firms.   The clay bank is a few rods east of the old house of
Kingman Thayer.   Shingles, butter firkins and cheese boxes have been made
to some extent.   Window sashes are at present manufactured by W. H.
Dyer.

Mineralogists and mining experts have pronounced the beds of black oxide
and silicious manganese in the west part of the town of rare value and quality.   One of these mines, situated on the present farm of W. H. Packard, was
successfully worked for a short time by a firm from Enfield.   The death of
one of the partners and the removal of the other to California prevented
further operations.

The manufactures of Plainfield never have been of much importance, owing,
doubtless, to the small size of the streams and the distance from business
centers.

ECCLESIASTICAL.

The Evangelical Congregational church was organized by an ecclesiastical
synod, August 31, 1786.   The society had fourteen members, and Rev. Moses
Hallock was their first pastor.   Their first house of worship was built in 1792.
The present structure was erected in 1846.   It will seat about 400 persons
and is valued, including grounds, etc., at $1,500.00.   The society now has
102 members, with Rev. F. G. Webster, pastor.   The church has also an
enviable missionary record.   It began early in this century, two years before
the formation of the American board.   The first missionary was James Richards.   He united with the church in 1805 and entered Williams college in 1806,
became acquainted there with Samuel J. Mills.   An intimate friendship existed between them.   In 1808, before the end of his third year in college, he
had come to the fixed purpose of spending his life among the heathen.   From
that time he severed from that purpose not for a moment.   His parents shared
the same spirit.   Properly, therefore, this foreign missionary record of the

church here began with that purpose of young Richards, in 1808, seventy-eight years ago. He entered Andover Theological seminary in 1809. The three years there spent, he did his utmost to promote a spirit of missions among the students. In October, 1815, he embarked for Ceylon, in company with other missionaries. He afterwards said, " The day on which I bade farewell to my native land was the happiest of my life." What follows will show that from 1815 this retired community has been represented abroad among the heathen, sometimes by two, three and four laborers, unceasingly to the present, an interval of seventy-one years. He died in 1822. Before the tid. ings of his decease had reached the home circle in Plainfield, his brother William, who had married Miss Clarissa Lyman, daughter of Levi Lyman, Esq., of Northampton, had already embarked at New Haven to join the mission at the Sandwich Islands. In 1838 he became associated with the government as the king's advisor, went on an embassy, 1842–45, to the United States, to England and France, which proved highly successful. In 1840 he became minister of public instruction, councilor and chaplain to the king. He deceased through over-work in 1847. The same year David Rood and wife, both of this town, sailed from Boston for the Zulus, South Africa. This is the fortieth year of their active missionary life. Still another in South Africa, Stephen C. Pixley, born in this town. Married Miss Louisa Healy, of Northampton. Sailed October, 1855, thirty-one years ago. In 1858, Miss Margaret Hallock, daughter of Homan Hallock, married Mr. Byington, missionary for over twenty years among the Bulgarians, and at Constantinople. Ill health has twice compelled him to discontinue labor and return to America. In 1826 a missionary printer was needed on the Mediterranean, at Malta, and some years after at Smyrna. Who should respond to this call but one of the sons of Plainfield, Homan Hallock, the youngest son of the first pastor here, Rev. Moses Hallock. Associated for some of his first years abroad with that superior oriental scholar, Rev. Eli Smith, the Arabic press at Malta did most valuable service. When the American Bible society commenced the publication of the Arabic Bible in the city of New York, it is said that only two persons in the world understood the difficult task of preparing molds for the printing of that Bible, viz.: an aged German, and Mr. Homan Hallock. When after a few years they transferred the work to Beyrout, Syria, to save expense, Samuel Hallock, inheriting his father's mechanical skill and nice workmanship, took the position his father had occupied and has filled it for sixteen years with much ability.

P PESCOTT, the youngest town in the county, lies in the northeastern corner of the same, and is bounded north by the county line, east ·by the county line and Greenwich, south by Enfield and Greenwich, and west by Pelham and the county line. It is shaped nearly in the form of an inverted letter L, and contains an area of about 12,706 acres.

The surface of the town is rough and broken, though there are many good farms, particularly in the valleys.   The soil is moist, fertile and strong.   The principal elevations are Mt. Ell, in the northeast part of the town, and Pres-cott hill and Rattlesnake mountain, in the western part.   The streams are the west branch of Swift river, which forms the western boundary of the town, and the middle branch of the same stream, flowing across the northeastern corner of the township.   Russ pond is a small body of water in the northern part of the town.

Formation and Settlement.—As we have said, Prescott is the youngest town in the county, its dating back to only 1822; and thus the early history of the territory belongs with that of the neighboring towns of which it formerly was a part.   The story of its formation is as follows :—

On December 31, 1734, a township of thirty-six square miles was granted to sixty proprietors, residents of Salem, to whom an additional grant of 4,000 acres was made June 17, 1742.   This territory took the name of New Salem, and lay just north of the old township of Pelham, most of it in Franklin county, an oblong town about thirteen miles in length.   It may readily be seen that such an inconvenient territory would not exist long without a desire on the part of its inhabitants for a division, that municipal business might be more centralized.   Many attempts were made from time to time for such division, but none were successful till January 28, 1822, when a tract about three miles in length was taken from the southern part of the town, annexed to the east parish of Pelham, and incorporated into a new township, which was given the name of Prescott, in honor of Col. William Prescott, of Peperell, who com-manded the American forces at the battle of Bunker Hill.

Who the first settler upon the present territory of Prescott was can not be definitely stated.   The southern part, or that which formerly belonged to Pelham was settled first, and its pioneers have been mentioned in connection with the sketch of that town.   Among these were the Conkeys, Mellens, (both of whom originally had a prefix of " Mc " to their names, and the Mellen was spelled with a ·" u,") Grays, Berrys, Crossetts, and Pierces.   To these may also be added the family of Obadiah Cooley, Seth Peibles, Peleg Aldrich, Jotham, Levi and Amasa Leach, Bennos Ayres, and many others.

Andrew Johnson, son of William, was born in 1781, and passed nearly all his life on a farm in the southern part of Prescott.   He married Judith Chase, and had born to him eleven children, viz.: Ansel, Adam, Henry, Joel, Jane, Lyman, Lucy, Maria, Rosalind, Rhoda and Shepard.   Of these only four are living, Ansel, Jane, Joel and Rosalind.   Ansel married Margaret Moulton, and has had born to him two children, Andrew and Henry.   Adam married Luzette Jennings, and reared two children, George and Marcia.   Henry married twice, first, Eliza Hunt, and second, Augusta Goodman, and had born to him five children, namely, Nina, Hattie M., Leo, Nettie and Theodore L.   Joel married Maria Washburn, who bore him five children, as follows: Adeline, Angenette, Frank, Andrew and Clara. Joel married for his second wife Harriet Voice.

John Pierce moved to Shutesbury from Middleboro, Mass., married three times, and his children were as follows: John, Nathan, Mary, Sarah, Peleg, Naba and Matilda. John married Sarah Haskins, and had born to him nine children, viz: Sarah, Joseph, Rounesville, Lucy, Asa, Appleton, Roxanna, Maria and Caroline. Appleton was born June 23, 1797, in what was then the town of New Salem, now Prescott, about one mile from the farm now owned by his son, Daniel T. He married Hannah Cole, April 16, 1820, and had born to him two children, Hannah A. and Daniel T. He learned the moulder's trade and worked at that for several years, then bought a saw-mill, which he run for sixteen years. He died May 20, 1881, aged eighty-four years. Hannah A. was born November 14, 1822, married Ellis White, of Barre, Mass., and has two children, Josiah E. and Anson A. Daniel T. was born November 23, 1829, married Ellen A. Pierce, in January, 1856, and has had born to him six children, five of whom are living, namely, Leslie M., who was born October 11, 1857, and married Lucy A. Soper; Adelaid E., who was born October 11, 1859, and married George Foote; Eudora H., who married George W. Brown, of Athol, Mass.; Carl M. and Lillie B.

Madison Pierce, son of Caleb, was born in that portion of Prescott which was formerly New Salem, March 31, 1809, and learned the blacksmith trade. He married twice, first, Elizabeth Lawless, who bore him two children, Elsie, who married Collis Vaughn, and Ellen, who married Daniel T. Pierce. The mother of these children died in 1842, and Mr. Pierce married for his second wife, Zuba Shaw, and had born to him five children, four of whom are living, namely, Cleora, Orinda, Emily and Lineus.

Elias Thayer, son of Calvin, came to this town with his father, from Leverett, Mass., when he was only four years of age. He afterwards moved to Orange, Mass., and in 1866 was killed by falling from a scaffold. His son, Addison, was born in this town in 1833, married Salinda M. Vaughn, November 18, 1856, and his children are Martha J., Minnie E., Ellis A. and Grace B. His oldest son, Milford, was killed by the falling of a limb, which struck him on the head. Mr. Thayer is engaged in the lumber business.

John Thrasher came to this town in 1823, and located about three-quarters of a mile from Prescott postoffice. He died at the age of eighty-seven years. His widow is now ninety-six years of age, and is in good health. His son Samuel, was born in 1822, and came here with his father when an infant.

Daniel R. Potter, son of Ezekiel, was born in Ludlow, Mass., April 10, 1818, and as his mother died at his birth, he was adopted by Levi Payne, of Belchertown, where he lived until he was ten years of age, until the death of Mr. Payne, and then went to live with an uncle in Connecticut. After three years he returned to live with Mrs. Payne. He married Maria L. (Newton) Cheeney, widow of Arnold W. Cheeney, and has had born to him two sons, Charles F., who died in 1869, at the age of nineteen years, and Frederick L., who was born July 31, 1854, and married Sarah F. Haskins, in 1885. Mr. Potter came to this town in 1867, and bought the place where he· now resides.

The population of the town has fluctuated as follows: 1830, 758; 1840, 786; 1850, 737; 1855, 643; 1860, 611; 1865, 596; 1870, 541; 1875, 493; 1880, 460.

The first hotel in the town was kept by William Conkey, in the old " Milo Abbott house." The first store-keeper, at least the first who kept a store of any account, was Peleg Canada. The first physician was Dr. Nehemiah Hinds, who located here as early as 1786. Among the men of distinction whom the town has sent out, may be mentioned Judge Peleg Aldrich and Hon. E. A. Thomas.

Organization.—The town was duly organized March 4, 1822, at which meeting the following officers were elected: Josiah Pierce, moderator; Chester Gray, clerk; Barna Brigham, Caleb Pierce and Nymphas Stacy, selectmen; and Moses Gray, Henry Haskins and Josiah Pierce, assessors.

In the late great war the town furnished sixty-seven men, a total of seven over and above all demands. It expended for war purposes $6,427.50, exclusive of $3,306.34, which was subsequently re-imbursed by the state.

VILLAGES.

PRESCOTT VILLAGE lies in the center of the southern part of the town, or that part formerly belonging to Pelham. Here is located the Congregational church, a few dwellings and a store and postoffice. The latter was established about 1822, with Barna Brigham, postmaster. Since then the following have served in this capacity: Stacy Lindsey, Dexter N. Richards, Charles Hodgkins. W. E. Johnson and Liberty Crossett.

NORTH PRESCOTT lies in the extreme northern part of the town, partly in New Salem. It has a Methodist church (over the line in New Salem), a store, postoffice and several dwellings. The postoffice was established here about 1844, and the postmasters have been Horace Hunt, S. L. Haskins, E. A. Thomas, Frank Sampson and L. K. Baker.

INDUSTRIES.

Marshall F. Brown's saw-mill, on road 12, was built about thirty-eight ago by Foster Brown, father of Marshall. It has the capacity for cutting 8,000 feet of lumber per day.

Brown & Harrington have a protable saw-mill, run by a thirty horse-power engine.

Asa Moore's shop, on road 21, was built for a grist-mill, by White & Hemenway, in 1826. Mr. Moore here does repairing and general wood work. The shop has bench saws and turning lathe.

Oscar Titu's cider brandy distillery, on road 17, was built in the spring of 1886. It has the capacity for distilling into brandy about 200 barrels of cider per month.

John E. Stowell's packing box factory gives employment to fifteen hands, and turns out about 1,000 boxes per day, using 600,000 feet of lumber per year.

James F. Wood, on road 13, is extensively engaged in breeding pure Italian bees and queens. He began as an apiarist in a small way in the spring of 1876. Since then he has gradually added to the business until he now has about 150 colonies which he uses entirely for breeding purposes. He ships his queens to all parts of the country by mail.

ECCLESIASTICAL.

The Congregational church, at South Prescott, is the only church within the limits of the town. On June 28, 1786, the eastern part of Pelham, with a part of New Salem, was incorporated as the East Parish of Pelham, and the church here was organized soon after. The first regular pastor was Rev. Matthias Cazier. The church was re-organized January 15, 1823. The present church building was erected in 1848. Rev. Augustus Alvord is pastor of the society.

SOUTHAMPTON is situated in the second tier of townships west of Connecticut river, in the southern part of the country, and is bounded north by Westhampton and Easthampton, east by Easthampton and the county line, south by the county line, and west by the county line and a small part of Huntington. It originally formed a part of Northampton, except a small addition, to "Additional Grant," so-called, which lay south of the original Northampton tract. It was also settled by Northampton people, thirty of whom in 1730, " proceded to divide up and settle the new precinct."

Physical Features.—In extent of territory Southampton may be classed among the first towns of the county, as it contains a little over seventeen thousand acres of land. The major part is comprised in the basin or valley that extends from the northern limits of the state to the shores of Long Island Sound, and is here termed the "third" or "great expansion." This valley is bounded both on the east and west by elevated ranges belonging geologically to the primary system. They approach each other closely on the north, recede towards the south, being farthest apart near the boundary line of Massachusetts and Connecticut, and then converge in the latter part of the last-named state. A greenstone ridge commences in the neighborhood of New Haven, extends nearly the whole length of this depression, and, with only occasional breaks, terminates abruptly in Belchertown. This trough or valley, reaching from the mountains on the north to the sea, between the greenstone ridge and the primary regions on the west, is nowhere, following the course of the now disused canal, more than one hundred and forty feet above the level of the river at Northampton.   Naturally, then, the Connecticut river should flow along this depression in the earth's surface, through Southampton and empty its waters into the sea at New Haven.   Instead of following this natural channel, it has worn a deep gorge in the mountain to the eastward through which it passes.   Geologists have been somewhat perplexed in arriving at the true course of the present physical aspects of this region.   The theory that it was once covered with water, and that the fertile meadows and the sites of beautiful and flourishing villages were once the bottom of a long and narrow lake has been given on another page.

There is not, probably, a single town in the Connecticut valley that surpasses Southampton in picturesque scenery.   People who penetrate its rural obscurity for the first time are apt to expand with rapture over the exquisite configuration of the landscape.   The surface is, with the exception of the plain lands, which are of no great extent, curiously diversified with endless undulations.   An artist once drew a waving line with his pencil across the corner of one of his pictures and designated it as the line of beauty.   This is finely illustrated in the physical conformation of this town.   The village occupies a position but little above the meadows that fringe the waters of the Connecticut.   On the west and northwest each succeeding ridge rises higher than the one immediately adjoining it, until the summit of Pomeroy mountain is reached.   The altitude of this eminence is more than twelve hundred feet above the level of the sea.   From its top there is presented a scene of rare loveliness.   The vision ranges over a vast expanse of hills and dales and mountains, while the river glitters beneath like molten silver under the rays of the summer sun.   At its base, in alternation of verdant fields and pleasant groves, the intervening country is arrayed in a drapery of rich and variegated colors.   A tower has recently been erected on the highest point of the mountain, and it has become a favorite resort in the summer season for the inhabitants of the valley.   With the top of the mountain something of a tragedy is connected.   In 1704, the hamlet of Pascommuck, an outlying settlement of Northampton, was attacked by the Indians and several persons slain, as detailed in the Easthampton sketch.   The assailants retreated to Pomeroy mountain, where they held a pow-wow during the night, and, on leaving, scalped Mrs. Janes, the wife of Benjamin Janes, whom they had brought with them as a prisoner.   Mrs. Janes was found alive on the mountains by her friends and eventually recovered.

But nature has not been so prodigal in her gifts to Pomeroy mountain—the origin of the name is involved in much obscurity, but is mentioned in the early records before the settlement of Southampton—as to neglect other sections of the town.   There is no part of its surface, with the exceptions previously mentioned, that may be termed exactly level.   It abounds in terraces and gentle slopes. Especially is this true of the elevation called Little mountain, at the foot of which the village quietly reposes. In many of its features it bears a striking resemblance to the far famed " Round Hill," of Northampton. There are charming sites for residences, and a natural adaptation for winding roads and paths. No prettier place can be found within a radius of fifty miles for homes of elegance and refinement. In the foreground is Mount Nonotuck rising abruptly towards the sky and prominently displaying its ribs of red sandstone. Just beyond it is its Cogener, Holyoke. Lower than either of the others, like a pigmy reposing under the shadow of giants, is White Loofe, a very modest eminence. Within the range of vision are the beautiful villages of Easthampton, Amherst, Hadley, the city of Northampton, as well as others of humbler pretentions, and the fertile and highly cultivated meadows of emerald hue, that lovingly embrace the broad river which with many curves and bends, gently flows through the valley. Little Mountain is really a gem in its way, and deserves more consideration than to be used indefinitely for cow-pastures.

As is befitting in a region so uneven and undulating, there is no deficiency of rivulets and brooks. They wind in all directions among the hills and meadows, and are generally tributary to the Manhan, the largest and principal stream within the limits of the town. Its source is in Westhampton, and its course southerly until it reaches the northern boundary of Westfield, where it turns with a sharp curve to the north and passes a little way east of the village to the Connecitcut, with which it mingles its waters. Inferior streams bear such local names as Triple, Moose, Alder, Meadow, and Red brooks.

Soil.—About two-thirds of Southampton are included in the new red sandstone formation of the Connectlcut valley, and possess the same general characteristics as neighboring localities embraced in the same geological system. The red rock, as it is locally designated, approaches in many places very near the surface, and when uncovered and exposed to the influence of the atmosphere and the action of frost, speedily disintegrates, and, when sufficiently comminuted, forms an excellent soil. Most of the arable land is of this description. When mingled in due proportion with organic matter, it assumes a dark color, is mellow and friable, and is worked with great facility. This view of red land, so prominent a feature in Southampton, may be distinctly traced through Connecticut, New York, New Jersey, Pennsylvania and Maryland to Virginia. The red lands are susceptible of the highest improvement.

The remaining territory rests upon granitic rock, covered with soil of varying degrees of thickness. A section of granite of triangular form, with its base in the towns on the north, is forced like a wedge in Southampton, between the sandstone on the east and the mica and the gneiss on the west. This is the true granitic region, and presents the general features that everywhere distinguish the primary formation. The surface is rugged and mountainous, and to the explorer with a purely utilitarian turn of mind, would probably offer few attractions.   Stones encumber the ground ; and although the huge rocks are not strown as thickly as "autumn leaves in Vallombrosa," they are sufficiently numerous to be reckoned by hundreds and even thousands on a single farm.   And yet this granite soil is strong and durable, and when properly cultivated will produce generous crops.   As may be inferred, tillage predominates in the eastern part of the town and grazing in the western.

Settlement and growth.—In 1730, the present township of Southampton was an unbroken, heavily-timbered wilderness without a single inhabitant, and included within the boundaries of Northampton.   The latter town had been settled about seventy-five years, but no clearings had been made nor houses erected on the south at a greater distance than three or four miles. Indian forays on the valley towns rendered all such enterprises extremely hazardous.   But despite this serious impediment to improvement and culti- vation, proprietary rights seem to have extended over nearly the whole territory, as the earliest known record relating to the subject states that on the tenth day of March of the year before mentioned, a meeting of the pro- prietors was held—being an adjourned meeting from the previous January— to decide upon the division of the lands and the formation of a settlement. The affirmative opinion prevailed, and a committee was appointed to make the distribution.   Hon. John Stoddard, Ebenezer Pomeroy, Deacon John Clark, Hon. Joseph Hawley and Ensign Ebenezer Parsons constituted this committee.   Two of them, John Stoddard and Joseph Hawley, were men of eminent ability and prominent members of the colonial government.   They made allotments to thirty individuals upon certain conditions.   The most important of these were that each settler should "till and fence five acres before next fall twelve months ; " build a house of at least one room within two years from the above date, either on Pomeroy mountain or on the town- plat hill, and remove with his famity and live there at least two years.

During the two following years little appears to have been done by the pro- prietors, except the clearing of small tracts, preparatory to the erection of dwellings.   In 1732 the two first houses built within the present limits of the town were those of Thomas Porter and Judah Hutchinson, and they are thus entitled to the distinction of being the first permanent settlers.   Both of these structures were of limited dimensions.   That of the former is still pre- served, forming a single room in the residence of the late Col. Elisha Ed- wards, and now occupied by his son, George K. Edwards.   Mr. Hutchin- son's house stood near the Joel T. Clapp place.   This is the current tradi- tion, and its authenticity has not been disputed until quite recently, when a claim was preferred that Ebenezer Kingsley was entitled to this honor, the only proof adduced to support it being the inscription upon his tombstone. This conflict of claims may, perhaps, be reconciled in this way :   Mr. Kings- ley might have been, and it is reasonable to infer that he was, the first person to make a clearing ; but as there is no mention of his house until two years after tradition affirms that Porter and Hutchinson erected their dwellings, it is equally reasonable to conclude that they were the pioneer builders of houses. It may be proper to observe, in this connection, that Samuel Pomeroy and Eldad Pomeroy, who always claimed to belong in the old town—Northampton—and never lived within the present limits of Southampton, had previously cultivated land in Pomeroy's meadow for nearly or quite a score of years.

During the next year (1733) fourteen settlers arrived, namely, Nathan Lyman, Phineas King, Joseph Clark, Ebenezer Kingsley, Nathaniel Searle, John Clark, John Wait, Ichabod Strong, Waitstill Strong, Samuel Danks, Stephen Root, Elias Root, Moses Wright and Ezra Strong. This was the first instalment of the holders of allotments of land who came to make permanent homes In the course of the three or four succeeding years fourteen others joined them, to wit, Jonathan Bascom, Samuel Bust, Roger Clapp, Aaron Clark, Elisha Clark, Jonathan Clark, Ebenezer French, Eleazer Hannum, Elias Lyman, John Miller, Noah Pixley, Israel Sheldon, Noah Sheldon and Stephen Sheldon.

By subsequent accretions, slowly during the continuance of the French and Indian wars, and more rapidly after their termination, the town attained a respectable degree of development, both in resources and population. The forest was cleared away on the best lands, which were divided into fields for tillage, pasture and meadows, and the soil, rich and strong, produced maximum crops, among which wheat, barley, rye, flax and corn occupied a conspicuous place. It may be observed that of the names enumerated above, nearly all can now be found in the town, and are borne by their lineal descendants. They belonged, without exception, to that sturdy class of Englishmen, who, in defence of the freedom of conscience, and in vindication of civil liberty, fought the battles of Edgehill, Naseby and Marston Moor, overturned a throne and brought a king to justice for his manifold encroachments upon their rights and privileges. To such men, Macaulay says, England is indebted for her constitutional liberties. They need no other or better eulogium. Southampton was organized as a Puritan town in a Puritan commonwealth, and its history has in no way disappointed the expectations and hopes of those who founded it.

In 1749 a tract containing three thousand acres, and bounded by Westfield on the south, called the "additional grant," was divided among the proprietors. This was an important and material addition to the area and resources of the settlement. There have also been at different periods, alterations in the boundary lines of the town. Most of them were unimportant. In one instance, however, Southampton was obliged to surrender considerable territory to the young, and when the transfer was made, feeble town of Easthampton.

The growth and fluctuations in the town's population may be seen by the figures set after the several years :   1776, 740 ; 1790, 829 ; 1800, 983 ; 1810,

1,171; 1820, 1,160; 1830, 1,244; 1840, 1,157; 1850, 1,060; 1855, 1,195; 1860, 1,130; 1865, 1,216; 1870, 1,159; 1875, 1,050; 1880, 1,046.

Organization.—In the course of ten years, after the first allotments of land had been made, there had been a gradual but gratifying increase in the population of the new settlement, and, as the distance to Northampton, where they were in the habit of attending Divine worship, was about eight miles, over roads rudely and imperfectly constructed, which rendered traveling in some seasons of the year tedious, difficult, and sometimes dangerous, it naturally occurred to their minds that some organization by which religious privileges could be instituted in their own secluded community, was both desirable and necessary. It does not appear from an examination of the early records that they were actuated by any other motive than this in the measures they adopted to obtain the passage by the general court of an act of incorporation of the settlement as a separate and distinct district, or precinct, to use the phraseology of the times. But this related only to religious matters. In all secular affairs the Second Precinct of Northampton, as the new settlement was called, remained an integral part of the present town. The inhabitants were empowered to assess and collect taxes for the erection of a meeting-house, the support of a preacher, and other purely religious purposes. The Second Precinct was regularly incorporated July 23, 1741, and on the 21st of the following September, the first precinct meeting was held at the house of Phineas King, one of the original fourteen settlers, when the following officers were chosen : Ebenezer Kingsley, moderator ; Phineas King, clerk ; Waitstill Strong, Ebenezer Finch and Aaron Clark, assessors; Stephen Sheldon, collector. A committee was also appointed, consisting of John Clark, Ebenezer Kingsley and Phineas King, to procure the services of a preacher of the Gospel. The precinct existed until January 5, 1753, when, with the assent of Northampton, it was incorporated as a town by the general court, with the name of Southampton. Under the town organization Ebenezer Kingsley was the first town-clerk, and Waitstill Strong, Stephen Sheldon and Ebenezer Kingsley constituted the first board of selectmen.

Indian Alarms and Depredations.—The ten years following the settlement of the town were measurably exempt from Indian alarms and incursions. But in 1743 the fear of savage raids became general, and measures were adopted to provide for the safety of the inhabitants in case an attack should be made. With this object in view a palisade, consisting of stakes driven into the ground, was constructed around the house of the Rev. Mr. Judd. On the west side and entered through a window in the second story, a watch-tower was built. From the top of this structure any indications of the presence of the enemy in the neighborhood could be detected.

During this period of uneasiness and apprehension, the work of clearing the land and cultivating the soil languished to some extent, as the settlers exercised the utmost vigilance, and when laboring in the field, stationed sentinels upon the borders of the forest to discover and avert any impending danger. No man ventured to any distance from his dwelling without carrying his gun in his hand. It was not, however, until 1746 that any Indians made their appearance and perpetrated any mischief, although it might have been previously suspected that they were covertly lurking in the woods waiting for a favorable opportunity to emerge from their concealment and murder the settlers. In the latter part of August of that year the houses of Aaron Clark and Elisha Clark were entered, the furniture injured or destroyed, and clothing and provisions stolen. As these houses were in an exposed situation, they had been abandoned by the families that respectively occupied them on the first intimation that the savages were in the vicinity. In the early part of September this party of dusky skulkers and marauders was again heard from. This time they lay in ambush near some bars between the houses of Ezra Strong and John Wait, through which cows were driven to pasture, the intention being to surprise and slay those who should come for the animals at the approach of evening. As the cows gradually drew near the bars, as was their habit towards the close of the day, an Indian was sent to drive them to the rear of the field and keep them there. Samuel Danks was sent to drive them home, and it so happened that, taking the nearest route to the pasture, he entered it on the side opposite the ambuscade. The restiveness of the animals aroused his suspicion that there might be something amiss, and presently discovering the Indians he fled, standing not upon the order of his flight, and gave the alarm. The savages, finding their ingenious scheme was thwarted, instantly took to the woods, and nothing more was seen or heard of them during the year.

The next year, 1747, the Indians made their appearance again, this time so slyly and stealthily that their presence was not suspected until they had murdered Elisha Clark, who was engaged in thrashing grain in his barn. Seven bullets had inflicted as many wounds upon his body. Hastily concealing the lifeless form in the straw, they speedily decamped, killing some cattle as they fled in a northwesterly direction, encamping the first night in Westhampton, where they left sixteen poles standing, which was supposed to be the number of those on the war-path. Nothing more was heard of them, the alarm subsided, and quietness prevailed during the winter months. It may be remarked that the barn in which Mr. Clark was killed stood near the present residence of Martin Clapp.

The enemy had disappeared only for a season. When the ice and snow had melted, the French, on the banks of the St. Lawrence, again set the red swarm in motion towards the settlements in the Connecticut valley, on a mission of pillage and murder. The ordinary route was to ascend the St. Francis to its source, then crossing the height of land between that stream and the Passumpsic, to descend the latter to its junction with the Connecticut, from which their progress to the outlying English plantations and hamlets was comparatively easy.

On the 9th of May, 1748, they unexpectedly appeared again in Southamp-

ton. About the middle of the day, as Noah Pixley was returning to his
house from the pasture, where he had driven his cows, and had nearly reached
the southern extremity of the village, he was fired upon by the Indians, who
were concealed among the bushes in a ravine, and although seven or eight
guns were discharged at him in quick succession, he received only a slight
wound in the arm. He had run but a few rods when he was overtaken, his
head crushed with a hatchet and his scalp torn away. The party then hastily fled along a path leading to the west part of the town, and stopped a short
time at the house of Samuel Burt, now known as the Stephen E. Searle
place ; but as Mr. Burt and his family had left it, they did not remain long
enough to materially injure it. The people immediately rallied and pursued
them, but, as usually happened on such occasions, they were too late to over-
take and punish the retreating foe.

It does nor appear that the danger was any greater at this time than in
some previous years, when the inhabitants courageously resolved to remain
and defend their homes. But a panic now prevailed, and panic-stricken men
rarely listen to reason or act with discretion and prudence. They abandoned
their houses and farms and retired to Northampton, where all, or nearly all,
had formerly lived. Mr. Judd repaired temporarily to Suffield. This step,
as the event proved, was entirely unnecessary, and entailed upon the people
much distress and inconvenience. The murder of Pixley marked the final
disappearance of the Indians ; their annual visits ceased, and the settlements,
so far as is known, was never again vexed with the presence of hostile, marauding bands of savages.

Towards the close of July of the same year seven families returned to
their homes, or to speak more definitely, under the cover of fortifications to
watch the motions of the enemy, should any appear, and protect as far as
possible the infant settlement from injury. In the course of the autumn most
of the people came back to their homes. The abandonment of the place, however, had left the wheat and rye crop unharvested, and no corn had been planted.
During this gloomy period the inhabitants were assisted to some extent by
the towns less exposed to danger, and where agricultural operations were not
interrupted by Indian incursions. Besides the suffering caused by the scarcity of provisions, the settlers lost by death three prominent men, namely,
Ezra Strong, Moses Wright and Noah Sheldon, who were among the thirty
persons to whom allotments of land were originally made.

Military.—In the subsequent wars with the French, which terminated in the
capture of Canada, Southampton contributed her full proportion of men, and
in the campaign conducted by Sir William Johnson, in which the reduction
of Crown Point seems to have been the primary object, two of them, Eliakim
Wright and Ebenezer Kingsley, Jr., were slain. When Fort William Henry
was surrendered to Montcalm, in 1757, owing to the cowardice or incapacity of
General Webb, the English commander, who remained inactive with his army
in the immediate vicinity of the fort, two others, Joel Clapp and Nathaniel

Loomis, were stripped of their clothing and chased by the Indians nearly four-teen miles through the forest, barely escaping with their lives. But the time was rapidly approaching when the dangers which constantly menaced the frontier settlements of New England were to disappear. Under the guiding hand of William Pitt, who had the sagacity to discern military capacity and ability and employ them in the execution of his designs and purposes, the valley of the St. Lawrence passed into the possession of the English, and ceased thereafter to be regarded as a nuisance and an annoyance. Tradition affirms that in the great enterprise which resulted so auspiciously, the citizens of Southampton bore an honorable part, but unfortunately their names have not been preserved in the records of the town.

It would expand the sketch of Southampton beyond the limits assigned to reproduce in detail from the records the action of the town during the Revolutionary war. It must suffice to state succinctly and briefly, the most important measures which were adopted with entire unanimity, as their were no loyalists or Tories here, to meet the exigencies of the times. As early as the 3d of October, 1774, at a town meeting called for the purpose, a committee of correspondence was appointed, consisting of Jonathan Judd, Jr., Samuel Burt, Aaron Clark, Elias Lyman, Jonathan Clark, Timothy Clark, Lemuel Pomeroy, Samuel Clapp and Israel Sheldon. At the same time Samuel Burt and Aaron Clark were appointed delegates to a convention of the several towns of Hampshire county to be held in Northampton, and at an adjourned meeting Elias Lyman was chosen delegate to the provincial congress to be held at Concord. Events followed each other rapidly, and the next month the town directed the constables to collect the " Province tax" immediately and pay it to Henry Gardiner, the gentleman designated by the provincial congress to receive it, instead of Harrison Gray, who was acting under royal authority This was promptly done and constituted an act of overt and flagrant rebellion. In the succeeding years the town voted liberal sums of money for supplying the soldiers with food and clothing, and bounties to enlisted men. It is quite evident that nearly every able-bodied man in the town was employed at some time in the Revolutionary struggle, in some capacity, in the service of the country.

In the war of 1812, the late Col. Elisha Edwards, then captain, was stationed for several months at Boston with his company. Massachusetts was not enthusiastically devoted to the prosecution of the war, and it is probable that Southampton sympathized with the prevailing sentiment in the commonwealth. Indeed, the town gave expression to its disapprobation of the policy of the general government by sending Luther Edwards and John Lyman as delegates to the anti-war convention at Northampton.

In the civil war, according to the statistics compiled by the authority of the state, Southampton furnished one hundred and twenty-seven men, being sixteen more than her quota, and of this number, five were commissioned officers. In the way of aiding soldiers and their families the sum of $10,808 was paid by the town, aside from $5,899.96 which was subsequently refunded by the state.

Liberal Education.—Probably no town in the state in proportion to population has furnished so many liberally educated men as Southampton. The colleges from which they graduated were, principally, Harvard, Yale, Williams and Amherst. The following is believed to be a complete list, with the year of graduation: Jonathan Judd, Jr., 1765; David Searle, 1784; Rev. Ashbel Strong, 1801; Rev. Lyman Strong, 1802; Rev. Sylvester Burt, 1804; Rev. John Woodbridge, 1804; Martin L. Hurlburt, 1804; Rev. Saul Clark, 1805; Theodore Pomeroy, 1808; Rev. Samuel Ware, 1808; Rev. Rufus Pomeroy, 1808; Rev. Thaddeus Pomeroy, 1810; Rev. Isaac Parsons, 1811; Rev. William Strong, 1811; Rev. Federal Burt, 1812; Rev. Sylvester Woodbridge, 1813; Rev. Rufus Hurlburt, 1813; Rev. Noble D. Strong, 1813; Rev. Aretus Loomis, 1815; Justin W. Clark, 1816; Rev. Medad Pomeroy, 1817; Rev. Chandler Bates, 1818; Rev. Lemuel P. Bates, 1818; Rev. Philetus Clark, 1818; Rev. Erastus Clapp, 1822; Rev. Jairus Burt, 1824; Rev. Bela B. Edwards, 1824; Rev. Abner P. Clark, 1825; Rev. Ralph Clapp, 1825; Joseph B. Clapp, 1829; Rev. Jeremiah Pomeroy, 1829; Alvan W. Chapman, 1830; Gideon Searle, 1830; Rev. Jesse L. Frary, 1831; Edward R. Thorp, 1831; Israel W. Searle, 1832; Mahlon P. Chapman, 1832; Rev. Philander Bates, 1833; Rev. Rufus C. Clapp, 1833; Daniel Gould, 1834; Rev. Sereno D. Clark, 1835; Rev. Justus L. Janes, 1835; Rev. Lemuel Pomeroy, 1835; Rev. Lewis F. Clark, 1837; Rev. William H. Sheldon, 1837; Spencer S. Clark, 1839; J. C. Searle, 1842; Rev. Henry L. Edwards, 1847; Austin Weeks, 1858; Rev. Henry Jones, 1857; Rev. J. B. Finch, date of graduation not ascertained; Rev. Andrew J. Clapp, 1857; Julius D. Phelps, 1874.

Biographical.—Rev. Jonathan Judd, in any sketch, however brief, of Southampton and of the men who have lived in the town at various periods in its history, must naturally be assigned a conspicuous position. He was a native of Waterbury, Conn., and a graduate of Yale college. He was fifth in descent from Deacon Thomas Judd, who was one of a company of one hundred persons who, under the guidance of the Rev. Mr. Hooker, made, in 1636, the memorable overland journey from Cambridge to the valley of the Connecticut, and settled Hartford. Very likely he was one of the number who transported the fair, fragile and delicate form of Mrs. Hooker "on their arms" during their long and wearisome progress to their place of destination. For a short time Mr. Judd preached to the people of Suffield, and while there had some correspondence with the committee appointed in Southampton to "seek out some meet person to preach the Gospel" in the new settlement. Proceeding to this town he was so fortunate as to meet Jonathan Edwards, the Northampton pastor, in Westfield, and the two gentlemen proceeded together on their journey. His ministrations were so acceptable that he was called to the pastorate with but one dissenting voice, and this dissentient soon became one of his most zealous supporters. His pastorate reached the term of sixty years, and during that long period he retained the respect, confidence and affection of his people. Theologically he coincided in opinion with Mr. Stoddard, the grandfather and predecessor of Mr. Edwards in the pastorate of the Northampton church, and, consequently favored the adoption of the " Half-way covenant," as it was called. When Mr. Edwards became involved in trouble with his church, Mr. Judd was a member of the council that dismissed that gentleman. In person he was tall, well-proportioned, and of imposing presence ; in deportment grave, dignified and courteous ; as a preacher clear, methodical and lucid. At his death he directed all his sermons, three thousand or more in number, to be burned. Certainly Mr. Judd must have possessed admirable qualities of mind to enable him to retain the unabated love and esteem of his people to the close of his life. He married, soon after his settlement, Miss Silence Sheldon, of Suffield. Children : four sons and three daughters—Jonathan, Sylvester, Solomon, Frederick, Silence, Sarah and Clarissa. Mr. Judd built and resided in the house now occupied by Colonel E. A. Edwards. There is a current tradition that after divine service one Sunday morning, as the minister was walking in a meditative mood along a narrow path in the thicket a few rods from his house, in the direction of High street, he was suddenly confronted by a tall and muscular savage, fully armed, evidently upon the war-path, and intent upon the perpetration of mischief. The appearance of the warrior was as abrupt as it was unexpected, and the pastor must have been greatly surprised as well as alarmed, as he was probably one of a band of marauders lurking in ambush in the vicinity ; but his self-command was perfect, he manifested no signs of fear, and calmly and steadily looked upon the immovable countenance of the dangerous and unwelcome intruder. For a few moments the gaze was mutual. Then, with backward steps, still keeping his eyes fixed upon the Indian, he slowly retreated towards his house. When he reached it, the dusky warrior, having apparently changed his purpose or gratified his curiosity, moved swiftly into the forest and disappeared. If there was preaching in the meeting-house that afternoon, the edifice probably bore more resemblance to a fortification than a house of worship.

Jonathan Judd, Jr., received a liberal education, having graduated at Yale college at twenty-one years of age. For two or three years he was the instructor of a grammar school in Hatfield. The first store in Southampton was opened by him, in 1769. The records of the town, while he was town clerk, are models of neatness and accuracy. He was moderately successful in business, and at his death his estate was estimated at $14,000.00. He was succeeded in business by his nephew, Asa Judd. Since 1769 the mercantile business has been conducted here without interruption by some member of the family, the present representative being A. G. Judd.

Sylvester Judd removed to Westhampton. His son, Sylvester, in 1822 became the editor and proprietor of the *Hampshire Gazette*, which he conducted with much ability for thirteen years. After his retirement from the

28*

Gazette, he spent three or four years in arranging in volumes the public papers and documents in the state house at Hartford, Conn. His tastes and inclinations were in the direction of historical and geneological researches, in which pursuit he has rendered invaluable service to the people of Hampshire county. His son Sylvester, the third of the name, graduated at Yale college in 1836, and became the pastor of the Unitarian church at Augusta, Me. His intuitions were lofty, elevating and ennobling, and his whole nature was eloquent with generous and magnanimous emotions and impulses. He was a man of genius, as well as of learning, as the story of " Margaret " fully attests.

Frederick Judd remained in Southampton and resided during a part of his life where Harris Nimocks now lives. He was a representative to the general court, selectman of the town and a magistrate of the commonwealth. He accumulated a handsome property, and was a citizen of character and influence in the community. Jonathan Judd, Jr., was town clerk ten years ; Jonathan N. Judd, son of Asa Judd, sixteen years ; and Frederick E. Judd, a grandson, ten years and the present incumbent of the office.

Rev. Vinson Gould was a native of Sharon, Conn., and was settled as the colleague of Mr. Judd in August, 1801, and dismissed in January, 1832, after a pastorate of thirty-one years. This gentleman was distinguished for his love of learning, and the schools of the town under his supervision and guidance attained to a high degree of excellence. It was owing to his encouragement more than to any other cause that so many young men in Southampton were induced to obtain a liberal education and embrace the clerical profession. He married Mindwell Woodbridge, daughter of Doctor Woodbridge. His son, David Gould, became a lawyer and practiced his profession in New York. One daughter, Mary, married Rev. A. W. McClure, and another, Mindwell, married Rev. John Patton, and resides in Delaware. After his dismissal, Mr. Gould was engaged for a while in teaching.

Elias Lyman was one of the original thirty who settled in the town, and was the descendant in the fifth degree of Richard Lyman, of High Ongar, Essex, England. His mother's name was Mindwell Sheldon. The name of Mindwell, used probably for its peculiar significance by the fathers, was a popular one for a long time in this region, and is, moreover, an euphoneous one. Caleb Strong, one of the most illustrious of the sons of Massachusetts, and one of the first senators in the congress of the United States, and governor of the commonwealth in a season of intense public excitement, was a nephew of Elias Lyman. He came to Southampton before he was eighteen years of age, and located in the west part of the precinct, being the first settler in that neighborhood, though Samuel Burt soon followed him. Eleven years afterward he left his forest home, traveled to Boston, and joined the army under General William Pepperell, for the capture of Louisburg, a strongly fortified town on the east side of the island of Cape Breton. He returned uninjured, and thereafter engaged in the peaceful pursuits of agriculture. Though in the decline of life he actively participated in the struggle for independence, and was elected a member of the provincial congress that met at Concord. He was a man of exemplary character, and filled many positions of trust and responsibility. Two of his sons were pioneers in the settlement of Chester. His daughter Eunice married Lemuel Pomeroy, and from her are descended the Pomeroy family of Pittsfield, long noted for business enterprise and wealth.

Col. Samuel Lyman, grandson of Elias Lyman, was a resident of Southampton for many years, and like his ancestor, filled many important civil positions in the town. He was a man of strong convictions and great firmness of character. Stephen Lyman, son of Colonel Lyman, besides attending to his farming and merchandise business, is also station agent of the Northampton & New Haven railroad. He has represented the town in the lower branch of the legislature, and at present is one of the deacons of the Congregational church. The honors and duties of the diaconate seem to seek this branch of the Lyman family. He is the fourth in lineal succession who has filled the office, the line of descent being Elias, Stephen, Samuel, Stephen. His daughter Harriet married Rev. William R. Stocking, who was for some time engaged in missionary labors in the neighborhood of Urumiah, in northwestern Persia. She died two or three years after her marriage, of cholera, in the valley of the Tigris, whither she had accompanied her husband on a visit. In all respects she was an estimable and accomplished young lady. Charles B. Lyman, another son, occupies the homestead, and is at present one of the selectmen of the town. He is an intelligent and progressive farmer, and makes a specialty of purchasing certain kinds of supplies for the Springfield market, a business he has followed for many years.

Isaac Parsons removed to Southampton from Northampton, in 1775. He was a descendant in the fifth degree of Cornet Joseph Parsons, who came to New England in the same year, and probably in the same ship that brought Henry Vane and Hugh Peters. He was one of the original settlers of Springfield, and his name is attached as a witness to the deed by which the Indians conveyed the territory comprised within the limits of the township to the English. Eighteen years afterwards he was one of the company that founded Northampton and organized the "Old Church." Isaac Parsons became the proprietor of what was denominated in the old maps of the precinct the "third square mile," situated in the extreme northwest corner of Southampton. This large tract remained nearly intact for one hundred years, and has never passed entirely ftom the control of the family. He married Mindwell King, of Northampton. Isaac Parsons, son of the preceding and second of the name, was born in 1790. His preparatory studies were pursued under the instruction of the Rev. Moses Hallock, of Plainfield, who was somewhat noted for fitting young men for college. He graduated from Yale, received theological instruction at Andover, and preached for a short time in Worcester and also in Northampton. He was finally settled over the Congregational church in East Haddam, Conn., and there he remained until his death.   He was a man of scholarly attainments, more than average mental endowments, and a perspicuous and vigorous writer.   His only son, Rev. Henry M. Parsons, was the colleague of Dr. Osgood, of the First church, in Springfield. Another son, Theodore Parsons, born in 1781, remained upon the homestead, the "third square mile."   He was a careful, prudent and industrious man. Sensible of the benefits which would inure to his children by affording them greater educational advantages than could be obtained in Southampton, he removed temporarily to Northampton, where they were instruced in the higher branches of learning.   His son Theodore entered Yale college, but died in his junior year.   Mr. Parsons died in 1854, leaving a good estate.   His son, Isaac Parsons, the representative of the family, has resided for the last few years in the village, and the town has no worthier citizen.   Of excellent abilities and well educated, he has often been selected to fill positions of honor and responsibility, the duties of which he has discharged intelligently and creditably.   He has often been chairman of the board of selectmen, the guiding mind in the school committee for nearly thirty years, and in 1866 a representative in the legislature from the first district of Hampshire county.

Samuel Edwards, in 1753, removed to this town from Northampton, and purchased the farm of Thomas Porter.   He was a teacher during the winter season for about forty years, and the chair which he occupied while engaged in that vocation is still preserved by the family, as well as a gun which he carried in the wars against the French and Indians.   This gun was also carried by his son Elisha in the Revolutionary war, and by his grandson Elisha in the war of 1812.   Elisha Edwards, commonly known as Colonel Edwards, grandson of Samuel Edwards, was among the prominent men who have lived and died in Southampton.   He was an intelligent man, prudent and conscientious in speech, and especially careful not to wound the sensibilities of any members of the community by ill-timed or hasty expressions.   In early life he manifested more than ordinary interest in public affairs and was repeatedly made the recipient of the public confidence and favor.   Seven times he represented the town in the legislature, was often one of the board of selectmen and a member of the last constitutional convention of Massachusetts.   His son, Elisha A. Edwards, was a captain in the 31st regiment, Massachusetts Volunteers, and was with General Butler in Louisiana.   He has been one of the county commissioners for the county of Hampshire eighteen years, during most of the time chairman of the board, and was recently elected for another term of three years.   Charles L. Edwards, another son, entered the military service soon after the commencement of the civil war as lieutenant in Company D, 37th regiment, was promoted to the rank of captain and then to that of major.   He was in the army of the Potomac and partici- pated in all the great battles in which that army was engaged.   He now resides in Kansas.   The third son, George K. Edwards, was also in the army with the rank of lieutenant.   His regiment was mostly employed in Virginia and about the defences of Washington. He resides upon the paternal home-stead and is noted for his enterprise in agricultural matters. Rev. Bela B. Edwards, grandson of Deacon Samuel Edwards, graduated from Amherst college in 1824, and adapted the ministerial profession. He was distinguished for his scholastic attainments and became widely known as a professor in the Andover Theological seminary, and as editor of various denominational periodicals. His mental habits were systematic and methodical, his love of learning intense, and his industry unwearied. In purely literary acquirements it may be said, without injustice to any, that he excelled all the other sons of Southampton. His labors were immense and he died at the meridian of his fame and in the full possession of his intellectual powers at the age of forty-nine years. Luther Edwards, second son of Deacon Samuel Edwards, settled about a mile west of the village. It is a tradition of the family that in the division of the paternal estate he received more acres of land than his brother Elisha, because a larger proportion of his share was hilly or mountainous. He was a prosperous and respected citizen, and served the town as selectman and member of the legislature. He married Clarissa, daughter of Rev. Jonathan Judd, and their daughter, Clarissa, became the wife of Major Harvey Kirkland, for many years register of deeds for Hampshire county. Luther Edwards, Jr., who succeeded to the homestead, was a man of vigorous mental powers, fixed opinions and strong convictions. He was studious in his habits and devoted his leisure moments to the perusal of works which tended to enlarge and improve the understanding. An anxious seeker after truth, he would unhesitatingly follow its teachings wheresoever it might lead regardless of personal consequences. It is said of him that at the advent of the temperance reformation he derived a considerable part of his income from a distillery. After examining the subject with his usual care, he came to the conclusion that the reform was a beneficial one to individuals and society, and that he would distill no more spirituous liquors. But he would not sell the equipment of the distillery to others to do what his conscience told him was wrong. The establishment was suffered to decay. He was a member of the legislature when the construction of the New Haven and Northampton canal was agitated. His excellent judgment clearly discerned that the enterprise would prove a disastrous failure—as it did—and he refused to countenance or promote the plans of its projectors. This adherence to the dictates of duty cost him his seat in the legislature, as he was defeated at the next election by a canal man. His son, Rev. Henry L. Edwards, graduated at Amherst college in 1847, studied theology at the Andover seminary, and for several years was the pastor of churches at South Abington and North Middleborough, but now resides in Northampton.

Noah Clarke came from Northampton, and settled in the west part of the town, on the banks of the Manhan river, at the foot of Montgomery mountain. The farm at the close of his life comprised about four hundred acres of land, which was inherited mainly by his son, the late Strong Clarke, who occupied the homestead nearly to the close of his life. Strong Clarke was in many respects a notable man. In his life he practiced the virtues of prudence and frugality, tempered with a judicious and well-directed charity. One of his prominent characteristics was his innate modesty and diffidence. He was in manner kind and sympathetic, and these qualities were exerted invariably to subdue and convince as well as to disarm and obliterate hostility and enmity. An admirable man in all the relations of life. His merits were appreciated by his townsmen, and he was twice elected to the legislature at a time when, owing to the multiplicity of parties, no other man, probably, could have obtained a majority in the constituency. His eldest son, Joseph S. Clarke, is a prominent citizen of Westfield; and the youngest, Jairus E. Clarke, is at the present time high sheriff of the county of Hampshire.

William S. Rogers was a useful and influential citizen, and served the town in various capacities. Was town clerk two years, a selectman fifteen years, and a representative in the general court three years.

Zeno E. Coleman, a son of Zeno and grandson of Samuel, was born on the old Coleman homestead, November 17, 1812, one of a family of eleven children. He married Aldula E. Babcock, of Franklin, Portage county, Ohio, September 13, 1838. Their children were Perry M., Henry E., Sumner O., Dwight D., Catharine E., Eugene A. and Sylvester P., four of whom, Henry E., Sumner O., Dwight D. and Sylvester P., are living. Mr. Coleman died April 8, 1882. He held the office of selectman several years, and in 1863-64 was chairman of the board, assisting materially in filling the town's quota. Perry M., their oldest son, was the first to enlist from the town, April 25, 1861, going out with Co. C., 10th Mass. Vols., and was killed at the battle of Fair Oaks, Va., May 31, 1862. His body was the only one of the Southampton boys that was brought home for burial. Zeno's widow now resides with her son, Dwight, on road 25.

Flavel K. Sheldon, a son of Capt. Silas, and descendant of Israel, was born on the present Benson farm, December 12, 1831. When about seventeen years of age his parents moved to the farm he now occupies, the old Vincon Gould farm, at the village. On August 8, 1862, he enlisted in Co. D, 37th Mass. Vols., as a private. In the spring of 1865 he re-enlisted, and was mustered out of service in July following. He was promoted on four different occasions, being mustered out as 1st lieutenant. Mr. Sheldon married Eunice C. Clapp, June 3, 1852, who bore him two children, Robert F. and Frank C., both of whom are living. Mrs. Sheldon died July 18, 1861, and for his second wife Mr. Sheldon married Adella S. Brown, daughter of Joseph Brown, of Westhampton. Their only child, Grace A., was born July 1, 1870. Mr. Sheldon was elected a state representative in 1884-85, from the 1st Hampshire district, and has held the office of vice-president of the Three-county Agricultural Society four years.

Alvan W. Chapman graduated from Amherst College in 1830, and adopted the medical profession. Eventually he removed to Florida and settled at Apalachicola, and was in the enjoyment of a lucrative practice at the outbreak of the rebellion. Being a northern man and entertaining strong union sentiments, he soon found his position one of embarrassment and even danger. Constantly menaced with the hostility of the more violent part of the community, he often found it necessary, to preserve his personal liberty, to pass the night in a boat among the numerous islands in the lagoon below the town. But he never could be induced to recognize the southern confederacy or render it any aid or comfort. When the rebellion was suppressed and the state reconstructed, he received the appointment of judge of probate for the county of Franklin, and discharged the duties of the office to the general satisfaction of the people. A few years afterwards he was commissioned by the general government to describe and clasify the plants, shrubs and trees of South Florida, and, making extensive explorations for the purpose, performed the work assigned him in an exhaustive and admiable manner. Although a modest and diffident man, averse to all notoriety, his fame as a scientist has extended beyond the limits of the United States, and he has been for many years an esteemed correspondent of scientific societies in Europe. A man of learning and of many acquirements in his special department, he is now passing the remnent of his life in retirement at Apalachicola.

Edson Hannum is one of the prominent citizens of Southampton. Always noted for his studious habits he may be ranked among men of more than the average intelligence. In the various reforms which have agitated society and the nation during the last half century, he has taken a deep interest. Especially was this true in regard to the anti-slavery cause, and so strong were his convictions on this subject that he severed his connection with the political party with which he had acted, and joined the party of freedom. Essentially progressive in the tendencies of his mind, he has always advocated such measures as seemed, in his judgment, just and proper, and designed to promote the greatest good of the greatest number. He has been often elected by the people to civil positions, and in 1864 was an active and efficient member of the legislature. Mr. Hannum was born on the old Hannum farm, May 26, 1815, and still resides there. He married Rosette Shadman, of Manchester, Conn., May 10, 1837, who bore him five children, four of whom, Ellen J., Frederick M., Hattie B. and Frank E., are living.

Lewis Hannum, son of Quartus, and brother of Edson, was born here March 26, 1817, on the old Hannum farm. He resided there until 1856, and sold it in 1861 to the present proprietor. In 1866 he removed to the village and built the house he now occupies. He married Nancy Robinson, April 4, 1839, and has one son, Melvin L., living in Brooklyn, and engaged in the furniture business in New York city.

Asahel Birge, commonly known as "Squire Birge," came from Connecticut, and during his whole life was a conspicuous figure in the affairs of the town, filling, at various times, the offices of town clerk, selectman, justice of the peace and representative in the legislature. He was the first person in the town to be inoculated for the small-pox. His son, Edward Birge, after a successful business career in Troy, has returned to the homestead to spend the residue of his life, and a grandson, Edward, is a professor in a western college.

Henry S. Sheldon is a son of Simeon Sheldon, was mainly instrumental in organizing the Methodist society, and is a person of note in the old town. He was first elected one of the selectmen in the second year of the civil war and continued in office until the rebellion was subdued. After an interval of a few years he was again elected and officiated as chairman of the board. In 1879 he was chosen a member of the general court.

Lyman C. Tiffany is a native of the town, and like Mr. Sheldon, was one of the selectmen in war times, and rendered the town efficient service in that trying and exacting period of its history. He has filled the office recently with great acceptance to the people. During several years he was town clerk. In 1861, when quite a young man, he was elected to the legislature, and proved an intelligent and capable representative. Mr. Tiffany is one of the most respected citizens of Southampton, and is distinguished for great clearness and accuracy of judgment. In this quality of the mind he is excelled by none, and is in every respect a useful and valuable member of society. For several years past he has been engaged in the whip manufacture, an industry in which, owing to judicious and careful management, he has been quite successful.

Sardis Chapman is an aged citizen, a brother of Dr. Alvan W. Chapman, now retired from business in the enjoyment of a competency acquired by industry during the active years of his life. Progressive in his ideas, he has been the consistent advocate of such reforms as seemed in his judgment beneficial to mankind. He is quite an antiquarian, and in geneological matters is an authority that may be relied upon with perfect safety.

Samuel B. Quigley was born in Chester, Hampden county, was educated in the schools of Fairfield, Conn., and in a printing office ; studied two years in the law offices of Hon. William G. Bates, of Westfield, and Messrs. Wells, Davis & Alvord, of Greenfield, but has followed through life the vocations of printer, teacher and farmer. Came to Southampton in 1861, and was one of the representatives in the legislature for the First Hampshire district in the years 1871 and 1872. He has been connected at different periods of his life as a writer with several newspapers, his first contributions to the press having been made when he was only sixteen years of age.

Dea. David B. Phelps, a native of Northampton, was for many years a resident of this town. In all matters of a public nature, both secular and religious, he manifested much interest, and was conspicuous for his advocacy of the temperance reform and the extension of the suffrage to women. He enlisted in the 52d regiment, and was a faithful soldier in the campaigns in Louisiana. In his death, a few years since, society lost a valuable member.

Deacon Timothy P. Bates, an intelligent citizen, has filled various town offices with credit, and has long been a deacon of the Congregational church, to whose welfare he devotes much time and attention.

Lemuel Pomeroy, one of the old-time worthies, lived on the Pomeroy homestead on the east side of White Loofe hill. It was on the old road from Northampton to Westfield, and was long known as the Pomeroy tavern. This family was included among the early settlers, and has produced some enterprising and capable men. Lemuel Pomeroy was one of the selectmen nine years, and a member of the general court ten or twelve years. In fact, during the active period of his life, but little business was transacted by the town in which he did not participate, and frequently control. Members of this family became noted in Berkshire county for their success in various manufacturing enterprises, and a descendant of this Southampton Pomeroy became the wife of the late General William Francis Bartlett.

Josiah A. Gridley was born in 1802, in Southington, Conn., but lived during his whole life, with the exception of the first two years, in Southampton. He attended the Pittsfield Medical college, and having a natural aptitude for therapeutics, embraced the medical profession and became a physician of the eclectic school. He was successful in his labors and secured a large and lucrative practice, which he retained until the infirmaties of age compelled him to relinquish it. Dr. Gridley was much more than an ordinary man, and analyzed all questions that came under his consideration with much mental acuteness. In the gift of language he was never excelled by any resident of the town, and was endowed with rare natural eloquence. As a talker and conversationalist he had few superiors. Of an inquiring and investigating mind, he was always a seeker after truth, and was never deterred from the pursuit from any apprehension that popular opinion would regard it with disfavor. A prominent attribute of his character was his moral courage. An earnest opponent of slavery he was early identified with the party of freedom and gave it a zealous support. The same may be said of the temperance cause with which he warmly sympathized.

Hon. Beman Brockway is the son of Gideon Brockway, who with his father Isaiah Brockway, settled on the extreme northwest part of the town adjoining the "third square mile" of the Parsons family one hundred or more years ago. The Brockway family came from Lyme, Conn., where most of those bearing the name of Brockway in this country originated. Beman Brockway was born in 1815, and spent the early years of his boyhood upon the paternal homestead and in acquiring the art "preservative of arts," in the office of the *Courier,* a newspaper published in Northampton. But his father was allured to the richer lands of Chautauqua county, New York, in 1832, and he followed him the next year, to be immediately solicited to undertake the publication of the *Sentinel,* a weekly newspaper at Mayville. The enterprise proved successful financially, and he remained as editor and proprietor eleven years when he sold the establishment and purchased the *Palladium*, a weekly paper at Oswego, which he soon converted into a daily. He sold the *Palladium* in 1853, having been invited by Horace Greeley to join the editorial staff of the New York *Tribune*. There he remained two years. His duties were laborious but were performed to the entire acceptance of Mr. Greeley, who, to the close of his eventful life manifested a strong personal and political friendship for Mr. Brockway. He returned to Oswego, and in 1858 was elected to the legislature where he served with distinction and usefulness, especially on questions affecting the canals, and was mainly instrumental in perfecting and securing the passage of an efficient law for the registration of voters. Soon after he removed to Watertown, resumed the profession of editor, and was so engaged when, in 1865, he was invited by Governor Fenton to accept the position of private secretary; but the Governor, who highly appreciated his capacity and ability, presently tendered him the resposible office of canal appraiser, the duties of which he discharged with signal success until the expiration of his term in 1870. In the course of that year he became connected with the Watertown *Daily Times* and *Weekly Reformer,* and by successive purchases soon acquired sole proprietary rights in these two journals of Northern New York. Under his judicious management, as editor-in-chief, these papers have attained a wide circulation and a commanding influence in that part of the state where they are published. Mr. Brockway has been a member of the editorial profession for more than half a century, and during all that time has been an able and efficient supporter of all measures devised to promote and enhance the prosperity and happiness of all classes of people, but particularly of the toiling millions. All official positions have come to him unsought and unsolicited, and all the obligations and duties attached to them have been performed by him with scrupulous fidelity. All things considered, Hon. Beman Brockway may be regarded as the most eminent son of Southampton now living. Mr. Brockway has been twice married, first, to a daughter of Solomon Warner, of Northampton, and second, to her cousin, Sarah Warner Wright, of Keene, N. H., and both were cousins of the late Oliver Warner, for many years secretary of state of Massachusetts.

Noah Burt was a faithful soldier and an ardent patriot during the war for independence. As tradition renders the story he was plowing in the field when the news arrived of the commencement of hostilities. Like Putnam on the same occasion, he unhitched his horses from the plow, and directing his boy to take charge of one of them, mounted the other, and with his gun and a few necessary articles, proceeded with all speed to Cambridge, where the patriots were gathering in force. During his absence the labor on the farm was performed by his wife with such occasional assistance as she was able to procure; and among other tasks which she imposed upon herself was the breaking of a colt to supply the place of the horse which had borne her husband to the army, and she succeeded in a short time in rendering the animal docile and obedient. At the conclusion of the war Mr. Burt found himself financially embarrassed, and tradition again affirms that he applied to his friend Governor Caleb Strong, of Northampton, for assistance, who generously loaned him half a bushel of silver dollars. In this last transaction tradition may have capriciously mingled fancy with facts, as it is doubtful if all the silver dollars in Northampton at the termination of the war would have filled a half-bushel.

Nathaniel Searle was one of the first settlers, and was noted as the richest man in the precinct. On that account, probably, his house was the only one that contained two rooms, and, before the erection of the meeting-house, religious services were held in it. Some of his descendants are still living in the town.

Samuel C. Pomeroy entered Amherst college but did not graduate. He was a representative in the legislature in 1852, went to Kansas where he became prominent, and served two terms in the United States senate.

Noah L. Strong also entered Amherst college, but like Mr. Pomeroy, did not graduate. He was a member of the lower branch of the legislature in 1848, and was subsequently elected one of the senators for the county of Hampshire.

Isaac S. Wolcott, son of Stephen, was born on the farm now occupied by L. C. Tiffany, March 30, 1806. He married Eliza Rust September 2, 1829, who bore him two children, Jairus B. and Lemuel P. Mrs. Wolcott died May 15, 1880, and Mr. Wolcott, at the age of eighty years, resides with his son Lemuel on road 12. The latter was born February 21, 1841, married Cornelia F. Shepard, of Westfield, October 14, 1880, and has two children, Alfred L. and Anna L.

Asa Southworth was born on the old homestead, in the northern part of the town, in 1793. He married Achsah Wood, in 1817. Mrs. Southworth now lives on the old homestead, aged eighty-eight years.

Luther Wright, from Northampton, came to this town in April, 1832, and located upon the old Wright homestead in the northern part of the town. He died here May 9, 1846, aged sixty-nine years. He brought with him his wife and two children, one of whom, Luther A., still resides on the farm at the age of seventy-seven years. He married Mirza Thompson, a native of Monterey, Mass., (then South Tyringham), who bore him one child, Samuel L., who carries on the farm. Mrs. Wright is still living, but has been a helpless paralytic fifteen years.

Joseph Russell came from Connecticut about 1809, and located at what is still known as Russellville, where he carried on for many years the business of carding and dressing cloth. He married Sylva Norton, August 29, 1805, who bore him nine children, Harriet E., Charles D., Mary, Almera, Joseph H., Sylva L., Isaac N., Martha A. and Augustus, all but three of whom are living. Isaac N. was born April 21, 1823, married Mrs. Ellen M. Luddington, April 2, 1878. Charles D. Russell was born here December 19, 1819, and has always resided here. He married Wealthy Upson May 23, 1836. Their children are Emily A. (Mrs. William Boyd), Alfred Z., Cynthia E. (Mrs. George Lyon).

Julius Boyd was born in what was a part of West Springfield in 1801, and came to Southampton about 1840. His son William D. was born there and was seven years of age when his parents moved here. William married Emily Russell, daughter of Charles D., in 1857, and has two children, Frank R. and Lillian E.

Nahum Shumway was born in Belchertown in 1812, and came to Southampton about 1841. He married Elizabeth Cook, who died in 1844. Mr. Shumway died in 1884. Their only child, Hattie E., occupies the old homestead on road 40.

Thomas J. Rawley, son of Thomas, was born on the E. Olds farm, December 2, 1812. He married Eliza Haskell, and they have had two children, Albert W. and Myron J. The latter died September 30, 1884.

Solomon A. Wolcott, residing on road 28, was born in Holyoke, May 29, 1811, and came to this town when five years of age. He married Louisa Pomeroy, who died in 1865; and in November, 1872, he married his present wife, Jane A. Elliott. They have two children, Louisa May and Anna J.

Gilbert Bascom, son of Elisha, was born here January 10, 1796, one of a family of seven children. He married Cynthia Clark, daughter of Oliver, April 25, 1822, and during the following years moved to the old homestead on road 23, where he resided until his death, April 4, 1883, and where his daughters, Elvira B. and Cynthia S. now reside. Mr. Bascom's children were Elvira B. (Mrs. Alford Warriner), Sophronia A. (Mrs. Silas D. Clark, of Northampton), Cynthia S. and Delia A., who died July 30, 1857, at the age of nineteen years.

Barney T. Wetherell was born in Middleborough, Mass., October 14, 1822. He married Adelia M. Stedman, born in Manchester, Conn., October 5, 1821, in Southampton, August 10, 1843. Their children are Georgianna E., born October 13, 1844, Helen A., born March 27, 1852, Arthur B., born February 2, 1855, and Louis S., born September 4, 1867. Mr. Wetherell is one of the prominent men of the town.

Dr. Sylvester Woodbridge was the first physician, and came to Southampton by the invitation of the town as expressed in a legal town meeting. He was quite successful in his practice, and accumulated a handsome property for those primitive times. He built the Woodbridge mansion, the most pretentious edifice in the town, which is in an excellent state of preservation, and may, with proper attention, last the greater part of another century.

Dr. Bela P. Jones, after the field had been occupied for two or three years by a Dr. Blair and then relinquished by him, settled in the town and remained about thirty years. He removed to Hudson, Michigan, where he died.

Dr. Artemas Bell succeeded Dr. Jones, and also practiced medicine in Southampton thirty years. He withdrew from practice on account of declining health and died a few years ago.

Doctors S. E. Thayer, G. W. Wood and H. P. Atherton followed each other in the order of their names, but did not practice long. Dr. E. Alden Dyer is at present the resident physician.

Dr. E. Alden Dyer was born at South Abington (now Whitman), Plymouth county, Mass., July 17, 1837. He studied in the common schools of South Abington, was three years at Phillips academy, Andover, one year in Amherst, then three years in Bellevue Hospital Medical college, N. Y., graduating in March, 1882. He then practiced in Northampton a little less than a year, and from there came to Southampton, succeeding Dr. H. P. Atherton, March 5, 1883.

The town never had but one lawyer, Charles F. Bates, and he remained only two or three years. He came from Westfield and was a brother of the late Elijah Bates, a lawyer of that town.

Among others than the ones we have spoken of, Joseph Kingsley, George D. Hannum, Elam Hitchcock, John B. Ewing, Lewis Graves, George H. Lyon, S. J. Hobbs, Alfred Woodward, George Clark, Charles D. Russell, Rufus Lyman, George Gorton, B. N. Norton, H. O. Strong, Newton Strong, Anson Swift, Charles P. Gridley, Harris Nimocks and Elijah Lyon may be mentioned as prominent citizens.

VILLAGES.

SOUTHAMPTON, the principal village, is situated at the foot of Little mountain near the center of the township, and contains about sixty dwellings, most of which are occupied by farmers whose estates consist of contiguous and outlying lands, which, under an improved system of agriculture, are generally increasing in productiveness. There are also two churches, Congregational and Methodist, an academy, three stores, a town hall and postoffice. The Northampton and New Haven railroad passes near the village on the east, and by its connections with other roads affords ample traveling facilities for the inhabitants. Most of the dwellings are neat and commodious, and some may even be termed elegant. The beautiful elm trees that surround the small open park or common in the center of the village, were planted by Asa Judd, a grandson of the Rev. Jonathan Judd, the first pastor of the church.

RUSSELLVILLE is a hamlet of a dozen or fifteen dwellings, in the southwest part of the township, and derives its name from the Russell family who have been engaged in business there for two or three generations.

MANUFACTURES.

Lyon Bros.' saw and grist-mill, on road 40, was built by them in 1882. The grist-mill has one run of stones and does both custom and merchant work, grinding about 40,000 bushels of grain per year. The saw-mill has a circular saw, shingle machine and planer, saws about 500,000 feet of lumber and 150,000 shingles per year. They employ four men.

B. T. Wetherell's saw-mill, on road 26½, operated by N. H. Lyman, was built in 1868, upon the site of the old John Lyman mill, which has been standing for more than half a century. The mill has a circular and bench-saw and shingle machine. It turns out about 200,000 feet of lumber, 100,000 shingles, and about 6,000 dozen whip-buts annually.

Herman Hupfer's elastic fabric mill, at Glendale, has just been put into operation by him. Mr. Hupfer has been in the employ of the Glendale Co. at Easthampton for the past twenty years, and together with his skill and knowledge of the business, he brings with him considerable skilled labor besides. The mill of the Glendale Co., which has been standing idle for some time, has been taken by him, a large, light, airy structure. He has at present three looms in operation, and employs five hands, though the capacity will doubtless soon be increased. They are now running entirely on elastic shoe goring after a patent of his own.

Charles Wait's saw-mill and cider-mill, at Russellville, has a circular saw, one bench-saw, slab-saw, and shingle machine. He employs two men and turns out 200,000 feet of lumber and 100,000 shingles per year. The cider-mill turns out about 3,000 barrels of cider per year.

Peck & Parsons's saw-mill, on r 19, was built by Allen C. Bartlett, about 1875. It has a circular saw, two bench-saws, planer, etc. They employ three men and cut about 200,000 feet of lumber per year.

William N. Graves's cider-mill, on road 2, was built by the Parsons family about half a century ago. Mr. Graves manufactures about 200 barrels of cider per year.

Charles D. Russell & Son's whip factory, at Russellville, was built by them in 1865. When in full operation they employ three men and turn out about $3,000.00 worth of business per year.

L. C. Tiffany's whip shop, on High street, was established by him in 1864. He manufactures, with his son, about 800 dozen per year, the machine part of the work being all done in Westfield.

Jesse F. Finch's blacksmith shop, on road 23, was built by his father, James B. Finch, about thirty years ago. He now does all blacksmith work, horse shoeing, jobbing, and general repair work.

George D. Hannum's cider-mill, on road 23, was originally built many years ago. It has the capacity for turning out about 1,500 barrels per year.

Philo J. Pomeroy has on his farm, on road 23, a valuable bed of fine blue pottery clay, covering an area of nearly forty acres, and averaging about twenty feet in depth.   He and his father, George Pomeroy, made brick here from this clay for about forty years, or up to the time of the latter's death, in 1881.   The deposit is in a desirable location, being only one and one-fourth miles from the depot at Easthampton, so that valuable potteries might be established here.

SHELDON ACADEMY.

This institution was incorporated by an act of the legislature passed January 27, 1829.   It was established by contributions, the principal donor being Silas Sheldon, who gave $1,500, and in whose honor the institution was named.   The original fund was $3,890.50.   The building was erected in 1829.   For a number of years past the trustees have given the town free use of the building, and it in turn maintains a high school therein.   The fund now amounts to $2,200.00.

ECCLESIASTICAL.

Congregational church.—There seems to have been preaching in the settlement as early as 1737; but it was not continuous and regular.   The names of two persons who officiated here previous to the precinct organization have been preserved.   They were David Parsons and John Woodbridge.   The services were conducted in private houses.   Mr. Parsons was subsequently settled over the church in Amherst, and Mr. Woodbridge over that in South Hadley.   As early as 1737 Northampton had voted in town-meeting that part of the tax assessed upon the new settlement should be appropriated for the erection of a meeting-house therein; but several years elapsed before it was finished.   Although an unpretending structure compared with the one in which the Congregational society now worship, its completion severely taxed the financial resources of the people.   When finished a committee was chosen to dignify the seats and pews, dignity not being very clearly defined as " in the compound ratio of age and property."   This structure was used until 1788, when the increase of population rendered it necessary to enlarge the building, or erect a new and more spacious house of worship.   The latter proposition was adopted and the present edifice was built.   It will be observed that it is nearly one hundred years old.   Forty-six years ago it was thoroughly repaired, and quite recently the interior was remodeled in accordance with modern ideas of taste and convenience.   The building itself is in a good state of preservation, and with care and attention may last the greater part of another century.   The first minister of the church in Southampton was the Rev. Jonathan Judd.   Mr. Judd was a native of Waterbury, Conn., and a graduate of Yale college in 1741.   He preached a few times to the people early in 1743, and with so much satisfaction that in June of that year they gave him an unanimous call to settle with them in the work of the ministry.   The following ministers constituted the council that installed the pastor : Jonathan Edwards, Northampton ; Samuel Hopkins, Springfield ; John Ballantine, Westfield ; John Woodbridge, South Hadley ; David Parsons, Amherst. Mr. Edwards preached on the occasion. The church thus organized numbered sixty-three persons, and it may be noted as a peculiarity of the time and the condition of thought that then prevailed, that it comprised nearly every adult inhabitant in the precinct. For settlement Mr. Judd was given two hundred acres of land, one hundred pounds old tenor in money, and one hundred and twenty-five pounds in work, probably in building a house and clearing land. His salary was to be £130 in money per annum for three successive years, and then to be increased £5 a year until it amounted to £170. The following is the ministerial record of Mr. Judd's successors, the respective dates denote the beginning and close of their labors : Rev. Vinson Gould, 1801–32 ; Rev. Morris E. White, 1832–53 ; Rev. Stephen C. Strong, 1854–59 ; Rev. Joseph E. Swallow, 1859–62 ; Rev. Alexander D. Stowell, 1863–64 ; Rev. Burritt A. Smith, 1865–68 ; Rev. Rufus P. Wells, 1869–74 ; Rev. Edward S. Fitz, 1874–76 ; Rev. E. L. Clark, 1877–86. Messrs. A. D. Stowell and E. L. Clark were acting pastors, as is Rev. D. W. Clark, who now supplies the pulpit.

Methodist church.—It is believed that Simeon Sheldon and his wife were the pioneer Methodists of Southampton. Previous to 1840 they had attended meetings of that denomination in the northern part of West Springfield—now Holyoke—and were so favorably impressed with the views and methods of the advocates of that ecclesiastical system in the prosecution of Christian effort and labor, that they invited Rev. Rufus Baker to visit their neighborhood and preach to the people. He complied with the request and religious services were held in the school-house in Foggintown, as the southeast part of the town is sometimes called. Others, mainly local preachers from various places in the vicinity, continued the work which Mr. Baker had begun, and a class was formed connected with the church in Westfield. These meetings, at the outset infrequent, gradually became regular, and were conducted for two or three years by Rev. Henry Battin. In 1842 a church organization was perfected, and two years afterwards the present meeting-house was erected. This is an unpretending, but handsome edifice, and sufficiently spacious for the wants of the society, which is in a prosperous condition. Rev. Tmomas Marcy was the first conference preacher, and he received his appointment the same year that the church was organized. In accordance with the usage and custom of the denomination, the pastors of the church have been changed at stated periods. Rev. A. W. Wood is the present minister.

SOUTH HADLEY lies in the southern part of the county, and is bounded north by Hadley, from which it is separated by the Mt. Holyoke range, east by Granby, south by the county line and west by the Connecticut river. It has an area of about 10,000 acres.

The surface of the town is picturesquely diversified and affords a large amount of good farming territory. The only streams of importance are Bachelor's and Stony brooks, flowing a westerly course across the township to the Connecticut, the former in the northern and the latter in the central part.

Settlement and Growth.—As this town was originally part of the town of Hadley, and included the township of Granby, it is not necessary to repeat the circumstances of its early grant. They are detailed in the sketches of those towns. In brief, South Hadley was set off as the second, or south precinct of Hadley, in 1732, and thus remained till April, 1753, when it was incorporated as a district. With this incorporation all the powers of a township were conferred, except that of sending a representative to the general court. In this privilege the district shared with Hadley and Amherst till 1775.

The settlement of the town was begun in the winter of 1726-27, and in November of 1727 the following persons are known to have been here: Daniel Nash (2d), Richard Church, Samuel Taylor, Samuel Smith, Samuel Kellogg, John Smith, John Preston, Nathaniel White, Thomas Goodman, Jr., John Taylor, Joshua Taylor, Joseph Kellogg, William Smith, Jonathan Smith, Luke Montague, Joseph White, Ebenezer Smith, Ebenezer Taylor, John Smith, Ephraim Nash and John Lane, the four last named in what is now Granby. The additions before 1731 were; William Gaylord, Nathaniel Ingram, Jr., Samuel Rugg, Samuel Taylor, Jr., Moses Taylor, Joseph Taylor, Daniel Nash (1st), William Montague, Ebenezer Moody, Ebenezer Moody, Jr., Peter Montague, Chileab Smith (2d), Timothy Hillyer; 1731 to 1740, John Smith, Falls Woods, Rev. Grindall Rawson, Benjamin Church, Jr., Moses White, John Alvord, John Alvord, Jr., Joseph Moody, Josiah Snow, Eleazar Goodman, Jabez Bellows, James Ball; 1740 to 1750, Jonathan White, John Gaylord, Gad Alvord, Daniel Crowfoot, Josiah Moody, Joseph White, Jr., Ebenezer Kellogg, Jesse Bellows, Reuben Smith, Moses Montague, John Stanley, Hugh Queen, Jonathan Preston, Josiah White, Joseph Cook, Daniel Moody, Thomas Judd, Rev. John Woodbridge, Silas Smith, Philip Smith, John Smith (4th), Thomas White, Nathaniel White, Jr., Ephraim Smith, Aaron Taylor, Samuel Preston, Elijah Alvord, John Hillyer, Timothy Hillyer, Jr.; 1750 to 1763, Phinehas Smith (2d), David Nash, Noah Goodman, Joseph Kellogg, Jr., Titus Pomeroy, Josiah Smith, John Rugg, Asahel Judd, Reuben Judd, Martin Wait, Josiah Snow, Jr., Gideon Alvord, John Woodbridge, Jr., William Wait, Jabez Kellogg, David Eaton, Israel Smith, John Chandler, Moses Alvord, Ebenezer Snow, Joseph Nash, John French, Benoni Preston, James Henry, Nathan Alvord, John Marshall, Elisha Church, Nathaniel Bartlett, Benjamin Pierce, Josiah Smith (2d),

William Taylor, Elisha Taylor, Job Alvord, William Brace, Reuben Taylor.

Moses Montague is a direct descendant of Richard Montague, who was the first settler of that name in America. He had born to him ten children, four of whom are living, namely, Mrs. E. Judd, of Southampton, Mrs. W. R. Kemp, of Holyoke, Col. G. S. Montague, of New Bedford, Mass., and C. Newton. The last mentioned was born on the homestead on road 4, which has been in the family for five generations, March 16, 1827, has always lived here, and married Lucy E. Judd, of Geneva, N. Y., in January, 1854. He has three children, Clara E., born September 3, 1858, Mary L., born July 17, 1869, and Wallace N., born December 1, 1871.

Gardner Powers is the son of John and Jerusha (Preston) Powers, and was born in this town, June 20, 1813. His mother was the great-grandchild of John Preston, one of the first settlers of this town, and whose death occurred March 4, 1827. He was probably the first adult buried in town. Neville, brother of Gardner, died in 1837, aged about twenty-seven years. Gardner married Esther, daughter of Levi Wilber, and has had born to him three children, only two of whom are living, Neville J. and Anna J., who was born in 1839, and is at home with her father. Neville J. was born August 4, 1837, married Elizabeth Davis, and has two children, Alice W. and Bertha E. He is a fresco painter, and lives in Troy, N. Y. The wife of Gardner Powers died December 30, 1883, at the age of sixty-eight years.

Josiah Smith was born in South Hadley, December 6, 1761, married Phebe Nash, in 1790, and reared nine children, viz.: Clarissa, Pamelia, Mary, Harriet, Harry, Nelson, Lowell, Clarissa, 2d, and Josiah. Mr. Smith died January 10, 1846, and his widow died in 1847. Nelson was born in Brookfield, Vt., May 18, 1801, married Rebecca, daughter of Dea. Selah Smith, March 20, 1823, and had born to him five children, as follows: Harriet S., born in 1825, Henry N., born in 1826, William, born in 1830, Clara L., born in 1834, and Jennie, born in 1836. Henry N. married Mary Cook, in 1856, and has had born to him two children, Mary J., born in 1857, and Arthur N., born October 17, 1859. Mary J. married John S. Barslow, in 1883, and has one child, Luther H.

Luther Smith was born in 1759, married Sylvia Judd, in 1792, and his children were as follows: Luther, Philip, Almira, Heman, Asaph and Asaph, 2d. Philip was born in 1797, occupied his father's farm nearly all his life, married Sarah, daughter of Jonathan Smith, of Leverett, Mass., and had born to him three children, namely, Sarah A., Philip H. and Newton. Mr. Smith died in 1867. Philip H., born in 1845, married Fannie, daughter of Charles Butterfield, in 1871, and has had born to him three children, Philip, Robert and Charles, who died in 1884. Mrs. Sarah Smith is now living with her sons Newton and Philip H.

Ephraim Smith, son of John, and a lineal descendant of Joseph Smith, of Hartford, Conn., was born in South Hadley, married Mary, daughter of John Preston, and had born to him seven children, as follows: Ephraim, Eli,

Darius, Simeon, Luther, Johanna and Lois. Eli married for his first wife, Lois, daughter of Ebenezer Kellogg, who bore him seven children, viz.: Johanna, Justin, Jehial, Lois, Sally, Eli and Leonard. He married for his second wife, Thankful Dickinson. Justin was born in South Hadley, married Rebecca Smith, of Williamstown, where he resided for a time, and had born to him five children, Nelson, of Granby, Giles, Justin, Eli, and Marilla, wife of George Moody. Nelson was born October 31, 1810, married Salena, daughter of Bela Burnett, resides in Granby, and has had born to him eight children, viz.: Mary S., wife of Watson Williams, of South Hadley, Osman, who died at the age of four years, Eliza B., wife of George Harris, Lewis B., of Springfield, Osman, of Springfield, Harvey G., of South Hadley Falls, Willard N. and Edson L., who live in Granby.

Broughton Alvord was born in this town in 1802, lived on the homestead most of his life, where his sister, Mary A., now resides. He died at the age of eighty-four years. He was the oldest of a family of five children, only one of whom, Ruth, married. The latter married Ellis Coney, who died in about four years, leaving one daughter, Harriet S., born October 2, 1827. Mrs. Coney married for her second husband, Estes Cummings, in 1829, and had one child. Mrs. Cummings died November 10, 1836.

Dexter Burnett, son of Arza, was born in this town, April 15, 1819, on the place now owned by Welcome Burnett, is a mason by trade, and married Clara M. Ainsworth, of Belchertown, in 1844. Soon after, he bought the land on road 16, where he now is, and built the house in which he resides at present. He has had born to him four children, namely, Lewis E., who died in 1847; Clara A., born in 1848, married Lucius B. Smith, in 1869, and has one child, Louie E.; Abby L., born in 1851, married Elliot Miller, of Greenfield, and has one child, Clara I.; and Louis Dexter, born in 1854, married Hattie Thurber, in 1881, and resides in Springfield. Mr. Burnett served in the late war, in Co. D, 27th Mass. Vols., was in nine engagements, was taken prisoner at Kingston, N. C., March 8, 1865, and was held a prisoner in Libby prison until Lee's surrender in April.

Eleazer Howard was born in Holyoke, September 13, 1810, and when he was two years of age his father, Pember, moved to Belchertown, where the latter died in 1841. At the age of twenty-one years, Eleazer moved to Enfield, and engaged with a company in the manufacture of shoe-pegs. He worked there about a year and a half, when he entered the employ of J. N. Hastings & Cutler in the sash, door and blind factory. In 1834 Mr. Hastings moved to South Hadley and built the factory now owned by Howard, Gaylord & Co. Mr. Howard married Sarah Smith, and has had born to him one child, Emory E. The latter was born July 9, 1850, and is now a practicing physician in Holyoke. He married twice, first, Clara M. Graham, in 1872, who bore him two children, and died in 1880, and second, Gertie Clifton, of Philadelphia.

William H. Moody, son of William and Emily (Harris) Moody, was born

May 15, 1844, and married Hattie M. Oppie, June 9, 1865. He served in the late war, in Co. D, 27th Mass. Vols., and served three years. His only brother, Josiah, was born in 1842, and also served in the late war, in Co. F, 44th Mass. Vols., and died at Newberne, N. C.. January 14, 1863. William H. located at Moody's Corners, where he has lived most of the time since. He has had born to him one child, Josiah, born October 30, 1884, and died February 26, 1886. They have an adopted daughter, Mary, born July 4, 1875.

Emerson Bates, son of John, was born in Westhampton, September 4, 1816, married Sarah A., daughter of David Edwards, of Northampton, and immediately moved on to the farm now occupied by him, on road 8. He has had born to him four children, viz.: Henry E., who died while serving in the late war, in 1863; Mary A., born in 1840, married T. C. Cooley, has one child, and lives in Springfield; John E., who married Hattie Wright, and has had born to him five children, namely, Clinton M., Edith W., Sarah E., Hattie I., and Lucy A; Nathan and Catharine, both of whom live at home. The farm now owned by Mr. Bates, and where he has resided forty-nine years, was the first piece of land for which a deed was given in South Hadley, and the house which was on the farm when he bought it was said to be 125 years old.

Isaac Abbey was an early settler of Enfield. His son Abner bought a farm in Wilbraham, but afterwards moved to Granby, where he died. Abner, Jr., lived in Boston, for a time, and then moved to south Hadley. His son Abner was born in this town, November 5, 1812, married Chloe A. Root, and has had born to him a large family of children, five of whom are living, namely, Emma, Arthur L., Charles C, Silas B. and Sibyl. Mrs. Abby died in February, 1874.

Sylvester Bryant located in this town, near South Hadley Falls, on road 32, in 1861. He engaged in the milk business, establishing a large and profitable trade. He continued in this business until 1885. He is now engaged in market gardening.

Joel Parsons was born in Easthampton in 1776, and is said to have made the first sleigh driven in the town. He married Rachel James, and thirteen children were born to him. His son Ralph was born January 13, 1805, spent his early days in Easthampton, and married twice, first, Hannah Thorp, who bore him three children, Abel T., who died in infancy, Jane E. and Abel H. He married for his second wife, Ruth, daughter of Perez Barker. The children of this marriage are, Alva E., Louis R. and George I. Alva E. was born February 13, 1846, and married Rebecca E. Hall. Louis was born in 1851, and married Annetta Scott.

Daniel Brainard came to this country, from England, and settled in Connecticut in 1662. He married twice, first, Hannah Spencer, and second, Mrs. Hannah Sexton, and died in 1715. Robert Brainard, a lineal decendant of Daniel, came to this town in 1805. He was the first Methodist in town, and settled on the farm now owned by Wells Brainard. He married twice, first, Abigail Spencer, who bore him Eight children, and died in 1815. He married for his second wife, Olive, daughter of Dea, Ezra and Jerusha (Smith) Brainard in 1813. Mr. Brainard died in 1831, and his widow died in 1844.

Joseph Emory Dickinson son of Asa, was born October 26, 1823, came to this town when he was twenty-one years of age, and married Mary A., daughter of Nathaniel Goodell in 1851. He had born to him two children, Lillian S., Born in 1854, and Joseph H., born in 1856.

John H. Preston, son of Gad Clark Preston, was born January 1, 1827, and married Sarah J., daughter of Moses Moody, in 1857. He spent three years in California, returning in 1855. He resides at South Hadley Falls.

Thomas T. Shumway, son of Binah and Philenda (Squires) Shumway, was born in Belchertown, December 11, 1822, and came to South Hadley about 1846. He served in the late war, in Co. I, 34th Mass. Vol., and was wounded in the right ankle in 1864. He married twice, first, Joanna Bishop, who bore him four children, and second, Jemima Weeks.

Moses Gaylord married Rebecca, daughter of Hiram Smith, and his children were as follows: James, born in 1844, Henry E., born in 1846, Lewis, born in 1849, Josiah, born in 1852, and died in 1858. and Fred born in 1859. Mr. Gaylord died in 1866, and his widow died in 1883. James married Mrs. Louisa Rose, January 1, 1885.

Moses Gaylord, of another branch of the family from the above, married Jerusha, daughter of Ephraim Smith, and had born to him seven children, viz: Lorenzo, John, Philotas, Moses, Roxanna, wife of Rockwell Wright, Simeon and William. John married Elizabeth, daughter of Elisha Moody, in 1838, and has one daughter, Elizabeth, living at home.

In 1776 the population of the town was 584. Its population for each decade since 1790 is shown by the following figures: 1790, 759; 1800, 801; 1810, 902; 1820, 1,047; 1830, 1,185; 1840, 1,458; 1850, 2,495; 1860, 2,277; 1870, 2,840; 1880, 3,538.

Organization.—The first officers chosen were those of the precinct, March 12, 1733, when Ebenezer Moody acted as moderator, and Daniel Nash, 2d, as clerk of the meeting. John Taylor, John Alvord and Samuel Smith were made assessors and committee; and John Smith, son of Ebenezer, collector. The administration of the affairs of the precinct were confined chiefly to matters of an ecclesiastical nature, the civil connection with Hadley not having been severed.

The first district officers were chosen April 30, 1853, at a meeting warned by Eleazar Porter, Esq., of Hadley, and were as follows: Dea. John Smith, moderator; Daniel Nash, clerk; Samuel Smith, Thomas Goodman, Dea. John Smith, Dea. John Smith, Jr., Luke Montague, selectmen; Samuel Smith, Dea. John Smith, Jr., Luke Montague, assessors; Moses Montague, Asahel Judd, constables; Dea. John Smith, Sr., treasurer; Josiah Moody, Experience Smith, Joseph Cook, hog-reeves; Reuben Smith, clerk of the market, sealer, packer, and gauger; Thomas Goodman, Job Alvord, fence-viewers;

Stephen Warner, Jr., Josiah White, surveyors of highways. Tithingmen, hay-wards, wardens, and deer-reeves were chosen in later years.

Military.—In the later French and Indian wars the town sent out about seventy-five men, though no troubles ever occurred here. In the Revolution-ary struggle, also, the township was not a whit behind its neighbors in furnish-ing men and means. In the late great war the town furnished 242 men, an excess of twenty-three over all calls, three of whom were commissioned offi-cers. It also furnished $24,668.52 for the cause, exclusive of $10,296.13, which was subsequently repaid by the state.

VILLAGES.

SOUTH HADLEY is a neat, substantial, quiet post-village, located near the center of the town. It has about 100 dwellings, one church, a high school building and several stores and mills, aside from the commodious buildings and elegant grounds of the famous Mt. Holyoke Seminary.

SOUTH HADLEY FALLS is a large, busy manufacturing village located in the southwestern part of the town, on the opposite side of the river from the City of Holyoke.

The only other thickly settled localities are Pearl City and Moody Corners, small hamlets in the northeastern part of the town.

Mount Holyoke Seminary was founded by Miss Mary Lyon, its first princi-pal, and incorporated February 11, 1836, and the corner-stone of the first building was laid on the 3d of the following October. This building is of brick, four stories and a basement, though greatly enlarged from its original dimensions, and other buildings have been erected, the largest and most ele-gant of the group being Williston hall, the corner-stone of which was laid June 1, 1875. Its cost was over $50,000.00. In the affairs of the seminary no domestics are employed. The members constitute one family, and by a proper division of labor, requiring a service from each of but one hour a day, perform all the needed household duties. While regarded as no part of the instruction proper, this daily service proves salutary as a means of promoting health and stimulating to system, order, and mutual helpfulness. The insti-tution has received considerable aid from private sources, but was never en-dowed. Rev. William S. Tyler, D. D., of Amherst, is president, and A. Ly-man Williston, of Northampton, treasurer. Miss Elizabeth Blanchard is principal, assisted by a large and competent corps of teachers.

MANUFACTURES.

The Carew Manufacturing Co., engaged in the manufacture of fine writing-paper at South Hadley Falls, was established in 1848. In 1873 their main building was burned, and immediately re-built. The company employs 100 hands and turns out three tons of paper per day. J. H. Southworth is presi-dent, and E. C. Southworth, treasurer.

The Hampshire Paper Co.'s mills are located at South Hadley Falls, and were built by the Glasgow Co. in 1860. The present company was organized and incorporated May 19, 1866, with a capital of $200.000.00. They employ 130 hands and turn out four tons of fine writing-paper and bristol-board per day. J. H. Southworth is president, and C. H. Southworth, treasurer.

The Glasgow Co.'s mills are located at South Hadley Falls, where they turn out about 70,000 yards of dress goods per week. The company was incorporated February 16, 1848, with a capital of $300,000.00, which was subsequently increased to $350,000.00.

Howard, Gaylord & Burnett's sash, door and blind factory, on road 16, was built by J. N. Hastings, in 1834, and came into the present company's possession in 1858. They employ eight hands and turn out 2,000 pairs of blinds, 2,700 sets of sash and 2,300 doors per annum.

Robert Laing's paper-mill, on road 5, was built by Laing, Afflick & Mortimer, in 1885, and operated by them under the name of the Mt. Holyoke Paper Co., until March 1, 1886, when Mr. Laing became sole owner. He employs eight hands in the manufacture of tissue and manilla paper.

Charles E. Marsh's saw-mill, on road 4, was originally built by Sylvester Moody, at a very early date. It has a circular saw and the capacity for cutting 7,000 feet of lumber per day.

Eugene J. O'Neil's tape and finding factory, on road 16, was built in 1885, upon the site of the old woolen-mill burned in 1883, The factory has eight Knowle's looms, finisher, etc., and gives employment to four hands.

F. A. Bogg's cider-mill, on road 17, makes about 1,000 barrels of cider per year, much of which is converted into vinegar.

CHURCHES.

The First Congregational church of South Hadley was formed as the "Second Church of Christ in Hadley." Its territory was known as the "South Precinct in Hadley," which then embraced what is now called South Hadley, and also the present town of Granby. The church was organized a short time previous to March 12, 1733. At that early date a meeting-house was in process of erection, and seems to have been commenced in 1732, though not completed until 1737. That house stood a little north of the present hay-scales, and is now known as the Judd dwelling-house, across the way from the north end of the green. The second house of worship, built in 1763, stood near where the present one does, with its main entrance at the south end, and the steeple at the north end. That was torn down to make a larger one for the accommodation of Mt. Holyoke seminary, in 1844. The cost of the new or third house was $10,000.00. It fronted west, and stood nearer the street than the present house, yet on nearly the same ground. The bell was moved across from the old to the new house, without being lowered in the earth. The third house was burned Sunday morning, January 17, 1875, and the present, or fourth house, costing about $33,000.00, was dedicated February 23, 1876. The parish was formed in 1825. Previous to that the town served as parish. The pastors of the church and the periods of their service have been as follows: Rev. Grindall Rawson, October, 1733–41; Rev. John Woodbridge, 1742–83, the time of his death, in the eighty-first year of his age; Rev. Joel Hayes, 1782–1827, the date of his death, in the seventy-fourth year of his age; Rev. Artemas Boies, 1824–34; Rev. Joseph D. Condit, 1835–47, the date of his death; Rev. Thomas Laurie, 1848–51; Rev. Eliphalet Y. Swift, 1852–58; Rev. Hiram Mead, 1858–67; Rev. John M. Greene, 1868–70; Rev. J. Henry Bliss, 1871–73; Rev. J. R. Herrick, 1874–78; Rev. William DeLoss Love, 1879. The present church membership is 336. The Sabbath school membership is about 200. The present estimated value of the parish property, including the parsonage, is $27,000.00.

The Congregational Church of South Hadley Falls was organized in 1824, with nineteen members, and Rev. John F. Griswold was their first pastor. Their first church building was erected in 1835. The present structure was built in 1864, at a cost of $20,000.00. It is a wooden structure, capable of seating 475 persons, and is now valued, including grounds, etc., at $25,000.00. The society now has 300 members, with Rev. W. S. Hawkes, pastor.

The South Hadley Falls Methodist Episcopal church was organized in 1829, with seventy-five members, and Rev. Hiram White was their first pastor. Their church building was built in 1832. It is a wooden structure, capable of seating 500 persons, and valued, including grounds, etc., at $10,000.00. The society now has 100 members, with Rev. E. S. Best, pastor.

St. Patrick's Roman Catholic church, located at South Hadley Falls, was organized by its first pastor, Rev. P. J. Harkins, with about 800 communicants, in 1868. The church building, erected that year at a cost of $15,000.00, is a wooden structure capable of accommodating 500 persons. The society now has about 1,200 communicants, with Rev. Eugene Toher, pastor.

———

WARE lies in the southeastern corner of the county, and is bounded north by Enfield, Greenwich and a part of the county line, east and south by the county line, and west by Belchertown, having an area of about 18,000 acres.

The surface of the town is rough and broken, as three ranges of hills traverse it from north to south. These are rough and rocky, but between them are productive valleys. The highest elevation is Coy's hill, in the eastern part of the town, having an altitude of about 500 feet. Ware river, the principal stream, enters the town at the northeast corner, and leaves it at the southwestern, keeping mostly along the eastern and southern boundaries. This stream furnishes a fine water-power, which has led to the town's being noted for its extensive manufacturing interests. Swift river forms the western boundary of the township. The other streams are Muddy, Flat and Beaver brooks, flowing through the valleys we have mentioned, into Ware river. Except on some of the sloping hillsides and the intervals of the valley, the soil of the township is not good, while all is difficult of cultivation.

Grant and Settlement.—A large portion of the present township of Ware, or about 10,000 acres, was a part of the "Equivalent Lands" grant, as described in the history of Belchertown. This covered nearly the whole of the western portion of the town. It took the name of "Read Manor," from John Read, Esq., of Boston, its purchaser. The southern part of the town, east of Read Manor, made up a part of the "Elbows" grant, so called. Five hundred acres in the southeastern part of the town, where the village now is, was granted to Richard Hollingsworth, of Salem, in 1673. The northeastern part of the town was granted to settlers in 1733, among whom were the Marsh and Clements families. These several grants, then, make up the town's present territory, and they were located as follows : The Read Manor, in 1713 ; the Hallingsworth grant, in 1715 ; the Elbows tract, in 1732 ; and the Marsh and Clements tract, in 1733.

The first settlement was made upon the Hollingsworth grant, at what is now the very center of the village. Capt. Jabez Olmstead, who came on that year and built mills at the falls, was the first settler. He was a man of means, had two sons and a daughter, but took little active part in public affairs. His house, known as the "great house," was standing till 1821.

Isaac Magoon was the first settler in the southeastern corner of the town. He came from Ireland with the colony that settled in Palmer in 1727. He and his son, Isaac, Jr., owned a tract of about seven hundred acres. The latter subsequently bought of Capt. Olmstead's heirs the mills and the land at the village. Jacob Cummings, from Killingly, Conn., came on soon after and became one of the most prominent men in the new settlement. Among others of the early settlers were the following : John Davis, William Brakenridge, Judah, Thomas, Ephraim, Samuel and Joseph Marsh, Samuel Sherman, Thomas Jenkins, Maverick Smith, Joseph Foster, Samuel Dunsmore, James Lemmon, John Downing, Daniel, David and Ebenezer Gould, William Paige, Phille Morse, William Coney, Oliver Coney, John Tisdale, Jeremiah Anderson, Thomas Andrews, James Lamberton, Dr. Edward Demond, Dr. Elias Bolton, Dr. Rufus King, William Bowdoin and others.

William Coney was born in Sharon, Mass., February 13, 1765, and came to Ware with his parents when about ten years of age. He married Hannah Marsh and reared nine children. His wife died April 10, 1829, and his death occurred May 24, 1848. His son, John, was born in Ware May 29, 1809, married Sophronia Allen October 5, 1842, and his children were as follows : Hubert M., born March 18, 1844, married Ellen Brainard, and has one

child, Edwin B.; George H., born October 23, 1847, married Alice Hine-
line, and is engaged in contracting and building; and Charles E., born in
1852, died November 5, 1875. In 1870, Mr. Coney built the place where
his widow now resides, and died March 29, 1884.

Ambrose Blair was born in Warren, December 18, 1802, and came to
Ware in 1824, when twenty-two years of age. He married Sarah Dunbar in
1835, who bore him two children, Francis and Almira. She died in 1874.
Mr. Blair says there is not a man now living in the town who was here when
he came.

In 1742 there were thirty-three families in the town. In 1776 the population numbered 773, and the census returns for 1790 give the same figures.
Since then the population has increased as follows: 1800, 997; 1810, 996;
1820, 1,154; 1830, 2,045; 1840, 1,890; 1850, 3,785; 1855, 3,498; 1860,
3,597; 1865; 3,374; 1870, 4,259; 1875, 4,142; 1880, 4,817.

Organization.—The territory was erected into a precinct December 7,
1742, and incorporated as a township November 25, 1761. The first town-
meeting was held March 9, 1762, when William Brakenridge was chosen
clerk; Samuel Sherman, William Brakenridge, John Davis, Jacob Cummings and Judah Marsh, selectmen and assessors; and Jacob Cummings,
treasurer.

The name Ware is derived from the "weirs" or "weares" formerly constructed in Ware river to aid in catching salmon.

Military.—In the war of the Revolution the town early took an active interest and sustained well her part throughout the great struggle. In the second
war with the mother country the town was not in sympathy, though several
of the citizens were drafted and marched to Boston. In the late great war
the town furnished 351 men, a total of twenty in excess of all demands, nine
of whom were commissioned officers. The town also raised $36,029.00
aside from $18,917.38 which was subsequently refunded by the state.

VILLAGES.

WARE VILLAGE has grown up about the magnificent water-power at the
site of the first settlement made in the town. It is a large, bright, busy,
flourishing manufacturing village, containing more than three-fourths of the
town's entire population. Formerly the town business was transacted at the
center of the town, and was transferred to the village in 1847. There is now
a large, elegant town hall here, recently erected. The village is also lighted
with gas, has a fine water supply, and all modern improvements.

WARE CENTER is now only a hamlet containing a few houses. It was formerly *the* village of the township.

MANUFACTURES.

The fine water-power at the village, where the river makes a sudden descent
of seventy feet, was, as we have stated, early utilized by Jabez Olmstead.

His heirs sold the property to Isaac Magoon, and it then passed to his son Alexander, in 1765. At this time there were a grist-mill and saw-mill here. In 1813, the whole property, comprising the site of the present village, was sold by James Magoon, grandson of Alexander, to Alpheus Demond, for $4,500.00. Mr. Demond came here the same year, built a dam, repaired the saw-mill and grist-mill, and started two carding machines, and the following year built a cotton-mill. But before this was completed he died, and the factory stood unused till 1821, when it was purchased by Holbrook & Dexter, of Boston, for $15,000.00. A company was soon formed, extensive building and repairs begun, and in 1823 the Ware Company was formed, with a capital of $600,000.00. But their plans were too vast and extensive for the times, or at least were ill-advised, for the company never made a dividend.

In 1829 the Hampshire Manufacturing Company was formed, with a capital of $400,000.00, who took all the property of the Ware Company. They went down with the great crash of 1837.

The Otis Company.—In 1839 the Otis Company was organized, with a capital of $350,000.00. They purchased all the property of the Hampshire Manufacturing Company on the north side of the river, and increased their capital to $500,000.00. In June, 1845, the mill built by the Ware Company in 1824 was destroyed by fire. The company immediately began the erection of a new brick mill on the same site, 200 feet long, by fifty feet wide, and five stories high. They also built one the same year, of stone, of the same size, on the falls below. In 1856–57 the old mills on the middle falls were taken down, and a new mill was erected, 200 feet long by fifty-three feet wide, and six stories high. In 1869 an addition of fifty feet in length was made to this mill, making it 250 feet long by fifty-three feet wide. In 1861 the Otis Company, in connection with Mr. Stevens, built a new dam of granite, at the middle falls. In 1864 they removed the looms from the new mill, and, replacing them with knitting-machines, began the manufatory of hosiery. They have at present on their pay-roll about 1,350 employees in their three mills and various finishing buildings. Two of the mills produce checks and denims, and the largest mill cotton underwear in a great variety of styles. The business is about equally divided between the two departments. In the weaving department there are 20,736 spindles and 660 looms; in the underwear department 12,016 spindles, and a large plant of knitting machinery. The average annual product is about 8,500,000 yards of checks and denims, 140,000 dozens underwear, and 35,000 men's half-hose, consuming about 3,800,000 pounds of cotton, and 180,000 pounds of yarn, purchased from other spinners, a part of which is imported.

These mills very rarely run on short time, and the product is generally in good demand. During the past season the company have built a large dye-house for the woolen goods department, and are also building an addition of about 72x52, five stories, to the underwear mill, which, when completed, will make this mill about 350 feet in length. It is expected that these additions will lead to some increase of product, and consequently the employment of more help. The employees of these mills come principally from about 450 families in the town, for which the company provide tenements for about 129 families. The tenement property is well cared for, particular attention being given to sanitary conditions.

The Palmer mill property, at Three Rivers, is also a part of the plant of the Otis Company. This mill contains 23,040 spindles, and 690 looms, producing about 8,000,000 yards of Otis checks, seersuckers and cantons, with about 625 employees.

The product of the company is sold by Messrs. Bliss, Fabyan & Co., Boston, New York and Philadelphia. George T. Fabyan, of Boston, is treasurer of the company, Edwin H. Baker, resident agent, with George E. Tucker, superintendent at Ware, and R. C. Newell, superintendent at Three Rivers.

Charles A. Stevens & Co.—In 1841 George H. Gilbert and Charles A. Stevens came from North Andover, in the eastern part of the state, and purchased of the assignees of the Hampshire Company all the property belonging to them on the south side of the river, including the water-power, land, woolen-mill, and machinery. These gentlemen formed a co-partnership under the name of Gilbert & Stevens, and began the manufacture of broadcloth. In 1846 they built a new mill on the falls below the one they then occupied, and put in four sets of woolen machinery. The mill was five stories high, and eighty feet long by fifty feet wide, and was built of granite taken from a quarry on the road to Warren. In 1844 this firm turned their attention to the manufacture of fine flannels, and so great was their success that their goods not only took the front rank in this country, but at the "World's Fair" held in London, in 1851, they were awarded the highest prize, (a gold medal) over all the competitors of the Old World. In 1851 the firm of Gilbert & Stevens was dissolved, and a division of the property was made, Mr. Gilbert taking the new mill, or, as it was called, the "Granite Mill," and Mr. Stevens receiving the old, or "Ware Woolen Mill." Mr. Stevens has made several additions and improvements to the property. He took his son, Charles E. Stevens, into parnership with him, and they do an extensive business in the manufacture of white and opera flannels and ladies dress goods, employing about 200 hands.

George H. Gilbert Manufacturing Co.—As we have said, in 1851, the Gilbert & Stevens Co. was dissolved, Mr. Gilbert taking the "new stone mill" and there with six sets of machinery continuing the manufacture of fine white flannels, etc. In 1857 Mr. Lewis N. Gilbert, a nephew, was admitted as a partner, and the firm became George H. Gilbert & Co., which title it retained until an act of the legislature in 1867 gave it its psesent name. In 1860 Messrs. George H. Gilbert & Co. purchased a water power in that portion of the adjoining town of Hardwick, which is now known as Gilbertville, and there erected a brick mill containing eight sets of machinery. In 1867 another mill was added, farther down the stream. Both these stand to-day and have grown to contain together forty sets of machines.

The product of the mills has been varied from time to time to meet the demands of trade, and at present consists principally of ladies' dress goods, although the fine white and opera flannels upon which the company obtained its reputation are still made. The corporation has now a capital stock of $600,000.00, forty-seven sets of woolen cards, 30,000 woolen spindles, about 540 broad looms, and the machinery necessary for furnishing the product of the same. The officers are Lewis N. Gilbert, president; Charles D. Gilbert, treasurer; and J. H. Grenville Gilbert, secretary.

The West Ware Paper Co.'s mill, on road 27, was built by a stock company with a capital of $30,000.00 and with the same officers as now in charge, in 1884. The company have four 1,000-pound engines, one seventy-two-inch Foudrinier. The mill is operated by both steam and water-power, and turns out about twenty-four tons of book, news and roll paper per week, employing thirty-five hands. The officers are S. P. Bailey, of Greenwich, president, and John B. Warren, treasurer.

R. C. Snow's grist and saw mill, on road 38, was built in 1886, upon the site of one destroyed by fire on January 27, 1886. The site has been in the family about thirty years. The grist-mill has two runs of stones, a large elevator, and grinds about two car-loads of grain per week. The saw-mill has a circular saw, planing machine, shingle-mill, etc., and cuts about 500,000 feet of lumber per year.

Jonathan I. Harwood's saw-mill and cider-mill, on road 22, was removed from farther up the stream and re-built by him in 1883. The saw-mill has a circular saw, bench saws, shingle machine, etc., and turns out about 50,000 feet of lumber and 40,000 shingles per year, and the cider-mill turns out about 600 barrels of cider per season.

William L. Brakenridge's saw-mill, on road 35, was built by him in 1874. It has a circular saw and shingle-mill, and saws about 20,000 feet of lumber and 15,000 shingles.

George Eddy's boot and shoe manufactory was established by him in 1873. The factory is located on Eddy street. He employs about thirty-five hands, making a specialty of boys', youths' and children's boots, and men's brogans. He turns out about 3,000 cases per year.

Charles W. Eddy has been located in the printing business at number 60 Main street for over fourteen years. In the spring of 1885 he added a plant for photo-mechanical printing—the art of producing illustrations on a press with printers' ink, giving all the minute detail and gradiation of light and shade seen in the photograph. He has made a specialty of publishing illustrations of the public buildings and places of interest in different towns, accompanying them with brief sketches. He has already published fourteen volumes of this kind. This is the only establishment in the county doing this work.

BANKS.

The Ware National Bank.—The Hampshire Manufacturers branch at Ware was incorporated February 26, 1825, with a capital of $100,000.00. At different times it was increased until it reached $350.000.00. Elnathan Jones, of Enfield, was president from 1825 to 1827 ; Joseph Bowman, of New Braintree, from 1827 to 1848 ; Orin Sage, of Ware, from 1848 to 1864. Homer Bartlett was cashier from 1825 to 1832 ; Henry Starkweather from 1832 to 1834 ; William Hyde from 1834 to 1864. This bank was re-organized as the Ware National Bank, December 10, 1864, and again December 10, 1884. It was started with a capital of $350,000.00, which was increased to $400,000.00, and reduced to $300,000.00 in March, 1879. William Hyde was chosen president and still continues in office. Henry Ives was chosen cashier, and resgined in 1867, when William S. Hyde was chosen to the position.

The Ware Savings bank was incorporated by an act of the legislature approved March 5, 1850. William Hyde, Henry Lyon, Charles A. Stevens and associates were the original incorporators. The first meeting of the corporation was held in the room over the Ware National bank, June 10, 1850, of which William Hyde was chairman and Charles A. Stevens secretary. The organization was finally perfected at an adjourned meeting by the choice of a board of trustees, of which William Hyde was made president, in which office he has been continued to the present time. Joel Rice was chosen secretary and treasurer. Of the first board of trustees William Hyde and Charles A. Stevens still continue in office. Joel Rice held the office of treasurer until his death, in 1857. Otis Lane was chosen June 1, 1857, as his successor, and continued to hold the office until January, 1886, a period of nearly thirty years, when he was succeeded by the present incumbent, Frederick D. Gilmore. The bank has now over $2,000,000.00 deposited with it.

CHURCHES.

The First church in Ware, Congregational, located at the center of the town, was organized May 9, 1751, and was long the only church in the township. It had about forty members at the time of its organization, and Rev. Grindall Rawson was the first pastor. The first church building was erected in 1750, a wooden structure which did service till 1800, when the present building was erected. It will seat about 250 persons and is valued, including grounds, at about $6,500.00. The society now has 111 members, with Rev. William G. Tuttle, pastor, the twelfth in succession since Mr. Rawson's partorate.

The East Congregational church is located at the village. In 1825, owing to the increase of population here, it was deemed advisable to establish a Congregational society. Accordingly, in April, 1826, a society was organized, and on April 12th the church was constituted. Rev. Parsons Cook, ordained June 21, 1826, was the first pastor. A church building was also erected that year and is still in use, though it has been several times remodeled and extensively repaired.

The Methodist Episcopal church, located at Ware village, was organized by its first pastor, Rev. Joshua Crowell, in 1825. The church building, erected in 1843, will seat 300 persons, and is valued, including grounds, at $8,000.00. The society now has 175 members, with Rev. Elwin Hitchcock, pastor.

The First Unitarian church, located at the village, was organized October 7, 1846, and the first pastor was Rev. George S. Ball. A church building was erected the followfng year, which was destroyed by fire, together with the town hall, November 6, 1867. The present fine church was built in 1869. The pastor of the society is Rev. B. V. Stevenson.

St. Wiliiam's Roman Catholic church, located at the village, about 1850, as a missionary enterprise connected with the church at Chicopee Falls. It became a separate parish in 1860, and Rev. P. Haley was the first pastor. The church building was erected in 1855. The parish is now a very large one, with Rev. William Moran, pastor.

Our Lady of Mt. Carmel Roman Catholic church, located at the village, was organized by its first pastor, Rev. L. G. Gagnier, in 1871. The church building, a brick structure capable of seating 750 persons, was built the same year, and is now valued, including grounds and other property, at $18,000.00. The society consists of about 150 families, with Rev. J. T. Sheehan, pastor.

———

WESTHAMPTON* lies in the western-central part of the county, has an area of about twenty-five square miles, and is bounded north by Chesterfield and Williamsburg, east by Northampton and parts of Easthampton and Southampton, south by Southampton and west by Huntington and a small part of Chesterfield. It originally formed a part of Northampton, as did the other two "Hamptons." After the latter were set off, a tract four miles wide in the western part of the old town still remained under the name of "The Long Division," which, in 1778, was incorporated into the present town of Westhampton. This name of Westhampton, however, appears in the Northampton records as early as 1774.

The town is drained to the southeast in a general sense, and mostly by tributaries that unite to form the north branch of the Manhan river. These are Turkey brook, Sodom brook and other streams. In the southwest part of the town, however, are found some small rivulets that, with others flowing from Huntington, form the south branch of the Manhan. In the northeast there are also found the head-waters of Roberts Meadow brook, a stream

*Prepared by Frederick H. Judd.

that finally unites with Mill river at Leeds, in the town of Northampton. The east branch of the Westfield river touches the northwest corner of Westhampton. In the north part of Westhampton, then, these three river systems—the Manhan, the Westfield, and the Mill river—have some of their sources very near each other, the high hills along the Chesterfield line forming the water-shed of the three valleys.

Westhampton may fairly be called a mountainous town. There are several distinct elevations with special names. Along the western side are Canada hill, Spruce hill, Gob hill, Breakneck mountain, and Red-Oak hill. In the center, north of the village, is Tob hill. Southeast of the reservoir is the eminence known as Hanging mountain, and near the middle of the east side of the town is Turkey hill. The names of two of these are evidently derived from the timber upon them, and a third from the number of wild turkeys found there originally, and even within the memory of some now living in town.

Settlement and Growth.—The first settlement in Westhampton was made in the southern part of the town, near the road now leading from Northampton to Huntington. That part of the latter town bordering on Westhampton was then called "Shirkshire," or "New Plantation," and that next beyond "Murrayfield." The people of Northampton wished to communicate with the people of Murrayfield, and so a road was laid out and called the Shirkshire road; this being essentially the same as that now leading from Northampton to Huntington, varying in the eastern part by taking a more southerly turn and crossing the stream just over the line, several rods lower down, thus reaching "King's Mill," near the site of which the brick paper-mill now stands. This road was simply a path through the woods, indicated by blazed trees. "It was laid out very wide so that travelers on horseback could wind their way among the rocks and trees."

Abner Smith made the first settlement in the town, coming from Connecticut to Murrayfield, and thence to Westhampton, about 1762, and locating near the old Enoch Lyman place, near where L. L. Rhodes now resides. He lived here a few years, and built again near the Fisher place, which he sold to Jonathan Fisher, about 1770. This place has remained in the Fisher family to the present day, descending from father to son, from Jonathan to Aaron, to Aaron, Jr., and to Jairus, the present occupant.

The second settlement was made by Ebenezer French, who located near the old tavern-stand of "Landlord" Ephraim Wright, a short distance from the Northampton line, on the Shirkshire road. This place descended to Martin, then to Lewis Wright, and was sold to Edmund Slattery, the present occupant. About 1767 Timothy Pomeroy came from Southampton, bought out Ebenezer French, and set up a tavern, which afterward passed into the hands of Ephraim Wright. This tavern was well patronized by the workmen in the lead mines then operated by the noted Ethan Allen and others.

At this time Nathaniel Strong, of Northampton, owned a large tract of land south of the Shirkshire road, near where William J. Lyman now lives. On this land was a large sugar orchard, and his boys used to come out yearly to make maple sugar. One of them, Noah Strong, Jr., located here, building about half-way between the Shirkshire road and Mr. Lyman's present residence. Here his son Lemuel was born, being the first child born in the town of Westhampton.

In 1765 Samuel Kingsley, of Southampton, deeded his two sons, Samuel and Joseph, farms on the Shirkshire road. The descendants of Joseph have lived in this town until the present day. His sons, Joseph, Jr., Ezra, Wareham and Marvel, all settled in this rown. Joseph, Jr.'s, children were Joseph S., Zenas and Lucy (Mrs Jesse Lyman). Of these, Joseph S. and Zenas lived in Northampton. Edward W., son of Zenas, now lives on the place near the church, occupied at first by Sylvester Judd, Esq., and afterward by Anson Chapman. Mrs. Lyman's children are Mary E. (Mrs. Edward Norton) and William E. Ezra's children were Wealthy (Mrs. J. A. Judd), Orin, removed to Northampton, Miriam (Mrs. Horace Baker), who lived in the place occupied by her father, in the south part of the town, Ezra M., who lives in New York city. Ezra was killed by lightning in his house in 1835. The children of Wealthy were Amoret (Mrs. Enoch Lyman), Jane W. (Mrs. Josiah Hooker), of Springfield, Harriet A. (Mrs. A. C. Shepard), who lives near the center of the town, Frederick H., who lives near the church, in the old "Centre schoolhouse," now re-modeled into a store and dwelling-house. Wareham's children are Alvin W., Roland, Almeron and Olive Jane. Alvin and his son William W. live on the place formerly owned by Nathan and Newman Clark, in the north part of the town. The other children of Wareham removed to Easthampton and Northampton. Marvel's children were Samantha (Mrs. J. M. Knight), of Chesterfield, Arlina (Mrs. George N. King), of Iowa, Elmina (Mrs. C. C. King), William M., killed in battle, Mary E., lives in Westfield, a music teacher. George E. Knight, son of Samantha, lives near the center of the town.

In 1768 Captain William Bartlett moved into town and was elected one of the first board of selectmen. He settled near where Captain Jared Bartlett lived so long, and where Samuel Williams now lives. Among his sons were Elihu and Jared. Elihu located further west on the road that leads to Enoch Lyman's old place, and there for many years was the only grist-mill for miles around. This place descended from Elihu to Elihu, Jr., to Christopher C., to O. Warren Bartlett, the present owner. Elihu P., son of Elihu, Jr., lives with his son, Edward A., on the place in the southeast part of the town, where Sylvester Judd and Orin Kingsley formerly lived. Elihu P. married Elsie, daughter of Orin Kingsley. It is said that the daughter of Parson Hale, as well as many other girls, used to come to the old grist-mill spoken of with their grist of corn and rye, on horseback, about the only mode of travel at that time.

In 1767 Jonathan Clark, of Southampton, deeded to his son, Jonathan, Jr.,

30*

a parcel of land in Westhampton, and in 1774 he came here and settled, about a mile west of the church, on the hill. The traces of these buildings are still to be seen. Mr. Clark left his family and joined the army, then at Ticonderoga and Crown Point, from which he returned a confirmed invalid. His son Jonathan, the third, relinquished his desire to complete his education, and, at the request of his parents, remained on the farm. His sons, Dorus and Festus S. both became ministers. Dorus preached, or lived in Blandford, Springfield, Boston and Waltham. He had a deep affection for his native town and visited it yearly if he could do so. At the time of the re-union he presented the Center school, of which he was a member in his boyhood, with funds to be called the " Clark Scholarship Fund," the income of which was to be given "to the best reader and speller in the first class, at the close of the winter term." It has accordingly been awarded up to the present time. Nathan Clark built the place, half a mile north of the church, where Dr. Orcutt afterwards lived and died, and where E. A. Howard now lives. It was in this house that Mr. Hale used to preach, and that the first town-meeting was held. Nathan's son Luther occupied the old place, and Theodore, another son, settled on the opposite side of the road, where his son Theodore, and afterward A. G. Jewett, lived. This place is now owned by Orville Flint. Nathan, Jr., settled in the north part of the town, where Alvin W. Kingsley now lives. Theodore married Mercy, daughter of Gideon Clark, and his sons were Theodore and Daniel W. The latter lived near the old place. His children, Emma, (Mrs. Samuel Williams) and Martha, (Mrs. A. K. Chapman), are both residents of this town.

Elijah Norton settled in the town in 1785, at the top of the hill, where Norton's tavern was so long kept, and where C. C. Bartlett now resides. His son Elijah continued the place after his death, and his son Joseph occupied the place at the foot of the hill, where Mrs. Moses Ludden, his daughter, now lives. Joseph's son, Joseph D., now lives in Loudville, near where the " King's mill" of early times stood. His son, Leonard M. Norton, lives with him and the firm of J. D. Morton & Son here, do a good business in wood-turning and manufacturing patent ladders. Elijah Norton, Jr., removed to the Centre, and his son, Benjamin H., continued to keep the tavern. Benjamin's son, Charles H., became a clergyman and preached and died in Becket. Edward, another son, kept a hotel in New York state. His son, Charles H., lived not far from where Asa Parsons formerly lived, near the Northampton line. George S., a third son of Benjamin, lived on the old place and sold it to C. C. Bartlett.

Timothy Phelps was one of the first settlers of this town, coming hither from Northampton. Coming out from there in the spring and working through the summer he would return to Northampton to winter. Timothy, his son, built the house on road 28½, now occupied by Strong A. Phelps, his brother, Milton F., and sister, Flora L. He married Lois Wright, of this town, and reared a family of four sons and four daughters. His son Jonathan succeeded him on the homestead. He married Lydia, daughter of Aaron Fisher, and granddaughter of Maj. Aaron Fisher, one of the first settlers of the town. They had a family of four sons and two daughters. The oldest son, Mahlon D., died at the age of nine years ; Jonathan W. enlisted in the late war in the 37th Mass. Vols., in 1864, and in six weeks contracted measles, and died of pneumonia, the effects of that disease, at Washington ; Strong A. and Milton F. are living on the farm occupied by their father and grandfather ; Christiana L. died at the age of twenty-three, after a lingering sickness of three years ; Flora L. resides with her brother as above.

Paul Clark settled about 1785, half a mile south of the center. Of his sons, Asher, Gains and Ira remained in town. Asher and Ira lived on the old place, and Gains removed to the southeast part of the town. His son Charles continued on his father's place, where Mrs. Charles Clark now lives.

Justin Edwards settled in town in 1778, on the place near where Francis Edwards now lives, but on the other side of the way. His son William continued on the old place, but built a new house. William's son Francis succeeded his father on the old farm, and Dea. William I. located on the old Alvord place, half a mile west. Dea. Edward entered the army in the late war. He was sent to the legislature in 1869.

Israel Bridgman located in the north part of the town. His son Spencer succeeded him. Spencer's son, Abner P., followed, and the place is now occupied by Dwight S., son of Abner. Israel's nephew, Clark Bridgman, located still farther north, and his sons Aretas H., Lucas and Franklin A. still reside in town. Franklin occupies the old farm, and Lucas is near by. Aretas H. lives in the house built by Dea. Eleazer Judd, on a part of the original farm of Solomon Judd. His son Fred D. lives with him.

In 1780 Solomon Judd, son of Rev. Jonathan Judd, of Southampton, settled about half a mile north of the Shirkshire road, toward the center. His sons Eleazer and John A. continued to live in town, Eleazer on the old farm, a part of which he sold to William S. Rust with the old house. He then built a new house on the opposite side of the street, in which he and his son Eleazer, Jr. lived, where A. H. Bridgman now lives. F. Pomeroy now occupies the old house. John A. removed to the Center and kept a store and the postoffice for many years, living in different places, but last in the first house south of the church, built by Captain F. Loud. His place is now occupied by his daughter, Mrs. A. C. Shepard. Fred H., son of John A., lives near the church in the old school-house building.

Thaddeus King settled about 1780, in the eastern part of the town. His son Luther succeeded him on the old farm. Elijah settled where Deacon Montague now lives. Elijah's sons, George N., who lived on the old place, but afterward removed to Illinois, Charles C. lived and died here. Luther's sons, Luther W. and J. Lyman, both lived on their father's place. J. Lyman at length removed to Illinois. Horace S., son of Luther W., now occupies the place first mentioned.

Jesse Lyman was a son of Azaria Lyman, who was one of the early settlers of this town. He built a house on road 39, about 1773, which he occupied all his life, as did also Jesse Lyman, and the same house was the home of William E. Lyman until 1851. It was occupied as a dwelling more than one hundred years, until the death of Jesse Lyman, in 1874. The old frame is this present year being newly covered and converted into a horse barn, on the premises occupied by William E. Lyman, for his use. William E. Lyman married Mary E., daughter of Dr. Hervey Orcutt, November 13, 1851, and has had a family of six children. Lillie Belle, born August 3, 1852, died February 1, 1855. Ella, born October 14, 1856, died May 27, 1857. Myra Elma, born May 10, 1858, married Stephen Rust, of Loudville. Annie Field, born November 21, 1862, married Perley L. Kimball, of Bellows Falls, Vt. William Hervey, born May 15, 1866, is at home with his father. Lizzie Rogers, born February 9, 1869, died November 14, 1869.

About 1775, Thomas Elwell settled, first near where E. P. Lyman now lives, but soon removed to the place which Theodore P. Elwell now occupies. His son, Amariah, succeeded him. Amariah's sons, Edmund, continued on the old farm, Jesse, built a little farther east, and Thomas, still farther, on the opposite side of the street, not far from the old Ephraim Wright place. Edmund's sons still live in town, Theodore P. on the old place, Myron L where Jesse formerly lived, and Amariah near the centre of the town.

About the year 1813 Lester Langdon settled in the north part of the town, near where F. Holdridge now lives, buying the place of John Brewer. His son Lester T. bought the Samuel Kingsley place, in the south part of the town, near Babcock's or Rice's corner, on the Shirkshire road. Here he now lives with his son, George K. His son, Franklin, removed to Iowa in 1865. Lester's sons, Chauncey and Albert, removed to Easthampton.

Matthias Rice bought the old Babcock corner about 1834, and lived there until his death, in 1881. He was one of the selectmen for a number of years. He was sent from the district to the state legislature in 1861. His son, Amos D., now occupies the old place.

Dea. Albert G. Jewett came here in 1846, and built the house next east of the Phelps place, now owned by Nelson A. Kingsley, and has since lived in several different places in town. He was one of the selectmen for sixteen years, and finally refused to serve, although he was again re-elected. He was sent to the state legislature from this district in 1881, and has long been a justice of the peace.

Dr. Hervey Orcutt came from Chicopee in 1835 and bought the old Nathan Clark place, where he lived until the time of his death, in 1873. He was the only practicing physician here for many years. His children are Mary (Mrs. William E. Lyman) and Helen A., both of this town.

In 1774, Rufus Lyman settled in the south part of the town, and the place has continued in the family to the present time, his son, Sereno, succeeding him and Edward Payson coming next, now occupies the place. Enoch, son of Rufus, located on or near the place where Abner Smith built the first house. His son, Enoch, succeeded him, and at length sold to Leander Rhodes. He was for many years one of the selectmen. He also served as county commissioner for several years, and was a justice of the peace. William J., son of Sereno, located north of the old place where Mr. Strong built, and where the first birth of a child occurred in the town. He and his son, Sereno D., still live here.

Dr. William Hooker, son of Rev. John Hooker, came to this town in 1878 and built the old house a little east of the church, where he lived until his death, at the age of ninety-three years. The house has always been occupied until three or four years since, when it was removed to make way for a more modern dwelling. Dr. Hooker was much loved by the people, and he ministered to the souls of his patients as well as to their bodies. His son, Anson, became a physician and practiced in Cambridge. Hugh T. lived with his father on the old place. Captain Henry located on Turkey hill, north of the center, and his son, Festus, bought just west of the church. Festus's son, Edward, served as color-bearer in the 37th regiment, and was in some of the severest battles of the late war, yet he returned home at the end of three years without having received so much as a scratch. He removed to Nebraska. Festus's son, Worthington, lives in Loudville, and his son, Charles H., lives on the old place west of the church. Mrs. Charles H. Hooker is a great-granddaughter of Parson Hale. Festus's daughter, Lucy, is Mrs. George E. Knight, of this town.

In 1797, Joel Burt came to town and settled in the western part. In a few years he removed to the place about one mile west of the place where Parson Hale formerly resided, and now unoccupied. His children, who remained in Westhampton, were Captain Levi, who located a mile and a half north of the center, and whose wife was a daughter of Parson Hale; Nathan, who continued on the old place for many years, then purchased the Parson Hale place, where he died. His daughter, Caroline Burt, now occupies the place. Levi's son, Lyman, lived and died on the old Wales place. Joel, another son, lived on the Willard Smith place; afterward removed to Sunderland, where he now lives with his son, Enoch Hale. George lived on his father's place until it was burned, then he bought the old Dr. Hooker place and built a new house, where he now resides. His son, Levi, lives with him. Enoch Hale, a son of Captain Levi, was lost at sea while returning from California. Martha, a daughter of Captain Levi, married W. F. Edwards and removed to Sunderland. Her daughter is Mrs. Charles H. Hooker. Captain Levi's daughter, Susan, (Mrs. R. W. Clapp), lives in Westhampton. Captain Burt is said to have owned a thousand acres of land in this town.

Joel Rust settled in the northwest part of the town, on the old turnpike road from Boston to Albany. His daughter Eliza, wife of Deacon Zenas S. Clark, lived on the old place. Deacon Clark removed to the old Claflin place just south of the church, where his daughter Cornelia now lives. Another daughter, Jane (Mrs. Edward Hooker), removed to Nebraska. Deacon Clark's son, Henry H., entered the army and was known to have been wounded in the battle of the Wilderness, but was never after heard from.

Azariah Lyman, one of the first inhabitants, settled here in 1771, and was succeeded by his son Jesse. William E., a son of Jesse, lives on the old farm, but built his house on the opposite side of the road. William E. has a saw-mill on his place, and does a large business in lumber, besides his large farm. He is a justice of the peace. Jesse's daughter, Mary E. (Mrs. Edward N. Norton), lives with her son, Charles H. Norton.

Jedediah Chapman came to this town about 1800, and bought the place opposite the Norton tavern, on the hill, where he worked at his trade as a blacksmith. His son Anson removed to the Center, and was a blacksmith for a time. Afterward he bought the Sylvester Judd place, and was a store-keeper until his death. He also was a justice of the peace. His daughters, Junia M. and Mary (Mrs. Edward W. Kingsley), still occupy the same place. Jedediah's son Linus removed to Norwich, but soon after returned to West-hampton and worked at his trade, a blacksmith, until his death. His son Arthur K. succeeds him, and lives on the place occupied by his father. Albert, another son of Linus, lives in Brooklyn, N. Y. Helen, a daughter of Linus, now Mrs. C. A. Clark, lives in Brookfield. Jedediah's son Hiram removed to Huntington. James M. located on the old Post farm, near Enoch Ly-man's. James' son Jerome lives in Westhampton. Homer G. removed to Williamsburg.

Dea. Joel Cook was born April 6, 1804, in the house on road 16, where all his life was spent, and where his daughter still resides. His father, Captain Noah Cook, was a native of Northampton, and came to this town, from there, more than one hundred years ago, settling on the same farm now occupied by the daughter of Dea. Joel Cook. Dea. Joel Cook married Harmony White, a native of Berket, Mass., and had a family of four children. The eldest died in infancy. Henry W. was born October 11, 1836, and died at the age of twenty-six, a physician at Bellevue Hospital, New York city. Noah B. is a printer in New York city. Sarah C. occupies the old homestead. Dea. Cook held various offices of responsibility and trust, was a selectman of West-hampton a number of years, one of the examining school committee, and was two terms representative to Boston. He was for many years deacon of the Congregational church. He always pursued the business of farming, and died in the house in which he was born, April 22, 1878.

Julius Cook was a son of Capt. Noah Cook, a Revolutionary soldier, who came to this town from Northampton. Julius Cook was born in this town in 1796, and always pursued farming for his occupation. He married, first, Mercy K. Hunt, of this town, and had two children, Clara and John. The latter married Sylvia Graves, of Hatfield. His second marriage was with Elizabeth Wells, of Northampton, who had one child, Eliza, who married

James Rutherford, a merchant at Mobile, Ala., and died there in 1870. His widow still resides there. John occupies the homestead on road 15. Julius Cook was a sergeant in the war of 1812, for which service, in his later life, he received a pension.

Dea. Samuel Edwards was a native of Southampton, a farmer with his father who was also named Samuel, who had removed from Northampton to Southampton, about 1760. He married Silence, daughter of Rev. Jonathan Judd, who was the first minister in Southampton, in 1780, and removed to this town, locating on road 50. They had a family of three children. One died at the age of five years. Silence married Enoch Lyman, who lived in the western part of the town. She has been dead about thirty years. The only son, Samuel, married Betsey, daughter of Dea. Asa Ludden, of Williamsburg, and succeeded his father on the farm. They had a family of ten, eight of whom are now living, only two residing in this town. Betsey, unmarried, and Theophilus, who now occupies the paternal estate. He married Sarah A., daughter of Levi Dole, of Shelburne, Mass., March 16, 1853. They have had born to them six children, viz.: Sarah A., born March 13, 1854, died January 12, 1878; Emily A., born June 27, 1855, married July 16, 1879, Clark F. Thayer, of Erie, Pa., now resident in Boston; Ella A. born November 18, 1857, married Homer G. Chapman, February 21, 1877, and died July 30, 1878; Clara E., born December 4, 1859, married Homer G. Chapman, April 28, 1880, and died October 30, 1882; Levi W., born March 30, 1862; and Arthur T., born September 26, 1871. Both sons are at home with their parents. Mr. Edwards has held the office of selectman of his town a number of terms, and on the board of examining school committee for three years. His son Levi holds the same office at present. He has often been called to superintend the Sunday-school of the Congregational church, and is one of the church committee.

Peter Montague was one of the very early settlers of this town, removing hither from South Hadley. He died here September 24, 1822, leaving a family of six. His son, David, settled on the farm now occupied by Henry W. Montague, at the center of the town. He married Lovicy, daughter of Enos and Hannah Janes, of Easthampton, born March 15, 1792, and died October 13, 1870. Of their family of thirteen, two died in infancy. Mary Ann, born January 1, 1814, married Theodore Clark, of this town, and died March 17, 1871, leaving no children. Sylvia was born March 2, 1816; Melzar V. was born May 5, 1818; Enos J. was born March 16, 1820; Hannah W. was born March 20, 1823; David S. was born February 1, 1825; Louisa, born January 21, 1827, died January 18, 1831; Alfred D., born March 6, 1829, married in 1858, June 17, daughter of Ansel and Eunice (Wright) Clapp, of this town. They have five children, three sons and two daughters, viz.: Francis C., who married Alice, daughter of L. M. Woodard, of Halifax, Vt., in 1882, and is a farmer with his father on road 25. Edward H., Lovisa J., Alfred D., Jr., and Harriet F., unmarried, resides at home. Mr. Montague has been on the town school board for a number of years. In 1876 he was chosen deacon in the Congregational church, which position he now occupies. Melzar, the eldest son of David, graduated at Williams college, studied theology at East Windsor, Conn., and became pastor of the Congregational church at Fort Atkinson, Wis. His voice failing, he became a successful teacher. He married Mary, daughter of Richard Hale, of this town, and died December 30, 1872, at Allen's Grove, Wis. He was the author of a poem read at the centennial reunion of his native town September 5, 1866. Enos Janes, son of David Montague, born March 16, 1820, graduated from Williams college in 1841, and from the Theological seminary at East Windsor, Conn., in 1845. He was ordained May 14, 1846, pastor of the Congregational church in Summit, Oconomowac and Fort Atkinson, Wis. He was a leading minister for thirty-four years. He married Faith Huntington, daughter of Rev. E. W. Hooker, D. D., of East Windsor, Conn. He died September 30, 1880, and was burried in his native town. Henry W. Montague, son of David, born April 17, 1831, married Achsah, daughter of Nathan Burt, of this town, and occupies the same farm on which his father settled. David S., born February 1, 1825, married first, Lucinda, daughter of Theodore Clark, and second, Asenath, daughter of Abner Parsons, of Northampton. By his first wife he had two children, May L., who died in infancy, and Myron H., who was born August 22, 1858. The latter married June 11, 1884, Emma Frances, daughter of F. A. Bridgman, of this town. He settled at farming with his father. January 5, 1885, he was driving a young colt, which became frightened and threw him from the wagon, killing him instantly. By his second marriage he has one daughter, Aurelia L., now a student at Mt. Holyoke Female seminary. Hannah L. married Elijah P. Torrey, a carpenter and joiner by trade, who resides near the Center. Nancy L., born May 7, 1837, died May 16, 1864. Sylvia M., born October 21, 1850, married Amos D. Rice, March 1, 1871, and resides on road 39.

Medad King was a native of Northampton. His father, also of the name Medad, being of the family from whom King street in Northampton was named. In an early day they owned a large tract along King street, their residence being on the lot where the French Catholic church now stands. Medad, when thirty years of age, settled in this town on road 16, in 1796 or 1797. He married Susanna, daughter of Daniel Warner, of Northampton, reared a family of eight children, five sons and three daughters, Sylvester, Elisha, Simeon, Medad, Gains, Susanna (1st), Dorcas and Susanna (2d). Dorcas died in childhood. Susanna (2d) lived to the age of thirty-eight, and was the wife of George Day, of Northampton. Sylvester died at the age of sixteen. Elisha was a blacksmith and worked at his trade in this town for many years. He married Elizabeth, daughter of Phineas Clark, of Easthampton, was for many years deacon in the Congregational church, and much respected for his piety and Christian walk. They reared a family of seven. Simeon died at the age of twelve. Medad succeeded his father on the homestead, married Lydia Clark, a sister of his brother Elisha's wife, and had one child, Amaranda, who died of scarlet fever at the age of six years. Fifty-four years ago was erected the house in which Medad now resides. His wife died February 3, 1836. Gains settled in Medina, N. Y., a tailor by trade. He married in New York, and of his family, George and Henry are still living, at Middleport, N. Y.

Zenas Kingsley was a native of this town, and carried on the trade of a clothier at Loudville just over the line in Northampton. He married Susan, daughter of Amariah Elwell, of this town. They reared a family of nine, of whom four daughters and four sons are now living. Susan M. married Henry Parsons, of this town. Edward W. married Mary E., daughter of Anson Chapman, a native and always a resident of this town. He has for a number of years carried on a lumber business at Columbia, N. H. He now occupies the former residence of Anson Chapman. He has one son, Edward A. Joseph H. married Elmina Norton, a native of Rochester, N. Y., and resides in Southampton. Zenas Mahlon enlisted in Co. A, 27th Mass. Vols., his name being the first enrolled for that regiment in 1861, served until his death, which occurred at Newberne, N. C., in 1862. Nelson H. is at Riverside, Cal., whither he went after having served through the late war. Ellen V. married Enoch Perkins, now living at Guildhall, Vt. Justus H., a farmer, now a resident of this town. Delia M., also a resident with her sister, Mrs. Charles Clark, on road 52.

Nelson A. Kingsley, son of Henry S., who has been treasurer of the town since 1877, was born at Ellicottville, N. Y., April 2, 1840. In 1862 he enlisted in Co. G, 154th N. Y. Vols. He was taken prisoner at the battle of Gettysburg, and was confined in Libby prison and at Belle Isle, Va. After the war he came to this town, where he has since resided.

Ansel Clapp was a direct descendant of Roger Clapp, who came to this country from Devonshire, England, May 30, 1630. He was born in Northampton, February 13, 1788 He married in 1818, Eunice, only daughter of Reuben Wright, one of the first settlers in Northampton. The same year he removed to this town, locating on road 11, where he passed the remainder of his life. His death occurred September 11, 1866, the result of an injury received in the harvest field a few weeks before. They had two sons and two daughters. Luther became pastor of a Congregational church at Wannatosa, Wis., and married Harriet P. Stedman, of Chicopee. The second son, Reuben W., married December 23, 1852, Susan T., daughter of Levi Burt, of this town, and granddaughter of Rev. Enoch Hale, first minister of Westhampton. To them were born eight children—Ellen L., born February 15, 1854, married Edward A. Allyn, of Holyoke, May 10, 1882 ; Laura H., born February 19, 1856, married September 30, 1885, Frederick A. Dayton, of Northampton ; George B., born November 3, 1857, a farmer in Easthampton ; Lyman W., born September 6, 1859, married June 8, 1886, Elizabeth C., daughter of William Ewing, of Easthampton, and is associated with his father on their large farm on road 11; Martha F., born March 30, 1862, died March 12, 1876; Edwin B., born May 17, 1864, a farmer; Susan M., born December 7, 1866, living with her parents; and Mary A., born November 25, 1868, died September 15, 1869. The eldest daughter, Harriet F., is unmarried and resides with her nephew, George B., in Easthampton. Sophia is the wife of Dea. Alfred D. Montague.

Horace F. Clapp was born in Southampton, May 16, 1825. His early days were spent in his native town on his father's farm, married Fidelia, daughter of Lemuel Thompson, of Monterey, May 2, 1854, and has five children living and buried one. Mary E. married Fred Freiday, now a resident of Iowa; Iretta married George A. Gorton, of Southampton; Chastina married Myron J. Rowley, who died in Florence in September, 1883. Mr. Clapp is a farmer on road 38.

Franklin J. Pomeroy was born in Southampton, in 1836, and his early life was spent on a farm with his father, Joshua, who was also a native of Southampton. He received a common school education, and attended Williston seminary, Easthampton. He has been a farmer nearly all of his business life. In 1881 he purchased a farm on road 33, where he now resides.

Erastus B. Pratt was born in Plainfield, October 24, 1842, where he remained with his father on a farm until the death of the latter in July, 1874. He then went to the state of Michigan, remaining there about one year. He married Betsey Poole, of Rockland, Mass., in March, 1876, removing soon after to Amherst, leasing a farm of Oliver Longley's estate. In April, 1877, he removed to this town, engaging in a general mercantile business, which he has ever since pursued. He received the appointment of postmaster in April, 1881, which he has held since that date. He has one child.

Charles N. Loud, son of Francis Loud, was born in September, 1839, in this town, attended the district schools here in his boyhood, three years in Hopkins academy, Hadley, and two years at Williston seminary, preparatory to a college education. In the early part of the late rebellion he enlisted from this town in Co. K, 52d Mass. Vols., and served a year. He was hospital steward, in charge of the United States barracks hospital at Baton Rouge, La. Returning home he went out as agent of the Christian Commission at Washington. He also taught in the New York Juvenile Asylum one year, having charge of a school of five hundred scholars. His father's health failing, he was called home to take charge of his business, and from that time gave up the idea of entering college. He has taught school many terms in this town, Northampton and Worthington. He was chairman of town school committee several years, and on the board for fifteen years. In 1869 he took charge of the manufactory business which had been established and carried on by his father a number of years, and is still in the same business. He has been selectman, town clerk, treasurer and collector, and has served on the jury of the United States court at Boston. He married first, Julia R., daughter of Franklin Strong, of this town, February 5, 1867, who died in December, 1869. His second marriage was with Susan C. Annable, of Worthington, September 5, 1871, and has three sons. Mr. Loud has been a member of the Congregational church the past twenty-eight years. He is now superintendent of the Sabbath-school.

Franklin Strong was a son of Paul Strong, who for many years kept tavern where Florence now stands. He was a miller by trade, owning and running a grist-mill in Easthampton, in the village of Loudville. He was also a farmer on road 52. He married Dorcas, eldest daughter of Dea. Elisha King, of this town, and had six children, of whom only Susan E. and Julia R. lived to womanhood. Julia married Charles N. Loud, of this town, and died December 16, 1869. Susan E. occupies the farm left by her father at his death, which occurred July 14, 1884. She also carries on the grist-mill left by him. Mrs. Strong died October 1, 1879.

Noah Parsons came to this town at an early day in its settlement from Northampton, settling on road 36. He reared a family of six children. Asa married Betsey, daughter of Aaron Hall, of Huntington, and had four children. One son was killed by the falling of a gate when a small boy, Aaron H., settled near his father after his marriage to Harriet N., daughter of Luther King. Henry M. married Susan M. Kingsley, of Northampton, and resides on the homestead. They have four children, having buried two in infancy. Susan E., Mahlon K., Edna H. and Lillian G., who reside with their parents. Asa Parsons died about fifteen years ago. His widow is still living, at the age of eighty-nine years, with her son Henry M. Chester, son of Noah, moved to Skaneateles, N. Y., and afterwards to Syracuse, N. Y., where he and his wife both died. She was a daughter of Benoni Clark, of this town. Noah went to Lima, N. Y., and died there. Spencer was engaged in the cabinet business at Syracuse, N. Y., when he died. Jared removed to South Onondaga, N. Y., and was a farmer there, and is now deceased. Edward located in Northampton, where his sons Edward and Spencer now reside.

The town's growth and fluctuations in population may be seen in the following figures, viz.: The population in 1790 was 683 ; 1800, 756 ; 1810, 793 ; 1820, 896 ; 1830, 913 ; 1840, 759 ; 1850, 602 ; 1855, 670 ; 1860, 608 ; 1865, 636 ; 1870, 556 ; 1875, 556 ; 1880, 564.

Organization.—The town was incorporated September 29, 1778, in accordance with an act of the general court, and Caleb Strong, Esq., of Northampton, afterward governor, was authorized to issue his warrant to the inhabitants of the new town to meet and choose their first town officers, " and transact such other lawful matters as shall be expressed in the warrant." In accordance with this act, Caleb Strong issued his warrant to Abner Claflin, one of the principal inhabitants of the town, to warn the inhabitants " to assemble and meet together at the dwelling-house of Nathan Clark, in said Westhampton, on Friday, the 19th day of November, to choose such officers as towns are authorized by law to choose." Also " to consider and determine whether the said town will request Mr. Hale to continue to preach in said town."

The officers chosen at the first meeting were Sylvester Judd, clerk; Dea. Martin Clark, treasurer; John Smith, Capt. William Bartlett and John Baker, selectmen ; John Parsons and Ephraim Wright, surveyors of ways; Azariah Lyman, tithingman; John Smith, warden; Abner Claflin, constable; Martin Clark, Azariah Lyman and Sylvester Judd were chosen a committee " to procure Mr. Hale, or some other person, to preach four Sabbaths after Mr. Hale's present engagement expires," preaching services to be held for " two Sabbaths at the house of Nathan Clark, and the remaining two Sabbaths at the house of Azariah Lyman, one house being situated south, the other north of the center."

Gideon Clark was chosen town clerk at the first annual town-meeting, in 1777, and was re-elected for thirty-five years, or until 1814, the year of his death. Sylvester Judd, Jr., served in 1814–15 ; Luke Phelps from 1816 to 1830, fourteen years ; John A. Judd, from 1830 to 1855, with the exception of one year (1837), when Francis Loud was chosen ; Daniel W. Clark served from 1855 to 1866; Charles N. Loud from 1867 to 1870; I. C. Davenport, in 1870. The present incumbent, Frederick H. Judd, from 1871 until the present time.

It is said that Parson Hale kept a very accurate account of births, deaths, and marriages, but they were all destroyed when his house was burned in 1816. The earlier records of these items in the town are very incomplete.

Westhampton Reunion.—The town issued letters of invitation to its former inhabitants and natives to meet at a reunion service on September 5, 1866, and about 1,200 persons responded to the call. The reporter of that day said : " It was, properly speaking, a centennial celebration of the settlement of the town, for the earliest inhabitants came in and began to fill the forest just about 100 years ago, although the town was not incorporated till some twelve years afterward, in 1778." Messrs. M. Rice, H. W. Montague, R. W. Clapp, E. H. Lyman and George B. Drury were chosen a committee of arrangements. The reporter again says : " The natives of the town compose a noble band of men and women, who would do honor to any locality. No town can boast a nobler ancestry or point to more celebrated descendants than the good old town of Westhampton. Among the clergymen were Revs. J. Lyman Clark, D. D., Dorus Clark, D. D., Tertius Clark, D. D., Calvin Clark, George Lyman, Chester Bridgman, Prof. Melzar Montague, Enos J. Monatague, Luthar Clapp, James Brewer, and Anson Clark. Physicians, Dr. Anson Hooker, son of Dr. William Hooker, and D. Jewett. Other professional and business men, C. P. Judd and Otis Clapp, of Boston ; E. M. Kingsley, of New York city ; Z. M. Phelps, of Riverdale, N.Y.; E. C. Bridgman, of New York city, and others. The poet of the day was Rev. Prof. Melzar Montague, of Ripon College, Wis., and Enoch H. Lyman was president ; the address of Welcome by R. W. Clapp ; historial address by C. Parkman Judd and Otis Clapp, from which many of these facts are drawn. After these addresses in the church, the throng repaired to the large pavillion in front of the church to refresh the inner man, at the bountifully spread tables. E. M. Kingsley presided at the tables. Rev. George Lyman, of Sutton, invoked the divine blessing. The banquet over the president "proceeded to uncork the natives." Rev. Tertius Clark of Cuyahoga was first called up.

"When he was a boy in Westhampton he like all other lads, was profoundly impressed by the great head of Squire Judd. The squire was the maker and expounder of the common law in town, and many looked up to him with the greatest veneration and awe. An incident occurred in the old meeting-house. Tithingmen had been appointed to keep the boys in order in the galleries. On one occasion his strong propensity to laugh came very near plunging him into the deepest disgrace and ruin. One of the tithingmen sported a large bandanna handkerchief, which he used to pull from his pocket on blowing his nose, which he did very frequently, and with a loud noise. One of the boys observing this frequent use of the immense wiper and wishing to have a little sport even 'in meeting time,' brought a pint of beans and poured them into the man's pocket, on the top of the handkerchief, one end of which was hanging outside. The explosion soon occurred. The bandanna was suddenly pulled, the beans flew in all directions, and the church was thrown into great commotion. The boy who put the beans into the pocket maintained the most imperturbable gravity, while the boy Tertius burst out into a shout of laughter, being utterly unable to 'hold in.' The tithingman soon appeared and arrested the laughing lad as the author of all the mischief. He was taken before Squire Judd in a state of awful fear and trembling. Most unexpectedly his life was spared, and he was let off with a reprimand never to do so again. He promised he would not, provided the boys did not bring any more beans."

The prayers of the good old men of those days were often an hour long. Rev. George Lyman said, "I remember hearing Deacon Edwards say when he had been obliged to stay at home from church on account of the snow drifts, that he had been absent from church before but once for more than twenty years." In speaking of Squire Judd, his grandfather, he said, "In his manner and general bearing he was a gentleman of the old school. To his minister, Parson Hale, of whom he was a fast friend he was uniformly respectful and differential, not forgetting to send him portions of the fattest of his herds and flocks. In his family prayers which were long and always offered in a standing posture, among other 'old-fashioned words and phrases' and 'sacred texts' which have fixed themselves in my memory, were the familiar words 'whom to know aright is life eternal.' I used to wonder in my boyhood, who that Noah Wright ('know aright') was, whose title to eternal life was secured."

Mr. E. C. Bridgman, of New York, said: "This is no ordinary entertainment to which the absent natives of Westhampton are invited. Nothing to be compared with it can we expect to enjoy again this side of the River. To show our appreciation of and gratitude for what has been done for us, I suggest that we take action in the formation of a town library. Some of us have

money; some have books, good books that we do not need; and all, I feel
sure, are disposed to do something. To set the 'ball in motion,' I offer for
this object one hundred dollars."

The whole subject of libraries was referred to a committee consisting of
Messrs. E. C. Bridgman, Otis Clapp, S. F. Phelps, Dr. Anson Hooker, E. M.
Kingsley and Rev. Mr. Allender. As the result of that "setting the ball in
motion," there is now a well selected public library of about 1,150 volumes
which is well patronized. Dr. Dorus Clark pronounced the benediction and
the assembly broke up.

Military.—In the war of the Revolution Westhampton took an honorable
part, though much that was done was in connection with Northampton, for it
must be borne in mind that the town was not organized until three years after
the war commenced. The following from the town records, however, shows
the spirit which prevailed :—

"Aug. 5, 1779.—At a town-meeting, voted, that the town would provide
such things for those men that went from us into the Continental army as the
town of Northampton desired of us.

"Aug. 11, 1779.—In the midst of Revolutionary difficulties, Massachusetts
having proceeded to call a State convention to form a constitution, Westhampton elected Sylvester Judd as a Delegate.

"Oct. 18, 1779.—The town voted to hire the three men required for the
Continental army. Gideon Clark, John Smith and Sheldon Felton were appointed a committee to assist the militia officers in hiring the men.

"Voted that the selectmen collect the clothing required of Westhampton
for the use of the army, deliver the same in Northampton, and take a proper
receipt therefor.

"Voted, that the men that went the month's campaign into Connecticut
be paid the same as those that went in June last, in proportion to their service.
Nathan Clark, Aaron Fisher and Sylvester Judd were appointed a committee
to attend to this.

"July 23, 1781.—Voted, to hire the three men now required of us for the
army, and that Capt. Azariah Lyman, Lieut. Aaron Fisher, and Lieut. Noah
Edwards be a committee to hire said men, expenses to be assessed upon
said town, and paid within one month.

"Sept. 18, 1781.—Voted, that the men that now hold themselves in readiness to join the army at the shortest notice shall be paid 2 pounds, 10 shillings per month for each month they shall be in actual service, twenty shillings
to be paid in advance when called upon to march.

"May 1, 1782.—Voted, that Mr. Sylvester Judd be a committee to hire
one man for the Continental army."

In the late great war the town furnished sixty-eight men; a surplus of four
over all demands. One was a commissioned officer. The town furnished
$9,454.50 for the cause, exclusive of $2,341.99 which was subsequently re-
imbursed by the state.

VILLAGES.

WESTHAMPTON, located in the central part of the town, has the town's only
postoffice. This is but a hamlet, and is locally known as the "Center." The
postmaster is Erastus B. Pratt.

LOUDVILLE is a small village in the southeastern part of the town, but most of it, including the postoffice, lies in Northampton.

MANUFACTURES.

Henry M. Parsons's saw mill is on road 36, on a branch of the Manhan river. The mill was originally built by Solomon Warner, about forty years ago. He, after running it about a year, sold out to Aaron H. and H. M. Parsons. The power is sufficient for business the year round. Mr. Parsons put in, a few years ago, a circular-saw with improved carriage.

William E. Lyman's saw-mill, located on road 33, upon Sodom brook, a branch of Manhan river, was built by his father, Jesse Lyman, in 1839. It has a circular saw and the capacity for sawing 5,000 feet of lumber per day.

Amos D. Rice's tannery, located at the corner of roads 39 and 40, was carried on by his father about forty years. It is the only small tannery for miles around.

S. A. Phelps's vinegar manufactory, on road 28½, was established by him in 1872. He has storage capacity for 300 barrels and turns out about sevty-five barrels per annum.

Charles N. Loud's saw-mill, on road 28½, was built and work commenced in it in 1869. It is run by water-power. He manufactures Sissons's patent clothes reels, tooth-powder boxes, and bobbins and quills. He employs five hands. He also contracts for furnishing and building, and manufactures lumber of all kinds.

Joseph D. Norton & Son have, on road 53, at Loudville, a manufactory for all kinds of wood-work. They employ five hands, their annual product being valued at $4,000.00. The works were established about forty years ago by the elder Norton.

CHURCH HISTORY.

Congregational church of Westhampton.—At the first town meeting the only other business than election of officers that came before the people was to secure the services of Rev. Enoch Hale to preach one-half the time at the house of Nathan Clark, and the other half at the house of Azariah Lyman. The church was organized September 1, 1779, by Rev. Solomon Williams, of Northampton, and Rev. Jonathan Judd, of Southampton, and Martin Clark and Reuben Wright were chosen deacons. Parson Hale was ordained its first minister September 29th of the same year, the service being held in an unfinished barn which stood close by where the barn of C. C. Bartlett now stands. Mr. Hale came from Coventry, Conn., and spent the remainder of his life here, dying at the age of eighty-four years, and the fifty-eighth year of his ministry. He was quite feeble for some years previous to his death, and Rev. Horace B. Chapin, from South Amherst, was installed as colleague pastor July 8, 1829, and was dismissed at his own request February 28, 1837.

Rev. Amos Drury, of Fair Haven, Vt., was settled June 28, 1837, and died at Pittsford, Vt., July 22, 1841. Rev. David Coggin, of Tewksbury, was ordained May 11, 1842, and died in Westhampton, April 28, 1852. Rev. Andrew Bigelow, of West Needam, was installed March 2, 1854, and was dismissed April 18, 1855. Rev. Roswell Foster, of Waltham, was installed November 10, 1856, and was dismissed December 28, 1858. Rev. Edwin Bissell, of Bolton, Conn., (now of Hartford Theological seminary) was ordained September 21, 1859. He enlisted in the army in 1862, in company with several of his people, and entered the 52d Regt. of this State, Co. K, and was chosen captain of the company. He was dismissed from the pastorate May 10, 1864. During his absence in the army the pulpit was supplied by Rev. Jesse Brush. Rev. Thomas Allender, of New London, Conn., was installed June 21, 1866, and died at New London, after a long and painful illness, September 17, 1869. Rev. Pliny F. Barnard, of Williamstown, Vt., was installed January 30, 1870, and was dismissed July 1, 1873. Rev. Joseph Lanman, of Lynn, was installed June 3, 1874, and dismissed September 11, 1876. Rev. Edwin S. Palmer, of Knoxville, Pa., was installed December 7, 1876, and was dismissed April 20, 1881. Rev. William C. Scofield, of Owego, N. Y., became the acting pastor October 1, 1881, and was released December 7, 1884. Rev. Alwyn E. Todd, of Chester, became acting pastor January 1, 1886. In 1853 Rev. Stephen C. Strong, of Northampton, (grandson of Gov. Caleb Strong) declined an invitation to settle, but supplied the place of pastor for some months.

In June, 1785, the first meeting house, 40x50 feet, was erected, and meetings were held in it, although it was not completed until some time after. The material for this building had been provided in 1779, but the contention over where it should be placed was so great that it did not find an abiding place in all these years. Tradition has it that the timbers were carried past Mr. Hale's house three times before it was allowed to assume the form of a building. This contention was a sore trial to the good parson, and it was due to his calm and patient bearing and influence that peace was the final outcome. At that time there came near being a separation of the north and south factions of the town over this vexed question. The house was finally located where the present church stands, being as near the geographical center of the town as it could be conveniently placed. It was taken down to make room for its successor in 1816, and a larger one was then built, being 70x50 feet. The building was said to be the finest church edifice in all the small towns of Western Massachusetts. This house was burned in February, 1829. Before the people went to their homes from the fire, they began to take measures to rebuild, and during that year the building now standing was erected, being some ten feet shorter than its predecessor. In 1860 the house was remodeled to some extent, the high pulpit was replaced by a lower and more modern one, the front of the galleries was lowered, also the doors of the pews, and the walls were painted. About this time the old square steeple was surmounted by a spire. In 1883 it was again extensively remodeled, at a cost of about $5,000.00, and the inside wholly changed. The gallery floor was extended over the whole, being now the floor of the main audience room up-stairs, the old lower floor divided into prayer room, ladies parlor, kitchen, library and dressing room. The organ is placed behind the pulpit, also the singers' seats, which are reached by a rear stairway, the pews put in circular form, the walls frescoed and floors newly carpeted, a new pulpit-set and chairs for the prayer room make it a very commodious and neat place of worship.

In 1828 and for several years after, the church was badly broken up and distressed by the secession of many of its members, who formed themselves into another church under the leadership of Rev. John Truair; but all this is now fully healed over and those most interested in the other church came back to their first love. The members now number about 300. Mr. Truair soon after left the town. His only surviving children, J. G. K. and Thomas S., reside in Syracuse, N. Y.

Parson Hale, in his time, took great interest in the education of children in the public schools and so imbued the minds of the people with his senti-ments that they have since been generally willing to provide liberally for the support of schools. A large number for so small a population have entered institutions for higher learning and several have graduated from colleges.

On May 3, 1879, the church in Westhampton voted that Caleb Loud, R. W. Clapp, William E. Lyman and Deacon William E. Edwards, with the pastor, be a committee to consider the matter of arranging for a centennial celebration of the church, and to report at a future meeting. On the report being made, the same individuals, with the addition of D. S. Montague to their number, were instructed to arrange for such a celebration, and on the third of September following the meeting was held. In response to invitations issued to former members and others, several hundred people were gathered here from all quarters. Rev. Mr. Palmer, the pastor, made an address of welcome. Dr. Dorus Clark, of Boston, in his eighty-third year, delivered the historical address, which was listened to with great pleasure. Following this address the sacrament was administered, Rev. E. J. Montague and Luther Clapp, from the west, ministering at the table; Deacons Edwards and Mon-tague being assisted by Deacons E. Kingsley and E. C. Bridgman, of New York; Elnathan Graves, of Williamsburg, and George L. Wright, of North-ampton. After this service the people gave their attention to the collation which had been prepared. E. M. Kingsley presided at table, and in re-sponse to his sentiments short speeches were made by Otis Clapp, Esq., of Boston, Rev. J. H. Bisbee, Rev. George Lyman, Rev. A. M. Colton, Rev. Luther Clapp, Rev. E. J. Montague and several others. Letters were read from others who were unable to attend, and as the memorable day was draw-ing to its close the people dispersed. William E. Lyman was president of the day.

31*

WILLIAMSBURG lies in the northern-central part of the county, and is bounded north by the county line, east by Hatfield and the county line, south by Northampton and Westhampton, and west by Goshen and Chesterfield. It was originally granted by the general court to Hatfield, a strip of country six miles long and three miles wide. The details of this grant are given in connection with the history of Chesterfield.

Occupying a pleasant location on the eastern slope of the Green Mountains, with a delightful climate and a beautifully diversified surface, Williamsburg is all that the lover of the beautiful in nature could desire. The general slope of the surface is south and west, and the whole town is drained by Mill river and its tributaries. The soil is warm and fertile, the land being excellent for pasturage, meadow, tillage and fruit. The land originally was heavily timbered with chestnut, hickory, walnut, oak, pine, rock-maple, hemlock, beech, cherry and sycamore, interlaced with grape vines and small fruits, including plums, blackberries, raspberries, whortleberries, strawberries, etc.; and now when cultivated, the apple, pear, peach, plum, grapes and berries flourish in abundant perfection. With wild animals the forests abounded. The bear, wolfe, moose, panther, deer, raccoon, beaver, otter, mink, sable, ermine, muskrat, black and red fox, rabbit, hare, elk, woodchuck, black, gray, red, ground and flying squirrels, and lynx and wild-cat were numerous. Brook trout were also plentiful in all the streams and were taken with the greatest ease.

The surface of the township, so charmingly diversified with hill and dale, presents landscape views unequaled. From many of the high hills in the north and west portions of the town, the whole valley of the Connecticut river, with Mount Holyoke and Mount Tom, are taken in at a glance, extending more than seventy miles up and down that noble stream. The church towers of many houses of worship may be seen at one view, besides meadows, fields, houses, forests and villages, which, combined, make up a panorama worthy of the pencil of the most skillful artist. Let one spend but a brief period of time among the hills of this town, in the warm season, and his mind will be stored with abundant diversities of nature in most of her charming forms. So well appreciated have the country retreats which the many old homesteads of the substantial people of the town become, that numbers of the natives of the place, whom business interests have called to localities far distant, yearly return to the scenes of their early life, with their families and acquaintances, to recruit in the bracing air, the unequaled waters and the unsurpassed scenery of this rural home. To them, wherever they go, there is "no place like home." Of late years the city stranger, too, has found his way thither each season.

Settlement and Growth.—It is generally conceded that the first settler upon the present territory of Williamsburg was John Miller, a "mighty hunter," who came on from Northampton in 1735 and located on the hill northwest of the present village of Haydenville. Here he spent many years alone, hunting and trapping. In 1752 he was joined by Samuel Fairfield, who built a hotel on the military road that had recently been built through the town. But the settlement thus begun progressed slowly. It must be remembered that the territory was a part of Hatfield, and the dangers from Indians the early settlers underwent is well set forth in the history of that town. The infant settlement at what is now Hatfield village was in a sense garrisoned and fortified, hence it is not to be expected that settlers would get far away from it till after the cessation of Indian alarms in 1759. The general period of settlement is assigned then between the years 1760–71, the district being incorporated during the latter year.

In 1772 the assessment list of the town shows the following residents, it being impossible to state chronologically the order of their settlement: Russell Kellogg, Elijah Wait, Joshua Warner, Jonathan Warner, George Andrews, William Dunton, Benjamin Blanchard, Joseph Tory, William Stephenson, Joel Warner, Paul Warner, Downing Warner, Jr., Smith Kennett, Mather Warren, Joseph Warren, Abner Cole, Samuel Fairfield, Amos Truesdell, John Wait, Samuel Day, John Nash, Elisha Nash, William Reed, Asa Thayer, Richard Church, John Meekins, Samuel Hontanton, Daniel May, Joseph Cary, John Burroughs, Silas Billings, Seth Tubbs, Daniel Hollis, William Bodman, James Smith, Simeon White, Thomas Lothing, Enoch Thayer, Ezra Strong, Thomas Warren, Seth Pomeroy, Josiah Pomeroy, John Miller, Seth Graves, Perez Graves, Silas Graves, James Porter, Thomas Fenton, Caleb Conant, Jesse Wild, Josiah Hadlock, Joshua Thayer, Andrew Gates, Asa Ludden, Ezra Ludden, Thomas Flow, Josiah Dwight, Anson Cheesman, Samuel Patridge, Simeon Burroughs, David Burroughs, Lucy Hubbard, Ebenezer Hill, Ichabod Hemenway, Abijah Hunt, Josiah Hadlock, Jr., Hezekiah Reed, Gaius Crafts, George Dunn, Thomas Fance, Ebenezer Paine, Thomas French, Lemuel Barber, Abel Thayer, Thomas Fenton, Jr., Benjamin Reed, Joseph Ludden, Lucy Ludden, Thomas Spafford, Jonathan Wolcott, Jonathan Wolcott, Jr., Thomas Meekins, Amasa Graves, Seth Hastings, Nehemiah Cleaveland, William Guilford, Asaph Wales, Eleazer Root, Aaron Hemenway, James Ludden, Seth Ludden, Asa Brown, Joseph Janes, James Janes, William Fenton, Thomas Beebe, Thomas Loring, Moses Carley, Josiah Hayden, Thomas How, Amasa Frost, Nathan Frost, Sampson Hill, Alexander Miller, Samuel French, Jacob Paine, Levi Ludden, Samuel Bagley, Edward Curtis, James Bangs, William Wales, Isaac Phinney and Benjamin Hadlock.

The origin of many of these early families was as follows: The Pomeroy family came from Northampton. The Hyde family came from the eastern part of Massachusetts. Josiah and Cyrus Hannum came from Belchertown, and were emigrants from Hartford. The Thayers came from Braintree and the Old Plymouth Colony. The Dwights came from Northampton, and the family was originally from Northampton, in England. The Nash family came from London, and are said to be originally from Lancaster. Thomas Nash, the original head of the family in America, on Connecticut river, came over with Mr. Davenport, to New Haven, as one of his congregation, in 1637. They had been residing at Leyden, in Holland. The Cleghorn family are of Scotch origin, and came from Martha's Vineyard. Indeed, at one time, just preceding and during the Revolutionary war, there were twenty families in Williamsburg that came from Martha's Vineyard. Thomas Mayhew and his brothers Constad and William, were direct descendants from the first Mayhews, father and son, who came to the Vineyard in 1651, from Northampton, in England. The Coffin family came from Nantucket; so did the Allens and the Butler family. The Bradfords came from Plymouth. The Williamses and Elisha Hubbard came from Hatfield, while Sylvanus and William Hubbard came from Sunderland. The Bodmans first came from Hatfield, but the family originally came from Devonshire, England. The Littles and Joseph Strong's family came from Simsbury, in Connecticut. William Steward, the grandfather of Senator Steward, of Michigan, as well as the Bartlett family, came from Martha's Vineyard. The Warner family came from Hatfield. The Washburn family came from the southeastern part of Massachusetts. Hosea Ballou, the Universalist divine in Boston, married a daughter of Nehemiah Washburn. The Starks family and Johnson family came from Haddam, Ct. The Ludden family, as well as Simeon Strong, came from Rehoboth, Mass. The Graves family came from Hatfield. The Cleveland families are said to have come from Northampton. The Hunt families came from Nantucket. The Hill families originally came from Hatfield; so did the Wade families. The Hayden families came from Hatfield, but were originally from Hartford. The Clark family came from Northampton. The widow Sarah Clark, whose maiden name was Sarah Hume, of Belchertown, married Deacon Elisha Nash, in 1812.

John Williams, one of the first settlers, came here from Middleboro, Mass., and settled on the farm now owned by Prescott Williams, May 15, 1773.

Rufus Hyde, a lineal descendant of William Hyde, whose name first appears in Hartford, Conn., in 1636, came to Williamsburg, from Norwich, Conn., and settled on the farm now owned by F. E. Hyde, the deed bearing the date of 1774. He married Mary, daughter of Jonathan Wolcott. His oldest son, Eleazer, was born December 27, 1772, married Keziah, daughter of Thomas Howes, of Ashford, Mass., and had born to him seven children. Lyman, second son of Eleazer, was born May 26, 1808, married Lucinda, daughter of Oliver Baker, for his first wife, of Chesterfield, and had born to him three children. Mrs. Hyde died August 31, 1855, and he married for his second wife, Sarah T., daughter of Chapin Thayer, of Hadley, and had born to him two children, Francis E. and Eugene.

Samson Hill came here from Hatfield, and made the first settlement in the northern part of the town, was a miller by trade, and run the first mill in town, being employed by Edmund Taylor. He married Prudence Ruggles, and reared five children. His son, Ephraim, married Sarah, daughter of

Samuel Bradford, and had born to him ten children, only two of whom are living, namely, Hiram, of this town, and Sarah, widow of Jeremiah Ward, and who lives in Springfield.

Jonathan Warner, a captain in the Revolutionary war, married Miss E. Sheldon, of Northampton, and had born to him eleven children, six of whom were sons, viz: Nathan, Silas, Job, Melza, Ebenezer and Jonathan. He was one of the early settlers of this town, located on the farm now owned by Francis Warner, was a carpenter by trade, and helped build the first church. Ebenezer was born in this town in 1776, was also a carpenter, married Sally, daughter of Samuel Graves, and reared five children, namely, Abigail, Ebenezer, Mary, Martha and Almond, the last three of whom are living. Almond married Sarah M. Codding, and has had born to him six children, as follows: Charles, who served in the late war, in 145th N. Y. Vols., Sarah J., Mary, Lewis H., Emily H. and Fidelia C.

Eliphalet Thayer, son of Oliver, was born in Braintree, Mass., in 1776, and when still a child his parents moved to the northern part of Williamsburg, locating on the farm now owned by A. W. Alexander. Eliphalet married Mary Sears, of Ashfield, and had born to him six sons and four daughters, of whom Marietta, Rhoda, Louisa, Rowland and William E. are living. The latter was born in Peru, Berkshire county, whither his parents had removed for a short time, October 11, 1816. Soon after this his parents removed to Charlemont, where they resided till William was ten years of age, when they returned to Williamsburg. At the age of twelve years he came to the village to reside with his brothers, Ezra and Willison, and with the exception of five years spent in Ithaca, N. Y., this has been his home since, and where for many years he has carried on the manufacture of tools. Mr. Thayer married Maria H. Dickinson, of Saybrook, Conn., October 20, 1840, who bore him five children, of whom Frederick W., Alice M. and George D. are living, the first being at home with his father, the second the wife of E. P. Blake, of Springfield, and the last a practicing physician in Northampton. Mrs. Thayer died August 14, 1859. On December 25, 1860, he married Harriet E. Dickinson, of Saybrook, Conn., who has borne him three children, Walter H., Edith E. and H. Winnifred. Eliphalet Thayer died November 10, 1840, aged sixty-four years.

Oliver Nash, son of Eliaha Nash, Jr., was born February 22, 1821, married Julia A. Strong, of Granby, Conn., and located on the homestead. Of his children, Alanson resides in the eastern part of the town, Ellen M. lives at home, and Emily E. (Mrs. Wilbur Smith) lives in Northampton.

Jonathan Luce married Mehitable, daughter of Nehemiah Bates, about 1793, and settled on the farm now owned by Mr. Barker. He reared fourteen children, viz.: Hannah, Ruth, Nehemiah, Loretta, Samantha, Minerva, Mehitable, Samuel, Nancy, Jonathan, Olive, Jonathan, 2d, Augustus and Eliza E. Augustus, the only son at present living, was born September 3, 1819, married Alvira C., daughter of Justus S. Clapp, of Huntington. He

came to Haydenville in 1843, where he learned the moulder's trade, and in
1854 took charge of the brass foundry of Hayden & Sanders, of which he has
been foreman ever since.   He has had born to him seven children, of whom
Clarence S. is an architect in New York city, Franklin is manager of a silk
store in Chicago, Alden S. is book-keeper in the same store, and Eleanor resides here with her parents.

John Wells came to this town, from Rutland, Vt., about 1790, and located
on the farm now owned by O. H. Everett.   He was a carpenter by trade,
and helped build the first church, which was located on the farm now owned
by Edwin Porter.   He had born to him two children, Cyrentha, who married
S. L. James, and John.   The latter married Eliza Graves, of Hatfield, and
had born to him five children, namely, Alma, William G., Alexis, Mary A.
and Sarah.   William G. married Maria, daughter of Joel Willcutt, of Chesterfield, and reared six children, viz.:   John A., Fred W., Lizzie M., Frank,
Martin G. and Jesse.

Sylvanus Hubbard was born in Sunderland, and came to this town in 1800,
where he learned the shoemaker's trade.   He located on land now owned by
Arthur Miller.   He married Abigail, daughter of Joshua Thayer, and had
born to him six children, only one of whom, Sylvanus, Jr., is living.   The latter married Joanna Nichols, of Charlemont, and has two children, Lizzie,
wife of Fred H. Judd, of Westhampton, and Mary F., wife of John Mc-
Calman.

Aaron Kingsley was an early settler of Northampton, and reared three
sons, Seth, Timothy and Supply.   Seth married Irene, daughter of Hart
Warren, of Williamsburg, and had born to him fourteen children, only one of
whom, Elbridge G., of Williamsburg, is living.   The last mentioned married
Elizabeth, daughter of Nehemiah White, and has had born to him three
children.

Asa Shaw moved to Chesterfield, from New Braintree, Mass., at an early
day, married Polly Vinton, and reared five sons and two daughters.   Asa,
Jr., who was three years of age when they moved to Chesterfield, married
Mehitable Beswick, and had born to him eleven children, only two of whom
are living, Martin, of Williamsburg, and Electa, wife of Edson Hayden, of
West Granby.   Martin was born in 1810, married Thankful, daughter of
Brewer Ball, and has had born to him three children, Emily T., Alvin M., of
this town, and Ira O., of Westhampton.

Joseph Bassett moved to Goshen, from Martha's Vineyard, in 1775, and
settled on the farm now owned by Frederick Rice, of that town.   He married
Mary Tilton, and reared a family of six sons and four daughters, of whom
only one of them is living, Ruth, the widow of Robert Rogers, aged eighty-
five years.   Mrs. Rogers reared a family of five children, viz.:   Martha,
Joseph, Emeline, Maria and Otis.

Jonathan Metcalf, of Williamsburg, is the son of Eli, Jr., and grandson of
Eli, Sr.   The last mentioned settled first in Worthington, at Ringville, near

the Chesterfield line, and subsequently moved across the line to Chesterfield. Eli, Jr., married Polly Higgins, and reared five children.

Dexter Tower was born in Cummington, March 12, 1816, married Irene B., daughter of Isaac Pierce, of Windsor, Mass., and had born to him four children, namely, Clinton B., of Northampton; Lizzie J., Climena B. and Pearly D. Climena B. married Alfred D. Sweet, and lives in Spencer, and Pearly also resides in the same place.

Thomas Nash, Jr., was born November 16, 1811, and married Lucinda King in 1838. He served as representative of this town in 1843 and 1866, and was selectman eleven years.

The last district meeting was held December 11, 1775, and the first town meeting February 12, 1776. The population was then 534 souls. In 1780 the number of polls had risen to 131, while in 1790 the population was 1,049. Since then the population has varied as follows: 1800, 1,176; 1810, 1,122; 1820, 1,087; 1830, 1,236; 1840, 1,309; 1850, 1,537; 1855, 1,831; 1860, 2,095; 1865, 1,976; 1870, 2,159; 1875, 2,029; 1880, 2,234.

Military.—In the Revolutionary war Williamsbnrg was generous in her contributions of men and means, performing well her part towards winning our common independence. The names of many who served in the war are on record, and we regret that our space does not allow their mention. The town also promptly responded to Governor Strong's call in the war of 1812–15. In the late great war the town furnished 250 men, a surplus of twenty-nine over all demands, four of whom were commissioned officers. The town also expended $20,000.00 for the cause, aside from $9,997.37, which was subsequently repaid by the state.

VILLAGES.

A large part of the population of the town is disposed in villages along Mill river and its tributary, Mill brook. Of these Haydenville and Williamsburg are the largest, and contain the postoffices.

HAYDENVILLE lies on both sides of the river in the southern part of the town. It has two churches, a savings bank, one hotel, a brass foundry, silk-mill, nine stores of different kinds, two barber shops, blacksmith shop, shoe shop, etc., and a number of fine residences.

WILLIAMSBURG village lies near the center of the town. It has two churches, six stores, two hotels, a tool shop, button factory, grist-mill, saw-mill, and other mechanic's shops. It lies about a mile from the terminus of the Williamsburg branch of the New Haven & Northampton railroad.

SKINNERVILLE is a hamlet lying midway between these two villages.

SEARLSVILLE is a hamlet about a mile northwest of Williamsburg village.

These villages, in common with all the property along Mill river suffered terribly in the great Mill river disaster of 1874. This was caused by the breaking away of the dam of the reservoir above, on the morning of Saturday, May 16th, when 1,000,000,000 gallons of water was sent whirling down the course of the stream spreading death, disaster and desolation in its wake. The most severe loss was sustained by the villages of Williamsburg and Haydenville and Leeds in Northampton. In this short course of only about eight miles, one hundred houses and factories were demolished, twenty iron and wooden bridges swept away and many miles of road obliterated, entailing a loss of over a million and a half of dollars—but no computation can set a price on the loss of the 136 human lives that were sacrificed. The loss of life was divided among the several villages, as follows : Williamsburg, 57 ; Skinnerville, 4 ; Haydenville, 24 ; and Leeds, 51.

MANUFACTURES.

The Haydenville Manufacturing Co., located at that village, is one of the largest manufactories of the kind in the world. They manufacture machinists' supplies and tools, and all kinds of brass work. The works were established in 1845. The officers are A. T. Foster, of New York, president; H. F. Peck, of New Haven, vice-president ; and John Peck, of New Haven, secretary and treasurer.

The Hill Brothers, at Williamsburg, are extensively engaged in the manufacture of buttons and button tassel and trimming molds, and do novelty wood-turning.

The W. E. Thayer Manufacturing Co.—This business was established in a small way, by Willison Thayer, brother of the present proprietor, about 1840. Subsequently the manufacture of buttons and furniture was added. Previous to this, he and his brother Ezra had manufactured clocks here for several years. Tool business was taken up by William E. in 1858, and he has since conducted it alone, having been for some time previous in partnership with Willison. He has built up the business till it now gives employment to twenty-five men in the manufacture of screw-drivers and various kinds or shelf-hardware. The goods are sent to most of the large cities of the United States.

H. G. Hill's grist-mill, at Williamsburg village, is operated by water power, has three runs of stones, and employs four men.

Morton & Davis are engaged in the manufacture of enameled pen-holders fancy wood-turning and lumber. Their works are operated by water-power.

Prescott Williams's cider-mill, on road 8, is operated by steam-power, and manufactures about 1,000 barrels of cider per. year.

G. M. Bradford's saw-mill is located on road 31, where he manufactures lumber, shingles and lath.

Henry L. James is extensively engaged in the manufacture of Union cassimeres.

The Haydenville Savings Bank was incorporated March 17, 1869, and began business January 2, 1870. The officers are Elnathan Graves, president ; F. B. Mason, secretary ; and B. S. Johnson, treasurer.

CHURCHES.

The Church of Christ, Congregational, located at Williamsburg, was organized July 3, 1771, with twenty-one members, and Rev. Amos Butler was the first pastor. In 1779 the first church building was commenced, and dedicated in 1787. The present church building, erected in 1836, will seat 500 persons, and is valued, including grounds, at $13,000.00. The society now has 204 members, with Rev. Thomas M. Price, acting pastor.

The Methodist church, located at Williamsburg, was organized in 1832, and Rev. D. Leslie, the first pastor, was appointed the following year. There had been meetings sustained of this denomination several years previous to this, however, presided over by laymen. The church building was erected during the year of organization, though it has several times been re-modeled and repaired. The present pastor of the society is Rev. A. W. Baird.

The Haydenville Congregational church was organized by Joel Hayden and others, with ten members, in January, 1851. Rev. Edward Swett was the first pastor. The church building was erected that year. It will comfortably seat 500 persons and is valued, including grounds, at $15,500.00. The society is now in a flourishing condition with 119 members.

The St. Mary's Roman Catholic church was built in 1864, upon a handsome site donated by Hon. Joel Hayden. The society was not formally organized until 1871, however, and Rev. Father Moyes was the first pastor. The church building will seat about 600 persons, and is valued, including grounds, at $15,000.00.

———

Worthington lies in the extreme western part of the county, and is bounded north by Cummington, east by Chesterfield, south by the county line, southwest by Middlefield, and west by the county line. It was originally called Plantation No. 3. On the second day of June, 1762, it was sold at auction in Boston, to Aaron Willard for £1,860. Subsequently it passed into the possession of Col. John Worthington, of Springfield, and Major Barnard, of Deerfield. At what date, or for what consideration, this transfer was made, does not now appear. At that time, it was, in territory, much more extensive than at present. When it was incorporated as a town, it extended from what is now Cummington, on the north, to Murrayfield, now Chester, on the south, and from Partridgefield, now Peru, on the west, to the north branch of the Westerfield river on the east. This embraced a portion of the territory now called West Chesterfield. In 1783 the town of Middlefield was incorporated. This was composed of the corners of several other towns. It embraced the southwest corner of Worthington, the northwest corner of Murrayfield, the northeast corner of Becket, the south side of Partridgefield, a part of Washington, and a piece of land called Prescott's Grant. Thus Worthington originally extended to what is now Middle-field Center, where it cornered on Becket. One or two lots, from the north-east corner of Chester were at some time annexed to Worthington, which accounts for the projection we find on the map below South Worthington. The reason for this annexation was that it was more convenient for the residents on this territory to attend church, and do business in Worthington, than in Chester. The town took its name from Col. Worthington.

The surface of Worthington is broken and picturesque. The scenery is of a varied character. Large and well-cultivated farms abound, while there are also mountain slopes still covered with forests, and beautiful, deep valleys, through which the streams flow southward with rapid current. The middle branch has a tributary from the east and one from the west, the former flowing in at the corner of Middlefield, the other at the school-house, farther north. In the south part of the town, midway between the middle branch and Little river, is the valley of the Kinney brook. The middle branch of the West-field river flows nearly north and south through the northwestern part of the town, and then forms the boundary line between Worthington and Middle-field, farther south. The northeast part of the town is drained by Stevens brook, which enters Chesterfield and flows some distance before effecting a junction with the Westfield. The southeast part is drained by Little river, which, uniting with other streams, finally becomes the eastern branch of the Westfield. An elevated range known as West hill lies east of the middle branch, and nearly parallel to it. A few separate elevations are of some note, as Parsons hill, Bashan hill, Knowles hill in the north, and White rock in the south.

Settlement and Growth.—The settlement was commenced in 1764, and progressed much more rapidly than the majority of the towns in its vicinity,—so rapidly, in fact, that, at the commencement of the present century, the town contained more inhabitants than it does at the present time. The names of those who are denominated the first settlers are numerous, but they were probably several years in accumulating. They are as follows: Nathan Leonard, Samuel Clapp, Nathaniel Daniels, Nahum Eager, Dr. Moses Morse, John Kinne, Ebenezer Leonard, Thomas Clemens, Benjamin Bigelow, Thomas Kinne, John Watts, Ephraim Wheeler, Mr. Collamore, Alezander Miller, Joseph Marsh, Amos Frink, Abner Dwelly, Jeremiah Kinne, Stephen and Davis Converse, Phinehas Herrick, Joseph Pettengill, Joshua Phillips, Gershom Randall, Daniel Gates, Asa Cottrell, Asa Burton, Zephaniah Hatch, Nathan Branch, John Buck, Timothy Meech, Samuel Crosby, Daniel Morse, Daniel Morse, Jr., John Skiff, James Benjamin, Beriah Curtis, Jonathan Prentice, Samuel Morse, James Wybourn, Israel Hoton, Col. Ebenezer Webber, Samuel, Robert and Amos Day, Joseph and Isaac Follett, Stephen Fitch, Ezra Cleaveland, Samuel Buck, Edmund Pettengill, James and John Kelley, Isaac Herrick, Joseph Prentice, John Patridge, Seth Sylvester, Amos Leonard, Elijah Gardner, Joseph Dewey, Luke Boney, Daniel Bronson, Asa

Spaulding, Hezekiah Maheuren, John Howard, Thomas Hall, Joseph Gardner, Miner Oliver, Constant Webster, Joseph Geer, Samuel Tower, Nathaniel Collins, Reuben Adams, John Drury, Matthew Fenton, James Bemis, Moses Buck, Thomas Buck, Samuel Pettengill, Noah Morse, Nehemiah Proughty, Seth Porter, Stephen Howard, Mr. Hickey, Elihu Tinker, William Burr, Jonas Bellows, Jonathan Eames, Mr. Wilkins, Mr. Rice, Mr. Ford, Samuel Wilcox, Rufus Stone, Moses Ashley, Joseph French, Samuel Converse, Thomas Butler, Simeon Lee, Samuel Taylor, Samuel Clay, Nathan Morgan, Lewis Church, John Ross, James Tomson, Lewis Porter, Moses Porter, Joseph Lee, Alexander Chillson.

Nahum Eager, born in 1740, was one of the first settlers of Worthington, and died January 15, 1805, aged sixty-five years. His son Nathaniel was born in this town, married twice, first, Mary Marble, who bore him two children, Nahum and Maria, and second, Sibyl Huntington, who bore him eight children, viz.: Samuel, Jennison, Mary, James, Jonathan, Julia, Joseph and Lucy. Jonathan H. was born in 1822, married for his first wife Mary E. Parsons, in 1843, who bore him six children, and for his second wife, he married Selina Buck, in 1876. His son James resides on the home farm.

John Tower was born in England in 1609, came to Massachusetts in 1637, and married Margeret Ibrook in 1629. Calvin B., and direct descendant of John, was born in Cummington, November 4, 1808, and lived on the farm now owned by luther tower, until he was twenty-five years of age. He then purchased a farm in this town on road 12, where he has lived fifty-two years. The house is one of the oldest in town, and is thought to be 115 years old. Mr. Tower married Amanda M. Higgins, and had born to him four children, namely, Lydia A., Alvira N., Angeline D. and Grace I. He died October 13, 1885. His widow resides on the homestead.

Rufus M. Wright was born in 1802, married Salima Parish, December 7, 1830, who bore him one daughter, and died January 22, 1876. The house in which Mr. Wright now resides on road 35 corner 30, is one of the first built in town, and was the one used for the parsonage for the first minister in town.

Benjamin Niles was an early settler of Worthington, married Fannie Elmore, and had born to him four children, Zilpha, Mary, Cynthia and John. The last mentioned married Theresa, daughter of Milton Adams, of Chesterfield, and reared two children, Charlotte, of Ware, and Jennette, wife of Willard Williams, of Williamsburg.

In 1776 the population of the town was 639; 1790, 1,116; 1800, 1,223; 1810, 1,391; 1820, 1,275; 1830, 1,179; 1840, 1,197; 1850, 1,134; 1855, 1,112; 1860, 1,041; 1865, 925; 1870, 860; 1875, 818; 1880, 758.

Organization.—In 1768 this territory was incorporated into a town, and called Worthington, in honor of Col. John Worthington, of Springfield, one of its proprietors, whose liberality towards the inhabitants was manifested by erecting for them, at his own expense, a meeting-house, and a grist-mill, and in assigning generous lots of land for ministerial and school purposes. He made the town a donation of twelve hundred acres of land. This was divided into twelve sections. One-half of these were called ministerial lots, the other half school lots. The object of the donor was to aid the town in the support of educational and religious institutions. The act of incorporation was passed June 30, 1768. The first town-meeting was held August 1, 1768, when the following officers were elected: Nahum Eager, clerk; Capt. Nathan Leonard, Capt. Nathaniel Daniels and John Kinne, selectmen; Thomas Clemmons, constable and leather sealer; Samuel Clapp, Dr. Moses Morse, surveyors of highways; Nahum Eager and Ephraim Wheeler, fence viewers; and John Watts, tithingman.

Military.—When the troublous times of the Revolution came, Worthington early took a decided stand, and immediately after the battle of Lexington, seventy-one men from this town and Ashfield marched to Cambridge. This vigorous action was pursued throughout the struggle, and the small mountain town has every reason to be proud of the record her patriotic ancestors has left.

In the second war with the mother country, the town took the common stand of its neighbors, a belief that the war was not necessary, but standing willing to do its share.

In the late great war the town raised 102 men, a surplus of nine over all demands, four of whom were commissioned officers. It also furnished $4,-462.00 for the cause, aside from $4,398.42, which was subsequently repaid by the state.

VILLAGES.

WORTHINGTON, or Worthington Corners as it is locally known, is a small post village located just north of the geographical center of the town. It has one hotel, a store, blacksmith shop, paint shop, basket shop, school-house and lyceum hall, and about eighty inhabitants.

WEST WORTHINGTON is a small post village located in the northwestern part of the town, on the middle branch of Westfield river. It has one church (Methodist Episcopal), one store, a school-house, saw and grist-mill, bedstead factory, broom fixture factory and about seventeen dwellings.

SOUTH WORTHINGTON is a post village located in the extreme southern part of the town. It has one church (Methodist Episcopal), it has a basket factory, grist-mill, school-house, and about fifteen dwellings.

RINGVILLE, a small post village located in the southeastern part of the town, has a sled factory and about ten dwellings.

WORTHINGTON CENTER, a small village in the central part of the town, has one church (Congregational) a town-hall, blacksmith shop and about fifty-five inhabitants.

MANUFACTURES.

A. Stevens & Sons's saw-mill and hoop factory is located on road 21, on Bronson's brook. About 1836, when the mill was the property of Aaron Stevens, Sr., it was burned, rebuilt in 1837 ; again burned in 1857, and rebuilt in 1858. The Messrs. Stevens have long conducted a prosperous business here.

William C. Sampson's mill, on road 7, was built by Fordyce and Philo Sampson in 1841. Fordyce died and Philo carried on the business alone till 1855, when his son, the present proprietor, became a partner. The facilities have been extended from time to time, and Mr. Sampson now carries on a good business in the manufacture of lumber, lath and factory supplies.

J. & H. Benton's saw and grist-mill, on road 1, was built in 1840, and came into their possession in 1871. The saw-mill has a circular-saw, planer and shingle machine, and the grist-mill one run of stones.

David Jones & Son's bedstead factory, on road 15, was built by Bartlett, Jordan & Co., for the manufacture of bench screws, in 1846. The factory has two planing machines, five circular saws and turning lathes. They manufacture bedsteads and lumber for agricultural implements.

Oliver B. Parish's factory is located on road 17. It was built in 1873-74. He does a prosperous business in the manufacture of loom fixtures and factory supplies of wood.

Hayden & Son's sled factory is located on road 53. The present factory was built in 1858, upon the site of one burned. E. & T. Ring long carried on the business here, hence the name Ringville. Mr. Hayden has been identified with the business since 1878. The firm employs about five hands in the manufacture of hand-sleds.

George H. Miller's saw-mill is located on road 46. It is fitted with circular saws, turning lathe, planer, etc., and Mr. Miller does a general woodworking business, and manufactures and deals in lumber.

Lyman Higgins's saw-mill is located on road 53. He does custom sawing.

Theron K. Higgins's basket factory, at South Worthington, was established in 1883. He employs four hands.

CHURCHES.

The Congregational church, located near the geographical center of the town, was organized April 1, 1771, and Rev. Jonathan Huntington was the first pastor. The first church building was probably built, or begun, the previous summer. It stood near the present residence of Spencer Stewart, on road 31. In 1792 it was moved and rebuilt. The present building was erected in 1824-25, and has since been remodeled and extensively repaired.

It is a wooden structure, capable of seating 600 persons, and is valued, including grounds, at about $10,000. The society now has 118 members, but at present no settled pastor.

The Methodist church at West Worthington was organized in 1849, and Rev. J. P. B. Jordan was the first pastor. The church building, a small structure, was built that year. The society now has forty-three members, with Rev. J. K. Thompson, pastor.

The Methodist church at South Worthington was formed in 1828, and a church building was erected the following year. The present building, a neat wooden structure, was built in 1847. Rev. J. K. Thompson is the present pastor.

INDEX TO PART I

BOND, D W 386 Daniel W 368 Elizabeth Powell 391 George 95 George W 371 H H 88 348 384 Henry H 367 M W 384 Mr 88 Nathan W 196 Nelson F 107 Sylvester 107 W 348

BONEY, Luke 478

BONNEY, Benjamin 204 205 207 Betsey F 293 Dr 293 Emma W 293 Franklin 293 Luke 219 Oliver 293 Priscilla P 293 Thomas 293

BOSWORTH, 239 E R 239 Luther H 373

BOURN, Benjamin 257 259

BOWDOIN, 127 Governor 127 233 James 127 William 84 445

BOWKER, Miss 226

BOWLES, Catherine 319 John J 319 Mr 356 Samuel 356

BOWMAN, Joseph 450

BOYD, Emily A 432 Frank R 432 Julius 432 Lillian E 432 Mrs William 432 Pliny S 3 265 272 William D 432

BOYDEN, James W 83

BOYNTON, S 243 W W 374

BRACE, William 438

BRACY, 311 Thomas 307

BRADFORD, 143 158 Ansel K 107 G M 476 Samuel 473 Sarah 472 473

BRADFORDS, 472

BRADISH, Dr 224 398

BRADLEY, B E 228 C M 228 H F 229

BRAINARD, Abigail 440 Daniel 440 Ellen 445 Ezra 441 Hannah 440 Jerusha (Smith) 441 Mr 441 Olive 441 Robert 440 Wells 440

BRAINERD, Sophronia 246

BRAKENRIDGE, William 445 446 William L 449

BRAMAN, Carrie 366 Curtis W 366 Daniel 233 Ellen 366

BRAMAN (continued) George A 366 Hattie L 366 James Henry 366 Maria 366 Martha A 366 Mattie L 366 Mina 366 Sally 235 Sarah 366 William W 366

BRANCH, Nathan 478

BRECK, Rev 172 Robert 83 172 232 233

BREDEN, Joseph 202

BRENNAN, Francis 179

BREWER, 394 Barzillai 233 James 464 John 456 Mr 233 Samuel 222 Stephen 383

BREWSTER, C H 375 Charles H 107 Charles K 84 Elisha H 83 84 J H 89 Jonah 222

BRIDGEMAN, Elliott 107 Malcolm 107

BRIDGER, Abner P 455

BRIDGES, Sarah 244

BRIDGMAN, 88 184 A H 455 Amy S 146 Aretas H 455 Arthur 185 Arthur M 146 Calvin 184 Chester 464 Clara A 146 Clark 455 Dwight S 455 E C 465 466 469 Ebenezer 182 184 Edward 107 153 Edward S 185 Emma Frances 460 Eugene 185 F A 460 Fannie R 153 Frank H 185 Franklin 455 Franklin A 455 Fred D 455 Frederick B 185 Gertrude L 146 Helen F 146 Helen M 184 Henry 184 Herbert L 146 Irene 184 Israel 455 James 77 184 339 Jane A 185 John 184 John B 184 Jonathan 184 Joseph 182 183 184 Lauren A 146 Lewis 331 Loraine H 146 Lucas 455 Malcolm 269 Martha 184 Mary 146 184 Mary C 184 Mary L 146 Mr 88 Oliver 184 Phineas S 184 Porter 184 Raymond L 146 Richard B 146 Ruth 184 Sarah 184 Sophronia S 185

BRIDGMAN (continued)
  Spencer 455 Theodore 184 William
  E 185 Wright 184 Wright 2nd 184
BRIGGS, 244 George N 139 James
  229 263 Lyman H 374 Mr 229
BRIGHAM, Barna 410 Julia 142
BROCKENBRIDGE, William S 83
BROCKWAY, 429 Beman 429 430
  Gideon 429 Isaiah 429 Mr 430
  Sarah Warner 430
BRONSON, Daniel 478
BROOK, Lord 180
BROOKS, ---- 233
BROS, Lyon 434
BROTHERS, Beemis 225
BROWN, 410 Aaron 309 Abel Jr 390
  Abner 204 206 Adella S 426 Anson
  272 Asa 471 C T 197 Clarence E
  373 Daniel 255 257 258 Ebenezer
  304 Eudora H 409 Foster 410
  George W 409 H J 322 Henry A
  107 Henry M 278 Jane 325 Jesse
  332 John 233 308 309 Jonas 309
  Joseph 426 L L 228 Levi 234 Lydia
  M 148 M V 194 Marshall F 410
  Martin V B 107 Mr 372 Rebecca
  309 Robert 182 184 Rodney 384
  Thomas 184 257 258 263
BROWNE, 260
BRUCE, Annie E 155 Charles 276
  Charles Crombie 155 Charles F
  155 D 196 E B 228 Frank C 236
  Josephine 155 Laura Bassett 155
  Martha P 155 Mary E 155
BRUSH, Jesse 468 William P 390
BRYAN, John T 326 327 330 Nora V
  326 328
BRYANT, 220 226 Ann 210 Anna 210
  Arthur 224 Asahel 359 Benjamin
  204 207 Betsey 208 210 Bricea 210
  Calvin 210 Celia 209 Consider 207
  Cyrus 224 Edgar 209 210

BRYANT (continued)
  Elizabeth 210 Frances 225 Ira 224
  Joanna 210 212 John 210 John
  Howard 224 Mr 225 Nathaniel 207
  208 210 212 Orrin 210 Patrick 210
  217 Patrick Jr 209 210 Peter 224
  225 Prince 207 Royal 210 Sarah
  225 Sarah M 359 Sylvester 440
  William Cullen 224 225
BUCK, Charles W 330 Cyrus 207
  Franklin 207 George 203 207 219
  Isaac 207 Isaac Jr 207 Joanna 209
  John 205 478 Matthew 207 Moses
  479 Otis 207 Otis H 208 Samuel
  478 Selina 479 Thomas 207 479
  Waterman 209
BUCKINGHAM, Jedediah 257
BUCKLE, Patrick 317
BUCKLEY, 331
BUGBEE, Catherine 295
BULFINCH, Caroline 290 S G 290
BULL, Lieut 307 Thomas 307 311
BULLOCK, Ex-Gov Of Massachusetts
  134
BUNDA, Peter 317
BURGER, Benjamin 257
BURGESS, Benjamin 255 256 260 263
  Mercy 260 Silas 260
BURK, Wait 257 259
BURKE, John B 332 Tilly 259
BURLEIGH, C A 294 Charles C 391
  Le Moyne 88 Mr 88
BURNELL, Francis 216 Joseph 204
  205 207 212 216 219 Joseph Jr 216
  Nancy 212
BURNET, Bela 270 Clarissa 270
  Jonathan 270 Mehetable 270
  Salena 270 Sally 270
BURNETT, 443 Arza 439 Bela 439
  Clara A 439 Clara M 439 Dexter
  439 Hattie 439 Lewis E 439 Louie
  E 439 Louis Dexter 439 Mr 439

CLARK (continued)

Jairus E 82 James 317 403 James W 107 Jane 458 Jason 234 Jemima 235 Job 234 John 234 394 414 415 416 John B 366 Jonas M 386 Jonathan 415 419 453 Jonathan 3d 454 Jonathan Jr 453 Joseph 415 Josiah Jr 367 Juliette 145 Justin W 420 L Maria 360 Lafayette 83 Lelia A 236 Lewis F 420 Lizzie L 146 Lois 234 Louisa M 145 Lucinda 460 Lucy 145 Luther 234 454 Luther A 107 Lydia 234 461 Maria 234 Martha 361 454 Martin 464 467 Mary 357 Mary Ann 459 Mercer 270 Mercy 454 Merritt 383 Minerva 401 Mr 332 337 401 417 454 Mrs 234 270 Mrs C A 458 Mrs Charles 455 Mrs Silas D 432 Myra 145 Myra A 366 Nancy W 401 Nathan 301 453 454 463 464 466 467 Nathan Jr 454 Newman 453 Noah 265 266 Obadiah 233 234 Oliver 432 Othinel M 357 Paul 455 Perkins K 323 Philetus 420 Philip 233 234 Phineas 460 Phinehas 233 President Of Massachusetts Agricultural College 135 Rebecca 145 Rowland 234 Roxa 270 Royal W 145 Samuel 266 Sarah 472 Sarah (Smith) 271 Sarah E 270 Saul 420 Sereno D 420 Seth 265 266 Seth W 401 Simeon 125 145 Solomon 3 397 Sophronia A 432 Spencer 270 Spencer S 420 Susanna 401 Tertius 464 Theodore 454 459 460 Tibbel 271 Timothy 419 Walter Edwin 146 William 181 270 271 337 339 William B 269 William Jr 84 William S 108 135 270 William Smith 146 Zenas S 457 Zilpha C 145

CLARKE, 212 Christopher 384 Edward 219 Fanny L 146 Henry 78 Jairus E 426 John 378 384 Joseph 397 Joseph S 426 Noah 425 Samuel 310 Strong 426

CLARY, John 299 Joseph 116

CLAY, Mr 349 Samuel 479

CLEAVELAND, Ezra 478 Nehemiah 471

CLEGHORN, 472

CLEMENTS, 445

CLEMMONS, Thomas 480

CLEVELAND, 472 John P 388 W M 406

CLIFFORD, 244

CLIFTON, Gertie 439

CLINTON, De Witt 74

CLOUGH, Olive 227

COATS, Jesse 234

COBB, 25 27-29 32-35 37 42 43 45 46 210 E G 391 Elizabeth 357 Lydia A 357 N A 22

CODDING, Sarah M 473

COFFIN, 472

COGGESHALL, Joseph G 334 390 Mr 335

COGGIN, David 468

COGSWELL, Clarence C 362 Laura P 362

COIT, Isaac 320

COLBURN, 244

COLE, 220 Abner 471 Amaziah 212 213 Amaziah Jr 213 Amos 213 Ansel 261 Betsy 213 Consider 212 213 Consider Jr 212 213 Ebenezer 210 212 Ebenezer Jr 212 Elijah 212 213 Elijah Jr 213 Ephraim 213 George 108 Hannah 409 Horace 211-213 220 Isaac 213 Joanna 210 212 John 115 213 307 318 Lydia 213 Nancy 213 Rachel 212 Ruth 318 Samuel 76 212 213 Sophia 213

FOOT, Enos 94

FOOTE, 115 Adelaid E 409 E N 373
George 409 Mrs 310 Nathaniel 307
311 Samuel 307 311

FORBES, Caleb 316 317 Charles E 81
349 Elijah 317 George W 384
Henry 276 Mr 349 384 William
317

FORBUSH, 244

FORD, Daniel 250 John 324 330
Maggie 326 Mr 479 Packard 250
Thomas 77

FORGUSON, John 393

FORTON, George A 462

FORTUNE, Lottie 151

FORWAR, Rev Mr 186

FORWARD, Justus 198

FOSGATE, Sally 150

FOSTER, A P 28 A T 476 George W
248 John 200 274 Joseph 445
Maria M 248 Roswell 468

FOWLER, Esther 137

FOX, Luther 159

FRANCIS, Marilla D 188

FRARY, Carrie A 235 E 311 Eleazer
307 Jesse L 420

FREEMAN, Ebenezer 317

FREIDAY, Fred 462 Mary E 462

FRENCH, Ebenezer 415 452 Henry F
135 John 437 Joseph 479 M M 386
Samuel 471 Thomas 471 William
317

FRIEND, Mr 329 332

FRINK, Amos 478

FROST, 24 29 31 34-36 38 44 64 65
Amasa 471 Charles C 22 Lucia M
235 Nathan 471 R S 322

FULLER, Dwight V 194 Mary 378
Zebulon 317

FULLERS, 274

FULTON, 92

GAGNIER, L G 451

GALLAGHER, William 240

GAMWELL, Julia M 189 Moses 332

GARDINER, Henry 419

GARDNER, Electa 318 Elijah 478
Francis H 269 Henry 123 Joseph
479 Louisa E 401 William 318

GATES, Aaron 178 Abigail 189
Andrew 471 Daniel 478 Ellen B
153 Horace 189 Lansford 153

GAY, 88 W B 1 4

GAYLORD, 439 443 Elizabeth 441
Flavel 84 Fred 441 Henry E 441
James 441 Jerusha 441 John 437
441 Josiah 441 Llewis 441 Lorenzo
441 Louisa 441 Mary M 296
Moses 441 Mr 441 Philomelia 318
Philotas 441 Rebecca 441 Roxanna
441 Samuel Jr 286 Sarah 141
Simeon 441 William 437 441
William M 82 368

GEER, E 317 Ebenezer 320 Elijah 317
Joseph 479

GEORGE II, King Of England 117

GERE, 86 Henry S 82 86 87 Mr 86
Salvina 319

GIBBS, 244 274 Abraham 274 276
Hannah 144 Thomas 274 276

GIDDINGS, Daniel 270 Huldah 270
James 270 John 270 Joseph 270
Mary 270 Patty 270 Sally 270

GIDDONS, 405

GILBERT, 244 448 Charles D 449
Ebenezer 228 Foster W 403 George
H 448 Helen L 142 J H Grenville
449 Lewis N 82 448 449 Mr 448
Susan H 140 W C 405

GILBERTS, 332

GILL, A G 88

GILLETT, 252 Catherine 248 Charlotte
E 248 Cornelius 248 Daniel 248
Daniel B 84 249 250 Edith 248
Edith B 248 Edward B 248

GILLETT (continued)
    Eliza 248 Elizabeth 248 Mary A
    248 Persis 249 Rufus W 249
    Samuel 307 311
GILLETTT, Daniel B 248
GILLFILLAIN, Thomas 225
GILMER, Jane A M 188
GILMORE, Eunice A 319 Frederick D
    450 James 317 393
GLEASON, Abigail 248 Esther 213
    Isaac 247 Mr 405 Ruth 247
GLOYD, 262 Joseph 403
GODDARD, Hannah 147
GOESSMAN, Charles A 135
GOFFE, 288 291 William 287
GOLD, 197 Levi W 197 Mr 197
    Thomas 94
GOLDTHWAIT, Loren E 269
GOODALE, Anna B 153 Austin A 153
    G L 24 25 28 41 George L 135
    Isaac 126 Mrs John 154 Robinson
    153 William F 153
GOODELL, Amanda 189 Charles S
    108 Dorothy 189 Julia A 189
    Lafayette 189 Lafayette W 197
    Marcus L 189 Mary A 441 Moses
    189 Mr 189 Nathaniel 441
GOODMAN, Augusta 408 Eleazar 437
    Mr 286 Noah 437 Richard 286 288
    Stephen 285 Thomas 441 Thomas
    Jr 437
GOODSELL, Dana 178
GOODWELL, Ruth 326
GOODWIN, 85 Mr 303 O 311 Ozias
    307 W C 373 William 281 302
GORTON, George 433 Iretta 462
GOSS, Elizabeth 247
GOUCH, Moses 233 234
GOULD, Daniel 420 445 David 422
    445 Ebenezer 445 Lurene S 360
    Mary 422 Mindwell 422 Mr 422
    Mrs 360 Solon N 360 Vincon 426

GOULD (continued)
    Vinson 422 436
GOVE, Dorothy 401
GRAHAM, Clara M 439
GRANGER, 301 Abraham 326 Daniel
    320 Jane 326 L N 300 Lorenzo N
    300 Luther 326 Miriam 326 Mr
    300 301 Paul 326 Rebecca 226 326
    Ruth 326 Sophronia 300
GRANT, Asa 255 257 Captain 259 399
    Christopher 257 259 John 258
GRAVES, 158 185 282 311 472
    Amasa 324 331 471 Amasa Sr 329
    Austin L 190 Clara L 327 Diantha
    358 Elijah 213 Eliza 474 Elnathan
    84 359 469 476 Esther 142 Fanny
    211 Hannah 190 Henry 189 190
    Henry B 359 Henry Jr 190 Isaac
    185 307 310 311 Isaac Jr 307 311
    Isaac Sr 310 Isaacc 312 Israel 211
    John 184 185 307 311 312 John Jr
    307 John Sr 310 Jonathan 181 184
    185 Joseph 183 Josiah H 358
    Lewis 309 433 Llizabeth C 296
    Louise 145 Maria L 325 Mary 359
    Mary J 359 Mary Smith 309 Moses
    Wales 190 Mr 190 434 Nancy 190
    Perez 471 Sally 473 Samuel 473
    Selina 189 Seth 471 Silas 471
    Sophia S 190 Sylvia 458 Thomas
    182 184 185 Thos 307 W B 327
    William 190 William N 434
GRAY, 26 30 Asa 24 Chester 410 Dr
    23 32 Harrison 123 206 419
    Horace 396 397 John 394 395 John
    Jr 393 Margaret 274 Mary 366
    Mathew 393 Moses 410 Nathaniel
    394 Oliver 394 Samuel 393 Wil-
    liam 366 394 395 William Jun 393
GRAYS, 408
GREELEY, Horace 430 Mr 430 R F
    322

506

HAYDEN, 220 221 224 384 472 474
481 Edson 474 Electa 474 Ex-lieut
Gov 384 Ida 358 Joel 84 87 358
477 Josiah 471 Mr 481 Mrs John
208
HAYES, Ex-President 215 Ezekiel 215
Joel 444 Rutherford 215 Sally 215
HAYWARD, Afton S 151 Betsey F
293 C 159 C F 159 Carrie S 151
Charles E 151 159 Daniel 252
Elijah 293 Elizabeth A 151 James
402 John 3 Loretta 151 Lucia B
151 Lucius F 151 Tilly Brown 402
HAZELTON, Jane 326
HEALY, 217 Joshua 211 219 Louisa
407 Parley 211 S A 217 218 Seth
211 Seth A 211
HELMSING, Margaritha 297
HEMENWAY, 410 471 Aaron 471 Mr
91
HENDERSON, Nancy 141
HENDRICK, Abbie I 235 Abby C 235
Arthur G 235 Charles Alfred B 235
Charles B 235 Cornelia 235 Daniel
N 235 Elisheba 235 Ella B 235
Ellen M 235 Frank H 235 Hildah J
235 Huldah 234 Israel 232 234
Jabez 234 James 234 James M 235
Jennie 235 Jesse 234 Joseph 234
Joseph N 234 235 Leslie N 235
Lester B 235 Lewis S 235 Lovina
234 Lovy 234 Martin V 235 Martin
V B 235 Mary 235 Mary B 235
Mary L 235 Mary V 235 Mr 235
Nancy 235 Oseola 235 Parmelia
235 Pearson 234 235 R J 235
Rachel 234 Reuben 234 Sarah B
235 Sarah L 235 Stephen 234 235
Theodore H 235
HENRY, Clarissa 151 James 437
Lizzie L 146 Luther 365 Margaret
365 Samuel 321

HENSHAW, 240 David 95 John 95
Samuel 82 367 383
HERRICK, Isaac 478 J R 444 Phinehas
478 William D 177
HERVEY, Sarah L 357
HIBBARD, 298 300 Albert 300 Elias
298 300 John 298 299 300 301
Truman 298
HICKEY, Mr 479
HIGGINS, 220 Almon 210 220
Amanda M 479 Barney 207 210
Billings 210 Catharine 210 Deliv-
erance 210 E H 218 Elijah 207 210
Eliza 210 Elmira 210 Elzina 210
Hiram 218 Jacob 210 228 Jonathan
210 Julia 210 Lewis 210 Lucy 210
Lucy E 210 Luther 210 Lyman 481
Mary 210 Nelson A 216 Polly 475
Rebecca 210 Ruth 210 Samuel 207
Simeon 210 Sophronia 210 Theron
K 481 William 210 Zilpah 210
HILL, 354 355 375 472 Abraham 126
Brothers 476 Ebenezer 471
Ephraim 472 H G 476 Hiram 473
Mr 126 Otis G 84 Prudence 472
Sampson 471 Samson 472 Samuel
L 378 Samuel Lapham 354 Sarah
472 473
HILLIARD, George S 367
HILLMAN, John R 108
HILLS, 160 Emily 150 Henry F 150
160 L D 150 L M 149 158 160
Leonard D 157 Leonard M 157 Mr
149
HILLYER, John 77 437 Mr 378
Timothy 437 Timothy Jr 437
Winthrop 378
HINCKLEY, 354 355 Henry R 108 S L
383 Samuel 82 367 Samuel L 82
354 383
HINDS, 274 Hopestill 274 Nehemiah
410 Timothy 277

HUSSEY, Albert C 362
HUTCHINSON, 125 414 415 Moses
231 Mr 414
HYDE, 218 471 Charles A 153 Charles
D 153 Eleazer 472 Esther R 153
Eugene 472 F E 472 Francis E 472
Harriet A 153 Keziah 472 Lucinda
472 Lyman 472 Mary 472 Mrs 472
Rosalind 191 Rufus 217 218 472
Sarah T 472 William 3 450 472
William S 450
IBROOK, Margeret 479
INDIAN, Awonusk 339 Callawane 341
Chickwollop 282 King Quabbin
273 Pacquollant 341 Quonquont
282 304 Umpanchella 282 Wife Of
Quonquont 304 Wulluther 339
Wuttowhan 341
INGHAM, Alexander 328 331 Erastus
325 328 329 Erastus J 326 331
Erastus John 326 James 328 Julia
326 Lillie C 326 Nora V 326 328
Solomon 324 328 329 Vesta 326
INGRAHAM, Daniel 405 Elisha 120
Mr 405
INGRAM, Aaron 148 Albert B 148
Betsey S 148 Caroline 148 Carrie
C 148 Cora L 148 Ebenezer 115
116 Elizabeth M 148 Frank 148
Harriet L 148 Jennie B 148 John
117 John Jr 115 161 John Sr 115 Jr
116 Lucia 148 Lucius 148 Lydia M
148 Mary B 148 Mary L 148 Mr 148
Nathaniel Jr 437 Peter 158 Robert
148 Sarah 148 Sarah B 148 Solo-
mon B 148 Susan C 148 William
148 Zacheus C 148
IVES, Henry 450
IVIE, Charles W 241
JACKSON, Francis 95 S 241
JAMES, 23 262 Cyrentha 474 Enoch
259 260 Henry L 476 J L 364

JAMES (continued)
John 255-257 260 262 L L 260
Luther 260 Lyman D 378 Moses
258 Mr 364 Rachel 440 S L 474
JANES, 231 Benjamin 231 412 Enos
459 Franklin W 234 Hannah 459
Harriet A 234 Harry L 234 James
471 Jonathan 233 Joseph 471
Justus L 420 Lois 234 Lovicy 459
Luke 234 Mrs 412 Samuel 231
William 339
JARVIS, Edward 375
JEFFERSON, A W 390 Mr 347 367
JENKINS, Thomas 445 William L 389
JENKS, Abbey 191 Arminda 191
Minerva 191 Russell 191
JENNINGS, Luzette 408 Mrs 310
Stephen 310 311
JEPSON, John 257
JEPSONS, 362
JEROME, E 390
JESUP, 25-27 30 32 35-38 40-48 H G
22
JEWETT, 394 A G 454 Albert G 456
Arthur C 395 Cecil 395 Charles P
395 Frank I 395 Fred S 395 Maria
395 Martha A 395 Mr 395 Sylves-
ter 395
JILLSON, Amasa 395
JOHN, Squire 261
JOHNSON, 472 Adam 393 394 408
Adeline 409 Andrew 408 409
Angenette 409 Ansel 408 Augusta
408 B S 3 476 C H 239 Clara 409
Clarinda B 212 Clarissa B 150
Daniel 202 Edwin H 150 Eliza 408
Frank 409 Frederick 150 G H 3 98
George 408 George H 112 177
Harriet 409 Hattie M 408 Henry
408 Hervey S 150 Jane 408 Joel
408 409 John 393 394 395 Judith
408 Leo 408 Louisa 150 Lucy 408

510

JOHNSON (continued)
Luzette 408 Lyman 408 Marcia
408 Margaret 408 Maria 408 May
150 Mr 178 Nettie 408 Nina 408
Rhoda 408 Rosalind 408 Shepard
408 Sir William 418 Theodore L
408 Theodosia 246 W E 410 William 393 408

JONES, 143 158 244 252 Albert 298
Bela P 432 Benajah 325 David 481
Dr 433 Elnathan 158 450 George N
108 H A 178 Henry 420 Henry A
397 James 320 John 324 325 328
Lewis Jr 299 Lizzie 360 M S 252
Marshall 252 Minerva 401 Nancy
W 401 Samuel 324 328 Susanna
401 T 252 Thomas 158 159 252

JORDAN, 481 J P B 482 J W P 221
JORDANS, 274
JOSELYN, John 73
JOSLYN, Abram 207 Sarah 394
JOWE, John 246
JOY, Asa 398 Cyrus 402 Isaac 398
Jacob 402 Royal 224 403

JUCHAN, George 264
JUDD, 312 A G 421 Amoret 453 Asa
421 422 Asahel 437 441 C Parkman 464 Clarissa 421 425 Eleazer
455 Eleazer Jr 455 Eunice 360 F H
3 Fred H 455 474 Frederic E 422
Frederick 421 422 Frederick H 451
453 464 Harriet A 453 Hophni 86
Jane W 453 John A 455 464 John
H 108 Jonathan 322 420 421 425
433 435 455 459 467 Jonathan Jr
419 420 421 422 Jonathan N 422
Lizzie 474 Lucy E 438 Mr 86 165
174 285 418 420 421 422 435 436
Mrs E 438 Mrs J A 453 Reuben
437 Rev Mr 416 Samuel 233 340
Sarah 421 Silence 421 459 Solomon 421 455 Squire 465

JUDD (continued)
Sylvester 3 421 422 453 464 466
Sylvester Jr 86 464 Sylvia 438
Thomas 77 340 420 437 Wealthy
453

JUDKINS, Mrs 290
JUDSON, C G 237
JUSS, Asa 433
KEENE, William 219
KEITH, Caleb 243 Ezekiel 249 Joseph
249 Josiah 252 Monroe 266 270
Myra 190

KELLEY, George 248 James 478 John
478

KELLOGG, 158 Aaron 130 Albert 143
Angeline 270 Bell 141 Carrie E
358 Catharine C 143 Charles 143
270 Charles H 143 Chester 266
Daniel 143 David 130 Ebenezer
115 116 437 439 Eleazer 143 Eliza
366 Elizabeth C 143 Ellen E 154
Elvira M 143 Ephraim 142
Ephraim Jr 142 Esther 143 Esther
M 143 Eugene G 277 Evenezer 166
Frank Bailey 358 Giles C 83 289
Ida 358 J Dwight 358 Jabez 437
James 159 Johanna 150 John 142
143 John E 143 Jonathan D 358
Joseph 310 437 Joseph Jr 437
Joseph M 143 Julia A 143 151
Justin P 108 Lois 439 Louisa M
145 Lucia 141 Martin 366 Mary
143 148 Mary E 153 Mary W 143
Mr 289 Nathaniel 142 202 Roxey
143 Rufus 143 Rufus M 143 Rus-
sell 471 S 311 Sally M 143 Sally
McCloud 143 Samuel 307 310 312
437 Sarah 310 Willard 143 153
Willard M 143 William 158 159
Willie A 143

KELLY, James 208 Martha 208
KELSEY, H S 272

KELSO, Edmund 330
KEMP, Mrs W R 438
KENNETT, Smith 471
KENT, Elijah 266 272
KENTFIELD, 244 Nellie R 147
KIBBE, Bros 325
KILBURN, Josiah 219
KIMBALL, Angie E 189 Annie Field
456 Arthur 225 Austin L 189 Clara
L 189 Edith L 189 Edwin 188 189
Edwin E 189 Ellen L 189 Fanny C
245 Henry E 189 Leila I 189 Mrs
William B 245 Nettie N 189 Perley
L 456 W B 195 245 William A 189
KING, A 147 373 Albert 373 Amaran-
da 461 Arlina 453 Catherine S 147
Charles C 455 Clara 147 Clarence
147 Cyrus 147 Dorcas 460 463
Ebenezer 317 320 Ebenezer A 147
Edward 329 Edward P 147 El-
bridge 405 Eleazar 204 Elijah 455
Elisha 460 461 463 Elizabeth 460
Ella C 147 Elmina 453 Emma C
147 Emory S 395 Flora J 147 Frank
A 147 Gains 460 461 George 461
George N 455 George W 405
Harriet N 463 Hattie J 147 Henry
461 Henry Ws D 147 Herbert F
147 Homer C 147 Horace S 455
Isaac 221 Isaac N 147 Israel 147 J
Lyman 455 Jennie A 395 Jessie M
395 John 77 257 339 Joseph 182
183 Julia 463 Julia R 463 Lucinda
475 Luther 455 463 Luther W 455
Lydia 461 Mary A 147 395 Mary E
147 Medad 460 461 Mindwell 357
423 Mr 147 405 Mrs C C 453 Mrs
George N 453 Paul 207 Phineas
415 416 Polly 141 Rufus 445 Silas
207 Simeon 460 Sophia 147 Susan
E 463 Susanna 460 Susanna (2d)
460 Sylvester 460 Thaddeus 455

KING (continued)
Thankful 187 Warren F 147 Wil-
liam 307 311 Woodbridge A 147
KINGLSEY, William F 360
KINGMAN, 394 Deacon 219 Isaac 255
257 Levi 228 262 Samuel 219
KING PHILIP, 201 254 273 341
KINGSBURY, Cyrus 263
KINGSLEY, Aaron 474 Albert H 360
Almeron 453 Alvin W 453 454
Arlina 453 Calvin 252 Calvin B
360 Caroline 360 Daniel 386 Delia
M 461 E 469 E M 465 466 469
Ebenezer 414 415 416 Ebenezer Jr
418 Edward 360 Edward A 461
Edward W 453 461 Elbridge 293
Elbridge G 474 Elizabeth 474
Elizabeth H 360 Ellen V 461
Elmina 453 461 Elsie 453 Enos
339 Ezra 453 Ezra M 453 Francis
360 George L 360 Harriet 360
Henry 360 Henry S 461 Irene 474
Joseph 433 453 Joseph H 461
Joseph Jr 453 Joseph S 453 Justus
H 461 L Maria 360 Lizzie 360
Lyman 360 Mahlon 461 Marvel
453 Mary 458 Mary E 453 461
Miriam 453 Mr 294 414 Mrs
Edward W 458 Nelson 461 Nelson
A 456 461 Olive Jane 453 Oliver
244 Orin 453 Robert M 360 Roland
453 Samantha 453 Samuel 453 456
Seth 474 Supply 474 Susan 360
461 Susan M 461 463 Timothy 474
Wareham 453 Wealthy 453 Wil-
liam M 453 William W 453 Zenas
373 453 461
KINNE, E S 210 211 219 Jeremiah 478
John 478 480
KINNEY, Albert C 366 Anna 367 C W
374 Charles M 366 Charles W 366
Edward 366 Ella 366 Fred 366

525

SEARS, 274 Lizzie E 148 Mary 473
Minnie 246 Roland 276
SEDGWICK, Judge 349
SEEGER, Charles L 368
SEELY, Sarah M 145
SEELYE, Julius H 133 Mrs S T 35
President 382 President Of Am-
herst College 134 S T 239 Samuel
T 238 239
SELDEN, Jonathan 265 266
SELLECK, Bradley 332
SEXTON, Hannah 440
SHADMAN, Rosette 427
SHATTUCK, C S 313 Mr 313 315 405
R W 228 William 406
SHAW, 224 Allen 209 Alvin M 474
Amy M 395 Asa 474 Asa Jr 474
Austin H 189 Calvin 270 Carl S
395 Charles 402 Charles A 153 154
Charles H 153 Dana 402 Electa
474 Ellen L 189 Elmer P 189
Emily T 474 Ethel E 153 Eva A
189 Fannie R 153 Fernando G 196
Frances 395 Francis 403 Francis H
189 Frederick B 153 G Washington
402 George F 189 George W 395
Hattie F 395 Huldah 270 Ida L 189
Ira O 474 John 223 Joshua 398
Josiah 403 Julia M 189 Larua A
189 Lillian J 189 Lovina 189 Mari
I 189 Martin 474 Mary 209 Me-
hitable 474 Myron A 189 Oziel 189
Polly 474 Samuel 224 402 403
Sarah Lodica 246 Thankful 474
Thomas 404 406 William 110 188
194 William B 189 William H 110
Zuba 409
SHAYS, 103 104 105 Daniel 103 395
SHEARER, 244 Charles 247 Elizabeth
247 Fanny 247 Field 247 Frances
247 James 247 Jane 247 John 247
Joseph 94 Lyman F 247 Pierce 247

SHEARER (continued)
Rachel 247 Reuben 246 247 Ruth
247 Seth 247 Sophia 247 Wm 247
SHEEDY, B DeForrest 362 Dr 363
SHEEHAN, J T 451
SHELDEN, Isaacc 77 Mary 358
SHELDON, 355 Adella S 426 Cather-
ine 187 E 473 Eunice C 426 Flavel
K 426 Flavel R 110 Frank C 426
Grace A 426 Henry S 428 Isaac
339 Israel 415 419 426 Mary 184
187 Mindwell 422 Mr 357 426 428
Mrs 426 Noah 415 418 Robert F
426 Silas 426 435 Silence 421
Simeon 428 436 Sophia 318 Ste-
phen 415 416 William H 420
SHEPARD, Cornelia F 431 Doct 257
Fannie Haskins 144 Harriet A 453
Mr 87 Mrs A C 453 455 Thomas
82 Thomas W 87 Thomas Watson
86
SHEPHERD, 105 Esther 274 Gen 104
Levi 383 Susan 360 William 104
SHERMAN, Abigail 188 Emily 362
Samuel 445 446
SHERWIN, Jacob 258
SHIPMAN, J D 261
SHORES, David 396
SHOULER, William 3
SHOVE, Edward 200
SHUMWAY, Austin 275 Binah 441
Elizabeth 432 Hattie E 432 Jemima
441 Joanna 441 Loren 145 Louise
275 Mr 161 432 Nahum 432
Nathan 196 Philenda (Squires) 441
Sarah E 145 Solomon C 110 194
Sophronia 275 Thomas T 441
SHUMWAYS, 274
SHURTLEFF, Flavel 110
SHUTE, J R 91 Mr 91
SILLSBEE, William 389
SIMPSON, 188 Sir G 399

526

SISSON, John 397
SKERRY, 298 Ebenezer W 298 Mr
  298
SKIFF, Ann 210 John 478 Obed 210
SKINNER, J L 89 J Leander 110 Mr 89
  William 329
SLATE, Sophia 147
SLATTERY, Edmund 452
SLOAN, Timothy W 110
SMITH, 195 244 281 298 301 315 329
  367 A 251 Aaron 115 116 Abby L
  439 Abner 182 183 452 457
  Adolphus 271 Alfred 251 Alice E
  145 Almira 438 Alva 271 Alvin
  251 252 Amelia 234 Andrew A
  144 Anna L 326 Arthur N 438
  Asahel 266 Asaph 438 Asaph 2d
  438 Atwell P 144 Austin 271
  Austin 2d 271 Azariah 329 Bath-
  sheba 256 Burritt A 436 C 301 C
  Edgar 83 Caleb 253 Calvin 271
  325 326 Caroline 297 Cephas 271
  Charles 438 Charles A 271 Charles
  H 360 374 Charles P 110 Charlotte
  J 245 Chester 267 271 298-300 361
  Chileab 285 Chileab (2d) 437 Clara
  A 439 Clara L 438 Clarissa 438
  Clarissa 2d 438 Cotton 145 298-
  301 Cyrus B 267 269 D 251 Daniel
  183 Darius 439 David 248 251
  David P 355 Dwight Ben 298 E P
  245 Ebenezer 326 332 437 441
  Edson L 439 Edward 248 251
  Edward C 326 Edward H 271
  Edward P 243 248 329 Edwin 269
  271 Edwin P 271 Electa 144 Eli
  407 438 Elias 118 Eliza 248 271
  Eliza B 439 Eliza Ellen 144 Eliza-
  beth 184 286 Elizabeth A 151 Ellen
  Eliza 144 Elliot 271 Emeline 271
  Emily E 473 Enos 248 285
  Ephraim 84 437 438 441

SMITH (continued)
  Erasmus 295 Erastus 299 Erastus
  2d 298 300 Erastus Jr 298 Ethan
  184 Eunice 360 Experience 265
  441 F 299 Fannie 308 438 Finley
  271 Francis 299 Frank H 367 Fred
  S 299 Frederick A 144 Frederick D
  300 G C 298 G M 298 302 G
  Myron 299 Geo C 298 George C
  271 300 George H 362 Gerald B
  326 Gideon 285 Giles 271 439 H B
  210 217 H H 251 H Lizzie 365 H
  Walworth 110 Hannah 263 Harriet
  146 438 Harriet L 326 Harriet S
  438 Harry 438 Harvey G 439
  Harvey J 87 Heman 438 Henry 248
  Henry J 87 Henry M 249 Henry N
  438 Henry W 279 Hezekiah 265
  Hezekiah Jr 265 Hilo J 360 Hiram
  441 Hiram Jr 83 Horace 365
  Howard 326 I P 219 Ichabod 286
  Irene 184 271 Israel 437 J 301 J G
  366 J Maria 360 Jacob 297 James
  265 267 395 471 James W 110
  Jane E 145 Jehial 439 Jennie 438
  Jerusha 441 Joanna 144 Joel 295
  Johanna 439 John 182-184 221 255
  257 258 263 265 310 325 328 329
  437 438 441 464 466 John (4th)
  437 John 2d 300 John Jr 441 John
  Sr 441 Jonathan 144 286 437 438
  Joseph 84 183 184 287 289 299
  438 Josephine 360 Josiah 437 438
  Josiah (2d) 437 Josiah W 87
  Judson 329 Julia 271 Julia E 144
  Justin 439 Kate W 326 Lawrence
  326 Leonard 439 Lewis 360 Lewis
  B 439 Lillie C 326 Lois 439 Loman
  271 Louie E 439 Louis C 326
  Lowell 438 Lucia M 144 Lucius B
  439 Lucy 271 325 Lurene S 360
  Luther 438 439 Luthera 360

SMITH (continued)

Luthera J 360 Lyman 144 195 M J
329 M Wilbur 360 Maggie 326
Marilla 439 Martha 300 Martha B
144 Mary 147 271 325 438 Mary E
144 145 Mary H 145 Mary J 327
438 Mary M 144 Mary S 271 439
Matthew 324-326 328-330 Matthew Jr 328 Maverick 445 Medad
271 Metcalf J 326 328 Milo J 374
Milo L 360 374 Minnie 309 Mr 87
144 195 248 326 361 438 Mrs
Wilbur 473 Myra A 366 Nancy B
300 301 Nathan 265 267 Nathaniel
115 161 Nellie E 362 Nelson 270
438 439 Nettie B 144 Newton 438
Newton A 144 Noah 144 Olive 2d
328 Oliver 84 308 328 332 378 383
Osman 439 Pamelia 438 Pelatiah
116 Phebe 438 Philip 286 437 438
Philip H 438 Phineas 271 Phineas
Jr 271 Phinehas 266 268 Phinehas
(2d) 437 Phinehas 1st 265 Phinehas
Jr 265 266 Rebecca 438 439 441
Reuben 437 441 Richard P 374
Robert 438 Robert C 271 Robert M
269 Rodney 302 Rodolphus 373
Russell 321 S C 267 Salena 270
439 Sally 144 439 Sally J 360
Samuel 267 285 328 437 441
Samuel C 269 272 Samuel E 326
Sarah 326 438 439 Sarah A 438
Selah 438 Selina 189 Sibyl 145
Silas 437 Silas M 378 Simeon 121
439 Simon 118 Sophia 295 308
315 378 Sophia S 326 Spencer 144
Stephen 115 Susan 271 Susan E
271 Susannah 271 Sylvester 285
Sylvia 438 Thaddeus 298 299
Thankful 439 Theodore W 326
Thomas E 217 Titus 271 W W 145
Walter A 225 Watson L 82

SMITH (continued)

Wayland F 326 Willard 327 Wil-
lard N 439 William 144 220 437
438 William A 144 267 269 437
William H 145 159 William W H
144 Willis A 271 Windsor 298
Worthington 289
SNELL, E S 133 Ebenezer 223 224
Samuel 257 Sarah 225 Squire 229
SNELLING, Samuel 178
SNOW, 244 C A 294 Ebenezer 437
Edwin 196 Josiah 437 Josiah Jr 437
Mr 196 R C 449
SNOWS, 274
SOPER, Lucy A 409
SOUTHWORTH, Achsah 431 Asa 431
C H 443 E C 442 J H 442 443 Mrs
431
SPAFFORD, Thomas 471
SPAULDING, Annie A 357 Asa 478
479 George E 230 Henry H 398
399 Mark H 110 368 Samuel T 82
368 T G 384
SPEAR, Asa A 110 Frank E 151 Mary
147
SPENCER, Abigail 440 George S 218
Hannah 440 Ichabod S 388 John
325 Mr 332 Orson 332 Sarah 366
SPERRY, Cornelia 235
SPOONER, Charles 269
SPROUT, Ezra 276
SPROUTS, 274
SQUIRES, Henry 246
STACKNEY, Julia 275
STACY, Nymphas 410
STANDLEY, Brother 285
STANLEY, John 437 Michael 330
STANTON, 220 321 A J 319 321 322
Abel 318 Adeline 319 Atherton J
321 Catherine 319 Dwight I 216
Edward W 319 Ella 319 Fanny M
319 Flora L 319 Fred P 319

536

WRIGHT (continued)
Rockwell 441 Roxanna 441 Rufus
M 479 Ruth 184 Salima 479
Samuel 77 285 339 357 Samuel L
431 Sarah 357 Sarah L 357 Sarah
Warner 430 Seth 383 Silas 285
Silas M 361 Stephen 231 233
Stephen Jr 232 233 Tryphena 234

WRIGHTS, 232 240
WYATT, Clara 148 Esther 148
WYBOURN, James 478
WYMAN, Daniel 257
YEOMANS, Elijah 286
YERRINGTON, James B 89
ZECHARIAHES, 116